OLD ENGLISH HOMILIES
FROM MS BODLEY 343

EARLY ENGLISH TEXT SOCIETY
O.S. 302
1993

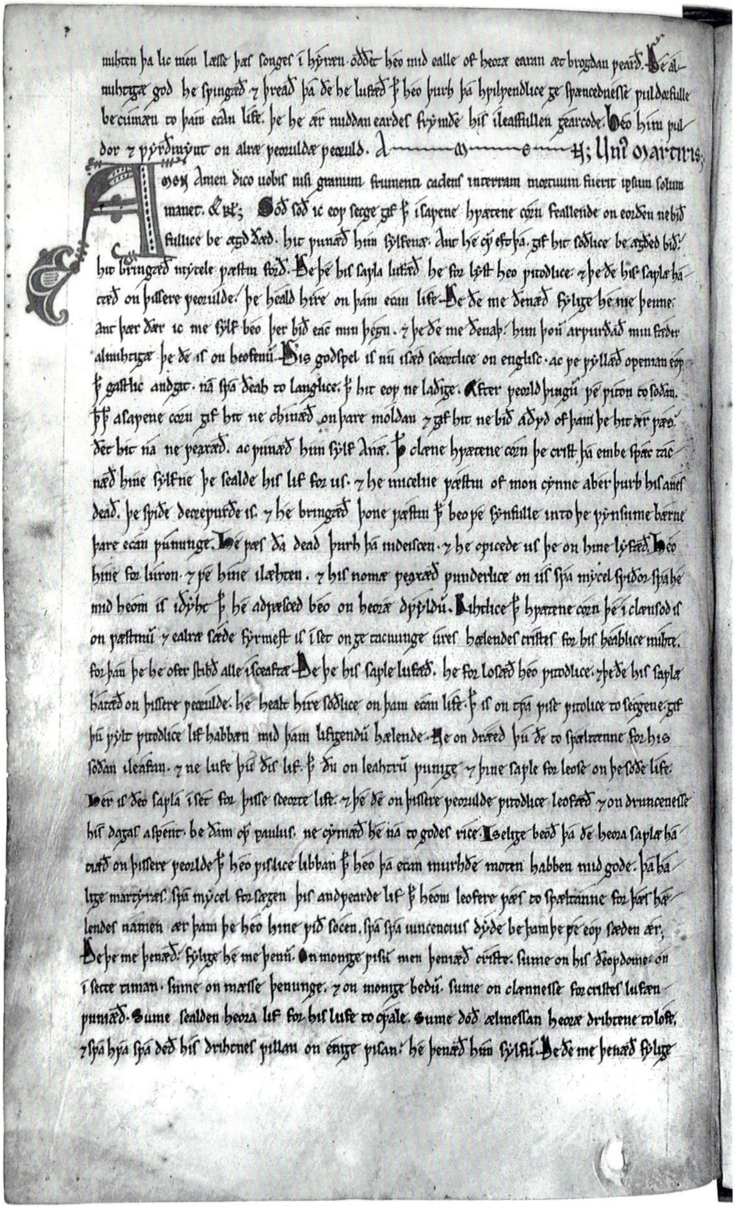

OLD ENGLISH HOMILIES FROM MS BODLEY 343

EDITED BY

SUSAN IRVINE

Published for

THE EARLY ENGLISH TEXT SOCIETY

by the

OXFORD UNIVERSITY PRESS

1993

Oxford University Press, Walton Street, Oxford OX2 6DP

Oxford New York Toronto
Delhi Bombay Calcutta Madras Karachi
Kuala Lumpur Singapore Hong Kong Tokyo
Nairobi Dar es Salaam Cape Town
Melbourne Auckland Madrid
and associated companies in
Berlin Ibadan

Oxford is a trade mark of Oxford University Press

British Library Cataloguing in Publication Data
Data available

ISBN 0-19-722304-4

Set by Joshua Associates Limited, Oxford
Printed in Great Britain by
Ipswich Book Company Ltd

PREFACE

This book began as a doctoral thesis for the University of Oxford. I should like to thank Professor Malcolm Godden and Professor Eric Stanley, joint supervisors of the project, who have been unstintingly generous in sharing with me their time and erudition. Miss Celia Sisam and Professor Jimmy Cross, my thesis examiners, offered me much useful advice and corrected many details. Miss Sisam and Professor Godden have also been extremely helpful in the transformation of thesis into book. Dr Bruce Mitchell made a number of valuable comments on my Textual Notes. Professor Peter Clemoes kindly lent me a copy of his unpublished doctoral dissertation.

I am grateful to the Bodleian Library, the Cambridge University Library, and the British Library, for allowing me to consult manuscripts in their possession.

The work for this project was undertaken while I was a graduate student at St. Hilda's College, Oxford, and then Fellow of Lincoln College, Oxford; I am indebted to both institutions for their generous support. The New Zealand University Grants Council and a Violet Vaughan Morgan Scholarship from the University of Oxford also provided financial assistance.

This book is dedicated to my parents, Robin and Bunty Irvine, who have always supported and encouraged me in every possible way. I also owe an inestimable debt to my husband, John Benger, who has provided knowledgeable advice and sympathy in equal measure.

CONTENTS

PLATES

:

ABBREVIATIONS AND SHORT TITLES

Anal. Boll.	*Analecta Bollandiana*
Archiv	*Archiv für das Studium der neueren Sprachen*
Assmann	*Angelsächsische Homilien und Heiligenleben*. Ed. B. Assmann. Bibliothek der angelsächsischen Prosa, III. Kassel, 1889; reprinted with a supplementary introduction by Peter Clemoes, Darmstadt, 1964
ASE	*Anglo-Saxon England*
Acta SS	*Acta Sanctorum*. Ed. Iohannes Bollandus and Godefridus Henschenius *et àl*. 67 vols. Antwerp, 1643–1770; Brussels, 1780–
Barré	Henri Barré, *Les Homéliaires Carolingiens de l'École d'Auxerre*. Studi e Testi, 225. Rome, 1962
Belfour	*Twelfth Century Homilies in MS. Bodley 343. Part I, Text and Translation*. Ed. A. O. Belfour. EETS, os, 137. London, 1909
Bethurum	*The Homilies of Wulfstan*. Ed. Dorothy Bethurum. Oxford, 1957
BHL	*Bibliotheca Hagiographica Latina Antiquae et Mediae Aetatis*. Ed. Socii Bollandiani. 2 vols. Brussels, 1898–1901. Supplementi editio altera (Subsidia Hagiographica, 12). Brussels, 1911
BL	British Library
Blickling	*The Blickling Homilies of the Tenth Century*. Ed. R. Morris. EETS, os, 58, 63, 73. London, 1874–80.
BT	Bosworth, Joseph, and T. Northcote Toller, *An Anglo-Saxon Dictionary*. London, 1898. Includes *Supplement* below unless there is explicit mention of BTS also
BTS	*Supplement* by T. Northcote Toller to *An Anglo-Saxon Dictionary*. Oxford, 1921
Campbell	A. Campbell, *Old English Grammar* (Oxford, 1959; reprinted 1977)
Camp. *Suppl.*	Enlarged Addenda and Corrigenda by Alistair Campbell to BT and BTS. Oxford, 1972
CCCC	Corpus Christi College, Cambridge

CCSL   Corpus Christianorum, Series Latina. Turnhout,
                  1953–
CH I   *The Homilies of the Anglo-Saxon Church: The First Part,*
                  Containing the Sermones Catholici, or Homilies of Ælfric,
                  I. Ed. B. Thorpe. London, 1844
CH II   *Ælfric's Catholic Homilies, The Second Series. Text.* Ed.
                  Malcolm Godden. EETS, ss, 5. London, 1979
Clemoes,   Clemoes, P. A. M., 'The Chronology of Ælfric's
  'Chronology'   Works'. In *The Anglo-Saxons: Studies in some Aspects of*
                  their History and Culture presented to Bruce Dickins. Ed.
                  P. Clemoes. London, 1959, pp. 212–47
Crawford   *The Old English Version of the Heptateuch, Ælfric's*
                  Treatise on the Old and New Testament and his Preface to
                  Genesis. Ed. Samuel J. Crawford. EETS, os, 160.
                  London, 1922
CUL   Cambridge University Library
EETS, os   Early English Text Society, Original Series
EETS, ss   Early English Text Society, Supplementary Series
Fehr   *Die Hirtenbriefe Ælfrics.* Ed. B. Fehr. Bibliothek der
                  angelsächsischen Prosa, IX. Hamburg, 1914;
                  reprinted with a supplementary introduction by
                  Peter Clemoes, Darmstadt, 1966
Förster   *Die Vercelli-Homilien, I.–VIII. Homilie.* Ed. Max
                  Förster. Bibliothek der angelsächsischen Prosa,
                  XII. Hamburg, 1932; reprinted Darmstadt, 1964
HBS   Henry Bradshaw Society
Ker, *Catalogue* N. R. Ker, *Catalogue of Manuscripts Containing Anglo-*
                  Saxon. Oxford, 1957
LS   *Ælfric's Lives of Saints.* Ed. W. W. Skeat. EETS, os,
                  76, 82, 94, 114. 2 vols. London, 1881–1900
MED   *Middle English Dictionary.* Ed. Hans Kurath and
                  Sherman M. Kuhn, and others. Michigan, 1954–
Microfiche   *A Microfiche Concordance to Old English.* Ed. Richard
  Concordance   L. Venezky and Antonette DiPaolo Healey. Toronto,
                  1980
Napier   *Wulfstan; Sammlung der ihm zugeschriebenen Homilien.*
                  Ed. Arthur S. Napier. Sammlung Englischer Denk-
                  mäler in Kritischen Ausgaben, 4. Berlin, 1883
NM   *Neuphilologische Mitteilungen*
OED   *Oxford English Dictionary*

OES	Bruce Mitchell, *Old English Syntax*. Oxford, 1985
PL	*Patrologiae cursus completus . . . Series Latina*. Ed. J. P. Migne. 221 vols. Paris, 1844–64
PMLA	*Publications of the Modern Language Association of America*
Pope	*Homilies of Ælfric: A Supplementary Collection*. Ed. John C. Pope. EETS 259, 260. 2 vols. London, 1967–8
RS	Rolls Series
Szarmach	*Vercelli Homilies ix–xxiii*. Ed. Paul E. Szarmach. Toronto, 1981
TH I	Temporale Homilies I
TH II	Temporale Homilies II

References to Old English texts are by short title, item number, and line number, unless otherwise stated, except for CH I, which is cited by homily and page number. Unless otherwise stated, translations are my own.

MANUSCRIPT SIGLA

I have retained the sigla adopted by Clemoes and Godden for the First and Second Series of *Catholic Homilies* and by Pope for the later homilies by Ælfric. The letter X followed by a superscript letter is used to represent manuscripts which include only a little of Ælfric's homiletic work, and the letter f followed by a superscript letter is used to represent fragments. The sigla were designed by Clemoes to reflect the position of the various manuscripts in the development of the First Series, with A representing the earliest stage.

A   BL MS Royal 7 C. xii
B   Bodleian Library MS Bodley 343
C   CCCC MS 303
D   Bodleian Library MSS Bodley 340 and 342
E   CCCC MS 198
F   CCCC MS 162
G   BL MS Cotton Vespasian D. xiv
H   BL MS Cotton Vitellius C. v
J   BL MS Cotton Cleopatra B. xiii and Lambeth Palace Library MS 489
K   CUL MS Gg. 3. 28
L   CUL MS Ii. 1. 33
M   CUL MS Ii. 4. 6
N   BL MS Cotton Faustina A. ix
O   CCCC MS 302
P   Bodleian Library MS Hatton 115 and University Library, Kansas, MS Pryce C2, item 2
Q   CCCC MS 188
R   CCCC MS 178
S   Bodleian Library MS Hatton 116
T   Bodleian Library MSS Hatton 113 and 114 and Junius 121
U   Trinity College, Cambridge, MS B. 15. 34
V   CCCC MSS 419 and 421
W   BL MS Cotton Julius E. vii
Z   Bodleian Library MS Laud Misc. 509
X^a CCCC MS 190
X^e BL MS Cotton Tiberius A. iii

X^g	BL MS Cotton Vespasian A. xxii
X^i	Lambeth Palace Library MS 487
f^a	CCCC MS 367
f^b	Jesus College, Cambridge, MS 15
f^d	Gloucester Cathedral MS 35
f^e	Koninklijke Bibliothek, The Hague, MS 133. D. 22
f^h	BL MS Cotton Otho A. xviii
f^i	BL MS Cotton Otho B. x
f^k	BL MS Cotton Vitellius D. xvii
f^m	Magdalene College, Cambridge, MS Pepys 2981 and BL MS Harley 5915
f^q	Brasenose College, Oxford, MS Latham M. 6. 15

GENERAL INTRODUCTION

This edition presents seven Old English homilies from one manuscript, Oxford Bodleian Library, MS Bodley 343.[1] Although the manuscript was itself written in the second half of the twelfth century, the homilies edited here were all composed over a century earlier. According to item numbering in Ker's *Catalogue* (which I have retained for ease of reference), the manuscript contains eighty-three Old English items altogether.[2] My reasons for selecting the seven items edited in this volume are pragmatic. The homilies are all unique to Bodley 343, and have therefore been neglected by scholars concerned with collating manuscript copies of Old English texts.[3] Much of the material in Bodley 343 survives elsewhere in earlier manuscript copies, and in any case is adequately dealt with in past or forthcoming editions.[4] These seven homilies have been printed only in the 1909 edition of A. O. Belfour, *Twelfth Century Homilies in MS Bodley 343*.[5] This supplies a text and translation; it is frequently inaccurate, however, in its recording of the texts, and, since the projected Part Two did not appear, we have no introduction, comments, or glossary.

Four of the homilies are by Ælfric. The attribution was first made by Peter Clemoes in a seminal article listing Ælfric's complete corpus and proposing a chronology for its composition.[6] Clemoes explains his criteria for identifying Ælfric as author of pieces not previously attributed to him:

in some cases cross-references to known works make identification certain; in others it depends either on immediate links with known works in subject-matter or expression, or on stylistic evidence in the widest sense—conformity to Ælfric's known intentions and habits of mind as well as to the characteristics of his way of writing.

[1] Ker, *Catalogue*, no. 310.

[2] There are also a small number of items in Latin, which are listed in Ker, *Catalogue*, p. 374.

[3] Pope, for example, excludes the four Ælfrician homilies from his edition on the grounds of their uniqueness; since they cannot be 'supplied with more Ælfrician texts', it is not possible to obtain improved readings for them (p. 5, n. 1).

[4] See, for example, CH II, Pope, Assmann, Fehr, and Bethurum.

[5] They appear as items iii, iv, vii, viii, x, xi, and xii in that edition. Like Belfour, I have retained the manuscript order of the homilies, but they are now renumbered i–vii respectively.

[6] Clemoes, 'Chronology'.

Clemoes cites homily iii as an example where cross-reference to a known work makes identification certain.[1] He does not make any specific comment on his attribution to Ælfric of homilies i, ii, or iv.

In order to confirm Ælfric's authorship of these four homilies, it is necessary to consider the evidence in more detail. There are two reasons why it is particularly important to do so for these homilies. First, the sole survival of the texts in a late twelfth-century manuscript obscures the type of evidence available for Ælfrician texts in earlier manuscript copies; whereas Pope was able to cite manuscript arrangement to support Ælfric's authorship of some of the homilies he edited, the compiler of Bodley 343 made no attempt to separate out Ælfric's texts from other works.[2] Various anonymous items, as I show below, are interspersed amongst those by Ælfric, more or less at random. Secondly, analysis of detailed stylistic points can be unreliable since it is clear from the homilies not unique to Bodley 343 that vocabulary and syntax were altered to conform to twelfth-century linguistic practice.

Despite such difficulties, sufficient incontrovertible evidence of Ælfric's methods remains. Most obviously, all four homilies are written in his distinctive rhythmical prose style.[3] In very general terms, this style consists of two-stress phrases linked in pairs by alliteration; it relates to the method of the alliterative poets, but is much less regulated. Thus an extra full stress or a secondary stress may occur, and alliteration is by no means consistent. Notwithstanding twelfth-century alterations, this rhythmical prose style is clearly recognizable in all four homilies. As Pope notes, 'this form is so distinctive that it is a strong indication of Ælfric's authorship wherever it appears'.[4]

Following Pope's example, I have printed the homilies in verse lines. Clearly this method has some drawbacks; Ælfric was not writing poetry, and at times rhythm and alliteration disappear altogether. As Pope argues, however, 'the form is too insistently regular to be disregarded and yet not quite clear enough to make its structure apparent at a glance without further guidance'.[5] A recognition of Ælfric's rhythmical prose style heightens an understanding of his method of composition: the advantages of marking out phrasal units seem to outweigh the disadvantages.[6]

[1] See p. xvii below.   [2] Pope, pp. 94–6.
[3] The features of this style are discussed in detail by Pope, pp. 105–36.
[4] Pope, p. 103.   [5] Pope, p. 135.
[6] Following Pope, I have not inserted an extra space or dot to mark the caesura; the lines flow more fluidly without a marker, and the position of the caesura is often unclear (if indeed one can be identified at all).

The alliterative prose style of the four homilies is not the only evidence of Ælfric's authorship. In their structure the homilies all consist of a verse-by-verse exegesis deriving from a variety of patristic sources such as Augustine, Gregory, Haymo, Alcuin, and Smaragdus. This is Ælfric's characteristic method of composition, as Pope's edition shows clearly in its juxtaposition of text and source material. Again the constant adaptation of the sources, omissions and independent additions, corresponds to Ælfric's method elsewhere. Ælfric characteristically paraphrases even the gospel-texts, so that there too his alliterative and rhythmical style is clearly evident.

In addition to these general features which suggest Ælfric's authorship, all four homilies contain specific material and ideas which appear elsewhere in his works. Sometimes Ælfric makes the link for us, sometimes we need to identify it independently. In homily i Ælfric does not refer explicitly to earlier works. He begins the homily, however, by acknowledging his audience's limited understanding and powers of concentration in words reminiscent of his Second Series homilies for Midlent Sunday and for the First Sunday in September.[1] Further on in the homily he includes two passages which are not in his source but which have close corollaries in his own writings elsewhere: the account of Archelaus' banishment and his replacement by tetrarchs, and the image of the sun's rays.[2] In homily ii Ælfric adapts Augustine so as to stress the doctrine of merit and reward rather than that of divine grace: he adds, for example, a reference to our gaining a hundredfold reward for our good deeds, an idea which appears several times elsewhere in his homilies. He also adds to his source a passage equating the kingdom of heaven with God's church, again a correspondence he makes frequently elsewhere. In homily iii Ælfric's phrase, 'swa swa we sædon hwilon ær' (l. 277), refers to his previous discussions of the Sabbath in CH II xii and Pope ii.[3]

The fourth Ælfrician homily edited here is divided into two parts. The first part, the Passion of St. Vincent, does not appear in Bodley 343, and is therefore edited here from its only surviving copy in another late twelfth-century manuscript, CUL Ii. i. 33. This piece was recognized by W. W. Skeat from its alliterative style to be the work of Ælfric, and he appended it to his edition of the *Lives of Saints*.[4] The

---

[1] CH II xii, 2–6; CH II xxx, 2–6.
[2] For further details, see pp. 14–16 below.
[3] See pp. 53–6 below.
[4] LS xxxvii.

second part of the homily is the pericope exposition found in Bodley 343. The connection between the two was identified by Clemoes,[1] and in this edition the two parts have been printed together as a whole for the first time. In his pericope exposition, Ælfric alludes to the narrative section of the homily: 'swa swa Uincencius dyde, be þam þe we eow sæden ær' (l. 338). Further evidence of Ælfric's authorship is the characteristically practical and everyday explanation of a biblical point at lines 300–3: a seed which remains whole on the ground will not germinate. Again apparently independently of the sources, Ælfric adds a warning against drunkenness with reference to St. Paul, an idea familiar from his other writings. Every indication points to Ælfric's authorship of this pericope exposition.

The other three homilies in this volume are anonymous. They are printed as prose since they exhibit no consistent rhythmic pattern. Although surviving only in this late manuscript, they are also pre-Conquest works, roughly contemporary with those of Ælfric. This can be ascertained first from their vocabulary and orthography which clearly derive from Old English, despite the updating by a twelfth-century scribe. In particular one of the homilies, v, is extremely similar in content and expression to other Old English homilies, one by Ælfric and one anonymous, for the same occasion, the First Sunday in Lent.[2] Moreover the latter half of homily vii does survive in other manuscripts; it corresponds to the last part (approximately one-third) of Vercelli Homily x.[3] Homily vii is a composite homily, and almost certainly its first half also derived from another Old English homily which has not survived.

THE MANUSCRIPTS

OXFORD, BODLEIAN LIBRARY, MS BODLEY 343

The manuscript, written in the second half of the twelfth century, is a substantial collection of works from the pre-Conquest period. It is probably the work of two scribes: the first is responsible for fols. vi–xxxix^v, the second, by far the larger contributor, for fols. 1–170.[4] The first scribe retains insular forms of *f*, *g*, *h*, *r*, and *s* in the Old English

[1] Clemoes, 'Chronology', p. 236, n. 1.
[2] See below, pp. 116–35 *passim.*
[3] Szarmach, pp. 14–16. See pp. 179–81 below for a discussion of the relationship and its significance.
[4] For the various characteristics of the two hands, see Ker, *Catalogue*, pp. 374–5.

items. The second scribe's neat and clear hand shows the following characteristics: *a, e, f, h*, and *r* are caroline; insular *g* is used for the spirant and caroline *g* for the stop, and a diagonal hairline is attached to the base of both forms; caroline *s* is used, but it sometimes descends below the line (particularly when doubled and before a *t*); *d* resembles *ð* without the cross-stroke; the ends of descenders generally turn to the left (except *þ*). Abbreviation of *n* or *m* is marked by a superscribed bar, usually straight but occasionally hooked; the superscribed bar or barred letter is also used to denote other abbreviations, for example, *cƿ* (for *cwæð*), *disciplis* (for *discipulis*), *drihī* (for *drihten*), *heteȝæ* (for *heretoȝæ*), *m̄* (for *men*), *scs* (for *sanctus*), *þ* (for *þæt*). The abbreviation *7* is used for *and*; a hooked *d* is found for *de*. Accents are used abundantly and without any apparent rationale; initials are decorative, usually in red, green or black; titles are written in the same hand and are in red or black.

The manuscript is foliated i–xxxix (vi–xxxix originally paginated 1–66, but 58 and 59 appear twice, and 52, 53, 54 appear for 62, 63, 64), 1–167, 169–74. Fols. i, ii, iv and v are post-medieval paper flyleaves. Fols. iv and v contain a list of contents of fols. 1–152. Some items are missing from the list (items 8, 12, 18, 55, 67, 69, 70, 71), and one is listed twice (item 40). Fol. iii was originally the final pastedown. It is now placed at the beginning, reversed and upside down. Writing on the inside of the leaf suggests that the manuscript derives from the West Midlands. This comprises a thirteenth-century rhymed antiphon for St. Wulfhad, and other words in the same hand. The flyleaf, fol. 173, boasts a drawing of a bishop and a cryptic inscription (apparently referring to St. Wulfstan of Worcester), probably thirteenth century.[1]

Some texts in Latin have been added in originally blank spaces, probably in the late twelfth or early thirteenth century.[2] Fols. 141ᵛ–143ᵛ are heavily glossed in a fifteenth-century hand.[3] The binding of the manuscript is eighteenth century.

The collation of the manuscript is as follows: i⁶ wants 3 and 4 after fol. vii, ii one (fol. x, preceded by missing leaves), iii–v⁸, vi⁶–1 (the first), vii⁸, viii⁴, ix–xiv⁸, xv⁴, xvi–xxiii⁸, xxxiv⁸ wants 3 after fol. 130 and 6

---

[1] C. Sisam suggests that the inscription reads 'wr (*for* ur) biscopen war wolstane god'; see 'Early Middle English *Drihtin*', in *Middle English Studies Presented to Norman Davis in Honour of his Seventieth Birthday*, ed. D. Gray and E. G. Stanley (Oxford, 1983), pp. 245–54. This would imply that the manuscript was at Worcester when the inscription was written.

[2] See Ker, *Catalogue*, p. 374.

[3] Angus F. Cameron, 'Middle English in Old English Manuscripts', in *Chaucer and Middle English Studies in Honour of Rossell Hope Robbins*, ed. Beryl Rowland (London, 1974), pp. 218–29.

after fol. 132, xxv^8, xxvi^8, xxvii^4, xxviii^8, xxix^8 wants 8 after fol. 170, xxx^2. The whole manuscript measures approximately 308 × 200 mm., the written space used is 240–60 × 135–60 mm. The pages contain 28–36 lines (ruled with a pencil, and varying within sections of the manuscript as well as from section to section); fols. xi–xxxix and 165–6 are in two columns. The size of the written space changes at fols. 65 and 155.

The manuscript divides into seven main sections. Each is formed by a group of quires which ends with a blank space before the next group begins with a fresh quire. The sections vary considerably in length and are made up as follows:

section (a), fols.vi–x (items 1–4);
section (b), fols. xi–xxxix^v (item 5);
section (c), fols. 1–20^v (items 6–12);
section (d), fols. 21–64 (items 13–31);
section (e), fols. 65–128^v (items 32–64);
section (f), fols. 129–54^v (items 65–76);
section (g), fols. 155–70 (items 77–85).

Bodley 343 is an extreme manifestation of an important phenomenon, the copying and collection of Old English texts up to two centuries after their original composition. More than thirty manuscripts containing pre-Conquest English texts survive from *c.* 1100 onwards, of which over a third are collections of homilies. By identifying and analysing the earlier history of Bodley 343's contents, we can elicit important information about how such texts were used and transmitted.

In undertaking this kind of analysis, I am heavily indebted to scholars who have already examined the complex network of relationships amongst the extant manuscript copies of Ælfric's *Catholic Homilies*, namely Peter Clemoes for the First Series and Malcolm Godden for the Second Series.[1] In his doctoral thesis, Clemoes describes six phases in Ælfric's development of the First Series. Four of these constitute successive stages in the issue of the First Series, two constitute a reorganization of the homilies therein. The four stages of issue and reissue correspond closely to Kenneth Sisam's earlier survey of four manuscripts containing the First Series homilies.[2] According to Sisam, each of the three manuscripts, Royal 7. C. xii (A), Gg. 3. 28 (K),

---

[1] Clemoes, 'Chronology'; Clemoes, 'Ælfric's *Catholic Homilies*, first series: the text and manuscript tradition' (unpubl. PhD diss., Cambridge, 1956); Godden, *CH* II.

[2] Kenneth Sisam, *Studies in the History of Old English Literature* (Oxford, 1953), pp. 148–98.

and CCCC 188 (Q), presented a different stage in the development of the text.[1] Bodley 340 and 342 (D) he saw as a transition between A and K, but closer to A. Clemoes assigns to D (along with CCCC 198 (E) and CCCC 162 (F)) a stage of its own. Hence for Clemoes, the four issues of the *Catholic Homilies* are represented by A; DEF; K; and Q.[2]

Between the stage presented in K and that presented in Q, Clemoes argues that the First Series underwent a different kind of development. At this interim stage, termed TH I (Temporale Homilies I) by Clemoes, the liturgical homilies for the Proper of the Season (Temporale) were arranged so as to provide a series for the Proper of the Season from Christmas to the Sunday after Pentecost.[3] Then, at some later period, after the last reissue of the First Series presented in Q, a further development took place, which Clemoes terms TH II; this comprised an extension of the TH I series throughout the year while confining it more strictly to pericope homilies. In Clemoes' forthcoming edition of the First Series, the six phases of development are distinguished in chronological order as follows: α (the phase presented in A); β (the phase presented in DEF); γ (the phase presented in K); δ (TH I); ϵ (the phase presented in Q); and ζ (TH II). I shall refer to these phases in the following discussion since they help to define the affiliations of the texts in Bodley 343 (B) with other manuscript copies.

In his edition of the Second Series, Godden analyses the texts of the Second Series homilies. He distinguishes first and second recension copies. The first recension is represented by K (although eighteen manuscripts altogether draw on the first recension).[4] The second recension signifies a version of the text substantially revised by Ælfric and belonging to a 'fairly late stage of his work'; the main witnesses for this recension are H, P, R, U, V, and f[b].[5] Godden notes that for the Second Series it is not possible 'to establish a chronological sequence

---

[1] Clemoes confirms Royal 7. C. xii's status as 'a unique witness to the earliest phase of which we know' in *Ælfric's First Series of Catholic Homilies British Museum Royal 7 C.XII fols. 4–218*, ed. Norman Eliason and Peter Clemoes, Early English Manuscripts in Facsimile 13 (Copenhagen, 1966), p. 28.

[2] The reissue represented by Q is discussed by Clemoes in 'Chronology', p. 234.

[3] Pope, pp. 47–8, questions whether Ælfric himself was formally responsible for TH I. He also differs from Clemoes in assigning the beginning of TH I to Septuagesima rather than Christmas (p. 47). Clemoes, however, in an appended note to 'Ælfric', in *Continuations and Beginnings*, ed. E. G. Stanley (London, 1966), pp. 176–209, p. 209, upholds his previous conclusions.

[4] CH II, p. lx.

[5] CH II, p. xxiii.

for the manuscripts based on the stages in the development of the text that they reflect, as Clemoes has done for the First Series'; Ælfric apparently did not have one single authoritative copy but rather 'made revisions to more than one exemplar . . . so that some variations probably indicate not the stage to which a manuscript belongs but the manuscript tradition within Ælfric's scriptorium from which it derives or simply its independence of other manuscripts'.[1]

Interspersed amongst the Catholic Homilies in Bodley 343 are various other texts apparently unrelated to them in textual history: other works by Ælfric, including several of his *Lives of Saints* and pastoral letters, homilies by Wulfstan, anonymous homilies, and a collection of Latin sermons. With the help of the various scholars who have examined the textual transmission of these works, I attempt to reconstruct through what lines of transmission they might have reached the compiler of Bodley 343, and hence the kinds of collections that might have been available to him.

A list of the contents of the relevant manuscript section precedes the discussion of the textual origins of its items. For each item the following information is offered: folio references, rubric (when provided), incipit (Latin and English where appropriate), occasion or subject of the text (where it is not evident from the rubric), and most recent edition of the text.[2] In the titles and incipits, abbreviations are silently expanded. The incipits of the Latin homilies of section (b) are printed here for the first time.

Section (a)

1. fols. vi–vii[v]. *Dominica .VIII. post pentecosten*. Cum multa turba . . . Marcus se godspellere cwæð on þissum dæʒe . . . CH II xxv. (Ends imperf.) . . . mid godes ʒewæpnuge onʒean (l. 132).

2. fol. viii[rv]. (beg. imperf.) habban god. þu wylt habban hælu . . . CH II xxvi (Ninth Sunday after Pentecost), l. 111 ff.

3. fol. viii[v]–ix[v]. In illo tempore. Dixit iesus discipulis suis. Ego sum pastor bonus . . . Ðis ʒodspel þe nu ʒeræd wæs cwyð . . . CH I xvii (Second Sunday after Easter), p. 238. (Ends imperf.) . . . embe eowerne biʒ[-] (p. 242, l. 11).

4. fol. x. (beg. imperf.) swyðor cepað. Ne cwæð he na . . . CH II xxxi (16th Sunday after Pentecost), l. 93 ff. [Fol. x, ll. 13–26 and whole of

---

[1] CH II, p. xxiv.
[2] Cited either according to the list of abbreviated short titles or otherwise by editor, date of edition, and item number (with full reference provided in a note).

fol. xv were originally blank, but were filled later with sequences and music (see Ker, *Catalogue*, item 86).]

Section (a) of B contains four homilies, all by Ælfric. Three (items 1, 2, and 4) are Second Series homilies for Sundays after Pentecost (the Eighth, Ninth, and Sixteenth), drawing on the first recension, with textual characteristics that link them to the predominantly south-eastern group of manuscripts, C, D, E, and F.[1] The fourth, Ælfric's First Series homily for the Second Sunday after Easter, which is placed third in the sequence, is unrelated textually as well as chronologically. It shows no connections with the CDEF group, but represents instead a slightly later phase of the text (Clemoes' γ phase).

The two quires of section (a) are far from complete. Four leaves survive of the first quire; at least two more, the central bifolium which would have contained the end of the first homily and the beginning of the second, are missing. The quire may also have had an outer bifolium (making it an eight-leaf rather than a six-leaf quire) of which the first leaf was perhaps detached because it contained the end of an unwanted homily, and the eighth leaf, subsequently lost, contained the remainder of CH I xvii (approximately one and a third sides).

Fol. x, a singleton, is all that remains of the second quire (and hence of the fourth homily). It was probably the last leaf of the quire since half the recto and the entire verso containing music and a sequence were originally blank. If this leaf was the end of the quire immediately following the first quire, other items must have intervened between items 3 and 4, since the end of the third homily and the beginning of the fourth which are missing would only take up altogether approximately two leaves (four sides). If such items had also shown links with the γ phase, then the apparently anomalous textual origin of item 3 in this section would look less strange.

It is possible that the singleton might have been preserved primarily because of the music and sequence which had been added to the verso. Thus the four leaves of quire one might have been end-leaves for binding.[2] Ker states that 'medieval binders often placed as many as four leaves and sometimes even more than four leaves of parchment at each end of the books they bound', and that although the leaves were

---

[1] Godden specifies more precisely that these homilies 'do not include all the CDF readings and hence must derive not from X(1), the common source of C(d), D, and F, but from an antecedent copy' (CH II, p. xxxviii). For the connections of C, D, E, F, and other first recension manuscripts with the south-east, see CH II, p. lx.

[2] I am grateful to Dr. M. B. Parkes of Keble College, Oxford, for this suggestion.

sometimes blank, they were also sometimes 'leaves of older manuscripts which had become useless'.[1] Although it would explain the
incompleteness of section (a) and its separation from the rest of the
English material of the manuscript, the theory has considerable drawbacks. First, it would seem a remarkable coincidence if four leaves of
Old English homilies were used to bind a manuscript itself consisting
mainly of Old English homiletic material, especially when these texts
do not appear elsewhere in the manuscript (except for an independent
extract from one in section (g)). Secondly, section (a), quires one and
two, and section (b), containing the Latin homilies, are all written in
the same hand.[2] Again, such a coincidence seems highly implausible
(though not impossible).

Section (b)

5. fols. xi–xxxix^v. (A sequence of short Latin homilies on the Gospels
for the year from Lent to Quinquagesima.)

(i) Intelligamus quid paulus apostolus commemorauit de caritate . . .;

(ii) In illo tempore. Ductus est ihesus in desertum . . . Triginta annis
fratres dilectissimi uenit dominus ad baptismum . . .;

(iii) Audistis fratres in lectione beati pauli apostoli superius lecta . . .;

(iv) In illo tempore. Interrogauerunt ihesum discipuli eius dicentes.
Interrogantes discipuli dominum fratres karissimi quod scribe dicebat . . .;

(v) In illo tempore. Erat ihesus eiciens demonium . . . Attendite fratres
karissimi quanta tribulatio erat . . .;

(vi) In illo tempore. Cum subleuasset oculos ihesus . . . Oportet nos
fratres karissimi primum audire . . .;

(vii) In illo tempore. Egressus inde ihesus secessit in partes tyri et sido-
nis . . . Ipse dominus noster ihesus christus de iudea egressus . . .;

(viii) Dixit ihesus turbis iudeorum et principibus sacerdotum . . .
Dominus ac redemptor noster nullam maculam habuit . . .;

(ix) In illo tempore. Cum appropinquasset ihesus ierosolimis . . . In
lectione euangelica fratres karissimi audiuimus. quia redemptor
noster misit . . .;

(x) Hodie uolumus fratres karissimi ad implere et uerbum dicere de
passione domini . . .;

(xi) Fratres. Expurgate uetus fermentum ut sitis noua conspersio sicut
estis azimi . . .;

---

[1] Ker, *Catalogue*, p. xli.   [2] Ibid., p. 375.

(xii) In illo tempore. Maria magdalene et maria iacobi et salome . . . In hac lectione euangelica hoc primum dicendum est . . .;

(xiii) In illo tempore. Tomas unus de .xii. non erat cum eis quando uenit ihesus . . . Tomas non erat cum eis illis apostolis . . .;

(xiv) In illo tempore. Dixit ihesus discipulis suis. Ego sum pastor bonus . . . Ille bonus pastor semet ipsum tradidit et animam . . .;

(xv) In illo tempore. Dixit ihesus discipulis suis. Modicum et iam non uidebitis me. Iterum modicum et iam uidebitis me. hoc fratres dominus ante passionem suam dixit discipulis suis . . .;

(xvi) In illo tempore. Dixit ihesus discipulis suis. Uado ad eum qui misit me . . . Quando dixit uado ad eum . . .;

(xvii) In illo tempore. Dixit ihesus discipulis suis. amen amen dico uobis . . . Fratres karissimi ante aduentum domini redemptoris nullus in nomine filii petebat . . .;

(xviii) Iste Iacobus filius alphei fuit quia et frater domini nominatur. Tres enim sorores fuerunt . . . [seven lines altogether];

(xix) Confitemini alter utrum peccata uestra . . . Confitebor enim est. equivocatum nomen . . .;

(xx) In illo tempore. Dixit ihesus discipulis suis. Quis uestrum habebit amicus. et ibit ad illum media nocte . . . Audistis fratres karissimi qualem significationem . . .;

(xxi) In illo tempore. Recumbentibus xi. apostolis aparuit illis ihesus . . . Dominus noster ihesus christus fratres post resurrectionem suam uenit coram discipulis suis . . .;

(xxii) In illo tempore. Cum uenerit paraclitus quem ego . . . Ad hanc causam fratres karissimi predicauit dominus ante passionem suam . . .;

(xxiii) In illo tempore. Dixit ihesus discipulis suis Si quis diligit me sermonem . . . Audistis fratres karissimi in lectione euangelica domino dicente . . .;

(xxiv) In illo tempore. Erat homo ex phariseis nichodemus nomine . . . Pharisei iudei sunt mali . . .;

(xxv) In illo tempore. Dixit ihesus discipulis suis parabolam istam. homo quisdam erat diues . . . Querendum est nobis fratres quarum dominus nomen mendici nominauit lazari . . .;

(xxvi) In illo tempore. Dixit ihesus discipulis suis parabolam istam. homo quidam fecit cenam magnam . . . Quis est iste homo fratres;

(xxvii) In illo tempore. Erant appropinquantes ad ihesum publicani . . . Pius et misericors ac redemptor noster fratres karissimi. non denegauit manducare cum peccatoribus . . .;

(xxviii) In illo tempore. Dixit ihesus discipulis suis. amen dico uobis nisi habundauerit iusticia ... Timeamus fratres ista. ne forte assimulemur illis phariseis ...;

(xxix) In illo tempore. Uenit ihesus in partes cesaree philippi ... In lectione euangelica audistis fratres karissimi ...;

(xxx) In illo tempore. Cum turba plurima esset cum ihesu nec haberent ... Pius et misericors semper miserebitur illius turbe ...;

(xxxi) In illo tempore. Atendite a falsis prophetis qui ueniunt ... Multi prophete falsatores fratres ...;

(xxxii) Fratres. Non simus concupiscentes malorum. sicut illi concupierunt. Paulus apostolus fratres dilectissimi doctor gentium ...;

(xxxiii) In illo tempore. Dixit ihesus discipulis suis. homo quidam erat diues qui habebat uillicum ... Quare exemplum dixit discipulis suis. fratres karissimi ...;

(xxxiv) In illo tempore. Cum appropinquasset ihesus ierusalem uidens ciuitatem illorum fleuit ... Fratres karissimi adtendite de flente domino ...;

(xxxv) In illo tempore. Duo homines ascenderunt in templum ut orarent ... Audistis fratres carissimi de lectione euangelica ...;

(xxxvi) In illo tempore. Exiens ihesus de finibus tyri. uenit per sidonem ... In lectione euangelica. audiuimus fratres karissimi quia exiens ...;

(xxxvii) In illo tempore. Dixit ihesus discipulis suis. Beati oculi qui uident que nos uidetis. Dico enim uobis quod multi prophete et reges cupiebant uidere ihesum ...;

(xxxviii) In illo tempore. Dum iret ihesus in ierusalem transiebat per mediam samariam et galileam ... Isti x. uiri leprosi fratres qui in euangelio commemorantur ...;

(xxxix) In illo tempore. Nemo potest duobus dominis seruire ... Dominus noster ammonet fratres et docet quod nullus potest seruire ...;

(xl) In illo tempore. Ibat ihesus in ciuitatem que uocatur naym. et ibant ... Multa mirabilia atque miracula fecit dominus fratres karissimi ...;

(xli) In illo tempore. Dixit ihesus discipulis suis. Simile est regnum celorum thesauro ... Thesaurus iste fratres karissimi de quo dominus ait ...;

(xlii) In illo tempore. Cum intrasset ihesus in domum cuidam principis ... Pius dominus ac redemptor noster non dignabatur ...;

(xliii) In illo tempore. Dixit ihesus discipulis suis. Arborem fici habebat quidam plantam . . . Arbor fici quam dominus noster ihesus christus fratres karissimi . . .;

(xliv) In illo tempore. Accesserunt ad ihesum saducei . . . Audiuimus fratres karissimi in lectione euangelica quod legis doctor . . .;

(xlv) In illo tempore. Ascendens ihesus in nauiculam . . . Secundum ystoriam fratres dominus in nauem ascendit . . .;

(xlvi) In illo tempore. Dixit ihesus discipulis suis. Simile est regnum celorum homini regi . . . Homo iste fratres qui fecit nuptias filio suo unigenito . . .;

(xlvii) In illo tempore. Erat quidam regulus cuius filius infirmabatur . . . Pius fratres karissimi rogabat centurio . . .;

(xlviii) In illo tempore. Dixit ihesus discipulis suis. Simile est regnum celorum homini regi . . . Audistis fratres dilectissimi quomodo dominus adsimulauit regnum celorum . . .;

(xlix) In illo tempore. Abeuntes pharisey inierunt ut caperent . . . Pessimi iudei fratres karissimi semper . . .;

(l) In illo tempore. Loquente ihesu ad turbas ecce princeps . . . Loquente dominum fratres. et predicantem et multa mirabilia facientem . . .;

(li) In illo tempore. Dixit ihesus discipulis suis. Simile est regnum celorum homini qui seminauit . . . Audiuimus fratres karissimi quod dominus assimilauit . . .;

(lii) In illo tempore. Ambulabat ihesus iuxta mare galilee . . . Dominus ac redemptor noster fratres karissimi uocauit et ait. Uenite . . .;

(liii) In illo tempore. Dixit ihesus discipulis suis. Erunt signa in sole et luna et stellis . . . Dominus ac redemptor noster fratres karissimi paratos nos . . .;

(liv) In illo tempore. Dixit ihesus discipulis suis parabolam hanc. homo quidam peregre proficiscens . . . homo iste fratres karissimi de quo audistis in lectione euangelica . . .;

(lv) In illo tempore. Cum audisset iohannes in uinculis opera christi . . . Querendum nobis fratres karissimi cur iohannes propheta . . .;

(lvi) In illo tempore. Miserunt iudei ab ierosolimis sacerdotes . . . Ex predicationei [sic] huius lectionis nobis uerbis iohannis . . .;

(lvii) In illo tempore. Dixit ihesus discipulis suis. Ecce ego mitto uos sicut . . . Ecce ego mitto uos in mundum. christianitatem facere . . .;

(lviii) In principio erat uerbum . . . In lectione euangelica fratres karissimi . . .;

(lix) In illo tempore. Postquam consummati sunt dies octo . . . Dominus ac redemptor noster fratres karissimi non uenit soluere legem sed ad implere . . .;

(lx) In illo tempore. Cum natus esset ihesus in bhetleem [*sic*] . . . Dominus ac redemptor noster fratres dilectissimi quando natus fuit in iudea . . .;

(lxi) In illo tempore. Cum factus esset ihesus annorum .xii. ascendentibus . . . Fratres dilectissimi dominus semper fuit et est et erit sine fine . . .;

(lxii) In illo tempore. Nuptie facte sunt in chana galilee . . . Dominus ac redemptor noster fratres karissimi inuitatus fuit ad nuptias . . .;

(lxiii) In illo tempore. Cum descendisset ihesus de monte: ecce leprosus . . . In diebus illis fratres karissimi multa turba ueniebat ad dominum . . .;

(lxiv) In illo tempore. [A]scendente ihesu in nauiculam secuti sunt eum discipuli eius . . . Querendum est istoria fratres karissimi quod dominus in nauicula fuit et discipuli eius . . .;

(lxv) In illo tempore. Dixit ihesus discipulis suis. Simile est regnum celorum homini patrifamilias qui exiit . . . Audistis fratres dilectissimi in lectione euangelica quali similitudinem . . .;

(lxvi) In illo tempore. Cum turba plurima conueniret. et de ciuitatibus . . . Dominus noster fratres karissimi dixit per similitudinem et postmodum . . .;

(lxvii) In illo tempore. Assumpsit ihesus .xii. discipulos suos. et ait illis. Ecce ascendimus iherosolimam . . . Dominus noster fratres karissimi commemorauit de passione sua quia appropinquabat . . .

Section (b) is a collection of sixty-seven short homilies all in Latin and arranged mainly in the order of the church year, running from Lent to Quinquagesima. The homilies are mostly for Sundays, but other occasions are occasionally treated. Two texts are sometimes supplied for one occasion, one on the Epistle and one on the New Testament pericope.[1] Although the texts do not derive from any known homiliary, they clearly rely heavily on the Church Fathers and, since they do not appear elsewhere, may be a fairly recent rewriting of inherited patristic teaching. Their brevity and simplicity suggest that they may have been intended for liturgical use, for preaching or reading aloud rather than for private reading. They may have been included in an otherwise Old English manuscript because they were

---

[1] For example, nos. xix (on Jas. v. 16–20) and xx (on Luke xi. 5–13) for *In Letania Maiore*, and nos. xxxii (on 1 Cor. x. 6–13) and xxxiii (on Luke xvi. 1–9) for the Tenth Sunday after Pentecost.

thought suitable for a readership or audience whose first language was English and whose knowledge of Latin was limited. Certainly the inclusion of a section written entirely in Latin argues strongly against an exclusively antiquarian motive behind the compilation of the manuscript.

Section (c)

6. fols. 1-4. *Incipit liber catholicorum sermonum anglice in anno .I. sermo ad populum de inicio creature*. An angin is alræ ðingæ . . . CH I i, p. 8.

7. fols. 4ᵛ–6ᵛ. Erat homo ex phariseis . . . Sum phariseisc mon wæs ihaten nichodemus . . . Pope xii (First Sunday after Pentecost).

8. fols. 6ᵛ–8. *Ewangelium*. Sume men nuten iwiss for heoræ nytennessæ . . . Pope viii (Fifth Sunday after Easter).

9. fols. 8–10. Erat quidam regulus . . . Ure hælend com hwilon . . . Irvine i (Twenty-second Sunday after Pentecost).

10. fols. 10–11ᵛ. Simile est regnum celorum homini regi . . . Cristes iwunæ wæs . . . Irvine ii (Twenty-third Sunday after Pentecost). [Fol. 11ᵛ, ll. 24 ff. is blank.]

11. fols. 12–14ᵛ. *De patientia Iob and Constantia. quomodo in dolore firmus in fide perseuerauerit*. Mine ȝebroðræ we rædeþ nu æt godes þenunge . . . CH II xxx (First Sunday in September).

12. fols. 14ᵛ–20ᵛ. Her onginnæð to sæcgæn be þam treowe . . . (Anonymous history of the holy rood-tree, ed. Napier, 1894).[1]

Section (c) consists of seven items (items 6–12). The first (item 6), the opening homily of CH I, a summary of Christian history, comes from a source representing the very earliest stage of the textual development of the First Series (the α phase). The next four (items 7–10) are a group of late homilies by Ælfric for the First Sunday after Pentecost, the Fifth or Sixth Sunday after Easter, and the Twenty-second and Twenty-third Sundays after Pentecost. Post-dating the *Catholic Homilies*, they probably represent the latest known phase in Ælfric's development of his homilies (TH II). Although items 7 and 8 belong as well to TH I (the earlier phase providing a series for the Proper of the Season from Christmas to the Sunday after Pentecost), they would have been retained for TH II. Items 9 and 10 must have belonged only to the TH II phase when new homilies for hitherto unfurnished Sundays after Pentecost were required. The four items

---

[1] Arthur S. Napier, *History of the Holy Rood-Tree*, EETS, os, 103 (London, 1894). For a recently discovered manuscript copy of this text, see N. R. Ker, 'A supplement to *Catalogue of Manuscripts Containing Anglo-Saxon*', *ASE*, v (1976), 121–31 (no. 73).

together, then, probably derive directly or indirectly from a copy of the
TH II collection, possibly one related to U, an eleventh-century
manuscript with Canterbury connections. TH II probably consisted
of two volumes dividing at Easter (since Easter was a standard
dividing-point in Latin homiliaries), and U is likely to be the second
volume (ending imperfectly) of a copy of the TH II set.[1] The four
items in B were not copied from that manuscript itself, but may have
derived from one very like it.[2] It is therefore surprising that the four
items do not include any of the *Catholic Homilies*, which must have
formed the bulk of a TH II set. Since most of the *Catholic Homilies*
items for Sundays after Pentecost appear elsewhere in the volume, it is
possible that B's compiler was selecting from TH II in the light of
those. But other evidence suggests this is unlikely: TH II included
several other new homilies as well as CH II xxiii (for the Third Sunday
after Pentecost), which do not appear at any point in this manuscript.
Probably only fragments of TH II had come down to the compiler.
This may suggest that the compiler of B had available to him for this
section only a small collection of texts at a time, perhaps in the form of
a booklet.[3]

The remaining two items show different origins again. Ælfric's
Second Series homily on Job (item 11) is quite different in character
from the others and derives from a source shared with the twelfth-
century manuscript G, going back in turn to the common source of
CDEF, possibly the same source as furnished the three Second Series
items in section (a). The final item is a copy of the anonymous *History
of the Holy Rood-tree*. The source of this copy has been identified by
Bertram Colgrave and Ann Hyde in three fragments of an eleventh-
century manuscript, Kansas University MS Pryce C2, item 1 (one
fragment) and CCCC 557 (two fragments).[4] The fragments apparently
come from Worcester, since they were glossed by the Worcester
'tremulous' hand, and their direct relation to B may indicate that B

---

[1] Clemoes, 'Chronology', p. 233.

[2] See the introduction to Pope xii: 'B, as in homily viii, shows greater affinity with U
than with M, but is not a direct descendant of U, for it sometimes supports readings in
M against U' (p. 476).

[3] For the type of booklets that might have been available, see Pam R. Robinson,
'Self-contained units in composite manuscripts of the Anglo-Saxon period', *ASE*, vii
(1978), 231–8.

[4] 'Two Recently Discovered Leaves from Old English Manuscripts', *Speculum*,
xxxvii (1962), 60–78. The CCCC 557 fragments were first identified by N. R. Ker in 'An
Eleventh-Century Old English Legend of the Cross before Christ', *Medium Ævum*, ix
(1940), 84–5.

itself is connected with Worcester.[1] The unsuitability of the item as a preaching text strongly argues against categorizing the manuscript as a primary resource for preachers.

Section (d)

13. fols. 21–3. Đe hælend crist syðöan he to þisse liue com . . . CH I xix, p. 258 (the Lord's Prayer).

14. fols. 23^v–26^v. *Passio sancti laurentii martyris .IIII^{to}. ides augusti*. On decies dæiʒe þæs wælreowan caseres . . . CH I xxix, p. 416 (St. Laurence).

15. fols. 26^v–30. *Passio sancti bartholomei apostoli .VIII. kl. septembris*. Wyrdwriteræs sæcgæð þet öreo leodscipæs . . . CH I xxxi, p. 454.

16. fols. 30–33^v. *Natiuitas sancte marie*. Men öa leofeste wuröie we nu . . . Assmann x.

17. fols. 33^v–35. *Passio sancti mathei apostoli .X. kl octobris*. þe apostol matheus and godspellere . . . CH II xxxii.

18. fols. 35–39^v. *Incipit uita sancti martini episcopi .III. idus nouembris*. Sulpicius hatte sum snoter writere . . . LS xxxi (with several sections omitted).

19. fols. 39^v–41. *Dominica X post pentecosten*. Dixit ihesus ad quosdam . . . Drihten sæde þis biʒspel bi sumum monnum . . . CH II xxviii (Twelfth Sunday after Pentecost).

20. fols. 41–42^v. *Euuangelium*. Men þa leofeste hwilon ær we sæden eow þo`ne´ pistol . . . CH II xxix (Assumption of the Virgin).

21. fols. 42^v–45. *Dominica III post epiphaniam domini*. Cum autem descendisset iesus . . . Matheus öe godspellere wrat on öissere godspellice redinge . . . CH I viii, p. 120.

22. fols. 45–47^v. *XXVII. idus. martii cathedra sancti petri apostoli*. We cwæöæö on ʒerimcræfte . . . LS x.

23. fols. 47^v–50. *Annuntiatio sancte marie*. Ure almihtiʒ s`c´uppend öe öe alle isceaftæ . . . CH I xiii, p. 192.

24. fol. 50^{rv}. *Dominica in septuagesima*. We wyllæö sæcgæn bi þisse andwearde tide . . . CH II v, ll. 234ff. (the note on Alleluia which follows the homily for Septuagesima).

25. fols. 50^v–52^v. *Simile est regnum celorum homini patrifamilias* . . . Se hælend cwæö þæt heofene rice . . . CH II v (Septuagesima).

26. fols. 52^v–54^v. *Dominica in sextagesima*. Cum turba plurima . . . On sumere tide þa þa mucel meniu . . . CH II vi.

---

[1] For an authoritative discussion of the tremulous hand, see C. Franzen, *The Tremulous Hand of Worcester A Study of Old English in the Thirteenth Century* (Oxford, 1991).

27. fols. 54ᵛ–56ᵛ. *Dominica in quinquagessima.* Assumpsit iesus duo-decim discipulos . . . Her is ired on þisse godspelle . . . CH I x, p. 152.

28. fols. 56ᵛ–58ᵛ. *Dominica .I. quadragessime.* Men þa leofeste ic cyðe eow þæt ðreo þing . . . Pr. Belfour v, p. 40; coll. Förster iii, p. 53 (Vercelli iii, elsewhere for the Second Sunday in Lent).

29. fols. 58ᵛ–60. *Dominica secunda in quadragessima.* Men þa leofeste we wyllæð her specan feawum wordum . . . Belfour vi, p. 50 (elsewhere for the Fourth Sunday in Lent).

30. fols. 60–2. *Natale sancti andree apostoli.* Ambulans iesus . . . Crist on sume tide ferde wið þare galileiscen sæ . . . CH I xxxviii, p. 576 (omits the *passio*). (Ends) ȝeornlice fylle; (p. 586, l. 27) beo wuldor and lof hælende criste a on alræ woruldæ woruld a buton ende amen.

31. fols. 62–4. *Natale sancti eadmundi regis et martyris.* Sum swyðe ilæred munuc . . . LS xxxii. [Fol. 64, ll. 15 ff. and fol. 64ᵛ were originally blank. They were filled later with a sermon by Augustine headed *Dedicatione ecclesie*, and a sequence with music; see Ker, *Catalogue*, items 87, 88.]

Section (d) contains nineteen items altogether: thirteen from Ælfric's *Catholic Homilies*, three from his *Lives of Saints*, two anony-mous homilies and an anonymous account of the Nativity of the Blessed Virgin Mary (from the Gospel of Pseudo-Matthew).

Items 14 (St. Laurence), 15 (St. Bartholomew) and 30 (St. Andrew) are First Series homilies from a late phase of development (the ϵ phase), a type that does not appear in DEF. Various other First Series homilies in sections (e) and (f) also belong to this phase.

Items 17, 19, and 20 are Second Series homilies showing the same textual origins as item 11 in section (c) (the Second Series homily on Job): they derive from a source shared with G, going back in turn to the common source of CDEF.

Items 23, 24–5, 26, and 27 are First and Second Series homilies deriving from a source shared with the first part of E (E(a)) and going back in turn to the common source of CDEF. Although the Second Series texts are not in G, other Second Series evidence suggests that a source shared with G intervenes between B and BE's common source.[1] (This may well be physically the same manuscript as the source of items 17, 19, and 20.) Only short extracts of the two First Series texts are in G,[2] and these offer no evidence for or against this

---

[1] CH II, p. xxxix.
[2] Ker, *Catalogue*, no. 209, items 52, 53.

intervening source shared with G. A simple stemma might be drawn up as follows:

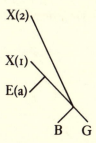

Items 28 and 29, the two anonymous homilies assigned to the First and Second Sundays in Lent, probably have the same immediate origins as items 23–7. Item 28's text is related to that of DEF, and is perhaps derived from the same copy as the one used by E and F.[1] In DEF, however, the homily is specifically assigned to the Second Sunday in Lent, not the First. D and E contain CH II vii for the First Sunday, and F contains both CH I xi and CH II vii for the First Sunday in Lent. For item 29, B is textually close again to D and E; probably B's item 29 descends, like item 28, from the copy used by E. Just as D and E assign item 28 to the Second Sunday in Lent, not the First, so they assign item 29 to the Fourth Sunday in Lent, not the Second.

The closeness in content of the whole sequence of items 23–9 to D and E(a) should be particularly noted. B, D, and E(a) all include the same homilies for the Annunciation, Septuagesima, Sexagesima, Quinquagesima, as well as for the First and Second Sundays in Lent (although the latter are assigned to different occasions in B). All three manuscripts also omit certain texts. None has Ælfric's First Series text for the First Sunday in Lent (E's copy is added in supplementary quires). It is interesting that G too, which relates closely to the DEF tradition, has no material for Lent (except for extracts from a homily for the Third Sunday in Lent).[2] Historical transmission must account for B's omission of Ælfric's homilies for Lent and inclusion instead of the anonymous texts; it is inconceivable that B's compiler would deliberately exclude Ælfric's homilies if they were available.

Items 13 and 21 are First Series homilies of the β phase, possibly

---

[1] See D. G. Scragg, 'The corpus of vernacular homilies and prose saints' lives before Ælfric', *ASE*, viii (1979), 223–77, p. 244.

[2] Ker, *Catalogue*, no. 209, item 20.

having the same origins as items 17, 19 and 20, that is, belonging to the DEF tradition but not in the same ways as items 23–7 because they do not derive from the source shared with E. A stemma incorporating Clemoes's discussion of CDEF may be useful here:

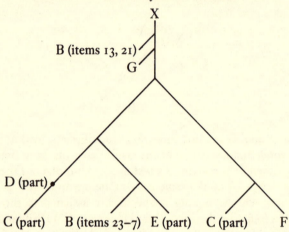

Items 18 (St. Martin), 22 (Throne of St. Peter), and 31 (St. Edmund) are three items from the *Lives of Saints*. It is difficult to ascertain how they might have reached B. They are unlikely to have come from the source shared with G or the DEF tradition: G's compiler shows an interest in saints' lives and biblical narrative but lacks these, and the *Lives of Saints* items in E and F seem to be supplementary texts, not part of the inherited collection. Possibly they came from a collection of pieces for saints' days which also provided items 14, 15, and 30, First Series homilies of a late phase for saints' days. Apparently Ælfric himself did not circulate such texts in a composite collection, but such combinations do appear in other manuscripts, for example, f[k].[1]

The same collection may have provided item 16 for the Nativity of the Blessed Virgin Mary (Assmann x). This is not, as one might have expected, Ælfric's First Series homily for the occasion, but rather a post-Ælfrician piece drawing on the Gospel of Pseudo-Matthew. Since the Ælfrician homily (Assmann iii) is in Q, a manuscript of the ε phase to which the First Series homilies in section (d) are related, it is particularly strange that the anonymous homily drawing on the apocryphal gospel appears in preference to it.[2] Possibly the compiler

---

[1] See Clemoes, 'Chronology', pp. 235–6.
[2] See supplementary introduction to Assmann by Peter Clemoes, p. xxix.

of the source-collection chose Assmann x in preference to Assmann iii because it was pure narrative not exegesis.[1]

Section (d), then, seems to be drawing on two main lines of transmission. Items 13, 17, 19–21, and 23–9 may all derive from a rather mixed collection drawing on the same manuscript tradition as DEF (via the last common source of B and G), and the others (items 14–16, 18, 22, 30, 31) mainly come from another mixed collection containing First Series and *Lives of Saints* items (and, probably, Assmann x).

The relationship between the groupings of the items by textual origins and their manuscript order appears quite arbitrary. There is one way, however, by which this might be explained. Short sequences chronologically ordered according to the church year are found throughout section (d) and these cut across the groupings by textual origins. Items 14–18, for example, are texts for saints' days chronologically arranged: Laurence (10 August), Bartholomew (24 August), Nativity of the Blessed Virgin Mary (8 September), Matthew (21 September), Martin (11 November). The chronological ordering cannot be coincidental, since items 14 and 15 at least are from a different line of transmission from the others. The subsequent two items, 19 and 20, which derive from the BG source, treat occasions falling within the period covered by the previous saints' narratives: the Twelfth Sunday after Pentecost and the Assumption (15 August). It seems that a compiler may have selected saints' narratives for occasions within a certain period (mainly August–September), then selected two other texts for occasions falling in that period. This type of grouping is parallelled in other manuscripts. In D, for example, texts for saints' days (St. Gregory (12 March), St. Cuthbert (20 March), St. Benedict (21 March), and the Annunciation (25 March)) are followed by texts for Sundays in the same period (Septuagesima, Sexagesima, Quinquagesima, the various Lenten Sundays, Palm Sunday, and so on).[2] In C, homilies for occasions in the first half of the year (excluding saints' days) are grouped together, followed by homilies for saints' days in the second half of the year, then homilies for the Common of Saints, then homilies for occasions in the second half of the year, excluding saints' days.

A new chronological sequence begins at item 21 and extends

---

[1] It is very unlikely that item 16 comes from the source B has in common with G, since G demonstrates much interest in Marian texts (with three homilies on the Assumption of the Virgin as well as a note on her parents and kindred), but lacks this piece.

[2] Ker, *Catalogue*, no. 309, items 11 ff.

through to item 29: the Third Sunday after Epiphany, St. Peter (22 February), Annunciation, Septuagesima, Sexagesima, Quinquagesima, First Sunday in Lent, Second Sunday in Lent. Here the items all probably have the same immediate origin, although item 22 (St. Peter) is from the First Series and *Lives of Saints* line, and must at some stage have been inserted because it was chronologically appropriate.

The compiler of B was clearly not himself concerned with chronological ordering, for the manuscript as a whole is not arranged at all consistently. It can be contrasted with C, for example, which has the same kind of complexity in its textual origins but is chronologically ordered throughout. We have to conclude that for section (d) the compiler of B was selecting from manuscripts (or a manuscript) already arranged chronologically.

Despite the compiler's own lack of concern with chronological ordering, section (d) presents a series of short chronological sequences which mingle material of different origins. In order to account for this, we need first to consider more closely the short sequence drawn from the DEF tradition via a source shared with E(a), items 23–9. Its relation to E(a) is particularly interesting. E(a), consisting of thirty-nine homilies, is the first two-thirds of a large, orderly two-volume homiliary more fully preserved in D.[1] (The last third may have been lost after E was produced or already missing from E's exemplar.) The common source of B and E(a), then, was a well-organized collection of at least thirty-nine homilies. B has only six of these, items 23–9, preserving a sequence present in E, but lacking three further Lenten items.[2] E(a) is written as three booklets, though derived from a single source; B's sequence corresponds to the end of the first booklet, with only one of the Lenten items (Assmann xii) to follow before the booklet ends. Since B's compiler proceeds to copy items for the immediate post-Lent period in section (e) without showing any parallels with the E(a) homiliary, although that period is covered at the beginning of E(a)'s next booklet, it looks probable that E(a)'s exemplar was itself written in booklets and that only the first booklet was drawn on for B (and not even the whole of that booklet, since B's compiler would probably have used the items before the Annunciation if they had been available).[3]

This sequence, as I suggested above, seems to have come to B via a

[1] See Sisam, *Studies*, pp. 154–6.
[2] Ker, *Catalogue*, no. 48, items 14–19, correspond to those in B.
[3] See further Robinson, 'Self-contained units', pp. 235–8.

source shared with G, a source which also contained a number of other homilies drawn from the DEF tradition by a different line of transmission. These included many Second Series homilies for the second half of the year, but also some from the First Series and some for the early part of the year. From this collection came items 1, 2, 4, 11, 13, 17, 19, 20, 21, the sequence of items 23–9, and possibly item 58 from section (e). Judging from their distribution in sections (a), (c), (d), and possibly (e) in B, they had already been broken up into small, not very orderly groups in the exemplar(s). Possibly items 12, 16, 18, and 22 (anonymous homilies and two of the *Lives of Saints*) came from this source too, but items 14, 15, and 30, from the ε phase of CH I, are more likely to have come from the source of section (e). Item 3 could also have come from the BG source, though its origins are different. It seems, then, that the short sequence of six items from E(a)'s source (that is, from the first booklet of a large well-organized homiliary) was one of a number of such short sequences, deriving ultimately from large collections, which came together in a composite but unordered collection subsequently drawn on for B sections (a), (c), and (d), and for G (which is as disordered as B). The texts with unconnected origins might at some stage have been added to the items from this BG collection wherever they were chronologically appropriate.

The most likely explanation seems to be that although the compiler of B himself has used a fairly large homiliary as his exemplar for this section, a previous compiler (or compilers) of that exemplar has worked from a whole series of smaller units or booklets. All the evidence suggests that at some stage an attempt has been made to put together chronological sequences from even smaller groups of texts. The booklets might have contained homilies in singles or doubles, perhaps already informally assembled in wrappers; sometimes several homilies might have been in one booklet (not necessarily chronologically arranged).

This hypothesis of the use of booklets in the course of transmission would account for both the short chronological sequences and the complexity of textual origins in section (d), and also for the complex and apparently arbitrary linking of items textually across the various sections of the manuscript. The idea is also supported by comparison with the make-up of other manuscripts. L, for example, seems to have been originally a number of distinct booklets which were gradually assembled into their present form. It consists of an original core (sermons on the lives of the apostles), then various additions with their own discernible order.[1] C includes texts which are related to the DEF line, some of which seem to be derived directly from F, some of which must have derived from D (though at least one copy must have intervened), and it also incorporates textually late Ælfrician homilies.[2] The complex textual origins of these two manuscripts can, as with B, best be explained by the use of booklets as exemplars. The scribes were apparently copying texts as they became available, rather than adhering to any obscure principle of selection.

Section (e)

32. fols. 65–6. *Dominica p[rima] de adue[ntu] domini.* þisses dæȝes ðenunȝ and ðissere tide mærð . . . CH I xxxix, p. 600.

33. fols. 66–67ᵛ. *Dominica secunda in adue[ntu domini].* Ðe Godspellere lucas awrat on ðissum dæȝðerlican godspelle . . . CH I xl, p. 608.

34. fols. 67ᵛ–69ᵛ. *In die natalis domini.* We willað to trumninȝe eowre leafa . . . CH I ii, p. 28.

35. fols. 69ᵛ–72. *Sermo in epiphania domini.* Ðes dæȝ is ihaten on bocum . . . CH II iii.

36. fols. 72–4. *Purificatio sancte marie.* Postquam impleti . . . God beadon ðære alde laȝe . . . CH I ix, p. 134.

37. fol. 74ʳᵛ. *De confessione.* Leofa man ic axie þe on drihtnes namen . . . Napier, lvi. A homily corresponding in part (pp. 289–90, *passim*) to a passage on confession printed most recently by Raith, p. xli,[3] and in part (p. 291, ll. 2–20) to the directions for a confessor in Oxford Bodleian Laud Misc. 482, fol. 46ᵛ (Ker, *Catalogue*, no. 343, item 17; compare also Napier xxix, p. 135, ll. 5–20).

38. fols. 74ᵛ–76ᵛ. *Dominica in ramis palmarum.* Cristes ðrowung wæs ired nu beforen us . . . CH I xiv, p. 206. [The words 'Circlice þeawæs forbeodoð to secgenne æniȝ spel on ðam ðrym swyȝdaȝas' (p. 218) follow the homily.]

39. fols. 76ᵛ–78ᵛ. *De resurrectione domini.* Maria magdalene et maria iacobi . . . Oft ȝe hyrdon embe ðæs hælendes ærist . . . CH I xv, p. 220.

40. fols. 78ᵛ–80ᵛ. *In letania maiore.* Ðas daȝas beoð ihatene letanie . . .

---

[1] W. Schipper, 'A Composite Old English Homiliary from Ely: Cambr. Univ. Libr. MS Ii. 1. 33', *Transactions of the Cambridge Bibliographical Society*, viii (1983), 285–98.

[2] CH II, pp. xxxv–xxxvi.

[3] J. Raith, ed., *Die altenglische Version des Halitgar'schen Bussbuches (sog. Poenitentiale Pseudo-Ecgberti*, Bibliothek der angelsächsischen Prosa, XIII (Hamburg, 1933, rpt. Darmstadt, 1964), pp. xli–xlvi; also printed in B. Thorpe, ed., *Ancient Laws and Institutes of England* (London, 1840), II, 130–6, and in R. Spindler, ed., *Das Altenglische Bussbuch (sog. Confessionale Pseudo-Egberti)* (Leipzig, 1934), pp. 170–5.

CH I xviii, p. 244. (The title *In letania maiore* is repeated after the Latin at fol. 79, l. 10.)

41. fols. 80ᵛ–83. *Sermo de ascensione domini.* Lucas þe godspelle us munode on ðisse pistol rædinge . . . CH I xxi, p. 294.

42. fols. 83–5. *In die sancto pentecosten.* Fram ðam halȝan æsterlican dæȝe beoð . . . CH I xxii, p. 310.

43. fols. 85–7. *Natiuitas Sancti iohannis Baptiste; VIII. kl. Iulii.* Ðe Godspellere lucas awrat on cristes bec be accænnednesse Iohannis . . . CH I xxv, p. 350.

44. fols. 87–8. *Passio sanctorum apostolorum petri et pauli.* Uenit iesus in partes . . . Matheus ðe godspellere wrat on ðære godspellicen isetnysse . . . CH I xxvi (first part), p. 364.

45. fols. 88–90. *De passione apostolorum petri et pauli.* We wyllað eafter ðisse godsplle [*sic*] eow ræccan . . . CH I xxvi (second part), p. 370.

46. fols. 90–92ᵛ. *Natale sancti pauli.* Godes laðung wyrðað þisne dæȝ . . . CH I xxvii, p. 384.

47. fols. 92ᵛ–95ᵛ. *De fide catholica.* Ælc cristene man sceal æfter rihte cunnan . . . CH I xx, p. 274.

48. fols. 95ᵛ–97. *Circumscisio domini.* Ðe Godspellere lucas beleac . . . CH I vi, p. 90.

49. fols. 97–98ᵛ. *Secundum Lucam.* Homo quidam erat diues et induebatur . . . þe wældendæ drihten sæde þis biȝspel . . . CH I xxiii, p. 328 (Second Sunday after Pentecost).

50. fols. 98ᵛ–100ᵛ. *Secundum Lucam.* Erant adpropinquantes . . . þæt haliȝe godspel us sæð þæt refan and synfulle men . . . CH I xxiv, p. 338 (Fourth Sunday after Pentecost).

51. fols. 100ᵛ–103. *Secundum Lucam.* Cum appropinquaret iesus . . . On summere tide wæs ðe hælend farende . . . CH I xxviii, p. 402 (Eleventh Sunday after Pentecost).

52. fols. 103–104ᵛ. *Secundum Lucam.* Ibat iesus in ciuitatem que uocatur naim . . . Ure drihten ferde to sumere buriȝ . . . CH I xxxiii, p. 490 (Seventeenth Sunday after Pentecost).

53. fols. 104ᵛ–107ᵛ. *Secundum Matheum.* Loquebatur iesus . . . Drihten wæs specende on sumere tide . . . CH I xxxv, p. 520 (Twenty-first Sunday after Pentecost).

54. fols. 107ᵛ–110. *Secundum Iohannem.* Preteriens iesus . . . Ure drihten ðe mildheortæ hælend . . . Irvine iii (Ælfric, Wednesday in the Fourth week of Lent).

55. fols. 110–13. *Assumptio sancte marie.* Hieronimus ðe halȝa sacerd wrat ænne pistol . . . CH I xxx, p. 436.

56. fols. 113–114ᵛ. *Festiuitas omnium sanctorum*. Haliȝe larweas sædon þæt seo ȝeleaffule ȝelaðung . . . CH I xxxvi (first part), p. 538.

57. fols. 114ᵛ–116. *Secundum Matheum*. Uidens iesus turbas . . . Ðæt haliȝe godspel þe lutle ær ætforen eow iræd . . . CH I xxxvi (second part of homily for All Saints), p. 548.

58. fols. 116–117ᵛ. *In octaua apostolorum petri et pauli*. Matheus þe god-spellere awrat on cristes bec . . . CH II xxiv.

59. fols. 117ᵛ–119ᵛ. *Iacobi apostoli*. On ðissum dæȝe we wurðiæð on ure lofsange . . . CH II xxvii.

60. fols. 119ᵛ–121ᵛ. *Plurimorum martyrum*. Cum audieritis . . . De hælend foresæde his leorningcnihtum . . . CH II xxxvii.

61. fols. 121ᵛ–122. *Unius martiris*. Amen amen dico uobis nisi granum frumenti . . . Soð soð ic eow secge . . . Irvine iv (Ælfric, second part of homily for St. Vincent).

62. fols. 122–4. *Unius confessoris*. Homo quidam peregre . . . Ure drihten sæde þis biȝspel his leorningcnihtæs . . . CH II xxxviii.

63. fols. 124–6. *Plurimarum uirginum*. Simile est regnum celorum decem uirginibus . . . þe hælend sæde biȝspel ilomlice be ȝehwilce þingum . . . CH II xxxix.

64. fols. 126–128ᵛ. *De doctrina sancti Gregorii*. Men ða leofeste cwæð sanctus gregorius . . . Old English version of the *Visio Sancti Pauli*. Napier, xlvi, p. 232.[1] [Fol. 128ᵛ, ll. 25 ff. is blank.]

Section (e) consists of thirty-three items (nos. 32–64). A large number of these have the same textual origin: items 32–4, 36, 39, 42–6, 48- 53, and 55–7 are nineteen First Series homilies all belonging to the ϵ phase.[2] Items 38, 40, 41, and 47 are four First Series homilies of an earlier type (probably between the α and β phases). Item 35, a Second Series homily of a late type, related to the second-recension manu-script R, is perhaps to be associated by transmission with the large group of First Series homilies of the ϵ phase, but its isolation suggests it derives from some other source, perhaps the exemplar of R (since it shares some errors and authentic revisions with R).[3] Item 54 is appar-ently a late composition of the TH I or TH II stage, and also might have the same immediate origin as those First Series items.[4]

Item 37, rubricated *De Confessione*, is a miscellaneous anonymous

---

[1] See also Scragg, 'The corpus of vernacular homilies', p. 251.

[2] The precise relations of each item within the ϵ phase First Series manuscripts, not relevant here, will be examined by Clemoes in his forthcoming edition.

[3] CH II, p. xxxix.

[4] See below p. 48 for a discussion of its textual origin.

text, presumably intended as a Lenten item. It resembles partly the passage on confession in the Pseudo-Egbert confessional, and partly the directions for a confessor in Bodleian MS Laud Misc. 482.[1] There are parallels also with the composite Napier xxix in T and the exhortations to confession in CCCC 320.[2] The item's textual origins are however obscure. The likely explanation for its inclusion here is its Lenten associations; it was probably inserted into the sequence at some stage in transmission owing to its appropriate subject-matter.

Item 58 is a Second Series homily probably having the same source as items 1, 2, and 4 in section (a), item 11 in section (c), and items 17, 19, and 20 in section (d), that is, deriving from a source shared with G, which goes back in turn to the common source of CDEF. Items 59, 60, 62, and 63 are Second Series homilies of a different textual origin, probably going back to another first recension archetype similar to K. Item 61 for the Common of a Martyr presumably derives from the same exemplar as the Second Series sequence for saints' days. Ultimately it probably goes back to a *Lives of Saints* collection. It does not appear in any other manuscript, but it is the second part of a homily whose first part, the *Passio*, is the narrative of St. Vincent in L.[3]

Item 64, rubricated *De doctrina sancti Gregorii*, is partly an Old English version of the *Visio Sancti Pauli*,[4] and partly a series of injunctions to perform good works and avoid evil, which survives independently elsewhere in T, where it is one of a number of texts inserted into a copy of *Polity*.[5] Item 64 seems to be a miscellaneous piece included, probably from another source, as a means of filling up the quire.

Once again chronology may provide the key to understanding the compilation of section (e) of B. The first close chronological sequence comprises texts for the First and Second Sundays in Advent, Christmas, Epiphany, and Purification (items 32–6). They are all First Series homilies belonging to the ϵ phase, except for the homily for Epiphany (item 35) which is from the Second Series. The next item is the miscellaneous *De Confessione*, probably interpolated at some stage as a Lenten text. The missing homilies for occasions from Septuagesima to

---

[1] Ker, *Catalogue*, no. 343, item 17.

[2] See K. Jost, *Wulfstanstudien* (Bern, 1950), p. 203, and Scragg, 'The corpus of vernacular homilies', p. 244. M. R. Godden, 'An Old English penitential motif', *ASE*, ii (1973), 221–39, discusses the relationship of the various texts in the context of a recurring motif.

[3] Clemoes, 'Chronology', p. 236n. See further pp. 77–98 below.

[4] Bethurum, p. 43.

[5] Scragg, 'The corpus of vernacular homilies', p. 251.

Lent may well have been deliberately omitted from the sequence by the Bodley compiler because they or equivalents were already in section (d). The chronological sequence is picked up again with the homily for Palm Sunday, proceeding through Easter, the Greater Litany and the Ascension to Pentecost (items 38–42); they are all First Series texts but items 38, 40, and 41 represent a different textual origin from those of the main ε phase sequence. Items 43–6 are a group of three saints' days, all First Series homilies textually linked to the main sequence, which follows chronologically from Pentecost: the Nativity of John the Baptist (24 June), Peter and Paul (29 June), Paul (30 June). The next two items (items 47 and 48) have been inserted with no heed to chronology; the texts are for Wednesday in Rogationtide and the Circumcision (1 January). Both are First Series homilies; the second, according to its textual origins, should belong to the main chronological sequence. The intrusion of these two texts may be the result of misplaced or unordered booklets at some stage in transmission.

The chronological sequence continues with a group of homilies for the Second, Fourth, Eleventh, Seventeenth, and Twenty-first Sundays after Pentecost (items 49–53). All of these belong textually to the original First Series sequence; all are rubricated *Secundum Lucam* or *Secundum Matheum* rather than assigned to a specific day.

With item 54, the chronological ordering is again interrupted: the homily's pericope is for Wednesday in the Fourth Week of Lent. The rubric pattern *Secundum Iohannem* suggests, however, that the homily may derive from the same immediate exemplar as items 49–53.

Items 55–7 show a return to homilies for saints' days: the Assumption (15 August), All Saints (1 November). Both belong textually to the main First Series group. They overlap chronologically with the earlier sequence for Sundays after Pentecost, and they represent most of the homilies for saints days in the latter part of the church year (after Paul (item 46 in B)) which have not already been included earlier in the manuscript.[1] Probably the compiler of B omitted them here because he had them already in section (d).

Items 58–63 are a series of texts for saints' days, some for the Proper, some for the Common of Saints. They are derived mainly from the Second Series: item 58, however, has a different textual origin from all the other Second Series texts, and item 61 is not from the Second Series but probably from a *Lives of Saints* collection. The texts are in

---

[1] The exceptions are Decollation of St. John the Baptist (CH I xxxii), St. Michael (CH I xxxiv) which is included in section (f) of B, and Clement (CH I xxxvii).

their usual Second Series order. They may represent selections from a fuller Second Series set, the scribe of B thereby omitting items already included in earlier sections of the manuscript.

Art. 64, *De doctrina sancti Gregorii*, stands independently, possibly acting as no more than a quire-filler.

If we relate this chronological analysis more closely to the textual origins of the various items, the following conclusions can be drawn. The original basis of section (e) seems to have been a sequence of eighteen First Series homilies running from Advent to All Saints; this comprises all those belonging to the ε phase except for item 48 (Circumcision) which is chronologically out of order. This sequence was gradually expanded in transmission by items from other sources: five more First Series items (consisting of item 48, and the four items (38, 40, 41, and 47) belonging to an earlier phase); one Second Series item from a source related to R (item 35); another Second Series item from a source related to DEF (item 58); four more Second Series homilies from yet another line of transmission (items 59, 60, 62, and 63); one item from the *Lives of Saints* (item 61); one late Ælfrician text (item 54); one Lenten text on confession (item 37); and the final composite item. The complete First Series items, twenty-three in all, themselves contain a very coherent sequence from Ælfric's revised First Series, and may derive from an otherwise unknown adaptation of the First Series. The sequence runs from Advent to All Saints, but omits occasions already covered in B and is filled out (by either B or a predecessor) with the various other items, mainly from the Second Series. The Second Series items could have come from a fuller set, with the scribe of B omitting from it items already included in earlier sections. The source of the last part of section (e), then, would not be just a group of Second Series homilies for saints' days, but a fairly complete set of the second half of the Second Series (lacking only CH II xxiii, xxxiii, and xxxiv, the last of which is made redundant anyway by LS xxxi (Martin)).

Section (f)

65. fols. 129–32. *De ueteri testamento et nouo*. Ðe ælmihtiȝæ scyppend þa þa he englæs isceop . . . Crawford, pp. 18–51 (Ælfric, summary of the Old Testament). A leaf is missing between fol. 130, ending 'wiðsette heoræ feondum', and fol. 131, beginning 'to chaldea londe'.

66. fols. 132–3. *Sermo de baptismate*. Leofe men ealle cristenum

manne is mycel neod þæt heo heora fuluhtes scead witan ...
Bethurum viii c.

67. fols. 133–7. Ælfricus abbas Wulfstano uenerabili archiepiscopo
salutem ... Us biscopum dafenað þæt we ða boclican lare ... Fehr,
Brief II, p. 69 [corrections on p. 269].

68. fols. 137–140ᵛ. *De secunda epistola quando diuidis crisma*. Ealæ
(*altered in red to* Eallæ) ᵹe mæssepreostas mine ᵹebroðre we secgæð
eow nu ... Fehr, Brief III, p. 147.

69. fols. 140ᵛ–141ᵛ. Spiritus sanctus septenaria operatione ... Isayas
þe witegæ wrat on his witegunge ... Napier 1883, Latin introduction
to vii and whole of viii [pp. 50, 56].

70. fols. 141ᵛ–143ᵛ. *Secundum marcum*. Interrogatus iesus a discipulis
de consummacione seculi dixit eis. Cum uideritis ... Leofa men Ure
drihtines apostoli axodon hine sylfne embe þissere weorlde endunge
... Coll. Bethurum, v, i b, and iv.

71. fols. 143ᵛ–144ᵛ. *Sermo*. Leofæn Men Gecnawæð þæt soð is ...
Bethurum, xx.

72. fols. 144ᵛ–146ᵛ. *Sermones*. Leofæ Men. Us is deope beboden þæt
we ᵹeornlice mynᵹian and læran scylan ... Bethurum, vi.

73. fols. 146ᵛ–149ᵛ. *Dedicatio ecclesie*. Mine ᵹebroþræ þa leofestan we
wylleð sume drihtenlice spæce ... CH II xl.

74. fols. 149ᵛ–152. *Dedicacio sancti michaelis*. Moneᵹum is cuð þeo
haliᵹe steow sancti michaelis ... CH I xxxiv, p. 502.

75. fols. 152–154ᵛ. Nuptie quidem facte sunt ... Iohannes þe godspellere cwæð on þam godspellice lare ... CH II iv.

76. fol. 154ᵛ. Sancta maria wes ðreo and sixti winter ða heo of
middenærde ferde ... (Three lines only in a late twelfth or early
thirteenth-century hand in a space left blank.) Cross and Hill,
pp. 80 ff.[1]

Section (f) contains twelve items altogether (nos. 65–76). Four are
works by Wulfstan, Bishop of Worcester and Archbishop of York: his
homily on baptism (item 66), a composite homily (item 70), the *Sermo
Lupi ad Anglos* (item 71) and another homily (item 72). Three of these
(items 66, 71, and 72) share a line of transmission with one other manuscript, V, and not with any other manuscript copies.[2] Item 71's textual
history is of particular interest. Three versions of the text exist. B's
version (along with V's) is the shortest; it differs from the others

---

[1] James E. Cross and Thomas D. Hill, *The 'Prose Solomon and Saturn' and 'Adrian and Ritheus'* (Toronto, 1982).

[2] See Bethurum's stemma (pp. 14, 17, and 22) for her nos. vi, viii c, and xx.

mainly in lacking both the rubric and a lengthy passage on the disgraces to which the English were subjected by the Danish invaders.[1] It seems likely that B's version is not only the shortest but also the earliest.[2] The clause '7 Æþelred man dræfde ut of his earde' (Bethurum, p. 258, l. 71) is required to complete the first part of the sentence both in substance and stylistically, but is not included in the other versions. It must have been deliberately deleted in the latter, probably for political reasons.[3]

The fourth of Wulfstan's works in this section, item 70, is a composite homily which adapts and amalgamates three homilies by Wulfstan (Bethurum v, i b, and iv). For all three texts, B's copy follows a quite different line of transmission from the other manuscript copies.

The rest of the section (except the final added item) comprises works by Ælfric, but in many cases links with Wulfstan continue to emerge. The first item of the section (item 65) is a letter by Ælfric for the layman Sigeweard, rubricated with its full title *De ueteri testamento et nouo* though only the Old Testament is included here. According to Clemoes, Ælfric composed the text somewhere between TH I and the ε phase of the First Series.[4] It appears elsewhere only in one other manuscript, Z, and the two copies are textually very close; as Crawford notes, they must descend from a common original.[5] There is one significant difference between the two manuscript copies. Either the scribe of B or, more likely, the scribe of a previous exemplar has omitted passages in which Ælfric addresses a correspondent directly, making the text a more thoroughly impersonal and objective piece of biblical summary than its predecessor.

Two items (67 and 68) are letters concerning the duties of clergy, written by Ælfric for Wulfstan's use. They were composed, according to Clemoes, between the ε phase of the First Series and Ælfric's latest stage in the development of his homilies, TH II.[6] Each derives from a quite independent line of transmission. Item 67 (Fehr, Brief II) shares a source with Xᵃ: item 68 (Fehr, Brief III) follows a different line of transmission from Xᵃ, sharing a source with T and Xᶜ.[7]

[1] See Bethurum, p. 22.
[2] S. Dien, '*Sermo Lupi ad Anglos*: The Order and Date of the Three Versions', *NM*, lxxvi (1975), 561 70, argues unconvincingly that B's version is a later one.
[3] See D. Whitelock, ed., *Sermo Lupi ad Anglos*, 3rd ed. (London, 1963), p. 6, and Bethurum, p. 22.
[4] Clemoes, 'Chronology', pp. 242, 245.
[5] Crawford, p. 12.   [6] Clemoes, 'Chronology', p. 245.
[7] The textual relationships of the items are examined by Clemoes in his introduction to Fehr.

Items 73 (*Dedicatio ecclesie*) and 75 (Second Sunday after Epiphany) are two Second Series homilies, both having the same textual origins: they show no significant links with the DEF group and agree fairly closely with K. In this they resemble items 59, 60, 62, and 63, and therefore perhaps draw on the source used for section (e). Item 73 is one of two homilies by Ælfric in section (f) of B which were elsewhere rewritten by Wulfstan.[1] The other item elsewhere adapted by Wulfstan is no. 69.[2] This is untitled in the manuscript, but known elsewhere as *De Septiformi Spiritu*. It is, as Pope notes, 'too narrow and brief for a homily . . . [and] is treated as a pendant to the homilies for Pentecost in the carefully arranged MS. U'.[3] According to Clemoes, the piece belongs to the TH II phase, though it was composed before TH I was developed (it was used in the TH I homily for the third Sunday after Easter).[4]

Item 74, *Dedicatio sancti michaelis*, is a First Series homily belonging, like the original sequence of First Series homilies in section (e), to the ε phase.

Section (f), then, is a miscellany of religious pieces with no apparent pattern in their arrangement. It has two unifying features which might help to explain the selection. First, almost half of the items relate to episcopal duties: a homily outlining each step in baptism (item 66), two consecutive pastoral letters written by Ælfric for Wulfstan concerning the clergy (items 67 and 68), and two consecutive homilies on the dedication of a church (items 73 and 74). Secondly, there are the persistent connections with Wulfstan himself: four items are his own compositions (items 66, 70, 71, and 72), two were elsewhere adapted by him (items 69 and 73), and two were written for his use by Ælfric (items 67 and 68). These two groups overlap, since Wulfstan himself was Bishop of Worcester. The contents of section (f), then, can be explained in two possible ways. The scribe of B may have been selecting the items especially with episcopal duties in mind, in other words compiling the volume primarily for the use of bishops or even a particular bishop. Not all the texts, however, are concerned with such duties (for example, item 69, *De septiformi spiritu*, and items 70–2, three of the homilies by Wulfstan). Given the strong connections with Wulfstan, the second possible explanation for the section's contents is

---

[1] The rewritten version of item 73 is Bethurum xviii, which is discussed by the editor on p. 35.

[2] Bethurum ix, discussed by the editor on p. 32.

[3] Pope, p. 142, n. 6.

[4] Clemoes, 'Chronology', pp. 228–33.

more plausible. The scribe of B may have been copying a group of texts compiled earlier for Wulfstan, though he himself had a different audience and function in mind. The group of texts copied might be related to the 'kind of theological commonplace book specially intended for a bishop's use' which we see in CCCC 265 and Xᵃ.[1] These manuscripts (amongst others) are collections of canonical and penitential material which are associated with Wulfstan and Worcester, and were indeed probably assembled by Wulfstan (perhaps with the Canons of Edgar in mind, as R. G. Fowler proposes).[2] It seems likely, then, that the Bodley scribe found this kind of collection assembled by Wulfstan, or someone associated with him, and thought the texts useful, perhaps for clergy and even for laity (as item 65 seems to suggest). The textual similarities to homilies in other sections may once again indicate that a compiler at some stage drew on the resources of a large monastic library, presumably Worcester, rather than on one particular manuscript.

Section (g)

77. fols. 155–8. Ala ȝebroðræ aræreð eowre heorte to ðam heofenlice gode . . . Belfour ix, p. 78 (rewriting of a homily for Christmas). Agrees with Skeat i, ll. 84–242 for fol. 156ᵛ, ll. 16 ff. [Belfour, p. 86, l. 25].

78. fols. 158–60. Men þa leofestæ we wullæð eow sæggæn bi þare halȝæ tide . . . Irvine v (anonymous homily for First Sunday in Lent).

79. fols. 160–3. Men þa leofeste sanctus matheus þe godspellere . . . Irvine vi (anonymous homily for Saturday before the Second Sunday in Lent).

80. fols. 163–164ᵛ. Ic eow bidde leofemen þæt swa ofte swa ȝe faren . . . Irvine vii (composite homily for (?)Tuesday in Rogationtide. Second part corresponds to last part of Vercelli x (Szarmach, pp. 14–16).)

81. fols. 165–166ᵛ. Pater noster qui es in celis . . . (Latin dialogues between student and teacher expounding the Lord's Prayer and Creed).

[1] See Mary Bateson, 'A Worcester Cathedral Book of Ecclesiastical Collections, Made C. 1000 A.D.', *English Historical Review*, x (1895), 712–31.

[2] '"Archbishop Wulfstan's Commonplace-Book" and the *Canons of Edgar*', *Medium Ævum*, xxxii (1963), 1–10. See further: B. Fehr, 'Das Benediktiner-Offizium und die Beziehung zwischen Ælfric und Wulfstan', *Englische Studien*, xlvi (1913), 337–46; D. Bethurum, 'Archbishop Wulfstan's Commonplace Book', *PMLA*, lvii (1942), 916–29; and D. Whitelock, 'Archbishop Wulfstan, Homilist and Statesman', *Transactions of the Royal Historical Society*, 4th series, xxiv (1942), 25–45.

82. fol. 166ᵛ. Auarus þæt is ȝytsere on englisc. auaricia is ȝytsunȝe . . . CH II xxvi, ll. 108 ff. (second part of homily for the Ninth Sunday after Pentecost).

83. fols. 166ᵛ–167ᵛ. Us sæȝð þeo haliȝe cristes boc. þæt ure hælend crist . . . Pope vi.

84. fols. 167ᵛ–170. *De uno confessore.* Matheus þe godspellere us sæde þis godspel . . . Assmann iv.

85. fol. 170, ll. 29–37. ðe wes bold [erasure] ȝebyld. er þu iboren were . . . (A fragment of verse known as *The Grave* which was added in a hand of s.xii/xiii to an originally blank space. Printed first by J. J. Conybeare.)[1]

Section (g) contains nine items altogether (items 77–85). Four of these are by Ælfric, all drawn from his later works. Item 77, the opening item of the section, is his revised version of the Christmas homily that begins the *Lives of Saints* collection (Clemoes assigns it to the period 1002–5, before TH I).[2] Item 82 is a short piece on avarice from CH II xxvi, with the same revised form of the text as is found in the second recension manuscript R, which contains the same extract. Item 83 is a passage on the types of sins represented by the three men resurrected from death, which is drawn from the late revised version of Pope vi appearing in H. Item 84 is Ælfric's second later homily for a confessor (Assmann iv), which was probably one of his last works (and, as Clemoes shows, must have been written by 1012).[3] The textual affiliations of these four items are surprisingly varied. Item 77 (Belfour ix) seems not to have been circulated as part of either TH I or TH II, or CH I; possibly it circulated separately or in an updated *Lives of Saints* collection. If so, it might then be associated with the homily *Unius Martiris* for St. Vincent (item 61 in section (e)). Item 82 (the excerpt on avarice), which corresponds textually to the same extract in R, presumably comes from the same late version of the Second Series on which R drew; B and R also share a source for item 35 (CH II iii) in section (e). Item 83 (the late version of Pope vi) apparently belongs to TH II.[4] Item 84 (Assmann iv) was circulated in late versions of the First Series, and possibly also individually.[5] This copy, like the passage on avarice, might derive from the source of R; textual evidence is

[1] 'Communication of an Inedited Fragment of Anglo-Saxon Poetry', *Archaeologia*, xvii (1814), 173.

[2] Clemoes, 'Chronology', p. 239.

[3] Ibid., p. 244.

[4] Ibid., p. 231.

[5] Ibid., p. 234.

inconclusive.[1] It is difficult to conceive of a single Ælfrician collection which could have provided all four pieces, especially since Belfour ix and Assmann iv are both ostensibly independent items, not readily forming part of homiletic collections.

Interspersed with these are three anonymous homilies, probably composed for Lent and Rogationtide, though not assigned to any occasion in the manuscript (items 78–80). Item 78 is a homily on the pericope for the First Sunday in Lent, not appearing in any other manuscript, though its conclusion is in the composite Napier lv (in T). Item 79 is a homily on the pericope for the Saturday before the Second Sunday in Lent, which does not appear elsewhere. Item 80 is a composite homily, probably for the Tuesday in Rogationtide; it draws in part on an anonymous homily which occurs in the Vercelli Book (Szarmach x) and several other manuscripts, and shows links with the copy in O though it probably does not derive from O itself.[2]

The Ælfrician and anonymous homilies in this section have two features in common. First, none of them shows the links with CDEF so common earlier in the manuscript. Secondly they are all similar in being homilies on general themes and not rubricated for particular occasions.

Amongst these English homilies is one Latin text, which is an exegesis of the Lord's Prayer in a catechetical form, questions being asked by D. (Discipulus) and answered by M. (Magister). The Latin sentences are generally short and simple, and express basic tenets of the Christian faith. Like section (b)'s Latin homilies, it would be appropriate for those whose knowledge of Latin was limited and may have been selected with that in mind.

Again the items in section (g) all have a long textual history behind them and a remarkable multiplicity of origins for such a small collection. The section, however, does have a kind of unity in its choice of items dealing with general themes and not necessarily tied to the church year. It is conceivable that the scribe of B made this selection from several exemplars, deliberately picking out those items which were not closely related to the church year in order to build up a *quando volueris* set. Given the rather haphazard organization of the rest of the manuscript, however, and the inclusion already of several *quando volueris* items, it seems unlikely that he had such a well-defined

---

[1] See supplementary introduction to Assmann by Clemoes, p. xxiv.

[2] James E. Cross, '"Ubi Sunt" Passages in Old English—Sources and Relationships', *Vetenskaps-Societetens i Lund Årsbok* (1956), 23–44, pp. 30–1.

aim in mind. It seems more feasible that he was sifting through an already existing, perhaps larger, *quando volueris* collection, picking out the items not already included in the manuscript. Section (g), then, may be a vestige of an already existing collection of homilies on general themes unrelated to the church year.

This still leaves unexplained the wide diversity of textual origins, and the availability of booklets would again provide a plausible explanation. The Ælfrician pieces are all late, yet each belongs to a quite different stage of Ælfric's development of his texts. A source shared with R may account for two of the items (82 and 84), but for item 84 the evidence is inconclusive. The anonymous texts are probably pre-Ælfrician, and item 80 at least seems to have had a different textual history from items 78 and 79. Several of the texts in the section could have circulated appropriately as independent items. Moreover the Latin text is unlikely to have been part originally of a set of Old English *quando volueris* items. At some stage, then, a variety of small exemplars must have been used for this selection. Either the scribe of B was working from a collection of booklets already informally assembled, or he was copying from a manuscript which directly or indirectly had been compiled from booklets with a *quando volueris* set in mind.

Conclusions

In B as a whole, the multiplicity of textual affiliations indicates the direct or indirect exposure to a considerable number of homiletic collections. Each of these collections individually would have furnished a scribe with most of the items he wanted, and yet in B only a few items have been taken from each, and even then sporadically. There seems to be no clear-cut principle of selection, whether chronological or thematic, which could explain this. The chronological sequences that do occur cannot have been the Bodley scribe's own work, for neither the manuscript as a whole nor any entire section are organized in any consistent chronological pattern. Similarly the sections that do seem to have a thematic unity, such as section (f) which is associated so closely with Wulfstan's work, and section (g) with its *quando volueris* set, are more likely to have been found by the scribe thus arranged than to have been compiled by him with those functions in mind.

The evidence of the whole manuscript points to faithful copying, probably at various stages of transmission, of many small collections which were themselves drawn from larger collections. Textual similarities across section boundaries therefore reflect not the scribe's repeated use of the same exemplar, but the fact that these small collections often drew ultimately on the same larger collections. A number of the large collections can be identified further back in the line of transmission: the collection which B shared as a source with G, furnishing much of sections (a) and (d) and occasional items in (c) and (e); a collection of First Series homilies, furnishing much of section (e) and some items in section (d); a collection of homilies from the second half of the Second Series, furnishing the last part of section (e); the Wulfstan-related collection drawn on for section (f); a *quando volueris* miscellany drawn on for section (g); and a small TH II run drawn on for section (c).

A consideration of the provenance of these collections may help towards identifying B's provenance, and towards understanding in what ways and how far copies of texts were interchanged in this period. The collection B shared as a source with G has strong south-eastern connections and probably originated there.[1] Neither of the two main groups of texts in section (e), however, has south-eastern connections, nor is there sufficient information on related manuscripts to speculate on their connections with any other area. One homily in section (e) (item 35 (CH II iii)) is related to the copy in R, a manuscript connected with Worcester;[2] otherwise the items from the First and Second Series are quite unrelated to the known Worcester material in the second part of E, R, and T. The collection of pieces associated with Wulfstan presumably derives from Worcester, but some of the items in it show links also with the south-east and with Exeter: items 66, 71, and 72 share a line of transmission with V, the original part of which (including these items) was probably written at Canterbury but which contains additions written at Exeter;[3] item 67 shares a source with X^a, which is from Exeter.[4] The small collections must have travelled widely; clearly texts were constantly interchanged amongst different collections in the course of copying.

Bodley 343's organization suggests that it was not written at one of the main monastic centres where the large known collections would have been available to its compiler. The manuscript, however, does

---

[1] CH II, pp. lx–lxii.

[2] Ker, *Catalogue*, p. 64.

[3] Ker, *Catalogue*, p. 118; see also Pope, pp. 82–3, and particularly n. 1 on p. 83, where he suggests that 'it looks as if U, B, and the pre-Exeter part of V were textually interrelated, and all at least partly derived from south-eastern exemplars'.

[4] Ker, *Catalogue*, p. 73.

show enough textual and other connections to suggest for its compiler proximity to Worcester and even limited access to the Worcester library. It was probably written somewhere near Worcester, though not at Worcester itself. This would fit with Ker's suggestion of a West Midland provenance which he deduced from fol. iii's rhymed antiphon for St. Wulfhad (who was associated with Stone in Staffordshire) and fol. 173's drawing of a bishop accompanied by an inscription containing the name 'wolstane' (dated s. xiii? so possibly referring to Bishop Wulfstan II of Worcester).[1] It would also tally with the scribe's linguistic traits, as I show below.[2]

The complexity of the manuscript's compilation and its reliance on so many lines of transmission provide evidence that from early in the eleventh century collections of homilies and related pieces must have been divided and recopied in great quantity. Smaller groups of material, that is, booklets, must frequently have been used by compilers. The collections of religious works now extant can only represent a tiny proportion of what was actually copied and available in the eleventh and twelfth centuries.

The function of such collections in the post-Conquest period, when the major theological, cultural, and linguistic changes would seem to render them obsolete and useless, has been touched on in the course of my analysis of B above.[3] Certain conclusions can be drawn about the motivation for B's compilation. First the inclusion of Latin material in B suggests that the interest in copying was more than the antiquarian one of preserving the Old English language and texts. Secondly, the compiler of B was clearly organizing his own collection from disparate sources. Even if he had only limited material available at any one time, he is at the very least taking care to select appropriate texts and ones which he has not previously copied in the manuscript. Thirdly B shows no sign of having played any direct role in preaching (although preaching in the vernacular did continue throughout the twelfth century).[4] It shows none of the omission marks, changes in punctuation, and marginal additions that appear in eleventh-century

[1] Ker, *Catalogue*, pp. 374–5.

[2] Here I disagree with Pope, who argues of B that 'to judge by the language, it was sent there after having been written in the south' (p. 18).

[3] On the English Church in the post-Conquest period, see, for example, Frank Barlow, *The English Church 1066–1154* (London, 1979); Dom David Knowles, *The Monastic Order in England*, 2nd ed. (Cambridge, 1963); R. W. Southern, *Medieval Humanism and Other Studies* (Oxford, 1970).

[4] See, for example, G. R. Owst, *Literature and Pulpit in Medieval England*, 2nd rev. ed. (Oxford, 1961), p. 4.

manuscripts like D and F, and which would be usual in a manuscript intended or used for preaching. Moreover the material is not uniformly suitable for preaching purposes. Section (c), for example, includes a long anonymous narrative, the *History of the Holy Rood-tree*, which is clearly unsuitable for preaching. Section (f), with its material related to Wulfstan and episcopal duties, also suggests that the demands of preaching were not the main concern of the compiler. Another argument against the direct use of the manuscript for preaching is that the texts of the homilies remain substantially unaltered; they are not adapted, whether by additions or omissions, to make them more appropriate for a twelfth-century audience.

One remarkable feature of B is that it contains no twelfth-century compositions amongst its Old English material. This is not always the case with the twelfth-century manuscripts: G, for example, includes some post-Conquest compositions alongside its Old English pieces, most of which are translations of twelfth-century Latin writings.[1] What it does suggest, however, since it is clear that the compiler of B did not have a purely antiquarian motivation, is that twelfth-century material written in English was not readily available. The most likely use of a manuscript like B would be devotional reading for English-speaking monks and nuns (G was clearly owned by a woman at the end of the twelfth century),[2] and a reading book for secular clergy which could be assimilated and adapted for use in preaching.[3] The twelfth century seems to have lacked not readers of English but writers in English. People wanting to read in English were obliged to rely mainly on the tenth- and eleventh-century compositions.[4]

---

[1] Ker, *Catalogue*, no. 209, items 27, 33, and 43–9, were probably written in the twelfth century.

[2] In a Latin prayer addressed to Mary written in a blank space in a late twelfth-century hand, the words 'ego ancilla tua' are used by the writer of the prayer; see Ker, *Catalogue*, no. 209, item 54. Compare Cotton Claudius D. iii (Ker, *Catalogue*, p. xix), an early thirteenth-century manuscript which contains a copy of the Rule of St. Benedict especially adapted for women, and Salisbury Cathedral 150 (Ker, *Catalogue*, no. 379), whose end-prayer has the masculine form 'famulum tuum' changed to feminine 'famulam tuam'; see Celia and Kenneth Sisam, eds., *The Salisbury Psalter*, EETS, 242 (London, 1959), p. 6.

[3] The flourishing of the cathedral monastery system in the twelfth century would have led to more frequent interchange between monks and secular clergy; see, for example, Knowles, *The Monastic Order*, pp. 619 ff. Many monasteries, for example Worcester and Rochester, took a particular concern in the pastoral welfare of the lay people; on Rochester, see Mary Richards, *Texts and their Traditions in the Medieval Library of Rochester Cathedral Priory* (Philadelphia, 1988), especially ch. 4.

[4] This lack of composition in English does not seem to have lasted beyond the end of the twelfth century. London, Lambeth Palace 487, and Cambridge, Trinity College

Clearly in the twelfth century there was a wider demand for reading material in English than we might expect given the historical circumstances, and indeed more of a continuity and conservative element in the Church. A manuscript like Bodley 343 seems to have fulfilled a crucial role in twelfth-century England, providing devotional reading material in English and a secondary resource for preaching at a time when composition in English had temporarily come to a virtual standstill.

CAMBRIDGE UNIVERSITY LIBRARY Ii. i. 33

Since this manuscript provides only part of one homily, I propose to include no more than a brief description here. Like B this manuscript was written in the second half of the twelfth century. It too is a collection of homiletic works, consisting largely of saints' lives from Ælfric's two series of *Catholic Homilies* and from his *Lives of Saints*. The manuscript's contents are listed in full in Ker, *Catalogue*, no. 18. The Passion of St. Vincent which forms the first part of Ælfric's homily on St. Vincent edited here in full is item 23. The foliation of the manuscript and its physical appearance are also described by Ker.[1] According to W. Schipper, 'three main hands are discernible in the manuscript': scribe A wrote fols. 3^r–36^v and 120^v–228^v; scribe B wrote fols. 53^r–120^v; and scribe C wrote 37^r–52^v.[2] On the basis of the way its contents are arranged, and in particular from the prominent position of Ælfric's homily on St. Æthelthryth, Schipper tentatively ascribes the manuscript to Ely.[3] As I noted above, the manuscript is especially interesting for its apparent reliance on booklets in its compilation. It is also important as evidence that even in the twelfth century compilers were building up their own collections of texts according to certain criteria; Schipper argues that the core-manuscript of L was probably an 'Apostolic Passional', and that scribe A by adding various items consciously reshaped the manuscript into a general passional for saints.[4] Finally, L's Ely provenance significantly suggests that although the importance of Worcester in preserving the Old English tradition has been rightly recognized, it may perhaps have been over-

B. 14. 52 contain adaptations of homilies by Ælfric alongside contemporary texts like the *Pater Noster* and *Poema Morale*.

[1] Ker, *Catalogue*, p. 27.
[2] 'A Composite Old English Homiliary', p. 286.
[3] Ibid., pp. 291–2.
[4] Ibid., pp. 290–1.

estimated, since the demand and conservatism clearly extended to places as far afield as Ely.

THE LANGUAGE OF THE HOMILIES

Bodley 343 provides valuable evidence for the language in its period of transition from Old to Middle English. Since it contains twelfth-century copies of pre-Conquest works, it allows us to see the actual processes involved in the development of the language.

The language of the homilies from Bodley 343 examined here shows many features of the late West-Saxon standard literary language.[1] Late West-Saxon was, however, becoming obsolete as a literary dialect through the twelfth century. Although we cannot tell whether his immediate exemplars were written in the twelfth century or earlier, we can say that the scribe of Bodley 343 is remarkably conservative linguistically for the third quarter of the twelfth century. Despite the scribe's obvious aim for linguistic fidelity, his texts show two main types of linguistic development. First, there is a further movement away from an ideal representation of individual phonemes by individual graphs: various graphs represent one Old English phoneme, and various Old English phonemes are represented by one graph. This orthographical confusion reflects a mixture of spelling traditions (late West-Saxon, Anglo-Norman and perhaps Latin), and a levelling of sounds originally distinct. Its effect was to widen the gap between spelling and pronunciation. Secondly, the scribe has introduced features reflecting his own regional dialect. The localization of this dialect is made difficult by the scribe's graphemic confusion (especially of ⟨æ⟩, ⟨e⟩, ⟨ea⟩), and by his use of some forms which, though apparently non-West-Saxon in Old English, became general in early Middle English.[2] The predominance of West Midland features shows, however, that it is a West Midland dialect. The language of two manuscripts, CCCC 402 and Bodley 34, is an important source of comparison. The close relationship in spelling and language between these two manuscripts was pointed out by J. R. R. Tolkien, who called

[1] The features of late West-Saxon are examined in Campbell.

[2] For general information on Middle English Grammar, I have had most frequent recourse to Karl Brunner, *An Outline of Middle English Grammar*, trans. Graheme Johnstone (Oxford, 1970), and Richard Jordan, *Handbook of Middle English Grammar: Phonology*, trans. and rev. Eugene Joseph Crook, Janua Linguarum, Series Practica, 218 (The Hague, 1974); hereafter cited as Jordan–Crook.

their common language the AB language.[1] The AB language has been described in some detail by S. R. T. O. d'Ardenne and Arne Zettersten, and I refer frequently here to their accounts.[2] Bodley 343's language, however, is not entirely consistent, and occasional significant linguistic variations between homilies suggest that not all deviations from late West-Saxon are the scribe's own. A thorough study of the language in the whole of Bodley 343, not possible within the scope of this volume, is required to establish which linguistic traits can, and which cannot, be ascribed to the Bodley scribe. I do, however, note where the important linguistic variations between homilies occur.

This study does not attempt to be a complete grammar of the stage of transition represented by the language of the texts. I shall describe only those aspects of the language which show deviation from the late West-Saxon literary standard, whether they arise from dialectal differences in Old English or from Middle English developments.

I discuss the language of the manuscript with reference only to the homilies edited here. The texts represent a wide cross-section of the manuscript: two are from section (c) (i and ii), two are from section (e) (iii and iv), and three are from the final section (g) (v, vi, and vii). (The first part of iv, which is in CUL Ii. 1. 33, is excluded from this discussion.) The occurrences of forms are indicated by the homily and line number (as in the glossary). Where it is the range of spellings that seems of particular importance, the frequency with which a form occurs is indicated by the multiplication sign (for example, i, 5×). Grammatical abbreviations correspond to those used for the glossary (except where they would be unclear).

ORTHOGRAPHY: VOWELS

1. OE *a* before a nasal

Although the scribe generally favours *o* before a nasal (see Phonology), he fluctuates between *a* and *o* in his spelling of some words. Examples: *ongan* ii. 118, v. 101, *ongon* ii. 114, v. 23, 26; *land* iii. 4, *lond*(-) i. 10, 42, 54, 82, 86, 141, 162, 164, *lang-* iii. 266, iv. 299, *long-* i. 35, 98, vi. 38, vii. 70, 90.

---

[1] '*Ancrene Wisse* and *Hali Meiðhad*', *Essays and Studies*, xiv (1929), 104–26.

[2] S. R. T. O. d'Ardenne, ed., *þe Liflade ant te Passiun of Seinte Iuliene*, EETS, 248 (London, 1961); hereafter cited as d'Ardenne, and Arne Zettersten, *Studies in the Dialect and Vocabulary of the Ancrene Riwle*, Lund Studies in English, 34 (Lund, 1965); hereafter cited as Zettersten.

2. OE *æ, e, ea*

(i) The scribe uses the two graphs ⟨æ⟩ and ⟨e⟩ interchangeably. ⟨æ⟩ often appears for ⟨e⟩, alongside forms with the original ⟨e⟩: *swælte* i. 17, *swelte* i. 90; (*ʒe*)*tel*(-) i. 150, ii. 106, 131, 138, *ʒetæle* ii. 108, 142, 144; *ælfremed* ii. 68, *ælfræmede* ii. 76; *godspellere* ii. 110, 114, *godspæl-lere* ii. 168.

Less commonly, ⟨e⟩ appears for ⟨æ⟩: *creft* ii. 207, *ibed* iii. 329, *aber* iv. 306, *ber* v. 59, *s*[*c*]*yncrefte* v. 124, *spec* v. 74, 114, vi. 2, 211.

(ii) ⟨ea⟩ appears occasionally for ⟨æ⟩: *healend* vi. 26, *eahtæ*(-*e*) vii. 133, 138. (See also Phonology: Short Vowels (3) and Long Vowels (1).) The initial *ea* of *eadleanes* (iii. 238) is an eME spelling (d'Ardenne, pp. 173, 182). (The IWS spelling *ætleanes* occurs just previously at iii. 236.)

⟨æ⟩ for ⟨ea⟩ is also rare; I have found the following instances: *scæde* iii. 214, 215, 216, but *sceadu* vii. 5; *læhtræs* vi. 35, but *leahtr-* iii. 121, 124, 126, iv. 326; *wældend* iii. 86, but *wealdend* i. 84; *ærming* iii. 92, but *earm-lice* iii. 116, *earmæn* iii. 260, *earme* vii. 10, 151; *ælle* v. 56, elsewhere *alle* except *ealle* vi. 21, *ealr-* iv. 317, vi. 41; *þæh* v. 73, elsewhere *þeah*. (See also Phonology: Short Vowels (3) and Long Vowels (1).)

3. OE *i/y*

The vacillation between *i* and *y* already present in IWS is found here in certain words (Campbell, §§317, 318). Examples: *ʒife* (n.) i. 88, vii. 151; *ʒyfe* (n.) i. 151; *forʒif-* ii. 38, 46, etc. (23×), *forʒyf-* i. 152, ii. 176, 178; *libb-* iii. 150, iv. 333, v. 77, 78, 166, 184 (vi, 5×, and vii, 2×), *lybbæn* v. 189.

Some common words show a remarkable consistency, for example, *bið* is always spelt with an *i*, not a *y*, and *syððan* is always spelt with a *y*, not an *i*. The adverb *ʒyt* is spelt almost exclusively with a *y*; *ʒit* occurs only once in these texts (ii. 132).

4. OE *u/y*

OE *y* (< u + i) is commonly written as *u*. Anglo-Norman influence is responsible for this spelling change (the sound remaining, as in OE, [y]).[1] Examples:

aʒulte ii. 213, *gultæs* ii. 208, *gult* v. 51, *gulteð* vi. 136. But *aʒyl*(*d*)*t-*/*agyl-*

---

[1] Forms such as *ʒewurpte, wurc*(*h*)*en, wurðe* (adj.), which exist alongside forms with ⟨y⟩ in these texts, are not included in discussion here, since the movement *wyr-* to *wur-* is already evident in WS texts. Also the forms *sunderlice, sundrie,* and *sundries* (from OE *syndriʒ*) are not included, since they can be explained by analogy with OE *sundor*. (There are no forms with ⟨y⟩ in these texts.)

ii, 7×, *ꝫylt* ii. 156, *ꝫylte* iii. 116, *gylt* ii. 211, *gylten* vi. 83, *gyltæs* ii. 84, vii. 145. So *u* 4× altogether, *y* 13×. (For the interchangeable use of *ꝫ* and *g*, see Orthography: Consonants (3).)

(ii) *sunegode* v. 53, *sunfulle* v. 89, 94, *sunnæn* v. 9, *sunne* v. 8, 54, vii. 12, *sunful* vi. 111. But *synnæ* i. 152, (*i*)*syn*(*n*)- ii, 13×, iii, 23×, iv, 1×, v, 4×, vi, 7×, vii, 7×. So *u* 8× altogether, *y* 56×. It should be noted that *u* is used only in the last three homilies.

(iii) *ifulled* v. 45, vi. 217, 250, vii. 67, *afulled* v. 141, *fulde* vi. 64, *ꝫefulde* vi. 146. But *ifylled* ii. 144, vi. 61, 71. So *u* 7× altogether, *y* 3×. Again all instances of *u* occur in the final homilies.

(iv) *bihud* v. 73, *bihuddest* vi. 61. But *bihydest* ii. 184, *bihyd* v. 121.

(v) *durstinesse* v. 26, 84, 92. (No instances of *dyrsti*-.)

(vi) *fure* vii. 29, 30, 111, *fures* vii. 47. But *fyre* iii. 249, *fyr* vii. 55.

(vii) *þulde* v. 168, *þuldelice* v. 74, 114, 117. But *ꝫeþyld* ii. 193.

(viii) *þuncþ* v. 82. But *þynce* (pres. subj. s.) i. 35, v. 177.

(ix) *wunsumlice* v. 24, vii. 8. But *wynsum*(-) iv. 309, 364.

(x) *onbrurdnesse* iii. 328, *endeburdnesse* v. 18. (No examples of -*b*(*r*)*yrd*-.)

(xi) *murhþe* iv. 334, v. 11, 125, vi. 43, etc. (11×), vii. 37, etc. (5×). (No instances of *myrhþe*.)

(xii) *lure* v. 113, vii. 112. (No instances of *lyre*.)

(xiii) Isolated examples in these texts: *uppon* (n.) v. 98, *luftlice* vi. 168, *lust* ('it pleases') vi. 174, *worldprude* vii. 4, *wunstræn* vii. 35, *lusten* vii. 131, *gute* vii. 146.

To this category also belong other words which show the reflex of OE *y* (as in some western dialects such as AB):

(i) *dude* (-*on*) v. 29, vi. 206, 225. But *dyde* i. 69, 93, ii. 32, iii. 151, iv. 338.

(ii) *muc*(*e*)*l*(-) ii. 48, iii. 81, v. 86, 95, 160, 168, vi. 82, etc. (9×), vii. 63 etc. (5×). But *myc*(*e*)*l*(-)/*mic*(*e*)*l*(-) i. 76, etc. (5×), ii. 58, etc. (6×), iii. 246, etc. (4×), iv. 306, etc. (4×), vi. 17, etc. (10×), vii. 46, etc. (4×)

(iii) *wul*(*l*)- (vb.) i. 33, etc. (3×), ii. 59, 187, v. 1, etc. (7×), vi. 182, 259, vii. 103, 140. But *wyl*(*l*)-/*wil*(*l*)- (vb.) ii. 91, 181, iii. 74, 86, 107, 267, iv. 298, 324, v. 159, vi. 19.

The negative form of the verb has not developed in the same way; its variant spellings are *e* and *y*, never *u* (Campbell §265).

It can be seen that in general, the number of instances of ⟨u⟩ for ⟨y⟩ increases dramatically in the final three homilies. This is probably the result of a different line of transmission for the last section of the manuscript.

The reverse spelling ⟨y⟩ for ⟨u⟩ occurs infrequently. Examples are *befrynnon* (*bi-*) i. 168, iii. 7, *wyndræ* iii. 12, 204, MS *cyðe* (with *y* corrected to *u*) iii. 327, *synne* ('sun') vi. 74, *cyðlycor* vi. 144. The forms *swytellice* (ii. 183, iii. 106) and *iswytelode* (iii. 12, 171) alternating with (-)*swutelode* (i. 125, 134, ii. 130, iii. 176) and *swutelice* (iii. 111, 364) may also show ⟨y⟩ for ⟨u⟩, but here *y* may be a rounded form of *i* retained without back mutation (in which case -*swutelode* and *swutelice* show ⟨u⟩ for ⟨y⟩).

5. OE *ā*

OE *ā* is still spelt ⟨a⟩ (as in the AB dialect and the *Ormulum*). Examples: *gast* (i. 150, etc.), *ham* (i. 30, etc.), *haliʒ* (i. 150, etc.), *lare* (i. 159, etc.).

ORTHOGRAPHY: CONSONANTS

1. The voiceless velar stop [k], spelt ⟨c⟩ in OE, is regularly spelt ⟨c⟩ before *a, o, u*, and consonants, and spelt ⟨k⟩ or ⟨c⟩ before *e* (*æ*), *i* and *y*. Clearly the scribe's orthography is moving towards the normal ME spellings of ⟨c⟩ before *a, o, u*, and ⟨k⟩ before *e, i, y*. The following examples show the distribution of ⟨k⟩ spellings:

(i) *kyneʒyrde* i. 56, *kynelice* i. 40, vii. 166, *kynerice* vii. 90, *kynestole* i. 50, *kyng*(-) i, 11✕, ii, 6✕, vi, 3✕, vii, 5✕. One exception: *cynedom* i. 38.

(ii) *lokinde* iii. 23, *loken* vi. 208, *lokiæn* vi. 113. Also note *loca*(-*æ*) i. 47, 86, vii. 6. Exception: *lociʒe* ii. 195.

(iii) *makæþ* i. 200, *makiʒe*(-*n*) i. 183, 191, *makyʒe* i. 171, *makede* iii. 18. Also note *macode* iii. 152. (No exceptions.)

(iv) *spæky* iii. 350, *speke* v. 126, *speke*(-*n*) vi. 20, 142, 184, *spæken* vii. 161. Several instances of ⟨c⟩ as final consonant and before *o* and *þ*. But also instances of ⟨c⟩ before -*e*(*n*) (i, 2✕, ii,3✕, iii, 4✕, v, 1✕, vi, 1✕, vii, 2✕).

(v) *þanken* vi. 173, *þankiende* vi. 171. But *þancian* iii. 300, *þonce* v. 170, vi. 137, *þoncæs* vii. 13, *þonciæn* vii. 98.

2. The voiceless palatal fricative [tʃ], also spelt ⟨c⟩ in OE, is here spelt ⟨c⟩ or ⟨ch⟩ (normal ME spelling ⟨ch⟩). The following examples show the distribution of ⟨ch⟩:

(i) *childræn* i. 49, *childe* ii. 190, *child* vii. 87. But *cildrum* ii. 13.

(ii) *neahlæchede* v. 64, vi. 26, 219. But *neahlæcedon* v. 151.

(iii) *chinæþ* iv. 301.

(iv) *ichærred* vi. 244. But *cyrren* vi. 258, *cerræn* vii. 158, *cerræð* vii. 145.

(v) *sechon* vi. 4. But *secea* vii. 159, *seceð* vii. 101.

(vi) *teachunge* v. 117, *tæche* vii. 149. But *tæcæð* ii. 207, 216, *tæcþ* iii. 162, *tæcinge* v. 166, 175, *tæcæn* vii. 130.

(vii) *wurchen* vi. 182. But elsewhere *wurc-*.

3. Continental (or Caroline) ⟨g⟩ is used for the OE voiced guttural stop, for example, *gode* iii. 15, *gan* iii. 20, 32, vi. 241, *gastlice* iii. 108, etc., *oferglad* iii. 213. In certain words, however, ⟨g⟩ and ⟨ȝ⟩ are used without distinction, for example, *gylt-/gult-* (nouns) and *(a)gylte-/ (a)gulte-* (verbs) are often spelt with ⟨ȝ⟩, and in vii *anginne* is spelt twice with ⟨g⟩, once with ⟨ȝ⟩.

⟨g⟩ is also used in the OE combination ⟨ng⟩ (occasionally, as in IWS, ⟨ngc⟩), for example, *leorningcnihtæs* iii. 74, etc., *ærming* iii. 92, *Englisce* iii. 132, 229, *tacnuncg* ii. 132. Exception: *cwylmynȝe* iii. 263. OE ⟨cg⟩ or, rarely, ME ⟨gg⟩ is used for [dȝ], for example, *sæcgæn* i. 33, etc., *sæggen(-e)* vi. 41, 249.

Again the scribe's dialect is showing the normal ME development in these spellings.

4. Insular ⟨ȝ⟩ is used for the OE voiced palatal spirant [j] initially, finally, and medially, for example:

(i) *ȝeorne* i. 11, ii. 16, etc., *ȝeldæn* ii. 25, *forȝifæn* ii. 71, 83.

(ii) *buriȝ* i. 7, 60, 158, v. 81, *wæȝ* i. 19, 100, etc., *dæȝ* i. 27, 148, etc., *læȝ* i. 8, 13, 60, 95.

(iii) *æȝhwær* i. 75, 81, *ætbroȝdon* iii. 200, *awariȝedan* iii. 249, *buriȝnes* vii. 7, 9, 17, 26, *diȝelices* iii. 112, *fyliȝe(-)* iv. 293, 339, 348, 349, vii. 12, *læȝde* ii. 23.

For the interchange of *iȝ* and *i*, see Campbell, §267. Examples: *awariȝed-* iii. 249, 250, 316, v. 15, 110, 130, 139, vii. 45, *awaried-* v. 62; *buriȝnes* vii. 7, 9, 17, 26, *burines* vii. 2; *lifiȝend-* i. 66, ii. 55, iv. 324, *lifiend-* v. 58, vii. 68; *moniȝ-* i. 113, 162, 166, iv. 340, 342, v. 83, vi. 245, *monie* v. 20, vi. 134. In general, spellings with *iȝ* are more common than those with *i*. Spellings with *i* occur more frequently in v and vii than in any of the other homilies.

For the tendency for *ȝ* to combine with a preceding front vowel to form a diphthong with *i*, see Campbell, §§243, 266. Examples showing frequency of the various spellings: *þeȝen(-)*, *þæȝen* ii. 10, etc. (10×), *þeȝn* iv. 294, 352, *þeines* (-æs, -um) v. 168, vi. 17, 58, 65, *þeiniendlice* v. 157, *þeiniȝen* v. 158, *þeiȝnæs* (-um) vi. 23, 234; *iseid* v. 103, *isæid* vi. 58,

isæd i. 32, iii. 106, iv. 297, vi. 236, 256; *imeind* vi. 55; *leiȝ* (noun, 'flame')
vii. 47, *liȝeum* vii. 30, *liȝæs* vii. 59. The diphthongs with *i* occur only in
v, vi, and vii; elsewhere ȝ is regularly retained (or omitted altogether in
the case of *isæd*).

5. The voiced guttural spirant [ɣ] is also normally represented by ⟨ȝ⟩,
for example, *laȝe* ii. 133, 144, etc., *aȝen-* ii. 54, 190, etc., *eaȝan* iii. 22,
155, etc. There is no sign of the ⟨w⟩ representing [w] from [ɣ] used
from 1200 onwards (Crook-Jordan, §186), nor of the ⟨h⟩ characteristic
of the AB dialect (d'Ardenne, p. 173). For examples of ⟨g⟩, see Phonology: Consonants (1).

6. Medial and final *ð* and *h* are occasionally confused. ⟨ð⟩ appears for
⟨h⟩ in the following examples: *þurð* v. 127 (numerous instances of *þurh*
elsewhere); *þoðtæs* vi. 264, *þuðten* vi. 180, elsewhere *þohte* v. 58, vi. 184,
þuhte vi. 197, 245.

Conversely ⟨h⟩ appears for ⟨ð⟩ in *wurhȝiæn* v. 133 (several instances
elsewhere of *wurð(-iæn)*). Note that the ⟨ȝ⟩ in this form is probably left
from *-iȝæn*.

⟨ð⟩ and ⟨h⟩ are combined in *þurðh* i. 83.

7. ⟨d⟩ and ⟨t⟩ are confused only occasionally. (This confusion is
frequent in the AB dialect; see d'Ardenne, pp. 196–7.) As in IWS, ⟨d⟩
sometimes appears for ⟨t⟩ in the pres. 3s. form of *healdan*, which twice
is spelt *heald* (iii. 271, iv. 292) and twice *healt* (iii. 44, iv. 322). Generally
syncopated pres. 3s. forms are spelt with ⟨t⟩: *bit* i. 80, *forlyst* iv. 290,
aspent iv. 330, *toglit* vii. 5. The form *send* (i. 82) is an analogical spelling
which is also found in OE (d'Ardenne, p. 197).

⟨d⟩ also appears for ⟨t⟩ in *unrodsoden* ii. 33 and *bed* ii. 213. ⟨d⟩ and ⟨t⟩
are combined (for ⟨t⟩) in *agyldtæþ* ii. 105 (several instances of *agylt-/
aȝylt-* elsewhere).

The ⟨d⟩/⟨t⟩ confusion may arise from the ME sound-change by
which final [d] was unvoiced to [t] (see Crook-Jordan, §200), but its
infrequency here would suggest that the sound-change was as yet
hardly integrated into the scribe's dialect.

8. ⟨c⟩ is doubled occasionally when it represents either [tʃ] or [k]:
weorcce iii. 111, 134, *wyrccenne* iii. 180, *eccenesse* vii. 93, *accenned* iii. 55.

Otherwise the doublings of consonants are derived from OE
(Campbell, §§453–4), for example, *æffre* iii. 183, iv. 366, *næffre* iii. 87,
spattle iii. 18, *brihttre* v. 108). The form *þonne* sometimes appears for
the masc. acc. sg. pronoun *þone* (e.g. iii. 151, 293, v. 118), and *þone* for

the conjunction with comparatives *þonne* (e.g. iii. 306). Where these forms are spelt with an *e* rather than *o*, the same confusion is found (*þenne* for *þene* at v. 112, vii. 36 and *þene* for *þenne* at vi. 99, 103, vii. 106).

PHONOLOGY: SHORT VOWELS

1. OE *a/o* before nasals

The texts show a preference for ⟨o⟩ rather than ⟨a⟩, as the examples listed in Orthography: Vowels (1) demonstrate. To these examples can be added the word *moni(ʒ)*-, which is always spelt with ⟨o⟩ not ⟨a⟩ (thirteen instances altogether).

In lOE, the sound [o] was characteristic of West Mercian (as earlier in the *Vespasian Psalter* [VP] dialect), and in Middle English [o] remained in the West Midlands (including part of Worcestershire).[1] All the other areas had in lOE [a] or, before lengthening groups, *a*, which became [ɔ:]. Since in the homilies treated here, the reflex of *a* (including lengthened *a*) is still spelt ⟨a⟩, the sound [o] before lengthening groups cannot be explained as the development of *a* to [ɔ:].

2. OE *æ, e*

For the orthographical confusion of these two graphs, see Orthography: Vowels (2). It is consequently impossible to differentiate the sounds represented by ⟨æ⟩ and ⟨e⟩. Spellings such as *creft* (ii. 207) and *scyncrefte* (v. 124) cannot safely be held to reflect West Mercian second fronting.

3. OE *ea*

The sound [ea] had been monophthongized to [æ]; ⟨ea⟩ is probably here an alternative spelling for ⟨æ⟩ or ⟨e⟩. (See Orthography: Vowels (2).) An isolated spelling such as *læhtræs* (vi. 35) cannot safely be held to reflect Anglian smoothing or lWS smoothing.

(a) *ea* before *l* + consonant

When no lengthening group follows: ⟨a⟩ is consistently found in the word *all*-. Exceptions are *ælle* v. 56, *ealr*- iv. 317, vi. 41, *ealle* vi. 21, 112, 166. In less common words, however, ⟨ea⟩ is often retained. Examples:

(i) *fallen* v. 133, but *feallend*- iv. 287, *feallendlic* vii. 124, *weallende* vii. 49, *fællæð* vii. 108, 112.

---

[1] For information on the Mercian dialect, see R. Vleeskruyer, ed., *The Life of St. Chad: an Old English Homily* (Amsterdam, 1953), and Paule Mertens-Fonck, *A Glossary of the Vespasian Psalter and Hymns, Part One: The Verb* (Paris, 1960); hereafter cited as Mertens-Fonck.

(ii) *healfæ* vii. 34, *healfe* vii. 35 (2×).

(iii) *tealte* vii. 137.

(iv) *psalme* vi. 61, but *sealmwurhte* i. 194, *psealmsonge* v. 186. (In this loan-word, however, ⟨a⟩ spellings are not infrequent elsewhere.)

The ⟨a⟩ spellings here could be attributed to the normal ME development of *ea* > *æ* > *a*, or to failure to have breaking.

Before the lengthening group -*ld*, both ⟨ea⟩ and ⟨a⟩ spellings again occur. Here, however, the ⟨a⟩ spellings are evidence of Anglian development, where *a* later underwent the change to *o* [ɔ:]. In the WS dialect, *ea* > *æ* equals ME *e* [ɛ:]. (See Crook-Jordan, §61.) I divide the following examples according to the homilies in which they are contained (with line numbers following the forms):

Homily i ⟨a⟩: *acwalde* 49, *aldor* 102, 108, 133; ⟨ea⟩: *an(d)weald(e)* 38, 55, 112, 171, 201, *seofenfealde* 151, *wealdend* 84.

Homily ii ⟨ea⟩: -*fealde* 94, etc., (*i*)*tealde* 110, 116, 117, 121, 126, 148.

Homily iii ⟨a⟩: *aldan* 274, *haldan* (-*æn*) 280, 310; ⟨ea⟩: *anfealdum* 107, *heald* (-*t*) 44, 271, (*i*)*tealde* 134, 183; ⟨æ⟩: *wældend* 86 (see discussion below).

Homily iv ⟨ea⟩: *heald* (-*t*) 292, 322, *sealde* (-*n*) 305, 344.

Homily v ⟨ea⟩: *anwealde* 115, *ealde* 36, 39, 173, *heald*- 79, 109, 162, *onstealde* 5, 116, *sealde* 39, 93, *weald* 61, 123.

Homily vi ⟨ea⟩: *ealdermonnum* 237, *healde*(-) 135, 263, *monifealde* 202.

Homily vii ⟨ea⟩: *beheald* 13, *eald*(-) 25, 86, *ealderdomes* 110, *ealdormen* 127, *healden* (-*on*) 43, 54, 64, 131, 159.

In general, ⟨ea⟩ spellings predominate. The complete absence of ⟨a⟩ spellings in the last three homilies is, however, striking, considering the number of spellings with ⟨ea⟩. This phenomenon may again reflect a different line of transmission for these homilies.

The ⟨æ⟩ of *wældend* (iii. 86) could reflect the monophthongization of ⟨ea⟩. E. G. Stanley's explanation of Orm's spelling *allwældennd* as an attempt to differentiate it from the verbal form is not likely to apply here directly.[1]

(b) *ea* before *r* + consonant

When no lengthening group follows, ⟨ea⟩ is most commonly used. Examples: *wearð* i. 101, 120, 149, etc., *cwearterne* ii. 30, *earmæn* iii. 260, *earmlice* iii. 116, *þearfæn* iii. 256, *earfoðlic*(-) v. 177, 185, *earfoðnesse* v. 66,

---

[1] 'Spellings of the *Waldend* group', in *Studies in Language, Literature and Culture of the Middle Ages and Later*, ed. E. Bagby Atwood and Archibald A. Hill (Austin, Texas, 1969), pp. 38–69, pp. 67–9.

vii. 67, *ȝearwode* vi. 68, *mearcode* vi. 192, *swearte* vii. 51, *þearf* vii. 95. The following exceptions occur: *ærming* iii. 92, *arfoþeste* iii. 267, *swarte* iii. 202, *erfoðnesse* vi. 247, *weorþ* vi. 84. The first three words show the normal ME development *ea* > *æ* > *a*. The -*er* form of *erfoðnesse* is characteristic of some West Midland dialects; see, for example, *Ancrene Riwle* manuscript, MS Cotton Nero A. xiv: *erm, herm, berme, kerf, ert* (Zettersten, pp. 232–3). But it could also be the result of *æ/e* confusion. The form *weorþ* is found also in the AB language. D'Ardenne, pp. 169f., explains the spelling as an indirect consequence of the past participle *geworpen* > *gewarpen*, and hence analogy with class VII (see also Zettersten, p. 245).

Before the lengthening groups *rd* and *rn*, ⟨ea⟩ is consistently found, even in words where reduced stress or failure to lengthen because of polysyllabic form might have led to *ea* > *æ* > *a*; for example, *earnode* i. 142, *hamweard* i. 21, 118, etc., *middaneard* i. 39, iii. 103, etc., *bearn(e)* ii. 193, iii. 134, etc., *heard(-)* iii. 80, 365, etc., *andweard(-)* iv. 336, v. 46, vi. 70, vii. 77.

(c) *ea* before *h* and *h* + consonant

⟨ea⟩ is commonly used, for example, *iseah* ii. 120, iii. 34, etc., *forseah* iii. 256, *leahtr-* iii. 121, 124, 126, iv. 326, *þeah* (shortened). Occasionally ⟨æ⟩ appears, for example, *læhtræs* vi. 35, *þæh* v. 73. (See also Orthography: vowels (2).)

4. OE *eo*

OE *eo* had become [ø] in the eleventh century, but in general the spelling ⟨eo⟩ is still used here, for example, *heofen-* i. 173, 175, etc., *eorþ-* iii. 17, 18, etc., *heorte* ii. 180, 182, etc., *feorran* i. 41. There is occasional evidence of unrounding to *e*, for example, *hundtentiȝ* beside *hundteontiȝ* (once each in homily iv) (lOE shortening). There is no evidence of Anglian smoothing, for example, *feoh* ii. 17, etc., and *weorc* ii. 85, etc., are always spelt with ⟨eo⟩. (The form *werces* occurs once (v. 171) but it is an addition by a later hand.) There are, however, other signs of Anglian influence:

(i) The Anglian form *seolf(-)* (as in the VP and the AB language) occurs beside the lWS form *sylf(-)*. Distribution is as follows:

	i	ii	iii	iv	v	vi	vii
seolf(-)	0	2	4	1	1	0	0
sylf(-)	13	14	6	7	4	4	6

(ii) The Anglian form *briht-* (VP *berht*, AB language *briht*) occurs alongside WS *beorht*. The word is used only in three homilies:

	iii	vi	vii
beorht(-)	1	10	0
briht(-)	0	19	2

(iii) The word *eornende* iii. 33 (WS *irnan*) is a distinctively Anglian form, occurring also in the VP and the AB language. Campbell (§155) explains that metathesis of *r* usually takes place too late for secondary *r*- groups to cause breaking but that in Anglian, when the vowel was *i*, metathesis of *r* was early enough for breaking to occur.[1]

In homily i *fefor* and *feofer/-or* each occur twice (i. 27, 28, 148, 153). This inconsistency probably stems from the Latin origin of the word ('febris'): back mutation does not seem to have occurred regularly in Latin loan words. Both forms are found in lOE: the *West-Saxon Gospels* of 1100 have *fefor*, the *Hatton Gospels* of 1160 have *feofer*. The AB language contains *feure* (Zettersten, p. 194).

5. OE *o*

In general ⟨o⟩ is found. The following exceptions should be noted:

(i) OE 1 & 3 pret. s. *wolde* often appears as *walde*. Altogether *wolde*(-) occurs twenty times, *walde* ten times (once altered from *wælde* v. 29). Distribution is as follows:

	i	ii	iii	iv	v	vi	vii
o	3	4	2	0	3	7	1
a	0	0	1	0	6	3	0

Clearly the use of *a* becomes much more frequent in the last three homilies, especially in homily v.

The ⟨a⟩ found in *walde* is characteristic of Anglian dialects; it is used consistently in the VP dialect (see Campbell, §156, Mertens-Fonck, p. 349), and in the AB language (see d'Ardenne, p. 188, Zettersten, p. 129). Whereas ⟨a⟩ in *walde* extended to Northumbria, the use of ⟨a⟩ also in *mareʒen* (i. 22, 143) allows the area to be narrowed further to the West Midlands (see Crook-Jordan, §35). The ⟨a⟩ spellings signify an opening of *o* between labials and liquids which is characteristic of the West Midlands. They also support a phonemic

[1] See also E. G. Stanley, 'The Chronology of *R*-metathesis in Old English', *English and Germanic Studies*, v (1952–3), 103–15.

status for [a] in late Mercian. If *walde* has a different ablaut grade from *wolde*, as certain scholars have argued, then this phonemic status is further substantiated (see Zettersten, pp. 130–1). It should be noted that *nolde* in these texts is always spelt with an ⟨o⟩, never with an ⟨a⟩ as in VP and the AB language.

(ii) OE *dorste* is spelt *durste* (iv. 367, v. 85, 153). Again *durste* is a consistently Anglian feature: it occurs in *Ru*[1] (see Campbell, §767) and in the AB language. Zettersten (p. 134) explains the ⟨u⟩ as being due to the influence of the indic. pret. p. and the subj. pret.

(iii) OE *sorg* appears both as *sorez-* (vi. 54, vii. 113) and as *seorez-* (vi. 94, vii. 59, 89). Zettersten (p. 124) notes that ⟨eo⟩ spellings in this word indicate an older rounded sound due to *i*-mutation (see also Crook-Jordan, §35).

6. IWS *y* < *ie*, arising (a) by palatal diphthongization of *ĕ*, (b) by *i*-mutation of *ĕa*, and (c) by *i*-mutation of *ĭo*.
Non-WS ⟨e⟩ often appears as well as IWS ⟨y(i)⟩. Examples:

(a) (i) *ʒif-*, *forʒif-*, *iʒif-* (or *-ʒyf-*) occur numerous times (i, 3×, ii, 26×, v, 3×, vi, 2×, vii, 2×). The form with ⟨e⟩ occurs only twice, both in vii: *forʒefenesse* vii. 148, *ʒefenæ* vii. 95.

(ii) In ii, *forʒylde* occurs 5×, *-ʒeld-* occurs 6× (*aʒeld-* ii. 25, *forʒeld-* ii. 28, *ʒeld-* ii. 8, 22, 25, 77). (The words do not occur in any other homily.)

(iii) *scyppend(e)* iii. 129, 287. (No instances of ⟨e⟩.)

(iv) *biʒete* v. 11, *biʒyte* vi. 49.

(b) (i) *cyrren* vi. 258. But *ichærred* vi. 244, *cerræn* vii. 158, *cerræð* vii. 145.

(ii) The form *dearne* (iii. 63) shows ⟨ea⟩ for Mercian ⟨e⟩. The same form appears in the AB language, which also has *wearnen* for OE *wiernan*/Anglian *wernan* (see Zettersten, pp. 54–5). These ⟨ea⟩ spellings suggest that in some Mercian dialects, and especially in the neighbourhood of the labial *w*, Primitive OE *æ* was retracted to *a* before *rn*, not broken to *ea*, and then mutated to [æ].

(c) *yrre* ii. 36, iii. 134, 135.

PHONOLOGY: LONG VOWELS

1. OE $\bar{e}$, $\bar{æ}$, $\overline{ea}$

As with the corresponding short forms, the graphemic confusion makes it impossible to draw any significant conclusion. (See Orthography: Vowels (2).)

In general, the three are spelt as in OE. The following exceptions occur.

OE $\bar{e}$ is often spelt $\langle æ \rangle$ (graphemic confusion).

OE $\bar{æ}^1$ (WGerm $\bar{a}$) is sometimes spelt $\langle e \rangle$. Examples:

(i) *sprece* (n.) ii. 52, *spece* (n.) v. 38, vi. 263, vii. 161, *specon* (v. pret. p.) vi. 16, 143, 145, 147), *speken* (v. pret. p.) vi. 20, 142. (10× altogether.) But *spæce* (n.) i. 20, 137, ii. 7, iii. 132, 207, 220, 229, *spæcon* (v. pret. p.) iii. 307. (8× altogether.)

(ii) *wældedum* iv. 355. But *dæd-/dæþ-* ii. 151, iii. 252, 291, v. 86, vi. 102, 134, 173, 194, 199, 258, 261, 264, vii. 146.

(iii) *iseliʒe* iv. 332, vii. 152. But *isæliʒe* vii. 56.

(iv) *tobrecon* (pret. p.) iii. 288. But *tobræce* (pret. subj. s.) ii. 146.

(v) *ormete* iii. 258.

I have not found any instances of $\langle ea \rangle$ for $æ^1$

OE $\bar{æ}^2$ (Germ. *ai* + *a*) appears sometimes as $\langle e \rangle$ and very occasionally as $\langle ea \rangle$. Examples:

(i) *æf(f)re* i. 76, ii. 111, 123, 198, 201, iii. 183, 225, 252, iv. 366, v. 8, 79, 84, 135, 174, vi. 36, 127, 171, 262, vii. 18, 22, 97. But *eafre* iii. 186, v. 56, vii. 144.

(ii) *næf(f)re* (-ræ) iii. 87, 303, v. 52, 54, 103, 108, vi. 67, 159, vii. 19, 51, 62. But *nefre* (-ræ) iii. 336, vii. 52.

(iii) *ælc-* i. 53, etc. (6×), ii. 47, etc. (6×), iii. 123, 284, v. 10, etc. (4×), vi. 37, 48, 209. But *ealc* v. 31, 102, *elc* v. 102.

(iv) *nænne* (mas.) ii. 29, vi. 29, 117, vii. 95. But *nenne* iii. 216, v. 166, vi. 119, 229.

(v) *ærest(-)* ii. 61, 100, 185, v. 142, 168, vi. 80, 99, 151, 244. But *ereste* v. 60, 63.

(vi) *ilædde* vi. 125, *iledde* vi. 170. Elsewhere *-læd-*.

(vii) *forʒæʒednysse* ii. 146. But *forʒeaʒednysse* ii. 145.

(viii) *healend* vi. 26. Numerous instances of *hælend* in each homily.

(ix) *teachunge* v. 117. But *tæcæþ* ii. 207, 216, *tæhte* ii. 221, *tæcð* iii. 162, *tæcinge* v. 166, 175, *tæhte* v. 163, *tæche* vii. 149, *tæcæn* vii. 130.

Whereas both $æ^1$ and $æ^2$ sometimes appear as $\langle e \rangle$, only $æ^2$ ever appears as ⟨ea⟩. A correspondence can be noted with the AB language, which shows a fairly consistent representation of $\bar{æ}^1$ (VP $\bar{e}$) by ⟨e⟩ and of $\bar{æ}^2$ (VP $\bar{æ}$) by ⟨ea⟩. (See d'Ardenne, pp. 191–2).

As with OE $\bar{ea}$, OE $\overline{ea}$ was monophthongized to [æ] about 1000. The spelling generally remains ⟨ea⟩, but there are occasional instances of ⟨æ⟩ or ⟨e⟩. Examples with ⟨æ⟩: æð v. 87, hænum vi. 38, scæwæde vi. 187. Examples with ⟨e⟩: elæ v. 133, asmeȝean vi. 45. In the AB language, $\overline{ea}$ also retains its OE spelling in general, though ⟨e⟩ occurs occasionally (see d'Ardenne, p. 192).

2. IWS $\bar{y}$, $\bar{\imath}$ (< īe, arising (a) by *i*-umlaut of $\overline{ea}$ or (b) by palatal diph- thongization of $\bar{e}$), Anglian $\bar{e}$

The appearance of ⟨e⟩ representing Anglian $\bar{e}$, as well as ⟨y⟩ repre- senting WS ie/y, establishes an Anglian influence in the course of transmission. There is no sign of SW ⟨u⟩ for [y]. Examples and distribution:

(a) (i) (ȝe)heran/(ȝe)hyran and its various forms:

	i	ii	iii	iv	v	vi	vii
-her-	1	1	1	0	2	6	4
-hyr-	1	5	7	1	1	2	0

It can be seen that the number of ⟨e⟩ spellings increases in the last three homilies.

(ii) (ȝe)lefan/(ȝe)lyfan and its various forms:

	i	ii	iii	iv	v	vi	vii
-lef-	2	1	2	0	0	–	–
-lyf-	13	0	8	1	4	–	–

(b) No instances of ȝet for IWS ȝyt/ȝit.

3. IWS $\bar{y}$ (< īe, arising by *i*-mutation of $\overline{\imatho}$), Angl. $\overline{eo}$ (< $\overline{\imatho}$/$\overline{eo}$). Both IWS ⟨y⟩ and Angl. ⟨eo⟩ appear. Examples:

(i) The verb styran/steoran and its various forms: -styr- ii, 4×, v, 1×. -steor- ii, 5×.

(ii) Noun ansyn appears as ansyne seventeen times altogether (v, 14×, vi, 3×), and as anseone once (vi. 12). (See Crook-Jordan, §86.)

PHONOLOGY: CONSONANTS

1. Medial [ɣ] is normally represented by ⟨ȝ⟩ (see Orthography: Consonants (5)). Occasionally, however, it appears as ⟨g⟩, not ⟨ȝ⟩, and this may be attributable to more than orthographical confusion. The ⟨g⟩ can be seen first in *witega(-æ(n)*)), which is spelt four times with ⟨g⟩ (i. 179, iii. 50, v. 41, vi. 148) and once with ⟨ȝ⟩ (vi. 61). (There is also an instance of *witegunge* at iii. 322.) The spelling ⟨g⟩ occurs regularly in *witege* in the AB dialect (d'Ardenne, p. 195). D'Ardenne explains this spelling as a natural change of *ȝ* to *g* after *d*, *t* and spirants *f*, *s*, *ð*, and notes that these combinations only arose naturally in the contracted forms related to adjectival *ig*.

The same use of ⟨g⟩ for ⟨ȝ⟩ occurs in *sunegode* (v. 53). Again the AB language can be compared, since it shows ⟨g⟩, not ⟨ȝ⟩, for *sunegin* and *sunegede*. D'Ardenne (p. 167) notes that the normal development of *syneȝian* is seen in ME *suneȝen, synewen, zeneȝi*, etc., but that 'in WM., where the type of derivative verb with stop *g*, as in *biblodgin, blodegin*, was developed [cf. *witege*], it is not surprising to find the *g* [of *syngian*] . . . transferred also to the disyllabic stems, producing AB *sunegin*'.

The single instance of *eagan* (iii. 364) beside the numerous instances of *eaȝan(-en)* is surprising and may be the result of scribal uncertainty. If, however, the ⟨ȝ⟩ here does represent the velar [ɣ] (as signified by Orm's *eȝhe*) rather than the palatal [j] (Crook-Jordan, §190, discusses the alternatives), then we have another example of the tendency for *ȝ* to become *g* and d'Ardenne's rule may need to be extended.

2. lOE metathesis by which *rht* becomes *r-ht* with the vowel after the *r* (Campbell §459) is regular, for example, *wrohte* i. 161, 165, etc., *bewrohtest* vi. 62, *wruhte* vi. 7.

The metathesis seen in MS *-hædfnesse* (v. 2) and in MS *huwhilce* (i. 42) can probably be ascribed to scribal error, and these have therefore been amended to *-hæfdnesse* and *ȝehwilce* respectively. Since the scribe does not elsewhere use ⟨wh⟩ for ⟨hw⟩, it is unlikely that in *huwhilce*, he is amalgamating ⟨hu⟩ of his exemplar with his own ⟨wh⟩.

3. *h* is regularly lost initially before *l*, *r*, as in the AB dialect (d'Ardenne, p. 201). Examples: *laforde* ii. 12, 18, etc., *lafes* v. 65, 66, etc., *lystæn* v. 79, vii. 160, *raðe* i. 30, ii. 25, vii. 136, *rofe* i. 110, *bireowsunge* ii. 152, *repunge* iii. 215, *rinæn* v. 93, *ætrinæn* v. 84, *rædlice* vi. 14, 169, vii. 73.

4. Long consonants are occasionally simplified. Examples: *fuluhte*

v. 5, *fulluht-* 10×; *sunendaȝæn* v. 181, *sunnendæȝ* 2×; *synum* iii. 92, *synn-* numerous times, *syðæn*, *-an*, *-on* v. 140, 141, 142, 143, vi. 83, 126, *syððan*, *-æn* 13×.

5. The form *iblesode* (vii. 36) may reflect the later ME development to *-bless-*. If so, it is the earliest example of this development. It may, however, be the result of scribal error. The following forms are found elsewhere in these homilies: *ibledsod* i. 196, *blætsung* iii. 317, *iblætsedon* iii. 240.

PHONOLOGY: UNSTRESSED SYLLABLES

1. All OE vowels in unstressed syllables were reduced, as usual in ME, to [ə], and often spelt ⟨e⟩ or ⟨æ⟩ instead of the normal OE spelling (see Accidence).

2. Final *n* arising from OE *-n* or *-m* is often lost, particularly in nominal forms (see Accidence).

3. Prefix written *ge-* in OE is spelt *ȝe-* or *i*, and is commonly used. Sometimes the two are combined: *ȝei-*.[1]

ACCIDENCE

Many inflections of lWS are correctly written, but there are signs that the levelling to [ə] characteristic of ME had occurred in the scribe's dialect (see also Phonology: Unstressed Syllables).

Nouns

The following orthographical confusion occurs in the inflections (with examples):

⟨æ⟩ for OE ⟨e⟩ is frequent: *lifæ* (str. ds.) v. 106, *larþeowæs* (str. gs.) v. 166

⟨a⟩ for OE ⟨e⟩ occurs occasionally: *dæda* (str. ds.) iii. 291, *apostolas* (str. gs.) iii. 214

⟨o⟩ for OE ⟨e⟩ occurs occasionally: *swæsendo* (str. ds.) v. 181, *wæredo* (str. ds.) vi. 5

---

[1] For the use of *ge-* in lOE and eME, particularly in nouns, see E. G. Stanley, 'The Prenominal Prefix *ge-* in Late Old English and Early Middle English', *Transactions of the Philological Society* (1982), 25–66.

⟨æ⟩ for OE ⟨a⟩ occurs frequently: *englæs* (str. np.) v. 105, *sawlæ* (str. gp.) v. 4, *heortæn* (wk. ds.) ii. 47

⟨e⟩ for OE ⟨a⟩ occurs quite often: *stanes* (str. np.) v. 65, *worde* (str. gp.) v. 76

⟨o⟩ for OE ⟨a⟩ in *uppon* (wk. ds.) v. 98

Final *n* is often omitted in the oblique cases of weak nouns. (This applies also to the dative plural of both weak and strong nouns, where occasionally *-en* < *-um*; see §(vi) below.)

The inflections differ from their OE counterparts in the following respects also:

(i) *-e* is occasionally added to an otherwise endingless form. Examples: *anseone* (fns.) vi. 12, *ansyne* (fns.) vi. 73, *blisse* (fns.) vi. 43, *murhðe* (fns.) vi. 43, *sawla* (fns.) iv. 328, *sunne* (fns. 'sin') v. 53, *stæfne* (fns.) vi. 255. The tendency for feminine nouns (for example, *unriht-wisnesse* iii. 120) which ended in a consonant in OE to have a final *e* in the nominative singular is common in ME. (Already in early texts, *-nesse* is sometimes extended to the nominative singular; see Campbell, §592 (f).)

(ii) Occasionally the normal OE inflexion is omitted altogether, as in the following examples:

as.: *ælmes* v. 12, *laðung* vi. 138.

gs.: *beorhtnes* vi. 87.

ds.: *beorhtnes* vi. 77, 168, *Crist* v. 53, *festen* v. 9, *lust* vi. 50, *wæsten* v. 15, *pistol* iii. 130

(iii) In some feminine and neuter nouns, the nominative and accusative plurals have occasionally been formed with *-en* (a feature which becomes more common in later ME, as in the AB dialect.) Examples:

np.: *limen* (n.) v. 88, 89, 90

ap.: *boden* (n.) vii. 127, *ȝebeden* (n.) v. 12, *honden* (f.) v. 94, *ricen* (n.) v. 122, *sunnæn* (f.) v. 9, *synnen* (f.) vi. 135, *wundæn* (f.) vi. 115

(iv) The gp. form *-ena* of the OE weak declension and of some fem. *o*-nouns (for example, *wracane* iii. 143 and *ȝefenæ* vii. 95) is occasionally used to express the gp. of other nouns as well: *daȝene* v. 180, 182, *toðene* vii. 50. This feature is found in other early ME texts, for example, in AB: *englene, kingene, dahene*. Here *dahene*, although genitival in form, is used in a dative context: *don ut of dahene*. D'Ardenne suggests in her glossary (p. 85) that it stands here for older *dahen* (VP *dægum*), surviving only in idiom with *don*, 'do away with'. She later adds that the substitution of *dahene* for **dahe* in this expression illustrates the equivalence of *e* and *ene* (p. 209). G. B. Jack offers a different explanation, that the gp. form *dagena* (found in OE as well as *daga*) gave rise to a new stem *dahen-* to which the prepositional inflection *-e* was added (derived from OE dp. *-um*).[1]

(v) In vii, the inflection *-es* is sometimes used to express the dp.: *mid weallende muðes* vii. 49, *mid teares* vii. 50, *mid þam feȝereste ȝymstanes* vii. 114–15, *ilic ... rænæs scuræs* vii. 135. The only example elsewhere is *bi Godes wordes* v. 78 (where *wordes* may be an error for ds. *worde*). In the AB dialect, *-es* is often used to express the dative case (d'Ardenne, 'case 3'), and is especially frequent after prepositions. D'Ardenne concludes that 'we must therefore assume an older stage, not far behind our AB, in which the dative *e* (*en*) derived from *um*, survived especially after prepositions, as did the singular dative in *e*. This *e* was then converted into *es*' (p. 205).

Cecily Clark notes that 'after prepositions rather more vestiges of dative inflexion survive' than do elsewhere, but adds that even then the nom./acc. form is used more often.[2] Since the regular nom. and acc. inflexion of all the nouns cited above is *-(a)s*, we may in fact have the regular nom. and acc. form being used in a dative position.

In any case, the use of *-s* to denote the dp. after prepositions, which appears only in vii, suggests that this homily may have derived from another copy where a more advanced dialect had already been included.

(vi) The dative plural is also sometimes denoted by *-en* (or *-æn*) which has developed from OE *-um* or from extension of the np. and ap. forms to the dp. Examples: *weaxbræden* ii. 134, *ȝebroðren* ii. 166, *leahtræn* iii. 124, *bræden* v. 40, *halȝæn* vi. 97, *honden* vi. 226, *eaȝnen* vi. 254.

The final *-n* is only rarely omitted: *costunge* v. 63, *engle* v. 162.

Conversely the inflection *-um* appears elsewhere for *-an/-æn* (e.g. MS *iferum* ii. 158, MS *heortū* ii. 167) and also for *-e* (e.g. MS *wifū* ii. 13, MS *childū* ii. 190, MS *bearnū* ii. 193). These spellings

---

[1] 'The Prepositional Plural in the AB Language', *NM* 82 (1981), 175–80. Jack compares AB words such as *ehnen* 'eyes' and *weane* 'misery' which have stem-forms derived from the OE gp.

[2] *The Peterborough Chronicle 1070–1154*, 2nd ed. (Oxford, 1970), p. liv.

imply that dp. *-um* was no longer distinct from np. and ap. *-an*, *-æn*, and *-e*.

Adjectives

In general, the OE inflexions are retained.

The orthographical confusion common to all unstressed syllables applies also to adjectival inflexions:

⟨æ⟩ for OE ⟨e⟩: *moniȝæ* (str. map.) i. 113, *soðæ* (str. fas.) ii. 176

⟨æ⟩ for OE ⟨a⟩:. *yfelræ* (str. gp.) v. 116, *godspellicæn* (wk. ds.) v. 22

⟨e⟩ for OE ⟨a⟩: *teoþe* (wk. mns.) v. 182, *eadmoden* (wk. ap.) i. 126

⟨o⟩ for OE ⟨a⟩: *forsædon* (wk. mas.) iii. 289

Final *n* is frequently omitted in oblique cases of weak adjectives (including dp. where *-en* < *-um*).

In accordance with development towards ME, there is a tendency for the inflexion of adjectives to be reduced to the addition of *e*. The signs of this development are as follows:

(a) in strong forms:

(i) mas. *-ne* > *-e* in *mycele wæstm* iv. 289, *æniȝe dæl* vi. 114.

(ii) m. and nds. *-um* > *-e* in, for example, *wið hearde stane* v. 108.

(iii) nap. takes *-e* in *swylce ðing* i. 171, *þeowtlice weorc* iii. 281.

(iv) dp. *-um* > *-e* in, for example, *on twam stænene weaxbræden* ii. 134, *fram weoruldlice weorcum* iii. 290, *on moniȝe wisum* iv. 340.

(b) in weak forms:

(i) as. and ds., and np. and ap. *-an* frequently appears as *-e* (*-æ*/*-a*), for example, *þone ilcæ ræstandæȝ* iii. 291, *þæs godspellice word* (ap.) vi. 256–7, *on ðare swarte nihte* iii. 202, *þa haliȝe martyræs* (np.) iv. 335, *þas syllice wundræ* (ap.) i. 170.

(ii) gp. *-ra* > *-æ* in *þare rihtwisæ monnæ* iii. 243, *heoræ arleasæ dædu* iii. 252.

(iii) dp. *-um* > *-e* in, for example, *on his mycle wundrum* i. 189, *for his aȝene synnum* iii. 11, 170.

The tendency to level inflexions to *e* does not seem to be governed by any factor in particular; it occurs in both prepositional and non-prepositional phrases, before both vowels and consonants, and with both polysyllabic and monosyllabic stems.

There are several occasions on which the scribe omits the OE inflexion altogether:

(i) str. fas. *-e* omitted in *æniȝ fare* v. 27, *æniȝ sunne* v. 8, *Cristes ansyne* (. . .) *swa briht* vi. 178, 195–6, *unasecgendlic lufæ* vi. 209.

(ii) str. ds. or dp. *-um* in *fram alle synlic lust* vi. 50.

(iii) wk. nas. *-e* omitted in *þæt gastlic andȝit* iv. 298, *on þisse deaþelic lif* vi. 84.

(iv) wk. ap. *-an* omitted in *þa haliȝ witegæn* vi. 148.

For the uninflected forms *æniȝ* and *haliȝ*, see d'Ardenne, who notes that in the AB language, 'adjectives ending in *i* (OE *ig*) after a long initial syllable are regularly indeclinable owing to the change of *ige* to *i*' (p. 217). Uninflected *briht* (in (i) above) may be the result of scribal carelessness, since the following phrase reads *and swa wlitiȝe*. The tendency to lose inflections seems to have to have been common in adjectives ending *-lic*.

Pronouns

1. *Personal Pronouns*

The first and second person pronoun forms are identical to the OE ones. The spelling *wæ* occurs once for *we* (see Orthography: Vowels (2)).

The following table shows the third person pronoun forms:

	m.	f.	n.	pl.
N.	he, hæ (vi. 145)	heo	hit	heo, hyo (vi. 27)
A.	hine	heo	hit	heom, heo, hi (ii. 65)
G.	his	hire	his	heoræ, -a, -e, hore (vi. 53)
D.	him	hire	him	heom

The fas. form *heo* (WS *hie*, *hi*) is probably based on the nominative form. This form also appears in the Mercian gloss to the Rushworth Gospels (Campbell, Ru.¹), and in the ninth-century Martyrology fragment (BL Addit. MS 23211) fas. *hio* appears.

The use of ap. *heom* beside *heo* is an early example of the ME replacement by the dative as the oblique case.

The spelling *hore* (vi. 53) once for gp. *heora* is probably an indication of the sound change to [ø] (see Phonology: Short Vowels (4)).

2. *Demonstrative pronouns*

The following tables show the various demonstrative pronoun forms:

(a) the simple demonstrative and definite article:

	m.	f.	n.	pl.
N.	þe, þeo, sæ	þeo	þæt	þa, þæ
A.	þon(n)e, þen(n)e, þane, þæne	þa, þæ, þæt	þæt	þa
G.	þæs, þes	þare	þæs	þare, þære
D.	þam	þare, þere, þære	þan, þam, þe	þam

The mns. form *þe* is generally used; it shows the levelling of initial *s* to the initial *þ* of other forms which is characteristic of ME. The form *sæ* is used only once (i. 140), and is combined there with the relative particle *ðe*. The occasional use of *þeo* for the mns. may perhaps be attributed to scribal confusion of gender. The instances are *þeo fefor/feofer* i. 27, 148, 153 (*þe fefor* occurs once at i. 28), *þeo wurðscipe* v. 160.

The same levelling of initial *s* to initial *þ* accounts for the fns. form *þeo*. There are no instances of *seo*.

For the various mas. forms, see Campbell, §380. For examples of *þonne* for *þone* and *þenne* for *þene*, see Orthography: Consonants (7) above.

The regular fas. form is *þa* (once *þæ* vii. 150). The use of *þæt* (once only) in *þæt ece eadiʒnesse* (vi. 265–6) may be an attempt by the scribe to avoid hiatus.

The form *þe* is occasionally used instead of *þam* to denote the nds.: *into þe wynsume bærne* iv. 309, *on þe soðe life* iv. 327, *mid þe deorewurðeste godewebbe* vii. 119.

The regular np. form *þa* once occurs as *þe* (*þe soðfæste* vii. 32), and once as *þæ* (*þæ rice caseres* vii. 126). Since, however, *þa* never occurs for mns. *þe*, we can assume that the plural was still pronounced with a distinct [a] and not [ə].

(b) the compound (emphatic) demonstrative pronoun:

	m.	f.	n.	pl.
N.	þes, þæs	þeos	þis	þas, þæs
A.	þesne, þisne, þæsne, þysne	þas, þis (v. 47)	þis, þisse (vi. 84)	þas
G.	þisses	þisre, þiss(e)re	þisses, þysses	–
D.	þissum	þisse, þiss(e)re, þis, þissen (vi. 51), þissum (v. 22)	þisse, þissum	þissum

There is no sign that *þeos* was extended to the fas. or the pl. as it was in the AB language (see d'Ardenne, pp. 226–7).

The fds. *þis* appears only once: *on þis ytemeste tide* (v. 47). The scribe's intention may be to avoid hiatus, but the reduced form *þis* is common in the AB dialect and in other ME texts.

3. *The relative pronoun*

The relative pronoun is expressed by the particle *þe* (once *þæ*), both by itself and in conjunction with the corresponding forms of the demonstrative.

There is one example of the use of *þæt* for *þe*: *ne nan synna þæt ne sceal beon forʒifen* (ii. 124).

In general, there is no sign of the replacement of *þe* by *þat* which was common in at least some texts of the thirteenth century, nor indeed of the distinction between animate and inanimate antecedents of *þe* and *þat* respectively, which Angus McIntosh identifies in the Katherine Group.[1]

Verbs

In general, the OE strong and weak conjugation forms are retained. The usual reduction of unstressed vowels to [ə] has clearly occurred (see Phonology: Unstressed Syllables (1)); it is accompanied by orthographical confusion of the graphs *æ*, *e*, *a*, and *o*, for example, infinitive *-an* spelt also *-æn*, *-en*, *-on*; pres. 2s. *-ast* spelt also *-æst*; pres. 3s. and pres. pl. spelt also *-æð* (and, rarely, *-oð*, for example, *acsoð* (pres. 3s.) ii. 103; pret. 3s. *-te*, *-de* also spelt *-tæ*, *-dæ*, and *-ode* also spelt *-ede*; pp. *-od* appears as *-æd*, *-ed*.

The scribe seems to respect in some degree the OE differentiation between weak class I and weak class II spelling: whereas weak II 2s. *-ast* commonly appears as *-æst*, weak I *-est* only occasionally does so, and whereas weak I *-að* is regularly spelt *-æð*, weak I *-eð* seems to remain *-eð*.

Significant deviations from the lWS standard are as follows:

1. Infinitive

The distinction between the infinitive and inflected infinitive is not always retained, e.g. *to lyfen . . . to witenne* v. 23–4.

---

[1] 'The Relative Pronouns *þE* and *þAT* in Early Middle English', *English and Germanic Studies*, i (1947–8), 73–87.

2. Present tense

(i) Syncope in weak I pres. 2s. & 3s. is not common, although some forms show it: *wurcð* i. 193 (beside *wurcæð* i. 197); *ʒehyrð* ii. 65, 67 (beside *ihyræð* ii. 62, 63); *ʒemænð* ii. 106; *forlyst* iv. 290; *aspent* iv. 330. The general dearth of syncopated forms suggests a link with the Anglian dialect where syncope is also rare (see Campbell, §751 (1)). (The AB dialect, however, has very frequent contraction; see d'Ardenne, p. 235.)

(ii) The ending *y* appears twice for pres. 3s., once for a strong verb, once for a weak verb: *spæky* iii. 350, *mismaky* iii. 123. The *y* for *þ* here may represent a scribal confusion of the two letters. (That both instances are in iii suggests a different exemplar for this homily.)

(iii) The inflectional -*i*- of weak II verbs (in, for example, the infin. and pres. pl.) is regularly retained, for example, *axiæn*, *earniæn*, *lufiæn*, *iaʒniæð*, *arwurðiæþ*, *blissiæð*, *halʒiæð*, *truwiæð*, *woniæð*. It is omitted rarely in the pres. p. (*þrowæð* vi. 92, 94, *earnæþ* vi. 199), and more commonly in the infinitive (e.g. *fanden* v. 49, *fonden* v. 59, *sceawen* vi. 46, *þanken* vi. 173, *loken* vi. 208).

(iv) A variety of forms is used for the pres. 1s. form of *beon* 'to be', for example, *am* i. 109, 112, iii. 16; *æm* iii. 16, 196; *eam* iii. 196; *eom* vii. 15. The form *eam* suggests Anglian influence; the form *am* (*æm*), used most frequently, is the normal ME form.

3. Past tense

(i) The past tense forms of strong verbs are regularly developed from the OE forms. (See Orthography and Phonology.)

(ii) The pret. pl. forms of *seon* are distinctively Anglian (see Mertens-Fonck, p. 270). Examples: *isæʒen* ii. 32, *iseaʒen* iii. 25, *iseʒon* iii. 362, 366, *iseʒen* iii. 364, vi. 28, 31, etc. The Anglian influence also extends to the past subjunctive, for example, *iseʒe* iii. 39, *isæʒe* iii. 99, 350, and to the past participle, for example, *isæʒene* vi. 144.

(iii) One irregular form is pret. p. *adroʒon* iii. 248 (for *adrugon*).

EDITORIAL PROCEDURE

Each of the homilies has a separate introduction, discussing its background, contents, and relation to sources and analogues. Each is also accompanied by an apparatus and explanatory notes. Latin sources are printed beneath the appropriate Old English material.

The text, in accordance with standard EETS practice, is printed with modern punctuation and capitalization. The spelling and word-order of the manuscript are generally retained. Where the manuscript is clearly in error, or where the scribe's inflections might be misleading, I have emended and annotated as necessary.[1] Abbreviations are silently expanded in the text, again in accordance with standard EETS practice, for example, *and* for *7*, *-um* for *-ū*, *þæt* for *þ*, *-de* for a hooked *d*.[2] Where abbreviations might be expanded in more than one way, I have expanded according to the appropriate Old English form.[3] Manuscript readings in the apparatus are given in their original and not expanded form. Accents are not here reproduced, since they seem to be used arbitrarily in the manuscript. Word-division and paragraphing are editorial, as is the metrical lineation in the first four homilies. Glosses to the main text are indicated in the footnotes. Folio references to the manuscript, and page references to Belfour's edition, are provided in the margin. Latin quotations are in italics.

The following signs are used in the main text:

( ) indicates an emendation other than a simple omission; the manuscript original is noted below in the apparatus.

[ ] indicates an omission in the manuscript.

Single quotation marks are used to indicate translation of the gospel-text expounded in the homily. Direct speech is not marked by quotation-marks.

In the apparatus the lemma, where supplied, is followed by a square bracket]; every word except the lemmata and variant readings is italicized. An interlinear or marginal insertion is indicated by ` ´; the material within these marks is italicized if the insertion is by a later hand (this applies particularly to homily iv).

The Latin sources are printed below the corresponding English text. Scriptural quotations are placed in single quotation marks. Otherwise I have followed the spelling and punctuation of the editor.

---

[1] The emendations which correspond to those made by Belfour are found on the following lines: homily i. 70, 84, 96, 116, 124, 132, 152; homily ii. 13, 38, 80, 146, 158, 167, 193, 207, 221; homily iii. 212, 221, 308; homily iv. 287, 288, 314, 360; homily v. 2, 40, 93, 148, 154, 155, 163, 171, 174; homily vi. 13, 18, 35, 52, 62, 81, 85, 90, 145, 168, 187, 207, 228, 237, 240, 259; homily vii. 17, 29, 31, 37, 39, 40, 46, 57, 68, 101, 102, 105, 107, 108, 113, 118, 124–5, 129, 147.

[2] For a list of abbreviations, see p. xix above.

[3] The abbreviation most often affected by this is *hī*. The occurrences of *hī* where *hine* has seemed to be a more appropriate expansion than *him* are all in homilies v, vi, and vii, and the line numbers are as follows: v. 15, 82, 114, 118, 130, 134, 153, vi. 8, 47, 135, vii. 71.

THE HOMILIES

I

THE HEALING OF THE KING'S SON

DATE AND AUDIENCE

The first homily in this collection, written by Ælfric, expounds John iv. 46-53, pericope for the Twenty-second Sunday after Pentecost. Manuscript evidence suggests that it was one of Ælfric's later compositions. Peter Clemoes argues from his examination of the manuscripts containing works by Ælfric that the homily was composed as an item for what he terms TH II, which refers to the second phase in Ælfric's development of his liturgical homilies for the Proper of the Season (Temporale). The first phase, TH I, is assigned by Clemoes to the period following the publication of the *Lives of the Saints* (1002-5); it provided a series for the Proper of the Season from Christmas to the Sunday after Pentecost. TH II (assigned to 1006 onwards) comprised an extension of this series throughout the year while confining it more strictly to pericope homilies.[1] The Twenty-second Sunday after Pentecost was an occasion for which Ælfric had not originally provided a homily, and this text was apparently designed to fill that gap.

The late date of the homily has implications for the identification of its intended audience. The TH II series was, according to Milton McC. Gatch, most probably designed for a monastic or clerical audience: TH II provides 'a new and more conventionally homiliarist organization of Ælfric's works for the Temporale which might have been intended for use in the Office by, say, seculars or canons who had inadequate Latin to follow the unenglished homilies of the Fathers or, more likely, for devotional reading'.[2] Mary Clayton has also noted 'a marked change in the character of Ælfric's later homilies for the Temporale: like the *Lives of the Saints*, they do not give the impression of being texts intended to be delivered to an ordinary lay congregation. They are pure homilies, consisting of exegesis only and lacking the

---

[1] Clemoes, 'Chronology', pp. 227-33.
[2] Milton McC. Gatch, *Preaching and Theology in Anglo-Saxon England: Ælfric and Wulfstan* (Toronto, 1977), p. 55.

sermon material found in the *Catholic Homilies*. There are, for example
none of the admonitions to the laity on subjects like tithes and sexual
behaviour which are such a marked characteristic of the *Catholic
Homilies*'. Clayton suggests that 'Ælfric's own conception of the
function of his work had changed . . . the *Temporale Homilies* were
intended largely for the religious element in his audience, who did not
need the kind of basic moral teaching which he had considered necessary in the *Catholic Homilies*'. In accord with Gatch, Clayton concludes
that 'the later homilies, saints' lives and Old Testament texts . . . are
reading pieces for those monks who had been in need of the kind of
material with which the *Catholic Homilies* had provided them, as well as
for the devout literate laity, who can always only have been a very
small group'.[1]

In homily i, exegesis of a gospel-text is certainly Ælfric's priority,
and he does not include any basic moral teaching. But neither does he
seem to have had a particularly learned audience in mind. In fact
Ælfric evokes a rather simple audience in his two direct addresses to
them. Early in his commentary he assures them that he will neither
overtax their understanding nor bore them:

> and we wullæð eow sæcgæn sum andʒit þerto
> of þare trahtnunge bi eowræs andʒites mæðe,
> na swa ðeah to longlice, þæt hit eow æðryt ne þynce.   (ll. 33–5)

This is exactly the same sentiment as that expressed in the opening
paragraph of Ælfric's homily on Job (CH II xxx, 2–6), and in his
Second Series homily for the Sunday *In media Quadragesime* (CH II xii,
2–6). The second direct address to his audience is an informal appeal
to them prior to his image of the sun's rays:

> Wen is þæt eower sum þisses wundriʒe nu
> hu ðe Almihtiʒæ God ælcne mon ihere,
> beo ðær ðe he beo, ʒif he bit his mildsunge.   (ll. 78–80)

Both of the references to his audience in this homily imply that Ælfric
expected from at least some of them only limited understanding, and
that he wished his commentary to be accessible to an uneducated, lay
audience as much as to a monastic or clerical one. Similarly the information about underkings and the organisation of the kingdom of
Judaea which Ælfric added to his main source might appeal especially

---

[1] Mary Clayton, 'Homiliaries and Preaching in Anglo-Saxon England', *Peritia*, iv
(1985), 207–42, pp. 240–1.

to a lay audience.[1] The image of the sun too, although deriving from patristic theology, is practical, rooted in the everyday world and easily assimilated. Moreover the structure of the homily is straightforward. Ælfric first translates the gospel-text, then treats it in the form of a running gloss on each verse in turn. He strives for simplicity and clarity in his exposition. Where he has the choice of interpreting literally or allegorically, as in the term 'underking' and in the story of Lazarus, he prefers the literal to the allegorical. An unsophisticated audience seems to be uppermost in Ælfric's mind. He is not just 'providing monastic material while still ostensibly addressing the people'.[2]

This does not diminish the importance to Ælfric of the religious element in his audience. But certainly he seems to have expected the laity to be amongst their number even on the less popular occasion of the Twenty-second Sunday after Pentecost, and to have intended his commentary to be accessible to them throughout. It might be conjectured that the homily is actually an earlier composition which Ælfric set aside then later included in his TH II series. Indeed, contrary to his normal practice, Ælfric makes no mention of previous discussions in this homily, although his material does overlap in places with that in other homilies. However the passages of repeated material which are not found in the homily's immediate source—the account of Archelaus' banishment and replacement by tetrarchs, and the image of the sun's rays—apparently derive from Ælfric's recollection of his previous renderings rather than from a first reading or rereading of the original Latin sources. The lack of reference to previous discussions might be explained partly by its inclusion in TH II. Ælfric's other account of Archelaus' banishment and its aftermath occurs in his homily for the Decollation of John the Baptist (CH I xxxii) which belongs to the Proper of the Saints and was therefore not included in TH I or TH II (it is not included in the manuscripts cited by Clemoes as witnesses for the two series). Clearly Ælfric would not have referred to a previous discussion if it did not belong to his current series. The image of the sun's rays, which I discuss below, appears elsewhere in two homilies (CH I xx and Pope viii), both of which were included in the TH I and TH II series. But Ælfric does not refer to CH I xx in Pope viii, even though the latter was certainly written later. The image evidently did not require any reference to previous usages.

Clemoes provides other manuscript evidence to suggest that homily i was a new composition at the TH II stage rather than carried over from TH I. The subject of the sevenfold gifts of the Holy Spirit (ll. 49–52) is raised without any reference to the TH I homily for the third Sunday after Easter (a compilation consisting of Napier viii, some of *De Doctrina Apostolica*, and a unique conclusion), 'whereas the TH I homily for the Sunday after the Ascension and *In Octavis Pentecosten* both have such a reference when they mention the same subject'.[1] The TH I homily for the third Sunday after Easter was discarded at the TH II stage and replaced by Assmann vi, and a TH II composition would therefore avoid any reference to it. The evidence all points to a late date for the homily despite the unsophisticated level of the commentary.

TRANSLATION OF THE GOSPEL-TEXT

The translation of John iv. 46-53 with which the homily begins tends towards amplification and interpretation while keeping always to the meaning of the original. Such non-scriptural phrases as 'ðær ðær he swyðest bodede', 'six fate fulle mid þam fyrmestan wine', 'ʒeorne', 'his lifes unwæne', 'and hopode to þan', 'on mareʒen', 'mid blisse', and 'mid fyrwetnysse sonæ' both enliven and dramatize the story. They also provide the alliteration and extra stressed syllables by which Ælfric creates his rhythmical prose, although as usual when translating a gospel-text Ælfric is not entirely consistent in his use of this style.[2] Ælfric is careful to make his text as relevant as possible to contemporary usage; he renders 'hora septima', for example, by 'swa ofer midne dæʒ' (where the West-Saxon gospels translate 'to þære seofoþan tide'). This adjustment of the biblical text by Ælfric means that he has to specify the connection between 'swa ofer midne dæʒ' and 'on ðare seofoðen tide' in order to make appropriate an interpretation of the number seven (ll. 149 ff.).

Ælfric had translated John iv. 46-53 once before in his homily for the Third Sunday after the Lord's Epiphany:

Iohannes se Godspellere awrat, þæt 'Sum under-cyning com to Criste, and hine bæd þæt he ham mid him siðode, and his sunu gehælde; forðan þe he

---

[1] Clemoes, 'Chronology', p. 232.

[2] Comparison of Ælfric's translation with that of the West-Saxon gospels reveals that while the latter may be more accurate, they exhibit none of the colourful individuality which emanates from Ælfric's version. See W. W. Skeat, ed., *The Gospel According to St. John*, vol. 4 of *The Four Gospels* (Cambridge, 1878), p. 42.

læig æt forðsiðe. þa cwæð se Hælend to ðam under-cyninge, Gewend þe ham, þin sunu leofað. He gelyfde þæs Hælendes spræce, and ham siðode. Ða comon his ðegnas him togeanes, and cyddon þæt his sunu gesund wære. He ða befran on hwilcere tide he gewyrpte. Hi sædon, Gyrstan-dæg ofer midne dæg hine forlet se fefor. þa oncneow se fæder þæt hit wæs seo tid on ðære ðe se Hælend him to cwæð, Far ðe ham, þin sunu leofað. Se cyning gelyfde ða on God, and eal his hired.' (CH I viii, p. 128)

Clearly this version is the earlier of the two: it is shorter and not written in Ælfric's rhythmical prose style. It does, however, show many similarities in phrasing and vocabulary to the later one: it too, for example, translates 'hora septima' as 'ofer midne dæg'.

SOURCES

From his translation of the gospel-text, Ælfric moves to its exposition. Characteristically, he has based his interpretation on the patristic teachings widely available in England at the end of the tenth century.[1] He does not specify, however, which patristic author (or authors) he has drawn on for this homily, noting only that he will tell 'sum andʒit þerto | of þære trahtnunge' (ll. 33–4). Although we can ascertain its various constituent parts, the precise identification of the main source must remain speculative.

James Cross observes that the homily 'has echoes of Gregory, *Homilia XXVIII in Evangelia*, a homily chosen for the Twenty-second Sunday after Pentecost in the version of Paul the Deacon's homiliary in P.L. 95'.[2] Paul the Deacon's homiliary, as C. L. Smetana has shown, was certainly a collection familiar to Ælfric,[3] although the Twenty-second Sunday after Pentecost was not an occasion included in the original homiliary.[4] The homily by Gregory, however, provides the

[1] For the patristic commentaries available in England at this time, see J. D. A. Ogilvy, *Books Known to the English, 597–1066*, Medieval Academy of America (Cambridge, Mass., 1967), and H. Gneuss, 'A preliminary list of manuscripts written or owned in England up to 1100', *ASE*, ix (1981), 1–60.

[2] 'The Literate Anglo-Saxon—on Sources and Disseminations', *Proceedings of the British Academy*, lviii (1972), 67–100, p. 84, n. 1.

[3] 'Ælfric and the Early Medieval Homiliary', *Traditio*, xv (1959), 163–204. More detailed information on the background to and contents of Paul the Deacon's homiliary is offered by the same author in 'Paul the Deacon's Patristic Anthology', in *The Old English Homily and its Backgrounds*, ed. Paul E. Szarmach and Bernard F. Huppé (Albany, 1978), pp. 75–97.

[4] The contents of Paul the Deacon's homiliary were first described by F. Wiegand, *Das Homiliarium Karls des Grossen auf seine ursprüngliche Gestalt hin untersucht*, Studien zur Geschichte der Theologie und der Kirche, 1 (Leipzig, 1897); they are also listed, with

material for the first part only of Ælfric's homily.[1] Like Gregory, Ælfric expounds John iv. 46-50, and in commentary on John iv. 50 introduces the story of the centurion (Matth. viii. 5-13) to illustrate how men should be judged according to their nature and not their worldly wealth. However where Gregory diverts to a lengthy discourse on the need to despise earthly abundance and glory, Ælfric continues with a verse-by-verse gloss of John iv. 51-3.[2]

There are several other expositions drawing on Gregory which cover the latter part of Ælfric's commentary and might have been known to Ælfric. These are by Heiric, Haymo, Pseudo-Bede, Alcuin and Smaragdus.[3] Ascertaining the relationship amongst these is not entirely straightforward, but comparison between them suggests that Gregory is drawn on by Alcuin, and that Alcuin is then copied by Pseudo-Bede, rewritten by Haymo and Heiric, and excerpted by Smaragdus.

The exposition of Heiric is found alongside Gregory's homily in the later version of Paul the Deacon's homiliary printed by Migne.[4] Since it omits commentary which appears in other expositions and which Ælfric has included, and since there is also very little evidence elsewhere to suggest that Ælfric ever drew on Heiric, it can be readily dismissed as a possible source here.[5]

Haymo, in a homily from his original collection, again draws on Gregory for the former part but not for the latter.[6] The text would have been known to Ælfric, whose dependence on Haymo as a source is well attested,[7] but Ælfric does not seem to have drawn on him here: nothing of relevance is unique to Haymo, and he lacks some material found both in Ælfric and other expositions.[8]

corrections and additions, by R. Grégoire, *Les Homéliaires du moyen âge: Inventaire et analyse des manuscrits*, Rerum Ecclesiarum Documenta, Series Maior, Fontes 6 (Vatican City, 1966), 71–114.

[1] Gregory's homily is printed in PL 76, cols. 1210–13.

[2] Gregory at PL 76, col. 1212; Ælfric at homily i, l. 137.

[3] Alcuin's commentary is found in PL 100, cols. 801–4, Pseudo-Bede's in PL 92, cols. 689–90. For Heiric, see PL 95, cols. 1438–42. For Haymo, see PL 118, cols. 726–8. For Smaragdus, see PL 102, cols. 495–6.

[4] Barré, pp. 160ff., provides an inventory of Heiric's homiliary, in which this homily is item 41.

[5] Pope finds 'only a few inconclusive resemblances' to suggest that Ælfric might have consulted the Migne homilies attributed to Heiric for his homilies for Fridays in Lent (p. 160).

[6] For a discussion of Haymo's original collection of homilies, see Barré, pp. 49–70.

[7] Cyril L. Smetana, 'Ælfric and the Homiliary of Haymo of Halberstadt', *Traditio*, xvii (1961), 457–69.

[8] At ll. 74–7, Ælfric's remark that the sub-king should have acknowledged God's ubiquity if he had had true faith, is found in other sources but not in Haymo, who

Pseudo-Bede's *In Iohannis Euangelium Expositio* is here identical with Alcuin, and since there is 'no evidence at all that Ælfric had seen the *Expositio* as distinct from the *Commentaria*', it can be discounted as a possible source.[1] Alcuin's *Commentaria in Iohannis Euangelium*, again drawing on Gregory for the first part of its exposition of John iv. 46-53, is closer to Ælfric's latter material than Gregory, Heiric, or Haymo. Alcuin would seem *prima facie* a likely source. But only scanty evidence exists elsewhere for Ælfric's knowledge of the Alcuin text: although Pope tentatively cites Alcuin's *Commentaria* as the source for seven pieces in his edition, he notes that all but one short passage from these appear in some other known collection.[2] The problem can, however, be side-stepped here, since Smaragdus, in his homily for the Twenty-second Sunday after Pentecost, offers an abridgement of Alcuin. All the Alcuin material used by Ælfric is also found in Smaragdus, and since we know that Ælfric drew on Smaragdus elsewhere, he seems altogether the most likely source.[3]

This solution, however, still leaves questions unanswered. Did Ælfric use Gregory for the first part of his commentary, then move to Smaragdus when Gregory abandoned a verse-by-verse treatment? Or did he use Smaragdus's exposition throughout as his main source? The simpler answer, that Ælfric drew on Smaragdus throughout, is preferred here, since Ælfric has nowhere used material from Gregory which is not included in that excerpted by Smaragdus.

TREATMENT OF SOURCES

Characteristically Ælfric is in no way restricted by his main source. This reveals itself in two ways. First, in passages where Ælfric is following his main source, he feels free to expand or condense material at will, and to alter the emphasis of the interpretation offered. Secondly, he adds independently several passages of commentary to the main source.

instead comments on miracles. At ll. 128–36, Ælfric's contrast of the sub-king and centurion stories is closer to other sources than to Haymo. At l. 142, the idea of the father deserving his son's healing occurs in other sources but not in Haymo, and at ll. 149–52 and ll. 160–7, Ælfric shows a greater degree of verbal correspondence with other sources than with Haymo.

[1] Pope, p. 161.
[2] Pope, pp. 161–2.
[3] Ælfric himself acknowledges his debt to Smaragdus in the list of sources found in his Latin Preface to the First Series, CH I, p. 1.

An example of Ælfric's adaptation of his source is found in lines 121–36 of homily i, which also affords a useful opportunity to examine the similarities and contrasts between this passage and an earlier representation of the same material in Ælfric's First Series of *Catholic Homilies*. The passage immediately follows a translation of Matth. viii. 5–10 (itself filled out by Ælfric according to the gospel-text), the story of the centurion whose faith is such that he rejects Christ's offer to visit his home to heal his servant, declaring that he will be healed by Christ's word alone. Ælfric, like Smaragdus, uses this as an opportunity to contrast the quality of faith of the centurion and that of the sub-king, arguing that it is a man's nature which should be admired and not his wealth. Ælfric independently stresses the message of humility. He adds the phrase 'for his eadmodnysse', placed ambiguously so that it could refer both to the centurion's humility in not wishing Christ to come to his house, and also to Christ's own humility in offering to visit the house. This phrase is connected linguistically with the subsequent exhortation to his audience to respect the humble ('we sceolen arwurðiæn þa eadmoden symle'), and here the word 'eadmoden' is used ambiguously by Ælfric to include both those who have the virtue of humility and those who are impoverished. Ælfric concludes this section of commentary by urging his audience to reveal their true humility ('þæt we sceolon . . . þa soðan eadmodnesse on us sylfe cyþan'). The nature of and need for humility is Ælfric's special concern here.

The contrast between the centurion's quality of faith and the under-king's is also drawn by Ælfric in his homily for the Third Sunday after Epiphany:

Drihten nolde gelaðod lichamlice siðian to þæs cyninges untruman bearne, ac unandweard mid his worde hine gehælde; and he wæs gearo ungelaðod to siðigenne lichamlice mid þam hundredes ealdre. Wel wat gehwa þæt cyning hæfð maran mihte þonne ænig hundredes ealdor, ac se Ælmihtiga Godes Sunu geswutelode mid þære dæde þæt we ne sceolon ða rican, for heora riccetere wurðian, ac for menniscum gecynde; ne we ne sceolon ða wannspedigan for heora hafenleaste forseon; ac we sceolon Godes anlicnysse on him wurðian. Se eadmoda Godes Sunu wæs gearo to geneosigenne þone ðeowan mid his andwerdnysse, and he gehælde þone æðeling mid hæse; be ðam cwæð se witega, 'Se healica Drihten sceawað þa eadmodan, and þa modigan feorran oncnæwð.' (CH I viii, p. 128)

The two passages show a close similarity in content. Both present a literal rather than allegorical interpretation. Both affirm the need to

love men for themselves and not for their wealth. Both emphasize our
need to manifest and esteem the quality of humility. They are,
however, independent in their phrasing and vocabulary. Assuming
that CH I viii was written at a much earlier period than homily i, they
provide valuable evidence for Ælfric's changing style and vocabulary.
In the earlier passage, there is no evidence of rhythmical prose; in the
later one, although it is not consistent, there is a rhythmic and
alliterative pattern, seen for example in the lines 'and þæs monnes
ȝecynd na his mihte wurðiæn' and 'ac þa welan we wurðiæþ wolice on
ðam ricum'. Some specific changes in diction can be observed (though
the possibility of scribal alteration should not be overlooked). Ælfric
uses the word 'lichamlice' twice in his earlier passage, and completely
avoids it in the later. The word for 'servant', 'ðeowa', becomes 'cnapa'
in the second version.[1]

The reason for the independence of the two passages becomes clear
when the available sources and their mutual relationships are taken
into account. Ælfric's source for his First Series homily for the Third
Sunday after Epiphany was a homily by Haymo expounding Matth.
viii. 1–13.[2] Haymo reproduces this material almost exactly in his
homily for the Twenty-second Sunday after Pentecost, but this homily
is, as I showed above, not Ælfric's source for his homily on John iv.
46–53.[3] The actual source Smaragdus, however, at this point resembles Haymo closely, which explains why Ælfric's two accounts are
so similar in content. In phrasing and organization, Ælfric is in fact
closer to Smaragdus than to his earlier homily. Not surprisingly it
seems that Ælfric's recollection of his previous rendering of the
underking and centurion contrast is rather hazy, and he has followed
Smaragdus independently of that account.

Although Ælfric relied on one source for the backbone of his
exposition, he fleshes it out by interpolating other passages of
commentary. Since these 'digressions' are important for identifying
Ælfric's own areas of interest, I shall consider each in turn.

Despite his opening emphasis on brevity, Ælfric's very first
passage of commentary is an addition to his main source. This is a
lengthy explanation of the term 'underking' (Ælfric's translation of
the Vulgate 'regulus') by reference to historical precedent. In this he

[1] See further my textual note to line 73.
[2] PL 118, homily xix, 137–47. The source was identified by M. Förster, 'Über die
Quellen von Ælfrics Exegetischen Homiliae Catholicae', *Anglia*, xvi (1894), 1–61, p. 45.
[3] PL 118, homily cxxxvi, cols. 726–8.

diverges from Smaragdus who offers a brief allegorical interpretation:

Regulus diminutivum nomen est a rege, et ideo forsitan regulus dicitur iste, qui salutem poposcit filio suo, quia plenam non habuit fidem.[1]

Ælfric's avoidance of allegory here is entirely in keeping with his stated intention to respect his audience's intellectual capabilities which are, he implies, distinctly limited ('bi eowræs andȝites mæðe'). However his determination to establish an historical authority for the concept of 'underking' needs further consideration. 'Underking' was not a particularly rare word in Old English,[2] and indeed Ælfric did not include any explanation of it in his homily for the Third Sunday after Epiphany (CH I viii). The discussion in homily i has two components: first, some general observations on the relation of underkings to the emperor, and second, a specific exemplum concerning Archelaus whose kingdom was divided into four parts after his banishment.

Ælfric begins the first part with a succinct definition of an underking: 'þe under þam casere rixæð'; he then stresses the awesome power of emperors in the period following Christ's birth. The long time-span of their rule is noted ('fela hund ȝeare') and also their wealth (acquired from gifts and tribute). At this point Ælfric curiously mentions that some emperors travelled to England, very many of whom died there. The statement, unusually for Ælfric, is not entirely accurate historically. Certainly some emperors did travel to England: as Ælfric would have read in Bede's *Historia Ecclesiastica* (Book I, chapters 2–9) and in Orosius' *History* (Books VI and VII), Julius Caesar, Claudius, Vespasian, Severus, Constantius and Maximus all visited Britain between 60 BC and the end of Roman rule in AD 409.[3] Only two of these, however, died in Britain: Severus (in AD 211) and Constantius (in AD 306). This makes Ælfric's claim that 'heoræ forwel felæ' died there seem rather exaggerated. In a discussion of Ælfric's

---

[1] PL 102, col. 495. Gregory does not comment on 'regulus' at all; Smaragdus's inclusion of this comment shows that he has excerpted from Alcuin, who added this comment to Gregory's exposition. (Smaragdus himself adds an interpretation of Carpharnaum which is in neither Gregory nor Alcuin and which Ælfric does not include.) Haymo's comments resemble those of Smaragdus: 'Sic ergo et iste regulus fortassis a qualitate mentis quam habebat interius, nomen traxit exterius. Regulus enim diminutivum nomen est a rege, quasi dicatur sub rege primus, vel parvus rex. Et ideo quia ex parte credebat, et ex parte non credebat, non rex, sed regulus meruit appellari' (PL 118, col. 726).

[2] The Microfiche Concordance includes numerous entries for the word 'underking'.

[3] Bertram Colgrave and R. A. B. Mynors, eds., *Bede's Ecclesiastical History of the English People*, Oxford Medieval Texts (Oxford, 1969).

vocabulary, Malcolm Godden notes how rarely 'forwel' is used as an intensifier by Ælfric in his later writings, and concludes that since the phrase 'heoræ forwel felæ' 'does not fit well with the sense of the sentence or with historical fact', it is 'perhaps a marginal comment by a misinformed reader, wrongly incorporated into the text'.[1] The phrase does, however, fit perfectly well with the sense. It also maintains the alliterative pattern of the homily, 'forwel felæ' alliterating with the previous 'forðfærdon'. The 'misinformed reader' would have had to be surprisingly at ease with Ælfric's style.

Why might Ælfric have felt justified in exaggerating the facts in this way? Indeed why should he refer at all here to the emperors' visits to England? Bede's influence might be partly responsible: the subject of his work required him to trace links between Rome and England. Ælfric may also have seen this as an opportunity to show patriotism: having stressed that the emperors had control 'over the whole world' in the early centuries AD, the importance of England could only be enhanced by noting that emperors both visited it and even died there. But possibly Ælfric had even more in mind. His reference to England at this point sets up an implicit connection between the situations in Rome and England in terms of kingship. In his subsequent comment he emphasizes how underkings were subordinate to the emperor in every respect. Ælfric is offering a precedent for the system of an omnipotent ruler who might nevertheless delegate limited responsibility to other leaders.

Elsewhere in his writings Ælfric recognizes that his audience can and will compare the political systems of other periods with their own. Two passages are particularly pertinent here. In the Preface to the *Lives of Saints*, Ælfric, attempting to reconcile his Latin source with the assumptions of his English audience, explicitly weighs the Roman ruling system against the English:

Unum cupio sciri hoc uolumen legentibus, quod nollem alicubi ponere duos imperatores siue cesares in hac narratione simul, sicut in latinitate legimus; sed unum imperatorem in persecutione martyrum ponimus ubique; Sicut gens nostra uni regi subditur, et usitata est de uno rege non de duobus loqui.[2]

Ælfric is worried that, if left unaltered, his source might affect his audience's belief in the absolute power of kingship. An even closer parallel can be drawn with the piece 'Wyrdwriteras us secgað ða ðe

[1] 'Ælfric's Changing Vocabulary', *English Studies*, lxi (1980), 206–23, p. 209.
[2] LS, I, pp. 2–4.

awritan be cyningum' (Pope xxii). This piece is identified by Pope as
'part of a lost composition pertaining to the defence of the kingdom'.[1]
In it Ælfric emphasizes the need for a king to delegate his authority to
generals, giving several historical examples of rulers (King David,
Constantine and other emperors) who successfully delegated their
military power in this way. According to Pope, this 'plea for a delega-
tion of the king's authority to generals ... is made nowhere else in
Ælfric's surviving works, so far as I can remember'.[2] I would suggest
that the passage in homily i is a more oblique example of just such a
plea. Interestingly, 'Wyrdwriteras us secgað' is also a late composition
by Ælfric, certainly written after the publication of the *Lives of Saints*
and possibly some time thereafter.[3]

Why might Ælfric have supported such a scheme whereby one ruler
could and should delegate responsibility to other leaders? Possibly it
stemmed from his observation of political activities in England in his
own lifetime.[4] Ælfric held in particularly high regard the reign of
Edgar (973–5), whose political success must have been highlighted by
Æthelred's subsequent failure to check disorder and Viking raids. In
Lives of Saints xiii, 147–77, Ælfric contrasts the peaceful and praise-
worthy time of Edgar's rule with that of Æthelred's (although neither
Edgar nor Æthelred are explicitly named). One particular incident in
Edgar's reign seems to have exemplified incontrovertibly for Ælfric
Edgar's regal ability. This was Edgar's acceptance of an offer of
allegiance from several other kings in Britain which took place in 973,
shortly after his coronation.[5] The event, recorded in three manuscripts of the *Anglo-Saxon Chronicle*, was recounted twice by Ælfric. In
his *Life of St. Swithun*, Ælfric, praising the tranquillity of Edgar's reign,
concludes:

> and ealle ða cyningas þe on þysum iglande wæron.
> cumera. and scotta. comon to eadgare.
> hwilon anes dæges eahta cyningas.
> and hi ealle gebugon to eadgares wissunge.[6]

---

[1] Pope, p. 725.

[2] Pope, p. 727.

[3] Pope, p. 726, argues for this late date: Ælfric refers at l. 79 to the epilogue to his
homily on *Judges* ('swa swa we awriton on sumon spelle hwilon'), and the use of
'hwilon' in that reference suggests that several years might have elapsed since then.

[4] See Pope, p. 373, for a list of passages testifying to Ælfric's concern for the political and military troubles of his day.

[5] W. H. Stevenson, 'The Great Commendation to King Edgar in 973', *English
Historical Review*, xiii (1898), pp. 505–7.

[6] LS xxi, 450–3.

He alludes to the incident again in the epilogue to his translation of the Book of Judges:

Eadgar, se æðela 7 se anræda cining, aræde Godes lof on his leode gehwær, ealra cininga swiðost ofer Engla ðeode, 7 him God gewilde his wiðerwinnan a, ciningas 7 eorlas, þæt hi comon him to buton ælcum gefeohte friðes wilniende, him underþeodde to þam þe he wolde, 7 he wæs gewurðod wide geond land.[1]

Edgar's success in controlling other rulers obviously impressed Ælfric. The incident was apparently symptomatic of Edgar's policy generally; he seems to have delegated responsibility successfully within England also, particularly in the Danelaw where the earls and bishops governed the Danes by royal appointment, but were offered autonomy in return for their allegiance.[2] The contrast with Æthelred's incompetent reign must have been striking.

To sum up, analogous material suggests that Ælfric uses his homily as an opportunity to exploit the parallel between the Roman emperors' appointment of underkings and Edgar's admirable control of various lesser kings and leaders. Although the parallel is far from explicit (no doubt for obvious practical reasons), Ælfric could have expected his audience to draw it for themselves with the help of his statement linking the two countries. The exaggeration of the number who died in England may even have been designed to alert his audience further to the intended comparison with Edgar whose ability to rule and delegate had so closely resembled that of the Roman emperors until he died in 975.

The second part of Ælfric's discussion of 'underking' offers a specific historical exemplum: the banishment of Archelaus and the establishment of tetrarchs in the Judaean kingdom. Ælfric derived this information from a homily by Bede for the Decollation of John the Baptist.[3] Its historical accuracy is again questionable, but this time Ælfric is not to blame. According to Bede, Archelaus, having succeeded to his father Herod (in AD 4), was deposed after ten years of rule (in AD 6), when his kingdom was divided into four parts to be ruled by his four brothers who were called tetrarchs. According to Josephus in *The Jewish War*, Herod named Archelaus king in 4 BC with his two brothers as tetrarchs subordinate to him. Immediately after 4 BC

[1] Crawford, pp. 416–17.
[2] See F. M. Stenton, *Anglo-Saxon England*, 3rd ed. (Oxford, 1971), pp. 370–2.
[3] Bede, Hom. II, 23, CCSL 122, pp. 349–57, pp. 350–1.

Augustus challenged Archelaus, and divided Herod's kingdom amongst the three sons, Archelaus being called an ethnarch, and the other two, tetrarchs. In AD 6 Archelaus was banished by Augustus and his territory was annexed as a Roman province with a Roman procurator. Bede, then, seems to have conflated two separate incidents concerning Archelaus: the division of his kingdom amongst him and his brothers just after 4 BC, and his banishment in AD 6. Ælfric incorporated this information in homily i and also in his own homily for the Decollation of John the Baptist where Bede's homily was his main source:[1]

þa wearð he [Herod] hreowlice and hrædlice dead æfter ðam ðe he ða cild acwealde for Cristes acennednysse. þa feng Archelaus his sunu to rice. Ða embe tyn geara fyrst wearð he ascofen of his cynesetle, forðan þe þæt Iudeisce folc wrehton his modignysse to ðam casere, and he ða hine on wræcsið asende. þa dælde se casere þæt Iudeisce rice on feower, and sette ðærto feower gebroðra: ða sind gecwedene æfter Greciscum gereorde, tetrarche, þæt sind, fyðerrican. Fyðerrica bið se ðe hæfð feorðan dæl rices.[2]

Ælfric makes no mention of this account in homily i. He also explains the meaning of 'fiðerrica' for the second time; this is hardly surprising, however, considering the rarity of occurrences of 'fiðerrica' in Old English.[3]

Of the two accounts the one in CH I xxxii must have been the earlier. A comparison with Bede shows the Catholic Homily to have drawn more directly on that source. It includes details from Bede which the later homily lacks: a time-period of ten years for the reign of Archelaus, the cause of his banishment (that is, the Jewish people condemning his pride), four brothers being chosen as tetrarchs, and the derivation of 'tetrarch' from Greek. The absence of detail in the later homily suggests that it may have been written in recollection of the earlier version.[4] Having drawn directly on Bede for CH I xxxii, Ælfric relied on his memory of that material for his TH II homily. One puzzling fact remains. Ælfric clearly knew the work by Josephus, since

[1] The source was identified by Förster, 'Über die Quellen', p. 23.

[2] CH I xxxii, p. 478.

[3] The only other extant instance besides the two in Ælfric is a gloss in Aldhelm's *De laude virginitatis* (gloss no. 1799) where 'fiðerrica' glosses 'tetrarcha'; see Arthur S. Napier, ed., *Old English Glosses*, Anecdota Oxoniensia, Mediaeval and Modern Series, 11 (Oxford, 1900), p. 48.

[4] See J. E. Cross, 'Ælfric—Mainly on Memory and Creative Method in Two *Catholic Homilies*', *Studia Neophilologica*, xli (1969), 135–55, for Ælfric's method of working by memory even when he is following a main source.

he refers to him by name later in the same Catholic Homily: 'Se wyrdwritere Iosephus awrat, on ðære cyrclican gereccednysse.'[1] Ælfric seems, however, to have overlooked the incompatibility between Bede's account of the fortunes of Archelaus and that of Josephus, perhaps deliberately because it suited his etymological linking of 'tetrarcha' and 'fiðerrica'.

The next passage which Ælfric has interpolated into his source is the image of the sun and its rays to describe God's omnipresence: just as the sun sends its rays to shine everywhere, so God sends His comforting rays to those with faith in every land (ll. 78–88). The image was apparently prompted by Smaragdus's comment: 'quia non esset locus, ubi non esset Deus'. The original source for Ælfric's analogy between the sun's rays and God's omnipresence has been identified by Cross as a passage by Augustine.[2] Ælfric also used the image on two other occasions, both independently of their main source. The first of these is in his homily *Feria IIII De Fide Catholica*:

Nu smeað sum undeopðancol man, hu God mæge beon æghwær ætgædere, and nahwar todæled. Beheald þas sunnan, hu heage heo astihð, and hu heo asent hyre leoman geond ealne middangeard, and hu heo onliht ealle ðas eorðan þe mancynn on-eardað. Swa hraðe swa heo up-asprincð on ærne merigen, heo scinð on Hierusalem, and on Romebyrig, and on ðisum earde, and on eallum eardum ætgædere; and hwæðere heo is gesceaft, and gæð be Godes dihte. Hwæt wenst ðu hu miccle swiðor is Godes andweardnys, and his miht, and his neosung æghwær. Him ne wiðstent nan ðing, naðer ne stænen weall ne bryden wah, swa swa hi wiðstandað þære sunnan. Him is nan ðing digle ne uncuð.[3]

This is the most extended and elaborate treatment of the image, and the closest to Augustine. Following Augustine, Ælfric explains that the sun sends out its rays over the whole world, but that since the sun itself is created by God, His power is even greater: accordingly His actual presence is everywhere and He can penetrate even a solid wall. Ælfric adds an interesting detail not in Augustine: he specifically cites Jerusalem, Rome and 'this country' as recipients of the sun's rays before resorting to 'all countries at once'. Possibly he is drawing in his own mind a contrast between the sun and the soul: in *De Anima Ratione*, Alcuin asserts that the soul cannot think of two things at once, using Jerusalem and Rome as his examples: 'Dum de Jerusalem

[1] CH I xxxii, p. 488.
[2] 'Ælfric and the Medieval Homiliary—Objection and Contribution', *Scripta Minora, Regiae Societatis Humaniorum Litterarum Lundensis*, iv (1961–2), pp. 24–9. The sermon is no. cxx in PL 38, col. 676.   [3] CH I xx, pp. 286–8.

cogito, non eo momento de Roma possum cogitare.'[1] Alcuin's text, including this passage, was used later by Ælfric as his source for LS i.[2]

Ælfric also used the image of the sun in his homily for the Fifth Sunday after Easter (Pope viii). Here the context is Christ's ability both to be man on earth and to exist in heaven, and the passage is briefer and more general:

> Gif ðu þises wundrast, hu he wunian mage
> mid mannum on eorðan, and eac swilce on heofenum,
> sceawa be þære sunnan, þe is Godes gesceaft,
> hu heo mage asendan hyre scinendan leoman
> fram hire upplican ryne ofer ealne middaneard.
> Se sunbeam bescinð þe swutellice eallne;
> and ne mæg se Eallwealdend, gif ðu hine lufast,
> his leoman þe asendan, and eac þe lufian?[3]

As Pope notes, its immediate source is clearly Ælfric's previous version rather than Augustine.[4] Various phrases reappear: 'gesceaft'; 'asent hyre leoman' becomes 'mage asendan hyre scinendan leoman'; 'geond ealne middangeard' becomes 'ofer ealne middaneard'. Some changes, however, can be observed. This time there is no suggestion that God's power is greater; although the sun is recognized as 'Godes gesceaft', its rays are compared to God's without qualification. The tone of the passage is also different. In CH I xx, Ælfric uses the image to show that God can see into all men's hearts and rewards or punishes accordingly; in Pope viii his emphasis is on God's love for all those who love Him.

The passage treating the image of the sun in homily i was probably written after these other two passages. It has echoes of both. It shares with Pope viii its brevity, lack of detail and beneficent tone; it recalls from CH I xx an acknowledgement of the superior power of God to that of the sun ('miccle swiðor' in CH I xx, 'mycele swyðor' in homily i), although in the later passage the sun's physical limitations are not mentioned explicitly.

The third passage interpolated by Ælfric is a brief account of the resurrection of Lazarus. This was probably prompted by Smaragdus's comment on the inadequacy of the underking's faith so that he

[1] PL 101, col. 642.

[2] LS i. 132–6. For Ælfric's use of Alcuin, see M. R. Godden, 'Anglo-Saxons on the mind', in *Learning and Literature in Anglo-Saxon England*, ed. M. Lapidge and H. Gneuss (Cambridge, 1985), pp. 271–98, especially pp. 278–85.

[3] Pope viii, 228–35.

[4] Pope, p. 371.

'morienti filio esse absentem putavit Deum'. Lazarus though already dead was healed by God. The story was a favourite exemplum for Ælfric; he used it as a basis for one homily (Pope vi), and referred to it in numerous others. In keeping with the general tenor of the homily, Ælfric has here used the Lazarus story purely for its literal value; frequently elsewhere he exploits its allegorical significance.[1]

The final interpolation made by Ælfric into his main source is an addition at the end. Apparently prompted by the preceding references to miracles and the disbelief of the Jews, Ælfric first recounts how the Jewish scribes who would not believe that John's baptism came from Christ were therefore not told who gave Christ power to work miracles. The story is not treated elsewhere in Ælfric's extant works. It appears in three gospel-texts: Matth. xxi. 23–8; Mark xi. 27–33; Luke xx. 1–8. Ælfric's account is closest to Luke's;[2] he follows Luke faithfully, adding only phrases such as 'we biddæð', 'ðas syllice wundræ', 'ðæt his fulluht beo', and changing one piece of indirect speech to direct. The translation displays very few characteristics of rhythmical prose style. There can be no doubt, however, that the passage is by Ælfric. His rhythmical prose is often irregular in rendering gospel passages, where he is obliged to remain as close as possible to his source. The diction is forceful and incisive, achieving a cumulative effect through repetition of phrases; important words, such as 'witæn' and 'witegæ', 'mihte' and 'makiȝe', are still linked by alliteration. The commentary which follows the gospel translation returns to rhythmical prose.

Ælfric may have welcomed the opportunity to include here a gospel-story which was the pericope for occasions he (like the Carolingian homiliarists) did not treat: according to the Sarum Missal, Luke xx. 1–8 was the pericope for the Wednesday after the Fifteenth Sunday after Trinity, and Matth. xxi. 23–7 for the Wednesday after the Second Sunday after Trinity.[3] Neither of these occasions is treated anywhere in the Old English homiletic corpus.

The subsequent commentary on this gospel-text (ll. 185–202) may derive from some unidentified source, or it may be Ælfric's own invention. Ælfric first accuses the scribes of spiritual blindness, a

---

[1] See, for example, CH I xxxiii, p. 496.

[2] Ælfric's statement, 'ȝif we þenne sæcgæþ þæt his fulluht is of monnum, | þenne wule al folc us oftorfiæn mid stanum' (ll. 177–8), corresponds to Luke xx. 6: 'Si autem dixerimus: Ex hominibus, plebs universa lapidabit nos'; Matthew and Mark express only the notion of fearing the crowd.

[3] F. H. Dickinson, ed., *Missale Sarum* (London, 1861–83), pp. 466, 508.

subject he treats fully in his TH II homily for Wednesday in the
Fourth week of Lent (homily iii below). He then discusses the power
behind Christ's miracles, that is, God. The subject of miracles, and by
what means they were performed, was clearly also of great interest to
Ælfric.[1] In this passage, he is evidently referring to physical not spiritual miracles. Physical miracles are still possible, Ælfric implies.
They originate from God, but others can perform them in His name.
Ælfric may be referring particularly to miracles performed at the
tombs of saints, since the passage bears a marked resemblance to the
close of his *Life of St. Edmund*:

> Synd eac fela oðre on angel-cynne halgan
> þe fela wundra wyrcað. swa swa hit wide is cuð
> þam ælmihtigan to lofe. þe hi on gelyfdon.
> Crist geswutelaþ mannum þurh his mæran halgan
> þæt he is ælmihtig god þe macað swilce wundra
>
> ·   ·   ·   ·   ·   ·   ·   ·   ·   ·
>
> ac crist geswutelað mannum hwær se soða geleafa is.
> þonne he swylce wundra wyrcð þurh his halgan
> wide geond þas eorðan.[2]

God produces the miracles though His saints execute them on earth.
    The closing discussion of miracles is entirely apt in the context of
homily i. Miracles of all kinds play a large part in its gospel-text and
commentary: the recovery of the underking's son and the underking's
subsequent 'conversion', the resurrection of Lazarus, the centurion's
servant's recovery, the Jewish scribes' question concerning miracles
and John's baptism. God's ability to perform at will both spiritual and
physical miracles has been effectively displayed, as has the necessity
for our belief in that power.

---

[1] See M. R. Godden, 'Ælfric's Saints' Lives and the Problem of Miracles', *Leeds
Studies in English*, N.S., xvi (1985), 83–100.
[2] LS xxxii, 264–8, 273–5.

Erat quidam regulus cuius filius infirmabatur Capharnaum, et
reliqua

'Ure Hælend com hwilon to Chanan þam tune
on Galileiscre scire, ðær ðær he swyðest bodede,
and on þam tune he awende hwilon water to wine,   5
six fate fulle mid þam fyrmestan wine.
Ða wæs sum underkyng on Capharnan buriȝ,
and his sune ða læȝ seoc to forðfore.
Ða axode þe underkyng embe þæs Hælendes fær,
þæt he from Iudea londe com to Galileam;   10
ferde þa | to þam Hælende and hine bæd ȝeorne   fol. 8ᵛ
þæt he sceolde faren and his sune hælen,
þe læȝ þa æt forðsiðe his lifes unwæne.
þa andswarde þe Hælend þus ðam underkynge:
Buton ȝe tacne iseon, nelle ȝe ilyfæn.   15
þe underkyng him andswarde eft: La, leof Drihten,
fare to mine sune ær þan ðe he swælte.
Ðe Hælend him cwæð þus to:
Fare ðe nu on þinne wæȝ, þin sune leofæð.
Ða ilyfde þe kyng ðæs Hælendes spæce,   20
and wende him hamweard, and hopode to þan.
Ða comen ðæs on mareȝen his men him toȝeanes,
and cydden him mid blisse þæt his sune leofede.
Ðe fæder heom befran þa mid fyrwetnysse sonæ

Bodley 343, fols. 8–10; Belfour, pp. 22–31.

SOURCES. The texts cited here (in addition to the Vulgate) are: (i) Smaragdus,
Collectiones in Evangelia et Epistolas, PL 102, cols. 495–6 (cited as Smaragdus); (ii) Bede,
Homeliarum Evangelii Libri II, CCSL 122, II, 23, pp. 349–57 (cited as Bede);
(iii) Augustine, *Sermones*, sermo cxx, PL 38, cols. 676–8 (cited as Augustine).
1–31 (*John iv. 46–53*) (46) Venit ergo iterum in Cana Galilaeae, ubi fecit aquam vinum.
Et erat quidam regulus, cuius filius infirmabatur Capharnaum. (47) Hic cum audisset
quia Iesus adveniret a Iudaea in Galilaeam, abiit ad eum. Et rogabat eum, ut
descenderet et sanaret filium eius: incipiebat enim mori. (48) Dixit ergo Iesus ad eum:
Nisi signa et prodigia videritis, non creditis. (49) Dicit ad eum regulus: Domine,
descende priusquam moriatur filius meus. (50) Dicit ei Iesus: Vade, filius tuus vivit.
Credidit homo sermoni quem dixit ei Iesus, et ibat. (51) Iam autem eo descendente,
servi occurrerunt ei, et nuntiaverunt dicentes quia filius eius viveret. (52) Interrogabat
ergo horam ab eis, in qua melius habuerit; et dixerunt ei: Quia heri hora septima reliquit
eum febris. (53) Cognovit ergo pater quia illa hora erat, in qua dixit ei Iesus: Filius tuus
vivit; et credidit ipse, et domus eius tota.

on hwylcere tide þe sune ȝewurpte.   25
Heo sæden him to andsware: Gyrstændæȝ he wurpte,
swa ofer midne dæȝ, þæt hine forlet þeo fefor.
þa oncneow þe fæder þæt hine forlet þe fefor
on þare ylcæ tide þe ðe Hælend him to cwæð:
Fare þe nu ham raðe, þin sune leofæð;   30
and he þa sylf ilyfde and all his hired þurh ðæt.'
      Ðis godspel is nu sceortlice isæd on Englisc,
and we wullæð eow sæcgæn sum andȝit þerto
of þare trahtnunge bi eowræs andȝites mæðe,
na swa ðeah to longlice, þæt hit eow æðryt ne þynce.   35
      'Underkyng' is ihaten þe under þam casere rixæð,
and on þam time wæron caseres on Rome
swa þæt heo ahton ða anweald and cynedom
ofer alne middaneard and ofer alle kyngæs
æfter Cristes acennednysse, and heo kynelice rixoden   40
fela hund ȝeare, and heom mon feorran | brohten   Bf. 24
of (ȝehw)ilce londe æȝðer ȝe lac ȝe gafol,
and heo sume eac comen to Englelonde hwilon,
and ðer forðfærdon heoræ forwel felæ.
      Ða wæron ða underkyngæs þam casere underðeode,   45
to ðam ðe h(e) wold(e), and heoræ wurðscipe wæs
bi þæs caseres willæn, loca hu he wolde.
      Ðæt cydde þe casere þam kynge Archelau,
þæs Herodis sune þe þa childræn acwalde;
he sette ut of kynestole, and sende hine on wræcsiðe   50
for his forwenednysse, and ȝesette for hine
feower oðre kyngæs þa wæren fiðerricæn,
for þan ðe heoræ ælc hæfde feorðen dæl þæs rices
on Iudea londe, and wæs swa ilytlod
heoræ ælces andweald, þæt heo unðances sceoldon   55
buȝan þam casere, to his kyneȝyrde.
      Nu wæs þes kyng þe com to Criste

---

42 ȝehwilce] huwhilce   46 he wolde] heo wolden   51 for¹] *written over*
erasure   53 feorðen] feoˈrˈðen

36–56 (*Bede, pp. 350–1*) Qui [Herod] cum post natiuitate dominicam pauco tempore
regnaret sicut euangelica testatur historai Archelaus eius filius successit in regnum; qui
cum uix decem annis potiretur accusantibus insolentiam eius Iudaeis pulsus est regno
ab Augusto ac perpetuo damnatus exilio. Deinde Augustus ut regni Iudaici minueret
potentiam diuisa in quatuor partes prouincia quattuor fratres Archelai eidem regendae
praefecit qui singuli a principatu quartae partis Graeco sermone tetrarchae uocati sunt.

underkyng ihaten on þa ylcan wisæn,
and he bæd his sune hælu, swa swa hær sæȝð þis godspel,
þe læȝ ða æt forðsiðe on Capharnan buriȝ.   60
    'Ða andswarde þe Hælend þus þam underkynge:
Buton ȝe tacnæ iseon, nylle ȝe ilefæn.'
Næs þe kyng alles buton Cristes ileafan,
ða ða he hine bæd þæt he hælde his sune,
ac he næfde swa ðeah alne ȝeileafan,   65
swa swa mon ilyfæn sceal on ðone lifiȝenden Hælend
þæt he mæȝ alle þing on ælcere stowe.
He mihte hælen mid his hæse his sune
swa swa he ða dyde, ðeah ðe he ne siðode
ham to his huse mid him and hine swa ȝehæl(de).   70
Ðe kyng nyste þa ȝyt þæt Crist mihte swa don,
and mid his worde hine hælen, and he forþy bed hine
þæt he ðer come and ðone cnapæn hælde.
Gif he rihtlice ilyfde, he sceolde ðonne witen
þæt God sylf is æȝhwær, on ælcere stowe,   75
þurh his mycele mihte, and mæȝ æfre hælpan
allum | ðe to him clypiæð on ælcere stowe.   fol. 9
    Wen is þæt eower sum þisses wundriȝe nu
hu ðe Almihtiȝæ God ælcne mon ihere,
beo ðær ðe he beo, ȝif he bit his mildsunge.   80
Ac ȝesceawæ þas sunnæn, hu heo scynæð æȝhwær,
and send hire leomen to alle londum endemes,

---

70 ȝehælde] ȝehælen   82 londum] *erasure of one letter before* l

61–77 (*Smaragdus, col. 495C*) Qui enim salutem quaerebat filio, procul dubio credebat, sed mementote quid petit, et aperte cognoscetis, quia in fide dubitavit, poposcit namque ut descenderet et sanaret filium ejus. Corporalem ergo praesentiam Domini quaerebat, qui per spiritum nusquam deerat, minus in illo credidit, quem non putavit posse salutem dare, nisi praesens esset corpore. Si enim perfecte credidisset, procul dubio sciret, quia non esset locus ubi non esset Deus. Salutem itaque filio petiit, et tamen in fide dubitavit, quia eum ad quem venerat, et potentem ad curandum credidit, et tamen moriente filio esse absentem putavit Deum.

81–8 (*Augustine, col. 676*) Ecce lux ista de coelo, quae solis nomine appellatur, cum processerit, illustrat terras, explicat diem, facit formas, coloresque discernit. Magnum bonum, magnum omnibus mortalibus Dei donum: magnificent eum opera sua. Si tam pulcher est sol; solis factore quid pulchrius? Et tamen videte, fratres: ecce diffundit radios suos per universam terram; patentia penetrat, clausa resistunt: lucem suam mittit per fenestras, numquid et per parietem? Verbo Dei totum patet, Verbum Dei nihil latet. Videte aliam differentiam, quam longe sit a Creatore creatura, maxime corporalis. Quando in oriente est sol, in occidente non est. Lux quidem ejus de illo grandi corpore effusa, pertendit usque in occidentem; sed ipse ibi non est.

and heo is ðeah ӡesceaft isceapen þurðh þone Hælend.
Mycele swyðor mæӡ þe Almihtiӡæ Wealdend
his leomen senden to his ileaffullum monnum   85
on ӡehwylcum londe, locæ hu he wulle,
and heom swa frefren, and his fultum heom don
þurh his mycele ӡife þe mæӡ alle ðing.

    'þe underkyng him andswarde: Efest, la leof Drihten,
far | to mine sunæ ær þan ðe he swelte.'   Bf. 26
Her him tweonode eft for his andӡitleaste.   91
He sceolde ilyfen þæt þe leofæ Hælend
mihte his sune hælen swa swa he Lazarum dyde,
þeah ðe he dead wære, þurh his drihtenlice mihte.
For þan ðe Lazarus læӡ on buriӡene feower niht   95
fu(l)e þa stincende, ac he forð stop sonæ
þa ðe ure Hælend hæt hine forþgan,
and he syððan leofede longe mid monnum.

    'Crist cwæð to þam kynge:
Far ðe nu on ðine wæӡ, þin sune leofæð,'   100
and his sune wearð swa from his seocnysse hal.

Sum hundredes aldor com to þam Hælende
hwilon on oðre stowe, and cwæð ðus to him þa:
Eala, ðu leofe Drihten, min cnapæ lið æt ham
al on paralisim, and he yfele þrowæð.   105
Ðe Hælend him cwæð to:
Ic cume me sylf to him, and ic hine hæle.
þa cwæð þe hundredes aldor:
Ne am ic na wurðe, Drihten, þæt ðu swa don sceole,
þæt ðu under mine rofe inӡonge mid fotum,   110
ac cwæð þin word, and min cnapæ bið hal.
Ic sylf am nu an mon on anwealde iset,
and ic habbe under me moniӡæ cnihtæs on fare,
and ic cwæðe to ðissum, Far ðu, and he færð,
al swa eft to oðrum, Cum þu, and he cymæð sonæ,   115
and to mine ðeow(e), Do þus, and he deþ.

84–5 Wealdend his] Wealdend he his   96 fule] fulle   116 ðeowe] ðeowum

91–8 (*Ælfric's own elaboration based on John xi*)
102–7 (*Smaragdus, col. 495D* [*though Ælfric has considerably expanded his source according to Matth. viii. 5–10*]) Qua in re hoc est nobis solerter intuendum, quod sicut alio evangelista testante didicimus, centurio venit ad Deum, dicens: 'Domine, puer meus jacet paralyticus in domo, et male torquetur.' Cui a Jesu protinus respondetur: 'Ego veniam et curabo eum.'

Ða wundrode þe Hælend his wordæ and ȝeleafen,
and on ende cwæð to him: Far ðe nu hamweard,
and ȝetimiȝe þe swa swa ðu ilyfdest;
and his cnapæ wearð ihæled on ðare ylcan tide.   120
  Ðe underkyng laðode Crist to his huse ham,
and he nolde swa ðeah nateshwon mid him faren,
and he wolde unlaðod to þam licgendæ cnapæ
þæs hundredes [aldres], swa swa ȝe ihyrdon nu,
for his eadmodnysse, þæt he eac swutelode   125
þæt we sceolen arwurðiæn þa eadmoden symle,
and þæs monnes ȝecynd na his mihte wurðiæn.
We ne cunnon wurðiæn witollice on monnum
þæt heo Godes anlicnysse habbæð on heom sylfum,
ac þa welan we wurðiæþ wolice on ðam ricum;   130
ac þe Hælend nolde siðiæn mid þam kynge, ðeah ðe he ibeden
    wære,
ac wæs ȝearu to farenne to þam bæddrædæn cn[a]pæn,
ðeah ðe ðe hundredes aldor hine þæs ne bede,
þæt he swa ȝeswutelode þæt we sceolon tocnawæn
hwæt we us sylfe beoð, na hwæt we sylfe habbæð,   135
and þa soðan eadmodnesse on us sylfe cyþan.
  'Ða ilyfde þe kyng þæs Hælendes spæce,
and | wende | him hamweard, and hopode to þam.'   fol. 9ᵛ, Bf. 28
On þæs Hælendes wordum he undernam ȝeleafan,
and sæ ðe mid twynunge com to ðam Hælende,   140
þe ferde ileafful to his londe hamweard,
and he forþan earnode swa his sune hæle.
  'Ða comen ðæs on mareȝen his men him toȝeanes,
and cyddon him mid blisse þæt his sune leofode.

130 ac] *preceded by* 7 *with deletion dot beneath*

121–5 (*Smaragdus, cols. 495–6*) Quid est quod regulus rogat, ut ad ejus filium veniat, et tamen corporaliter ire recusat? Ad servum vero centurionis non invitatur, et tamen se corporaliter ire pollicetur; reguli filio per corporalem praesentiam non dignatur adesse, centurionis vero servo non dedignatur occurrere.

125–30 (*Smaragdus, col. 496A*) Quid est hoc, nisi quod superbia nostra reconditur, qui in hominibus ron naturam, qua ad imaginem Dei facti sint, sed honores et divitias veneramur.

131–6 (*Smaragdus, col. 496A*) Redemptor vero noster, ut ostenderet, quia quae alta sunt hominum, sanctis despicienda sunt, et quae despecta sunt hominum, despicienda non sunt, ad filium reguli ire noluit, ad servum autem centurionis ire paratus fuit.

139–42 (*Smaragdus, col. 496A*) Incipiebat enim fidem habere in sermone Jesu, et qui ex parte dubius venit, fidelis recessit, et ideo sanitatem filii meruit.

þe fæder heom befran ða mid fyrwytnysse sonæ   145
on hwylcere tide ðe sune wurpte.

Heo sæden him to andsware: Gyrstendæȝ he wyrpte,
swa ofer midne dæȝ, þæt hine forlet þeo feofer.'

On ðare seofoðen tide wearð his sune ihæled,
and þæt ȝetel is haliȝ þurh ðone Halȝæ Gast   150
on his seofenfealde ȝyfe, ðe ure sawle onlihtæð,
and he us dæþ forȝyfennysse alræ ure synn(æ).

'Ða oncneow þe fæder þæt hine forlet þeo feofor
on ðare ylcan tide þe ðe Hælend him to cwæð:
Fare þe nu ham ræðe, þin sune leofæð;   155
and he þa sylf lyfde and all his hired þurh ðæt.'

þeo Cristes boc us sæȝð þæt Crist sylf bodede
tweȝen daȝes on an (on) Samarian buriȝ,
and heo ða ilyfdon þurh his lare on God.

Nu ilyfde þes kyng on Crist, mid his hirede,   160
þurh ðæt an wundor þe he wrohte on his sune.

For þan ðe moniȝe ilyfæþ of alle londe on Crist
of hæðenum ðeodum, þurh his halȝ(an) apostlæs
þe þæs Hælendes æ ofer lond seowon.

Ða Iudeisce isæȝen hu he wrohte tacnæ   165
mycele and moniȝæ him sylfe tomiddes,
ac swa ðeah to feawæ of þam folce ilyfdon.

Ða Iudeisce boceræs bifrynnon hine hwilon:

152 synnæ] synnum   158 on] preceded by erasure of s (of samarian?)
163 halȝan] halȝum   apostlæs] s[2] above an erasure

149–52 (Smaragdus, col. 496B) Septenarius numerus sanctificatus est in donis sancti
Spiritus, in quo sanitas omnibus credentibus datur, constat. Quia in sancto Spiritu, qui
est donum Dei, remissio est omnium peccatorum credentium. [Followed by a short discussion of the significance of the numbers three and four, not included by Ælfric.]
157–9 (John iv. 40–41)
160–7 (Smaragdus, col. 496C) Quia nuntiatus est ei filius sanus, ad solum ergo
sermonem crediderunt plures Samaritani, ad illud autem miraculum, sola domus illa
credidit, quae res protendit in multitudinem fidem gentium, et in paucitate fidei
Judaeorum. Gentes vero solo sermone, id est, praedicatione apostolica crediderunt,
Judaei vero signa viderunt ipsum Dei filium facientem, et tamen pauci crediderunt ex
eis.
168–84 (Luke xx. 1–8 [independent addition by Ælfric]) (1) Et factum est in una dierum,
docente illo populum in templo et evangelizante, convenerunt principes sacerdotum, et
scribae cum senioribus, (2) et aiunt dicentes ad illum: Dic nobis in qua potestate haec
facis, aut quis est qui dedit tibi hanc potestatem? (3) Respondens autem Iesus dixit ad
illos: Interrogabo vos et ego unum verbum; respondete mihi: (4) Baptismus Ioannis de
caelo erat, an ex hominibus? (5) At illi cogitabant intra se dicentes: Quia si dixerimus de
caelo, dicet quare ergo non credidistis illi? (6) Si autem dixerimus: Ex hominibus, plebs

Sæȝe us, we biddæþ,
on hwæs mihte ðu wurcæst þas syllice wundræ,   170
oððe hwa ȝeaf þe ðesne andweald þæt ðu swylce ðing makyȝe?
Ðe Hælend heom andswarde: Sæcgð me nu an þing,
wæs Iohannis fulluht of heofenum oððe of mannum?
Ða smeadan ða boceræs betwyx heom, þus cwæðende,
Gif we him nu sæcgæð þæt his fulluht beo of heofene,   175
þenne andswaræþ he us, Hwi nolde ȝe him ilefen?
Gif we þenne sæcgæþ þæt his fulluht is of monnum,
þenne wule al folc us oftorfiæn mid stanum,
for þan ðe heo witæn to soðe þæt Iohannes is witegæ.
Heo cwæden þa to andsware: 180
Nute we na to sæcgenne hwanon Iohannis fulluht beo;
and þe Hælend heom andswarde: Ne ic eac eow ne sæcge
on hwylcere mihte ic makiȝe þas wundræ;
and heo letæn þa swa.
þa boceræs wæron ablende on mode   185
þa þa heo nolden sæcgen soð be | Iohanne,   Bf. 30
ðonne heo wæl wiston þæt his fulluht wæs of Gode;
and heo dweloden swyðe þa ða heo swylces axoden
hwanon Cristes miht wære on his mycle wundrum,
for þan ðe heo mihten icnawæn, ȝif heo cyðen æniȝ god,   190
þæt nan mon ne mihte makiȝen swylce tacnæ
butan Gode sylfum oððe on Godes nome,
þe ðe ane wurcð wundræ ðurh his mihte.
Swa swa ðe sealmwurhte song hwilon bi Gode:
Benedictus Dominus | Deus Israelis qui facit mirabilia solus,   fol. 10
Ibledsod is þe Drihten Israele ðeodæ God   196
þe ðe ane wurcæð wundræ þurh his mihte.
For þan ðe nan mon ne mæȝ nane mihte fremmæn
buton God wurce þa wundræ ðurh þone mon,
þe ðe him sylf makæð mihte and wundræ   200
butæn ælcum men; ðam is anweald and wuldor
and wurðment on ecnysse a to worulde.
AMEN.

176 he] *lower part of* e *smudged into top part*   188 dweloden] w *altered from another*
letter (e?)

---

universa lapidabit nos; certi sunt enim Ioannem prophetam esse. (7) Et responderunt se
nescire unde esset. (8) Et Iesus ait illis: Neque ego dico vobis in qua potestate haec
facio. (*The subsequent commentary discussing miracles is apparently Ælfric's own.*)

NOTES

9. *axode*: Ælfric normally uses *geaxian* rather than *axian* to mean 'discover, learn'. It is likely that a twelfth-century scribe has omitted an initial *ge-* here.

10. The alliteration of this line is interesting. It seems to depend on *Iudea* and *Galileam* (though the *l* in *londe* and *Galileam* may provide a secondary correspondence). In general Ælfric tends to separate the palatal and guttural *g*, so that each alliterates with itself only. Sometimes, however, mixtures of the two are found; see Pope pp. 130–1 (including examples).

14, 16, etc. *andswarde*: *Andwyrde* is the form Ælfric normally uses for 'answered'. The scribe has consistently replaced the verb *andwyrdan* by *andswarian*.

27. *swa ofer midne dæȝ*: Ælfric discusses the significance of the various hours of the day in his homily for Septuagesima Sunday (CH II v). The day is divided at the third hour, the sixth hour (midday), the ninth hour (3 p.m.), and the eleventh hour. Since the sixth hour corresponds to midday, the seventh hour is accurately rendered by *swa ofer midne dæȝ*. Ælfric also uses *ofer midne dæȝ* to render 'the seventh hour' in CH I viii, p. 128.

27, 28. The use of the feminine form *þeo* for the definite article preceding the nominative singular masculine *fefor* (again at 148 and 153) probably results from scribal confusion of gender. The use of *þe* with the same function in 28 suggests that this scribe had little concern for consistency of gender.

46. *to ðam ðe he wolde*: The phrase probably refers to the wishes of the emperor rather than those of the underkings. I have therefore emended MS *to ðam ðe heo wolden* to the singular form shown above. Compare a similar use of the phrase in Ælfric's epilogue to the Book of Judges: '7 him God gewilde his wiðerwinnan a, ciningas 7 eorlas, þæt hi comon him to buton ælcum gefeohte friðes wilniende, him underþeodde to þam þe he wolde, 7 he wæs gewurðod wide geond land' (Crawford, p. 417).

47. *loca hu*: For this construction, see T. F. Mustanoja, *A Middle English Syntax* Part I Parts of Speech (Helsinki, 1960), pp. 476–7. Compare *loc(a) hwa*, *loc(a) hwæt*, *loc(a) hwæþer*, *loc(a) hwelc* listed as forms of the relative in *OES* §520.

52. *fiðerricæn*: The word is rare in Old English. Apart from two other uses by Ælfric (CH I xxvi, p. 364, CH I xxxii, p. 478), it appears only as a gloss to the word 'tetrarcha' in the MS Digby 146 version of Aldhelm's *De Laude Virginitatis* (Napier, *Anecdota Oxoniensia*, gloss 1799). The gloss belongs to the latter part of the eleventh century (see Napier, p. xxvii).

73. *cnapæn*: In this homily *cnapa* is used to refer both to the underking's son (John iv. 46–53) and also to the centurion's servant (Matth. viii. 5–13). In CH I viii, his earlier rendering of the same gospel-texts, he does not use *cnapa* at all,

denoting the centurion's servant by *cniht* and *þeowa*, and the underking's son by *bearn* and *æðeling* (pp. 126–8). The distinction between *cnapa* and *cniht* is one made by Ælfric elsewhere:

> þonne þæt cild wyxt, and gewyrð eft cnapa,
> and eft syððan cniht, oþþæt he swa
> becymð to þære ylde þe him geann his Scyppend.
> (Pope xii, p. 484)

Since in Matth. viii. 5–13, the centurion's servant is called 'puer', *cnapa* would seem to be more appropriate than *cniht*. Indeed in his writings, Ælfric tends to render the Latin 'puer' by *cnapa*, reserving *cniht* for 'adulescens' or 'iuvenis'. H. Gneuss has argued ('The origin of Standard Old English', *ASE* 1 (1972), p. 76) that the use of *cnapa* rather than *cniht* for 'boy' seems to have been a characteristic of the Winchester texts. It may have been a distinction which Ælfric became more concerned with in his later writings (Pope xii belongs to what Clemoes, 'Chronology', calls TH I, that is a fairly late phase in Ælfric's development of his homilies). Certainly there is a much greater variety of vocabulary used to denote the various categories in CH I viii than in homily i. It may also be the case that *cniht* was beginning to shift towards its modern meaning of 'knight' by the time homily i was written: in the latter, Ælfric has used *cnihtæs* to refer to the centurion's soldiers (called *cempan* in CH I viii).

75, 77. *on ælcere stowe*: The repetition of this phrase is rather clumsy. But since the phrase fits the rhythmic pattern on both occasions, Ælfric must be deliberately emphasizing God's omnipresence.

96. *fule*: Although MS *fulle* makes perfectly good sense, Belfour's emendation to *fule* is accepted, since Ælfric in another homily twice uses *fule* in a similar context. He refers first to each person who is buried in sin, 'he fule þonne stincð on his fracodum dædum' (Pope vi, p. 319, l. 169), and then to Lazarus specifically:

> Se þridda deada (wæs) þe ure Drihten arærde
> Lazarus (se Iudeisca), se læg bebyrged
> fule þa stincende, swa swa we her beforan sædon.
> (Pope vi, p. 321, ll. 196–8)

105. *al on paralisim*: Ælfric is closer here to the Latin 'paralyticus' of Matth. viii. 6 than in his previous rendering of the word in CH I viii (*bedreda*, p. 126). The word *paralisim* is common in Old English, and Ælfric uses it several times elsewhere: CH II xxxvii, l. 179; LS I x, l. 235, I xxi, l. 178, II xxv l. 724, II xxvi l. 214, II xxxi l. 488.

107. *me sylf*: The function of *me sylf* in this context is ambiguous: it is being used either emphatically or as a reflexive accusative. See *OES* §§276–7.

124. *hundredes aldres*: The word *hundredes* is never used elsewhere to stand for *hundredes aldor*; the omission of *aldres* must be the result of scribal error, and Belfour's emendation is accordingly accepted here.

150-2. The notion of the sevenfold gifts of the Holy Spirit is frequently incorporated by Ælfric in his homiletic writings. See, for example, CH I xxii, p. 326 (the Holy Spirit 'onbryrt ure mod mid seofonfealdre gife'); CH II xvi, p. 167, ll. 201-3 ('ða men becumað to his ecan gereorde þe on andwerdum life ðurh geearnungum becumað to seofonfealdre gife þæs halgan gastes').

157-67. Smaragdus draws a clear distinction here between the Samaritans and the king's subjects: Christ's words alone are sufficient to win the Samaritans over to faith in God, whereas an actual miracle gives rise to faith only amongst the king's immediate household. Smaragdus thereby contrasts the respective faiths of the Gentiles (who believed in God from hearing the apostles preach) and the Jews (who saw actual miracles but refrained from believing). Ælfric likewise contrasts the Gentiles and the Jews in terms of their willingness to believe. But the initial basis of this contrast is less clear than in Smaragdus. Where Smaragdus's phrase 'sola domus' emphasizes that only the Jews in the king's immediate household were converted by the miracle, Ælfric's phrase 'an wundor' (applying 'sola' to the miracle rather than the household) excludes any implication that more Jews should have been converted. This does not seem to be a deliberate change of meaning on Ælfric's part, since he proceeds to the same contrast of the Jews and Gentiles as in Smaragdus. He presumably either misread the Latin, or was translating from a corrupt reading ('solum' for 'sola').

The contrast between the Jews and the Gentiles in terms of faith was a popular subject for Ælfric, who always implies that his own people are to identify exclusively with the Gentiles. See, for example, CH II viii, 49-51, 89-93; CH II xiv, 258-62; CH II xxv, 58-63.

163. *ðurh his halgan apostlæs*: The manuscript reading *ðurh his halʒum apostlæs* is clearly incorrect. Since Ælfric stopped using *ðurh* with dative early in his career (Sisam, *Studies*, pp. 180ff., and M. R. Godden, 'The Development of Ælfric's Second Series', *English Studies*, 209-16), Belfour's emendation of *apostlæs* to *apostlum* is unjustified. It is more likely that MS *halʒum* is a scribal error for *halʒan*, and the text has been emended accordingly.

164. *æ*: It is tempting to emend *æ* to *lagu*, which would better fit the alliterative pattern, and which was frequently used in a religious sense by Ælfric later in his career (see Godden, 'Ælfric's Changing Vocabulary', p. 215). But *æ* is likely to be the correct reading since no twelfth-century scribe would have altered *lagu* to the more outdated *æ*. See A. Fischer, 'Lexical Change in Late Old English: From *æ* to *lagu*', in *The History and the Dialects of English: Festschrift for Eduard Kolb*, ed. A. Fischer (Heidelberg, 1989), pp. 103-14.

195. The scriptural reference is to Ps. lxxi. 18.

THE SERVANT'S FAILURE TO FORGIVE

DATE AND AUDIENCE

This homily has many features in common with the previous one. Since the homilies follow one another in Bodley 343, and both appear only in that manuscript, their textual history is closely connected. The manuscript evidence cited by Clemoes suggests that both belong to the late TH II phase of Ælfric's development of his series.[1] The two are associated not only textually but also in their content. They celebrate consecutive occasions: homily i expounds the pericope for the Twenty-second Sunday after Pentecost, and the text of homily ii, Matth. xviii. 23–35, is the pericope for the Twenty-third Sunday after Pentecost. Since both also offer fairly straightforward verse-by-verse expositions of the gospel, it seems possible that they were written in close succession.

Like homily i, homily ii was apparently designed for preaching to a congregation; we find direct addresses to an audience in 'her is mucel andʒit eow monnum to witenne', 'we al swa hit sæcgæð on Engliscere sprece eow', 'swa swa we hwene ær eow sæden on Englisc', and 'be ðam ðe ʒe sylfe herdon'. Elsewhere in the homily, however, Ælfric uses the second person singular pronoun rather than the second person plural: lines 103–5 stress that 'þu' must forgive all who sin against 'þe', and at the end of the homily (ll. 181 ff.) the need to reconcile deeds and thoughts and to combine discipline with mercy is urged on a singular audience. Ælfric may be slavishly following his source in its preference for the second person singular rather than plural. But it seems possible that Ælfric intended these parts of his text to apply primarily to a small, exclusive group from amongst his audience, that is the monks and clerics. This would fit well with Clayton's argument for Ælfric's *Catholic Homilies* that he had in mind when writing, a situation 'where the laity would have been preached to in the monastic

---

[1] Clemoes, 'Chronology', p. 231.

church, with the monks also present'; such a situation would explain 'the non-exclusive character of homilies directed chiefly at one section of his audience but which never exclude the other sections'.[1] The whole homily moreover fits with the 'increasing emphasis on providing instruction for this [religious] element in his audience' which Clayton identifies in the *Temporale Homilies*.[2] It includes more complex material than homily i, for example its explication of the significance of the number seven. Ælfric assumes that his audience prays on a daily basis: 'ælce dæȝe we biddæþ ure synne forȝifennysse on þam paternoster'. Finally in the last section of his commentary Ælfric implies that his audience is responsible for disciplining others, addressing them as 'ðu þe styran scealt', and emphasizing that the role should be performed with mercy: 'ðe ðe monhatæ bið, ne mæȝ he wæl styræn; forþan ðe þa halȝa weræs ðe weron iu lareowæs beoð nu iherode ðurh heoræ liðnysse'.

SOURCE

Ælfric informs his audience early in his commentary that he has derived his material from Augustine: 'we nimæð herto to ðissere trahtnunge Augustinum ðone wisæ, ðe we wæl truwiæð' (ll. 49–50). In the course of the homily he twice more reminds us that he has the authority of Augustine for his exposition: 'Nu sæȝð us Augustinus' (l. 107) and 'ac Augustinus us sæȝð' (l. 189). The source to which Ælfric is referring is identifiable as Augustine's homily lxxxiii.[3] As with homily i, the source is found in the late Migne version of Paul the Deacon's homiliary for the same occasion, though this occasion is not one included in the original homiliary.[4]

TRANSLATION OF THE GOSPEL-TEXT AND OTHER BIBLICAL PASSAGES

Ælfric has slightly restructured Augustine's text (where the pericope is included in the midst of the exposition), making it conform to the usual pattern of his homilies with the gospel-text first and all the exposition following. His translation of the pericope derives from the

[1] 'Homiliaries and Preaching', p. 239.
[2] Ibid., p. 242.
[3] PL 38, cols. 514ff. The source was first identified by Cross in 'The Literate Anglo-Saxon', p. 84, n. 1.
[4] See the introduction to homily i, p. 5, n. 4.

Vulgate rather than Augustine's paraphrase. As usual, Ælfric has tended to expand the gospel-text: words and phrases are added which give the passage his distinctive rhythmical and alliterative style. In the following examples of single lines, the material added to the gospel-text by Ælfric is placed in square brackets: 'þa feol ðe þæȝen adun [to his lafordes fotum]' (l. 15); 'sumne oðerne mon of his [aȝenum] iferum' (l. 21); 'and ilæhte hine sonæ [and læȝde hine adun]' (l. 23); 'aȝeld nu [swiðe raðæ] þæt þæt ðu me ȝeldæn scealt' (l. 25); 'ac sette hine on cwearterne [mid swiðlicum gramæ]' (l. 30); 'and cwæð ðus [mid yrre]: Ealæ ðu yfelæ ðeowæ' (l. 36); 'þam [stiðum] witnerum, [þe hine witniæn sceolden]' (l. 41). As a result of his addition of 'and læȝde hine adun' in line 23, Ælfric has to interpolate a line 'ða ȝeælnode ðe oðer hine up swa ðeah' (l. 26) to make sense of the following statement 'and feol to his fotum' (rendering the Latin 'procidens').[1]

For his translation of other biblical passages where Augustine and the Vulgate differ, Ælfric recalls the Vulgate at least for longer passages. This is in keeping with his general practice: according to Pope, 'Ælfric's pericopes and other extended translations from the gospels clearly follow the Vulgate' while a brief citation is frequently 'borrowed from a commentator, and Ælfric may quote it in the commentator's form'.[2] In his translation of Matth. xviii. 15–17, for example, Ælfric follows the Vulgate, not Augustine (ll. 60–8). The Vulgate has 'adhibe tecum adhuc unum vel duos', in contrast to Augustine's 'adhibe tecum duos vel tres': Ælfric translates 'hafe ðe to ȝewitæn ænne broðor oððe tweȝen'. In lines 69–72, Ælfric's use of direct speech for both Peter and Christ also suggests that he has recalled the Vulgate for Matth. xviii. 21–2 (the passage immediately preceding the pericope in the Bible) rather than following Augustine. Again in lines 165–7, where Ælfric translates Matth. xviii. 35 (without including the Latin), he seems to have turned to the Vulgate: for Augustine's 'Pater vester coelestis', Ælfric has 'min heofenlice Fæder' corresponding to the Vulgate 'Pater meus caelestis'.[3] For the brief quotation from Luke vi. 37–8 in line 87, however, Ælfric is probably

---

[1] The meaning of 'ȝeælnode' seems in this context to be 'pulled himself together'; see my textual note to l. 26.

[2] Pope, p. 152.

[3] The evidence is otherwise inconclusive. Augustine has 'fratribus vestris ex cordibus vestris' (two second person pronouns), the Vulgate 'fratri suo de cordibus vestris' (one third person and one second), and Ælfric 'eowrum ȝebroðren, ælc an of his heort(æn)' (one third person and one second but applying to alternate nouns).

following Augustine rather than the Vulgate; his wording of 'dimitte et dimittetur vobis' is the same as Augustine's whereas the Clementine recension of the Vulgate appears as 'Dimittite, et dimittemini'.[1]

TREATMENT OF SOURCE

In general Ælfric's aim was to abbreviate Augustine's rather lengthy exposition.[2] At times this merely entails cutting out unnecessary filler material. For example, at lines 96–7 Ælfric omits a large passage in which Augustine expands the idea that one must forgive all sins: ten thousand talents correspond to ten thousand sins, and God expects all of these to be forgiven; indeed even in sleep, Augustine continues, we have need of talents, since we are still subject to sinfulness. The idea that one must forgive not only seventy-seven but all sins is repeated elsewhere, and Ælfric's omission of this material in no way detracts from his argument.

Elsewhere Ælfric has actually added extra material to his source. Sometimes this material merely clarifies Augustine. For example, Ælfric reminds his audience of the relevance of the multiples of ten in relation to the pericope: the mention of ten thousand prompts him to add 'swa fela ðusend pundæ sceolde þe ðæʒen þam kynge' (l. 139); the reference to a hundred pence leads him to add 'swa mycel sceolde þe mon þam þeʒene' (l. 141). Slightly more substantial an amplification is Ælfric's independent explanation of why Christ might be said to have begun His ascension at His baptism: at this event the heavens were opened, as witnessed by John the Baptist (ll. 119–20). This is presumably a reference to John i. 32, the descent from Heaven of the Holy Spirit at John's baptism, with a reminder also of John i. 51, where Christ subsequently promises that 'videbitis caelum apertum, et angelos Dei ascendentes, et descendentes supra Filium hominis' (you will see heaven open, and the angels of God ascending and descending upon the Son of man).

[1] I have used the word 'probably' here, since 'dimittetur uobis' is cited as a variant wording in *Nouum Testamentum ... Latine*, ed. J. Wordsworth and H. I. White, Pars prior: Quattuor Euangelia (Oxford, 1889–98). Pope notes that for his edition he has normally quoted the Clementine recension 'since it is generally satisfactory', but that on rare occasions he has found reason to cite the recension of Wordsworth and White 'for punctuation or a likely variant' (p. 152). We cannot be sure of the exact wording of Ælfric's Bible here.

[2] For Ælfric's techniques of stylistic abbreviation in his treatment of Augustine elsewhere see Ann E. Nichols, 'Methodical Abbreviation: A Study in Ælfric's Friday Homilies for Lent', in *The Old English Homily*, ed. Szarmach and Huppé, pp. 157–80.

Certain independent additions and omissions, however, suggest that Ælfric had a more complex attitude towards his source. These passages show a conscious deviation on his part from the Augustinian emphasis on salvation by grace rather than by merit. Where Augustine focuses on divine grace as the means by which men are to receive salvation, Ælfric is much more interested in the doctrine of merit and reward: only by good deeds shall we receive salvation in heaven.

As with homily i the opening passage of exposition is an addition to the main source: Ælfric equates the kingdom of heaven with God's church (ll. 53-9). The added material here and elsewhere in this homily repeats ideas included in earlier compositions and Ælfric is probably recalling these rather than turning to other Latin sources. This parallel was drawn by Ælfric previously in, for example, his First Series homily for the Twenty-first Sunday after Pentecost and his Second Series homily for Septuagesima.[1] The link between the heavenly kingdom and the church congregation is used here as a means of introducing the theme of forgiveness: Ælfric suggests that God wishes us to forgive others just as He forgives us. The implication is that forgiving others enables us, indeed is necessary for us, to be forgiven by God.

At lines 75-95 Ælfric reveals clearly his emphasis on salvation by merit. First he omits Augustine's description of every man as a debtor of God, presumably to concentrate on the relation between man and man and hence to play down the possibility of salvation by God's grace. When Augustine introduces the idea of mendicancy, suggesting that we are all beggars of God when we pray, Ælfric diverges from him altogether. He elaborates instead on Luke's words 'forgive and you will be forgiven; give and gifts will be given to you', explaining that our good deeds will be rewarded in heaven a hundred times over. The notion of a hundredfold reward, biblical in origin (Matth. xix. 29), clearly appealed to Ælfric, since he used it several times elsewhere, often likewise independently of his main source.[2] It fits well with the doctrine of merit and reward which Ælfric substitutes for Augustine's emphasis on divine grace.

In his commentary on the eleven goats' hair curtains of Exod. xxvi. 7, Ælfric adds a phrase stressing the need to do severe penance

---

[1] CH I xxxv, p. 520; CH II v, 36-9. Earlier uses of the parallel often derive from Ælfric's immediate source.

[2] See, for example, CH I xviii, p. 256; CH II vii, 110-12; Pope xiii, 106-8; Pope xvi, 155 ff. Pope notes that the similar statement in his homily xiii is independent of the sources (p. 509).

for sins ('and he sceal mid stiðnysse his synne ʒebeten' (l. 154)), instead of following Augustine who expatiates on the significance of the number seven (col. 518). The theme of penance is further brought into prominence by Ælfric when he adds independently the biblical passage 1 John i. 8–9, which affirms that God will forgive us if we confess our sins.[1] Ælfric also comments on this text, stressing that we must forgive others from our hearts so that God may be merciful to us. Again Ælfric is emphasizing that meritorious conduct on earth is essential for our salvation.

Like Augustine, Ælfric ends with a discussion of the need to use discipline to persuade wrongdoers to amend their ways. The image of the merciful father at line 201 is Ælfric's own: it picks up the earlier reference to governing 'his aʒenum childe' by discipline and love, but it also suggests the mercy of the omnipotent 'Milde Fæder'. The comparison of the relationship between one who must chastise and a wrongdoer and that of doctor to his patient (ll. 203–7) derives from Augustine.[2] Ælfric included a similar idea in an earlier homily on St. Bartholomew; here God is compared to the doctor who

ðurh mislice swingla his folces synna gehælð. Nis se woruld-læce wælhreow, ðeah ðe he þone gewundodan mid bærnette, oððe mid ceorfsexe gelacnige. Se læce cyrfð oððe bærnð, and se untruma hrymð, þeah-hwæðere ne miltsað he þæs oðres wanunge, forðan gif se læce geswicð his cræftes, þonne losað se forwundoda. Swa eac God gelacnað his gecorenra gyltas mid mislicum brocum; and þeah ðe hit hefigtyme sy ðam ðrowigendum, þeah-hwæðere wyle se goda Læce to ecere hælðe hine gelacnigan.[3]

In that homily the passage is independent of Ælfric's main source, the apocryphal *Passio S. Bartholomaei apostoli*.[4]

---

[1] Ælfric may be recalling another sermon by Augustine, no. cxv (PL 38, cols. 652–4). The gospel-text for this sermon is Luke xvii. 3–4, which corresponds to Matth. xviii. 21–2 in its reference to forgiving a brother's sins seven times (the latter is cited by Ælfric at ll. 69–72). In his sermon cxv Augustine cites 1 John i. 8–9 as an apposite text.

[2] Allen J. Frantzen, *The Literature of Penance in Anglo-Saxon England* (New Brunswick, New Jersey, 1983), p. 159, notes that Ælfric, in using the medical metaphor, is 'reworking images commonplace in the penitentials'. Ælfric may also be recalling Gregory's *Cura Pastoralis* which frequently upholds the importance of wounding for the purpose of healing (see, for example, Part I, ch. ix; Part II, chs. vi and x; Part III, Prologue, chs. ii, xxiv–xxvi, xxx, xxxvii). The metaphor also appears in a sermon by Caesarius of Arles (CCSL 103, *Sermo* v, p. 29).   [3] CH I xxxi, p. 472.

[4] See B. Mombritius, ed., *Sanctuarium seu Vitae Sanctorum* 2nd ed. 2 vols. (Paris, 1910), I, 140–4 (*BHL* 1002). See Patrick H. Zettel, 'Ælfric's Hagiographic Sources and the Latin Legendary preserved in B.L. MS Cotton Nero E i + CCCC MS 9 and other manuscripts' (unpubl. D.Phil. diss., Oxford, 1979), pp. 181–2, for a discussion of Ælfric's use of this source.

Ælfric then proceeds to distinguish secret sins which are to be corrected secretly and public sins which are to be corrected publicly (ll. 208–15). Despite remaining fairly faithful to Augustine in this passage, he explicitly refers to other sources as well: 'swa swa us sæcgæð bec' (l. 208). The phrase is a convenient half-line filler within the homily's rhythmical prose style, but Ælfric's care and accuracy elsewhere in reference to his sources makes it unlikely that this is the full explanation. The identity of the 'bec' needs to be considered. Ælfric made the same distinction between different types of sins in his earlier homily for the Seventeenth Sunday after Pentecost:

þa diglan gyltas man sceal digelice betan, and ða openan openlice, þæt ða beon getimbrode þurh his behreowsunge, ðe ær wæron þurh his mandæda geæswicode.[1]

For this passage he is also following his main source for the homily which was Bede's Commentary on Luke:

Sed et hoc notandum, quod quia publica noxa, publico eget remedio, levia autem peccata leviori et secreta queunt poenitentia deleri, puella in domo jacens, paucis arbitris exsurgit, eisdemque ne miraculum vulgarent indicitur.[2]

Bede's homily may be one of the other books which Ælfric had in mind. But Ælfric does seem to have had a particular interest in penitential practice, as Allen Frantzen has shown.[3] As well as the two passages cited above, Ælfric elsewhere stresses the importance of proper penance. In his First Series homily for the Third Sunday after the Epiphany he states explicitly that penance must entail confession to a priest and that repentance alone is insufficient: 'Swa sceal eac se ðe mid heafod-leahtrum wiðinnan hreoflig bið cuman to Godes sacerde, and geopenian his digelnysse ðam gastlican læce.'[4] In his First Series homily for Shrove Sunday he again expresses the necessity of private penance for secret sins:

cume forði gehwa cristenra manna to his scrifte, and his diglan gyltas geandette, and be his lareowes tæcunge gebete.[5]

Ælfric's interest in penance generally suggests that his reference to 'bec' may refer to literature other than patristic. Penitential manuals

---

[1] CH I xxxiii, p. 498.
[2] PL 92, col. 445. The source for the homily was identified by Förster, 'Über die Quellen', p. 25.
[3] *The Literature of Penance*, especially pp. 158–61.
[4] CH I viii, p. 124.
[5] CH I x, p. 164.

were apparently popular and readily available in tenth-century England.[1] The two-fold system of penance espoused by Ælfric, private penance for secret sins and public penance for open sins, had been developed by the Carolingians, a compromise resulting from their limited success in attempting to re-introduce public penance.[2] Ælfric would certainly have read the Carolingian writings on penance,[3] and he may have had some of those in mind with his reference to other 'bec'.[4]

The category of 'bec' might also have included books of the Bible. This possibility is supported by Ælfric's comment a few lines later, after he has elaborated on the way secret sins should be corrected in private and open ones should be corrected publicly so that others may be guided: 'þus tæcæð us þæt godspel and þe Godes apostol' (l. 216). The apostle is 1 Timothy v. 20, a passage which was echoed by Augustine in 'ut caeteri timeant' (translated by Ælfric as 'þæt oðre beon isteoredæ' (l. 210) and then expanded to 'and oðre beon istyrede ðe þa steor ihyræð' (l. 215)). The gospel is Matth. xviii. 15–17 which Ælfric translated at the beginning of his exposition; in this he was following Augustine who referred explicitly to his sermon for the previous day: 'Hesterna die sanctum Evangelium admonuit nos.' For the last part of his homily Ælfric may have had in mind this previous sermon by Augustine, particularly its discussion of the need to discipline children out of love and to avoid hatred.[5] Ælfric incorporates these ideas in his last section independently of the later sermon by Augustine which is his main source. His conclusion criticizes the 'monhatæ' and emphasizes that we should show kindness and mercy in the manner of the saints and of God.

---

[1] Frantzen, The Literature of Penance, ch. 5.

[2] See C. Vogel, Les 'Libri Paenitentiales', Typologies des Sources du Moyen Âge Occidental, fasc. 27 (Turnhout, 1978), pp. 39–43.

[3] Fehr, p. cxviii, posits Hrabanus Maurus, De institutione clericorum, as a likely source for Ælfric in some passages.

[4] Examples of passages which may have been recalled by Ælfric are as follows: Theodulf of Orleans, Capitulary II (PL 105, cols. 211 D and 215 A and D); Hrabanus Maurus, De clericorum institutione, Book II, ch. xxx (PL 107, cols. 342–3); documents from ninth-century Frankish Councils, Monumenta Germaniae Historica, Concilia II. 1 (Hannover, 1906), p. 253 (no. xxvi), p. 256 (no. xxxi), p. 278 (no. xxv), Capitularia II (Hannover, 1890), pp. 183–4 (no. xxxi), p. 189 (no. x); Preface to Halitgar's De Poenitentia, Book V (PL 105, cols. 655–6); Hincmar, De Divortio Lotharii Regis et Tetbergae Reginae, Interrogatio v and xxii (PL 125, cols. 653 and 739), Epistola xxxiii (PL 126, col. 246 B).

[5] Sermon lxxxii (PL 38, cols. 506–14), especially cols. 506–7.

Simile est regnum celorum homini regi et reliqua.

Cristes iwunæ wæs ðæt he wolde oft spæcæn
on deopum biȝspellum to his discipulis;
ða sæde he hwilon biȝspel to heom:
'Heofene rice is ilic ane kynge,   5
he ðe hæfde mot wið his men hwilon,
and wolde mid ȝesceade settan his spæce.
He spæc þa wið ænne mon þe him ahte to ȝeldene
ten þusend pundæ, and manode him þæs feos.
Ða næfde þe ðeȝen nane mihte to þam,   10
þæt he ðam laforde his lane forȝylde,
ac þe laford het þa lædon ðone þæȝen
mid wif(e) and mid alle his cildrum, and syllæn wið feo,
þæt hure his lan wurde him forȝolden.
þa feol ðe þæȝen adun to his lafordes fotum,   15
and bæd hine ȝeorne, mid þissum worde cwæðende:
La leof, let me fyrst and ic þin feoh forȝylde.
Ðe laford þa mildsode þam ðeȝene þerrihte,
and læt hine faren, and all þæt feoh him forȝeaf.
Ða eode þe ðeȝen ut, and he efne þa imette   20

Bodley 343, fols. 10–11ᵛ; Belfour, pp. 30–41.

---

13 wife] wifū

SOURCES. The text cited here (in addition to the Vulgate) is Augustine, *Sermones, sermo* lxxxiii, PL 38, cols. 514–19.

1–47 (*Matth. xviii. 23–35*) (23) Ideo assimilatum est regnum caelorum homini regi, qui voluit rationem ponere cum servis suis. (24) Et cum coepisset rationem ponere, oblatus est ei unus qui debebat ei decem millia talenta. (25) Cum autem non haberet unde redderet, iussit eum dominus eius venundari, et uxorem eius et filios et omnia quae habebat, et reddi. (26) Procidens autem servus ille orabat eum, dicens: Patientiam habe in me, et omnia reddam tibi. (27) Misertus autem dominus servi illius, dimisit eum, et debitum dimisit ei. (28) Egressus autem servus ille invenit unum de conservis suis, qui debebat ei centum denarios; et tenens suffocabat eum, dicens: Redde quod debes. (29) Et procidens conservus eius, rogabat eum, dicens: Patientiam habe in me, et omnia reddam tibi. (30) Ille autem noluit, sed abiit, et misit eum in carcerem, donec redderet debitum. (31) Videntes autem conservi eius quae fiebant, contristati sunt valde; et venerunt, et narraverunt domino suo omnia quae facta fuerant. (32) Tunc vocavit illum dominus suus, et ait illi: Serve nequam, omne debitum dimisi tibi, quoniam rogasti me; (33) nonne ergo oportuit et te misereri conservi tui, sicut et ego tui misertus sum? (34) Et iratus dominus eius tradidit eum tortoribus, quoadusque redderet universum debitum. (35) Sic et Pater meus caelestis faciet vobis, si non remiseritis unusquisque fratri suo de cordibus vestris.

sumne oðerne mon of his aȝenum iferum,
þe ahte him to ȝeldenne hundtentiȝ peneȝæ,
and ilæhte hine sonæ, and læȝde hine adun,
and hine ofðryhte, ðus cwæðende him to:
Aȝeld nu swiðe raðæ þæt þæt ðu me ȝeldæn scealt.   25
Ða ȝeælnode ðe oðer hine up swa ðeah,
and feol to his fotum fyrstes him biddende;
bihet þæt he wolde al his feoh him forȝeldæn.
þa nolde þe ðeȝen læten | him nænne fyrst,   Bf. 32
ac sette hine on cwearterne mid swiðlicum gramæ,   30
oððet he him forȝylde unðances his feoh.
Ða isæȝen þa hiredmen hu ðe þeȝen dyde
embe ðone oðerne, and unrodsoden swiðe,
and cyddon þam kynge hu he idon hæfde.
Ðe kyng het þa sonæ hine clypiæn him to,   35
and cwæð ðus mid yrre: Ealæ ðu yfelæ ðeowæ,
ic forȝeaf þe ðone sceat swa swa ðu me bæde,
and ðu noldest forȝifæn swa þinum ȝefer(æn),
and him swa mildsiæn swa swa ic ðe mildsode.
Ða yrsode ðe laford, ant læt hine bitæcen   40
þam stiðum witnerum, þe hine witniæn sceolden,
oððet he forȝylde al ðæt feoh him seolfum,
for his arleasnesse, þæt þæt he him forȝeaf.'
Nu sæȝð us þis godspel þæt þe Hælend þa sæde:
'Al swa deþ to soðan min heofenlice Fæder eow,   45
ȝif ȝe ne forȝifæð eowrum ȝebroðrum,
ælc an of his heortæn, þæt þæt he aȝylte.' |
    Her is mucel andȝit eow monnum to witenne,   fol. 10ᵛ
and we nimæð herto to ðissere trahtnunge
Augustinum ðone wisæ, ðe we wæl truwiæð,   50
swa swa he hit ȝeloȝode on ðare Ledenspæce,
and we al swa hit sæcgæð on Engliscere sprece eow.
    'Heofene rice' is ihaten on ðissere stowe
Godes aȝene laðung, þæt is, al Godes folc,
ðe rihtlice ilefæð on ðone lifiȝende God;   55
and on þare laðunge ȝewurð þeos ȝelicnesse,

33 unrodsoden] *glossed by* ungledodon *in the same hand*   38 ȝeferæn] ȝeferũ
39 mildsiæn] mi'l'dsiæn   41 witniæn] n² *altered from another letter*   47 aȝylte]
3 *altered from* g

48–59 (*Ælfric's independent addition*)

for þan ðe God sylf is þe soðæ kyng
þe us monnum mildsæð for his mycele cyste,
and wule þæt we mildsien oðrum monnum al swa.
Ðe Hælend cwæð hwilon to þam halȝan Petrum ðus: 60
Gif þin broðor synegæð wið þe, cyð him onsundron ærest.
Gif he þe ihyræð, swa ðu strynest hine Gode.
Gif he þe ne ihyræð, hafe ðe to ȝewitæn
ænne broðor oððe tweȝen, and ðrea hine eft swa,
ant ȝif he hi ne ȝehyrð þæt he hine ȝerihtlæce,   65
sæȝe ðenne openlice on alle ȝelaðunge.
Gif he ðonne ne ȝehyrð ða halȝa laðunge,
beo he ðenne ælfremed, swa swa hæðen mon from ðe.
Ða axode Petrus: Hu ofte sceal ic forȝifæn?
Bið inoh seofen siðum? and him sæde ðe Hælend: 70
Ne sæcge ic na seofen siðum, ac ðu scealt forȝifan
seofon siðon ȝewis, and hundseofentiȝ siðon.
Ða sæde him ðe Hælend syððan þis biȝspel,
swa swa we hwene ær eow sæden on Englisc,
for þan ðe he us lærde mid þare | licnesse,   Bf. 34
and nolde þæt we loseden, from his lufe ælfræmede.   76
Ælc mon eornestlice ah to ȝeldene sum þing,

71 ac] *top part of* a *smudged into loop*

60–8 (*Augustine, col. 514*) Hesterna die sanctum Evangelium admonuit nos non negligere peccata fratrum nostrorum: 'Sed si peccaverit', inquit, 'in te frater tuus, corripe eum inter te et ipsum solum. Si te audierit, lucratus es fratrem tuum. Si autem contempserit, adhibe tecum duos vel tres: ut in ore duorum vel trium testium stet omne verbum. Si autem et ipsos contempserit, dic Ecclesiae. Quod si Ecclesiam contempserit, sit tibi sicut ethnicus et publicanus.'

(*Ælfric has also recalled Matth. xviii. 15–17*) (15) Sed si autem peccaverit in te frater tuus, vade et corripe eum inter te et ipsum solum; si te audierit, lucratus eris fratrem tuum. (16) Si autem te non audierit, adhibe tecum adhuc unum vel duos, ut in ore duorum vel trium testium stet omne verbum. (17) Quod si non audierit eos, dic ecclesiae; si autem ecclesiam non audierit, sit tibi sicut ethnicus et publicanus.

69–70 (*Augustine, col. 514*) Cum enim dixisset hoc Dominus Jesus Petro, subjecit et interrogavit Magistrum, quoties ignosceret fratri qui in illum peccasset; et quaesivit utrum sufficeret septies.

70–2 (*Augustine, col. 514*) Respondit illi Dominus: 'Non solum septies, sed etiam septuagies septies.'

73–4 (*Augustine, col. 514*) Deinde narravit similitudinem valde terribilem: quia simile est regnum coelorum homini patrifamilias . . . (*The parable*)

75–6 (*Augustine, col. 515*) Ergo hanc similitudinem ad nostram instructionem proposuit, et admonendo perire nos noluit.

77–81 (*Augustine, col. 515*) Quia omnis homo et debitor est Dei, et debitorem habet fratrem suum. Quis est enim qui non sit debitor Dei, nisi in quo nullum potest inveniri peccatum? Quis est autem qui non habeat debitorem fratrem, nisi in quem nemo

ant hæfð oðerne mon þe him sceal sum ðing;
for þon ðe nan mon nis ðe næbbe sume synne,
ant nan mon nis eft aht eað[fynd]e on life,   80
þe næbbe oðerne mon ðe wið hine aʒylte.
Nu sette God sylf us þesne reʒol betwyx us,
þæt we þam forʒifan þe wið us aʒyltæð,
þæt God us forʒife ure gyltæs wið him.
Twa weorc beoð þare soðan mildsunge   85
þe us alysæð be Cristes sylfes lare:
Dimitte et dimittetur uobis, date et dabitur uobis.
He cwæð: Forʒife ʒe, and eow bið forʒifen,
doð god oðrum monnum, and eow bið god iʒifen.
Ðu bist mildsunge æt Gode, mildsæ ðu oðre men.   90
Ðu wylt underfon god, tyðæ ðu oðre men,
na for ðissum life ane, ac for þam ece life,
ðær ðe bið forʒolden be hundfealde iwiss
swa mycel swa ðu bi anfealde her monnum tyðæst
for þæs Hælendes lufæn, ðe ðe het don swa.   95
Nu maʒe we axiæn swa swa Petrus axode,
hu ofte we sceolon oðrum monnum forʒifæn.
Ælce dæʒe we biddæþ ure synne forʒifennysse
on þam paternoster swa swa Crist sylf us ʒesette þæt ʒebed,

peccavit? Putasne, quisquam in genere humano reperiri potest, qui non et ipse aliquo peccato obstrictus sit fratri suo? Debitor est ergo omnis homo, habens tamen et ipse debitorem.

82-4 (*Augustine, col. 515*) Ideo Deus justus constituit tibi regulam in debitore tuo, quod faciet et ipse cum suo.

85-7 (*Augustine, col. 515*) Duo sunt enim opera misericordiae, quae nos liberant, quae breviter ipse Dominus posuit in Evangelio, 'Dimittite, et dimittetur vobis; date, et dabitur vobis.'

88-90 (*Augustine, col. 515*) 'Dimittite, et dimittetur vobis', ad ignoscendum pertinet. 'Date, et dabitur vobis', ad praestandum beneficium pertinet. Quod ait de ignoscendo; et tu vis tibi ignosci quod peccas, et habes alium cui tu possis ignoscere. Rursus quod pertinet ad tribuendum beneficium; petit te mendicus, et tu es Dei mendicus. (*Followed by a passage emphasizing that we are all beggars of God when we pray.*)

91-5 (*Independent of Augustine*)

96-7 (*Augustine, col. 515*) In remissione ubi venia petitur, et ab ignoscente debetur, hoc potest movere, quod et Petrum movit. 'Quoties debeo', inquit, 'ignoscere?' (*Followed by an elaboration: one must forgive all sins.*)

98-105 (*Augustine, col. 516*) Ergo quotidie petimus, quotidie divinas aures orando pulsamus, quotidie nos prosternimus et dicimus: 'Dimitte nobis debita nostra, sicut et nos dimittimus debitoribus nostris' (*Matth. vi. 12*). Quae debita tua? Omnia, an aliquam partem? Respondebis, Omnia. Sic ergo et tu debitori tuo. Hanc ergo regulam ponis, hanc conditionem loqueris: hoc pacto et placito quando oras, commemoras, ut dicas, 'Dimitte nobis, sicut et nos dimittimus debitoribis nostris.'

ærest his apostolis, and heo syððan us forþ,   100
þæt God sylf us forȝife ure synnæn wið hine,
swa swa we forȝifæð þam ðe wið us aȝyltæð.
Nu acsoð God þe hu felæ synna he forȝife þe,
þenne sæȝest ðu alle; do þu al swa ðe sylf,
forȝif allum þam monnum ðe wið þe agyldtæþ.   105
Hwæt ȝemænð þonne ic cwæðe þæt moniȝfealde ȝetel
seofen and hundseofentiȝ? Nu sæȝð us Augustinus
mycele tacnunge be ðam ȝetæle þus.
Ða þa ure Hælend wæs her on life ifullod,
þa tealde þe godspellere Lucas from Criste sylfum   110
upweard to Adame alle þa fæderæs æfre,
from men to oðrum, and he funde þa ·
seofen and | hundseofentiȝ fæderæs—þæt beoð swa fæla
    mæȝða—   fol. 11
ant Matheus þe godspellere ongon to tellenne
fram Abrahame duneweard oððet Cristes acennednysse.   115
He tealde niðerweard hu Crist com to middanearde,
and Lucas tealde upweard fram Cristes fulluhte,
for þan ðe his upstiȝe ongan on þam fulluhte.
On his fulluhte wæron heofenæs iopenode,
ðæt iseah Iohannes, þe hine fullode,   120
and Lucas tealde þanon, swa swa we sædon ær,
upweard to Adame seofen and hundseofentiȝ mæȝða.
Nu næs nan mæȝð forlæten æfre from men to oðrum,
ne nan synna þæt ne sceal beon forȝifen,
for þan ðe on | ðam fulluhte beoð alle synna forȝifenæ,   Bf. 36

115 acennednysse] *followed by erasure of* s

106–22 (*Augustine, cols. 516–17*) Quid sibi ergo vult 'septuagies septies'? Audite, fratres, magnum mysterium, admirabile sacramentum. Quando Dominus baptizatus est, Lucas evangelista sanctus ibi commemoravit generationes ejus, quo ordine, qua serie, quo stemmate ad illam generationem ventum fuerit, qua natus est Christus (*Luke. iii. 21–38*). Matthaeus coepit ab Abraham, et venit usque ad Joseph descendendo (*Matth. i. 1–16*): Lucas autem ascendendo coepit numerare. Quare ille descendendo, ille ascendendo? Quia Matthaeus generationem Christi commendabat, qua descendit ad nos; ideo quando natus est Christus, coepit numerare descendendo. Lucas autem quia tunc coepit numerare, quando baptizatus est Christus; ibi est initium ascensionis: iste ascendendo numerare coepit, numerando autem complevit generationes septua-ginta septem. (*Followed by further explanation of the significance of the number seventy-seven.*)

123–31 (*Augustine, col. 517*) Si ergo nulla generatio praetermissa est, nulla culpa praeteritur, ubi non debeat ignosci. Nam ideo ipsius septuaginta septem generationes enumeravit, quem numerum Dominus in peccatorum remissione commendavit; quoniam a baptismo coepit enumerare, ubi omnia peccata solvuntur.

ðanon þe Lucas tealde þa mæ3racan upweard.   126
Đa ða ðe Hælend wolde her on life beon acenned
on þare seofan mæ3ðe and ðare hun(d)seofenteoðan mæ3ðe,
and bead syððan Petrum þæt he swa oft for3ife,
ðæt he 3eswutelode þæt alle synna   130
sceolen beon a for3ifene be ðam ylcæ tele.
Git þær is oðer tacnuncg al swa deop swa ðis.
Godes la3e wæs isett, þurh hine sylfne iwriten,
on twam stænene weaxbræden mid tyn ealicum wordum,
þæt is Decalogus icwæden on Leden;   135
ða he bitæhte Moysen on ðam munte Synay,
his folce to steore, and forð swa us alle.
Nu is þæt tynfealde 3etel on ðam tyn ðusendæ:
swa fela ðusend pundæ sceolde þe ðæ3en þam kynge;
and hundteonti3 pene3æ bið tyn siðes tene: 140
swa mycel sceolde þe mon þam þe3ene,
bi þam ylce 3etæle be þam tyn bebodum,
þe God sylf sette his monnum to steore.
On ðam tenfealde 3etæle bið Godes la3e ifylled,
and on endlyfænfealde bið þeo for3ea3ednysse   145
þæt mon Godes [la3e] tobræce mid for3æ3ednysse,
and synna 3efræmme on his 3esetnysse.
Forþy3 weron itealde on þam Godes itælde,
þe Moyses wrohte on þam wæstene,

---

127 ða] a *altered from* e   128 hund-] hunð-

132–43 (*Augustine, col. 517*) Et in hoc, fratres, adhuc accipite sacramentum majus ...
Deinde paulo diligentius interroga ipsius numeri secretum, latebrasque ejus inquire:
pulsa diligentius, ut aperiatur tibi. Justitia lege Dei constat: verum est. Nam lex in
decem praeceptis commendatur. Ideo ille debebat decem millia talentorum. Ipse est ille
memorabilis Decalogus scriptus digito Dei, traditus populo per Moysen famulum Dei.
Debebat ergo ille decem millia talentorum: omnia peccata significat, propter numerum
legis. Debebat et ille centum denarios: non minus ab eodem numero. Nam et centies
centum fit decem millia; et decies deni, centum. Et ille decem millia talentorum, et ille
decies denos.

144–54 (*Augustine, cols. 517–18*) Observet ergo ipsum peccatum: quia numerus
undenarius transgressio legis est. Lex enim denarius, peccatum undenarium. Lex enim
per decem, peccatum per undecim. Quare peccatum per undecim? Quia transgressio
denarii est, ut eas ad undenarium. In lege autem modus fixus est: transgressio autem
peccatum est. Jam ubi transgrederis denarium, ad undenarium venis. Adeo magnum
mysterium figuratum est, quando jussum est tabernaculum fabricari. Multa ibi
numerosa dicta sunt, in magno sacramento. Inter caetera vela cilicina jussa sunt fieri,
non decem, sed undecim (*Exod. xxvi. 7*): quia per cilicium ostenditur confessio peccatorum. (*Followed by further observations on the significance of number seven.*)

þa alles endlyfæn wæbb betwyx þam oðrum webbum.   150
þa endlyfæn wæron hærene for ðare dæþbote
and for þare andetnysse mid bireowsunge,
þe ðe mon don sceal, þe Godes laȝe tobræcð,
and he sceal mid stiðnysse his synne ȝebeten.
Nu forȝeaf þe kyng, swa swa ðis godspel cwæð ær,   155
alne þone mycele ȝylt mildelice þam þeȝene,
ðeah þe he wurðe nære, ac he nolde forȝifæn
his aȝenum ifer(æn) ðæt ðæt he him sceolde,
mycele læsse ȝesceat þonne him sylfum wæs forȝifen.
He nolde ȝetyðian ðæt ðæt him wæs ityðod,   160
and he wearð þa bitæht to tintreȝienne
þam stiðum witnerum, þe hine witniæn sceolden
oððet he forȝylde alne þone sceat.
Nu sæȝð us þis godspel þæt þe Hælend þa sæde:
All swa deþ to soðan min heofenlice Fæder eow,   165
ȝif ȝe ne forȝifæð eowrum ȝebroðren,
ælc an of his heort(æn), ðæt þæt he agylte wið hine.
Iohannes þe apostol, ðe wæs eac godspællere,
awrat on his pistole, ðissum wordum cwæðende:
Si dixerimus quia peccatum non habemus   170
ipsi nos seducimus et ueritas in nobis non est, et cetera.
Gif we sylfe sæcgæð þæt we synnan næbbæð,
we bipæceð us sylfum, | and soðfestnysse ne bið on us.   Bf. 38
Gif we ðonne andetteð ure synnæn ȝeornlice,
God bið us itreowe, and eac swiðe rihtwis,   175
and forȝyfæð us ure synnæn þurh his soðæ lufe,
and eac | us afeormæð fram unrihtwisnesse.   fol. 11ᵛ
We sceolon forȝyfæn ðam ðe wið us agyltæð,
swa swa ðe Hælend sæde be ðam ðe ȝe sylfe herdon,
of inneweardre heortæ, þæt he us mildsiȝe.   180

---

158 iferæn] iferum   167 heortæn] heortū   hine] h *altered from another letter*
(þ.?)   179 ȝe] `ȝe´

155–63 (*Augustine, col. 517*) Uterque debitor, et uterque veniae deplorator et
impetrator: sed ille servus malus, servus ingratus, iniquus, noluit rependere quod
accepit, noluit praestare quod illi indigno praestitum fuit.

164–7 (*Augustine, col. 518*) Si enim imitari non vis, exhaeredari disponis, 'Faciet' ergo
'ita vobis', inquit, 'Pater vester coelestis, si non remiseritis unusquisque fratribus vestris
ex cordibus vestris.'

168–80 (*Independent of Augustine*)

Ac ne cwæð þu na mid wordum þæt þu wylle mildsiæn,
and ælciȝe swaðeah wiðinnæn ðinre heortan;
for þan ðe God isihð þin inȝehyd swytellice,
þeah ðe men nyten hwæt ðu on mode bihydest.

God cwæð eft nu to þe: Ic forȝife nu ærest þe,   185
forȝif þu hure syððan, and ȝif ðu swa ne dest on eornost,
ic wulle habban eft æt þe þæt þæt ic ðe ær forȝeaf;
ðis is to understandenne, mid inneweardre heortan.

Ac Augustinus us sæȝð ðæt mon steoræn sceal
his aȝen(um) child(e) mid æȝe and mid lufe,   190
hwilon mid wordum, hwilon mid swingelum,
ȝif he ælles ne mæȝ his dysiȝ alecgæn.

Ðæt bið yfel ȝeðyld, þæt ðu iðafiȝe þin(um) bearn(e)
þæt he on fræcednesse fare mid his dysiȝe,
and þu lociȝe on hwylce þe licie;   195
þenne bið þeo lufe him al to hatungæ awend,
ȝif þu nelt his ȝehælpæn and him steoræn on ær.

Ðam stuntum monn(e) mon sceal steoræn æfre
butæn ælcere hatunge, and hine rihtlæcen,
ða ðe styræn sceolon, na to stiðlice swa ðeah,   200
ac swa swa milde fæder mid mildheortnysse æfre,
þæt þe mon beo irihtlæht, na mid ræðnesse fordon.

All swa ðe læce deþ ðe læcnæð þene mon,

---

184 bihydest] b *altered from* h   190 aȝenum childe] aȝene childū
193 þinum bearne] þine bearnū   198 monne] monnū

181–4 (*Augustine, col. 518*) Ne dicas in lingua, Ignosco, et corde differas. Supplicium enim ostendit tibi Deus, minando vindictam. Novit Deus ubi dicas. Vocem tuam homo audivit: conscientiam tuam Deus inspicit. Si dicis, Dimitto; dimitte. Melius est cum clamas ore, et dimittis in corde, quam blandus ore, crudelis in corde.

185–8 (*Augustine, col. 518*) Dicit enim Deus, Dimitte, et dimittetur tibi. Sed ego prior dimisi: dimitte vel postea. Nam si non dimiseris, revocabo te; et quidquid tibi dimiseram, replicabo tibi. Non enim mentitur Veritas; non enim fallit, aut fallitur Christus, qui subjecit, dicens: 'Sic et vobis faciet Pater vester, qui in coelis est.'

189–202 (*Augustine, col. 518* [*freely paraphrased by Ælfric*]) Jam ergo obsecrant pueri indisciplinati, et nolunt vapulare, qui sic praescribunt nobis, quando volumus dare disciplinam: Peccavi, ignosce mihi. Ecce ignove, et iterum peccat. Ignosce: ignovi. Peccat tertio. Ignosce: tertio ignovi. Jam quarto vapulet. Et ille: Numquid septuagies septies te fatigavi? Si hac praescriptione severitas disciplinae dormiat, repressa disciplina saevit impunita nequitia. Quid ergo faciendum est? Corripiamus verbis, et si opus est, et verberibus: sed delictum dimittamus, culpam de corde abjiciamus. Ideo enim Dominus subdidit, 'de cordibus vestris', ut si per charitatem imponitur disciplina, de corde lenitas non recedat.

203–7 (*Augustine, col. 518*) Quid enim tam pium quam medicus ferens ferramentum? Plorat secandus, et secatur: plorat urendus, et uritur. Non est illa crudelitas; absit ut

þe pinæð on ða wundæ ðæt heo wurðæ ihæled.

For þan ðe ðe mon losæð, þe liȝeð yfele forwundod,   205
ȝif þe læce him aræð, and nyle mid stiðnesse
þa wunde hælen, mid þam ðe his c[r]eft tæcæð.
Nu beoð sume gultæs, swa swa us sæcgæð bec,
ðe mon diȝollice sceal mid ȝesceade betan,
and sume openlice þæt oðre beon isteoredæ.   210
Gif ðe gylt beo diȝle, bet þu hine diȝollice,
and ne mælde þu nateshwon hine oðrum monnum;
and ȝif openlice aȝulte, bed þu hine openlice,
ðu þe styran scealt, þæt he seolf beo irihtlæht,
and oðre beon istyrede ðe þa steor ihyræð.   215
þus tæcæð us þæt godspel and þe Godes apostol.
Ðe ðe monhatæ bið, ne mæȝ he wæl styræn,
for þan ðe þa halȝa weræs ðe weron iu lareowæs,
beoð nu iherode ðurh heoræ liðnysse; | Bf. 40
ant God sylf is liðe ant mid liðnysse us steoræð,   220
and lufæð mildheortnysse ant (ð)a he tæhte us.
Beo him a a wurðmynt and wuldor.
Amen, Amen.

---

207 creft] c`e´ft   221 ða] da

---

saevitia medici dicatur. Saevit in vulnus, ut homo sanetur: quia si vulnus palpetur, homo perditur. (*Followed by further passage on necessity of discipline.*)

208–10 (*see discussion at pp. 35–6 above*)

211–15 (*Augustine, col. 519*) Si peccatum in secreto est, in secreto corripe. Si peccatum publicum est et apertum, publice corripe: ut ille emendetur, et caeteri timeant.

216–end (*independent of Augustine*)

NOTES

3. *discipulis*: The word is a Latin borrowing, and the Latin dative plural inflection has here been retained. Elsewhere Ælfric uses the Old English inflection -*um* not the Latin -*is* to form the dative plural, for example, Pope xx, l. 282 (*discipulum*).

6. *he ðe*: The normal Old English form we would expect here for the relative pronoun is *se ðe*. However the pronouns do not follow a sufficiently regular pattern to justify emendation.

7. *settan his spæce*: *spræc* meaning a 'case, cause, suit, claim' (BT meaning no. X) can be used both in a general sense and as a legal term. BT cites an example from an Old English charter where *settan* and *spræc* are combined in

a legal context: *ðæt ðis æfre gesett spræc wære* ('that this for ever should be a settled suit').

10. *ðeȝen*: Ælfric's use of *ðeȝen* rather than *ðeow* to translate the Latin 'servus' is uncharacteristic. Elsewhere Ælfric uses *ðeȝen* to translate Latin nouns such as 'minister' and 'sacerdos' (for God's thanes), which imply a higher status. See, for example, the translation of John xii. 26 in Pope xi. Ælfric seems to consider that a king's servant is of sufficient status to be a *ðeȝen* and not a *ðeow*. We can compare his version of John iv. 46–53 in CH I viii, where he uses *ðegn* for both the centurion and for the servants of the underking, reserving *ðeowan* for the centurion's servant (pp. 126–8). (*Cniht* is Ælfric's usual word for the centurion's servant in CH I viii (translating Latin 'puer'), but his uses of *ðeowan* (p. 126, l. 33; p. 128, l. 1) suggest that the two words denoted equivalent status. See my discussion of *cniht* and *cnapa* in the note to line 73 of homily i). Note, however, that in homily ii, the servant is demoted in terms of diction when his wickedness has been revealed: the king addresses him as *yfelæ ðeowæ* (36).

13. *wif(e)*: The emendation from -*um* to -*e* (suggested by Belfour) is justified by the Vulgate *uxorem*.

26. *geælnode*: This must be a form of the verb *elnian* (BT spelling) 'to strengthen' (from *ellen* 'strength'). Its precise meaning here is difficult to ascertain; presumably *hine* acts as an accusative reflexive pronoun and *up* as an adverb modifying the verb so that the phrase can be rendered as 'picked himself up' or 'pulled himself together'. The specification of upwards movement is necessary because the man has been knocked down but then has to fall at his attacker's feet almost immediately (27).

65. *hi ne*: Belfour's emendation to *hi[m] ne* is unnecessary, since *hi* here is the accusative plural pronoun acting as direct object to *ȝehyrð*. It is possible that the scribe was confused about the meaning here, since the manuscript form is *hine* as if it were one word and itself the direct object of *ȝehyrð*.

68. *beo he ðenne ælfremed, swa swa hæðen mon from ðe*: Ælfric is translating here the Vulgate 'sit tibi sicut ethnicus et publicanus'. Although the most accurate translation of Latin 'publicanus' is Old English *gerefa*, this clearly did not have the derogatory connotations of 'publicanus'. Elsewhere too Ælfric avoids translating 'publicanus' by *gerefa*, choosing instead the more explicitly critical *synful* or *manful*. In his translation of Luke xviii. 9–14, for example, Ælfric translates 'publicanus' first by *openlice synful* and then by *manfulla* (CH II xxviii, ll. 6–7, 9). In his translation of Matth. ix. 9–13, Ælfric initially renders 'publicani' as *gerefan*, but later translates 'cum publicanis et peccatoribus' as *mid ðisum manfullum mannum and synfullum* (CH II xxxii, ll. 8, 13). The West-Saxon gospels also translate 'publicanus' variously as *manfulla*, *sinfullen*, *yfelwyrcendum*.

In homily ii, 68, Ælfric has apparently avoided translating 'publicanus'

II THE SERVANT'S FAILURE TO FORGIVE 47

altogether, choosing rather to translate 'ethnicus' twice, first as *ælfremed* and then as *hæðen mon*.

80. *eað*[*fynd*]*e*: The corresponding word in the source, 'reperiri', makes this a convincing emendation by Belfour.

146. *Godes* [*laȝe*] *tobræce*: The addition of *laȝe* suggested by Belfour is convincing; compare *Godes laȝe* (144), and *þe Godes laȝe tobræcð* (153).

151. *dæpbote*: Belfour emends MS *dæpbote* to OE *dædbote* here and at vii. 150 (also at Belfour, p. 50, l. 32, and compare *dædbetendum* at Belfour p. 138, l. 14). The recurrence of the MS spelling *dæp-* suggests that this was the scribe's regular form (perhaps associated with *deaþ*, 'death') and therefore not an error requiring emendation. Compare *deaðbote* in the Bodley 34 copy of *þe Liflade ant te Passiun of Seinte Iuliene*, d'Ardenne, p. 65, ll. 710–11.

190. Belfour retained the dative plural *-um* of MS *childum* and accordingly emended MS *his* to *heoræ* (my 192). The alteration of *-um* to dative singular *-e* and consequent retention of MS *his* seems to me more convincing. First, we have already encountered in homily ii a scribal alteration of dative singular noun inflection *-e* to *-um* (13 *wifum* for *wife*). Secondly, the Augustinian source explicitly cited at this point by Ælfric (189) alludes to the child in the singular not the plural.

198. *monn*(*e*): The corresponding form *hine* (199) suggests that this is another occasion where the scribe has changed a dative singular noun to dative plural (compare 13 and 190).

208. *swa swa us sæcgæð bec*: See pp. 35–6 above for a discussion of which books Ælfric might have had in mind here.

217. *monhata*: This word is not recorded in BT. It occurs in Pope xiii, l. 70 (*mannhatan*) and in Pope xv(a), l. 19 (*manhata*). Pope notes the variety and ambiguity of the MS spellings in his note to xiii, l. 70.

III

THE HEALING OF THE BLIND MAN

This homily expounds John ix. 1–39, the gospel-text traditionally associated with Wednesday in the fourth week of Lent. Like the two previous homilies here edited, this was assigned by Clemoes to Ælfric's TH II series, since it does not appear in the TH I manuscripts, CUL Ii. 4. 6, CCCC 302 or BL Cotton Faustina A. ix, but does appear in Bodley 343. Because, however, Wednesday in the fourth week of Lent lies within the scope of TH I (from Christmas to the Sunday after Pentecost), Clemoes notes that the homily 'may well have been part of TH I though we lack the evidence to prove it today'.[1] If it originally formed part of TH I, it might have been excluded from the surviving TH I manuscripts because a homily for the fourth Wednesday in Lent was rarely needed.[2]

The intended audience for this homily was evidently the well-educated clergy or monks rather than the ignorant laity. This would tally with recent views on the changed function of Ælfric's later texts which I outlined above.[3] Ælfric has included the Latin original of the majority of his biblical quotations as well as the English translation, suggesting that he is anticipating a relatively learned audience. The remark, 'ðis godspel is langsum, and hæfð longne traht. | Nu wylle we eow secgan þæt arfoþeste andʒit; | þæt oðer ʒe maʒon eow seolfe understanden' (ll. 266–8), is clearly directed at a learned audience. Ælfric expresses uncertainty about who can perform miracles in the comment 'we nyton, þeah he mende þæt micele wundor, | þæt nan synful man ne mihte swylce tacnæ wyrcæn' (ll. 333–4), a confession which would seem to be inappropriate for an unlearned lay audience.

---

[1] Clemoes, 'Chronology', p. 232.

[2] Clemoes, 'Chronology', p. 228, suggests that Ælfric's five homilies for the Fridays in Lent, which he tentatively assigns to TH I, might have been omitted from the extant manuscripts because they were 'of relatively minor usefulness'.

[3] Gatch, *Preaching and Theology*, p. 55, and Clayton, 'Homiliaries and Preaching', pp. 309–10 (see pp. 1–2 above).

Finally, Ælfric's conclusion, 'we hine iseoð nu mid soðæ ȝeleafan' (l. 367), referring to the Christians in contrast to the Jews, might apply more appropriately to an enlightened audience.

TRANSLATION OF THE GOSPEL-TEXT

The gospel-text, unusually long, is given in full in a form fairly closely corresponding to the Vulgate. Although conveying faithfully the sense of the Latin original, Ælfric characteristically does not translate it word for word, frequently adding, omitting or altering phrases in order to clarify and even interpret the text.[1] At one point, Ælfric omits a whole gospel-verse (John ix. 23) when it merely restates the material of the two previous verses. Most commonly, Ælfric adds adjectives and adverbial phrases to embellish the biblical text: 'deorce', 'soðlice', 'ful ȝeare', 'wodlice', 'þus huxlice', 'wislice', 'mid ȝeleafan'. These often seem to have been added with rhythmic or alliterative patterns in mind. Although Ælfric has not consistently translated the biblical text in his rhythmic prose style, he was clearly concerned to enhance its rhetorical effect by such phrases. He often converts the direct speech of the Latin into indirect speech, thereby creating a more fluid style.

Ælfric has treated this gospel-text once elsewhere, though in a much more cursory fashion. In his homily for the Passion of St. Bartholomew, he offers a catalogue of the reasons for which men are afflicted by God, and summarizes John ix. 1 ff. to show that men can be afflicted for God's miracles:

Sume menn beoð geuntrumode for Godes tacnum, swa swa Crist cwæð be sumum blindan men, ðaða his leorning-cnihtas hine axodon, for hwæs synnum se mann wurde swa blind acenned. þa cwæð se Hælend, þæt he nære for his agenum synnum, ne for his maga, blind geboren, ac forði þæt Godes wundor þurh hine geswutelod wære. And he þærrihte mildheortlice hine gehælde, and geswutelode þæt he is soð Scyppend, ða ða ungesceapenan eahhringas mid his halwendan spatle geopenode.[2]

Ælfric does not use this text in any other work, although the same theme of the healing of a blind man (Luke xviii. 31–43) forms the basis of his Shrove Sunday homily (discussed below).

---

[1] Despite Ælfric's characteristic paraphrase, an arbitrary alteration such as that at l. 78, where he renders 'Moysi locutus est deus' as 'Moyses spæc to þone Almihtiȝa Gode', is puzzling. Ælfric may have been following an unrecorded variant, or even mistranslating since no such reading is recorded in the various biblical versions; see *Nouum Testamentum*, ed. Wordsworth and White, p. 575.

[2] CH I xxxi, p. 474.

SOURCES AND ANALOGUES

For the source for his exposition of John ix. 1–39, Ælfric seems to have turned to Augustine's commentary *In Ioannis Evangelium, Tractatus xliv*, a text which he used frequently without resorting to Paul the Deacon.[1] In this he follows the pattern established in his homilies for the Fridays in Lent, assigned by Clemoes to the TH I stage of development, which also (with the exception of Pope iii which expounds a gospel-text from Matthew) have Augustine's commentary as their main source.[2] For his homily on John ix. 1–39, Ælfric has not, so far as I can tell, derived material from any other patristic expositions of the same text. Augustine's two other sermons on the text, for example, have not been used.[3] An anonymous homily in Paul the Deacon's collection resembles Augustine in much of its doctrine, but Ælfric at no point seems to have followed its wording or organization in preference to Augustine.[4] The collections of Alcuin, Pseudo-Bede, Haymo and Smaragdus all contain commentaries on John ix. 1–39; these, however, consist largely of excerpts from Augustine's tractates, and there are no indications to suggest that Ælfric used any of them.[5]

Ælfric relies on Augustine for the arrangement of his homily and for the bulk of the material included in it. Like Augustine, Ælfric confronts the paradox suggested by the gospel-text of being physically blind whilst having spiritual sight and of seeing physically whilst being spiritually blind; both authors propose faith in God as the solution to the latter. Ælfric, however, does diverge from Augustine in several important respects.

Stylistically Ælfric adapts Augustine's commentary in various characteristic ways.[6] He prefers a concise and matter-of-fact style to Augustine's eloquent and repetitive one. Ælfric does not entirely eschew rhetorical questions and exclamations in this homily.[7] But he shows a definite tendency to turn Augustine's elaborate stylistic

---

[1] CCSL 36, pp. 381 ff. Pope, p. 159, discusses Ælfric's use of this text.

[2] The homilies are Pope ii, v, and vi, and Assmann v. The sources for the homilies edited by Pope are discussed in his individual introductions; the sources for Assmann v are discussed by Nichols, 'Methodical Abbreviation', p. 175, n. 5.

[3] PL 38, nos. cxxxv (cols. 746–50) and cxxxvi (cols. 750–4).

[4] PL 95, cols. 1293 ff.

[5] Alcuin, PL 100, cols. 877 ff., Pseudo-Bede, PL 92, cols. 757 ff., Haymo, PL 118, cols. 305 ff., Smaragdus, PL 102, cols. 159 ff.

[6] See Nichols, 'Methodical Abbreviation', for an analysis of Ælfric's methods of abbreviating Augustine in the Friday homilies for Lent.

[7] See, for example, ll. 197–201.

devices into simple declarations.[1] He writes, for example, that 'nes ðe blindæ man swa þeah buton synnum on life, forþan ðe moniჳ blind mon bið swiðe manful' (ll. 172–3), when rendering the following ornate and verbose passage by Augustine:

Quanta mala committunt caeci! A quo malo abstinet mens mala, etiam clausis oculis? Non poterat uidere, sed nouerat cogitare, et forte concupiscere aliquid quod caecus non posset implere, sed in corde iudicari in cordis perscrutatore.

Secondly, despite their general correspondence in theme, Ælfric has subtly altered Augustine's perspective. Whereas Augustine lays stress on the role of God's grace, the emphasis of Ælfric's homily is that salvation depends on personal conduct. At the beginning of his exposition (ll. 114 ff.) Ælfric, like Augustine, draws a parallel between blindness and original sin. However Ælfric then proceeds independently to decry the extent of sinfulness in contemporary society ('leahtras . . . on us beweoxon iwunelice to swiðe' (ll. 121–2)), and to suggest that each man who 'mismaky his lif' (l. 123) is in a state of blindness equivalent to being born blind but that this blindness of the heart can be cured by faith. Ælfric follows Augustine by quoting Eph. ii. 3 (l. 131), but he again changes the emphasis of the material. Whereas for Augustine the quotation demonstrates the workings of original sin (he expounds the word 'natura' to show man's innate sinfulness), Ælfric focuses on man's individual responsibility for his actions. First in his translation of Eph. ii. 3 he adds the phrase 'mid teonfulle weorcce' to show that through their wrongful deeds mankind could appropriately be described as 'yrres bearn' ('on ure ჳecynde' is not a sufficient explanation for Ælfric's purposes). Next Ælfric explains that a child of wrath is anyone with whom God is angry, then adds independently that the term 'child of death' applies to anyone who is worthy of death.[2] Like Augustine, Ælfric extends the idea of 'filii irae' with a list of analogous terms: '*Filius diaboli, filius iniquitatis, filius uindicte, filius gehenne, et his similia*' (ll. 139–40). Only two of the four terms overlap with Augustine's (*filius uindicte* and *filius gehenne*), and in fact Ælfric apparently has in mind a separate set of sources: 'Man cwæð on bocum' (l. 137). He is probably referring to the books of the Bible: *filius gehenne* is biblical (Matth. xxiii. 15) as are Ælfric's own

---

[1] Nichols, 'Methodical Abbreviation', p. 160, notes that Ælfric's preference for statement over rhetorical question extends also to his handling of other patristic authors.

[2] The phrase 'child of death' is not biblical, and, as far as I can tell, must be Ælfric's own extension of the notion of 'child of wrath'.

additions, *filius diaboli* (Acts xiii. 10) and *filius iniquitatis* (Ps. lxxxviii. 23; 2 Sam. vii. 10; 1 Chron. xvii. 9; Hos. x. 9). Ælfric's explanation of these terms again reveals his concern to appeal to his audience's own sense of responsibility. Whoever performs the devil's work is 'deofles sunu', whoever lives in an unrighteous manner is 'unrihtwisnesse sunu'. The idea of just deserts for one's behaviour is stressed in Ælfric's description of the other two terms: one who deserves punishment is 'wracane sunæ', one who deserves hell is 'helle sunu'. As in homily ii the Augustinian emphasis on salvation by grace is replaced by a doctrine of merit and reward. To conclude this section Ælfric returns to the notion of original sin, explaining that all the evil implied by the various categories of progenitors was dwelling amongst us before Christ's coming; he contrasts this period with the one after Christ's coming when redemption has become possible for those with true faith.

Elsewhere in the homily Ælfric again adds material which exemplifies his own point of view as distinct from Augustine's. In a passage describing the scene on Judgement Day Ælfric independently emphasizes that each man's final judgement will depend on his earthly deeds. After quoting (as Augustine does) Matth. xxv. 34 where Christ receives the righteous into heaven, Ælfric specifically states that this is the reward for righteousness: 'þis is þæt edlean þare rihtwisæ monnæ þe rihtlice leofedon, and mid gode weorce Gode icwæmdon' (ll. 242–4). Similarly after quoting Matth. xxv. 41 where Christ sends the unrighteous into hell, Ælfric explains independently of Augustine why they deserved such a fate: 'þonne underfoð heo edlean on ecere pine heora arleasæ dæda þe heo æfre adruȝon oð heoræ lifes ende, and heoræ Drihten forsæȝon' (ll. 251–3). At this point in his homily Ælfric, prompted by Augustine, cites the example of Lazarus (ll. 254–65), following Augustine's account quite closely. Elsewhere Ælfric has written a homily expounding the story of Lazarus and the rich man;[1] his commentary there, however, emphasizes that one must befriend the poor since the righteous and unrighteous will see each others' fates after death, not, as here, that it is too late to act righteously after the Day of Judgement.

One further passage added by Ælfric to his source significantly contributes to his emphasis on the need to live righteously on earth. John ix. 14 states that the blind man was healed 'on þam halȝan ræstendæȝe'. In his exposition of this Ælfric first provides his

---

[1] CH I xxiii.

audience with general information, not in Augustine, concerning the Jewish custom of celebrating Saturday not Sunday (ll. 272ff.). He explains carefully and clearly the background to the Sabbath, and then its significance in terms of the actual lives of his audience. The Jews were not allowed to do servile work on Saturday, because it was their holy Sabbath. Independently of Augustine again, Ælfric interprets the Sabbath as our span of life during which we must avoid sins, sins therefore being prefigured by the servile work which the Jews avoided. Ælfric distinguishes between the Jews who kept the Sabbath free of servile deeds but nevertheless sinned, and Christ who, although He healed the blind man on the Sabbath, kept the Sabbath because He was free of sins. Ælfric explains that Sunday is now celebrated because it was the day of Christ's resurrection. He comments independently on the second half of John ix. 24, using it as an opportunity to emphasize the difference between the Jews and Christ, and to spell out its significance for his contemporary audience:

> Ðe restandæჳ wes ihalჳod on ðes Hælendes ðrowunge
> fram ðeowtlicum weorce, ac we ne ðurfon na leng
> lichamlice haldæn, ac on ure lifes ðeawum
> on gastlice andჳite, and on gode weorcum.
>
> (ll. 308–11)

The 'restandæჳ' is now to be kept spiritually rather than bodily by refraining from sins.

This passage is interesting not only as an example of Ælfric's concern with his audience's everyday behaviour but also for its relationship to Ælfric's previous works. As the phrase 'swa swa we sædon hwilon ær' suggests, Ælfric has discussed the subject before. First in his homily for Midlent Sunday he expounds the third commandment as follows:

þæt ðridde bebod is; Beo ðu gemyndig. þæt þu ðone restendæg gehalgige; On six dagum geworhte god ealle gesceafta. and geendode hi on ðam seofoðan. þæt is se sæternesdæg. þa gereste he hine. and ðone dæg gehalgode; . . . Se sæternesdæg wæs ða gehaten restendæg. oð cristes ðrowunge. on ðam dæge læg cristes lic on byrigene. and he aras of deaðe on ðam sunnandæge. and se dæg is cristenra manna restendæg. and halig ðurh cristes ærist; þone dæg we sceolon symle freolsian. mid gastlicere arwurðnysse; Se sæternesdæg wæs gehalgod mid micelre gehealdsumnysse on ðære ealdan .æ. for ðære getacnunge cristes ðrowunge. and his reste on ðære byrgene. Ac se sunnandæg is nu gehalgod þurh soðfæstnysse his æristes of deaðe; Oðer restendæg is nu eac toweard. þæt is þæt ece lif. on ðam bið an dæg buton ælcere nihte. on þam we us gerestað ecelice. gif we nu ðeowtlicera weorca. þæt sind synna geswicað;[1]

Ælfric explains, then, that although under the old law Saturday was celebrated, now Sunday is kept holy because Christ's resurrection took place on that day. The passage offers an interesting alternative interpretation to the other one. In homily iii, Ælfric concentrates on a tropological interpretation, limiting his exposition to the present only: the Sabbath denotes 'ures lifes timæ, | on þam we sceolon simle synne forbuʒon, | swa we selost maʒon, ure Scyppende to lofe, | and ʒif we hwæt tobrecon, beton þæt ʒeorne' (ll. 285–8). In his Second Series text, however, Ælfric shows that he was aware of an anagogical as well as the tropological interpretation: there the Sabbath represents the eternal life 'on ðam we us gerestað ecelice. gif we nu ðeowtlicera weorca. þæt sind synna. geswicað'.

Another discussion of the subject appears in Pope ii:

> and is n(u) se Sunnan-dæg syþþan gehalgod
> þurh ures Driht(nes) ærist, þe on þam dæge aras,
> and we hine wurþiað (Gode to) wyrðmynte,
> and syþþan geswac þæs Sæte(rnes-dæges fre)ols.
>   On þam ealdan resten-dæge, þe we (ær embe spræcon,)
> ne worhton þa Iudei nan þeowtlic (weorc,
> and se an) getacnode eal ure lif,
> þe is gastlic (ræsten-dæg, on þam) we Gode sceolon
> symle þeowian, and sy(nna forbugan,)
> þe synd þeowtlice weorc, and on þeowte (gebringað
> heora) wyrcendras a to worulde.
> þa Iu(deiscan freolsodon) þone foresædan resten-dæg,
> and oft (bemændon þa ða) men wæron
> gehælede on þam dæge fram (urum Hælende.)[2]

It is most likely, as Pope suggests, that this passage rather than the CH II one is in Ælfric's mind when he writes 'swa swa we sædon hwilon ær'.[3] Both the Pope and homily iii passages emphasize that the Jews prohibited servile work on the Sabbath; both interpret the Sabbath tropologically as our whole life in which we must avoid sins (in contrast to CH II xii which interprets it anagogically as the eternal life).

Ælfric explains the Sabbath and Sunday distinction in one other work, his Second Old English Letter to Wulfstan (Fehr, Brief III),

---

[1] CH II xii, 273–7, 300–11.
[2] Pope ii, 252–65.
[3] Pope, p. 245.

written, according to Clemoes, late in his career (about 1006).[1] There
are some striking similarities with the passage in homily iii:

Under Moyses æ men halgodan þa þone sæternes-dæg mid swiðlican
weorðmynte fram ðeowetlicum weorcum, and we sculon us healdan fram
ðeowetlicum weorce, þæt sindan sinna gewiss, þe gebrincgað on ðeowete þa
ðe hi swyðost begað, swaswa se hælend cwæð on his haligan godspelle:
'Omnis qui facit peccatum, seruus est peccati.' Ælc þara ðe sinna gewyrcð, is
ðara sinna ðeow. We sculon gastlice healdan Godes resten-dæg, swa þæt we
silfe beon fram sinnum æmptige and se dæg beo gehalgod on us sylfum swa.
Fela þincga getacnað se fore-sæda restendæg. Ac we healdað nu æfter þæs
hælendes æriste ðone sunnan-dæg freolice, forðon-ðe he of deaðe aras on
ðam easterlican sunnan-dæge, and se sunnan-dæg is on ge-sceapennisse
firmest and we sculon eac hine æfre weorðian, Gode to wyrðminte, on
gastlicum ðeowdome.[2]

The authority for the change from Saturday to Sunday for the
'ræstendæg' seems to have been assigned traditionally to the so-called
Sunday Letter. The Letter is dated before 584 and is hence 'the oldest
document in the Western Church setting forth, in a mythological
form, a theory which teaches the substitution of the Lord's day for the
Jewish Sabbath'.[3] Clare Lees notes that it 'urges strict enforcement of
the observance of Sunday, accompanied by dire threats for those who
fail to comply'.[4] The change to the Lord's day from the Jewish Sabbath
was acknowledged by Bede in his *Historia Ecclesiastica* and translated in
the Old English version; it is related that Bishop Aidan always kept
Easter on Sunday:

for þam geleafan þære Dryhtenlican æriste, þa æriste he gelyfde on anum þara
restedaga beon gewordene, 7 eac for þam hyhte ure toweardan æriste, þa he on
anum þara restedaga, se nu Sunnandæg is nemned, soðlice towearde mid
þære halgan 7 mid þære rihtgeleaffullan gesomnunge gelyfde.[5]

The *Excerptiones Ecgberti* decree that one ought to keep the Sabbath
spiritually:

Requievit in sepulchro per sabbatum, et sanctificavit Dominicam diem resurrectione sua; nam Dominica dies prima dies seculi est, et dies resurrectionis

---

[1] Clemoes, 'Chronology', p. 245.
[2] Fehr, pp. 194–6.
[3] Robert Priebsch, ed., *Letter from Heaven on the Observance of the Lord's Day* (Oxford,
1936), p. 29.
[4] 'The "Sunday Letter" and the "Sunday Lists"', *ASE*, xiv (1985), 129–51, p. 129.
[5] *The Old English Version of Bede's Ecclesiastical History of the English People*, ed. Thomas
Miller, 2 vols., EETS, os, 95–6 (1890–1), 110–11 (1898), I, 206–8.

Christi, et dies Pentecostes, et ideo sancta est; et nos ipsi debemus esse spiritaliter sabbatum sabbatizantes, id est, vacantes ab operibus servitutis, id est, peccatis, quia 'Qui facit peccatum, servus est peccati.'[1]

The *Excerptiones*, a motley collection of religious pieces, were probably compiled in England in the late Anglo-Saxon period. This passage on the Sabbath bears a remarkable similarity to Ælfric's CH II discussion, making it more than likely, as Malcolm Godden has suggested, that Ælfric was the author of both pieces.[2] The significance of the Sabbath was clearly a concern central to Ælfric.

The wider Ælfrician corpus also acts as a useful context for another section of the homily (ll. 188 ff.). John ix. 4 contains a contrast between the day when Christ performs God's works and the night when no works can be performed. Apart from the occasional omission, Ælfric follows Augustine's exposition for this gospel-text. Both authors stress that Christ's ascension cannot have marked the beginning of the period of darkness, since the apostles continued to work miracles after it. Ælfric cites the same examples as Augustine: the Holy Spirit gave all earthly languages to the apostles (Acts ii. 4), and Peter healed men by his shadow (Acts v. 15). Ælfric, again following Augustine, quotes both John xiv. 12 ('maiora horum faciet') and John xv. 5 ('sine me nihil potestis facere').[3] Like Augustine, Ælfric contrasts a day of this world and the Lord's 'day' (ll. 222 ff.), quoting Matth. xxviii. 20 to show why the Lord's day continues to the end of the world. Ælfric interprets night as 'helle dimnes', the darkness of hell in which no-one who ignores the light Christ promised us by dwelling amongst us may prosper (ll. 232–5). Again he follows Augustine in this ('Nox ista impiorum erit'). It is, however, quite different from Ælfric's usual interpretation of darkness. In his other homily on the healing of a blind man which expounds Luke xviii. 31–43, Ælfric suggests that the darkness pertains to this life on earth because men are deprived of the heavenly light:

þes an blinda man getacnode eall mancynn, þe wearð ablend þurh Adames gylt, and asceofen of myrhðe neo[r]xena-wanges, and gebroht to ðisum life þe

---

[1] *Ancient Laws*, ed. B. Thorpe, II, 102–3 (no. xxxvi).

[2] 'Anglo-Saxons on the mind', in *Learning and Literature*, ed. Lapidge and Gneuss, pp. 271–98 (especially p. 283).

[3] The first quotation Ælfric presents only in English translation, 'maran wundræ ȝe wurcæð'; the second appears in both Latin and English. Since the Latin of the first is rather obscure without an explanation of 'horum', Ælfric's decision to omit it is understandable.

is wiðmeten cwearterne. Nu sind we ute belocene fram ðam heofenlican leohte, and we ne magon on ðissum life þæs ecan leohtes brucan.[1]

In this homily, then, Ælfric compares life on earth to prison where we are locked out from the heavenly light, in contrast to his homily on John ix. 1–39, where he suggests that the light of Christ has remained in the world and the dark night represents the dimness of hell. Darkness in CH I x contrasts with that light 'þe we magon mid englum anum geseon, þæt ðe næfre ne bið geendod';[2] in the later homily, it contrasts with 'þe drihtenlicæ dæʒ, þæt is ures Drihtnes midwunung', which 'bið us æfre astreht oð ende þissere weorulde'. Elsewhere too, Ælfric interprets darkness as life on earth. In another homily Ælfric explains that night betokens the ignorance of this world:

Se halga Augustinus trahtnode þis godspel, and cwæð, þæt seo niht getacnode þa nytennysse þisre worulde. þeos woruld is afylled mid nytennysse. Nu sceal forði gehwa arisan of ðære nytennysse, and gan to his frynd, þæt is, þæt he sceal gebugan to Criste mid ealre geornfulnysse.[3]

In his *Life of St. Maurice*, Ælfric recounts how Maurice lamented as he gazed up to heaven:

> Eall middan-eard is mid miste befangen
> deopre nytennysse buton us drihten crist
> oþþe his leoht forgife. oþþe us læde onweg.[4]

In his homily *In Natale Sanctorum Virginum*, Ælfric comments on that hour of midnight when Christ calls the wise and foolish virgins:

Hwæt getacnað seo midniht. buton seo deope nytennys. for ðan ðe seo geendung þyssere worulde cymð þonne men læst wenað. swa swa se apostol cwæð; Dies domini sicut fur in nocte. ita ueniet; Drihtnes dæg cymð. swa swa ðeof on niht;[5]

Finally, Ælfric explains of Nicodemus that he 'com nihtes to Criste, and seo niht getacnode | his agene nytennysse'.[6] Clearly darkness more often represents the ignorant state of men on earth than it does the dimness of hell.

Ælfric's departure from his usual interpretation of darkness is designed to support his particular viewpoint here. Instead of distinguishing mankind in terms of dark ignorance and bright faith, Ælfric defines two periods of time, one when Christ's influence enlightens

---

[1] CH I x, p. 154.   [2] CH I x, p. 158.
[3] CH I xviii, p. 248.   [4] LS xxviii, 108–10.
[5] CH II xxxix, 107–11.   [6] Pope xii, 69–70.

the world (that is, the present), and one when that influence is entirely withdrawn (that is, after Judgement). Ælfric, then, emphasizes the fundamental change wrought by redemption; he shows, by his interpretation of darkness, that Christ's coming has brought a light to mankind whose influence continues until Judgement Day and which makes salvation possible for those who live righteously.

Returning now to the ways in which Ælfric diverges from his main source, I have shown so far that Ælfric adapts Augustine both stylistically and thematically throughout his homily. One other more specific change should be mentioned here. Ælfric adapts Augustine in such a way as to make the commentary relevant to current religious practice. The passage in question occurs at lines 155–65, where Christ's physical healing of the blind man is linked to the rite of baptism. Augustine explains in his commentary how the double process of anointing with clay then washing with water represents the two stages of becoming a full Christian. He presents a hypothetical dialogue in which a catechumen who 'inunctus est, nondum lotus' (is anointed but not yet washed) is being questioned; the next stage for catechumens is that they 'festinent ad lavacrum, si lumen inquirunt' (hasten to a bath if they are seeking light). Ælfric, too, distinguishes anointing, when a person is christened and taught faith, and washing, when he is baptized and receives sight. Ælfric, however, avoids two of the assumptions made by Augustine, first that a period of some time separates christening and baptism, and secondly that the person being baptized can speak on his own behalf. According to the older practice, baptism followed christening after an interval of some years, during which time a catechumen was taught his faith. This practice is assumed by Augustine in his commentary; it is also witnessed in, for example, accounts of the *Life of St. Martin*. The following passage from an anonymous Old English Life (Vercelli xviii) stresses that Martin's christening and baptism were quite distinct:

7 þa fleah he [Martin] to Godes cirican 7 bæd þæt hine man þær gecristnode—þæt bið sio onginnes 7 se æresta dæl þære halgan fulwihte ... ða wæron þreo gear ær his fulwihte þæt he woruldlicu wæpen wæg ... 7 þeah he þa gyt ne wære fullice æfter cierican endebyrdnesse gefullad—ac he wæs gecristnod, swa ic ær foresægde—hwæðre he þæt geryne þæs halgan fulwihtes mid godum dædum heold 7 lufade ... ða he ða hæfde eahtatyne wintra, ða gefullade hine man æfter cirican endebyrdnesse.[1]

[1] Szarmach, pp. 57–8.

Ælfric wrote his own life of St. Martin (LS xxxi), relating how Martin was christened when he was ten but not baptized until he was eighteen (although his behaviour meanwhile was as impeccable as if he had been baptized).

These accounts, describing as they do events long past, naturally cannot be considered indicative of Anglo-Saxon practice. Indeed Anglo-Saxon baptismal rites seem to have been quite different. First, baptism entailed only one ceremony in which both rites were performed successively. Wulfstan's homily on baptism, for example, implies one ceremony only:

And ðonne þis gedon bið eal fullice wel swa to ðære cristnunge gebyreð, þonne is æfter eallum þisum mid rihtum geleafan to efstanne wið fontbæðes georne.[1]

Moreover, child baptism had become the normal practice in the Anglo-Saxon period. During the fourth and fifth centuries, adult baptism had been common, even in a Christian family. After the sixth century, however, it became much more rare. In 418, the Council of Carthage had decreed that infants must be baptized so that the sin contracted in generation (that is, original sin) might be remitted through the sacrament of regeneration.[2] The traditional rites of the catechumenate continued to be used for infants. Both Ælfric and Wulfstan assume child baptism to be standard practice. In his Second Series homily for the Epiphany Ælfric takes it for granted that his audience will have been baptized while too young to understand fully what was being pledged:

Uton beon gemyndige hwæt we gode beheton. on urum fulluhte; Nu cwepst ðu. hwæt behet ic ða ða cild wæs. and sprecan ne mihte? . . . Nu stent ðeos gesetnys on godes gelaðung. þæt man ða unsprecendan cild fullige. and hi beoð gehealdene þurh oðra manna geleafan. swa swa hi wæron þurh oðra manna synna geniðerade. for ðan ðe hit bið twylic hwæðer hit on life aðolige. oð þæt hit þam lareowe mid geleafan andwyrdan mage;[3]

Wulfstan, in his homily on baptism, places the burden of responsibility on the child's friends:

And ðeah þæt cild to ðam geong sy þæt hit specan ne mæge, þonne hit man fullað, his freonda forspæc forstent him eal þæt sylfe swylce his sylf spæce.[4]

[1] Bethurum viii c, 69–71.
[2] See *New Catholic Encyclopedia* (Washington D.C., 1967), III, 239 (under 'catechumenate'), and F. L. Cross and E. A. Livingstone, *The Oxford Dictionary of the Christian Church*, 2nd ed. (London, 1974), under 'baptism' and 'infant baptism'.
[3] CH II iii, 245–7, 257–61.   [4] Bethurum viii c, 126–9.

In another piece on baptism (*Dominica IIIIa vel quando volueris*), Wulfstan several times refers without comment to the 'cild' being baptized:

þonne se mæssepreost cristnað ærest þæt cild, þonne orðað he þry on an on hit ... And þæt sealt þe se sacerd þam cilde on muð deð, þæt getacnað godcundne wisdom.[1]

Ælfric, then, aware that Augustine's exposition assumes the old practice of adult baptism by two separate ceremonies, rephrases it so that the interpretation fits both the old practice and the new one of child baptism by one ceremony.

Ælfric's conclusion to this homily draws out the paradox underlying the gospel-text—that one can be both blind and also have sight. The physical sight but spiritual blindness of the Jews is contrasted by Ælfric with his contemporary audience's physical blindness (in not seeing Christ in person) but spiritual sight. The link between assuming that one is seeing clearly and in fact being blind (ll. 361–3) derives from Augustine, but the explicit contrast of the Jews and the Christians is Ælfric's own. Such a conclusion must have been most encouraging for Ælfric's own enlightened Christian audience.

[1] Bethurum viii b, 15–16, 22–4.

Secundum Iohannem: Preteriens Iesus uidit hominem cecum a natiuitate
et reliqua.

'Ure Drihten, ðe mildheortæ Hælend, þa þa he mid monnum
wæs lichomlice wuniȝende, ant he ȝeond land færde
fela wundræ wyrcende for ðæs folces ileafan,   5
þa ofseah he sumne mon ðe wæs blind acenned.
þa befrynnon his apostoli hine and cwædon:
For hwæs synnæ wæs ðæs mon swa blind acenned,
hwæðer þe for his aȝene, oððe for his maȝæ?
Ða cwæð ðe Hælend heom sonæ to andsware: 10
Næs he blind acenned for his aȝene synnum, oððe for his maȝa,
ac ðæt Godes wyndræ wyrdon on him iswytelode.
Me idafenæð to wyrcenne his weorc þe me sende,
þa hwile ðe dæȝ bið, for ðan þe ðeo deorce niht cymæð,
þonne nan mon ne mæȝ naht to gode don.   15
Ic am middaneardes liht, þa hwile ðe ic on middanearde æm.
Mid þam ðe he ðis ȝecwæð, þa spætte he on þa eorðan,
and makede of ðam spattle and of ðare eorðe lam;
and smirede mid þam lame ofer þæs blindan eaȝen,
and het hine ða gan to ane wæterscipe þe wæs ðær onhende,   20
þe hatte Syloe, þæt is icwæden, | Asend.   Bf. 60
He eode þa sonæ, and his eaȝan aþwoh,

Bodley 343, fols. 107ᵛ–110; Belfour, pp. 58–75.

---

6 ofseah] s *altered from* f *by erasure of cross-bar*

---

sources. The material quoted here (other than biblical) is from Augustine, *In Iohannis*
Euangelium Tractatus CXXIV, *Tractatus* xliv, CCSL 36, pp. 381–8 (cited as Augustine
with section and line numbers).

1–105 (*John ix. 1–39*) (1) Et praeteriens Iesus, vidit hominem caecum a nativitate. (2) Et
interrogaverunt eum discipuli eius: Rabbi, quis peccavit, hic aut parentes eius, ut
caecus nasceretur? (3) Respondit Iesus: Neque hic peccavit, neque parentes eius, sed ut
manifestentur opera Dei in illo. (4) Me oportet operari opera eius qui misit me donec
dies est; venit nox, quando nemo potest operari. (5) Quamdiu sum in mundo, lux sum
mundi. (6) Haec cum dixisset, expuit in terram, et fecit lutum ex sputo; et linivit lutum
super oculos eius, (7) et dixit ei: Vade, lava in natatoria Siloe (quod interpretatur
Missus). Abiit ergo, et lavit, et venit videns. (8) Itaque vicini et qui viderant eum prius
(quia mendicus erat) dicebant: Nonne hic est qui sedebat et mendicabat? (9) Alii
dicebant: Quia hic est; alii autem: Nequaquam, sed similis est ei. Ille vero dicebat: Quia
ego sum. (10) Dicebant ergo ei: Quomodo aperti sunt tibi oculi? (11) Respondit: Ille
homo, qui dicitur Iesus, lutum fecit et unxit oculos meos, et dixit mihi: Vade ad
natatoria Siloe, et lava. Et abii, et lavi, et video. (12) Et dixerunt ei: ubi est ille? Ait:

and com aȝean lokinde. Ða cwædon his neahȝeburæs:
La, hu næs þæs þe blinde mon þe swa iboren wæs,
þe we iseaȝen sittæn simle wædliende?   25
Sume men þa sædon þæt hit ðe ylcæ were,
and sume sædon þæt hit wære sum oðer him ilic,
ac he him seolf sæde þæt he were ðe ylcæ.
Heo þa axoden him: Humetæ isixst þu nu?
He heom andswyrde and cwæð: Ðe þe is ihaten Hælend,   30
þe wrohte lam of eorðan, and mine eaȝen smirode,
and het me syððan gan and me sylfne aðwean
on ðam eornende wætere þe is ihaten Syloe.
Ic eode and weosc me, and ic sonæ iseah.
Heo axodon him ða: And hwær is he nu?   35
He cwæð þæt he nuste. And heo læddon hine sonæ
to þam synderhalȝan for þam sellice wundræ.
And þe mon wæs ihæled on þam halȝan ræstendæȝe.
þa axodon þa synderhalȝan eft hu he iseȝe.
He cwæð ða to þam unleaffullum: 40
Mid lame he me smirode ofer mine eahringæs,
and ic weosc me and iseah.
þa sædon sona sume þa synderhalȝan:
Nis þes mon na from Gode, þe þone ræstændæȝ ne healt.
Heom andswyrdan þa oðre: 45
Hu mæȝ æniȝ synful man þas tacnæ wyrcæn?
And þa wearð þær flit betwyx þam synderhalȝan.
And heo syððan axodon eft þone ihælede mon,
hwæt he be þam Hælende sæde.

42 weosc] aþwoh *written above in the same hand*   44 ræstændæȝ] s *altered from another letter* (d?)

Nescio. (13) Adducunt eum ad pharisaeos, qui caecus fuerat. (14) Erat autem sabbatum quando lutum fecit Iesus et aperuit oculos eius. (15) Iterum ergo interrogabant eum pharisaei, quomodo vidisset. Ille autem dixit eis: Lutum mihi posuit super oculos, et lavi, et video. (16) Dicebant ergo ex pharisaeis quidam: Non est hic homo a Deo, qui sabbatum non custodit. Alii autem dicebant: Quomodo potest homo peccator haec signa facere? Et schisma erat inter eos. (17) Dicunt ergo caeco iterum: Tu quid dicis de illo, qui aperuit oculos tuos? Ille autem dixit: Quia propheta est. (18) Non crediderunt ergo Iudaei de illo, quia caecus fuisset et vidisset, donec vocaverunt parentes eius qui viderat. (19) Et interrogaverunt eos, dicentes: Hic est filius vester, quem vos dicitis quia caecus natus est? quomodo ergo nunc videt? (20) Responderunt eis parentes eius, et dixerunt: Scimus quia hic est filius noster, et quia caecus natus est; (21) quomodo autem nunc videat, nescimus: aut quis eius aperuit oculos, non nescimus: ipsum interrogate, aetatem habet, ipse de se loquatur. (22) Haec dixerunt parentes eius, quoniam timebant Iudaeos; iam enim conspiraverant Iudaei, ut si quis eum confiteretur esse Christum,

He cwæð þæt he were sum hali3 witega.   50
þa nolden þa Iudeiscen ilyfan be þam men
þæt he were blind acenned | ant wyrde ihæled,   fol. 108
ac clypodon þa his mæ3es. And cwædon heom ðus to:
þes mon is eower sunæ, þe þe 3e secgæð þæt wære
soðlice blind accenned, and hu isihð he nu la?   55
His ma3as sædon þa: We witan soðlice
þæt he ure sunu is, and þæt he wæs blind acenned;
ac we nyten swa þeah hu he isihð nu,
ne hwa his ea3en 3eopenode. Axiæð him sylfne;
he hæfð þa yldæ þæt he andswyriæn mæ3.   60
þis sædon þa ma3as for þan ðe heo heom asæton
þæt heo wyrden iutla3ede of ðare 3esamnunge,
for þam ðe þa Iudeiscæn on heoræ dearne þeohte
hæfdon icwæden, þæt swa hwa swa Crist andette,
wyrde iutla3od of heoræ 3esamnunge.   65
þa forleton heo þa ma3as, and to þam men cwædon:
Do wulder Gode; we witan ful 3eare
þæt ðes mon is synful. He sæde heom to andswyre:
Nat i(c) 3if he synful is, ac ic wat swa þeah,
þæt ic blind wæs, and ic | wislice nu iseo.   Bf. 62
Heo axodon hine ða 3yt: Ant hu ihælde he ðe?   71
Ða cwæð ðe ihælede mon heom to andsware þus:
Hwene ær ic eow sæde; hwæt sceal hit eow eft iheræd?

69 ic] ic'c'r

---

extra synagogam fieret. (23) Propterea parentes eius dixerunt: Quia aetatem habet,
ipsum interrogate. (24) Vocaverunt ergo rursum hominem qui fuerat caecus, et dixerunt
ei: Da gloriam Deo; nos scimus quia hic homo peccator est. (25) Dixit ergo eis ille: Si
peccator est, nescio; unum scio: Quia caecus cum essem, modo video. (26) Dixerunt
ergo illi: Quid fecit tibi? quomodo aperuit tibi oculos? (27) Respondit eis: Dixi vobis
iam, et audistis: quid iterum vultis audire? numquid et vos vultis discipuli eius fieri? (28)
Maledixerunt ergo ei, et dixerunt: Tu discipulus illius sis; nos autem Moysi discipuli
sumus. (29) Nos scimus quia Moysi locutus est Deus; hunc autem nescimus unde sit.
(30) Respondit ille homo, et dixit eis: In hoc enim mirabile est, quia vos nescitis unde
sit, et aperuit meos oculos. (31) Scimus autem quia peccatores Deus non audit; sed si
quis Dei cultor est et voluntatem eius facit, hunc exaudit. (32) A saeculo non est audi-
tum quia quis aperuit oculos caeci nati. (33) Nisi esset hic a Deo, non poterat facere
quidquam. (34) Responderunt et dixerunt ei: In peccatis natus es totus, et tu doces nos?
Et eiecerunt eum foras. (35) Audivit Iesus quia eiecerunt eum foras; et cum invenisset
eum, dixit ei: Tu credis in Filium Dei? (36) Respondit ille et dixit: Quis est, Domine, ut
credam in eum? (37) Et dixit ei Iesus: Et vidisti eum; et qui loquitur tecum, ipse est. (38)
At ille ait: Credo, Domine; et procidens adoravit eum. (39) Et dixit Iesus: In iudicium
ego in hunc mundum veni, ut qui non vident videant, et qui vident caeci fiant.

La, wylle ȝe beon his leorningcnihtæs?
Heo wariȝedon þa wodlice hine and cwæædon:
Beo þu his leorningcniht; we habbæð ure lareow
Moysen þone heretoȝæ, and we his leorningcnihtæs beoð.
We witen þæt Moyses spæc to þone Almihtiȝa Gode,
ac we ne cunnon þisne mon ne hwanon he icumen is.
Ða andswarede þe ihælede mon þam heardheortan and cwæð: 80
On ðam is mucel wunder, ðæt ȝe nyten hwanon he beo,
and mihte ȝeopeniæn swa þeah mine eaȝen.
Soðlice we witan þæt ðe soðfestæ God
þa synfullen ne ȝehyrð to swylcere bene;
ac ðe þe his beȝenga bið and his willæn wyrcæð,   85
þonne wille ihyran þe heofenlicæ Wældend.
Fram þissere weorulde anȝinne, ne wearð næffre ihyred
þæt æniȝ man mihte þone mon ȝehælen,
and his eaȝen iopeniæn ðe ær wæs blind acenned.
Buton he fram Gode were, ne mihte he þis don.   90
þa andswaredon þa Iudei him þus huxlice and cwædon:
þu eart ærming al acenned on synum,
and þu lærst us ðus? And heo belucon hine þa wiðuton.
Ða ihyrde ðe Hælend þæt heo hine ut adræfdon;
and he hine þa imette, and him þus to cwæð: 95
Ðu ilyfest on Godes Sunu? And he mid ileafan him andswyrde:
Laford, la, hwylc is he þæt ic ilyfe on hine?
Ðe Hælend him andswyrde:
And þu hine ær isæȝe, and he is ðe ylca ðe þe to spæcð.
He cwæð þa mid ȝeleafan: Ic ilyfe, Drihten;   100
and he hine ða astræhte to þæs Hælendes fotum.
þa cwæð ðe Hælend him eft þus to:
Ic com hider on dome on ðisne middaneard,
þæt ða men ȝeseon þe ne mihten ær iseon,
and ða þe iseoð sceolon beon blinde.'   105
     Ðis godspel is nu isæd swytellice on Englisc
anfealdum anȝite, ac we willæð eow sæcgen
þæt gastlice anȝit, mid Godes fultume,
be þam ðe ðe wisæ Auȝustinus hit awrat on bocum.
For þan ðe Cristes wundræ þe he wrohte on þisse life   110

<hr/>

106–13 (*Augustine, 1, 7–10*) Breuiter ergo caeci huius illuminati commendo mysterium. Ea quippe quae fecit Dominus noster Iesus Christus stupenda atque miranda,
et opera et uerba sunt: opera, quia facta sunt; uerba, quia signa sunt.

wæron soðlice ȝefremede and swutelice mid weorcce,
and swa ȝetacnoden þeah sum þing diȝelices;
for ðan ðe his weorc beoð wunderlice on tacnum.

Ðes foresæde blinde mon, ðe swa iboren wæs,
tacnode al moncynn on þisse middanearde,   115
þe wearð earmlice ablend for Adames ȝylte,
and þæs ecan lihtes yfele bedæled,
of ðam we alle men ordfrymæn habbæð. |
And þurh ðæs deoflæs onde ðe Adam beswac,   Bf. 64
us becom dæð to, and eac unrihtwisnesse; | 120
and us for icynde comæn leahtras to,   fol. 108ᵛ
and on us beweoxon iwunelice to swiðe.
Nu ælc þare monnæ þe mismaky his lif,
and on fulum leahtræn lið unȝeleaffullice,
his mod is ablend swylc he blind ȝeboren beo.   125
Ne bið ðe mon na ileafful, þe on leahtrum wunæð.
þeo unleaffulnesse is þare heortæ blindnysse,
and þe soða ȝeleafa onliht þone mon,
þe mæȝ mid his mode his Scyppend iseon.
Be þam cwæð ðe apostol Paulus on sumon his pistol: 130
Fuimus et nos aliquando [*natura*] *filii ire sicud et ceteri,*
þæt is on Englisce spæce,
We weron eac hwilon on ure ȝecynde swa swa oðre men
yrres bearn itealde, mid teonfulle weorcce.
Yrræs bearn bið þe ilcæ ðe Godes yrre hæfð,   135
and ðe bið deaðes bearn þe deaþes wyrðe bið.
Man cwæð on bocum ȝehu be þissum bearnteame,
þæt ȝehwa beo icwædon þæs sunæ þe he folȝæð:
Filius diaboli, filius iniquitatis,
filius uindicte, filius gehenne, et his similia,   140
þæt is, he is deofles sunu, ðe þe deofles weorc wyrcð,
and unrihtwisnesse sunu, ðe þe unrihtlice leofæð.
Eft he bið wracane sunæ, þe ðe wracæ iearnæð,

111 weorcce] weoˊrˊcce   115–16 middanearde, þe] -eardeþe *with space-bar added*
between e *and* þe   126 bið] i *altered from* e *by erasure of loop*

114–29 (*Augustine, 1, 10–14*) Si ergo quid significet hoc quod factum est cogitemus,
genus humanum est iste caecus; haec enim caecitas contigit in primo homine per peccatum, de quo omnes originem duximus, non solum mortis, sed etiam iniquitatis.
130–44 (*Augustine, 1, 16–18*) Quandoquidem apostolus natus in gente prophetarum
dicit: 'Fuimus et nos aliquando natura filii irae, sicut et ceteri'. Si 'filii irae', filii uin-
dictae, filii poenae, filii gehennae.

and he bið helle sunu, þe ðe helle ʒeearnæð.

Nu alle ðeos yfelnesse wæs on us wuniʒende   145
ær þam ðe þe mildheortæ Crist, þe is middaneardes liht,
niðer asteah of heofenum, and her on life wunode
xxxiii ʒeare; and ða ðe on hine ʒelyfæð,
he mid his soðan ʒeleafan soðlice onlihte,
and þa ðe ne ʒelyfæð, libbæð on blindnesse.   150

Hwæt dyde þe Hælend þa ða he hælde þonne blindne?
'He spætte on þa eorðan, and of þam spatle macode lam';
for þan ðe his godcundnesse underfeng þa menniscnesse
ure eorðlicen cyndes, and us mid þam alysde.

He smirode his eaʒan eac mid þam lame,   155
ac he wæs þeah swa blind oððet þæt wæter hine aðwoh,
þe is ihaten Siloe, þæt is icwædon, Asend.

Ðe Hælend wæs asend soðlice to us
to ure alysednesse fram his Almihtiʒæ Fæder;
and buton he wyrde asend, nere ure nan   160
alysed fram synnum, ne fram helle pine.

Ðenne ðe mon bið icristnod, and me him tæcð his ileafan,
þonne beoð his eaʒan ismirode; ac he ne isihð swa þeah,
ær þam þe he beo ifullod mid fulle ʒeleafan
on þæs Hælendes namæ, þe hider asend wæs.   165

'His leorningcnihtæs befrunnon hine, and cwædon:
For hwæs synnum wæs ðes mon swa blind acenned,

145–50 (*Augustine, 1, 18–23* [*But Ælfric not close to Augustine*]) Quomodo 'natura', nisi quia peccante primo homine, uitium pro natura inoleuit? Si uitium pro natura inoleuit, secundum mentem omnis homo caecus natus est. Si enim uidet, non opus habet ductore; si opus habet ductore et illuminatore, caecus est ergo a natiuitate.

151–65 (*Augustine, 2*) Venit Dominus; quid fecit? Magnum mysterium commendauit. 'Exspuit in terram', de saliua sua lutum fecit; quia Verbum caro factum est. Et inunxit oculos caeci. Inunctus erat, et nondum uidebat. Misit illum ad piscinam quae uocatur Siloe. Pertinuit autem ad euangelistam commendare nobis nomen huius piscinae, et ait: 'Quod interpretatur Missus'. Iam quis sit missus agnoscitis; nisi enim ille fuisset missus, nemo nostrum esset ab iniquitate dimissus. Lauit ergo oculos in ea piscina quae interpretatur Missus, baptizatus est in Christo. Si ergo quando eum in seipso quodammodo baptizauit, tunc illuminauit; quando inunxit, fortasse catechumenum fecit. Potest quidem aliter atque aliter tanti sacramenti exponi profunditas et pertractari; sed hoc sufficiat Caritati uestrae; audistis grande mysterium. Interroga hominem: christianus es? Respondit tibi: 'Non sum', si paganus est aut Iudaeus. Si autem dixerit: Sum; adhuc quaeris ab eo: Catechumenus, an fidelis? Si responderit: Catechumenus, inunctus est, nondum lotus. Sed unde inunctus? Quaere, et respondet; quaere ab illo in quem credat; eo ipso quo catechumenus est, dicit: In Christum. Ecce modo loquor et fidelibus et catechumenis. Quid dixi de sputo et luto? Quia Verbum caro factum est. Hoc et catechumeni audiunt; sed non eis sufficit ad quod inuncti sunt; festinent ad lauacrum, si lumen inquirunt.

hwæðer þe for his aȝene, oððe for his maȝæ?

þa cwæð | ðe Hælend heom sonæ to andsware: Bf. 66

Næs he blind acenned for his aȝene synnum, oððe for his

 maȝe,   170

ac þæt Godes wundræ wyrdon on him iswytelode.'

Nes ðe blindæ man swa þeah buton synnum on life,

for þan ðe moniȝ blind mon bið swiðe manful,

ac he nes for his synnæ, oððe for his maȝæ,

blind acenned, swa swa Crist sylf sæde,   175

ac þæt Godes wundra wyrdon on him iswutelode.

'Me ȝedafenæð to wyrcenne his weorc ðe me asende.'

Nu ȝe maȝen ihyren hu ðe Hælend wearð asend

fram his Almihtiȝa Fader, swa swa we ær cwædon.

He cwæð þæt him ȝedafenode to wyrccenne his weorc, 180

for þam ðe he is his Sunu of þam soðan Fæder,

Almihtiȝæ Alesend, of þam Almihtiȝa Fæder,

and he æffre his weorc and al his wuldor tealde

to his heofenlice Fæder, þe hine asende.

For þan ðe he of him is al þæt he is,   185

eafre acenned | Sunu unaseȝenlice,   fol. 109

and þe Fæder nis na of nanum oðrum.

 'Crist cwæð:

þa hwile þe hit dæȝ bið, for þam ðe þeo deorce niht cymð,

þonne nan mon ne mæȝ noht to gode wyrcean.'   190

Hwilc is ðe dæȝ, oððe hwæt is þeo niht?

172–6 (*Augustine*, *3*, *11–29*) Quid est quod dixit? Si nullus homo sine peccato, numquid parentes huius caeci sine peccato erant? Numquid ipse uel sine originali peccato natus erat, uel uiuendo nihil addiderat? An quia oculos clausos habebat, concupiscentiae minime uigilabant? Quanta mala committunt caeci! A quo malo abstinet mens mala, etiam clausis oculis? Non poterat uidere, sed nouerat cogitare, et forte concupiscere aliquid quod caecus non posset implere, sed in corde iudicari a cordis perscrutatore. Si ergo et parentes eius habuerunt peccatum, et iste habuit peccatum; quare Dominus dixit: 'Neque hic peccauit, neque parentes eius', nisi ad rem de qua interrogatus est, 'ut caecus nasceretur'? Habebant enim peccatum parentes eius, sed non ipso peccato factum est ut caecus nasceretur. Si ergo non peccato factum est parentum ut caecus nasceretur, quare caecus natus est? Audi magistrum docentem; quaerit credentem, ut faciat intellegentem. Ipse causam dicit quare ille caecus sit natus: 'Neque hic peccauit', inquit, 'neque parentes eius; sed ut manifestentur opera Dei in illo.'

177–87 (*Augustine*, *4*, *1–6*) Deinde quid sequitur? 'Me oportet operari opera eius qui misit me.' Ecce est ille missus in quo faciem lauit caecus. Et uidete quid dixerit: 'Me oportet operari opera eius qui misit me, donec dies est.' Memento te quomodo uniuersam gloriam illi dat de quo est; quia ille habet filium qui de illo sit, ipse non habet de quo sit.

191–221 (*Augustine*, *5*, *1–5*, *13–28*) Quae est illa nox, quae cum uenerit, nemo poterit operari? Audi quid sit dies, et tunc intelleges quae sit nox. Unde sumus audituri

Crist cwæð him sylf þæt he is ðeo soðe liht
þisses middaneardes, and he is ure dæȝ,
þe us mid ȝeileafæn onliht fram blindnesse.
'He cwæð: 195
Ic eam middaneardes liht, þa hwile ðe þe ic on
     middanearde æm.'
Hwæt, wene we, la, broðræ, þæt he were þa mid monnum,
þa þa he on menniscnesse on middanearde wæs,
and æfter his æriste and upstiȝe to heofonum,
us wyrde ætbroȝdon and his beorhte liht,   200
and þeo deorce niht come æfter Drihtnes upstiȝe?
Nis hit na swa þeah swa we on ðare swarte nihte
ure lif adreoȝon, buton Cristes lihte.
His apostoli wrohten fela wyndræ and tacnæ
æfter his upstiȝe, and eac heom becom to   205
ðe Haliȝe Gast of heofenum, and heom alle ȝeaf
alle þeodæ spæce þe on þissere worulde beoð.
Heo wrohten eac þa wundræ þe Crist sylf ne wrohte;
for þan þe he sæde to heom ær his ðrowunge:
Maran wundræ ȝe wurcæð; and hit wearð eac swa,   210
swa þæt ða leaffulle men lædden ða untruman men
on heoræ læȝerbe(d)dum, and læȝdon heom bi þere stræte
þer þer Petrus eode; and heom oferglad þa
ðæs apostolas scæde, and heo sona wurdon hale
fram al untrumnesse for his scæde repunge.   215
Ne hælde þe Hælend nenne mon þurh his scæde,
ac þeos miht com of him swa þeah,
for þan | ðe he cwæð ær to heom: Bf. 68
Sine me, nichil potestis facere,

---

205 heom] ʻhˊeom   212 læȝerbeddum] læȝer bendū

---

quisnam sit dies iste. Ipse dicat: 'Quamdiu in hoc mundo sum, lux sum mundi.' Ecce ipse
est dies. Lauet oculos caecus in die, ut uideat diem.... Putamus eum, fratres, fuisse hic
tunc, et modo non hic esse? Si ergo hoc putamus, iam ergo post adscensum Domini facta
est nox ista metuenda, ubi nemo possit operari; si post adscensum Domini facta est nox
ista, unde apostoli tanta operati sunt? Numquid ista nox erat, quando Spiritus sanctus
ueniens, et omnes qui in uno loco erant adimplens, dedit eis loqui omnium gentium
linguis? Numquid nox erat quando claudus ille ad uerbum Petri saluus effectus est, immo
ad uerbum Domini habitantis in Petro? Numquid nox erat quando transeuntibus discipulis aegri cum lectulis ponebantur, ut uel umbra transeuntium tangerentur? Dominus
autem cum hic esset, neminem transiens umbra sua saluum fecit; sed ipse discipulis
dixerat: 'Maiora horum facietis.' Dixerat quidem Dominus: 'Maiora horum facietis'; sed
non se extollat caro et sanguis; audiat dicentem: 'Sine me nihil potestis facere.'

þæt is on ure spæce,   220
Ne maȝe ȝe nan þin[g] don buton me.
þes weoruldlice dæȝ þe us ȝewunelic is,
bi'ð iendod mid þan onsiȝendum æfne;
ac þe drihtenlicæ dæȝ, þæt is ures Drihtnes midwunung,
bi'ð us æfre astreht o'ð ende þissere weorulde,   225
swa swa Crist sylf behet þam 'ðe hine lufiæ'ð:
Ecce ego uobiscum sum omnibus diebus usque ad consummationem
saeculi,
þæt is on Englisce spæce,
Efne ic beo mid eow alle daȝum heonon for'ð   230
o'ð þissere weorulde endunge.

Hwæt is 'ðeo deorce niht buton helle dimnes,
on þære nan mon ne mæȝ naht to gode wyrcean,
þe 'ðe nu on his life þes lihtes ne ȝem'ð,
þe Crist us behet þurh his midwununge?   235
O'ðer is weorces timæ, o'ðer is ætleanes timæ.
Nu is weorces timæ o'ð þissere weorulde endunge;
and æfter ure life bi'ð eadleanes timæ,
þonne Crist on his domsetle clypæ'ð to his icorenum:
Cumæ'ð nu to me, mines fæder iblætsedon,   240
and iaȝniæ'ð þæt rice, þe eow iȝearcod wæs
fram middaneardes anginne. þis is þæt edlean
þare rihtwisæ monnæ þe rihtlice leofedon,

---

223 iendod] *final* d *altered from another letter* (n.?)

222-53 (*Augustine, 6, 1-5, 7-26*) Quid igitur? quid dicemus de nocte ista? Quando erit, quando nemo poterit operari? Nox ista impiorum erit; nox ista eorum erit quibus in fine dicitur: 'Ite in ignem aeternum, qui paratus est diabolo et angelis eius.' Sed nox dicta est, non flamma, non ignis. Audi quia et nox est. . . . Operetur ergo homo dum uiuit, ne illa nocte praeueniatur, ubi nemo possit operari. Modo est ut operetur fides per dilectionem; et si modo operamur, hic est dies, hic est Christus. Audi promittentem, et ne arbitreris absentem. Ipse dixit: 'Ecce ego uobiscum sum.' Quamdiu? Non sit in nobis sollicitudo qui uiuimus; si fieri posset, de hac etiam uoce posteros qui futuri sunt, securissimos faceremus. 'Ecce', inquit, 'ego uobiscum sum usque in consummationem saeculi.' Dies iste qui circuitu solis huius impletur, paucas horas habet; dies praesentiae Christi usque in consummationem saeculi extenditur. Post resurrectionem uero uiuorum et mortuorum, cum positis ad dexteram dixerit: 'Venite, benedicti Patris mei, percipite regnum', positis autem ad sinistram dixerit: 'Ite in ignem aeternum, qui paratus est diabolo et angelis eius', ibi erit nox ubi nemo potest operari, sed recipere quod operatus est. Aliud est tempus operationis, aliud receptionis; reddet enim Dominus unicuique secundum opera sua. Cum uiuis, fac, si facturus es; erit enim tunc nox ualida, quae inuoluat impios. Sed et modo omnis infidelis, quando moritur, illa nocte suscipitur; non est ut illic aliquid operetur.

and mid gode weorce Gode icwæmdon.

Ðeo dimme niht bið ðonne ure Drihten clypæð   245
on þam miclan dome to þam manfullæ heape,
þe mid yfele weorce hine ær gremoden,
and on unrihtwisnesse heora lif adroзon:
Gewitæð fram me, зe awariзedan, into þam ece fyre,
þe is deofle iзearcod and his awariзedum gaste.   250
þonne underfoð heo edlean on ecere pine |
heora arleasæ dæda þe heo æfre adruзon   fol. 109ᵛ
oð heoræ lifes ende, and heoræ Drihten forsæзon.

On ðare nihte cwylmde, swa swa Cristes boc us sæзð,
þe wælзa rice, ðe walde þa habban   255
Lazarum þone þearfæn, þe he on his life forseah,
þæt he mid his fingræ hure his tunga drypte
for þan ormete bryne þe he on cwylmode.
Ac him wæs þæs wætan forwyrnd,
swa swa he forwyrnde ær þa crumen þam earmæn Lazare.   260
Him com þa to зemynde his зebroðræ on life;
wolde þa god wyrcan, and heom warniзæn
þæt heo ðider ne comen to þare cwylmynзe.
Ac þa nes na weorces timæ, ac wæs edleanes,
and he wæs þa on þare nihte þær he wyrcen ne mihte.   265
   Ðis godspel is langsum, and hæfð longne traht.
Nu wylle we eow secgan þæt arfoþeste andзit;
þæt oðer зe | maзon eow seolfe understanden.   Bf. 70
   'Ðe mon wæs ihæled on þam halзa ræstendæз.
þa sædon sonæ sume þa sunderhalзan: 270
Nis ðes mon na fram Gode, þe ðonne restandæз ne heald.'
þa Iudeiscan heoldon heom to freolsdæзe

_____

263 cwylmynзe] cwylm`ynзe´, *with* `ynge´ *written above an erasure*

_____

254–65 (*Augustine, 6, 26–33*) In illa nocte diues ardebat, et stillam aquae de digito
pauperis requirebat; dolebat, angebatur, fatebatur, nec ei subueniebatur, et conatus est
benefacere. Ait enim Abrahae: 'Pater Abraham, mitte Lazarum ad fratres meos, ut dicat
illis quid hic agatur, ne et ipsi ueniant in hunc locum tormentorum.' O infelix! quando
uiuebas, tunc erat tempus operandi; modo iam in nocte es, in qua nemo possit operari.
269–97 (*Augustine, 9, 8–17*) 'Non est hic homo a Deo, qui sabbatum non custodit.' Ipse
potius custodiebat, qui sine peccato erat. Sabbatum enim spiritale hoc est, non habere
peccatum. Denique, fratres, hoc admonet Deus, quando commendat sabbatum: 'Omne
opus seruile non facietis.' Haec sunt uerba Dei sabbatum commendantis: 'Omne opus
seruile non facietis.' Iam superiores lectiones interrogate, quid sit opus seruile; et
Dominum audite: 'Omnis qui facit peccatum, seruus est peccati.' Sed isti nec uidentes,
ut dixi, nec inuncti, sabbatum carnaliter obseruabant, spiritaliter uiolabant.

þonne Sæteresdæʒ, and na ðone Sunnendæʒ,
on þa aldan wisæn æfter Moyses æ,
swa þæt heo on þam dæʒe nan ðeowtlic weorc   275
wyrcan ne mosten, for þare micclan tacnunge
ðe þe dæʒ tacnode, swa swa we sædon hwilon ær.
Ðe Sæteresdæʒ, þe heo swa swiðe freolsoden,
is ure gastlice freols, þe we for Gode sceolon
haldan on ure life on ðare neowen ʒecyðnesse,   280
and warniæn us wið synnæ þe beoð þeowtlice weorc.
Swa swa Crist seolf cwæð on sumne godspelle:
Omnis qui facit peccatum seruus est peccati,
Ælc ðare þe synnæ ʒewyrcæð is ðare synne ðeow.
Is nu þe ræstandæʒ ure lifes timæ,   285
on þam we sceolon simle synne forbuʒon,
swa we selost maʒon, ure Scyppende to lofe,
and ʒif we hwæt tobrecon, beton þæt ʒeorne.
þa Iudeiscan freolsoden þone forsædon ræstandæʒ
fram weoruldlice weorcum, ac heo ʒewemdon swa ðeah   290
þone ilcæ ræstandæʒ mid unrihte dæda,
and mid þam ðe heo wiðcwædon þæt Crist nære fram Gode.
He heold þonne restandæʒ þeah ðe he ihælde þonne blindan,
for ðan ðe he leofede his lif buton synnum;
and we halʒiæð nu him þone halʒan sunnandæʒ,   295
for þan ðe he on ðam dæʒe of deaþe aras,
ða þe he us alysde fram þam ecan deaðe.
   'Heo cwædon to ðam men: Do wuldor Gode';
swylc heo cwædon þæt Crist nære God,
and he sceolde þancian þam heofenlican Gode.   300
'We witen ful ʒearæ þæt ðæs mon is synful':
ðis sædon þa Iudeiscan be þam soðfestæn Hælende,
þe ne wrohte næfre on þisse weorulde synnæ.
Ac heo weron synfulle, ðeah ðe heo swa ne wendon;
and heom wære bætere þæt heo wrohton alle dæʒ   305
on þam halʒan restandæʒ, þone heo be þam Hælende

---

285 lifes] *line ʹʹnder* li *may cover an erasure*   298 Gode] g *altered from* ʒ *by addition of loop*

298–300 (*Augustine, 11, 1–4*) 'Uocauerunt ergo rursum hominem qui fuerat caecus, et dixerunt ei: Da gloriam Deo.' Quid est: 'Da gloriam Deo'? Nega quod accepisti. Hoc plane non est gloriam Deo dare, sed Deum potius blasphemare.
301–11 (*Ælfric's independent addition*)

swa huxlice spæcon, heom seolfum to wite.

Ðe restandæȝ wes ihalȝod o[n] ðes Hælendes ðrowunge
fram ðeowtlicum weorce, ac we ne ðurfon na leng
lichamlice haldæn, ac on ure lifes ðeawum 310
on gastlice andȝite, and on gode weorcum.

'þa Iudeiscan wariȝedon wodlice ðone blindan'
syððan he ihæled wæs, þa he be þam Hælende spæc
and befran hwæðer heo | wolden his leorningcnihtæs
beon. fol. 110, Bf. 72

'Heo sædon him to andsware: Beo ðu his leorningcniht,' 315
swylce he wære awariȝed ȝif he cristene wære.

Ac þæt nis na wariȝung, ac witolice blætsung,
þæt mon Criste folȝie mid soðæ cristendome.

Heo temdon to Moysen þam mæran lareowe,
þæt heo his leorningcnihtæs weron and his lare folȝodon, 320
ac ȝif heo his lare folȝedon, þonne lyfdon heo on Crist;
for þam ðe Moyses awrat witegunge be Criste,
and þa Iudeiscan noldon nowþre folȝian
ne Moysen ne Criste mid nane soðfestnesse.

Ðe ihælede mon cwæð þæt God nele ihyran 325
þa synfulle men, ac he ne sæde na riht.

For þan ðe he ne c(u)ðe þa ȝyt þa halȝa Cristes boc,
þe sæð hu þe manfulle, mid mycele onbrurdnesse,
binnon Salomones temple hine sceortlice ðus ibed:
Deus propicius esto michi peccatori, 330
þæt is, God Almihtiȝæ, mildsiȝe me synfulle;
and he wearð irihtwisod, and wende him ham.

313 ihæled] d *altered clumsily in red from another letter* (r, t, s?) 323 nowþre] þ *has*
unusually high and large loop 327 cuðe] u *written above a* y halȝa] ȝ *imperfectly*
formed 329 ibed] i *added later*

312–24 (*Augustine, 12*) 'Maledixerunt ei, et dixerunt: Tu discipulus eius sis.' Tale
maledictum super nos, et super filios nostros. Maledictum enim est si cor discutias, non
si uerba perpendas. 'Nos autem Moysi discipuli sumus; nos scimus quia Moysi locutus
est Deus, istum autem nescimus unde sit.' Utinam sciretis 'quia Moysi locutus est
Deus'; sciretis quia per Moysen praedicatus est Deus. Habetis enim Dominum dicentem: 'Si crederetis Moysi, crederetis et mihi; de me enim ille scripsit.' Itane sequimini
seruum, et dorsum ponitis contra Dominum? Sed nec seruum sequimini; nam per illum
ad Dominum duceremini.
325–34 (*Augustine, 13, 1–10*) 'Respondit ille homo, et dixit eis: In hoc mirabile . . . hunc
exaudit' (vv. 30–1). Adhuc inunctus loquitur. Nam et peccatores exaudit Deus. Si enim
peccatores Deus non exaudiret, frustra ille publicanus oculos in terram demittens et
pectus suum percutiens diceret: 'Domine, propitius esto mihi peccatori.' Et ista confessio meruit iustificationem, quomodo iste caecus illuminationem.

We nyton, þeah he mende þæt micele wundor,
þæt nan synful man ne mihte swylce tacnæ wyrcæn.

'Ðe ihælede mon cwæð to þam heardheortum Iudeiscum: 335
Fram þissere weorlde anginne, ne wearð nefræ ihyred
þæt æniȝ mon mihte þone mon ihælen,
and his eaȝan openiæn, þe ær wæs blind acenned;
buton he fram Gode were, ne mihte he þis don.'
Freolice he spæc her, and ful andrædlice.   340
Hwa mihte openiȝan þa unsceapenæ eaȝen
and him sihðe ȝifen, buton ðe ðe ȝeisceop ær
Adam of eorðan and Euam of his ribbe?

'Ða yrsodan þa Iudeiscan, and hine utdrifon.
Ac Crist hine underfeng þa þa heo hine forsæȝen,   345
and him sonæ cwæð to: þu ilefest on Godes Sunu?
He andswyrde mid ileafan:
La, hwylc is he, laford, þæt ic ilefe on hine?
And þe Hælend cwæð him to:
þu hine isæȝe ær, and he is ðe ilcæ þe þe to spæky.   350
He cwæð þa mid ileafan: Ic ilyfe, Drihten,
and feol to his fotum,' for þan ðe he oncneow
ðet hit idafenlice wæs, ðæt he to his Drihtne
mid astreahtum limum and ȝeleafan hine ȝebede.

'Ða cwæð ðe Hælend him eft to þus: 355
Ic com hider on dome on þisne middaneard,
þæt ða men iseon þe ne mihten ær iseon,
and þa ðe iseoð sceolon beon blinde.'
þes mon wæs blind iboren, ac he iseah þurh Criste,

345 Ac] *lengthened ascender on* a   353 idafenlice] *half-stroke of* ð *added later to* d

---

335–43 (*Augustine, 13, 10–15*) 'A saeculo ... facere quidquam' (vv. 32–3). Libere, constanter, ueraciter. Haec enim quae facta sunt a Domino, a quo fierent nisi a Deo? Aut quando a discipulis talia fierent, nisi in eis Dominus habitaret?

359–*end* (*Augustine, 17* [*Ælfric not close to Augustine*]) Commoti sunt ergo uerbis istis 'quidam ex pharisaeis, et dixerunt ei: Numquid et nos caeci sumus?' Audi iam quid est quod mouebat: 'Et qui uident, caeci fiant. Dixit eis Iesus: Si caeci essetis, non haberetis peccatum.' Cum sit caecitas ipsa peccatum. 'Si caeci essetis', id est, si uos caecos aduerteretis, si uos caecos diceretis, et ad medicum curreretis; 'si' ergo ita 'caeci essetis, non haberetis peccatum', quia ueni ego auferre peccatum. 'Nunc uero dicitis: Quia uidemus, peccatum uestrum manet.' Quare? Quia dicendo: 'Uidemus', medicum non quaeritis, in caecitate uestra remanetis. Hoc est ergo quod paulo ante non intellexeramus quod ait: 'Ego ueni, ut qui non uident, uideant'; quid est: 'ut qui non uident, uideant'? Qui se non uidere confitentur, et medicum quaerunt, ut uideant. 'Et qui uident, caeci fiant'; quid est: 'qui uident, caeci fiant'? Qui se putant uidere, et medicum non quaerunt, in sua caecitate permaneant. Ergo istam discretionem uocauit iudicium,

æȝðer mid eaȝan and mid ȝeleafan.   360
þa Iudeiscan wendon þæt heo weron hale,
ac heo ne iseȝon na Crist mid soðæ leafæ,
ne his | lihtes ne bedon, for þan ðe heo blinde weron.   Bf. 74
Heo hine iseȝen swutelice mid eagan,
and mid hearde heortæ huxlice forseȝon.   365
We hine ne iseȝon mid lichamlicere ȝesihðe,
ac we hine iseoð nu mid soðæ ȝeleafan.
Heo þurhwunedon on blindnesse, and we wurdon onlihte
ðurh ðone lyfiȝendan Drihten, þe leofæð a on ecnysse.
AMEN.   370

cum ait: 'In iudicium ueni in hunc mundum', quo discernit causam credentium et
confitentium a superbis, se uidere putantibus, et ideo grauius excaecatis, tamquam
dixerit ei peccator confitens et medicum quaerens: 'Iudica me, Deus, et discerne
causam meam de gente non sancta'; illorum scilicet qui dicunt: 'Uidemus', et eorum
peccatum manet. Non autem illud iudicium iam intulit mundo, quo de uiuis et mortuis
in fine saeculi iudicabit. Secundum hoc enim dixerat: 'Ego non iudico quemquam';
quoniam prius uenit, 'non et iudicet mundum, sed ut saluetur mundus per ipsum'.

NOTES

3. The opening phrases do not fit into any regular metrical pattern, mainly
because *Ure Drihten* is superfluous to metrical requirements.

24. *hu* acts here as an interjection which is introducing a negative question
and expecting an affirmative answer. Compare, for example, Pope v, l. 77.

61. *asæton*: MED cites the verb *asitten* 'to be afraid of or fear (sth.)', citing
only this instance. The verb derives from OE *onsittan*, and *asæton* may be a
twelfth-century scribal alteration.

73. *hwæt*: On the basis of the Vulgate, this word probably has the function
of an interrogative meaning 'why' rather than an interjection meaning 'what!'.

110ff. The similarity of this passage to Ælfric's other homily on the healing
of a blind man (CH I x) should be noted:

þeahhwæðere þa wundra þe Crist worhte, oðer ðing hi æteowdon þurh
mihte, and oðre ðing hi getacnodon þurh geryno. He worhte þa wundra
soðlice þurh godcunde mihte, and mid þam wundrum þæs folces geleafan
getrymde; ac hwæðre þær wæs oðer ðing digle on ðam wundrum, æfter
gastlicum andgite. þes an blinda man getacnode eall mancynn, þe wearð
ablend þurh Adames gylt, and asceofen of myrhðe neo[r]xena-wanges, and
gebroht to ðisum life þe is wiðmeten cwearterne. Nu sind we ute belocene
fram ðam heofenlican leohte, and we ne magon on ðissum life þæs ecan
leohtes brucan. (p. 154)

For a discussion of this passage in relation to Ælfric's explanation of *ðeo deorce niht*, see pp. 56–8 above.

112. *swa ʒetacnoden þeah*: It is possible that the phrase represents a scribal error for *ʒetacnoden swa þeah*. However since *þeah* as an adverb meaning 'however' often appears on its own in Ælfric's writing, and since the phrase makes sense as it stands, I have resisted the temptation to emend. Compare 156 *þeah swa blind* which is probably to be translated as 'nevertheless thus blind' rather than emended to *swa þeah blind*.

123. *mismaky*: *mismacian* is a verb not found in Old English, and its use here is probably a twelfth-century scribal substitution. The earliest example in the OED is of *c.* 1400: 'Be stille, good wyff, quoth they, there of mysmake you noght.' The MED cites the Bodley 343 example, but its next example is from a text over two centuries later (1394). Under the prefix 'mis-', the OED notes that 'a great extension of the use of the prefix took place, mis- being freely combined with words of indigenous and of foreign origin alike. Many of the new compounds appear to have been suggested by French formation with mes-' (p. 491). This occurrence of *mismaky* is apparently the earliest extant use of the verb. The 3rd person pres. sg. indic. -*y* for -*þ* perhaps results from an Anglo-Norman confusion of the letters *y* and *þ*; compare *spæky* in 350.

131. The omission of the word *natura* from the Latin quotation of Eph. ii. 3 must be a scribal error, since Ælfric includes the word in his translation, and I have therefore emended the text to include it.

151–65. For a discussion of the two stages of becoming a Christian, 'icristnod' and 'ifullod', see pp. 58–60 above.

161, 232. *helle pine, helle dimnes*: In printing these as two separate words, not as compounds, I have followed Campb. *Suppl.* (p. v), which treats groups consisting of genitive plus noun, including those with *helle*, as independent words. For the word *pine*, see note to 251.

162. *me*: An early Middle English form of the indefinite pronoun *man*, probably a scribal alteration to distinguish it from *ðe mon* earlier in the line.

197. *broðræ*: The single term of address *broðræ* is unusual for Ælfric who usually writes *leofan gebroðra, eala ge gebroðra* or *mine gebroðra* (e.g., CH II xiii, l. 277). Concern for metrical regularity may have influenced Ælfric here.

200. *ætbroʒdon*: The word is the past participial form of Old English *ætbre(g)dan*. For the spelling of this form, see my section on language. For a discussion of the meaning of the verb, see E. G. Stanley, ed., *The Owl and the Nightingale* (p. 142, note to l. 1380). The alternative which he rejects for that poem is more appropriate here, that is, 'taken away from' with the idea of spoliation.

213. *oferglad*: A rare compound not otherwise found in Old English (though *glidan* is fairly common).

251. *pine*: The noun *pine* meaning 'pain, torment' is not found in Old English. The verb *pinian* was common from an early period, but the noun does not appear until the twelfth century. The use of *pine* here and at 161 is probably the result of a twelfth-century scribal substitution for *wite* or *susle*.

255. *wælʒa rice*: In his earlier homily which relates the story of the rich man and Lazarus (CH I xxiii), Ælfric refers to the *dives* as *ðæs rican* (p. 330) and *se rica* (p. 332). Clearly the word *rica* could imply 'prosperous, rich', rather than just 'powerful'. In homily iii, Ælfric has avoided any ambiguity by including both *wælʒa* and *rice*. *Wælʒa* also alliterates with the following *walde*. The OED notes that 'in many OE and ME passages, it is difficult to decide whether this sense [powerful] or sense 2 [wealthy] is mainly intended'. See M. R. Godden, 'Money, power and morality in late Anglo-Saxon England', *ASE* xix (1990), 41–65.

255–7. The pronoun *he* in 257 refers to *Lazarum* in 256. The phrase *habban Lazarum . . . þæt he . . . his tunga drypte* means 'to have Lazarus . . . moisten his tongue'.

277. *swa swa we sædon hwilon*: A reference to Pope ii, ll. 252–65. See pp. 53–6 above for a fuller discussion.

333–4. These two lines follow Ælfric's summary of the story of the sinful man who prayed for mercy and was justified by God (Luke xviii. 10–14). Their meaning is obscure. Belfour's translation is clearly incorrect: 'We do not know—although he meant the great miracle—why any sinful man should not be able to perform such miracles' (p. 73). The word *þeah* may also be rendered as 'whether' (see *OES* §§3416–17), and the lines could therefore mean either (a) 'We do not know whether he meant that great miracle, in that no sinful man could perform such miracles' (with 'he' referring to the blind man and 'that great miracle' referring to the healing of the blind man); or (b) 'We do not know whether he meant that great miracle—that no sinful man could perform such miracles' (where 'he' again refers to the blind man who, when he said that God will not hear sinful men, might have meant that sinful men could not perform miracles). The latter seems to me the more convincing alternative. The hesitant tone of the lines makes it tempting to see them as a marginal note incorporated by a scribe into the main text, but their alliterative and rhythmic pattern suggests that they did in fact belong to the original homily. The question of miracles and who could perform them was one of particular interest to Ælfric. His homilies assume that sinful men could perform physical miracles, although he would naturally deny that such physical miracles give them any kind of spiritual authority. See M. R. Godden, 'Ælfric's Saints' Lives and the Problem of Miracles', *Leeds Studies in English* n.s. xvi (1985), 83–100.

340. *andrædlice*: The adverb meaning 'in awe' probably derived from OE *ondrædendlice* 'to be feared, awe-inspiring'. The word did not carry through into ME (MED cites only this instance).

IV

ST VINCENT'S DAY

STRUCTURE OF THE TEXT

The fourth homily edited here survives only as two separate pieces, and is printed in its original form for the first time.[1] The first part, an account of the passion of St. Vincent of Saragossa, is found in one late manuscript, CUL Ii. 1. 33, written in the second half of the twelfth century.[2] This manuscript contains a large proportion of saints' lives by Ælfric, belonging mainly to his two series of *Catholic Homilies* and his *Lives of Saints*. The passion of St. Vincent, from its alliterative style, reveals itself also to be the work of Ælfric. Since it was appended by Skeat to his edition of the *Lives of Saints*, it has generally been treated as part of that collection, although there is no evidence that Ælfric himself ever added it to that set.[3]

A reference to St. Vincent also appears in a short homily in Bodley 343. The homily is an exposition of the gospel passage John xii. 24–6, and is included in a section of the manuscript which collects homilies for the Common of the Saints (mostly from the Second Series of *Catholic Homilies*).

Peter Clemoes has argued convincingly that these two items, the Passion of Vincent and the exposition of John xii. 24–6, must originally have formed one homily.[4] First, both pieces are too short to stand independently. Secondly, the gospel exposition refers to an account of Vincent already given to the audience: 'swa swa Uincencius dyde, be þam þe we eow sæden ær' (l. 338). Lastly, CUL Ii. 1. 33 frequently

---

[1] I am grateful to Cambridge University Press for permission to use here material originally published in my article 'Bones of Contention: the Context of Ælfric's Homily on St. Vincent', *ASE*, xix (1990), 117–32.

[2] For a description of the manuscript, see Ker, *Catalogue*, no. 18 (the Vincent Passion is item 23). Its piecemeal assemblage and possible Ely provenance have been discussed by Schipper in 'A Composite Old English Homiliary'.

[3] LS xxxvii. Skeat's other texts are taken from the only complete manuscript of the *Lives of Saints*, BL, Cotton Julius E. vii. For Skeat's attribution of the Vincent piece to Ælfric, see LS II, p. xviii.

[4] Clemoes, 'Chronology', p. 236. Clemoes's argument is endorsed by Pope, p. 140.

includes only the *passio* or narrative section of homilies for which
Ælfric provided both *passio* and pericope exposition.[1]

The combination of gospel exposition with narrative in the homily
on St. Vincent makes it somewhat anomalous in the corpus of Ælfric's
writings. In his two series of *Catholic Homilies*, Ælfric provided works
for those saints' days celebrated by the whole English church, as he
explains in a preface: 'þæra anra þe angelcynn mid freolsdagum
wurðað'.[2] For these he often used expositions of the gospel-text as
well as narratives of the saint's life and/or death. In his later collection, the *Lives of Saints*, he provided texts for a large number of saints
celebrated in monastic services. Again Ælfric outlines his intention in
his preface to that collection: 'þu wast leof þæt we awendon on þam
twam ærrum bocum þæra halgena þrowunga and lif . þe angel-cynn
mid freols-dagum wurþað. Nu ge-wearð us þæt we þas boc be þæra
halgena ðrowungum and life . gedihton þe mynster-menn mid heora
þenungum betwux him wurðiað.'[3] The *Lives of Saints* are all narrative
reading pieces, not homilies in the strict sense, with no gospel expositions, and apparently not designed as preaching texts. The feast of
Vincent did not qualify for inclusion in the *Catholic Homilies*, and the
saint seems to have been of such slight importance that Ælfric did not
even include him in his *Lives of Saints* collection (at least in its original
form). At some later stage, however, Ælfric was clearly prompted to
compose a text on Vincent, and this was not merely a reading piece but
a homily in the strict sense, with both *passio* and gospel exposition.

THE CULT OF VINCENT

Although Vincent's life remains almost entirely obscure, the details of
his death on a gridiron in Valencia in about AD 304 captured the attention of hagiographers, so that both his fame and relics were dispersed
throughout Europe and beyond from the fourth century onwards.
Augustine, in an early fifth-century sermon, exclaims: 'Quae hodie
regio, quaeve provincia ulla, quo usque vel Romanum imperium, vel
christianum nomen extenditur, natalem non gaudet celebrare Vincentii?'[4] Louis de Lacger, in a detailed examination of the cult of

---

[1] The *passio* only is included of Ælfric's texts for Paul (CH I xxvii), Peter and Paul
(CH I xxvi), Andrew (CH I xxxviii), and Matthew (CH II xxxii). See Ker, *Catalogue*, no.
18, items 7, 9, 10, and 16.

[2] CH II, p. 2.

[3] LS, p. 4, 41–5.

[4] *Sermo* cclxxvi, PL 38, col. 1257.

Vincent, remarks on 'cette exceptionnelle faveur de la piété populaire' towards Vincent, an interest which was manifested in the wide geographical spread of his cult: he was the dedicatee of churches in Italy, Gaul, Spain, Africa and Illyria.[1] From the ninth century onwards, he became a patron also of cathedrals.

The earliest surviving accounts of the martyrdom of Vincent are a verse panegyric by Prudentius written in about 400, and six sermons by Augustine which date from the early fifth century.[2] The story was also transmitted through a lost late fourth-century *passio*. The extant versions of this original *passio*, three separate prose accounts known as the *passio amplissima*, the *passio fusior*, and the *passio brevior*, were written during or after the seventh century.[3]

The alleged survival of Vincent's body was vital for the dissemination of his cult. According to the *passio amplissima*, the body was buried in a tomb on the outskirts of Valencia: 'sub sacro altari extra muros eiusdem civitatis Valentiae ad quietem reponitur'.[4] It is known from other sources, assembled by de Lacger, that at some time in the fifth century this tomb was opened and the distribution of the relics began.[5] From the early sixth century, Vincent's relics are reported in all regions of the West.[6] Childebert, King of Paris, purportedly obtained Vincent's stole as a trophy from a siege of Saragossa in 531. Gregory of Tours, who reported this incident, mentions other relics of Vincent housed in various parts of France. A reference to Vincent's relics in Ravenna in 550, and an inscription pointing to them which has been found in Algeria, show that the relics had also reached Italy and Africa. De Lacger suggests that most churches dedicated to St. Vincent

---

[1] 'Saint Vincent de Saragosse', *Revue d'Histoire de l'Église de France*, xiii (1927), 307–58, pp. 308–9. An account of the various places in which churches were dedicated to Vincent is provided by A. de Waal, 'Zum Kult des hl. Vinzenz von Saragossa', *Römische Quartalschrift für die christliche Alterthumskunde und für Kirchengeschichte*, xxi (1907), 135–8.

[2] The work by Prudentius is *Peristefanon* V, CCSL 126, pp. 294–313. The sermons by Augustine are identified amongst other later sermons by B. de Gaiffier, 'Sermons latins en l'honneur de S. Vincent antérieurs au Xᵉ siècle', *Anal. Boll.*, lxvii (1949), 267–86. Four of the sermons are in PL 38, cols. 1252–68; one is in PL 38, cols. 33–52; the last is in *Sancti Aurelii Augustini, Hipponensis episcopi, Operum supplementum* I, ed. A. B. Caillau (Paris, 1836), pp. 67–8.

[3] See *BHL*, where further bibliography is to be found. For the *passio amplissima* (*BHL* 8627–33), see *Acta SS*, Jan., II, 394–8. The *passio brevior* (*BHL* 8638) and the *passio fusior* (*BHL* 8639) are printed in *Anal. Boll.* i (1882), 260–2 and 263–70 respectively. The names distinguishing the three versions were assigned by de Lacger, who also offers tentative dates for each, in 'Saint Vincent de Saragosse', pp. 325–7.

[4] *Acta SS*, Jan., II, 397. The *passio brevior* and *passio fusior* do not designate a place for the burial of the body.

[5] 'Saint Vincent de Saragosse', pp. 328–30.   [6] Ibid., pp. 331–2.

probably managed to procure some item or other from amongst his bones.[1] At some point, relics of Vincent apparently travelled across to England. In tenth-century England, as D. W. Rollason has shown, 'relic-collecting was actively pursued as a normal and accepted royal occupation and in fact the kings seem deliberately to have set out to amass treasures of relics'.[2] King Athelstan's notoriously avid pursuit of relics makes it likely that the acquisition of Vincent's relics can be ascribed to his reign (925–39): an Old English Exeter relic-list from the late eleventh century includes relics of Vincent amongst those which were allegedly given by Athelstan to Exeter (though the reliability of this list is questionable, as I show below).[3]

One of the most interesting features of Vincent's cult is its connections with that of the Roman saint Laurence. Laurence, also a deacon martyr, was tortured to death in 258 (about half a century before Vincent). Controversy surrounds the method by which he died. Traditionally he, like Vincent, was thought to have been roasted on a gridiron. Research by H. Delehaye has shown, however, that this manner of death is entirely contrary to the Roman tradition.[4] Delehaye argues convincingly from textual evidence that the story of roasting on a grill must be a later addition to the legend of St. Laurence. He traces it back to a Phrygian source which recounts the roasting of three Christians on a grill during the mid fourth-century persecution instigated by Julian.[5] The attribution of this manner of death to Laurence, however, probably derives more directly from the legend of Vincent.[6] Laurence, with his powerful base in Rome, seems to have escalated in popularity, rapidly surpassing Vincent. Dom Gregory Dix notes that there was a complete service for St. Laurence's Day (August 10) three or four centuries before provision was made for the ordinary Sundays of the year.[7]

---

[1] 'Saint Vincent de Saragosse', p. 333.

[2] 'Relic-cults as an Instrument of Royal Policy c. 900–1050', *ASE*, xv (1986), 91–103, p. 92.

[3] On Athelstan's relic-hunting, see J. A. Robinson, *The Times of St. Dunstan* (Oxford, 1923), pp. 71–80, and Rollason, 'Relic-cults'. Evidence of his interest in manuscripts as well as relics is discussed by S. Keynes in 'King Athelstan's Books', in *Learning and Literature*, ed. Lapidge and Gneuss, pp. 143–201. The OE Exeter relic-list is printed by M. Förster, *Zur Geschichte der Reliquienkultus in Altengland*, Bayerische Akademie der Wissenschaften, phil.-hist. Abt., VIII (Munich, 1943); Vincent's relics are mentioned on p. 73.

[4] 'Recherches sur le légendier romain', *Anal. Boll.*, li (1933), 34–98, pp. 49–50.

[5] Ibid., pp. 55–6.

[6] The connection between the two is discussed further by P. F. de' Cavalieri, 'A proposito della *Passio S. Vincentii Levitae*', Studi e Testi, lxv (Vatican City, 1935), 115–25.

[7] *The Shape of the Liturgy*, 2nd ed. (London, 1945), p. 368.

Other correspondences can be traced between Vincent and Laurence. The two saints were associated in litanies of the saints.[1] Even their relics seem at times to have belonged together: the biographer of St. Domnolus, bishop of Mans who died in 581, reports how, after building a monastery in honour of the deacon saints Vincent and Laurence, Domnolus solemnly placed in it the head of Vincent and a large portion of the grill on which Laurence was burnt.[2]

This link is particularly evident in the use of the gospel reading John xii. 24–6. Ælfric's use of this text for Vincent appears to be the earliest recorded example. Other extant sermons on Vincent, including those by Augustine, are, as de Gaiffier shows, designed to be used after the reading of the *passio*;[3] unlike Ælfric's, however, they all treat aspects of Vincent's life rather than expounding a gospel-text. Paul the Deacon's homiliary and the Carolingian homiliaries, from which Ælfric derives the bulk of the material for his commentaries, provide no material at all for St. Vincent's Day, which was clearly not considered an important feast at the time of their compilation.[4] These homiliaries, however, do have texts for St. Laurence, and regularly use John xii. 24–6 for the occasion. Paul the Deacon's homiliary, for example, draws on Augustine's commentary on John xii. 24–6 for its homily *De Sancto Laurentio Martyre*.[5] In the original homiliary of Haymo, the pericope John xii. 24–6 belongs to the feast *In Natale Sancti Laurentii*.[6] Smaragdus's homily on John xii. 24–6, which consists of excerpts from Alcuin's *Commentaria in S. Ioannis Evangelium*, is again assigned to the feast of St. Laurence.[7]

The use of the reading for Vincent as well, however, is in evidence

---

[1] See Michael Lapidge, 'Litanies of the Saints in Anglo-Saxon Manuscripts: a Preliminary List', *Scriptorium*, xl (1986), 264–77. Of the litanies listed by Lapidge, the following contain invocations to both Laurence and Vincent: nos. 1, 2, 3, 5 [separated by one saint], 6, 8 [separated by one saint], 9, 12 [separated by one saint], 13, 16, 18, 19, 21 [separated by one saint], 22, 23 [widely separated], 24 [widely separated], 29 [widely separated], 32, 33, 34, 36, 37 [widely separated], 38 [separated], 39, 40, 42 [separated by one saint], 44 [widely separated] and 45. The following litanies contain an invocation to Laurence, but none to Vincent: 4, 7, 10, 11, 26, 28, 30 and 31. I am grateful to Michael Lapidge for help with this reference.

[2] See de Lacger, 'Saint Vincent de Saragosse', pp. 332–3.

[3] 'Sermons latins', p. 268.

[4] For Paul the Deacon's homiliary, see p. 113, n. 11. For the Carolingian homiliaries, see Barré, *passim*. (Barré's use of the term 'Carolingian' is questioned by Clayton, 'Homiliaries and Preaching', p. 211.)

[5] *Sermo* xlii (PL 95, col. 1490). Augustine's commentary is *In Ioannis Euangelium Tractatus*, li. 9–12, CCSL 36, pp. 442–5.

[6] Barré, p. 156 (no. 34); the whole homily is printed in PL 118, cols. 763–5.

[7] PL 102, cols. 437–9.

soon after Ælfric's time. Later authors or compilers associate John xii. 24–6 with Laurence, Vincent and also the Common of a Martyr. In the Missal of the New Minster, Winchester, from the second half of the eleventh century, the reading for the feasts of Vincent, Laurence and *In Vigilia Unius Martyris*, is John xii. 24–6.[1] The Sarum Missal, probably compiled in the late twelfth or thirteenth century, likewise assigns John xii. 24–6 to the feasts of Vincent, Laurence and *unius martyris*.[2] The homiliaries reflect this multiple use. In the only three homiliaries from the period 1150–1350 in which John xii. 24–6 is assigned to the feast of St. Vincent, it is also assigned to the feast of St. Laurence.[3] In numerous other homiliaries from the same period, the text is assigned to Laurence's feast but not to Vincent's (which is often absent altogether).[4] John xii. 24–6 is frequently assigned to the Common of a Martyr in these homiliaries. The association between the reading and this feast may explain why the second part of the Vincent homily survived independently. A compiler, perhaps even Ælfric himself, recognized that this gospel exposition might be appropriately assigned to the Common of the Saints, and hence it came to circulate separately with texts for the Common of Saints. Its rubric in Bodley 343, *unius martiris*, far from being arbitrary, surely derives from this traditional identification of John xii. 24–6 with the Common of a Martyr.[5]

The association of Vincent and Laurence with the same gospel-text helps to explain Ælfric's choice of John xii. 24–6 for the feast of St.

---

[1] *The Missal of the New Minster Winchester*, ed. D. H. Turner, HBS, 93 (1962), pp. 64, 140, and 197. According to its editor, the manuscript, Le Havre, Bibliothèque Municipale, 330, was written for the New Minster, Winchester. N. R. Ker, *Medieval Libraries of Great Britain: A List of Surviving Books*, 2nd ed., Royal Historical Society Guides and Handbooks, 3 (London, 1964), p. 200, ascribes it to the Old Minster, Winchester, on liturgical evidence.

[2] *The Sarum Missal*, ed. J. Wickham Legg (Oxford, 1916), pp. 242 (Vincent), 304–5 (Laurence) and 360 (a martyr). Wickham Legg dates the work between 1150 and 1319 (pp. v–vii).

[3] See J. B. Schneyer, *Repertorium der Lateinischen Sermones des Mittelalters für die Zeit von 1150–1350*, 9 vols. (Munster Westfalen, 1969–80), I, 712, 713 (nos. 89 and 97); IV, 138–9, 143 (nos. 200 and 258); V, 41, 42 (nos. 86 and 90).

[4] See, for example, Schneyer, *Repertorium der Lateinischen Sermones* I, 485 (no. 168); II, 402 (no. 405a), 561 (no. 376); III, 347 (no. 157); IV, 34 (no. 282), 615 (no. 222); V, 545 (no. 286).

[5] The West-Saxon Gospels, in a marginal note, assign John xii. 24–6 to a different occasion again, 'tywes dæg on þære palmwucan' (Tuesday in the week following Palm Sunday). The usual pericope for this occasion is John xii. 1–36 (not just John xii. 24–6). But the West-Saxon Gospels assign John xii. 1–23 to the Monday after Palm Sunday. See *The Gospel According to St John*, ed. Skeat, pp. 114, 118.

Vincent.[1] Given the influence of the Vincent legend on that of Laurence, it is possible that the gospel reading was originally applied to
Vincent and later transferred to Laurence, and that this link with
Vincent has somehow survived down to Ælfric's time. The absence of
earlier evidence for it suggests, however, that the reading in fact
originated with Laurence and was transferred to Vincent because of
the similarity of the legends. If so, it is unlikely that Ælfric himself
initiated the transfer, for the reading is used for Vincent in continental
texts after his time. He presumably followed the practice of those
English monasteries which had already developed a cult of St. Vincent
in the tenth century.

ÆLFRIC'S REASONS FOR WRITING A HOMILY ON VINCENT

In general, Vincent seems not to have held any special status in Anglo-
Saxon England. He appears in the *Old English Martyrology*, but this
source is so eclectic that no particular significance should be attached
to his inclusion.[2] Similarly, although in early eleventh-century English
calendars, Vincent's name invariably appears beside his feast (22 January), it is only rarely marked out as being more than an ordinary saint's
day. Other saints are awarded a high ranking much more often. It
seems most likely, therefore, that a homily on Vincent was specially
commissioned. Evidence that such commissions did occur is found,
for example, in Ælfric's Latin Preface to his *Sermo in Natale Unius
Confessoris*, which, as he tells us, was undertaken at the request of
Bishop Æthelwold II.[3] Two main types of evidence, calendars and
accounts of relics, can be examined in order to discover whence such a
commission might have derived.

In four contemporary calendars, Vincent's feast is awarded first or
second class status. The two calendars marking it with an 'S' (denoting second class importance) are Oxford, Bodleian Library, Bodley
579 (the Leofric Missal), 39ʳ-44ᵛ, and BL, Add. 37517 (the Bosworth

---

[1] Since in his First Series homily on Laurence (CH I xxix), Ælfric had restricted
himself to narrative only, he was therefore free to expound John xii. 24–6 in a homily on
St. Vincent.

[2] *Das altenglische Martyrologium*, ed. G. Kotzor, 2 vols., Bayerische Akademie der
Wissenschaften, Abhandlungen, phil.-hist. Klasse, N.S., 88 1/2 (Munich, 1981) II, 23–4.
The entry for Vincent is discussed by J. E. Cross in 'Saints' Lives in Old English: Latin
Manuscripts and Vernacular Accounts: The *Old English Martyrology*', *Peritia*, i (1982),
38–62.

[3] Assmann iv, p. 49 (Latin note preceding homily).

Psalter), fols. 2–3.[1] The Leofric Missal calendar was written at Glastonbury, probably in AD 979, that in the Bosworth Psalter at St. Augustine's, Canterbury, between 988 and 1012.[2] The two manuscripts awarding it first class rank ('in cappis' and 'in albis' respectively) are BL, Cotton Vitellius E. xviii, 2ʳ–7ᵛ, and BL, Arundel 155, 2ʳ–7ᵛ.[3] Vitellius E. xviii was written at Winchester, s. xi[1]; Arundel 155 is from Christ Church, Canterbury, written between 1012 and 1023.[4]

At first glance, the widespread provenance of these manuscripts seems to undermine any attempt to pinpoint a particular centre at which Vincent might have held a special status. But this apparently random distribution is deceptive. The Bosworth Psalter, although written at Canterbury, derives originally from a Glastonbury text. This immediately connects it with the Leofric Missal. Comparison of the two calendars by Gasquet and Bishop has shown that they both derive independently from a common Glastonbury source: the Bosworth Psalter compiler 'had before him a Glastonbury calendar but not that which is now found in the Leofric Missal'.[5] If the 'S' beside Vincent was copied from the Glastonbury source, then Glastonbury can be identified as one centre with particular respect for Vincent at the end of the tenth century.

The two calendars which award Vincent first class status are also more closely related than at first appears. Although Arundel 155 was written at Christ Church Canterbury, the calendar is derived from a Winchester manuscript. Its links with the late eleventh-century BL, Arundel 60 of Winchester were observed by Gasquet and Bishop: 'Arundel 155 is the post-Conquest calendar of Winchester represented in a calendar of . . . Arundel MS. 60; which last named calendar itself is substantially the same as that in use before the Conquest as preserved in Cotton MS. Vitellius E XVIII.'[6] Ker confirms the similarities between the calendars of Arundel 60 and Vitellius E. xviii, and compares them also with the calendars in two other manuscripts, Cambridge, Trinity College R. 15. 32 (s. xi[1]) and BL, Cotton Titus D.

---

[1] *English Kalendars Before A.D. 1100*, ed. F. Wormald, HBS 72 (London, 1934), nos. 4 and 5. The provenance and dates of the manuscripts are Wormald's, unless otherwise noted.

[2] A. G. Watson, *Catalogue of Dated and Datable Manuscripts c. 435–1600 in Oxford Libraries*, 2 vols. (Oxford, 1984) I, 19, most recently supports '979?' for the date of Bodley 579.

[3] *English Kalendars*, nos. 12 and 13.

[4] Ker, *Catalogue*, p. 298, dates Vitellius E. xviii to s. xiᵐᵉᵈ.

[5] F. A. Gasquet and E. Bishop, *The Bosworth Psalter* (London, 1908), p. 21.

[6] *The Bosworth Psalter*, p. 30.

xxvi (s. xi[1] (1023–35)).[1] By using manuscripts whose provenance is known, Ker is able to establish that the calendars all derive from the New Minster rather than the cathedral priory of Winchester. The attribution of first class markings to Vincent in the Vitellius E. xviii and Arundel 155 calendars thus suggests that Vincent was held in high regard at the New Minster, Winchester, as well as at Glastonbury.

The special status of Vincent at Winchester and Glastonbury seems to have been linked in both cases with the possession of relics, at least according to the testimony of later documents. In a twelfth-century addition to the eleventh-century *Liber Vitae* of New Minster, Winchester (also known as the Hyde Register), Vincent is mentioned twice in a list of relics: 'brachium Sancti Vincentii leuite et Martyris' and 'reliquie Sancti Vincentii'.[2] According to Geffrei Gaimar's *L'Estoire des Engleis*, written in about 1135–40, Æthelred was pronounced king (in 978) before the altar of St. Vincent at Winchester.[3]

In documents associated with Glastonbury, relics of Vincent also play a prominent role. William of Malmesbury, in his twelfth-century account *De Antiquitate Glastonie Ecclesie*, reports that a large vessel, 'argento et auro coopertum, cum ymaginibus ex ebore decenter intersertis, continens reliquias sancti Uincencii et capud sancti Apolinaris', was given by King Edgar to Glastonbury.[4] In an annal for 1052, William of Malmesbury records that, after the desecration of his tomb, Edgar's bones were placed in the same shrine above the altar at Glastonbury as the relics of Vincent and Apollinaris.[5] William tells the same story in his *Gesta regum*.[6] John of Glastonbury, in his mid fourteenth-century Chronicle based partly on William of Malmesbury's *De Antiquitate Glastonie Ecclesie*, also claims that substantial

---

[1] Ker, *Catalogue*, pp. 167, 301. The resemblances between Vitellius E. xviii and Titus D. xxvi are also observed by T. A. M. Bishop in *English Caroline Minuscule* (Oxford, 1971), p. 23 (no. 26).

[2] *Liber Vitae: Register and Martyrology of New Minster and Hyde Abbey, Winchester*, ed. W. de Gray Birch (London and Winchester, 1892), pp. 147 and 149.

[3] Ed. A. Bell, Anglo-Norman Text Society, nos. 14–16 (Oxford, 1960), p. 129, ll. 4071–5. I have not been able to find the source for this claim. The *Anglo-Saxon Chronicle* enters Æthelred's coronation twice, once in 978 and once at Kingston ('æt Cinges tune') in 979; see *Two of the Saxon Chronicles Parallel*, ed. C. Plummer, 2 vols. (Oxford, 1892–9) I, 122. The 'Epistola Adelardi' in *Memorials of Saint Dunstan Archbishop of Canterbury*, ed. W. Stubbs, RS (London, 1874), p. 61, notes that both Edward and Æthelred were crowned and anointed by Dunstan, but gives no further details.

[4] *The Early History of Glastonbury: An Edition, Translation and Study of William of Malmesbury's 'De Antiquitate Glastonie Ecclesie'*, ed. J. Scott (Woodbridge, 1981), p. 130.

[5] *The Early History of Glastonbury*, p. 134.

[6] William of Malmesbury, *De Gestis Regum Anglorum*, ed. W. Stubbs, 2 vols., RS (London, 1887–9) I, 181.

relics of St. Vincent are to be found at Glastonbury: 'Ibi quoque sunt reliquie . . . Sancti Vincencii archidiaconi et martiris pro magna parte, quas perquisiuit pius rex Edgarus.'[1] The actual relics are listed in Cambridge, Trinity College R. 5. 33 (724), written in the thirteenth and fourteenth centuries, and containing miscellaneous items mainly relating to Glastonbury: 'In feretro apostolorum . . . continentur reliquiae beati Vincencii martiris, videlicet hanchia una, costa una, quatuor mustelli, de brachiis et tibiis, septimum os, et majus est extra.'[2]

Other places in England also laid claim to relics of Vincent, for example Peterborough (in a twelfth-century list in a Chronicle), and Exeter (whose late eleventh-century Old English relic-list I cited above).[3] However, these claims are late and therefore unreliable: in the case of Exeter, Rollason notes that the list cannot be an accurate account of the relics given by Athelstan to Exeter since 'it includes relics of three saints who lived after Athelstan's time'.[4] It is possible that this particular list is another manifestation of the history of 'replacing lost documents' at Exeter after Leofric moved the Devon bishopric there in 1050; Frank Barlow points out that whereas 'in a charter which Cnut gave to St Peter's in 1019 it is stated that the monastery's ancient charters had been destroyed by fire, . . . by the end of Leofric's episcopate his muniment room contained at least five charters in favour of the monastery attributed to King Athelstan, all clumsy fabrications'.[5]

---

[1] *The Chronicle of Glastonbury Abbey: An Edition, Translation and Study of John of Glaston-bury's 'Cronica sive Antiquitates Glastoniensis Ecclesie'*, ed. J. P. Carley (Woodbridge, 1985), p. 18. For information on the date and sources of the Chronicle, see the introduction to this edition.

[2] The manuscript was printed by T. Hearne as the 2nd vol. of his edition of the Chronicle. See *Johannis Glastoniensis Chronica sive Historia de Rebus Glastoniensibus*, 2 vols. (Oxford, 1726) II, 446. The exact meaning of the passage is obscure; I suggest the following: 'In the reliquary of the apostles . . . are kept the relics of the blessed martyr Vincent, namely one thigh-bone, one rib, four pieces from the forearms and shin-bones, the seventh bone (which) is externally larger.' I am grateful to Richard Sharpe of the Medieval Latin Dictionary and Timothy Hobbs of Trinity College Library, Cambridge, for their helpful comments.

[3] A full catalogue of the English religious houses whose relic-lists include Vincent's relics is given by I. G. Thomas, 'The Cult of Saints' Relics in Medieval England' (unpubl. PhD diss., London, 1974), p. 470. For Peterborough, see *The Chronicle of Hugh Candidus*, ed. W. T. Mellows (Oxford, 1949), pp. 54, 56; for Exeter, see Förster, *Zur Geschichte*, p. 73.

[4] 'Relic-cults', p. 92.

[5] F. Barlow, K. M. Dexter, A. M. Erskine, L. J. Lloyd, *Leofric of Exeter* (Exeter, 1972), p. 12.

One centre, however, offers more convincing evidence of its association with Vincent and his relics in the relevant period: the monastery of Abingdon.[1] Vincent's connection with Abingdon can be traced
in three documents. Two of these were written to record the history of
Abingdon abbey; they are also late, but include a curious diversity of
references. The first is the *Chronicon monasterii de Abingdon*, which
survives in two manuscripts, one from the late twelfth and one from
the late thirteenth century.[2] The second is entitled *De abbatibus
Abbendoniae*, and is a short account of the abbots of Abingdon, extant
in one early thirteenth-century manuscript.[3] From these two documents we can trace a chronological series of references to St. Vincent.
Shortly after AD 940, a chapel dedicated to St. Vincent was apparently
built by a woman from Culham: 'Sepulta est Ælfida matrona iste in
capella quam in honore sancti Vincentii aedificaverat.'[4] Even if, as
seems likely, the actual site of the chapel were Culham rather than
Abingdon, the proximity of the two makes a connection indisputable.[5]
This is valuable evidence for an early interest in Vincent at Abingdon,
although the reason for the dedication is unclear: the chapel probably
pre-dated Abingdon's acquisition of Vincent's relics. The actual relics
of Vincent claimed by Abingdon are listed in its Chronicle: 'De Sancto
Vincentio brachium et hance, et pars spatulae et costa ejus.'[6] The
Abingdon records offer two accounts of how these relics came to
Abingdon. The Chronicle suggests that the bones were given to
Abingdon by Edgar (who reigned 959–78): 'cujus sacrae reliquiae a

[1] The association of Vincent with Abingdon has been discussed also by A. Thacker,
'Æthelwold and Abingdon', in *Bishop Æthelwold: His Career and Influence*, ed. B. Yorke
(Woodbridge, 1988), pp. 43–64, pp. 60–1.

[2] *Chronicon Monasterii de Abingdon*, ed. J. Stevenson, 2 vols., RS (London, 1858) (not
including the Appendices); hereafter cited as *CMA*. The two manuscripts are BL,
Cotton Claudius C. ix (s. xii^ex), and BL, Cotton Claudius B. vi (s. xiii^ex); the text in the
edition is mainly from the latter. The dates are those assigned by Ker in *Medieval
Libraries of Great Britain*, p. 3. F. M. Stenton, *The Early History of the Abbey of Abingdon*
(Reading, 1913), pp. 4–6, also notes that the editor conflates a twelfth-century account
with a thirteenth-century one.

[3] Appendix II in *Chronicon Monasterii de Abingdon*, ed. Stevenson II, 268–95; hereafter
cited as *AA*. The manuscript, BL, Cotton Vitellius A. xiii, is dated s. xiii^in by Ker,
Medieval Libraries of Great Britain, p. 3.

[4] *CMA* I, 92.

[5] The issue of the chapel's site is raised by M. Biddle, G. Lambrick and J. N. L.
Myres, in 'The Early History of Abingdon, Berkshire, and its Abbey', *Medieval
Archaeology*, xii (1968), 26–69. Lambrick takes the view that the chapel was at Culham,
noting that Culham Church 'constituted what was virtually a "peculiar" of Abingdon
Abbey' (p. 47, n. 66). Biddle, however, concludes from the dedication to St. Vincent that
the chapel was an Abingdon building (p. 64, n. 157).

[6] *CMA* II, 156.

tempore Eadgari regis maxima habentur veneratione hoc in monas-
terio, ab ipso . . . exquisitae'.[1] This account would allow for the
possibility that Edgar shared out relics of Vincent between Abingdon
and Glastonbury. According to *De abbatibus Abbendoniae*, however, the
monks of Abingdon stole the relics of St. Vincent and the head of St.
Apollinaris from monks of Glastonbury during Osgar's abbacy at
Abingdon (963–84): 'In cujus tempore furati sunt monachi Aben-
doniae reliquias Sancti Vincentii, et caput Sanctae Apollinaris, et
multas alias reliquias, [a] monachis Glestoniae.'[2] The practice of
stealing relics seems to have been common in the Anglo-Saxon
period. Indeed, as P. J. Geary has shown, great pride was taken in their
theft.[3] Relics were regarded not as attributes of the saints but as the
saints themselves, who moved from place to place only voluntarily;
stealing a relic was therefore possible only if the saint consented to his
or her transfer. Other arguments were put forward to justify such
despoliation. The relics would benefit the community to which they
were translated; also the new guardians of the relics could give the
bones the protection they deserved, a degree of security manifestly not
afforded by their previous owners. All this, however, does not in itself
authenticate the account of the theft of Vincent's relics. Given the
existence of such sanctions for relic theft, a monastery might well
fabricate evidence to support its claim to particular relics. Similarities
between the Glastonbury list of relics of Vincent and the Abingdon
one (both include a thigh-bone, fore-arm and rib) suggest that they
may have been describing one set of bones to which they had com-
peting claims, rather than discrete collections. The theft story
recounted by Abingdon was perhaps an attempt to discredit the
Glastonbury claims, by acknowledging that although Glastonbury
may originally have possessed relics of Vincent, these were transferred
to Abingdon at a fairly early date. Two other factors point to the
apocryphal nature of the Abingdon account in *De abbatibus Abbendoniae*. Stenton comments on the general unreliability of this work; it
comprises a 'romantic narrative' by an 'imaginative' author, which
strikingly illustrates 'the practice of mediaeval chroniclers to multiply
fictitious detail'.[4] And Thomas argues that 'in this form at least the
story is fictitious, for although at Glastonbury the head of S. Apol-

---

[1] *CMA* II, 48.   [2] *AA*, p. 280.
[3] *'Furta Sacra': Thefts of Relics in the Central Middle Ages* (Princeton, 1978), pp. 132–57.
See also D. Sox, *Relics and Shrines* (London, 1985), pp. 41–60.
[4] *Early History*, pp. 1–2.

linaris was always mentioned in connection with the relics of S. Vincent there, the former saint is not mentioned in the Abingdon relic-list or anywhere else in the chronicle, so that Abingdon's claim to relics of him was obviously not of long standing'.[1]

Even if the account of the theft were no more than a twelfth-century fabrication, Vincent's high status in Abingdon from an early date is supported by several other references in the Abingdon documents. In 1016, according to the Chronicle, King Cnut gave a reliquary to Abingdon to house Vincent's relics; later, in the time of Abbot Ingulf (1130–59), the reliquary was sold to help the poor during a great famine.[2] Vincent's feast was elevated to the status 'in cappis' by Abbot Faritius at the beginning of the twelfth century.[3]

These Abingdon claims to have possessed relics in the tenth and eleventh centuries are recorded, like those of Winchester and Glastonbury, only in documents of the twelfth century or later. One other text, however, provides more important and more contemporary evidence for linking Vincent with Abingdon. This is the Old English tract on the resting-places of the saints.[4] The tract is another sign of the important role of relics in the Anglo-Saxon period; as D. W. Rollason suggests, 'resting-place lists were perhaps a celebration of the saintly wealth of the Anglo-Saxons'.[5] It survives in two eleventh-century manuscripts, one of which is the *Liber Vitae* of New Minster, Winchester.[6] According to Liebermann, it was compiled some time between 1013 and 1030.[7] The document states that Vincent's remains, or at least the bulk of them, lie at Abingdon: 'Ðonne resteð on Abbandune sanctus Uincentius martir.'[8] Clearly relics of Vincent were associated closely with Abingdon in the early eleventh century.[9]

The writer who might have been expected to give the earliest and

---

[1] 'The Cult of Saints' Relics', p. 151.

[2] *CMA* I, 433–4, 443, II, 214; *AA*, p. 291.

[3] *AA*, p. 287. In a further document outlining arrangements for the provision of wine, Vincent's feast has been elevated with an octave; see *Chronicon Monasterii de Abingdon*, ed. Stevenson, II, 315.

[4] *Die Heiligen Englands*, ed. F. Liebermann (Hannover, 1889).

[5] 'Lists of Saints' Resting-places in Anglo-Saxon England', *ASE*, vii (1978), 61–93, p. 82.

[6] CCCC 201 (Ker, *Catalogue*, no. 49b, items 54–5), and BL, Stowe 944 (Ker, *Catalogue*, no. 274, item (d)); the latter is printed by Birch, *Liber Vitae*, pp. 87–96.

[7] *Die Heiligen Englands*, p. xiii.

[8] Ibid., p. 15.

[9] The *Chronicle* of Hugh Candidus, whilst claiming relics of Vincent for Peterborough, includes also an amplified version of the OE tract on the resting-places of the saints which assigns Vincent to Abingdon; see Mellows' edition, p. 59.

most reliable testimony on this subject is Ælfric: he was in a position to know about the various claims, and he often ends his saints' lives with details of the resting places of the saint's bones. But in this case he is strangely silent. Although the earliest extant accounts of Vincent's martyrdom offer no information about the distribution of his bones, Ælfric used a later version of the legend as his source. This source, identified by Patrick Zettel, belongs to a collection of saints' lives known as the 'Cotton-Corpus Legendary' (probably composed in the late ninth century).[1] It combines material from the *passio amplissima* and the *passio fusior*, and also adds a few details of its own.[2] Ælfric's conclusion to his narrative follows the Cotton-Corpus account which provides an epilogue on the dispersal of Vincent's bones.[3] This epilogue does give some indication of the distribution of the relics: such was Vincent's popularity 'ut reliquiae eius non solum apud Hispanias sed etiam apud Galliarum provincias miro excolantur affectu'.[4] Ælfric, however, whom we might expect to have reproduced these details about Spain and Gaul, substitutes a vague statement: 'and his halȝan ban wurdon wide todælede, and mid mycelre lufe hi man wyrðaþ ȝehwær' (iv. 279–80).[5] This apparent reluctance to specify a location for Vincent's relics may suggest that Ælfric knew of other claims to them nearer home, but was unwilling to commit himself. This would be especially likely if he had no reliable account as to how they could have reached England. His uninformative account does at least leave open the possibility that the bones survived in an English monastery.

If, as I have argued, Ælfric's homily on Vincent was specially commissioned, the question arises as to which monastic centre might have been responsible for this commission. The New Minster at Winchester and Glastonbury are both possible candidates. Certainly Ælfric had close connections with Winchester, but the calendar evidence is not consistent in giving Vincent special status there (only

---

[1] 'Saints' Lives in Old English: Latin Manuscripts and Vernacular Accounts: Ælfric', *Peritia*, i (1982), 17–37.

[2] The Cotton-Corpus *vita* of Vincent is edited by A. Fábrega Grau in *Pasionario Hispanico II*, Monumenta Hispaniae sacra, serie Litúrgica 6 (Madrid, 1955), 187–96.

[3] This epilogue is not found in the *vita* proper as printed by Fábrega Grau, but is provided by the manuscripts of the Cotton-Corpus collection; see Zettel, 'Saints' Lives in Old English', p. 30.

[4] BL, Cotton Nero E. i, part 1, 121ᵛ. The passage is printed in full by Zettel in 'Saints' Lives in Old English', pp. 30–1.

[5] Elsewhere, for example in his *Life of St. Oswald*, Ælfric adds the current resting-place of the bones (LS xxvi, 283–5).

two out of the five New Minster calendars discussed above mark out his feast), and the list of saints' resting-places shows that the New Minster did not claim to possess the relics of the saint at that time, but believed them to be at Abingdon. Glastonbury, on the other hand, had no known connection with Ælfric, and its claims to relics are also not recorded till the twelfth century. 'The evidence suggests', Rollason notes, 'that from the tenth century onwards the monks of Glastonbury were increasingly forceful in claiming for their monastery a high antiquity and the possession of important relics.'[1]

It was perhaps Abingdon that had in Ælfric's lifetime the best claim to, and special interest in, the saint, and also strong reasons for eliciting Ælfric's assistance. Ælfric must have developed a connection with Abingdon during his time at Winchester, and through his association with Æthelwold. Æthelwold had been granted Abingdon by King Eadred, and remained abbot there from 954 to 963. In 963 he was elevated to the bishopric of Winchester, a post which he held up to his death in 984. During that period Ælfric was Æthelwold's pupil. In his Latin *Vita S. Æthelwoldi* (written in 1006), Ælfric stresses Æthelwold's revitalizing influence on Abingdon, noting how dilapidated it was prior to Æthelwold's abbacy: 'erat tunc destitutum ac neglectum, uilibus edificiis consistens et quadraginta tantum mansas possidens'.[2] Moreover it was monks from Abingdon who in 964 replaced the expelled clerks at the Old and New Minsters at Winchester, probably under Æthelwold's initiative.[3] In his *Vita S. Æthelwoldi*, Ælfric states that the clerks were driven out by the bishop with the king's licence, and his English *Life of St. Swithhun* records that the clerks were 'adræfed | for heora unþeawum þurh æðelwold bisceop'.[4] Whether Æthelwold or Edgar was responsible, the influx of Abingdon monks into the New Minster again testifies to a close link between those two centres during the time of Ælfric's residence.

The homily on Vincent was not written till much later in Ælfric's career. Clemoes tentatively assigns it to the period 1002–5, after the publication of the *Lives of Saints* but before Ælfric's reorganization and expansion of his series of liturgical homilies (TH I and TH II).[5] Many of Ælfric's occasional pieces, however, were being written around

---

[1] 'Relic-cults', p. 101.

[2] *Three Lives of English Saints*, ed. M. Winterbottom, Toronto Medieval Latin Texts (Toronto, 1972), p. 20.

[3] See Stenton, *Anglo-Saxon England*, p. 451.

[4] *Three Lives*, p. 23; LS xxi, 27–8, see also 83–5.

[5] Clemoes, 'Chronology', pp. 244–5.

1005 (between TH I and TH II), the date of Ælfric's move to Eynsham, and it is tempting to see the close proximity of Abingdon and Eynsham as providing the opportunity for the Abingdon monks to seek his help.

The reasons why the Abingdon monks might have requested such a homily in the vernacular remain to be considered. It is clear that enhancing a saint's importance in any way was considered beneficial for the centre of that saint's worship; Rollason notes that 'reformed monasteries sought to reinforce their claims to be the spiritual leaders of late Anglo-Saxon England by presenting themselves as promoters of the cult of saints and guardians of their relics'.[1] To that end every monastery observed a number of feasts on its own account, and these feasts were often 'those of the patron saints of the abbey, or of any whose bodies or other relics rested there'.[2] The Abingdon monks might well have seen many advantages in celebrating more fully a saint whose relics were associated with their monastery. The composition of the homily in the vernacular implies that its audience was intended to include the laity, probably in the context of the mass.[3] In keeping with this, Ælfric assures his audience he will not write at too great a length, and begins his exposition of John xii. 24–6 with a simple agrarian image (ll. 300–3). Like Assmann iv, however, the homily was probably actually commissioned by a bishop or monks. Certainly Ælfric seems to expect monks and probably secular clergy to be amongst the audience, since he includes items appropriate to them in his list of the ways men serve God (ll. 340–5). Ælfric also adds, independently of his source, a warning against drunkenness, a vice which he characteristically regards as being particularly prevalent amongst the clergy.[4]

The circumstances leading to Ælfric's composition of this homily on St. Vincent provide a fascinating witness to the curious ways of hagiography. The initial popularity of this fourth-century Spanish saint is unquestionable. But his cult was apparently overshadowed by

[1] 'The Shrines of Saints in Later Anglo-Saxon England: Distribution and Significance', *The Anglo-Saxon Church: Papers on History, Architecture, and Archaeology in Honour of Dr H M Taylor*, ed. L. A. S. Butler and R. K. Morris (London, 1986), 32–43, p. 38.

[2] Knowles, *The Monastic Order in England*, p. 542.

[3] For a discussion of the context in which Ælfric's homilies might have been preached, see Gatch, *Preaching and Theology*, pp. 40–59, and Clayton, 'Homiliaries and Preaching'.

[4] See, for example, Assmann i, 140–50; CH II, p. 2 (Latin *Ammonitio*); Fehr, Brief I, p. 18, ll. 1–6. Bethurum, p. 344, notes that there were repeated contemporary accusations against the English for drunkenness.

his Roman counterpart Laurence, who acquired part of Vincent's legend and shared with him a gospel lesson. By the late tenth and early eleventh centuries, Vincent's cult had travelled across to England, possibly reinforced by a collection of his relics: certainly several Anglo-Saxon monasteries came to restore some prominence to Vincent, and to believe that they possessed these relics. It was such an interest, probably in the form of a commission, that prompted Ælfric to write his account of the saint and the accompanying gospel exposition. Although Ælfric is cautious enough not to commit himself on any particular location for the relics, his reference in the final lines of the *passio* to the wide distribution of Vincent's bones does allow for the possibility that some may have been translated as far afield as the Anglo-Saxon centre of Abingdon.

SOURCES AND ANALOGUES

Ælfric derived the two parts of his homily from quite separate sources. With the *Lives of Saints* fresh in his mind, it is not surprising that for the *passio* section of his Vincent homily Ælfric turned to the Cotton-Corpus Legendary which had been the main source for his Lives.[1] Zettel allows that Ælfric may have drawn on another source to complete his Life, as yet not conclusively identified.[2] In this edition of the Vincent *passio*, I cite the passages from the Cotton-Corpus Life which Ælfric has rendered into English and also the *additamentum* to the *passio amplissima* which, although not in the *vita* proper as printed by Fábrega Grau, is 'provided by the manuscripts of the Cotton-Corpus collection in the concluding sentences of their version of Vincent's life'.[3]

Ælfric is generally conservative in his treatment of his source for the Vincent *passio*. The opening section (ll. 1–21), therefore, which is not at all close to the main source, is most likely, as Zettel suggests, to have derived from a second source. Ælfric is closer here to the *passio amplissima* and *passio fusior* version (quoted in source material), but there are no verbal correspondences between the two passages. None of the central details included in the Latin is found in the Old English (for example, the names of Vincent's parents, Vincent's noble ancestry, Valerius' speech impediment), though this is not in itself evidence; as

---

[1] See p. 90 n. 2 above.
[2] Zettel, 'Saints' Lives in Old English', p. 30.
[3] Ibid.

a general principle in his Lives, Bethurum has noted, Ælfric 'omits doctrinal matter, historical detail, and names that would be unfamiliar to his hearers'.[1] It is most likely, however, that some other secondary source was used, or that Ælfric composed the opening independently.

Ælfric's tendency is to abridge and compress his source, par-ticularly towards the end where he omits large passages. He adds very little, except for occasional explanatory comments; the most notable addition is his image of a web: 'and hine [Vincent] hetelice tihton | swa swa man web tiht' (ll. 102–3). Occasionally Ælfric is closer to the *passio amplissima* or to the Cotton-Corpus manuscripts than to the text as printed in Fábrega Grau; these instances are at lines 144–5 and line 191, and at the very end of Ælfric's homily where he follows the *additamentum* in his reference to the distribution of Vincent's relics.

For the second part of his homily on St. Vincent, the exposition of John xii. 24–6, the identification of sources is by no means straight-forward. Four patristic authors contain material close to Ælfric's commentary: Augustine, Smaragdus, Haymo, and Alcuin.[2] Of these, Alcuin corresponds to Ælfric more extensively than any of the other authors. Alcuin's *Commentaria*, supplemented occasionally by mater-ial from Haymo's homily (generally close in meaning to Alcuin though with little direct verbal correspondence), would account neatly for nearly all of Ælfric's homily. According to Pope, however, Alcuin's *Commentaria* was rarely, if ever, used by Ælfric as a source, and Ælfric may never have encountered it as a separate work.[3] Moreover, all the material included by Alcuin would have been available to Ælfric else-where. Alcuin's commentary consists largely of excerpts from Augus-tine's Tractate on John, and Smaragdus draws on Alcuin for his homily on St. Laurence. Neither Augustine nor Smaragdus alone can have been Ælfric's source; some of Ælfric's material exists only in one or other of these texts. If Ælfric did draw on Augustine and Smarag-dus, he must again have supplemented their commentaries from the Haymo homily.

The choice, as with homily i, is between a larger number of well-known Ælfrician sources or a smaller number of sources which include an uncertain Ælfrician source. Either Ælfric drew on Augus-

---

[1] D. Bethurum, 'The Form of Ælfric's *Lives of Saints*', *Studies in Philology*, xxix (1932), 515–33, p. 520.

[2] Augustine, *In Ioannis Euangelium Tractatus*, li. 9–12, CCSL 36, 442–5; Smaragdus, PL 102, cols. 437–9; Haymo, *Homiliae de Tempore*, PL 118, cols. 763–5; Alcuin, *Commentaria in S. Ioannis Evangelium*, PL 100, cols. 911–13.

[3] Pope, pp. 161–2.

tine and Smaragdus, with occasional recourse to Haymo, or he drew
mainly on Alcuin, again supplementing him occasionally from
Haymo. The selection and ordering of material is here crucial. Since
Alcuin was predominantly a derivative writer, he can only be identified as a main source through his similarity to Ælfric in arrangement
of material. The source material from Alcuin which I provide for
Ælfric's exposition derives from other patristic authors as follows:

for lines 304–12 and 323–7 Alcuin corresponds to Augustine;
for lines 328–34 the first sentence of Alcuin corresponds to Augustine and the rest of the section to Smaragdus;
for lines 335–8 Alcuin corresponds to Smaragdus;
for lines 340–7 and 349–51 Alcuin corresponds to Augustine;
for lines 352–7 Alcuin corresponds to Augustine, except for the
sentence beginning 'Merces est . . .' which resembles Haymo;
for lines 358–68 Alcuin corresponds to Augustine.

Is it likely that Ælfric selected independently a passage from Augustine, then one from Smaragdus, then another from Augustine, then
one from Haymo, then finally back to Augustine, when the whole
sequence of these particular excerpts is found ready-made in Alcuin?
The similarity in arrangement seems too striking to be coincidental.
Did Ælfric after all have direct access to Alcuin, perhaps only late in
his career, after he had already composed the majority of his homilies?

This kind of evidence is by no means conclusive, but it does make
Alcuin's *Commentaria* the most likely source for the homily.

The complex relationship between this second part of the Vincent
homily and its sources may make a sequential comparison of the two
useful, particularly since Ælfric diverges from his sources in matter
and emphasis at various points. He opens his commentary with a
characteristic assurance to his audience that he will not write at too
great a length (ll. 297–9), perhaps particularly appropriate here after
the reading of Vincent's *passio*. Following this Ælfric, again independently of his sources, inserts an explanation of John xii. 24 from an
agricultural point of view: a seed which remains whole on the ground
does not germinate (ll. 300–3). The everyday, practical explanation is
typical of Ælfric. Like Alcuin (and Haymo), Ælfric now compares
Christ to a grain of wheat, 'mortificandum et multiplicandum', that is,
'þe sealde his lif for us' (l. 305), and 'he micelne wæstm of moncynne
aber þurh his anes deað, þe swiðe deorewurðe is' (ll. 306–7). Ælfric
extends the analogy, equating the crop from the grain of wheat with
sinful mankind, and the barn with heaven: 'and he bringæð þone

wæstm, þæt beo we synfulle, into þe wynsume bærne þare ecan wununge' (ll. 308–9). For this, Ælfric is probably recalling the parable in Matth. xiii. 24 ff., which distinguishes the tares which are to be burned from the wheat which is to be gathered into the barn; the tares represent the wicked and the wheat the righteous. In this whole passage, Ælfric differs slightly in his interpretation from Alcuin (and Haymo). For Alcuin the wheat represents the name of Christ and the crop represents the faith. For Ælfric, however, the wheat represents Christ himself and the crop represents the righteous people. Alcuin's emphasis is typological, Ælfric's anagogical.

Ælfric now, like Alcuin (and Haymo), distinguishes between the Jews and the faithful; 'mortificandum infidelitate Judaeorum, multiplicandum fide omnium populorum' is rendered fairly closely by 'he was ða dead þurh þa Iudeiscan, and he cwicede us þe on hine lyfæð' (ll. 310–11). At lines 313–15 Ælfric emphasizes the contrast and here his source seems to be Haymo:

Nam ejus nomen tanto magis crescit in fide credentium, quanto per mortem in perfidia Judaeorum est exstinctum.

Similarly his next point that the grain of wheat aptly represents Christ since it excels all other grains (ll. 316–19) has an equivalent only in Haymo:

Et pulchre Dominus grano triciti comparatur, quia sicut in omnibus annonis nihil frumento pulchrius, nihil est delectabilius: ita ipse omnes creaturas excellit, quia nihil eo suavius, nihil dulcius invenitur.

Ælfric's choice of the term 'iclænsod' to describe the grain of wheat (where Haymo uses 'pulchrius' and 'delectabilius') may derive from the parable cited above where the wheat was 'purified' from the tares at the time of harvest.

For his next section (ll. 323–34), Ælfric returns to Alcuin's commentary. He reorders Alcuin in order to stress the theme of gaining happiness in the eternal life, and he adds a specific reference to St. Paul's warning against drunkenness (1 Cor. vi. 10).

Ælfric, like Alcuin, explains that 'ðeo sawla' of the gospel-text means 'þisse sceorte life', and he blesses those who hate this life and 'wislice libban' in order to attain eternal happiness with God. Again like Alcuin, Ælfric turns to praise of the holy martyrs for adhering to this doctrine: they 'swa mycel forsæȝen þis andwearde lif, þæt heom leofere wæs to swæltanne for þæs Hælendes namen ær þam þe heo hine wiðsocen' (ll. 335–7). The specific reference to Vincent (l. 338) is, of course, Ælfric's own, a relic of the text's original function as the second part of a Vincent homily.

Ælfric begins his commentary on the first part of John xii. 26 with a description of ways in which men serve Christ (ll. 340–5). Five different ways are outlined: divine service at appointed times, mass and prayers, living in purity, giving up one's life, and almsgiving. He concludes that 'swa hwa swa deð his Drihtnes willan on eniȝe wisan he þenæð him sylfum' (ll. 346–7). An equivalent list appears in Alcuin, though Ælfric has not followed Alcuin very closely. First, the location of the list is not Alcuin's, since his is found only in the final section of his commentary on John xii. 24–6, not otherwise used by Ælfric. Secondly, Ælfric's list only partially corresponds to Alcuin's in its components. Alcuin recommends three ways of serving Christ: living well, almsgiving, and preaching Christ's name and doctrine. Of these, only the second corresponds closely to Ælfric.

It is instructive to note here some curious parallels between Ælfric and Haymo. Haymo also describes ways in which men serve Christ, and the location of his list does correspond to Ælfric's. Moreover some of Haymo's items which are not in Alcuin appear in Ælfric. Haymo, in his list, distinguishes those who speak well (confessors), those who die in Christ's name (martyrs), and those who give alms (the faithful laity). The second and third categories directly correspond to Ælfric (the third overlapping with Alcuin). Ælfric, then, seems indebted to Haymo rather than Alcuin at this point in his commentary, although he has not kept particularly close even to Haymo.

Ælfric's divergence from Alcuin may suggest that he had a different audience in mind. His omission of Alcuin's reference to preaching and his independent addition of three items are particularly interesting. The three items added are divine service at appointed times, mass and prayers, and living in purity. These represent a distinct shift of emphasis towards the monastic life. There is no evidence that Ælfric expected his audience to have much direct contact with the laity: he has omitted Alcuin's reference to preaching and Haymo's choice of 'confessores'. This section of exposition, then, gives us a valuable insight into the audience to which Ælfric directed the homily; it is monks and, perhaps, secular clergy, who are in his mind when he outlines the various ways in which men serve Christ.

For the rest of this homily, Ælfric remains close to Alcuin. His tendency is to clarify and elaborate Alcuin's commentary. In lines

350–1, he explains independently, for example, that to follow Christ's example means 'on rihtwisnesse and soðfestnessæ simle þeniæn'. At line 353, Ælfric, like Alcuin, emphasizes the heavenly reward to be gained by following Christ; Ælfric describes expansively the bliss of heaven. Alcuin continues to expound what it means to serve Christ, but Ælfric omits that final section of his main source and ends here with a closing prayer.

XI KAL FEBR, PASSIO SANCTI VINCENTII MARTYRIS.

On Ispanian lande þære Speoniscan leode
wæs se halʒa martir þe hatte Uincentius
to menn ʒeboren, and mid his maʒum afedd,
on mycclum (cristen)dome, and he on Cristes lare   5
wel þeonde wæs, oðð æt he wearð ʒehadod
to halʒum diacone, þam Helende þeowiende
mid þam mæran bisceope Ualerium,
se wæs þa mære lareow on Ispanian lande,
swa swa seo ʒereccednysse us seʒð on Ledenum ʒereorde.   10
þa aras seo ehtnys þæra arleasra cwelleræ
wide ʒeond þas world wodlice swiðe
onʒean Cristes ʒeleafan, and onʒean þa Cristenan menn,
for þan þe se deofol wolde adwæscan þone ʒeleafan
mid þam mycelam ehtnessum, and þam ormetum witum;   15
ac swa man ma ofsloh þara martira þa,
swa þær ma ʒelyfdon þyrh þa mycclan wundra
þe þa halʒan ʒeworhtan, þurh þæs Helendes mihte;
for þam þe soða ʒeleafa þæs soðfestan Godes

CUL Ii. 1. 33, fols. 128ᵛ–132ᵛ; LS II, pp. 426–43. From l. 284, Bodley 343, fols. 121ᵛ–122; Belfour, pp. 74–7.

---

4 maʒum `fæʒere´    5 mycclum `þeawum´   cristendome] cristen cristen dome, *with first* cristen *underlined and* 7 *on written opposite in the LH margin*   he `eac´ 7 halʒum `ercan´   13 menn `ðe God lufedon´   19 soðfestan] n *altered from another letter* (s?)

SOURCES. 1. *The* Passio

The texts cited here are: (i) Fábrega Grau, *Pasionario Hispanico*, II, 187–96 (cited as Fábrega Grau); (ii) *Anal. Boll.*, I (1882), 263–70; (iii) *Acta SS*, 22 Jan., II, 394–8; (iv) BL MS Cotton Nero Ei, part 1.

1–13 (*Ælfric here is closer to the* passio fusior *and* passio amplissima *text than to Fábrega Grau*)

(*Anal. Boll., I, 263* [*cf. Acta SS, 394*]) Beatus Vincentius extitit patre Euticio progenitus, qui fuit Agesi nobilissimi consulis filius: mater vero ejus Enola ex Osca urbe noscitur procreata. Qui a pueritia studiis litterarum traditus, superna providente clementia, quae sibi eum praevidebat vas electionis futurum, gemina scientia, sub beato Valerio Caesareae Augustae civitatis episcopo efficacissime claruit; a quo etiam sanctitate insignis diaconii apicem suscepit. Et quoniam idem episcopus impeditioris linguae fuisse dignoscitur, tradito doctrinae ministerio venerabili Vincentio, ipse orationi et divinae contemplationi sedulus insistebat. At vero memoratus archidiaconus vices saepe dicti pontificis diligenter et opportune exequebatur.

14–21 (*Probably Ælfric's independent elaboration*)

ne byð næfre adwæsced, þurh þa deofollican ehtnysse,   20
ac byð swiðor ʒeeacnod swa swa us seʒað bec.

On þam daʒum wæs þa sum heretoʒa wælhreow,
Datianus ʒehaten, swiðe hetol ehtere
on anre heafodbyriʒ on þam foresædan lande,
þe beʒeat | æt þam casere þæt he acwellan moste   fol. 129
þa halʒan Cristenan menn mid mislicum witum.   26

Him ʒeuþe þa se casere, swa swa us cyþað bec,
þæt se wælhreowa ehtere þone anweald hæfde,
þæt he moste acwellan þa Cristenan mid witum,
for þam þe hi beʒen wæron mid bealowe afyllede,   30
Criste wiðerwinnan mid wodlicre reðnysse.

Hwæt þa Datianus, se deofollica cwellere,
on þam anwealde þe he underfanʒen hæfde,
ʒecydde his wodnysse ofer þa Cristenan menn,
and beʒan to dreccenne mid dyrstiʒum anʒinne   35
þa halʒum bisceopas, and þa ʒehadodan preostas.

Wolde ærest þa heafodmen þæs halʒan ʒeleafan
mid witum oferswiðan, þæt he syððan mihte
þa læssan ofercuman and fram heora ʒeleafan ʒebiʒan.

þa efste se bisceop and se eadiʒa Uincentius   40
to þam æðelan martirdome;
þohtan þæt hi wurdon witodlice ʒesæliʒe,
ʒif hi mid estfulnesse eardlice underfenʒon
þone wuldorfullan cynehelm heora martyrdomes,
þurh þa andætnysse þæs Hælendes ʒeleafan.   45

---

21 seʒað `ure'     29 Cristenan `men'   31 Criste] `and' criste`s'
36 preostas `and þa diacones'

21–30 (*Fábrega Grau, p. 187, §3*) Igitur quum apud Cesaragustanam civitatem, ut multorum sinceritas et signata veritatis verba testantur, Datiano cuidam presidi gentili et sacrilego, ex dominis et principibus suis seviendi in christianos exobtata offula cecidisset, et ob latranti profane crudelitatis, famelico cani sua rabies adspirasset;

32–6 (*Fábrega Grau, p. 187, §3*) episcopos, clericos, et omnia sancta corpora, temtamentis diaboli magis Deo probanda, spiritu nequitie sue rabie precipitanter incubuit.

40–5 (*Fábrega Grau, p. 187, §3*) Protinus pervolantes, episcopus gloriosissimus Valerius et Vincentius beatissimus martyr, perniciter in sue laudis titulo cucurrerunt, feliciores se in ipsa futuros confessione credentes, si coronam statim preco quam suis virtutibus et meritis, pro sua devotione rapuissent.

(*For 43–4, Ælfric is closer to the Cotton-Corpus manuscripts than to Fábrega Grau*)
(*Nero Ei, fol. 119ʳ*) . . . si coronam martyrii statim praecones quam suis virtutibus et meritis pro sua devotione rapuissent.

Datianus þa, se deofollica ehtere,
het ȝebrinȝan þa halȝan
ȝebundene mid racenteaȝum into anre buriȝ
and hi beȝen belucan on leohtleasum cwearterne.

Let hi liȝȝan swa on meteleaste, 50
micclum ȝehefeȝode mid þam heardan isene;
hopode þæt hi sceolde þurh þa wita
abuȝan fram Godes ȝeleafan.

Æfter lanȝsumum fyrste he het hi ȝebrinȝan him to;
wende þæt hi wæron mid þam witum fornumene, 55
and mid þære meteleaste | mihtlease ȝedone; fol. 129ᵛ
wolde hi ȝewitnian mid marum witum,
þæt hi swa eaðelice ȝeendian ne sceoldan.

Hi comon þa beȝen mid bliðum andwlitum
and ansundum lichamum to þam ȝeleafleasan deman; 60
and he wearð ofwundrod þæt hi wæron ansunde
and fæȝeres hiwæs on fulre mihte;
and axode þa weardmen humeta hi dorston
hi swa wel fedan mid wistum and drencum.

He ne mihte na tocnawæn þæt Crist sylf hi afedde, 65
and befran þa mid ȝraman þone foresædan bisceop:

---

49 beȝen `het´ 50 `and´ let 51 `swiðe´ micclum 57 marum] um
deleted and replaced by an 59 `bliðum mode and mid fægerum´ (*at end of line and in LH*
margin) 65 `hi cwædon þæt hi hym on naþor ne dydon.´ He ne ... 66 bisceop
`þus axian´

46–53 (*Fábrega Grau, pp. 187–8, §4*) Sed enim ille artifex sevus, ut vexatione itineris
magis illos frangeret, et facilius afficeret iniuria, quos videret superari non posse de
pena, ad civitatem Valentiam sanctos Dei pertrahi mox precepit. Cum summa pena
carceris, famis inopia, stridore catenarum, ut manibus et collo vix ferri pondera
sustinerent, et per omnes artus iam tunc mortis supplicia paterentur, que illi graviora
cumulatius pro sua laude portarunt.

54–8 (*Fábrega Grau, p. 188, §4*) Sed ubi iam defecisse eos crederet, iugi iniuria
fatigatos, timens ne ipsorum preventus occasu sue sevitie damna pateretur, produci
iussit e carcere, quum putaret eos, tamdiu a communi publice conversationis luce
seclusos, nec corpore iam nec ipsum spiritum prevalere; mori tamen eos ante tormenta
nolebat, quibus proponebat etiam nec mortuis temperare.

59–65 (*Fábrega Grau, p. 188, §5*) Sed pabefactus Datianus a conspectu eorum, quod
integri corpore et viribus essent: Quid, inquit, istos indulgentiori pastu, et potu largiori
propinastis? Et mirabatur furor cecus robustiores esse, quos Deus paverat.

66–9 (*Fábrega Grau, p. 188, §5*) Irascens igitur malignitatis sue presagus spiritus, quod
videbat inter sua supplicia fortiores, qui eum vincerent superesse, mox inflata vox
serpentis insibilat: Quid agis, inquit, tu, Valeri, qui sub nomine religionis contra
principes facis, extimans inimicus, quod si ipsut caput conturbare et percutere potuis-
set, id est episcopum, reliqua quoque subiectiora facilius membra confoderet?

Eala þu Ualerius, ic þe befrine nu,
hwæt dest þu, mid þam þæt þu durre winne
onȝean þone casere, swilce þurh eawfæstnysse?
Ac þe bisceop ne ȝeandwearde þam wælhreowum swa hraðe,   70
for þan þe God wolde þæt he wurde oferswiðed
þurh þone diacon on þam martirdome,
þe þa ȝearo wæs to þam wuldorfullan siȝe;
and þæt se manfulla mihte eac tocnawan
þæt se bisceop mihte mid ȝebyldum ȝeleafan   75
his wita forseon, þa ða he wearð oferswiðed
þurh þone diacon mid his drihtnes ȝeleafan.

þa cwæð Uincentius to þam arwyrðam bisceope:
Andweard þam arleasan mid anrædum ȝeleafan,
þæt his wodnys swa wurðe tobrut,   80
mid ealdordome ures Drihtnes mihte.
Seo ylce nædre specð nu þurh þises arleasan muð,
þe þa frumsceapenan men ȝefurn forlærde,
and mid niðfullum andan him benæmde þæs wuldres
þe him God forȝeaf, ȝif hi him ȝehyrsumodon.   85
He ne ȝeearnode nanes wuldres, ne he ne wunode on
    soðfæstnesse,
ac þone deað þe he scencte þam frumsceapenum mannum,
þone he dranc ærest him sylfum to bealowe.
Winne he wiþ me on þisum ȝewinne nu,

69 casere `oððe onȝean us'   70 Ac] a *altered to* A   ne] *deleted and replaced by*
nolde   72 diacon `Uincentius'    75 ȝebyldum `and ȝodum'   77 his
`leofan'    ȝeleafan] *crossed out and replaced by* `mihte'   78 bisceope `þus, la leof, ȝe'
andweard   81 Drihtnes `soðlice'    83 men `Adam and Euan'   85 forȝeaf
`on neorxnawanȝe'

70–81 (*Fábrega Grau, p. 188,* §6) Sed Deus unus voluit, eum etiam ab inferioris
ministerii nomine superari, ut adverteret quid facturus aut acturus esset ille, qui in
capite sacerdotii erat, quum posset eum etiam levita eius, qui habebat minora offici-
orum ministeria, vincere. Quid submurmuras, inquit episcopo suo Vincentius sanctus,
cuius iam erat spiritus in corona, et contra canem leviter musitus; exclama in magna
virtute, o christicola!, ut conterrita rabies, que contra sanctum Dei mysterium latrat,
divine percussa protinus vocis auctoritate frangatur.

82–94 (*Fábrega Grau, pp. 188-9,* §6) Iste enim ille est venenatissimus serpens, qui in
protoplastis gloriam ab omnibus traditam, quam ipse perdiderat, invidit. Statimque
insatiabilis homicida, ut occideret, quod Deus inmortalis fecerat mori, et ipse
contemtus gustu, quem aliis tradebat, prior ipse propinatus est. Iste ille est quem
exigimus e corporibus humanis invocatione divina et Christi nomine; mecum decertet,
pugnet, si prevalet. Confidentia videbit, me plus posse dum torqueor, quam ille dum
torquet: quia, dum punit, gravius ipse punienda patietur. Unde iam singulariter gaudeo,
quia dum patior, vindicabor.

and he wið me feohte on his feondlicum truwan,   90
and he ȝesyhð soðlice þæt | ic swyþor mæȝ   fol. 130
þone ic beo ȝewitnod, þonne he þe witnaþ,
for þan þe he sylf sceal swærran witu þrowian,
and he byð oferswiðed on minre ȝeswencednysse.

þa ȝeanȝsumode sona se arleasa Datianus,   95
and cwæð to his ȝinȝrum and to his witnerum þus,
Forlætað þysne bisceop and ȝebrinȝaþ on witum
Uincentium þone wiðercoran, þe us mid wordum swa tynð.
Ahoð hine on þære henȝene, and hetelice astreccað
ealle his lima, þæt þa liþa him toȝaan.   100
þa ȝefæstnodon þa cwelleras þone Cristes þeȝn
on þære heardan henȝene, and hine hetelice tihton
swa swa man web tiht, and se wælhreowa him cwæð to:
Hwæt seȝst þu nu, Uincentius? Hwæt þinȝ þe be þe sylfuum
and be þinum earman lichaman on þysum laþum witum?   105
Se halȝa wer þa cwæþ to þam wælhreowan þus:
þises ic ȝewilnode and ȝewiscte æfre.
Nis me nan þinȝ leofre þæt me on minum life ȝetimode,
and þu swiðost ȝeþwærlæcst mines sylfes ȝewilnunȝe.
Nelle ic þæt þu ȝeswice, for þan þe ic sylf ȝearo eom   110
witu to ðrowienne, for þam wuldorfullan Drihtne.
Nelle ic þæt ðu waniȝe min wuldor for Gode,
and þonne þu me witnast, þu bist sylf ȝewitnod.

---

95 ȝeanȝsumode] *glossed by* bealh hine   99 hine `ic hate´   107 ȝewiscte] i
over erasure   112 Gode `and mine ȝesælða´

95–100 (*Fábrega Grau, p. 189, §7*) Exarsit diabolus adversus christianam fidem, et dum
contemni se ac despici videt, ingemuit: Amovete, inquit Datianus, episcopum istum;
Vincentium graviorem rebellem, qui in publicam contumeliam venit, adplicate tor-
mentis. Animositati eius maiora iubebat inferre supplicia, et quicquid illi accessurum
erat pro gloria, vincere presumebat ex pena, sibi potius inferens diabolus, que illi
crudelitatis spiritu minabatur, et supplicia, que inferebat ipse passurus. Adplicate,
inquit, ad eculeum: membris extendite, et toto corpore dissipate; penam ante ipsa sui
tormenta sustineat.

104–13 (*Fábrega Grau, p. 189, §8*) Tunc Datianus: Quid dicis, inquit, Vincenti, ubi istut
corpus tuum miserabile conspicis? At ille subridens, ait: Hoc est quod semper obtavi:
nemo mici amabilior, nec familiarior fuit. Tu solus maxime ad mea vota concordas.
Ecce iam et in sublimibus ago, et te, et ipsos principes tuos, in seculo altior, despicio.
Ne cesses, diabole, crudelitate qua adspiras; prestabis mici gloriam, si inter ipsa
graviora supliciorum meorum exitia vincaris. Nolo cesses: insurge, diabole, et toto
malignitatis tue spiritu debacchare. Ne gloriam meam minuas, ne damna inferas laudi:
paratus est Dei servus ad omnia pro nomine salvatoris sustinenda, ut dum devotionem
meam punis, gravius ipse puniaris.

Datianus þa deofollice yrsode,
and beȝan to sleanne swiðe mid ȝyrdum   115
his aȝene witneras, þe þone halȝan witnodon,
þæt hi swiðor sceolde hine ȝeswæncan.
Se halȝa wer þa cwæþ: Nu þu ȝewrecst on him
ða witu þe ic þrowiȝe for þinre wælhreownysse,
swilce þu sylf wille ȝewrecen me on him.   120
He hrymde þa swiðor and mid reðnysse ȝrymetode,
and ȝyt swiðor wedde sleande his cwelleras
mid saȝlum and mid ȝyrdum; het hi swiðor witnian |
þone halȝan wer on þære henȝene.   fol. 130ᵛ
þohte þæt he mihte his mod ahnexian   125
þurh þa ormætan wita, ac he wann on idel,
for þan þe hi ateoredon on þære tintreȝunȝe,
þæt hi lenȝ ne mihton þone martir ȝewitnian,
and he anræde þurhwunode on þam witum swa þeah.
Datianus þa axode mid æblæcum andwlitan   130
his reðan cwelleras, þus cweðende him to:
Hwar is nu eower miht and eower mæȝen becumen?
Ne oncnawe ic eowere handa þe æfre hetole wæran,

114 yrsode `and wæs gram on his mode´   121 Erasure of þa after hrymde (end of MS
line)   ȝrymetode `swa leo´          124 halȝan] ha`l´ȝan   131 reðan] followed by a
space (end of MS line)   132 and eower] repeated in MS

114–20 (Fábrega Grau, p. 189, §9) Clamare Datianus cepit, et inter tortores suos et
carnifices ipsos illo furore bacchari virgis, fustibus milites cedere, et in suos amplius
desevire. Dum sevit ingemuit, dum adversus Christi servum devotissimum venit, prius
ipse diabolus suos occiderat, et vere quos in potestate habebat, christiano a pena tuto, et
Dei eternitate securo, illos magis, qui in illius erant dicione, vexabat. Quid dicis, inquit
Vincentius sanctus, Datiane? Ecce iam de apparitoribus tuis vindicor; ultionem mici in
penam ipse fecisti.

121–9 (Fábrega Grau, pp. 189–90, §10) Summa voce diabolus fremere cepit, rabidiori-
bus intonare sermonibus, stridore dentium frendere, et in suis amplius desevire; ut dum
martyrem Dei lacerat, seipsum potius laceraret. Fessi, cessere carnifices, et defatigata
lictorum manus, dum per latera martyris pendet, victa defecit. Expalluit torquentium
vultus, siquidem sudoris rivolis liquescentia membra tabuerunt; anhelum fessis pectus
extabuit, putans se potius ipsos inter martyris sancti tormenta torqueri.

130–40 (Fábrega Grau, p. 190, §10) Exsanguis et ipsius Datiani facies tremere cepit.
Trepidum pectus, evanescentes hebetantesque lumine oculi quasi in sua morte confusi:
Quid agitis! suis militibus exclamat; non agnosco manus vestras obsistentes perti-
naciter: homicidas sepe vicistis, parracidarum magorumque silentia alta rupistis,
arcana ipsa adulterorum vobis in conventibus patefacte sunt: et quisquis confitendo
mori timebat, in mortis confessione perductus est. O milites principum meorum, quod
in contumelia imperatorum nostrorum dicitur non possumus prohibere, ut vel pro
nostro solo pudore taceatur; alteros in confessionem mortis sue loqui cogimus: huic
silentium pro nostra contumelia non possumus imperare.

swa oft swa ȝe ȝewitnodon þa ðe wæron forscyldeȝode
oþþe þurh manslihte oððe þurh morþdæda,   135
oððe þurh drycræft oððe dyrne forliȝer.
Æfre ȝe ȝewyldon mid witum hi ealle,
and hi heore diȝlan dæda eow bedyrnan ne mihton.
Ac ȝe nu ne maȝon þusne mann oferswiðan
þæt he huru suwiȝe on þysum scearpum witum.   140
þa smercode se halȝa wer and to þam hetolan cwæð:
þis is þæt awriten is witodlice on Godes æ
þæt ða ȝeseondan ne ȝeseoþ ne þa ȝehyrendan ne ȝehyrað.
Drihten Crist ic andette, þæs ælmihtiȝan fæder sunu,
mid þam halȝan ȝaste, anne soðne God.   145
Ac witna me ȝyt swiðor for þissere soðan andetnysse
þæt ðu on eallum þinȝum þe oferswiðedne oncnawe.
Datianus þa cwæþ to þam Drihtnes cyþere:
Gemilsa þe sylfum and ne amyr þine ȝeoȝuþe,
and þin lif ne ȝescyrt on þisum suslum þus,   150
þæt þu hure ætberste þisum heardum witum,
huru nu æt ende, þeah þu ær noldest.
Uincentius him cwæþ to mid cenum ȝeleafum þus:
Ne ondræde ic þine witu ne þine wælhreowan tintreȝo,
ac ic swiðor ondræde þæt þu ȝeswican wylle   155

---

135 manslihte] man slihte`s′   140 suwiȝe] ȝ *altered from* e   141 hetolan
`Datianus þus′      150 ȝescyrt] ȝes`c′yrt   152 þeah] *erasure before* þ, *and* e *altered*
from another letter   154 ic `me′

142–7 (*Fábrega Grau, p. 190, §11*) Tunc demum Vincentius sanctus subridens, ait. Hoc
est quod in sancta lege prescribitur: Videntes non videbunt, et audientes non audiunt.
Dominum Iesum Christum confiteor Filium Dei Patris altissimi uniti unicum, et cum
Patre unum Deum esse protestor, et negare me asseris quia, que sunt vera confiteor?
Plane debes torqueri, si mentior, si principes tuos deos dicam; sed torque diutius
confitentem, nec a pena mea cesses, ut vel sic possis probatam sacrilego spiritui tuo
respirare veritatem.
    (*For 144–5, however, Ælfric is closer to the* passio amplissima)
    (*Acta SS, 395*) Dominum enim Christum confiteor, filium altissimi Patris vnici
vnicum, ipse cum Patre et Spiritu sancto vnum solum Deum esse profiteor. (*Ælfric omits
some lines from Fábrega Grau describing Datian's extreme physical reaction.*)
    148–52 (*Fábrega Grau, p. 190, §12*) Misere, inquit Vincentio Datianus, tui: ne florem
perdas nunc primum vernantis etatis; in primis annis positus, ne vitam minuas
longiorem. Parce iam supplicibus tuis, ut vel sera, que supersunt, tormenta lucreris.
    153–6 (*Fábrega Grau, p. 191, §13*) At ille prescius sanctitate, ait: ... Non timeo sup-
plicia tua, quecumque iratus impeleris; hoc magis mici formidinis est, quod fingis te
velle misereri. (*Ælfric omits a few more lines from Fábrega Grau, in which Vincent continues to
plead for further torments.*)

þinre reðnusse and swa me ȝemiltsian.

Dacianus þa het hine ȝedon of þære henȝene,
and hine | eft ahon on heardum ȝealȝan sona;   fol. 131
and hine man þa swanȝ and mid saȝlum beot,
and mid blysum ontende his bare lic eall,   160
astrehtum limum, ac his ȝeleafa swaþeah
on his Drihtenes andetnysse æfre þurhwunode.

Man ledde to his breostum brade isene clutas
swiðe ȝlowende þæt hit sanȝ onȝean,
and hi þa teartan wita mid witum ȝeeacnodon,   165
and his ærran wunda mid wundum ofsettan,
and into his innoðum hine ȝewundodon,
swa þæt on his lichaman nan dæl ne belaf
þe nære ȝewundod on ðære witnunȝe.

Him fleow þa þæt blod ofer ealne þone lichaman,   170
and him se innoþ eac ȝeopenode onȝean
and his liþa toslupon on þam laðum tintreȝum.

Ac he eall þis forbær mid bliþum andwlitan
and mid stranȝum ȝaste on Godes andetnysse,
to þam Helende clypiende þe he on ȝelyfde.   175

Wa la wa, cwæþ Datianus, we synd oferswiðede.

---

161 swaþeah `ne ateorode´     163 breostum `feower´   169 witnunȝe `soðlice´
170 blod `ut´        171 him `eac´   172 liþa `eall´        174 mid `godes´

157–8 (*Fábrega Grau, p. 191, §14*)Datianus dixit: Transferatur Vincentius ad legitimam questionem; percurrant omnium latronum homicidarumque convictorum, etiam parracidarum, violentiora tormenta: si tamdiu, inquit, durare anima potest, inter supplicia vel membra deficiant. (*Ælfric omits Vincent's joyful response from his source.*)

159–72 (*Fábrega Grau, p. 191, §15*) Hinc ad patibulo raptus, immo ex eculeo depositus, tortores suos ipse percurrens, moras carnificum urguendo, in sevitia sua diabolum pudore tarditatis onerabat. Torquitur, tunditur, flagellatur, exuritur, et distentis membris crescebat corpus ad penam, sed spiritus, qui Christum Dominum fatebatur, in victoriam perdurabat. Inprimuntur ardentes pectori lamine, et liquefactus inter ipsas candentes ferri acies, licor guttis, flama stridente, respergitur. Vulnera vulneribus inprimuntur, et supra tormenta tormenta deseviunt; sales ignibus adsparsis, crepitantibus minutis, per membra dissiliunt: et iam non ad artus tantum, sed ab ipsius viscera suppliciorum tela iaciuntur. Et quia integri corporis pars nulla superesset, que primum fuerat inlata, iam et ipsa pena punitur. (*Ælfric omits a few lines here describing Datian's reaction.*)

173–6 (*Fábrega Grau, pp. 191-2, §16*) Renuntiatur ipsi Datiano a dilectis et militibus suis, percurrisse Vincentium universa supplicia hilari vultu, spiritu fortiori, pertinaci magis professione, qua ceperat Dominum Iesum Christum fateri. Heu! inquit Datianus, vincimur. (*Ælfric omits a few more lines of speech by Datian.*)

Ac secaþ nu, ic bidde, an blind cweartærn
þær nan leoht ne maȝe inn, and on þam myclum þeostrum
strewiað ȝeond eall tobrocene tiȝelan
scearpe ȝeecȝode, and þæron astreccaþ   180
þysne wiðercoran, þæt he hine bewend(e)
fram wite to wite and symble ȝearewe habbe.
Belucað hine þonne fæste þæt he licȝe þær ana
leohtes bedæled on þam laðum bedde.
Secȝað me swa sona swa ȝe oncnawaþ   185
þæt he cucu ne byð. And þa cwelleras swa dydon,
ȝebrohton þone halȝan wer on þam blindan cwearterne,
and besæton hine syþþan, wakiȝende.

Mid þam ðe þa weardmen wurdon on slæpe,
þa com þær heofonlic leoht into þam halȝan were   190
on þam blindan cweartearne swilce beorht sunbeam,
and him wearð ȝebed|dod mid hnescre beddinȝe,   fol. 131ᵛ
and he sylf þa sanȝ his sealmes bliðe
his drihten heriende mid incundre heortan.

þa wundrode þa weardmen þæs wynsuman leohtes,   195
swiðe afyrhte for þam færlican tacne.

---

181 bewende] bewendan   191 swilce `an'   192 wearð] weard   bed-
dinȝe `swiðe ænlice'       195 `þa ða weardmen awocan' þa wundrode   196 tacne]
followed by erasure of letter in red ink

177–86 (*Fábrega Grau, p. 192, §17*) Querite, inquit, locum tenebrosum oppressumque,
urgente tectura, ab omni publica luce sepositum, et perpetua nocte damnatum: reatui
huius peculiarem, extra carceres carcerem patiatur. Ibi fragmentis testule passim
exasperatos congerite mucrones, ut ex omni parte male incisa fractura, elimatis aculeis,
iacentis corpus, quod tetigerit, infigat, et ipsa conversio laterum iterum innovetur ad
pena; ut quod, comutatis artubus, membra evadere se credunt, semper offendant.
Divaricate preterea distentum roborem, quodadusque discerpi pene artus possint, ut
per singula membra rebellis nostrorum principum expiret. Inde clausum relinquite
tenebris, ne vel oculis respirent ad lucem; nullus ibi hominum relinquatur, ne vel
consortio alicuis sermonis animetur. Clausa et obserata sint omnia: solliciti tantum
estote, ut quando defecerit, nuntietur.

185–95 (*Fábrega Grau, p. 192, §18*) Nec mora: quum prima quies fessos custodum
artus, somno vincente, laxaverat, quod Datianus pene gravissime mortis intulerat,
divinitus commutatur in gloria. Carceris illius nox tetra novam accepit lucem: flagrant
cerei ultra solitum fulgorem radiantes. Ipse sanctus Vincentius, stramentis mollioribus
iam refectus, psalmum Domino canit, et hymnum letus exultat, vocis organo modulata
suavitate concinens. Tota autem vicina, que ad eius supplicia mesta pendebat, pro
suavitate sonitus demulcet auditus. Trepidi subito expavere custodes, et evasisse per
fugam, quem acceperant, putaverunt.

[*For l. 191, Ælfric is closer to the Cotton-Corpus manuscripts version.*]
(*Nero Ei, fol. 120ᵛ*) . . . ultra solis fulgore radiantes.

þa cwæþ se hal3a wer: Of þam heofonlican leohte
ne beo 3e afyrhte. Ic heom nu 3efrefrod
mid en3ellicre þenun3e. Gað in and sceawiað.

Ge 3ebrohton me on þrystrum, and ic blissi3e nu on leohte;   200
mine bendas sund tolysede, and ic blissi3e mid san3e.
Ic eom nu 3estran3od and hnesce understreowod.
Wundriað þises, þæt se þe wurðaþ God
mid soþre andetnesse, þæt he si3efæst byþ æfre.

Cyþaþ nu ardlice eowerum arleasan hlaforde   205
hwilces leohtes ic bruce, and hwilcere beddin3e,
þæt he 3yt ma3e asmea3an sum syllic wite
to minum wuldre ne wani3e he nan þin3,
þæs þe minum martirdome ma3e to wuldre becuman.

His mildheortnesse ane ic me ondræde swiðost,   210
þæt he beo awend swilce he wille mildscian.

Hi cyddon þa þis þam hetolan cwellere,
and he wearð 3ean3sumod
and æblæce on nebbe cwæþ him to andsware:
Hwæt ma3e we him mare don, nu we synd oferswiðede?   215

---

197 þa] *erasure of a stroke above* a   199 sceawiað `*hu me is*´   200 þrystrum] s
over erasure   202 under-] e *over erasure*   205 arleasan] *erasure beside* l
206 hwilcere] r *altered from another letter*   207 sum `*þin3*´          208 wuldre `*ic
bidde*´   209 þe `*he*´          210 ane] e *altered to* c          211 wille `*me 3e*´ mildscian
213 3ean3sumod `*on his mode*´   215 oferswiðede] *altered to* ofercumene (cf. l. 233)

197–211 (*Fábrega Grau, pp. 192–3, §19*) Tunc beatus Vincentius exclamans, ait: Nolite
timere: pro vobis laudes meas ipse non fugio. Propere, si potestis, inrumpite, et solacia
martyris, angelico obsequio ministrata oculis, aurite securi; ubi relinqueratis tenebras,
gaudete lucem; quem ingemescentem in suspiriis credebatis, in laudem Dei veri, et cum
Patre unici exultare gaudete. Laxata sunt vincula, crevere vires, corpus stramento
molliori reficitur; miramini potius, et plenis pia voce asserite preconiis, confessorem
Dei semper esse victorem. Euntes renuntiate quin potius Datiano, qua perfruar luce;
comentetur adhuc, si potest, diabolus, et aliquid superaddat ad gloriam meam. Si quid
potest, de laudis titulo nicil defraudet, sed exerceat quicquid adhuc furor bacchantis
invenerit. Solam eius misericordiam timeo, ne videatur ignoscere.

212–28 (*Fábrega Grau, p. 193, §20*) Ad renuntiationem omnium, exsanguis, trepidus et
pallidus, Datianus etiam ipse sibi male conscius, in se penam sensit, dum in famulum
Dei sevit. Tandem vox vera, etsi invita simplicitate, prorupit: Et quid, inquit, amplius
faciemus? Iam victi sumus. Deferatur ad lectulum corpus, stramentis mollioribus
reponatur: nolo gloriosiorem eum facere, si inter tormenta defecerit. Fertur ad lectulum
gaudentium manibus, et letantium humeris, qui oscularentur vestigia eius, et omne
corpus lacerum lamberent, et ipsum sanguinem profluentem in sue salutis remedia
distringerent. Et qui in ipsius fuerant supplicia crassati, utitur eorum obsequiis
baiulorum: Dei servus beatissimus accipere inimicorum suorum meruit servitutem. Hic
vero statim spiritus, iam victo diabolo, cruento consilio emisit e seculo.

Beraö hine nu, ic bidde, of þam blindan cwærterne
to suman softan bedde þæt he swa hine reste.
Nelle ic hine wyrcan wuldorfulran ȝyt,
ȝif he on þam witum ȝewitnod ateoraö.
Hi hine þa bæran bliþelice on æarmun 220
þe hine ær witnodon on þam wælhreowum tintreȝum.
And hi his fet cystun, and his flowende blod
ȝeornlice ȝaderodon him sylfum to hæle,
and ȝeleddon hine | swa on þam softan bedde fol. 132
swa swa se arlesa het and forleetan hine swa. 225
  Hit ȝelamp þa sona æfter litlum fyrstum,
þæt se halȝa ȝewat of worlde to Gode
mid siȝefæstum martirdome, oferswiödum deofle,
to þam ecan wuldre mid þam welwillendan Drihtene,
þæt þæt he þam behet eallum þe hine lufiaö 230
and þam þe his ȝeleafan healdaþ oö ende.
Datianus þa cwæþ, se deofollica cwelleræ,
ofsceamod swaþeah: Gif ic oferswiöan ne mihte hine
ær cucene, ic hine witniȝe deadne.
Awyrpaö nu his lic on anum widȝillum felda, 235
fuȝelum to æse, and fulum hundum to mete,
and þam wildeorum; and his wælhreowan þeȝnas swa dydon,
sona ȝeferedan þæt lic to þam feldan middan,
and hit þar awurpon wildeorum to mete.
Hit ȝelamp þa sona þur Godes foresceawunȝe 240

216 `ut´ of    217 he `maȝe´   `ȝe´ reste    220 hi `namon´ hine þa `and´
bæran   222 flowende] e over erasure   224 ȝeleddon] ȝe`le´ddon
227 halȝa `diacon´   232 deofollica] erasure between first o and f
233 oferswiöan] altered to ofercumen (cf. l. 215)   234 witniȝe `þus´
237 wildeorum] wild`e d´eorum    239 wildeorum `and fuȝelum´

232–7 (Fábrega Grau, p. 193, §21) Renunciato igitur recessu eius, iam victus atque con-
fusus, Datianus dixit: Si non potui, inquit, superare viventem, puniam vel defunctum:
non est spiritus, qui repugnet, non etiam anima, que vincat.... Proicite, inquit, illum
in apertum campum nullo defendente obstaculo: ibi cadaver exanime feris avibus et
canibus consummetur, vel, quod solum inferre mortuo possum, non habeat sepulturam.
240–50 (Fábrega Grau, p. 194, §22) Corvus haud procul residens, avis lenta et
pigerrima, cute tetra, specie decolor, puto ut funebrem habitum vel lamento quasi
lugentis ostenderet, quum abigeret reliquas aves magnificas pinnisque pernicies,
adveniente subito lupum in curribus suis, terrens, exegit e corpore, quum ille, reflexa
cervice, non quod corvi illius impetu terreretur, sed in aspectu corporis stupefactus
hereret, credo, aliquam custodiam mirabatur angelicam. Reddita est antiquitatis storia,
per avem similem, ut, que ante ad Elie plenos messorum portaverat cibos, nunc sancto
Vincentio martyri iussa obsequia ministraret.

þæt an sweart hrem þær fleah sona to,
and bewerode þæt lic wið þa wildan fuӡelas,
and hi ealle afliӡde mid his fiðerum aweӡ,
and eac þa reðan deor mid his onræsum.

Se ælmihtiӡa God þe þe Eliam his witeӡan   245
þurh þone sweartan hræm asende hwilon mete,
and hine þa afedde þur þæs fuӡelas þenunӡe,
swa swa on cyninӡa bocum fulcuð is be þam;
þe ylca ӡeheold nu þæs halӡan weres lic,
þurh þæs hremmes weardunӡe wið þa oðre fuӡelas.   250

þis wearð eft ӡecydd þam arleasan Datiane,
and he þa ӡeanӡsumod þus cwæþ:
Ne mæӡ ic hine oferswiðan forðon swa deadne?
Swa ic his swiðor ehte mid swiðlicre ehtnysse,
swa ic hine swiðor wyrce wuldorfulran symle.   255

Ac ӡif þeo [eo]rðe ne mæӡ þone mann forniman,
be he besenced on | sælicum yðum,   fol. 132ᵛ
þæt us swa oft ne sceamiӡe for his anes siӡe
on manna ӡesihþum, þe hit eall ӡeseoð,
beo he huru bediӡlod on þære deopen sæ.   260

Be he besiwod on anum sæcce mid hefeӡum stanum,
and awurpað hine on þære widӡillan sæ,
þam fixum to mete þeah þe þa fuӡelas noldon.

Ða reþan cwelleras þa raþe swa dydon,
awurpan þæs halӡan lic on þære widӡillan sæ,   265
inid þam hefeӡum stanum, swa swa hi het þe dema,
þæt he huru ne sceolde þære sæ ætberstan,

---

246 mete `on þam westene ðe he onwunode'          247 afedde] `dær' (for ðær)
249 ylca] `God' (at end of MS line)          259 ӡeseoð `and witon'   261 hefeӡum]
altered to hefieӡum   266 hefeӡum] altered to hefieӡum

251–63 (*Fábrega Grau, p. 194, §23*) Territus tali nuntio Datianus: Iam, inquit, vincere
nec mortuum possum, et per diversa sevitia mea, dum acrius persequor, gloriosiorem
feci. Sed si consumere eum terra non potuit, mergatur pelago, ne erubescamus quotidie
in oculis hominum: victoriam eius vel maria celabunt. Insuatur fiscinule quasi in
culleum parracide, immo in eronis angustiis cum gravissimo lapidum pondere corpus
lacerum constipetur. Et ubi spatia naute longa processerint, inprimatur fluctibus corpus, ut in pastibus pisces, si quid forte superest laceri vulneris, vel lambendo
consumant. (*Ælfric omits here a fairly large passage from his source, in which further details of
the disposal of Vincent's body are given.*)
264–8 (*Fábrega Grau, p. 195, §24*) . . . et ubi oculis absconditi montes atque omne litus
evanuit, ubi iam defessis satis visum est, timentes ne ad aliam provinciam eripiendum
forte portarent, medio mari inmersum fluctibus inpresserunt.

þeah þe he þære eorðan æror ætburste.
And reowan him hamweard mid healicre blisse.

Ac þæs halȝan weres lic, þurh þes Hælendes mihte,   270
to þam strande becom ær þam þe hi stopon on land,
and on þam ceosole ȝelæȝ, oðþæt sum ȝeleafful wudewa
swutele ȝebicnunȝe be þam underfenȝ
hwær se halȝa lichama læȝ on þam strande,
beworpen mid þam ceosole þurh þa sælican yþa,   275
swilce he bebyrȝed wære þurh Godes wissunȝe.
His lic wearð þa ȝeferod to ȝeleaffulre cyrcan
mid mycelre arwyrðnesse, and þar on innan bebyriȝed;
and his halȝan ban wurdon wide todælede,
and mid mycelre lufe hi man wyrðaþ ȝehwær   280
swa swa us secȝað bec, for his soðan ȝeleafan,
þam Hælende to lofe þe leofað a on ecnesse.
AMEN.

Unius Martiris Amen Amen dico uobis nisi granum frumenti cadens
in terram mortuum fuerit ipsum solum manet et reliqua.   285
'Soð, soð, ic eow secge: Gif þæt isawene hwætene corn

268 ætburste 'ða hiȝ swa ȝedon hæfdon swa ðe dema hi het'   270 Ac 'soðlice'
275 þam 'sand' ceosole

269–76 (*Fábrega Grau, p. 195, §25*) Et redeuntes iam ad Datianum hilares. . . . Sed ecce,
licet fortissimos remiges, velociori tamen Dei manu gubernante, martyris ad litus
prevenerat corpus. . . . Qui dum trepidus vel lentior venit, comonita in somnis vidua
quedam, etate et sanctitate plenissima, vera signa accepit quiescentis: ubi corpus
reciprocatum lenior fluctus iam molli arena tumulaverat, et elementi ipsius prolabente
congerie ad honorem famulatus lambendo servierat sepulture.

277–8 (*Fábrega Grau, p. 195, §27*) Hinc ad basilicam sanctum corpus adlatum est
venerabile omnibus, et beatum iam de honorificentia sepulture securum. (*For the final
part of his homily, describing the distribution of Vincent's relics (279–80), Ælfric seems to have
followed an extra passage in the Cotton-Corpus MSS which BHL classes separately as an Additamentum.*)

279–80 (*Nero Ei, fol. 121ᵉ*) Tantam autem gratiam beato martyri Vincentio post
triumphos post coronam victoriae contulit, ut reliquiae eius non solum apud Hispanias
sed etiam apud Galliarum provincias miro excolantur affectu.

2. *The Gospel-Exposition*
The texts cited here (in addition to the Vulgate) are: (i) Alcuin, *Commentaria in S. Ioannis Evangelium*, PL 100, cols. 911–13 (cited as Alcuin); (ii) Haymo, *Homiliae de Tempore*,
PL 118, cols. 763–5 (cited as Haymo).
286–96 (*John xii. 24–6*) (24) Amen, amen dico vobis, nisi granum frumenti cadens in
terram mortuum fuerit, (25) ipsum solum manet; si autem mortuum fuerit, multum fruc-
tum affert. Qui amat animam suam, perdet eam; et qui odit animam suam in hoc mundo,

feallende on eorðen ne bið fullice beæʒ(ð)æd,
hit wunæð him sylf (a)næ; ant he cwæð eft þa:
Gif hit soðlice beæʒðed bið, hit bringæð mycele wæstm forð.
Ðe þe his sawla lufæð, he forlyst heo witodlice;   290
and þe ðe his sawlæ hatæð on þissere weorulde,
þe heald hire on þam ecan life.
Ðe ðe me ðenæð, fyliʒe he me þenne;
ant þær ðær ic me sylf beo, þer bið eac min þeʒn;
and þe ðe me ðenaþ, him þonne arwurðað   295
min Fæder Almihtiʒæ þe ðe is on heofenum.'
Ðis godspel is nu isæd sceortlice on Englisc,
ac we wyllæð openian eow þæt gastlic andʒit,
na swa ðeah to langlice, þæt hit eow ne laðiʒe.
Æfter weorldþingum, we witon to soðan   300
þæt þæt asawene corn, ʒif hit ne chinæð on þare moldan,
and ʒif hit ne bið aðyd of þam þe hit ær wæs,
ðet hit na ne weaxæð, ac wunæð him sylf anæ.
þæt clæne hwætene corn þe Crist þa embespæc
tacnæð hine sylfne þe sealde his lif for us,   305
and he micelne wæstm of moncynne aber
þurh his anes deað, þe swiðe deorewurðe is;
and he bringæð þone wæstm, þæt beo we synfulle,
into þe wynsume bærne þare ecan wununge.
He wæs ða dead þurh þa Iudeiscen,   310
and he cwicede us þe on hine lyfæð.
Heo hine forluron, and we hine ilæhten;
and his nomæ weaxæð wunderlice on us
swa mycel swiðor swa he mid heom is ið[r]yht,
þæt he adwæsced beo on heoræ dwyldum.   315
Rihtlice þæt hwætene corn, þe iclænsod is on wæstmum

287 beæʒðæd] beæʒdðæd   288 sylf anæ] sylfenæ

in vitam aeternam custodit eam. (26) Si quis mihi ministrat, me sequatur; et ubi sum ego, illic et minister meus erit. Si quis mihi ministraverit, honorificabit eum Pater meus.

304-12 (*Alcuin, cols. 911-12; cf. Haymo, col. 763C*) Se autem dicebat ipsum esse granum mortificandum et multiplicandum: mortificandum infidelitate Judaeorum, multiplicandum fide omnium populorum.

313-15 (*Haymo, col. 763D* [*? perhaps Ælfric's own expansion of Alcuin*]) Nam ejus nomen tanto magis crescit in fide credentium, quanto per mortem in perfidia Judaeorum est exstinctum.

316-19 (*Haymo, cols. 763-4*) Et pulchre Dominus grano tritici comparatur, quia sicut in omnibus annonis nihil frumento pulchrius, nihil est delectabilius: ita ipse omnes creaturas excellit, quia nihil eo suavius, nihil dulcius invenitur.

and ealræ sæde fyrmest, is iset on ʒetacnunge
ures Hælendes Cristes for his heahlice mihte,
for þan þe he oferstihð alle isceaftæ.

'Ðe þe his sawle lufæð, he forlosæð heo witodlice; | 320
and þe ðe his sawlæ hatæð on þissere weorulde,   Bf. 76
he healt hire soðlice on þam ecan life.'

þæt is on twa wise witolice to secgene:
ʒif þu wylt witodlice lif habbæn mid þam lifiʒendum Hælende,
ne ondræd þu ðe to swæltænne for his soðan ileafan;   325
and ne lufe þu ðis lif, þæt ðu on leahtrum wuniʒe
and þine sawle forleose on þe soðe life.

Her is ðeo sawla iset for þisse sceorte life,
and þe ðe on þissere weorulde witodlice leofæð
and on druncenesse his daʒas aspent,   330
be ðam cwæð Paulus, ne cymæð he na to Godes rice.

Iseliʒe beoð þa ðe heora sawlæ hatiæð
on þissere weorlde, þæt heo wislice libban
þæt heo þæ ecan murhðe moten habben mid Gode.

þa haliʒe martyræs swa mycel forsæʒen   335
þis andwearde lif, þæt heom leofere wæs to swæltanne
for þæs Hælendes namen ær þam þe heo hine wiðsocen,
swa swa Uincencius dyde, be þam þe we eow sæden ær.

'Ðe þe me þenæð, fyliʒe he me þenne.'
On moniʒe wisum men þeniæð Criste: 340

323-7 (*Alcuin, col. 912A*) 'Qui amat', inquit, 'animam suam, perdet eam.' Quod duobus
modis intelligi potest: 'qui amat, perdet', id est, si amas, perdes: si cupis vitam tenere in
Christo, noli timere mori pro Christo. Item alio modo: 'qui amat animam suam, perdet
eam'. Noli amare in hac vita, ne perdas in aeterna vita. Hoc autem quod posterius dixi,
magis habere videtur evangelicus sensus; sequitur enim: 'Et qui odit animam suam in
hoc mundo, in vita aeternam custodit eam.' Ergo quod supra dictum est: 'qui amat',
subintelligitur, in hoc mundo; ipse itaque perdet: 'Qui autem odit', utique in hoc
mundo, in vitam aeternam ipse custodit eam. Magna et mira sententia, quemadmodum
sit hominis in animam suam amor ut pereat, odium ne pereat! Si male amaveris, tunc
odisti: si bene oderis, tunc amasti.

328-34 (*Alcuin, col. 912B [reordered by Ælfric]*) Felices qui oderunt custodiendo, ne
perdant amando. Hic animae nomine vita praesens designatur; vel etiam hujus vitae
delectatio, quae perdenda est ut feliciter invenias voluntatem tuam in regno Dei, quam
fortiter vicisti in hoc saeculo.

(*Also 1 Cor. vi. 10*) '. . . neque fures, neque avari, neque ebriosi, neque maledici, neque
rapaces regnum Dei possidebunt.'

335-8 (*Alcuin, col. 912B*) Nam sancti martyres odio habuerunt hanc praesentem vitam
pro Christi nomine, dum magis voluerunt hanc praesentem vitam perdere, quam
Christum negare.

340-7 (*Alcuin, col. 913B*) 'Si quis mihi ministrat'; omnis enim quicunque bene agit,
Christo ministrat. Unde unusquisque pro modulo suo ministret Christo, bene

sume on his ðeowdome on isette timan;
sume on mæsseþenunge and on moniʒe bedum;
sume on clænnesse for Cristes lufæn wuniæð;
sume sealden heora lif for his lufe to cwale;
sume doð ælmessan heoræ Drihtene to lofe;   345
and swa hwa swa deð his Drihtnes willan
on eniʒe wisan, he þenæð him sylfum.
'Ðe ðe me þenæð, fyliʒe | he me þenne.'   fol. 122
Gif we Criste ðeniæð, we sceolen him fyliʒen.
We sceolon faran on his weʒas,   350
þæt is, on rihtwisnesse and soðfestnessæ simle þeniæn.
      'And þer ic beo seolf, þær bið eac min þeʒn.'
Her we maʒen ihyren hwæt he deð us to leane,
ʒif we him þeniæð on eawfestum life
and on wældedum: þæt we wuniæn moten   355
þær þær he sylf bið on þam soðe life
on ece wuldre a to weorulde.
      'And þe ðe me þenæð, hine þone arwurðæþ
min Almihtiʒa Fæder þe ðe is on heofenum.'
Mid hwylce wyr(ð)mente arwyr(ð)æð þe Fæder   360
þone mon þe þenæð on þisse life his Sunu,
butan mid þam wyrðmente þæt he wuniæn mote
on þam ecan life þær þær he sylf bið,
and his wuldor iseon, and þare wynsumnesse
a butæn ende brucæn mid alle his halʒum?   365

---

355 moten] *erasure (of accent?) above* t   360 wyrðmente arwyrðæð] wyrdmente
arwyrdæð   365 a butæn] MS `a´ butæn   brucæn] æ *formed from long ascender on* a

vivendo, eleemosynas faciendo, nomen doctrinamque ejus, quibus potuerit praedi-
cando.

(*Also compare Haymo, col. 765A*) Variis enim modis fideles Christo ministrant. Alii bene
dicendo, ut confessores; alii pro ejus nomine moriendo, ut martyres; alii juste
eleemosynas tribuendo, ut fideles laici.

349–51 (*Alcuin, col. 912C*) 'Si quis mihi ministrat, me sequatur.' Quid est, 'me
sequatur', nisi me imitetur? Christus enim pro nobis passus est, ait Apostolus Petrus,
relinquens nobis exemplum, ut sequamur vestigia ejus (*I Petr. ii. 21*).

352–7 (*Alcuin, col. 912C*) 'Si quis mihi ministrat, me sequatur.' Quo fructu, qua
mercede, quo praemio? 'Et ubi sum', inquit, 'ego, illic et minister meus erit.' Merces est
amoris, et operis pretium, quo ministratur Christo, esse cum illo cui ministrat. Ubi
enim bene erit sine illo? Aut quomodo [male] esse poterit cum illo?

358–65 (*Alcuin, col. 912C*) 'Et si quis mihi ministraverit, honorificabit eum Pater
meus.' Quo honore, nisi ut sit cum Filio ejus? Quod enim superius ait: 'Ubi ego sum,
illic et minister meus erit': hoc intelligitur exposuisse, cum dicit: 'Honorificabit eum
Pater meus.'

Hwa mæʒ æffre wilniæn mare wyrðmente,
oððe hwa durste þisses wilniæn, ʒif þe Almihtiʒa Hælend
þisses ne behæte þam ðe hine lufiæð?
Ðe ðe leofað on ecnesse mid his Almihtiʒæ Fæder
and þam Halʒan Gaste on anre godcundnesse, 370
on ane mæʒenðryme, on anum ʒecynde a on ecnesse.
AMEN.

366–8 (*Alcuin, col. 912D*) Nam quem majorem honorem accipere poterit adoptatus, quam ut sit ubi est unicus; non aequalis factus divinitati, sed consociatus aeternitati? (*Alcuin continues to expound what it means to serve Christ, but Ælfric ends at this point with a closing prayer.*)

NOTES

92. *þe*: Skeat (LS xxxvii. 91) translates this as the acc. sg. of *þu* ('When I am tormented, then he will torment thee'). The passage makes more sense if *þe* is rendered as the relative pronoun ('I can do greater things when I am tormented than he who torments'). This reading is supported by the Latin source: 'Confidentia videbit, me plus posse dum torqueor, quam ille dum torquet.'

95. *ʒeanʒsumode*: This intransitive use of the verb (Glossary, sense (b)) is not cited in BT.

245–8. The scriptural reference is to 1 Kings xvii. 6.

287, 289. *beæʒðæd (-ed)*: The past participle of a verb not attested elsewhere. It means 'harrowed', and derives from OE *egeþe, egþe* ('rake, harrow'). The noun *eithe* (or *aithe*) meaning 'harrow' carries over into Middle English.

314. *iþ[r]yht*: This emendation suggested by Belfour is convincing. The word is past participle of the verb *geþryccan* 'to repress, restrain, suppress'. The other possibility, that *-þyht* represents OE *-þeaht*, past participle of the verb *þeccan*, 'to cover', is not so appropriate in the context.

329–31. The scriptural reference is to 1 Cor. vi. 10. For Ælfric's special concern with drunkenness, see p. 92 (incl. n. 4) above.

V

THE TEMPTATION OF CHRIST

CONTEXT OF THE HOMILY

This homily, the first of the three anonymous ones edited here, offers an exposition of Matth. iv. 1–11, the Temptation of Christ in the wilderness. The homily's origin is obscure, its author and date of composition being unknown. It survives only in the late copy of Bodley 343, where it is item 78 in that manuscript's final section. Although Bodley 343 does not specify by a rubric the occasion for which the homily was intended, it can be assigned from other evidence to the First Sunday in Lent: Matth. iv. 1–11 was traditionally the pericope for that date, and the commentary mentions that the holy period in which fasting is customary is approaching (ll. 1–3). In Bodley 343, the homily is preceded by Ælfric's homily for Christmas (Belfour ix), and followed by the anonymous homily (homily vi below) on Christ's Transfiguration, pericope for the Saturday before the Second Sunday in Lent.

I have argued (pp. xlix–l above) that in this final section of the manuscript the compiler was drawing on a larger homiliary and selecting the items needed to supplement his existing collection. Much of the earlier part of Bodley 343 draws on a source shared with D (Bodley 340 and 342) and E (CCCC 198). Since D lacks Ælfric's homily for the First Sunday in Lent, and E includes it only as an addition in supplementary quires, it was probably absent from the collection(s) on which these manuscripts largely drew. Bodley 343 therefore would have lacked any homily for the First Sunday in Lent, making this anonymous homily for that occasion an appropriate acquisition.

SOURCES AND ANALOGUES

Although there is no other extant copy of the homily, a remarkably close version of its final section (from l. 162) does survive in the composite homily Napier lv.[1] The relationship between Napier lv and

[1] Napier, p. 283, l. 18–p. 284, l. 17.

the Bodley 343 homily has been examined by Michael Cummings.[1] Cummings argues convincingly that the close connection between the passages in Napier lv and homily v implies that they must have derived from a common Old English source. Since Napier lv is clearly a composite homily, amalgamating several homiletic sources, the common passage is most likely to have derived from a source similar in content to the Bodley 343 homily.[2]

Two homilies by different authors also show a remarkably close relationship to the Bodley 343 text. One is Ælfric's First Series homily for the First Sunday in Lent, the other is the third Blickling Homily, again for the First Sunday in Lent.[3] Both the homilies also expound Matth. iv. 1–11. Ælfric, like the Bodley homilist, offers a verse-by-verse exposition; the Blickling homilist probably also treated the gospel-text in sequential order (though this pattern is broken at p. 33, l. 2 where the homilist recapitulates the gospel-text then supplies a more discursive commentary), but its missing leaf only a little way into the commentary (at p. 29, l. 23, after 'costung') makes this impossible to confirm.[4] The similarity of the three homilies in structure is matched by much overlapping in the substance of the three commentaries.

The close correspondences amongst the three homilies must immediately arouse speculation that all three derive from the same Latin source. That the Bodley homily and Ælfric's homily might derive from the same source has been suggested by John Pope.[5] Although Pope does not specify a source, he probably had in mind Gregory's *Homelia in Evangelia xvi*, which was identified by Max Förster as the main source for Ælfric's CH I xi.[6] Förster elsewhere proposed this as the basis also of Blickling iii.[7] More recently James Cross has pointed out that homily v is based on the same work by Gregory.[8]

The most likely conclusion would seem to be that all three Old

---

[1] 'Napier Homily 55 and Belfour Homily 10 on the Temptations in the Desert', *NM*, lxxx (1979), 315–24.

[2] Cummings, 'Napier Homily 55', p. 322.

[3] CH I xi, pp. 166–80; Blickling, pp. 26–39.

[4] The lost leaf is convincingly proposed by Marcia A. Dalbey in 'A Textual Crux in the Third Blickling Homily', *English Language Notes*, v (1968), 241–3. Its likelihood is confirmed by D. G. Scragg, 'The homilies of the Blickling manuscript', in *Learning and Literature*, ed. Lapidge and Gneuss, p. 300.

[5] Pope, p. 16.

[6] 'Über die Quellen', pp. 11–12. Gregory's homily is PL 76, cols. 1135–8. It was in Paul the Deacon's homiliary as PD 76; see p. 5, n. 4 above.

[7] 'Zu den Blickling Homilien', *Archiv*, xci (1893), 179–206, pp. 180–2.

[8] 'The Literate Anglo-Saxon', p. 84, n. 2.

English homilies have derived their expositions from Gregory's homily. Each could independently have incorporated supplementary material from other sources; this would account for the passages of commentary independent of Gregory but available in other patristic texts. For Ælfric's homily, for example, Förster has suggested debts to Bede, Jerome, or Smaragdus, and Smetana has found parallels in Haymo.[1]

There are, however, some difficulties with this conclusion. On several occasions the Old English homilies agree in incorporating commentary which is not in Gregory but is in some other patristic source. Such evidence suggests not that their authors were using Gregory and independently incorporating material from other sources, but that either the homilies must depend directly on one another, or they must have had a common origin which had already incorporated material from various sources. The possibility that one or other of the Old English versions could have descended from another can be immediately dismissed; even if each were not closer to Gregory in various passages, the lack of significant verbal similarity would make direct dependence most unlikely.[2] The extent to which the three homilies have material in common and the nature of the resemblances would seem to suggest therefore that all three were drawing on a common Latin source consisting of a conglomeration of passages from various patristic authors.

By comparing the surviving Latin material with the Old English versions and the Old English versions with each other, a fairly complete idea of what an original common source might have contained can be constructed. Almost all of Gregory's rather short homily must have been included in it. The next most important contributor was probably Haymo, whose homily xxviii for the First Sunday in Lent accounts for a significant part of the shared commentary not in Gregory.[3] Haymo's lengthy homily includes almost all of the material in Gregory, though not always word-for-word. The homily cannot itself, however, be the source for the Old English

---

[1] 'Über die Quellen', p. 12; Smetana, 'Ælfric and the Homiliary of Haymo of Halberstadt', p. 462.

[2] For example, my ll. 82–96 are closer to Gregory, col. 1135, ll. 27–40 than to CH I, p. 168, ll. 4–9; CH I, p. 174, ll. 24–9 are closer to Gregory, col. 1136, ll. 31–7 than my ll. 112–17 or Blickling, p. 33, ll. 17–24; Blickling, p. 33, l. 32–p. 35, l. 2 are closer to Gregory, col. 1136, ll. 47–55 than my ll. 150–5 or CH I, p. 174, ll. 18–22.

[3] PL 118, cols. 190–203. According to Barré (pp. 49–70), this homily was an original one in Haymo's collection.

writers, for several reasons: first, sometimes the three Old English homilies are closer to the original Gregory than to its rendering in Haymo; secondly, two or three of the Old English versions occasionally agree in offering an interpretation which is at variance with Haymo's; finally, the Old English versions do have in common supplementary material which is not in Haymo.[1]

This proposed common source, then, would probably have consisted of Gregory's homily, supplemented by passages from Haymo, Pseudo-Jerome, and at least one other source. A similar kind of amalgamation (though not itself the source for the Old English authors) was undertaken by Smaragdus, whose homily on Matth. iv. 1–11 is a selection of passages from such authors as Gregory, Bede, Ambrosius, and Fulgentius.[2]

Despite the attractiveness of the idea of a lost common Latin source for all three Old English homilies, certain caveats should be borne in mind. These concern their arrangement of material and the relationship of their contents to known sources. Despite the similarity of structure and content in all three homilies, the variation in the arrangement of material within each one is remarkable. In order to postulate a common source, we need to argue that Ælfric, the Bodley homilist, and/or the Blickling homilist, altered drastically the placing of both brief and lengthy passages of commentary.

Taking first Blickling iii, its bipartite structure is clearly related to its source material. The origin of its second part (from p. 33, l. 2) can be readily ascertained; in both content and order it follows Gregory's homily from beginning to end. It omits certain sections, which might already have been included in the first part of the homily; the words 'mid þrim gemettum seo costung' immediately preceded the homily's missing leaf, and the omissions from Gregory include his discussion of the threefold nature of temptation (instigation, pleasure, and consent) and of how the three temptations of greed, vainglory, and covetousness were offered both to Adam and to Christ. The first part of Blickling iii apparently draws ultimately on a variety of sources. Charles D. Wright has recently argued that a Hiberno-Latin text, incorporating material from the commentaries of Jerome on Matthew and of Ambrose on Luke, may have been a source for at least this opening section of Blickling iii.[3]

[1] One instance of the latter can be traced to an identifiable source; see below p. 131 n. 3.
[2] PL 102, cols. 122–9.
[3] 'Blickling Homily III on the Temptations in the Desert', *Anglia*, cvi (1988), 130–7.

There is no evidence, however, to suggest that such an Irish compilation was used by Ælfric or the Bodley homilist; none of the
passages in Blickling iii which Wright traces to Hiberno-Latin texts
finds any parallel in CH I xi or homily v. Perhaps then the Blickling
author was using two separate immediate sources: for its first part a
Hiberno-Latin commentary on Matth. iv. 1–11 which drew on the
same patristic texts used by Ælfric and the Bodley homilist, and for its
second part Gregory's homily for the First Sunday in Lent.

This seems to me a plausible solution. Blickling iii has drawn on
two separate immediate sources. The source for its first part is itself
conglomerate and might even have drawn on the common Latin
source (whose existence we are still assuming) for CH I xi and homily
v (this would explain the rare occasions where all three homilies agree
but no patristic source has been identified).

But there does exist a Latin homily which includes the whole of
Gregory's homily as one piece, and appends to it a verse-by-verse
exposition composed of passages from various other patristic authors.
This is the homily by Smaragdus mentioned above. Smaragdus's
homily itself is not the Blickling homilist's source. But it does not
seem impossible that another Latin text might have been constructed
in a similar way, but in reverse order: a verse-by-verse exposition
followed by Gregory's homily.

If this were the case, and if such a text were the source of Blickling
iii, could it also have been the source of CH I xi and homily v? Three
important points are relevant to this question. The first is that the
material from Gregory which is rendered as a block at the end of
Blickling iii is to be found incorporated into the verse-by-verse
expositions of Ælfric and the Bodley homilist. The second point is
that CH I xi and homily v are nevertheless strikingly different in their
respective arrangements of the material drawn from Gregory, selecting similar passages but for exposition of different verses of the gospel-
text. This would be in keeping with a common source which contained an amalgamation of selected patristic passages followed by
Gregory, which was independently reworked by Ælfric and the
Bodley homilist into a verse-by-verse sequence. It would also help to
explain why Ælfric and the Bodley homilist vary so markedly in their
arrangement of the material. The third point is that Ælfric himself
does include a large section from Gregory at the end of his homily.
Like the Blickling homilist, though less abruptly, he departs from his
verse-by-verse exposition (p. 174, l. 30), turning to a separate piece of

commentary drawn from Gregory. But the similarity ends there. The material which Ælfric selects from Gregory for special consideration is the threefold nature of the devil's temptation (instigation, pleasure, and consent), and the parallels between the devil's three temptations of Adam and of Christ (by greed, vainglory, and covetousness). In other words, what Ælfric includes from Gregory as a kind of appendage to his verse-by-verse exegesis is exactly equivalent to the material that the Blickling homilist has omitted from Gregory in the second part of his homily. It is difficult to know what significance, if any, should be attached to this; Ælfric is unlikely to be filling in from Gregory what a source common to the Old English homilies had not included, since much of this material was probably covered in the missing leaf of the Blickling homily. But Ælfric might have chosen the material on the nature of temptation as being of particular interest and hence worthy of separate consideration; if he had before him a source which itself separated a verse-by-verse exegesis and more discursive commentary from Gregory, then an appended passage drawn from Gregory might have seemed all the more justifiable. Following his general discussion of temptation, Ælfric returns to the subject of fasting, and thence to an exhortation to tithing and almsgiving, a conclusion common to all three Old English homilies as well as Gregory.

If there were one immediate common Latin source for all three Old English homilies, then Blickling iii must have been closest to it, at least in structure; it is inconceivable that an Old English homilist would have picked out from a composite Latin verse-by-verse exegesis the material derived from Gregory and collected it together as the second part of his homily. I offer this common source as a hypothesis and not as a conclusion. It would help to explain the similarities in content amongst the homilies, their closeness at times to each other as opposed to any identified patristic text, and yet their vast discrepancies in the arrangement of material.

One further possibility should be considered as a way of accounting for such factors, but sufficient external evidence is not yet available to argue a convincing case. We tend to think of a 'common source' as one text. The period of Lent was a particularly important one for preaching, and it is reasonable to assume that more Latin sermons appropriate for that time would have been available and circulating amongst clergy than for other times of the year. It is possible that collections were made of several different sermons for one occasion, and that these might have circulated in such groups. If so, then Ælfric, the Bodley homilist, and the Blickling homilist, might each have been drawing independently on one such group of sermons for the First Sunday in Lent. A 'common source' might not have been just one text but a whole group of patristic texts collected together.

In the following pages, Bodley 343's anonymous homily for the First Sunday in Lent is analysed in terms of its relationship to known ultimate sources and analogues. Although we do not have the immediate source(s) from which the homily is derived, it is clear that this Old English homilist was using his source material intelligently to present a clear and coherent exposition of Matth. iv. 1–11.

The homilist begins with an introduction which is probably his independent composition (ll. 1–16). No equivalent is to be found in any of the existing Latin source material, nor in the Old English analogues, CH I xi or Blickling iii. The homilist exhorts his audience to fast assiduously in the approaching period of Lent, following Christ's example. Fasting must be accompanied by almsgiving and frequent prayer, if one is to earn heavenly bliss, and the vices of greed, drunkenness, and lust must accordingly be avoided. The homilist has introduced here the themes of fasting and avoiding temptation which he will develop later in the homily.

With 'Sanctus Matheus wrat' at line 17, the homilist turns to direct translation of and commentary on the gospel-text Matth. iv. 1–11. Matth. iv. 1 is cited in Latin as well as English, the only occasion on which Latin is used in the whole homily (perhaps suggesting that the intended audience for the homily was not necessarily well-educated). The first part of the commentary for this verse is a faithful rendering of Gregory (except that the homilist has omitted Gregory's proleptic references to Matth. iv. 5 and 8).[1] The homilist, like Gregory, confirms that the Holy Spirit (and not the devil) was responsible for Christ's journey to the desert; he stresses particularly that the action was voluntary on Christ's part ('and þæt he sylfwilles þider ferde').

At line 26, the homily departs from Gregory in content and order.[2] For this second part of the commentary on verse 1 (ll. 26–32), the homily exhibits some similarity to Haymo in ideas, although it is not

[1] PL 76, col. 1135, 20–7.

[2] In this the homily can be contrasted with CH I xi. Ælfric begins with a brief summary of Gregory, ll. 20–7, then proceeds to a rendering of Gregory's immediately following passage (ll. 27 ff.), a passage which the Bodley homilist has inserted much later (ll. 82 ff.). Here we see Ælfric following Gregory in order more closely than the Bodley homilist.

close enough in wording to suggest Haymo as the direct source.[1] No closer equivalent is to be found in the Old English analogues. Both Haymo and the Bodley homilist argue that the reason why Christ deliberately underwent temptation was to convince human beings of their own ability to overcome the devil by behaving righteously. Although the homilist refers twice to 'overcoming' the devil, he does not otherwise resort to the military diction employed by Haymo ('exemplum pugnandi', 'impugnandi contra diabolum'). In fact his emphasis is rather on the constructive ways in which man and Christ can interact; Christ allows the devil to tempt Him 'for ure lufe', and the word 'rihtwisnesse', which occurs twice, refers once to Christ and once to mankind.

Following his translation of Matth. iv. 2, the homilist first comments that Christ's hunger proves His physical reality, then compares Christ's fast to the two Old Testament precedents of Moses and Elijah (ll. 35–48). The idea of Christ's physical reality being proven by His hunger may derive ultimately from Haymo: 'Additum est, postea esuriit, ut vera in illo humanitas esse ostenderetur.'[2] The comparison to the fasting of Moses and Elijah appears in all the equivalent Latin material, and either Gregory or Haymo might have acted as the ultimate source.[3] Gregory includes only a brief reference to Moses and Elijah; Haymo discusses their significance in more depth. The Bodley homilist, like Haymo, treats the subject at greater length than Gregory, and like Haymo he alludes to Elijah's role as a prophet. But whereas Haymo proceeds to discuss how Moses and Elijah foreshadow Christ's fulfilment of the law and the prophets, the Bodley homilist fills out the account with further information probably drawn directly from the Old Testament. From Exod. xxxiv derives his comment that Moses wrote the Old Law 'mid his aȝene fingre . . . on twam stænene bræden, and þam folce sende, and het þæt heo alle þeræfter lyfedon' (ll. 39–41), from 1 Kings xix, the role of the angel in providing food for Elijah, and the foreknowledge which results from his fasting.[4]

Ælfric, like the anonymous Bodley homilist, suggests that Christ's

---

[1] PL 118, col. 191B.

[2] PL 118, col. 196A.

[3] PL 76, col. 1137A; PL 118, col. 193A.

[4] An interesting contrast can be made with Ælfric's rendering of the biblical passage in his homily for Midlent Sunday: 'þa awrat se ælmihtiga god him twa stænene wexbredu mid his agenum fingre. on ðam wæron awritene tyn word. þæt sind tyn ælice beboda' (CH II xii. 135–7).

humanity is revealed through His hunger, then moves directly to a discussion of Moses and Elijah.[1] Unlike the Bodley homilist, he does not include any additional biblical information; rather he stresses that the fasting of Moses and Elijah was only possible through God's power. Ælfric's reference to Moses and Elijah in CH I xi comes not as part of the verse-by-verse exegesis (as in homily v, and indeed in Haymo's homily) but amongst the material drawn from Gregory contained in the separate section towards the end of the homily. Blickling iii in its extant form contains no reference to Moses and Elijah, but its missing leaf may explain this.

At line 48, the Bodley homilist moves to the devil's motivation for his temptation of Christ. Having shown how the fasting of Moses and Elijah and that of Christ compare to one another, he now contrasts Moses and Elijah with Christ in terms of sin. Whereas Moses and Elijah are sinful both innately because of original sin ('Adames gult') and also through their own sinful actions, Christ is entirely without sin (ll. 48–53). The contrast of Moses and Elijah with Christ may have been suggested by Haymo, but the context of sin shows Gregorian influence.[2] The same passage from Gregory is drawn on by Ælfric: he too contrasts humans who are born of sinful flesh, and Christ who was born of a virgin without sin.[3]

At lines 54–9, the Bodley homilist shows some similarity to Haymo in the idea of the devil wanting to test whether Christ was divine.[4] But whereas Haymo asserts that the devil presumed to tempt Christ as if He were a man because he saw Him hungry, the Bodley homilist relates how the fact that Christ was without sin led the devil to test whether He was indeed the Son of God. Here homily v can be compared more closely to Ælfric's account:

þam deofle wæs micel twynung, Hwæt Crist wære? His lif næs na gelogod swa swa oðra manna lif. Crist ne æt mid gyfernysse, ne he ne dranc mid ofer-flowendnysse, ne his eagan ne ferdon worigende geond mislice lustas. þa smeade se deofol hwæt he wære; hwæðer he wære Godes Sunu, seðe mann-cynne behaten wæs. Cwæð þa on his geðance, þæt he fandian wolde hwæt he wære. (CH I xi, p. 168)

Again it is Christ's sinless nature which prompts the devil to test Him (though Ælfric has categorized more precisely than the Bodley

---

[1] CH I xi, p. 178, ll. 8–15.
[2] PL 118, col. 196A; PL 76, col. 1135D.
[3] CH I xi, p. 176, ll. 1–5.
[4] PL 118, col. 196D.

homilist what distinguishes Christ from other men). But immediately following this passage Ælfric adds that it is Christ's hunger which made the devil doubt His divinity and therefore tempt Him. Ælfric, like Haymo but unlike the Bodley homilist, has explicitly linked Christ's hunger with the devil's determination to tempt Him.

The Bodley homilist proceeds to describe how the devil enticed Christ with the same temptations as those he used to beguile Adam and Eve, that is, by gluttony, avarice, and vainglory (ll. 59–63). The ultimate source for this is Gregory.[1] Ælfric includes a similar passage, again clearly based on Gregory:

Se ealda deofol gecostnode urne fæder Adam on ðreo wisan: þæt is mid gyfer-nysse, and mid idelum wuldre, and mid gitsunge; and þa wearð he oferswiðed, forðon þe he geðafode ðam deofle on eallum þam ðrim costnungum. (CH I xi, p. 176)

Ælfric is closer than the anonymous homilist to Gregory here, since he, like Gregory, proceeds to elaborate on how Adam succumbed to the three temptations of gluttony, avarice, and vainglory. In CH I xi this passage is part of the separate section drawn from Gregory which Ælfric has added at the end of his verse-by-verse account (it is framed by a passage on the three-fold nature—instigation, pleasure, and consent— of the devil's temptation, and a passage showing how the devil tempted Christ in the same ways that he did Adam). In homily v the passage is brief and has been included within the verse-by-verse sequence, at the end of commentary on Matth. iv. 2.

At line 64 the Bodley homilist moves to translation of, and commentary on, Matth. iv. 3. Although none of the extant Latin texts contains an equivalent passage of commentary, a corresponding passage can be found in Ælfric's homily.[2] Both Ælfric and the anonymous homilist state that Christ could easily have changed the stones into bread. Ælfric describes God as 'seðe awende wæter to wine, and seðe ealle gesceafte of nahte geworhte'; the Bodley homilist has (probably independently of any source) amplified the idea of Christ as God the Creator, using repetition for emphasis: the phrase 'he alle sceafte isceop and wrohte' is repeated within two lines, and 'hit wære sone iworden' is followed closely by 'þenne weron heo sonæ'.[3] The Bodley

---

[1] PL 76, col. 1136, ll. 1–4, 18–19, 25–6. Haymo has a similar passage at PL 118, col. 200, but its context is quite different; Haymo is discussing the different orders of the temptations as they are presented in Matthew and Luke.   [2] CH I xi, p. 168, ll. 23–6.

[3] Pseudo-Bede's incidental reference to the Creation, 'Dixit Deus, Fiat lux, et facta est lux' (PL 92, col. 19), is the only such reference amongst the relevant patristic texts.

homilist explains that Christ refused to change the stones into bread in order to conceal his divine power from the devil (ll. 71–4). For this Haymo is the closest of the available Latin sources: 'Ita enim Dominus noster Jesus Christus sua opera temperavit, ut diabolus ejus adventum cognoscere non posset, et per virtutem miraculorum suorum se Deum esse mundo manifestaret.'[1] Ælfric states that Christ did not wish to do anything on the devil's instructions (not that he wished to conceal his divine power): 'ac he nolde nan ðing don be ðæs deofles tæcunge'.[2] The Blickling homilist provides a closer analogue: 'Drihten on þære costunge nolde his þa myclan miht gecyþan.'[3] The Bodley homilist emphasizes Christ's determination to keep His divine power concealed from the devil later in the homily within his exposition of Matth. iv. 7: 'Hwæt, Crist mihte eaðe mid ane worde þenne deofel senden on ece lure, ȝif he him his godcundæn mihte cuþen wolde' (ll. 112–13).

The homilist translates Matth. iv. 4, and comments on it briefly (ll. 74–80). Haymo may be the source from which the passage was derived, but since Ælfric's equivalent passage ('swa swa þæs mannes lichama leofað be hlafe, swa sceal his sawul lybban be Godes wordum, þæt is, be Godes lare, þe he þurh wise menn on bocum gesette') is much closer to the Bodley homilist's, it seems likely that another source (perhaps drawing on Haymo) was used by both.[4] The distinction between bodily and spiritual food was a traditional one: the idea recurs in Ælfric's homilies, for example, and is also found in Blickling v.[5]

Translation of Matth. iv. 5 at line 81 is followed by commentary derived ultimately from Gregory.[6] The homilist has followed Gregory fairly closely, although he does diverge from Gregory in interesting ways. The idea of the devil actually touching Christ is introduced and reiterated by the homilist, presumably to emphasize the distinction between the physical contact and the spiritual salvation that ultimately

[1] PL 118, col. 196C. Gregory's commentary on Christ's refusal to respond to the devil's temptations with anything other than words contrasts Christ's patience with mankind's impatience (PL 76, col. 1136C).

[2] CH I xi, p. 168, ll. 25–6.

[3] Blickling, p. 33, ll. 17–18.

[4] PL 118, col. 197B; CH I xi, p. 168, ll. 28–30; Förster cites Pseudo-Bede, PL 92, col. 19, as the source for this passage in CH I xi, but the number of similarities to Haymo elsewhere makes him the more likely source here too.

[5] See, for example, CH I, p. 248; CH II, pp. 233, 258, 269; Blickling, p. 56.

[6] PL 76, col. 1135, ll. 27–40. The same passage is found in Haymo, PL 118, col. 191, Smaragdus, PL 102, col. 122, Bede, PL 94, col. 358.

ensued for mankind: 'hu deofel æfre þa durstinesse hæfde þæt he Cristes lichame ætrinæn durste, oðer forðen þæt he him on neawste cumen moste' (ll. 84–5), 'his lichame rinæn moste' (l. 93), 'deofles ætrine' (l. 96). To Gregory's assertion that the devil is the head of all sinful men and all sinful men are his limbs, the homilist adds the corresponding statement (from Col. i. 18) that Christ is the head of all holy men and all holy men are His limbs (ll. 87–8). The idea is one found frequently in homiletic literature.[1]

Both CH I xi and Blickling iii provide analogues for this passage. Its location varies widely from text to text. In CH I xi, as in Haymo, the passage is included in commentary on Matth. iv. 1. In Blickling iii, it is found near the beginning of the second half of the homily (corresponding to its position near the beginning of Gregory's homily). In homily v, it functions as commentary on Matth. iv. 5. It is possible, however, that the Old English authors are drawing here on a later text derived from Gregory; all three have independently introduced explicitly the notion of humility ('eadmod(-)') with reference to Christ.[2] If this is the case, however, the Latin text drawing on Gregory must have remained fairly faithful to him, judging by the relationship between Gregory and the three Old English texts: Ælfric has drastically summarized Gregory; the Blickling homilist has rendered him more faithfully than the Bodley homilist, but only the latter has included Gregory's reference to the Jews and Pilate.

At line 97 the homilist moves to Matth. iv. 6: the devil tempted Christ to throw Himself off a pinnacle, citing the scriptures (Ps. xc. 11–12) as evidence that He would be helped by angels. The subsequent commentary explains how the devil lied in his citation of scripture since it was written that angels would come to the help of holy men, not of Christ. For this the homilist shows some resemblance to Haymo.[3] Close analogues in both CH I xi and Blickling iii, however, suggest that all three may have drawn on an intermediary.[4]

---

[1] Ælfric, for example, uses it at CH I, pp. 238, 260, 272, 368, 390; CH II, pp. 157, 225.

[2] Homily v, ll. 86 and 95 'eadmodlicre'; Blickling, p. 33, l. 6 'eadmodlican'; CH I, p. 168, l. 5 'eadmod'.

[3] PL 118, col. 198A/C.

[4] CH I xi, p 170, ll. 4–9; Blickling, p. 29, ll. 29–32. The link between these three passages is discussed by Wright, 'Blickling Homily III', p. 131. As ultimate source for the passage in Blickling iii, Wright cites Jerome: 'Verum ibi non de Christo sed de uiro sancto prophetia est. Male ergo interpretatur scripturas diabolus' (CCSL 77, p. 21), and compares later commentators such as Bede, *In Lucae evangelium* (CCSL 120, p. 97), and Smaragdus, *Expositio Libri Comitis* (PL 102, col. 127). He notes, however, that Jerome's comment probably reached the Blickling homilist through an intermediary, owing to its

The Blickling homilist is closest to Haymo of the three, and could
have derived his commentary for this passage directly from Haymo.
However Ælfric and the Bodley homilist are certainly closer to each
other than to Haymo here; they at least must have been drawing on a
common intermediary, and the nature of the resemblances shown
elsewhere amongst the three homilies suggests that the Blickling
homilist may also have been drawing on this. The three Old English
homilies can be contrasted with the Latin in several ways.

Ælfric and the Bodley homilist agree in their material against the
Latin in several respects. First, both independently develop the idea
of the devil as a liar by nature.[1] Secondly, the Bodley homilist actually
conflicts in interpretation with Haymo at one point, and in this he is
probably matched by Ælfric. Whereas Haymo interprets the stone as
'legem quae in tabulis lapideis scripta est', the Bodley homilist
specifically applies the stone to the devil. Ælfric does not offer any
explicit interpretation of the stone, but his repeated comments that
angels support holy men against the devil and that they sustain all
mankind against devils implies that in the context of Matth. iv. 6 the
stone corresponds to the devil.[2] An interesting parallel can be
observed in Ælfric's homily on the Dedication of the Church of St.
Michael; here Ælfric's comments also imply that the stone of Ps. xc is
to be interpreted as the devil:

ælcum geleaffullum men is engel to hyrde geset, þe hine wið deofles syrwunge
gescylt, and on halgum mægnum gefultumað. (CH I xxxiv, p. 516)

Ælfric's source for this latter homily is a different homily by Haymo;
the relevant passage in Haymo is: '... quia unusquisque fidelium,
angelum ob sui custodiam deputatem habet, qui et eum a tentationibus defendit, et in virtutibus juvat'.[3] Haymo's comment, however, is
not directly within the context of Ps. xc (which he quotes later). Ælfric
has made the connection between the stone and the devil more
explicit, and it is certainly possible that for CH I xxxiv he was recalling
an interpretation of the stone from his source for CH I xi, a source

similarity here to CH I xi and homily v. For the comment in Blickling iii (as in CH I xi
and homily v) that angels act as guardians of men (not in Jerome), Wright (n. 7, pp. 131–
2) notes the similarity to Haymo's homily which I have cited as nearest to the source for
homily v. Haymo seems to me to be closer to all three Old English homilies than
Jerome.

[1] Homily v, ll. 101–3; CH I xi, p. 170, ll. 5–6.
[2] CH I xi, p. 170, ll. 8–9, 10–12.
[3] PL 118, cols. 770–6, col. 776. The source is identified by Förster, 'Über die
Quellen', pp. 45–6.

shared with the Bodley homilist and possibly also with the Blickling homilist.

Thirdly, both Ælfric and the Bodley homilist expand Haymo's comment that angels act as guardians of the life of holy men.[1] They follow different directions, however, in their expansion of this comment. Ælfric moves from the angels' support of holy men to stress the angels' support of all mankind, thus showing that the devil has no power to force man to evil if he wishes to resist. The Bodley homilist writes that angels will help holy men and holy souls, and proceeds to comment that angels will help the souls of holy men not only in life but also against the devil after death (ll. 104–9). Ælfric, then, emphasizes the impact of the angels' guardianship on all mankind in this life, the Bodley homilist emphasizes that the angels will guard holy men both in this life and after death.

Significantly, however, the Bodley homilist returns later in his commentary to the way that angels help men in the world. This occurs within his exposition of Matth. iv. 11. Having affirmed (following Gregory, col. 1136D) that the angels would not have served Christ if he had not been true God (as opposed to true man), the Bodley homilist then states, as if contradicting his previous statement, that angels often have been and still are sent into the world to help mankind (ll. 155–7). In support of this, he paraphrases Hebr. i. 14, assuring his audience that the angels will minister to all men who are endeavouring to deserve eternal salvation and who keep God's commands (ll. 157–62).[2] Two points should be made here. First, Haymo, immediately after his comment on Matth. iv. 6 discussed above ('quia ad custodiendam sanctorum vitam angeli deputantur'), cites Hebr. i. 14. Secondly, and more importantly, a parallel can be found in Blickling iii. In the second part of that homily, the Blickling homilist, following Gregory, states that angels would not have ministered to Christ if He were not true God. Like the Bodley homilist at line 155, the Blickling homilist, independently of Gregory, proceeds at this point to remark that angels minister to all Christians when they have overcome the devil.[3] It seems

---

[1] The Blickling homilist includes only a brief remark, 'forþon þe englas beoþ aa halgum mannum on fultume swa swa scyld'. His choice of the word 'scyld(-)' is interesting since it appears also in homily v. Such a verbal link, although possibly coincidental, could signify a common intermediary with wording altered from Haymo's.

[2] Hebr. i. 14: 'Nonne omnes sunt administratorii spiritus, in ministerium missi propter eos, qui haereditatem capient salutis?'

[3] A close parallel appears in Blickling xvii (the Dedication of St. Michael's Church): 'Englas beoð to ðegnunge gæstum fram Gode hider on world sended, to ðæm ðe þone

as though the link between Gregory's statement and the role of angels in the world is not picked up independently by the Bodley homilist, reminded of his earlier account of how angels help holy men, but was present in some intermediary source on which both the Bodley homilist and Blickling homilist drew.

At line 110 of homily v, Matth. iv. 7, containing Christ's answer to the devil in which He too cites scripture (Deut. vi. 16), is translated (with the independent addition of the emotive qualifier 'oferiȝend-lice'). It is followed by commentary (ll. 112–17) derived ultimately from Gregory.[1] Close analogues are to be found in CH I xi and Blickling iii;[2] Ælfric is particularly close to Gregory in this passage. The Bodley homilist is alone amongst Gregory, Ælfric, and the Blickling homilist, in not introducing the concept of vengeance, even as an alternative to be avoided.[3] The passage is variously placed in the Latin and Old English texts. In the Blickling homily, it appears in the second part and therefore follows Gregory's ordering. Haymo includes it in commentary on Matth. iv. 4. Ælfric places it in the context of verse 11. In homily v, it functions as exegesis for Matth. iv. 7.

The ensuing section of commentary (ll. 118–31) demonstrates the freedom with which the Old English homilist felt able to treat his Latin source(s). Matth. iv. 8 is translated, and followed by a passage describing first the omnipotence of Christ and then the power of the devil to create illusions. The first part concerning the glory of this world and the omnipotence of Christ may derive originally from Haymo, and has an analogue, though again not very close, in Blickling iii.[4] The second part (from l. 124) shows the homilist independently developing Haymo's commentary. Haymo claims that the devil could only show all the glories of the world simultaneously to Christ because Christ Himself allowed it. The Bodley homilist states that the devil, through his deceptive powers, could have shown any man all the glories of the world as an illusion. The phrase 'þonne him ilyfed bið' (l. 129), implying that the permission of Christ is needed to sanction the devil's deceptions, shows that the two passages are not contradic-

---

ecean eðel mid mode & mid mægene to Gode geearniað, þæt him syn on fultume ða þe wið þæm awergdum gastum syngallice feohtan sceolan' (Blickling, p. 209, ll. 22–6).

[1] PL 76, col. 1136C. I have also cited Haymo, PL 118, col. 197A in my source material, since it may represent the kind of intermediary on which the Bodley homilist drew.

[2] CH I xi, p. 174, ll. 24–9; Blickling, p. 33, ll. 17–24.

[3] Haymo similarly has no reference to vengeance, but minor coincidences in omission of material cannot be treated as significant for source identification.

[4] PL 118, col. 99 ('nec mirum . . . videre possent'); Blickling, p. 31, ll. 1–11.

tory. But the emphasis on the devil's ability to make his illusions visible to all men as well as to Christ is the Old English homilist's own. Of particular interest is his assertion that the devil can appear in the guise of an angel (ll. 129–31). The use and origin of the image of the devil in disguise has been examined by Rosemary Woolf:

In *Juliana* and, presumably, in *Genesis B*, the devil disguises himself as an angel of light in order to make his temptation more convincing . . . The angel-of-light disguise is of specifically Christian origin, as it appears, for instance, in the *Vita Adae et Evae* and the *Apocalypse of Moses*, and is stated as a doctrine with biblical support by Gregory I in his *Moralia* (Lib. xxix, Cap. xxx): 'Transfigurat enim se velut angelum lucis (ii Cor. xi, 14) et callida deceptionis ante plerumque proponit laudabilia, ut ad illicita pertrahat.'[1]

Although Ælfric does not refer to the devil's deceptive powers in CH I xi, he does treat the subject in a different work, his *Life of St. Martin*.[2] Ælfric relates how a devil disguised as a monk claimed that in the middle of the night God would clothe him with a heavenly garment, by which means he would reveal God's power. The 'monk' duly appears before the other monks in a mysteriously luminous garment, but refuses to visit St. Martin. When he is dragged to Martin, the garment vanishes. The implication here is that the devil can deceive ordinary men with his illusions though saints can see through them. The Bodley homilist's emphasis on the devil's ability to deceive mankind is in keeping with this. Moreover the Fall itself, the origin of sin amongst mankind, happened as a result of the devil's ability to appear in disguise; since the Bodley homilist has earlier compared the devil's temptations of Christ with those of Adam, he may have an implicit reference to the Fall in mind.

After translating Matth. iv. 9, the Bodley homilist skilfully creates a linguistic link between the devil's request to Christ to fall physically at his feet and the horror of the fall—presumably both metaphorical and physical (into hell)—which results from submitting to the devil (ll. 133–4). The closest Latin parallel is found in Hiberno-Latin commentaries including Pseudo-Jerome: 'Vere cadit, qui adorat diabolum.'[3] The Blickling homilist makes a similar link, translating Matth. iv. 9, then exclaiming 'Eala soþlice se afealleþ se þe deofol weorþeþ'.[4] At ll. 134–7, homily v's author independently elaborates

---

[1] 'The Devil in Old English Poetry', *Review of English Studies*, N.S., iv (1953), 1–12, pp. 2–3.   [2] LS xxxi, 792–830.

[3] PL 30, col. 542. See further Wright, 'Blickling Homily III', p. 135 and nn.

[4] Blickling, p. 31, l. 1 (with 'weorþeþ' for 'weorþaþ'). Wright, 'Blickling Homily III', p. 135, relates this passage in Blickling iii to several Hiberno-Latin commentaries.

on and clarifies the idea, describing effectively the malicious nature of the devil, who delivers ever more cruelty in return for ever greater obedience.

For commentary on Matth. iv. 10, the homilist explains, independently of any extant Latin source, how the devil's powers were diminished after Christ ordered him away, and Christ's doctrine flourished by various means: first through Himself, then through His apostles, then through holy teachers (ll. 140–3). He then urges his audience to pray only to God and serve Him alone (ll. 143–9). Ælfric has an analogous passage in which he acknowledges the scriptural authority for this (Deut. vi. 13): 'hit is awriten on ðære ealdan æ'.[1] Haymo and other Latin texts offer a lengthy discussion on the different types of 'service' according to the etymology of the relevant Greek words. Since Ælfric and the Bodley homilist are closer to each other than to the Latin—both authors distinguish praying for intercession from saints and praying to God—a different source common to the Old English authors offers a likely explanation.[2]

A translation of the final verse of the pericope (Matth. iv. 11) is followed by a passage of commentary which can be divided into two parts. The first (ll. 150–5) is derived from Gregory: Christ's dual nature is proven in that the devil tempted Him as a man and angels ministered to Him as God.[3] The homilist then moves to consider the function of angels in the world, citing Hebr. i. 14 to show that angels will minister to all men who desire to earn eternal salvation and who keep God's commands (ll. 155–62). I have discussed above (in the context of ll. 104–9 of homily v) the connections between these two parts, arguing that although the second part relates closely to lines 104–9 of homily v, an intermediary source (also drawn on by the homilist of Blickling iii) was probably responsible for both parts of the commentary on Matth. iv. 11.

The scriptural citation at lines 163–4 is from 2 Cor. vi, and for this the Bodley homilist is clearly indebted to Haymo (col. 195). From Haymo too is derived the list of virtues which prepare one for eternal salvation though the Old English homilist has slightly expanded it, mainly by repetition and varying vocabulary (ll. 164–72). This list has

[1] CH I xi, p. 174, ll. 4–6.
[2] In his homily on the Nativity of our Lord (CH I ii, 19–32), Ælfric explains that the Old and New Testaments differed in their attitude to prayer; whereas before Christ men were permitted to pray to angels, afterwards this was forbidden and only prayer to God Himself was allowed.
[3] PL 76, col. 1136D.

also been used (and slightly adapted) by Ælfric.[1] Again the common source must have supplied the Old English homilists with such a list. Evidence of reordering of the source by one or other of the Old English homilists is found here again: in Ælfric's homily, this list of virtues is placed after, not before as in homily v, the passage in which the number of days for abstinence are calculated.

The passage encouraging the audience to tithe their goods and to fast a tenth part of their days brings us to the close of the homily (l. 173 to end). This probably derives from Gregory;[2] Ælfric and the Blickling homilist also contain fairly close renderings of the Latin source. The striking feature which distinguishes the Bodley homilist's account from that of any of the other versions is his willingness to allow compromise, to adapt God's requirements to human nature. Twice the homilist stresses that a man does not have to do what seems too onerous to him: first, if tithing a tenth part of his possessions seems too difficult, he should at least try to fast the tenth part of his days (ll. 176–8); secondly, if living with austerity and abstinence for the whole of this tenth part seems too severe, he should try to keep the fast as well as he can (ll. 184–8). This tolerant attitude does not seem to have been widespread. The Laws are consistently adamant that tithing is absolutely necessary and that non-compliance will be severely punished, as the following examples show:[3]

(i) I Cnut 8. 2: '7 gyf hwa þonne þa teoþunge gelæstan nelle, swa we gecweden habbað, þæt is se teoða æcer, ealswa seo sulh hit gega, þonne fare þæs cingces gerefa to 7 þæs bisceopes 7 þæs landrican 7 þæs mynstres mæssepreost, 7 nime unþances ðone teoðan dæl to þam mynstre, þe hit to gebyrige' (p. 292);

(ii) IV Eadgar, 1. 4: 'Ðonne beode ic 7 se ærcebisceop, þæt ge God ne grymman, ne naþer ne geearnian ne þone færlican deað þises andweardan lifes, ne huru þone toweardan ecere helle mid ænegum oftige Godes gerihta; ac ægðer ge earm ge eadig, þe ænige tylunge hæbbe, gelæste Gode his teoðunga mid ealre blisse 7 mid eallum unnan' (pp. 206–8);

(iii) VIII Æthelred, 7: 'And wite Cristenra manna gehwilc, þæt he his Drihtene his teoþunge, a swa seo sulh þone teoðan æcer gega,

---

[1] CH I xi, p. 178, ll. 30–4.

[2] PL 76, col. 1137, ll. 27–40. Haymo includes exactly the same material (PL 118, cols. 193–4), but within commentary on verse 2.

[3] Felix Liebermann, ed., *Die Gesetze der Angelsachsen*, I (Halle, 1903).

rihtlice gelæste be Godes miltse 7 be þam fullan wite, þe Eadgar cyningc gelagode' (pp. 264–5);

(iv) I Eadmund: 'Teoðunge we bebeodað ælcum Cristene men be his Cristendome and ciricsceat 7 Romfeoh 7 sulhælmessan. And gif hit hwa don nelle, si he amansumod' (p. 184).

This kind of legal rather than moral obligation to tithe is also absent from the Ælfric and Blickling homilies. In this they can be compared with Blickling iv, a homily on tithing. According to Rudolph Willard, Blickling iv reflects its source, Caesarius of Arles, which in turn reflects the thought of the early sixth century in which 'tithing was being taught as morally, though not canonically, binding'; he concludes that the Old English translation must have been made 'either before the tithing legislation of Edgar was enacted, or in total unconcern as to its existence'.[1] Clearly this explanation is not satisfactory for all the homilies, since Ælfric's homily at least must have been written after this legislation obtained. The references to tithing in the three homilies indicate that laws on tithing were not readily enforceable despite the presence of legislation. The Bodley homilist implies that tithing was not even morally, let alone legally, binding if it entailed undue personal hardship.

At this point in their works, both Ælfric and the Blickling homilist follow Gregory in emphasizing that fasting in itself is not sufficient virtue and must be accompanied by other merciful and charitable actions.[2] Homily v ends, however, without such an elaboration but with the promise of happiness for those who act appropriately, and with the formulaic reminder of the Lord's eternal rule.

Bodley 343's anonymous homily for the First Sunday in Lent derives, then, from a lost Latin source which it may have shared with Ælfric's and Blickling's homilies for the first Sunday in Lent. This common Latin source was based mainly on Gregory, but included material from other patristic authors such as Haymo and Jerome. Although the immediate source has not survived, it is possible for us to gain some idea of the Bodley homilist's methods of composition by examining his treatment of Gregory and of the Bible, and by comparing his text with the other Old English homilies using the same or a

[1] 'The Blickling-Junius Tithing Homily and Caesarius of Arles', in *Philologica: The Malone Anniversary Studies*, ed. Thomas A. Kirby and Henry Bosley Woolf (Baltimore, 1949), 65–78, pp. 67, 71.

[2] CH I xi, p. 180, l. 2; Blickling, p. 37, l. 15.

similar source. The following conclusions can be drawn. Some of the material seems to be the homilist's own independent composition. He offers his own fairly lengthy introduction to the gospel-exposition, and his conclusion too is apparently based only loosely on any source. He often orders material independently, thereby achieving emphasis on different aspects of commentary. He seems to have been particularly concerned to provide a systematic verse-by-verse exegesis of the gospel-text. He exhibits a confident knowledge of the Bible, apparently introducing independently, for example, additional biblical information on Moses and Elijah, and freely paraphrasing Old Testament quotations. He devotes particular attention to the devil's ability to deceive by means of visual illusions. Given that this is an age where originality was not a high priority, the Bodley homilist shows a considerable independence in his rendering of source material; he offers an organized and straightforward, if not ambitious, account of Christ's Temptation in the wilderness.

Men þa leofestæ, we wullæð eow sæggæn bi þare halȝæ tide þe nu
toweard is, þe we onsundren mare fæsten and mare for(hæfd)nesse on
habbað, þonne on oðre tide ȝemænelice. þonne do we þæt to bote and
to clænsunge ure sawlæ, and eac for þam þe Crist sylf us þæs fæstenes
5 bysne onstealde. Hit is iwriten þæt þe Hælend sonæ æfter his fuluhte
ferde on sume wæsten and þær festæ feowertiȝ daȝe and feowertiȝ
nihtæ togædere ær þam þe he moncyn ofer all openlice lærde. Ne
fæste he na forþan ðæt he æfre æniȝ sunne wrohte þæt he mid þam
festen beten þurfte. Ac he feste þæt he walde monncynnes sunnæn
10 hælen and alesæn, and us bisne onstællæn, þæt wæ witen þæt ælc þare
mannæ þe ðencþ þæt he ða heofenlice murhþe biȝete, þæt he sceal nu
þurh festen, and þurh ælmes, and þurh lomlice ȝebeden, and þurh
lichamlice forhæfdnesse her on weorlde earniæn, and na þurh
ȝifernesse, ne ðurh druncennesse, ne ðurh lichamlice lustæs. Crist
15 þolede eac on þam wæsten þene awariȝede deofel hine fandiæn, swa
we nu heræfter secgæn wullæð.

Sanctus Matheus wrat, þe godspellere, þis dæȝþerlice godspel
æfter þissere endeburdnesse, þus cwæðende: *Ductus est Ihesus in
desertum a Spiritu ut temptaretur a diabolo*. He cwæð: 'þe Hælend wæs
20 ilæd fram Gaste on wæsten þæt he were ifondod of deofle.' Monie
men tweoniæð fram hwylce gaste Crist wære on þæt westen ilæd nu
hit swa cuðlice on þissum godspellicæn lare sæȝð þæt ðe wariȝede
deofel hine þær swa openlice costniæn ongon. Hit is buton tweon to
fol 158ᵛ lyfen and ȝeare to witenne | þæt ðe Haliȝe Gast him wunsumlice on
25 þæt wæsten lædde, and þæt he sylfwilles þider ferde þæt he wolde

Bodley 343, fols. 158–60; Belfour, pp. 96–107.

---

2 forhæfdnesse] for ouer hædfnesse

SOURCES. The sources referred to here are: (i) Gregory, *Homiliae in Evangelia*, PL 76,
cols. 1134–8 (cited as Gregory); (ii) Haymo, *Homilia de Tempore*, PL 118, cols. 190–203
(cited as Haymo); (iii) Pseudo-Jerome, *In Evangelium Secundum Matthaeum*, PL 30, cols.
541–2 (cited as Ps.-Jerome); (iv) Pseudo-Bede, *In Matthaei Evangelium Expositio*, PL 92,
cols. 18–20 (cited as Ps.-Bede).
1–16 (*Independent of sources*)
20–6 (*Gregory, col. 1135 B*) Dubitari a quibusdam solet a quo spiritu sit Jesus ductus in
desertum, propter hoc quod subditur: 'Assumpsit eum diabolus in sanctam civitatem.'
Et rursum: 'Assumpsit eum in montem excelsum valde.' Sed vere et absque ulla quaes-
tione convenienter accipitur ut a sancto Spiritu in desertum ductus credatur, ut illuc
eum suus Spiritus duceret, ubi hunc ad tentandum malignus spiritus inveniret.
(*Haymo, cols. 190–1, reproduces this material, but also has extra commentary between 'ductus
credatur' and 'ut illuc'. No equivalent in OE analogues.*)

deofle þa durstinesse ȝyfæn þæt he him þær costniæn ongon, na for
þam þæt þe deofel hæfde æniȝ fare to ure Hælende oðer his mæð
wære þæt he him ahwær on neawste come, ȝif he hit for ure lufe | ne Bf. 98
ȝeðafede. Ac he hit dude ure life to bisene þæt he walde þæt we wisten
hu eaðelice he þene deofel ofercom, na mid his godcunlice mihte ane, 30
ac mid þare mænniscæ rihtwisnesse. Swa eac nu mæȝ ealc mon deofel
ofercumen, ȝif he on rihtwisnesse and on gode weorcum his lif adrihð.

'Ða sonæ þa ðe Hælend on þæt wæsten becom, þa fæste he
feowertiȝ daȝa and nihte togædere; and æfter þam he sæȝde þæt hine
hingrede.' Witerlice on þam hit wæs ful cuð þæt he hæfde soðne 35
lichame þa him hingriæn mihte. Hit is iwriten on þare ealde laȝe þæt
twæȝe men her biforen þis festen festen. Moyses feste feowertiȝ daȝe
and nihte togedere þa he wæs on Synai þære dune æt Drihtines spece;
and Drihten him sealde þa ealde laȝe þe he mid his aȝene fingre wrat
on twam stænene bræden, and þam folce send(e), and het þæt heo alle 40
þeræfter lyfedon. Elias þe witegæ feste eac þæt ilce festen feowertiȝ
daȝe and nihtæ tosomne, æfter þan ðe he æt þene mæte ðe þe engel to
him brohte, and he wearð þa þurh ðone mete istrongæd swa þæt he
þæt fæsten feste. And æftær þam fæsten he wearð mid wisdomes gaste
ifulled, and him þa toweardæn þing unwreah and swytelode, þæt he 45

26 costniæn] t *altered from another letter*   29 walde] *altered from* wælde
31 deofel] *stroke above* o (*probably accidental*)   32 adrihð] d *altered from another letter*
34 feowertiȝ] *erasure between* o *and* w   40 sende] senden   42 æt] *glossed by*
þiȝede

26-32 (*Haymo, col. 191B* [*Similar in idea but not in wording*]) Dandus enim erat diabolo
locus tentandi, ut fieret Christo occasio superandi. Permisit enim se a maligno spiritu
tentari, ut nobis exemplum pugnandi ostenderet. Quod apostolus Paulus in Epistola
sua ad Hebraeos, cum de Domino loqueretur, dicit: 'Non enim habemus pontificem,
qui non possit infirmitatibus nostris compati, tentatum autem per omnia pro similitu-
dine absque peccato' (*Hebr. iv*). Adeamus ergo ad thronum gloriae cum fiducia, ut
misericordiam consequamur, et inveniamus gratiam in auxilio opportuno. Sed cum
mens humana creatorem suum et redemptorem, qui nullum omnino peccatum habuit, a
diabolo audit tentatum, metu fragilitatis suae expavescit. Sed qui ex humana fragilitate
terretur, ex conditoris sui compassione fiduciam resumere debet. Qui enim propter nos
homo fieri dignatus est, in humana natura se tentari pro nobis permisit, ut sua tenta-
tione nostram excluderet: nec solum impugnandi contra diabolum audaciam tribueret,
sed etiam vincendi fiduciam restauraret.
35-6 (*Haymo, col. 196A*) Additum est, 'postea esuriit', ut vera in illo humanitas esse
ostenderetur.
36-48 (*Gregory, col. 1137A*) Moyses enim ut legem acciperet secundo diebus quadraginta jejunavit (*Exod. xxxiv. 28*). Elias in deserto quadraginta diebus abstinuit (*3 Kings
xix. 8*). Ipse auctor hominum ad homines veniens, in quadraginta diebus nullum omnino
cibum sumpsit (*Matth. iv. 2*).
(*Also compare Haymo, col. 193A*) Quorum alter [Moses] legislator fuit, alter [Elias]
eximius prophetarum. Per Moysen ergo lex, per Eliam prophetia significatur.

heom wiste swa ȝeare swa þa ðe he on andweardnesse iseah. Nu eft on
þis ytemeste tide þe Hælend hine eadmedede to þam þæt he þis ylce
fæsten feste feowertiȝæ daȝæ and nihtæ togadere. For hwon nolde þe
deofel fanden Moysen and Heliam swa he ure Hælend fondode, buten
50 for þon ðe he underȝeat þæt heo mennisce men wæren, and þurh
Adames gult ibundene, and eac þæt heo on summe þinge isyngod
hæfden? For næs næfræ nan mon on þisse middænearde swa haliȝ,
þæt he on summe þinge ne sunegode buten Crist ane, þe ðe is soð
God and soð mon; him næs næfre nan sunne on. Ac þa ðe deofel com
55 to him, þa iseah he þæt he hæfde soðne lichame and þæt he wæs unilic
ælle oðre monnum þe he on middænearde eafre imette, and þæt on
him næs nare synne wem. þa ondredde þe deofel þæt hit wære, swa
swa hit wæs, þæs lifiende Godes Sune, and þohte þa þæt he walde mid
þare costunge fonden hu hit wære. Ber þa to him þa ylce costungæ þe
60 he þam ereste men Adam and Euam mid forcostode and biswaac, and
Bf. 100 his | wylles weald on him æhte: þæt wæs þurh ȝifernesse, and ȝytsunge,
and ydel ȝylp. þa wolde Crist þone awariede deofel ofercumen on
þam ylce þrem costunge þe ðe deofel ær þa ereste men mid biswaac.

'Ða neahlæchede þe deofel to þam Hælende and cwæð to him:
65 Gyf þu eart Godes Sune, hat þæt þæs stanes to lafes wurðen.' Næs
Criste nan earfoðnesse þæt he þa stanes mid his worde to lafes wrohte;
for ȝif he hit icwæde, hit wære sone iworden, and þenne wiste ðe
deofel ful wisslice þæt he wære þe ylce Drihten þe þe æt frymðe wæs,
þa þa he alle sceafte isceop and wrohte; and he cwæð, Gewurðe liht,

54 deofel] d῾e´ofel   60 he] e *probably altered from another letter*

48–54 (*Haymo, col. 196A*) ['Postea esuriit'] Hoc enim de Moyse et Elia scriptum non
legimus, quia nulli dubium, quod post jejunium ut puri homines esurierint: sed de illo,
qui ita Deus erat, ut etiam homo esset, dignum fuit ut scriberetur. Vel certe post
jejunium esuriit, ut occasio tentandi diabolo praeberetur.
(*Also Gregory, col. 1135D*) Et nos cum tentamur, plerumque in delectationem, aut etiam
in consensum labimur, quia de carnis peccato propagati, in nobisipsis etiam gerimus
unde certamina toleremus. Deus vero qui, in utero Virginis incarnatus, in mundum sine
peccato venerat, nihil contradictionis in semetipso tolerabat.
54–9 (*Haymo, col. 196D*) Sed quia ejus divinitatem voluit explorare, ideo accedens ad
tentandum, dixit: 'Si Filius Dei es', etc.
[*But closer to CH I xi, p. 168, ll. 10–16.*]
59–63 (*Gregory, col. 1136A, B*) Antiquus hostis contra primum hominem parentem
nostrum in tribus se tentationibus erexit, quia hunc videlicet gula, vana gloria et avaritia
tentavit . . . Sed quibus modis primum hominem stravit, eisdem modis secundo homini
tentato succubuit . . . Sed eisdem modis a secundo homine vincitur, quibus primum
hominem se vicisse gloriabatur.
65–71 (*Ps.-Bede, col. 19B* [*cited here because it is the only Latin text to refer to the Creation. The
OE text is close here to CH I xi, p. 168, ll. 23–5.*]) 'Dic' non fac dicebat, quia scriptum
noverat, 'Dixit Deus, Fiat lux, et facta est lux.'

and þa wæs sone iworden liht. And swa he | alle sceafte iscop and fol. 159
iwrohtæ; þenne he walde þæt heo weren, þenne weron heo sonæ. þa 71
nolde þa ȝyt Crist haten þæt ða stanes to lafes wurðen, ac he walde
þæt his godcundlice miht wære ȝyt þam deofle bihud, þæh heo wære
him æft ful stronge iopenod. 'And he þa þuldelice to him spec and þus
cwæð: Hit is iwritæn þæt monnes lif ne bið na on lafe ane, ac bið on 75
ælc þare worde þe of Godes muðe forþstepð.' Hwæt we witen þæt
monnes lichame sceal bi mete libban þa hwile þe he on þisse life bið;
swa sceal eac þeo sawle libbæn bi Godes wordes, þæt is þæt heo sceal
Godes lare ȝeorne lystæn, and his bode æfre healden ȝyf heo sceal þæt
ece lif habben.   80

'Ða nam þe deofel þene Hælend on þære halȝan buriȝ, and sette
hine ofer þæs temples yppan þær þære larþeawselt wæs.' Hit þuncþ
moniȝe monnum wunderlice to herenne, and eac uneaðelic to lyfene,
hu deofel æfre þa durstinesse hæfde þæt he Cristes lichame ætrinæn
durste, oðer forðen þæt he him on neawste cumen moste. Ealæ, ȝif we 85
wullæþ iþencean his oðre dæde þe mucele mare and eadmodlicre
beoð, þenne maȝe we þisses þe æð ilyfæn. Crist is alle haliȝe monnæ
heafod, and alle haliȝe men beoð his limen; and deofel is eac alle
synfulle monnæ heafod, and alle sunfulle men beoð his limen. Soðlice
þa Iudeus wæren alle deofles limen, þa ðæ ure Hælend to deaþe 90
demdon. Pilatus wæs eac deofles lim, þe ðe ure Drihten lichamlice
ahon hæt. Hwylc wunder wæs þenne þeah Crist ða durstinesse

---

72 þæt ða] þæt `ða´     82 þuncþ] þuncþ     87 haliȝe] `h´aliȝe   88 is] s
altered from c   90 wæren] æ altered from a   ure] ascender erased above u

---

71–4 (*Haymo, col. 196C* [*not close*]) Ita enim Dominus noster Jesus Christus sua opera
temperavit, ut diabolus ejus adventum cognoscere non posset, et per virtutem miraculorum suorum se Deum esse mundo manifestaret.

76–80 (*Ps.-Bede, col. 19B*) Qui sicut corpus terreno vivit cibo, sic anima Dei verbo quod
de ejus ore procedit, dum suae voluntatis consilium per sacras Scripturas revelare
voluerit nostrae fragilitati.

(*Also Haymo, col. 197B*) Et sicut corpus moritur, si non pascitur cibo carnali, ita moritur anima, nisi reficiatur verbo Dei: non ut non sit, sed ut mala sit.

82–96 (*Gregory, col. 1135B–C* [*also in other Latin texts*]) Sed ecce cum dicitur Deus
homo vel in excelsum montem, vel in sanctam civitatem a diabolo assumptum, mens
refugit, humanae hoc audire aures expavescunt. Qui tamen non esse incredibilia ista
cognoscimus, si in illo et alia facta pensamus. Certe iniquorum omnium caput diabolus
est, et hujus capitis membra sunt omnes iniqui. An non diaboli membrum fuit Pilatus?
An non diaboli membra Judaei persequentes, et milites crucifigentes Christum fuerunt?
Quid ergo mirum si se ab illo permisit in montem duci, qui se pertulit etiam a membris
illius crucifigi? Non est ergo indignum Redemptori nostro quod tenari voluit, qui
venerat occidi. Justum quippe erat ut sic tentationes nostras suis tentationibus vinceret,
sicut mortem nostram venerat sua morte superare.

deof(le) sealde þæt he his lichame rinæn moste, þa he walde þurh
Bf. 102 deofles lime, þæt is þurh sunfulle monnæ honden, lichamlice | deaþ
95 ðrowiæn? Ealæ hwæt, þæt wæs mucele mare and eadmodlicre þonne
þæs deofles ætrine, and he hit þeah for monnæ hæle þrowode.

'þa cwæð þe deofel to Criste: Gif þu eard Godes Sune, þenne
asend þu nu þe adun of þissere uppon; for þam hit is iwriten bi Godes
Sune þæt he beodeþ his englum bi þe, þæt heo þe on heoræ handen
100 habbæð þæt ðin fot ne ðurfe forðon æt stane spurnen.' On þesne
ænne godspel we rædæþ þæt deofel ongan haliȝe bec to reccan, ah he
þa sone þone forme cwide leah, swa him ealc lyȝe and elc leasunge
bilimpð. Næs hit næfre sunderlice bi Criste iseid þæt him sceoldon
englæs on fultume cumen, ac hit wæs isungen and iwriten bi haliȝe
105 men and bi haliȝe sawlen, for þan þe englæs beoð heom on fultume
hær on weorlde. And æft þenne heo of þisse lifæ faræð, þonne cumæð
heo þær sonæ þam sawle to hælpe and to burȝene, and heom scyldæþ
wið hearde stane, þæt is deofel, þæt heo næfre æt þam ne spurneð, ac
þa englas healdæþ heom wið his yfel and wið his niþes grymnesse.

110 'Ða andswerede Crist þam awariȝede gaste and cwæð to him: Hit
is iwriten þæt mon ne sceal to [o]feriȝendlice his Drihtin God
fondiæn.' Hwæt, Crist mihte eaðe mid ane worde þenne deofel
senden on ece lure, ȝif he him his godcundæn mihte cuþen wolde; ac
he to him þuldelice spec and hine ofercom mid mennisce rihtwis-
fol. 159ᵛ nesse, na mid þam anwealde his godcundnesse. | Ac he us þa bysene
116 onstealde þæt we sceolon yfelræ mannæ hate and heora niþæs
ðuldelice forberæn, and symle Godes bocæ teachunge ȝeorne fylȝean.

'Eft þe deofel nam þonne Hælend and lædde hine on ane swiðe
heahne dune, and sceawede him alles middæneardes rice and his

93 deofle] deofel   111 to oferiȝendlice] to feriȝendlice

100–9 (*Haymo, col. 198A, C*) Ex quo loco cognoscimus quia diabolus male Scripturas
interpretatur. Hoc enim non de persona Domini scriptum est, sed in persona justi viri
canitur, qui adjutorio indiget angelorum, ne offendat ad lapidem, hoc est, in legem quae
in tabulis lapideis scripta est.

112–17 (*Gregory, col. 1136C*) . . . et qui eo verbo quod erat tentatorem suum mergere in
abyssum poterat, virtutem suae potentiae non ostendit, sola divinae Scripturae
praecepta dedit, quatenus suae patientiae praeberet exemplum, ut quoties a
pravis hominibus aliquid patimur, ad doctrinam excitemur potius quam ad vindictam.

(*Also Haymo, col. 197A*) Magna est Domini potentia, sed non minor ejus declaratur
patientia. Qui enim solo verbo tentatorem suum, aut in lapidem convertere, aut in
abyssum poterat mergere, ejus tentationes sustinuit, ostendens nobis non esse
timendum cum tentamur, sed cavendum ne tentationibus consentiamus . . . Nec
potestate, sed auctoritate diabolum Dominus voluit superare, ostendens nobis quo-
tiescunque a diabolo tentamur, ad auctoritatem Scripturarum semper esse recur-
rendum.

blisse.' Witerlice næs Criste noht wurð þisses middeneardes rices, ne 120
þysses witiȝendæn wuldres þissere weorlde, bihyd oþer forstolen, ac
he alle ricen, æȝþer ȝe heofenlice ȝe eorþlicen, wissæð, and alle
isceaftæ on his weald hæfð, and heom alle æfter his willæn reccæð and
styreð. Ac þe deofel hæfde þeah mid leasunge þurh his s[c]yncrefte
middaneardes murhþe and all weorldlice feȝernesse togædere 125
æthiwod. þeah hit ðenne allungæ mon wære þe him þære wið speke,
þenne mihte he þeah alle weorldlice feȝernesse togadere iseon þurð
deofles hywunge; for þam ðe ðe deofel mæȝ felæ þingæ dwymorlice
hywiæn before monnæ eaȝum, þonne him ilyfed bið. | Hwilon he Bf. 104
sceawæð hine seluen on engles hywe, and bið þeahweðere awariȝed 130
gast swa swa he ær wæs.

'Ða cwæð þe deofel to Criste: Alle þas ðing ic þe ȝyfe and sylle ȝyf
þu wult fallen to mine fotum and wurhȝiæn me.' Elæ hwæt, ælc þare
monnæ sarlice ȝefalleð þe hine nu to deofle ȝeeadmodeþ. Nis nan
mon þæt æfre þam deofle ȝeorne ihyre, þæt he æft æt him þe bætere 135
are finden maȝe, ac æfre swa he him nu ȝeornere hereð, swa he eft him
grimmere wurð a, þæt he hine on ende on ecere yrmþe bringæð.

'þa cwæð Crist to þam deofle: Ga heonne [on]hinderling, þu
awariȝedæ sceoccæ. Soðlice hit is iwritæn þæt mon sceal to Drihten
ane him biddæn, and him ane þeowiæn.' þa syðæn weron deofles 140
mihtæ onhinderling afulled, and Cristes lare wæs a syðæn waxende
ȝeond þæsne middaneard, ærest þurh him syluen, and syðan þurh his
apostolas and þurh þa haliȝe larþeowæs þe syðon wæren. Crist cwæð
þæt mon sceal to Gode Almihtiȝ ane biddan and him ane þeowian.
Soðlice ne sceole we us biddæn naþor ne to englum ne to oþre haliȝe 145

121 forstolen] *after* n, *the letter* t *has been blotted out*   129 hwilon] l *altered from*
another letter

120-4 (*Haymo, col. 199D*) Non putandum est autem omnia regna mundi et gloriam
eorum simul Domino ostendere potuisse ab alio, nisi a seipso; sed qui omnia creavit per
Divinitatem, ipse omnia, juxta quod voluit, simul vidit per humanitatem: sive totum, ita
ut est, sive in sphaeram collectum, ut scilicet (sicut supra jam diximus) diabolo daretur
occasio tentandi. Nec mirum, si Dominus sic totum mundum prospicere potuit, qui
etiam quibusdam sanctis hoc in munere praestitit, ut eum in sphaeram collectum videre
possent.
124-31 (*No source found*)
133-4 (*Hiberno-Latin texts, e.g., Ps.-Jerome, col. 542B*) Vere cadit, qui adorat diabolum;
quicumque monachus principi propter mercedem curaverit, se diabolo mancipatur.
134-7 (*No source found*)
140-3 (*cf. CH I xi, pp. 172-4*)
145-9 (*Haymo, cols. 201D–202A* [*Similar in idea but not in wording*]) Quomodo ergo
Domino soli servire praecipitur, cum servitium commune dicitur? ... Apud Graecos
servitus duobus modis dicitur: dicitur enim λατρεία, dicitur et δουλεία.... Sed

monnum, buton to ure Drihtne ane þe þe is soð God. Ac we sceolen
þeah ælcne Godes halʒe biddæn to fultume and to þingunge, and
þeahhwæ[þ]re to nan oðre us ne biddan, buton to þam ane þe is soð
God.

150 'Ða forlet þe deofel þene Hælend and awæʒ awat, and engles him
sone neahlæcedon and him seruedon.' On þis we maʒen openlice
underʒyten ure Hælendes cynde, þæt he is æʒðer ʒe soð God ʒe soð
mon. Iwislice ne durste þe deofel fondien hine ʒif he ful ʒeare ne
cneowæ þæt he (w)ære soð mon; ne eac him englæs ne þenedon ʒif he
155 nære soð God. Ofte (sið)æs hit ilamp, and nu ʒyt deþ, þæt englæs
beoð ofte hyder on middanearde isende monnum to hælpe and to
fultume. Be þam cwæð þe apostol: Englæs beoð þeiniendlice gastes;
and heo beoð hider on middænearde isende to þeiniʒen allæ þam
monnum þe nu earniæn wyllæð mid gode weorcum þæt heo to þære
160 eadiʒnesse þe ece is bicumen moten. Mucel is þeo wurðscipe þe God
Almihtiʒ us hafð iʒyfen, ʒif we moten beon his bearn icwædene and
fol. 160 engle ilice ʒif we nu his bodu | healdæn wullæð. Uten ʒemunen hu þe
ap(ostol) us munede and tæhte and lærde, and þus cwæð: Nu is þe
Bf. 106 anfenge tid, and nu beoð þe halwende | daʒes, þæt ælc mon mæʒ him
165 seolfen þæt ece lif earniæn mid ure Drihtne ʒif he his lif rihtlice
libbæn wule æfter larþeowæs tæcinge. Ne sceole we nenne mon

---

154 wære] nære   155 siþæs] þissæs   160 wurðscipe] s *altered from* c
163 apostol] apła

λατρεία illa servitus est quae soli Deo debetur per culturam et venerationem, qua
auctori et conditori omnium. Unde et εἰδωλολατρείας nomen compositum est ex
εἴδωλος et λατρεία: eo quod honorem et servitutem soli Deo debitam, homines stulti
idolis deferre voluerunt; δουλεία autem illa servitus dicitur quae communis est, et
invicem a fidelibus exhibenda. Unde et servus δοῦλος apud eos appellatur. Jubemur
ergo et per charitatem servire invicem, quod pertinet ad δουλείαν: et jubemur iterum
soli Deo servire, quod pertinet ad λατρείαν, ut ejus honorem nulli creaturae deferamus.

150–5 (*Gregory, col. 1136D*) Notandum vero quod subditur, quia, recedente diabolo,
angeli ministrabant ei. Ex qua re quid aliud quam unius personae utraque natura
ostenditur? Quia et homo est quem diabolus tentat, et idem ipse Deus est cui ab angelis
ministratur. Cognoscamus igitur in eo naturam nostram, quia nisi hunc diabolus
hominem cerneret, non tentaret. Veneremur in illo divinitatem suam, quia nisi super
omnia Deus existeret, ei nullo modo angeli ministrarent.

155–7 (*Haymo, col. 198C [and cf. lines 104–9 above, and CH I xi, p. 170, ll. 9–12.*]) In quo
loco et illud cognoscimus, quia ad custodiendam sanctorum vitam angeli deputantur.

157–60 (*Cf. Blickling iii, p. 35, ll. 2–4*)

160–2 (*Independent of sources and OE analogues*)

162–72 (*Haymo, col. 195B*) Quapropter secundum Apostolum, qui ait: 'Ecce nunc
tempus acceptabile, ecce nunc dies salutis' (2 Cor. vi), dignum est ut in his diebus
exhibeamus nosmetipsos sicut Dei ministros, in multa patientia, in jejuniis, in vigiliis,
in castitate, in charitate non ficta.

byl3en læs þe ure bene ne beo noht; ac on alle þinge 3earwie we us sylfe swa swa Godes þeines, þæt is ærest on mucele þulde, and on dræfednesse, and on hali3e wæcce, and on festene, and on clænnesse, and on þolemodnesse, and on clæne þonce, and on soðe lufe Godes 170 and monnæ. þas mæ3nu lædeþ þæs monn(es) sawle on heofene rice þe heom on him hæfð.

Soðlice hit wæs iboden and ihaten on þare ealde æ þæt ylc mon sceolde æfre embe twelf monðe þone teoðe dæl his weorldæ(h)tæ Gode syllen; and hit is nu eac on þare niwæ la3e æfter bocæ tæcinge 175 rihtlic and Gode cwæmlic to donne. Gif hit þonne hwylcum men on his mode to earfoþlic and to uneaþelic þynce, tylie he þæt he hyre þone teoþe dæl his da3e for Gode feste. Hwæt we witen þæt on twelf monþe beoð þreo hundred da3æ and fif and sixti3 da3e and six tidæ, and þisses festenes is twea and feowerti3 da3ene. And 3if we þa six 180 sunenda3æn of adoþ þe we swæsendo on habbæþ, þonne ne beoð þær buton six ant þritti3 da3ene þæs fæstenes, þonne bið þæt þe teoþe dæl þare twelf monþe. Swa hwylc mon swa wule on ylce tid heardlice and forwyrnedlice libbæn, þe bið fulfremed. Gyf hit þonne hwylcum men to earfoþlice þince, tilie he þenne þæt he hure þis fæsten selost feste, 185 æ3þer 3e on psealmsonge þe þe ðæt cunne, 3e on ælmesdæde, 3e on hal3e bedum and wæccum, and on ælce þære gode, þe he for Gode to gode don ma3e, þæt we alle moten on þis hali3e tid æ3þer 3e for Godæ 3e for weorlde þe bliþelycor lybbæn, þam Drihtne fultumiende, þe ðe leofæð and rixæð a a on ecenesse. AMEN. 190

---

171 mæ3nu] *glossed by* werces *in later hand* monnes] monū 174 weorldæhtæ] weorld æltæ 175 eac] *upper part of* c *like a* t 180 twea] a *altered from* o feowerti3] feowwerti3 188 tid] *written over erasure of another word* 189 weorlde] w *altered from another letter*

173–83 (*Gregory, col. 1137B-C* [*cf. Haymo, cols. 193D–194A*]) A praesenti etenim die usque ad Paschalis solemnitatis gaudia sex hebdomadae veniunt, quarum videlicet dies quadraginta duo fiunt. Ex quibus dum sex dies Dominici ab abstinentia subtrahuntur, non plus in abstinentia quam triginta et sex dies remanent. Dum vero per trecentos et sexaginta quinque dies annus ducitur, nos autem per triginta et sex dies affligimur, quasi anni nostri decimas Deo damus, ut qui nobismetipsis per acceptum annum viximus, auctori nostro nos in ejus decimis per abstinentiam mortificemus. Unde, fratres charissimi, sicut offerre in lege jubemini decimas rerum (*Levit. xxvii. 30ff.*), ita ei offerre contendite et decimas dierum.

183–90 (*An independent conclusion*)

NOTES

42. *æt*: In the manuscript the word *þiȝede* is written above this word. The OED, *s.v. Thig*, states that the OE verb *þicg(e)an* was lost *c.* 1150, and its place was taken in the north by the Norse form, with modification of sense to 'receive'. It seems possible therefore that *æt* was a scribal substitution for *þiȝede*, and that the scribe then wrote the original word *þiȝede* above its replacement.

57. *wem*: This form stems from either OE *wam* or OE *wen(n)*. Campb. *Suppl.* cites one other example (in Cotton Vespasian D. xiv) of the spelling *wem*.

60. *forcostode*: The form derives from OE *costian*; it is cited in Campb. *Suppl.* but not in BT. The word does not appear elsewhere in OE.

78. *wordes*: I have retained the MS form rather than emending to dat. sg. *worde*, since it may be an example of the inflection *-es* being used to express the dat. pl., which is found otherwise only in homily vii (see Accidence: Nouns (v), p. lxxii above).

82. *þære larþeawselt*: *Larþeawselt* is a cognate of OE *lareowsetl*, a neuter noun, here in the nominative case. The immediately preceding pronoun, *þære*, is a feminine form, either genitive or dative, and therefore inappropriate. It probably results from scribal confusion, either from original *þær þær* ('there where') or from *þæt* (neuter nominative form of *se*). I have refrained from emending the text either way, since the scribe is frequently inconsistent in his pronominal forms.

98–100. The scriptural cross-reference is to Ps. xc. 11–12.

107. *to hælpe and to burȝene*: The form *burȝene* suggests that we have here two inflected infinitives which govern the dative object *þam sawle* (rather than two dat. sg. nouns after *to*, as in *to hælpe and to fultume* at 156–7). On the irregularity elsewhere of inflected infinitive endings, see p. lxxvi above.

111. *to oferiȝendlice*: This emendation of MS *to feriȝendlice* is suggested by the MED (under the entry *oferhiȝendlice*). It is more plausible that the scribe should have omitted a second consecutive *o* than that he should have altered *oferh-* to *to fer-* (the latter is suggested by Belfour who emends to *ofer[h]iȝend-lice*).

119. *sceawede*: The meaning 'show' is usually found in Old English with the prefix *ge-*. Campb. *Suppl.* (under *sceawian*) cites this instance without the prefix and one other occurrence (in Cotton Vespasian D. xiv, another late twelfth-century manuscript). See Glossary for other examples in the homilies edited here (v. 130, vi. 46, etc.).

124. *s[c]yncrefte*: This emendation suggested in Campb. *Suppl.* under the entry *æthiwod* is accepted here.

126. *æthiwod*: The word is included in Campb. *Suppl.* under the entry *æthiwian*. Campbell's translation, however, 'to transform', does not fit the context; *æthiwian*, according to its context, must mean 'to present as an illusion' (hence a cognate of OE *hiwian*). Ælfric, in his continuation to the *Life of St. Swithun*, discusses such illusions:

> Mannum is eac to witenne þæt manega dry-men
> maciað menig-fealde dydrunga þurh deofles cræft.
> swa swa wischeras oft doð. and bedydriað menn
> swylce hi soðlice swylc þincg don.
> ac hit is swa ðeah dydrung mid deofles cræfte.
> and gif hwa hit bletsað þonne ablynð seo dydrung.
>
> (*LS* xxi, p. 470)

144–9. The homilist distinguishes between two usages of the verb *biddan* in this passage. The construction *biddan* (*us*) *to* (144, 145–6, 148) is specifically restricted to praying to God; *biddan* + acc. of person asked and *to* of thing sought (147) is used to mean praying for help from others such as God's saints.

151. *seruedon*: This verb represents a scribal substitution for OE *þeowodon* (or similar form). Compare Assmann x, p. 118. The copy in Bodley 343 reads 'He sealde ... oðernedel þæm þe gode ane seruedæn' (col. 2, ll. 46–9); *seruedæn* here corresponds to OE *þeowodon* preserved in the Hatton 114 copy (col. 1, l. 54). The verb *seruian* does not appear elsewhere in Old English; it is not included in BT, and Campb. *Suppl.* cites this as an isolated instance. It is used, however, several times in twelfth-century texts, for example, in the *Lambeth Homilies*: 'Hu me sulde godalmihti serue and his wille wurche in orðe' (cited in OED). In homily v, the scribe is inconsistent in his diction: he substitutes *seruedon* here, but retains *þeowian* at 140 and 144. This variation suggests that both forms were still in use at the time of copying, although *þeowian* was clearly becoming obsolete.

157. The scriptural reference is to Hebr. i. 14.

163. *munede*: Campb. *Suppl.* notes that the infinitive of this form is *mynian* meaning 'exhort'. He suggests that there may have been some confusion with *mynegian* which was the usual OE verb meaning 'exhort'.

163–4. The scriptural reference is to 2 Cor. vi. 2.

VI

THE TRANSFIGURATION OF CHRIST

CONTEXT AND AUDIENCE

This homily, like v above, is anonymous and found only in the last section of Bodley 343. It provides an exposition of Matth. xvi. 27–xvii. 9, the Transfiguration of Christ, a gospel-text not expounded elsewhere in the extant Old English homiletic corpus.[1]

The occasion for which the homily was intended is not identified in Bodley 343 (no rubric is provided), nor does the homily itself specify an occasion. In the manuscript it is preceded by an anonymous homily whose pericope is for the First Sunday in Lent (homily v above), and followed by a composite homily for Lent or Rogationtide (homily vii below). As I argued in the general introduction, the compiler seems in this final section of his manuscript to have been selecting from a larger homiliary items needed to supplement his existing collection. The three homilies edited here may have derived from a group of items appropriate for Lent, since Matth. xvi. 27–xvii. 9 was the pericope for the Saturday before the Second Sunday in Lent.[2]

The Saturday before the Second Sunday in Lent is not an occasion on which a large lay congregation would have been expected to have attended Mass. No other Old English homily expounding this gospel reading or designated for the Saturday before the Second Sunday in Lent has survived. The existence of a vernacular sermon on the pericope for this occasion is therefore rather puzzling. Two potential functions of homily vi should be considered.

---

[1] Ælfric's summary of the story in his homily for Palm Sunday (CH II xiv) acts only as an introduction to his account of Christ's Passion.

[2] Various homiliaries available in Anglo-Saxon England assign Matth. xvi. 27–xvii. 9 to the Saturday before the Second Sunday in Lent: see, for example, the homiliary of Haymo of Auxerre (PL 118, col. 221). The West-Saxon gospels provide tangible evidence of its continued association with that occasion during the Anglo-Saxon period in England: beside the text is noted 'ðys sceal on sæternes-dæg on þære forman lencten wucan'.

First, the association between Matth. xvi. 27–xvii. 9 and the Saturday before the Second Sunday in Lent does not necessarily imply that the Old English text was written specifically for that occasion. It might rather have been intended for preaching or reading in the Lenten season generally. The homily's main source is a homily by Bede, whose title, *In Quadragesima*, suggests a general application.[1] Bede's homily was in Paul the Deacon's original homiliary, where it was placed between homilies for the First Sunday in Lent and the Second Sunday in Lent, but with no specific occasion identified.[2]

If the homily was written for a more general purpose than the Saturday before the Second Sunday in Lent, then what kind of preaching context might the homilist have had in mind? Ælfric provides a useful analogy in his Second Series homily for Easter Day, where he comments:

Sume his geswutelunge we eow sædon on oðre stowe. sume we willað eow nu secgan. nu ge her gegaderode syndon; We wenað þæt ge ealle on andwerdnysse her ne beon to ðam dæge. þe we þæt godspel rædan sceolon;[3]

Although the gospel-text which Ælfric proceeds to expound is that associated with the Wednesday in Easter Week, the implication is, as Godden has shown, that 'a much larger congregation would be present than could be expected on the Wednesday'.[4] Godden argues convincingly from this that the homily was written for Easter Day itself, not for the Wednesday in Easter Week. The bipartite division of his audience implied by Ælfric presumably refers to the monks or secular clergy who will be present at the reading of the gospel on its appropriate day and the laity who are present only on more popular occasions.[5] The passage provides important evidence that vernacular

---

[1] D. Hurst, ed., *Bedae Venerabilis Opera*, CCSL 122, *Homelia 24*, pp. 170–7. On the title, Hurst notes that 'in serie lectionum quae Romae antiquitus recitari solebant sabbato post dominicam primam quadragesimae assignata est', p. 170. The Bede source for homily vi was identified by James Cross, '*De Ordine Creaturarum Liber* in Old English Prose', *Anglia*, xc (1972), 132–40, pp. 138–9.

[2] Paul the Deacon's original homiliary contained two homilies on the Transfiguration, one by Leo the Great (PL 54, col. 308) and the aforementioned one by Bede, both for unspecified occasions. Leo's sermon was PD 86, Bede's was PD 87; they are preceded by PD 85 which is assigned to the First Sunday in Lent, and followed by PD 88 which is assigned to the Second Sunday in Lent. See Grégoire, *Les Homéliaires du Moyen Âge*, p. 89.

[3] CH II xvi, 100–4.

[4] 'The Development of Ælfric's Second Series of *Catholic Homilies*', p. 210.

[5] Mary Clayton's argument in 'Homiliaries and Preaching' that 'Ælfric, when writing, had the Winchester or Cerne type situation in mind, where the laity would have

homilies were written to be preached on occasions other than those with which their pericopes were associated. Homily vi might have been intended for one of the more popular occasions in Lent where laity as well as monks would have been present. Certainly Lent was a period when the laity might be assumed to have attended Mass more frequently than usual, and hence have created more demand for homilies in the vernacular. This would seem to be supported by Ælfric's provision of five homilies for the Fridays in Lent, though the actual function of these latter is also uncertain.[1] Clemoes assigns them tentatively to the first stage of Ælfric's reorganization and expansion of his Temporale homilies (TH I), noting that 'most of them might well be omitted from our extant selections, *being of relatively minor usefulness* [my italics]'.[2] Gatch questions their function more explicitly: 'Whether Ælfric expected the laity to be present on Fridays in Lent or planned to read these sermons on Sunday or designed them for devotional uses or for reading in a *familia* of canons or monks is not finally ascertainable.'[3]

Gatch's list of options leads conveniently to the second possible intended function of homily vi. This is that the homily was written specifically for the Saturday before the Second Sunday in Lent, and hence for a monastic rather than a lay audience. But defining the context for such a sermon within a monastic environment is not straightforward. Gatch, in discussing the context for Ælfric's vernacular sermons, suggests that they may have been 'monastic rather than secular, and it is at least remotely conceivable that they had a place in the Night or the Capitular Office. Their use at meals or as *lectio divina* is more likely.'[4] Clayton, whilst arguing that the two series of *Catholic Homilies* were written for a mixed audience of monks and laity, suggests that Ælfric's later *Temporale Homilies* (which include homilies for all of the Sundays after Easter, most of those after Pentecost, and for the five Fridays in Lent) would have been preached on occasions when the laity would not have been present, and 'were intended largely for the religious element in his audience', that is, monks whose command of Latin may often have

been preached to in the monastic church, with the monks also present' (p. 239) would explain Ælfric's comment in CH II xvi.

[1] Pope ii, iii, v, vi, and Assmann v.
[2] Clemoes, 'Chronology', p. 228.
[3] *Preaching and Theology*, pp. 54–5.
[4] Ibid., p. 53.

been limited.[1] The context, according to Clayton, would still have been reading in connection with the Mass, though they could also have been used for private reading. As with Ælfric's homilies, more than one designated usage is possible for homily vi: it might well have been intended for devotional reading as well as preaching, whether by monks and clerics or by the laity.

Homily vi offers no direct information as to its primary intended function. It is possible that the phrase 'þe ðis godspel wrat' (ll. 1–2) refers to a gospel reading immediately preceding the homily, which would indicate that it was meant for preaching on the occasion on which the gospel-text was read (that is, the Saturday before the Second Sunday in Lent). But the phrase might equally look forward to the translation of the gospel-text which the homilist is about to undertake.

In its content homily vi certainly makes no allowances for a less educated audience. It is unusually lengthy, ambitious and intellectually sophisticated in comparison with other extant Old English anonymous homilies (such as homily v above). The homily's author uses complex allegorical exegesis without hesitation, and deals competently with the finer points of doctrinal interpretation. Homily vi is a homily of a particularly high quality, worthy of comparison with the works of Ælfric and Wulfstan.

The homily's relationship chronologically to Ælfric's and Wulfstan's writings is difficult to ascertain. Ælfric himself, so far as is known, did not write a homily for this occasion or on this gospel reading, and it is tempting to see it as the work of an anonymous author belonging to a 'school of Ælfric', who is intending to complement Ælfric's corpus. But there is no sign of direct influence by Ælfric, and in doctrine the homilist's emphases are often different from Ælfric's. This is particularly evident in his treatment of eschatology. The homilist returns constantly to the Day of Judgement, building up a vivid and elaborate picture which differs in detail from both Ælfric and other English homilists of the period (the author of homily vii, for example). It seems more likely that the author of homily vi, like the Blickling and Vercelli authors, was writing before rather than after Ælfric's period of composition.

---

[1] 'Homiliaries and Preaching', pp. 240, 241.

SOURCES AND ANALOGUES

The homily's main source, as I noted above, is a homily by Bede entitled *In Quadragesima*. The homilist follows Bede in his verse-by-verse exposition of the gospel reading. He does not always do so closely, however, his main tendency being towards amplification of Bede's commentary. He feels no compunction in incorporating other sources or his own ideas, particularly when they shed light on his favourite subject of Doomsday. Throughout the homily, the writer's individuality is evident, and the result is an intelligent and detailed reading of the Transfiguration story. The following sequential examination of the homily concentrates on the homily's relationship to Bede and its other identifiable sources.

In his rendering of the pericope which opens the homily, the homilist omits none of the biblical material. He adds various explanatory phrases (for example, 'swa þæt heo hit aberon ne mihten', l. 25) and helpful extra comments: he identifies Moses, for example, as 'þe hal3æ þe þe ifyrren worlde ær wæs forðfæren' (ll. 15–16) and Elijah as 'þe prophetæ' (l. 16).

For the first part of his commentary (ll. 33–57), the homilist is not very close to Bede. He may have had another source, but the extra material is mostly general and unspecialized and could well be the homilist's independent insertion. Although the theme of the transience of earthly things is initially common to both Bede and the Old English homilist, the latter has inserted extra material in preference to some of Bede's commentary. He emphasizes by repetition the transience of life, then, omitting Bede's reference to the eternal reward ('dulcedine futurae retributionis') offers instead an explanation for the Transfiguration: that Christ 'walde þurh þæt heoræ bileafe festniæn, and ealre þare monnæ þe hit iheren sæggen' (ll. 40–1). He also employs for emphasis an inexpressibility topos, declaring that, however brief the gospel-text, the joy experienced on that single day is quite indescribable and inconceivable.[1]

The second explanation for the Transfiguration (ll. 48–51) derives from Bede: Christ demonstrates by it that each man who wishes to attain heaven must refrain from indulging earthly desires. Where Bede, however, proceeds to list the virtues which qualify a man for

[1] On inexpressibility topoi, see E. R. Curtius, *European Literature and the Latin Middle Ages* (Bern, 1948, transl. W. R. Trask, London, 1953), pp. 159–62.

salvation (cleanness, piety, peace, love, and justice), the Old English homilist emphasizes the hardship, brevity and sorrow of life on earth for those aiming for heaven. To support this, he independently includes a paraphrase of Matth. vii. 14: 'Quam angusta porta et arcta via est quae ducit ad vitam.'

At lines 55–7 the homilist paraphrases Phil. iii. 20, which Bede has quoted verbatim in his commentary. He does not elaborate on this gospel-text as Bede does, mentioning only that we must come to the bliss and joy of heaven 'þurh Gode'.

The homilist then comments on Matth. xvii. 1 specifically. He omits Bede's first idea (that the righteous are separated now from the faithless in mind if not in body), and concentrates instead on the future, stating specifically that 'þa soðfæste men beoð isceadde feor fram yfele monnæ neawiste on þam towearde weorlde' (ll. 59–60). This is the first indication of the homilist's particular interest in the end of the world and its aftermath. He concludes with a paraphrase of Ps. xxx. 21: 'Abscondes eos in abscondito faciei tuae a conturbatione hominum, proteges eos in tabernaculo tuo a contradictione linguarum' (also quoted by Bede).

Like Bede, the homilist then discusses the significance of the six days before Christ fulfilled his promise of transfiguring Himself before His disciples (ll. 64–72). Both source and Old English rendering interpret this as evidence that holy ones will go to heaven at the end of the world, the world being made up of six ages which are nearing completion. The Old English homilist does not follow Bede in quoting Matth. xxv. 34 specifically or in elaborating on the idea of the six ages of the world as they relate, for example, to the six days which God took to create the world. There is also no attempt by the homilist to stress the urgency of repentance within this sixth age, a feature of other Old English homilies, particularly the Blickling collection.[1] Homily vi's author merely notes that the sixth age has arrived, and that after its completion the holy will rejoice.

The homilist turns at line 73 to exposition of Matth. xvii. 2. He repeats (again independently) his previous explanation for the Transfiguration (at ll. 40–1), that is, it was intended to confirm and strengthen the faith of His disciples and of others who heard of it. In his next

---

[1] The motif of six ages in the world was one commonly used by Old English homilists; see, for example, CH II iv, 82–91, where the six water vessels betoken the six ages of this world. For eschatology in the Blickling Homilies, see Milton McC. Gatch, 'Eschatology in the Anonymous Old English Homilies', *Traditio*, xxi (1965), 117–65.

passage, however, the homilist follows Bede closely in suggesting that Christ's Transfiguration foreshadows the metamorphosis of all the holy on Judgement Day and by citing Matth. xiii. 43: 'Tunc iusti fulgebunt sicut sol in regno Patris eorum. Qui habet aures audiendi, audiat.'

Diverging temporarily from Bede, the homilist explains how the stars, sun and moon are now less bright than hitherto, but will have their luminosity restored at the end of the world when they, along with holy men, will take their rest (ll. 80–94). Cross has traced this passage to Pseudo-Isidore's *De Ordine Creaturarum Liber*, ch. v, *De sole et luna*, and suggests that the collocation of Matth. xiii. 43 and Isa. xxx. 26 in Isidore may have prompted the Old English homilist's inclusion of the passage.[1] Cross cites two other passages which are similar in idea to Isidore. Jerome, in his *Commentaria in Isaiam Prophetam* (lib. ix, PL 24, cols. 349–50), had referred to Isa. xxx. 26 to explain the brightness of the sun in Matth. xiii. 43, but since, unlike *De Ordine*, he did not mention the original loss of light, he was clearly not the anonymous homilist's source. Haymo, in his *Commentaria in Isaiam* cites Pseudo-Isidore specifically for his comment on the original loss of light, but he does not even refer to Matth. xiii. 43. Although these other Latin authors are not closer to the Old English homilist, there is evidence to indicate that Pseudo-Isidore himself is not the homilist's source. Cross has noted a close relation between this passage and the *Old English Martyrology* entry for 21 March, Fourth day of the Creation:

On ðone an ond twentegðan dæg bið se feorða worolde dæg. On ðæm dæge God gesette on heofones rodor sunnan ond monan: þa wæs seo sunne seofon siðum beorhtre ðonne heo nu is, ond se mona hæfde ða ða beorhtnesse þe seo sunne nu hafað. Ac þa Adam ond Eua on neorxnawonge gesyngodan, ða wæs þæm tunglum gewonad heora beorhtnes, ond hi næfdon na siððan butan þone seofoðan dæl heora leohtes. Ac on Domesdæge þonne ure Drihten edniwað ealle gesceafte, ond eall mænnisc cynn eft ariseð ond hi næfre ma ne gesyngiað, þonne scineð seo sunne seofon siðum beorhtre ðonne heo nu do, ond heo næfre on setl gangeþ. Ond se mona scineð swa swa nu seo sunne deþ, ond he næfre ma wonað ne ne weaxeð on his endebyrdnesse, ac þenden þa tunglu her lyhtaþ on ðysse deadlican worolde. Symble ðonne se mona gangeþ æfter ðære sunnan, ðonne weaxeð his leoht; [þonne he byð beforan hyre, þonne wanað hys leoht.] Ond swa he bið þære sunnan near, swa bið his leoht

---

[1] Cross, '*De Ordine Creaturarum Liber*', pp. 139–40. *De Ordine Creaturarum Liber* is printed in PL 83, cols. 913–54.

læsse; ond swa he bið hire fyrr, swa bið his leoht mare; ond hwæðre he bið symble þurh þa sunnan onlyhted.[1]

This *Martyrology* passage and the homily vi passage are in fact closer to each other in some respects than to Isidore, and it is possible that some other intermediary, drawing on Pseudo-Isidore, was the homilist's source. Neither passage can derive from the other, since each contains material which the other lacks but which Pseudo-Isidore contains. The statement in the Old English homily that the brightness will increase when holy men receive their final reward (ll. 92–4) is in Isidore (§7) and not in the *OE Martyrology*. The idea in the *OE Martyrology* that when the moon follows the sun its light increases, and the nearer to the sun it is the dimmer its light becomes, and vice versa, is in Pseudo-Isidore (§8), but is not used by the Old English homilist. There are sufficiently close resemblances between the two Old English passages to suggest that they stem from a source closer to both than Isidore. Both the Old English texts, independently from the Latin, refer to the sun and moon by the general term 'stars' ('tunglæ'/'tunglum'). Both specify Adam and Eve instead of merely translating 'homines', and both refer specifically to 'domes dæg(e)' as the time when the restoration of brightness will occur. Both omit the same large portions of Isidore (all of §5, for example). The similarities of both vocabulary and material seem too striking to be coincidental.

The notion presented in Isa. xxx. 26 that the sun was to become seven times brighter and the moon to assume the sun's light is also used by Ælfric in three homilies.[2] In each case, it is an addition to Ælfric's immediate Latin source. In Pope xxi, Ælfric considerably extends the quotation, interpreting it in a similar way to Pseudo-Isidore:

> Eac swylce seo sunne, and soðlice se mona
> wurdon benæmde heora wynsuman beorhtnysse
> æfter Adames gylte, na be agenum gewyrhtum.
> Be seofonfealdan wæs seo sunne þa beorhtre
> ær þam se mann agylte, and se mona hæfde
> þære sunnan beorhtnysse, swa swa heo scinð nu us.
> Hi sceolan eft swaþeah æfter Domes-dæge habban
> be fullan heora beorhtnysse, be þam þe hy gesceopene wæran;

[1] Kotzor, *Das altenglische Martyrologium*, Part II, pp. 38–9.
[2] CH I xl, p. 618; Pope xi. 513–15; Pope xxi, 56–65.

  and se mona ne ealdað æfter þam dæge,
  ac bið ansund scinende, swa swa seo (sunne) deð nu. (56–65)

The idea is also found in another Old English text, the *Dialogue of Salomon and Saturnus*, where Salomon describes Pater Noster's eyes as follows:

and his eagan sindon xxi ðusendum siða beorhtran ðonne ealles middangeardes eorðe, ðeah he heo sy mid ðæra beorhtestan lilian blostmum ofbræded, and æghwylc blostman leaf hæbbe xii sunnan, and æghwylc blostma hæbbe xii monan, and æghwylc mona sy synderlice xii ðusendum siða beorhtra ðonne he geo wæs ær Abeles slege.[1]

At line 94, the homilist returns to his main source, emphasizing with it that Christ still shines more brightly than any other light. The homilist paraphrases 1 Cor. xv. 41 (quoted by Bede): 'Efne swa þe steorræ oferscineð oðerne on brihtnesse þæt he bið brihtre þene þe oþer.' His subsequent comment that men shall be distinguishable in brightness on Doomsday, is independent of his source, although it is probably prompted by Bede's quotation of the first part of 1 Cor. xv. 42: 'sic et resurrectio mortuorum'. The homilist applies the variable brightness of stars directly to men's bodies on the Day of Judgement, suggesting that they too will differ in brightness. Each man's brightness, according to the homilist, will be in proportion to his moral worth, and the more good deeds he performs the greater the reward he shall receive on Judgement Day. The suggestion that one's moral worth will be reflected by the brightness of one's body on Judgement Day is rare in vernacular homiletic literature. Ælfric incorporates the idea once, in his homily for the Nativity of the Blessed Virgin Mary:

  Bið swa ðeah toscead, swa swa se apostol sæde:
  'Stella autem ab stella differt in claritate, et cetera.'
  þæra steorrena beorhtnyss ne bið on eallum gelice.
  Oðer is soðlice þære sunnan beorhtnyss
  and oðer þæs monan on ðisum middanearde
  and oðer þæra steorrena, beþam ðe hi standað.
  Swa bið eac on domes dæg, þær nan ðing dyrne ne bið,
  þonne þa halgan scinað, ælc be his geearnungum,

---

[1] John M. Kemble, ed., *The Dialogue of Salomon and Saturnus*, Ælfric Society (London, 1848), p. 148. The text is also printed by Robert J. Menner, *The Poetical Dialogues of Salomon and Saturn* (New York and London, 1941), p. 169. Kemble (p. 177) compares this passage with the one cited above from the *OE Martyrology*.

æfter þam æriste, and on þære beorhtnysse
hi beoð æfre wunigende buton ateorodnysse.[1]

Elsewhere his accounts of the Last Judgement do not include this idea.[2]

The ensuing section (ll. 104–10), explaining that Christ's appearance was compared to the sun because nothing brighter could be found, is loosely based on Bede. The homilist independently stresses by repetition that Christ's appearance far surpasses the brightness of the sun, and he omits Bede's reference to the saints who are also compared to the sun (in 1 Cor. xv. 41).

In his next section (beginning at l. 110), the homilist follows Bede in idea, adding explanatory statements where he deems necessary. He states with Bede that no sinful man shall be able to see Christ's face, then adds 'ac þæt toȝescead bið wunderlice iworden þurh þa mucele mihte þæs Almihtiȝæ Godes sune' (ll. 111–12). The homilist elaborates on Bede in his description of what the sinful ones will see: 'tantum uidebunt in quem transfixerunt' becomes 'ac þa synfulle men sceolen iseon þa wundæn and þa sar on ure Drihtne and þære næȝlæ swaðe, þe he wæs on rode mid inæȝlod' (ll. 115–16). The homilist also spells out the reason for this punishment: 'for þan þe heo nu her on worlde his mycele eadmodnesse wæron unþongfulre þonne heo sceoldon' (ll. 117–18). Again, when the homilist has intimated the glorious vision of Christ in store for the righteous, he independently explains: 'for þon þe heo her on worlde his ðrowunge and his eadmodnesse mid worde and weorcum him þoncfulle wæren' (ll. 121–3).

The idea that on Doomsday Christ's wounds will be visible is common in vernacular homilies.[3] As Dorothy Bethurum has noted, it has a scriptural justification, deriving from the prophecy of Zach. xii. 10: 'et aspicient ad me, quem confixerunt'.[4] Less common, however, is

---

[1] Assmann iii, 486–95. The source for Assmann iii has been identified as Augustine's *De sancta virginitate* (PL 40, cols. 395–428) by Mary Clayton in 'Ælfric and the Nativity of the Blessed Virgin Mary', *Anglia*, civ (1986), 286–315. This particular passage by Ælfric derives from §26 (col. 410); referring to John xiv. 2, Augustine notes that 'in multis ... mansionibus honoratur alius alio clarius'.

[2] See, for example, CH I xl, pp. 616–18; Pope xi.

[3] See, for example, Bethurum ii, 65–73. For further examples, see Bethurum, p. 286, and Joyce Bazire and James E. Cross, eds., *Eleven Old English Rogationtide Homilies*, 2nd ed., King's College London Medieval Studies (London, 1989), p. 130, n. 11 (includes reference to homily vi).

[4] Bethurum, pp. 286–7. The prophecy is repeated in John xix. 37, and fulfilled in Luke xxiv. 39–40 and John xx. 27. Bethurum adds that 'this figure as described in Apoc. i. 7 is transferred to the Day of Judgement in patristic writing'.

the development of this idea found in homily vi, that the sinful shall see only God's wounds and the holy shall see only His beauty. Two instances of it can be found elsewhere in vernacular literature. One is in Vercelli ii:

On þam dæge ure Dryhten in his þam myclan mægen-þrymme, 7 his onsyne ætyweð 7 his lichoman. þonne bið seo wund gesewen þam firen-fullum, 7 þam soð-fæstan he bið hal gesewen. 7 þonne Iudeas magon ge-seon, þone-þe hie ær cwealdon 7 hengon.[1]

The other is in the poem *Christ*:

> Her bið þam godum glædmod on gesihþe,
> wlitig, wynsumlic, weorude þam halgan,
> on gefean fæger, freond ond leoftæl,
> lufsum ond liþe leofum monnum
> to sceawianne þone scynan wlite,
> weðne mid willum, waldendes cyme,
> mægencyninges, þam þe him on mode ær
> wordum ond weorcum wel gecwemdun.
> He bið þam yflum egeslic ond grimlic
> to geseonne, synnegum monnum,
> þam þær mid firenum cumað, forð forworhte.[2]

Independently of Bede, the homilist includes a brief description of the Last Judgement (ll. 123–7) which is based on Matth. xxv. Again his own particular interest in the end of the world is apparent. He closes this section with a paraphrase of Phil. iii. 21 (following Bede), indicating that the bodies of the righteous will become bright like Christ's.

Like Bede, the homilist interprets the white garments at Christ's Transfiguration as the congregation of holy ones (ll. 129–34). He omits Bede's subsequent scriptural quotations (Isa. xlix. 18, Gal. iii. 27, and Mark ix. 2). Perhaps prompted, however, by the references to baptism, he explains how the congregation becomes white 'þurh fulluhtes bæðe', and also 'þurh monie haliʒe dæde'.

The next section of the homily (ll. 134–40) derives its ideas from Bede. None can entirely refrain from sin, but God will purify the holy. The Old English homilist diverges slightly from Bede in interpretation: Bede suggests that God performs the cleansing of the congregation in heaven ('dominus faciet in caelo emundans ecclesiam

---

[1] Förster, p. 45.
[2] George Philip Krapp and Elliott Van Kirk Dobbie, eds., *The Exeter Book*, The Anglo-Saxon Poetic Records, III (New York and London, 1936), p. 28, ll. 910–20.

uestem uidelicet suam'), whereas the Old English homilist states that God purifies the holy congregation, then leads them to heaven (ll. 137–40). This moment of cleansing or purifying of the holy congregation probably refers to the fire of judgement, and is presumably the same purification to which Ælfric refers in his homily *In Octavis Pentecosten Dicendus*:

> Ða leohtan gyltas and ða lytlan synna
> beoð þonne afeormode þurh ðæt witniendlice fyr,
> and nis nanes cynnes wite on þyssere worulde swa teart
> swa swa þæt foresæde fyr þe afeormað þa gymeleasan.[1]

and again in his *Sermo de Die Iudicii*:

> and þæt fyr þonne afeormað þas eorðan,
> and hi geedniwað to ænlicum hiwe,
> and heo ne bið na forburnen, ac bið geclænsod
> from eallum þam fylþum þe hyre fram frymðe becomon,
> and heo swa on ecnysse eall scinende þurhwunað.[2]

At the end of the poem *Elene*, Cynewulf too describes a fire of judgement which will purify the two groups of men not destined for hell:

> Bið þam twam dælum
> ungelice. Moton engla frean
> geseon, sigora god. Hie asodene beoð,
> asundrod fram synnum, swa smæte gold
> þæt in wylme bið womma gehwylces
> þurh ofnes fyr eall geclænsod,
> amered ond gemylted. Swa bið þara manna ælc
> ascyred ond asceaden scylda gehwylcre,
> deopra firena, þurh þæs domes fyr.
> Moton þonne siðþan sybbe brucan,
> eces eadwelan.[3]

The purification of the righteous, though clearly integral to eschatological tradition, is rarely introduced in homiletic literature; once again this anonymous homilist's particular interest in all facets of Doomsday is revealed.

The homilist then quotes Matth. xvii. 3 (ll. 141–2), and turns again

---

[1] Pope xi, 225–8.
[2] Pope xviii, 81–5.
[3] *The Vercelli Book*, ed. George Philip Krapp, The Anglo-Saxon Poetic Records, II (New York and London, 1932), p. 102, ll. 1306–16.

to Bede for interpretation. He converts Bede's indirect questions ('quales apparuerint et quid locuti sunt cum eo') into direct questions addressed to his audience: 'Leofe men, hwylce scawedon heo heom? oððe hwæt specon heo to him?' (ll. 142–3). Like Bede, he refers to the corresponding text in Luke ix. 13 for clarification. He also follows Bede in interpreting Moses and Elijah as the Law of God and the prophets. The Latin describes 'oracula legis et prophetiae' as 'quae in domino conpleta et nunc doctis quibusque patent et electis omnibus in futuro manifestius patebunt', and the Old English homilist specifies more elaborately what this means. God revealed to Moses and Elijah first 'alle þa ðing ðe towearde weron', namely Christ's coming to the world, His Passion, Resurrection and Ascension, and secondly 'alle þa ðing þe us haliȝe bec nu ȝyt towearde secgæð', namely Judgement Day, the Lord's coming again into the world, the resurrection of mankind and the future life. The Old English homilist independently assures his readers that 'buton tweon all þis sceal iwurðæn' (ll. 155–6). The homilist has preferred his own elaboration to Bede's comments on the aptness of Moses and Elijah being visible 'in maiestate', and once again he has independently introduced the subject of Judgement Day.

The homilist then follows Bede in commenting further on the significance of Moses and Elijah (ll. 156–66). His allegorical interpretation is derived from Bede, but he independently elaborates on Elijah's present circumstances before proceeding to what he signifies. Elijah is still living in the flesh 'on þam stowe þe God him hæfð isæt', and there he will wait until the time of Antichrist, when God will restore him to earth to proclaim His commands and suffer martyrdom. The final comment on Elijah's significance, 'þa þe nu ær domes dæȝ libbende beoð imette', closely matches Bede's 'hi qui in aduentu iudicis uiui inueniendi sunt in carne'.

The ensuing passage describing the Last Judgement (ll. 166–70) ultimately derives from 1 Thess. iv. 16–17, although the Old English homilist's immediate source is Bede's paraphrase. Like Bede, the homilist adds to the Bible specific references to judgement and to the reward of eternal life. Bede's 'qui utrique pariter' is spelt out by the homilist: 'ealle men, æȝþær þa ðe ær forðiwitene wæron, ȝe þa ðe þenne on lichame libbende beoð'. 'Rapti in nubibus' is paraphrased as 'ahofene up ofer þysne luftlice heofen'; the unusual phrase 'þysne luftlice heofen' is apparently designed to distinguish the sky above from heaven where the righteous are taken. For Bede's 'in uno eodemque momento', the homilist recalls a phrase from another biblical text, 1 Cor. xv. 52, which tells how we shall all be changed 'in ictu oculi' at the last trumpet. The homilist incorporates this phrase (rendering it as 'on anes eaȝæn beorhtnes') into his account, creating a vivid and dramatic image of the instantaneous transposition to Christ.

The second part of Bede's sentence, 'peracto iudicio ad uitam inducuntur aeternam', raises some difficulties of interpretation. Whereas the biblical passage makes no reference at all to judgement, Bede implies that judgement takes place in the air, and the Old English homilist states this explicitly. According to the biblical passage, only the righteous are lifted up to meet Christ; Bede is more ambiguous, but seems to imply that all those lifted up are led to heaven; the Old English homilist unhesitatingly assures his audience that although all men are lifted up for judgement, only the holy ones will be led to eternal life: 'and syððæn bið þe mycele dom rædlice iendod, and alle Godes halȝæn beoð þenne to þam ece lif iledde' (ll. 169–70).

There is, in fact, no clear consensus in biblical tradition about where the Last Judgement would take place. The problem is that biblical accounts do not make explicit the order of events on Doomsday. Certainly most references, for example those in Matth. xxiv, suggest that the Lord will come to perform judgement at the end of the world. But does the destruction of the world occur before or after the judgement? And are all men raised up for judgement or only the righteous? Does judgement occur before the resurrection of the righteous or afterwards? The Book of Revelation seems to suggest that the Last Judgement occurs in a kind of vacuum after earth and sky have disappeared:

Et vidi thronum magnum candidum, et sedentem super eum, a cuius conspectu fugit terra et caelum, et locus non est inventus eis. Et vidi mortuos magnos et pusillos stantes in conspectu throni; et libri aperti sunt, et alius liber apertus est, qui est vitae: et iudicati sunt mortui ex his quae scripta erant in libris, secundum opera ipsorum.[1]

It has been suggested that the Bible is employing symbolic language, and that the place of the gathering of all men was not an important issue.[2] But most biblical commentators, including those from the Old English period, have attempted to be more precise.

[1] Apoc. xx. 11–12.
[2] *New Catholic Encyclopedia*, VIII, 39.

Some cite 1 Thess. iv. 16–17 as definite evidence that the Last Judgement took place in the air and not on earth. The homilist of vi is one who holds this view. Ælfric is another; he states quite specifically that the Judgement will not be on earth, and cites the passage from 1 Thess.:

Ne bið se dom on nanum eorðlicum felda gedemed, ac bið swa swa se apostol her wiðufan on þyssere rædinge cwæð, þæt we beoð gegripene on wolcnum togeanes Criste, geond þas lyft; and þær bið seo twæming rihtwisra manna and arleasra.[1]

The homilist of vii below seems to hold both views simultaneously: he states that on Judgement Day the Lord will seek 'þisne middæneard', but proceeds to describe the actual judgement as taking place after 'all þæs middæneard byð mid fure aræred' (l. 30). The problem is whether 1 Thess. iv. 16–17 was ever actually intended to refer to the Last Judgement itself. It seems most unlikely that resurrection of the wicked was ever visualized. Moreover the passage mentions only those who are to be with the Lord forever. In his commentary on the Epistles of St. Paul to the Thessalonians, James E. Frame states that this passage is obviously not meant to be a detailed description of the *Parousia*, and that Paul would have admitted various other points including the judgement of all men without the resurrection of the wicked.[2] It seems that Paul's concern was only with the final reunion of the saints and God, rather than with the Last Judgement as a whole. The Last Judgement itself then could have taken place on earth, or at least in a kind of vacuum where earth had originally been. Other biblical commentators seem to assume that this was the case. Norman Cohn cites a passage by the fourth-century writer Lactantius, which expresses this point of view:

When peace has been brought about and every evil suppressed, that righteous and victorious King will carry out a great judgment on the earth of the living and the dead.[3]

Some Old English writers also thus visualized the Last Judgement. The author of the poem *Be Domes Dæge* suggests that the Last Judgement will take place 'here':

---

[1] CH I xl, p. 616.
[2] *The Epistles of St. Paul to the Thessalonians*, The International Critical Commentary (Edinburgh, 1912), pp. 177–8.
[3] *The Pursuit of the Millenium* (London, 1957), p. 12.

oþþe hu egeslic and hu andrysne
heah-þrymme cyningc her wile deman
anra gehwylcum be ærdædum.[1]

And in the poem *Christ*, all people are described as gathering on Mount Sion for the final arrival of the Lord.[2]

The question of whether the Last Judgement took place on earth or up in the air was by no means a straightforward one, and the author of homily vi has once again illustrated his independence of mind by depicting a universal aerial resurrection for judgement, after which only the righteous will be led to heaven.

The Old English homilist addresses his audience directly again at line 171, exhorting them to remember Christ's suffering and give due thanks. Although the basic idea (our debt of gratitude to God for His suffering) is from Bede, the homilist has simplified it and applied it more pertinently to his audience.

The homilist then proceeds (at l. 173) to follow Bede fairly closely. The first sentence is the author's own idea, but is constructed according to the same pattern as the ensuing material from Bede: the homilist emphasizes to his audience the advantages of love for God. The next sentence (ll. 175–7), with its contrast between the sweetness of divine life and the so-called pleasures of earthly life, renders Bede closely: 'Verum quia quo amplius quisque uitae caelestis dulcedinem degustat eo amplius fastidit omnia quae placebant in infimis.'

With Bede, the homilist then turns to Matth. xvii. 4: St. Peter's reaction to the glorious vision (l. 177). The homilist follows Bede closely here. He first explains how Peter forgot all earthly things because of the joyous sight, and then quotes the gospel-text (Peter's suggestion that three tabernacles should be built in that place). With Bede he declares that Peter is misguided here since there is no need for a house in heaven. He omits Bede's further description of heaven as a haven of peace admitting no adversity, but includes the evidence of Apoc. xxi. 22: 'Et templum non vidi in ea; Dominus enim Deus omnipotens templum illius est, et Agnus.' The homilist slightly expands Apoc. xxi. 22, but conveys its meaning accurately.

The anonymous homilist's interpretation here, it should be noted, differs from Ælfric's elsewhere. The variation is possible because other biblical texts do imply that Heaven contains various dwellings.

[1] J. Rawson Lumby, ed., *Be Domes Dæge*, EETS, os, 65 (London, 1876), p. 8, ll. 94–6.
[2] *The Exeter Book*, ed. Krapp and Dobbie, pp. 27–8, ll. 867–98.

John xiv. 2 reads: 'In domo Patris mei mansiones multae sunt. Si quo minus dixissem vobis, quia vado parare vobis locum.' In 2 Esdras vii. 94 the righteous are gathered into their own chambers. Hence Ælfric interprets the idea of heavenly dwellings literally in, for example, his homily for the Fourth Sunday after Pentecost:

He cwæð on sumere stowe, 'On mines Fæder huse sind fela wununga'; forðan gif sume beoð strengran on geearnungum, sume rihtwisran, sume mid maran halignysse geglengede, þæt heora nan ne beo geælfremod fram ðam micclan huse, þær ðær gehwilc onfehð wununge be his geearnungum.[1]

and in his homily for the Assumption of the Blessed Mary:

Drihten cwæð ær his upstige, þæt on his Fæder huse sindon fela wununga: soðlice we gelyfað þæt he nu to-dæg þa wynsumestan wununge his leofan meder forgeafe.[2]

Ælfric does not cite Apoc. xxi. 22 anywhere in his homilies.

The homilist, at line 191, follows Bede in returning to the first part of Peter's speech. In his commentary on this, the homilist emphasizes that 'mid gode dæde' we shall be able to see God eternally. The Old English homilist omits Bede's comment that the man who has not performed any good deed will never see his Creator's face. At lines 195–8, the homilist, like Bede, comments in a general way on Peter's reaction, but with a slight difference in emphasis: whereas Bede notes that Peter felt such joy that he did not wish to be separated from that sight, the Old English homilist reminds us of his earlier comment at lines 180–1 that Peter could imagine no joy except the sight of Christ's countenance, implying comparison with the inadequacy of earthly pleasures.

Like Bede, the homilist again addresses his audience directly ('fratres carissimi'/'leofæ men'), asking them to consider the happiness of those who deserve to see the extent of the Lord's glory. He specifies independently of Bede that the righteous will see eternally Christ's divine glory (ll. 205–9). Following Bede, he then poses a rhetorical question, asking which man can conceive how great are the joys and beauties of the righteous in heaven (a reminder of the rewards in store for the righteous). Like his source, he refers not only to the vision by the righteous of 'twæȝræ monnæ wuldor' (the two men being Moses and Elijah), but also to their yet more glorious beholding of the multitude of God's angels and saints, and Christ

---

[1] CH I xxiv, p. 350.
[2] CH I xxx, p. 446.

Himself. The Old English homilist does not quote 1 Petr. i as Bede does, but his reference to looking on Christ's face 'mid alle murhðe and mid alle blisse' was perhaps suggested by the biblical 'exultabitis laetitia inenarrabili et glorificata'. The ensuing description of heaven as a place where 'hæfð ælc to oðre unasecgendlic lufæ, and ylc blissæþ on oðres gode and on oðres murhðe swa on his aȝene' (ll. 209–10) is inserted independently of the homilist's source: the homilist stresses the desirability of aiming for this harmony in heaven. Ælfric describes heaven in a similar manner in his homily for the Assumption of Mary:

Godes gecorenra wuldor is gemetegod be heora geearnungum, and nis hwæðere nan ceorung ne anda on heora ænigum, ac hi ealle wuniað on soðre lufe and healicere sibbe, and ælc blissað on oðres geðincðum swa swa on his agenum.[1]

At line 211, the homilist translates Matth. xvii. 5. He omits a passage from Bede concerning the protecting nature of God's cloud. He does not follow Bede closely in his commentary on God's words, although both consider Christ's dual nature, His simultaneous humanity and divinity, and the need for the disciples to understand that He was both true man and divine. The comment 'for þon alle soðfeste men on him ifulled standeþ' (l. 217) is the Old English author's own addition.

In his next section (ll. 217–23), the Old English author loosely paraphrases Bede. He states independently that Christ showed His disciples the vision 'for mucele arfestnesse'. The idea that Christ wished to strengthen the faith of His disciples by this vision before His suffering is in both commentaries. Both refer to the glorification of Christ's body after His death ('æfter his upriste' in the Old English).

The homilist then paraphrases Matth. xvii. 6–9, adding his own interpretative comments: 'for heoræ mennisce tydernesse . . .' (l. 224), and 'swa þe arfeste larþeow don sceal . . .' (ll. 225–6). The latter significantly implies that the homily's audience may have been expected to include secular clerics who had the task of instructing the laity.

After translating Matth. xvii. 6–8, the homilist, like Bede, resumes commentary with Matth. xvii. 9. He begins with a rhetorical question asking why Christ forbade his disciples to tell anyone about the

[1] CH I xxx, p. 446.

vision. His two reasons correspond to Bede's. The first is that people would have resisted more fervently the persecution of Christ if they had known its aftermath. The subsequent explanation, that Christ wished it to happen in this way so that the faith His suffering induced in men should not be diminished, also derives from Bede (although Bede's reference to human salvation is omitted): 'et sic humanae salutis effectus qui per sanguinem eius erat futurus, retardaretur'. The second reason is that people would have believed, and undergone profound shock at His suffering: 'Ac he wiste þæt hit þuhte eft æfter þam moniȝe tyddrum modum swiðe eȝeslic þenne heo his hearde þrowungæ seȝen, and all þæt edwit and þa erfoðnesse þe he for monnæ hæle þolede' (ll. 244–7). As usual, the Old English author is more expansive stylistically than Bede.

In the next section (ll. 247–55), the Old English author paraphrases Bede's commentary: maximum impact on mankind is achieved by first accomplishing the Passion, Resurrection, and Ascension, and only then divulging them, along with the disciples' vision. Both authors are concerned to explain why all this was revealed *after* the Passion.

The Old English homilist's final address (ll. 256–68) is extremely close to Bede. Only one noteworthy distinction occurs: in the opening exhortation where Bede urges his readers to turn back to themselves ('ad nostram . . . conscientiam'), the Old English homilist exhorts his readers to turn 'to ure Drihten'. Both authors, however, enjoin their audiences to act righteously. Both exhort their audiences to refrain from idle speech, and refer to the rewards for such good deeds at the Resurrection, the chief of which is to see the Saviour Himself.

The anonymous Old English homily for the Saturday before the Second Sunday in Lent consists of a lengthy exposition of Matth. xvi. 27–xvii. 9, largely based on Bede's homily *In Quadragesima*. Whilst the Old English homilist generally eschews thematic divergence from the source, he does show a particular interest in the Day of Judgement. Several references to Doomsday are inserted independently of the source. At lines 99–104, the homilist notes that men shall differ in brightness on Doomsday, and that judgement will be meted out according to deeds. In lines 123–7, he inserts a brief description of the Last Judgement. He includes 'domes dæȝ' in his list of things which are to come (l. 154). The passage from Isidore may have particularly appealed to this homilist because of its discussion of the restoration of brightness to the moon, sun and stars at the time of judgement.

The length of the homily may account for the dearth of surviving copies. It is more likely, however, judging from the lack of any other Old English homily for this occasion, that the occasion was not considered important for preaching purposes in the Anglo-Saxon period, and that the homily was therefore of only limited use. The high quality of the homily, due in part to the willingness of its author to treat complex doctrinal issues, makes it a valuable contribution to the corpus of Old English works.

Men þa leofeste, sanctus Matheus þe godspellere þe ðis godspel
wrat, sæde þæt 'þe Hælend spec to his leorningcnihtæs bi domes
dæȝe, and hæt heom alle þam monnum cuþæn þæt he him sylf on
þissere weorlde endunge hider on middænearde us eft sechon walde

Bf. 108   on his | mæȝenþrymme mid engle wæredo, and he þenne walde ylce
6   men ȝe rice ȝe heane demen, and heom ædlean syllæn æfter heore
aȝene wruhte. And cwæð ða ȝyt, þæt summe þa ðe þær weron ne
sceolden deaþæs onfon ær þam þe heo seȝen hine sylfen on his rice
cumende. Ða embe six niht æfter þan þe Crist heom þas word sæde,
10   he nom mid him þa his þreo leorningcnihtæs, þæt wæs Petrus,
Iacobus, and Iohannes, and lædde heom uppon summe dune
onsundræn. þa feringe wearð Cristes anseone swiðe wunderlice fæȝer
iworden before(n) heom þrym, swa þæt his wlite scean swa sunnæ,
and his claðes weron iworden swa hwite swa snaw. þa rædlice
15   ætsceawede him þær Moyses þe halȝæ þe þe ifyrren worlde ær wæs
forðfæren and Heliæs þe prophetæ, and specon þær wið þone
Hælend. Sona swa þa haliȝe þeinæs þæt wundor swa mycel isæȝen, þa
sæde Petrus to Criste: Drihten, god is us þæt we hær beon, ȝif (ð)u

fol. 160ᵛ wylt, | þæt we her wurcean þreo inn, þe an, and Moyse an, and Helie
20   an. þa imong þæt heo þus speken þa com þær færinge swiðe beorht

Bodley 343, fols. 160-3; Belfour, pp. 106-23.

---

7 wruhte] h *altered from another letter*   13 beforen] be forem   18 ðu] du
20 þæt heo þus] þ 'heo' þus

SOURCES. The texts cited here (in addition to the Vulgate) are: (i) Bede, *Homeliarum Evangelii Libri II*, CCSL 122, I, 24, pp. 170-7 (cited as Bede followed by line numbers); (ii)
Pseudo-Isidore, *De Ordine Creaturarum Liber*, PL 83, cols. 923-5 (cited as Ps.-Isidore).

1-32 (*Matth. xvi. 27-xvii. 9*) (27) Filius enim hominis venturus est in gloria Patris sui
cum angelis suis, et tunc reddet unicuique secundum opera eius. (28) Amen dico vobis,
sunt quidam de hic stantibus qui non gustabunt mortem, donec videant filium hominis
venientem in regno suo. (1) Et post dies sex assumit Iesus Petrum et Iacobum et
Ioannem fratrem eius; et ducit illos in montem excelsum seorsum. (2) Et transfiguratus
est ante eos; et resplenduit facies eius sicut sol, vestimenta autem eius facta sunt alba
sicut nix. (3) Et ecce apparuerunt illis Moyses et Elias cum eo loquentes. (4) Respondens autem Petrus dixit ad Iesum: Domine, bonum est nos hic esse; si vis, faciamus hic
tria tabernacula, tibi unum, Moysi unum, et Eliae unum. (5) Adhuc eo loquente, ecce
nubes lucida obumbravit eos, et ecce vox de nube dicens: Hic est Filius meus dilectus,
in quo mihi bene complacui; ipsum audite. (6) Et audientes discipuli ceciderunt in
faciem suam, et timuerunt valde. (7) Et accessit Iesus, et tetigit eos, dixitque eis: Surgite,
et nolite timere. (8) Levantes autem oculos suos, neminem viderunt, nisi solum Iesum.
(9) Et descendentibus illis de monte praecepit eis Iesus dicens: Nemini dixeritis
visionem, donec Filius hominis a mortuis resurgat.

ʒenip, and heom ealle ofersceadewæde; and an stæfne wæs iworden
on þam miste, þus cwæðende: þis is mi leofæ sune þe me wæl licæð;
ʒehyræð him. Sonæ swa þa Cristes þeiʒnæs þæt mycele wundor
isæʒen and þa fæderlice stefne ihærdon, þa wæren heo swiðe afyrhte
swa þæt heo hit aberon ne mihten, ac feollen on þam eorðæn swiðe 25
ofdredde. Ða neahlæchede heom þe Healend and ran heom and heom
up ahof, and cwæð to heom: Arisæð and ne ondredæþ eow. þa hyo
heoræ eaʒen up ahofæn and arison, þa ne iseʒen heo neoþer ne
Moyses ne Helias, ne nænne mon buton Crist ane. þa ðe heo eft nyðer
of ðare dune eoden, þa bead Crist heom þreom þe þa wunderlice 30
sihðe iseʒen, þæt heo hit nane men ne sæden ær þam þe he for monnæ
hæle iþrowed hæfde, and of deaþe arise.'
  Leofe men, ure Drihten mid his aʒene wordum þurh his halʒæn
godspellere us munæð and læreð þæt we us warniæn wið | synne ant Bf. 110
wi(ð) mandæde, and þisses manfullen middaneardes læhtræs 35
forlæten, and þæt we æfre on ylce tide ʒeorne þencean hu læne, and
hu witende þas weorldlice þing beoð; and is swiðe uncuð ælce men,
æʒþær ʒe rice ʒe þam hænum, hu longe he þisses lænen lifes brucon
mote. Hwæt we nu iherdon hwylc wunder he ætywde his leorn-
ingcnihtes on þissere gastlice isihðe, for þam þe he walde þurh þæt 40
heoræ bileafe festniæn, and ealre þare monnæ þe hit iheren sæggen.
þeah ðe godspellere þas haliʒe race mid lyt worde write,
þeahhwæðere þæt blisse and þeo murhðe þe heo ðer iseʒen on anes
dæʒes hwile wæs mare þenne æniʒ mennisc mon sæcgen maʒe oþðe
forþan asmeʒean. Ðe godspellere cwæð þæt Crist wolde her on 45

21 ʒenip] *glossed by* ł mist   ofersceadewæde] d *altered from* w   22 miste]
glossed by ł nipe   23 swa] s *formed by extension of wynn*   26 ofdredde] o *written
above an* a *with deletion dot beneath*   35 wið] wid   45 asmeʒean] *glossed by*
beþencean (*in same hand*)

33–45 (*Bede, 1–9* [*not close*]) Quia dominus ac redemptor noster electos suos per huius
uitae labores ad illam quae laborem nescit uitam futurae beatitudinis introducere
disposuit modo per euangelium suum sudores certaminum temporalium, modo
aeternorum describit palmam praemiorum ut auditis uidelicet agonum necessitatibus
meminerint sibi requiem in hac uita nequaquam esse petendam audita rursum
dulcedine futurae retributionis leuius ferant mala transeuntia quae bonis sperauerint
remuneranda perpetuis.

45–57 (*Bede, 64–76* [*also not close, and order of ideas changed*]) Ostensurus gloriam suam
discipulis in montem ducit eos excelsum ut doceat omnes qui hanc uidere desiderant
non in infimis iacere uoluptatibus non inlecebris seruire carnalibus non cupiditatibus
adhaerescere terrenis sed aeternorum amore ad superna semper erigi angelicae
munditiae pietatis pacis dilectionis et iustitiae uitam quantum mortalibus possibile est
semper imitari debere iuxta eum qui dixit: 'Nostra autem conuersatio in caelis est unde
etiam Saluatorem expectamus Iesum Christum dominum nostrum. Ostensurus

worlde sceawen his aȝene ansyne his leorningcnihtæs swa beorhtlice
and swa þrymlice swa hine alle haliȝe on heofenæ rice iseon sceolden;
and he wolde læren us mid þam þæt we wisten þæt ælc þære monnæ
þe þenceþ þæt he þa heofenlice rice biȝyte, þæt he sceal þa hwile þe
50 he her on weorlde bið his lif sceadæn fram alle synlic lust, and fram
þissen eorþlice ȝytsunge. We sceolen ȝemunæn þæt Crist sæde þæt
þe wæȝ is swiðe heah and swiðe stæȝ(er) þe lædeþ us to heofenæ;
þene wæȝ faræð þa men þe hore hyht to heofenum habbæð and þencð
hu ateoriendlic þis eorðlic lif is, and hu swiðe hit is all mid soreȝe
55 imeind. Uten ȝemunen hwæt þe apostol cwæð: Ure murhþe, and ure
wuldor, and ure blisse is on heofene. To þam murhðe and to þam
blisse we sceolen becumen þurh Gode.

Wel þæt is isæid þæt 'Crist his haliȝe þeinæs lædde up on þa heaȝe
dune onsundron'; þæt tacnæð þæt þa soðfæste men beoð isceadde
60 feor fram yfele monnæ neawiste on þam towearde weorlde. þenne bið
ifylled þæt ðe witeȝæ cwæð on þam psalme: Drihten, þu bihuddest
þine halȝæn on þines andwlitæn wuldr(e), and þu heom bewrohtest
on heofenæ rice, and heom scyldest wið alle yfele þingum.

þe godspellere sæde þæt Crist 'æfter six daȝum' fulde þæt he his
fol. 161 þeinum bihet, | þæt heo his ansyne swiðe wunderlice iseon sceolden.
66 On þam is bitacnæd þæt alle haliȝe sceolen æfter þisse weorlde to
þam heofenlice blisse bicumen þe ðe Drihten heom bihet, þe ðe næfre
ne leah, and hit heom ȝearwode ær þan þe middæneard isceapen
Bf. 112 wære. | We rædeð on bocum þæt þissere weorlde tide stondæþ on six
70 ylde. Nu beoð þe fiue forð igan, and þeo sixte is nu andweard. Nu æft

---

51 ȝemunæn] *glossed by* understonden (*in same hand*)   52 stæȝer] stæȝre
62 wuldre] wuldres   69 þissere] þ *altered from* ꝥ (*stroke through ascender erased*)
70 æft] *superscript* 7 *added later in red*

---

gloriam suae maiestatis in montem discipulos ducit ut discant ipsi discant omnes qui
hanc uidere sitiunt non eam sibi in huius saeculi profundo sed in regno supernae
beatitudinis esse quaerendam.

(*Also Matth. vii. 14*) Quam angusta porta et arcta via est quae ducit ad vitam.

58–63 (*Bede, 76–82*) Et bene cum diceret quia 'ducit illos in montem excelsum' addidit
'seorsum' quia iusti etsi nunc cum prauorum uicinia premuntur animo tamen sunt toto
atque intentione fidei separati ab illis et in futuro funditus seorsum abducuntur ab eis
cum abscondit eos in abdito uultus sui a conturbatione hominum protegit eos in tabernaculo suo a contradictione linguarum.

64–72 (*Bede, 82–97*) Quod autem post dies sex ex quo promisit discipulis claritatem
suae uisionis ostendit significat sanctos in die iudicii regnum percepturos quod eis
'promisit qui non mentitur Deus ante tempora saecularia'. Tempora quippe saecularia
sex aetatibus constant quibus conpletis audient ipso dicente: 'Venite benedicti patris
mei possidete paratum uobis regnum a constitutione mundi.' [*The ensuing material is
omitted by the OE homilist.*]

þonne þeos ifylled bið̄ and iendod, þenne iheræð̄ alle haliȝe ure
Drihten and iseoð̄, and þenne blissiæð̄ a on ecnesse.

Hwi sæde þe godspellere þæt 'þæs Hælendes ansyne wære
scinendæ and swiþe wunderlic iworden, and scean swa synne'? For
þan þe ðe Hælend w(o)lde festnen and strengæn heore bileafe þe þæt   75
iseȝen, and eac eft alræ þare þe hit ihyrden secgæn, þæt we alle
mihten underȝyten, þæt swa swa his ansyne wearð̄ on beorhtnes
iturnd, swa beoð̄ alle his halȝæn on wlite and on wuldor ihwærfod on
domes dæȝ swa he him sylf sæde: Soð̄feste men scineð̄ swa beorhte
swa sunne on heore fæder rice. Leofe men, ær þam þe ðe æreste men   80
Adam and Eua agulten and Gode wreð̄ædon on neorxnawo[n]gæ, ær
þan þa tunglæn, sunne and monæ hæfdæn mucele mare beorhtnesse
þenne heo nu habbeð̄; ac syð̄æn heo gylten þurh unhersumnesse, and
God heom weorp of þam mucele murhð̄e on þisse deaþelic lif hider
on middæneard, þa sceolden þa (t)unglæ þæs wite þrowiæn, for þam   85
ðe heo þare menniscen cunde onfon sceoldon, and heo þa for þon
worden heoræ beorhtnes muceles dæles benumene. Hit ilimpð̄ þeah
on þissere weorlde endunge on domes dæȝ, þæt God ȝyfð̄ heom æft
heoræ fulle brihtnesse. þenne underfehð̄ þe mone þare sunne
brihtnesse, and þeo sunne [bið̄] seofen siðe brihtre þenne heo nu is.   90

---

75 wolde] o *written above* æ   77 swa²] s *formed by adding ascender to wynn*
81 neorxnawongæ] neorxnawogæ, *with* n² *altered from another letter*   85 tunglæ]
ȝunglæ   87 worden] *inserted above by another hand*

73–6 (*Independent of sources*)
76–80 (*Bede, 100–6*) Transfiguratus est ante discipulos dominus et sui corporis
gloriam qua per resurrectionem erat inlustrandum significat et electorum omnium
quantae claritatis post resurrectionem sint corpora futura manifestat. Nam et de illis
alibi dicit: 'Tunc iusti fulgebunt sicut sol in regno patris eorum'; et hic in exemplum
futurae clarificationis ipsius resplenduit facies eius sicut sol.
80–7 (*Ps.-Isidore, §3*) Haec enim dum humanis usibus ministrare a Deo creatore
destinata sunt, cum homines inculpabiliter vixissent, et sub Creatoris, quo conditi
fuerant, lege perseverarent, etiam sui luminis plenitudine decorata ministrabant; cum
vero homines, quibus in ministerio sociata primitus rutilabant, propter transgressionem
dejecti, paradisi beatitudinem amiserunt, ipsa quoque luminaria, quamvis non sua
culpa, sui luminis detrimenta non sine suo dolore pertulerunt, sicut Paulus apostolus
contestatur, dicens: 'Quoniam omnis creatura congemiscit, et dolet usque adhuc' (*Rom.*
viii. 22).
87–90 (*Ps.-Isidore, §4*) Sed quia per Redemptoris adventum humano generi pristinae
beatitudinis in melius restauratio promittitur, etiam creatura suum antiquum decorem
accepturam non dubitatur. Unde propheta Isaias de sole specialiter, et luna, illustratus
spirituali famine, inquit: 'Et erit in die illa, cum ceciderit turris, erit lux lunae sicut
lux solis, et lux solis erit septempliciter, sicut lux septem dierum, cum alligaverit
Dominus vulnus populi sui, et percussuram plagae ejus sanaverit' (*Isa. xxx. 25ff.*)

Heo moten eac þenne heom resten þæs runes and þæs ȝewinnes þe
heo nu ðrowæð. þis bið iworden þenne þa tid cymæð þæt þa Godes
bearn, þæt beoð alle haliȝe men, underfoð eac reste heore mucele
winnes and seoreȝæs þe heo nu dreaȝæð and þrowæð. Ne mæȝ þeah
95 þare tunglæ ne þare haliȝræ wlite and fæȝernesse beon ilic Cristes
beorhtnesse, for þan þe his wlite and his beorhtnesse oferscinæð alle
oðre liht. Sanctus Paulus þe apostol cwæð be þam Cristes halȝæn:
Efne swa þe steorræ oferscineð oðerne on brihtnesse þæt he bið
brihtre þene þe oþer. Swylc bið þe mon ærest on domes dæȝe swa
100 mucele wundorlycor and brihtræ þenne he þer scinæð for þene
oðerne. For þam swa mycele mare swa ðe mon her on weorlde to gode
Bf. 114 deþ | toforen þam oðre, and swa mucel swa he bið on his dæde bætere
þene þe oðer, swa mycele mare mæde and ædlean he sceal underfon
æt ure Drihtine on domes dæȝ. Hwæt we witæn soðlice þæt ðe wlite
105 and þeo feȝernesse þare drihtenlice ansyne feor oferstihð þare sunne
brihtnesse, swa hit rihtlic is; ac for hwan ȝemet þe godspellere þare
drihtenlicæ ansyne to þare sunne brihtnesse, buton for þam þe he ne
mihte nane brihttre ne wlitiȝre ifinden? Ac þeah, swa ic ær sæde, þe
fol. 161ᵛ wlite and þeo feȝernesse Cristes ansyne | alle þare sunne beorhtnesse
110 oferstihð. þæsne wlite and þis wuldor þare drihtenlice ansyne ne mot

91 eac] ea'c', *with* c *written above an erasure*

91–4 (*Ps.-Isidore*, §§6, 7) Cessante namque mutabilitate humani status, cui serviunt, et
sui cursus mutabilitas cessabit. Quod enim inquit, 'Sol in orto suo', hoc indicat quod
nunquam inclinabitur in occasu suo; et in eo quod dicitur: 'Luna stabit in ordine suo',
hoc insinuat quod mutationes incrementi et decrementi sui non patietur, sed in suo
ordine semper stabit. Hoc autem erit, 'quando', ut Apostolus loquitur, 'ipsa creatura
liberabitur a servitute corruptionis in libertatem gloriae filiorum Dei' (*Rom. viii. 21*).
Cum enim sancti pro mercede sui laboris, quo Deo servierint, immutati fuerint, et
fulserint sicut sol justitiae, cujus est sanitas perennis, tunc et ipsi corporeo huic soli pro
mercede sui ministerii, quo servituti corruptionis subjecta est, in septuplum fulgoris
rutilatio restituetur.

94–9 (*Bede, 106–9*) Non quia domini et sanctorum eius aequalis possit esse claritas et
gloria cum et eisdem sanctis dicta apostolus: 'Stella autem ab stella differt in claritate,
sic et resurrectio mortuorum.'

99–104 (*Independent of sources*)

104–10 (*Bede, 109–12*) Sed quia nihil sole clarius uidere nouimus non solum domini
sed et sanctorum in resurrectione gloria solis aspectui conparatur quia clarius sole
aliquid unde exemplum daretur hominibus minime potuit inueniri.

110–29 (*Bede, 112–21*) Hanc autem glorificam dominici corporis maiestatem hanc
sanctorum corporum claritatem nullus in iudicio reproborum uidere putandus est.
Tantum 'uidebunt in quem transfixerunt, et plangent se super eum omnes tribus
terrae'. At cum peracto iudicio sublati fuerint impii ne uideant gloriam Dei tunc iusti ad
contemplandam perpetuo gloriam regni eius et ipse pro modulo suo incorruptionis luce
transfigurati intrabunt. Unde dicit apostolus: 'Qui reformauit corpus humilitatis
nostrae configuratum corpori claritatis suae.'

nan sunful mon iseon, ac þæt toȝescead bið wunderlice iworden þurh
þa mucele mihte þæs Almihtiȝæ Godes sune. Ealle we sceolon on
þam dæȝe, gode and yfele, on ure Drihten lokiæn; ac ne bið þenne nan
deofles mon þæt þæs wuldræs and þæs wlites æniȝe dæl iseon
mote. Ac þa synfulle men sceolen iseon þa wundæn and þa sar on ure 115
Drihtne and þære næȝlæ swaðe, þe he wæs on rode mid inæȝlod, and
nænne dæl þæs blisses þe ic ær sæde, for þan þe heo nu her on worlde
his mycele eadmodnesse wæron unþongfulre þonne heo sceoldon.
Ðonne ne maȝen þa Cristes halȝæn nenne dæl þæs sares ne þare
wundæ on þam drihtenlice lichame iseon, ac heo iseoð þær on him 120
þæt blisse, and þone wlite, and þa fæȝernesse, for þon þe heo her on
worlde his ðrowunge and his eadmodnesse mid worde and weorcum
him þoncfulle wæren. Ðenne on domes dæȝ wurð ȝeiscead atwa alle
soðfeste men and synfullæ; þenne æfter þam beoð þa synfulle men on
ece wite isend, and soðfeste men beoð to heofene rice ilædde, þær heo 125
moten þa scinendæ Cristes ansyne a ecelice iseon, and heo þær syðan
æfre on brihtnesse libbæð and scinæð. Be þam sæde ðe apostol:
Drihten ȝehywæð þa eadmodnesse ures lichames, and hine ȝedeþ
wlitiȝne ant brihtne æfter his aȝene anlicnesse. Hwæt sæcge we þæt
his claþæs tacnoden þe ðe godspellere bisæde þæt heo wæren 130
iworden 'swa hwite swa snaw', buton þa halȝæ laþungæ, þæt is, alræ
haliȝre heap and samnung? Soþlice þa gædering bið hwit iworden
þurh fulluhtes bæðe, and heo scinæð hwite and brihte beforen Godes
eaȝum þurh monie | haliȝe dæde. Wæl we witen þæt nis nan mon þe Bf. 116
hine wið alle synnen healden maȝe þa hwile þe he her on weorlde bið, 135
þæt he on summe þingæ ne gulteð, oððe on worde, oððe on weorce,

---

113 dæȝe, gode] dæȝegode, *with space-bar inserted between* dæȝe *and* gode
123 atwa] t *altered from another letter* (c?)   124 þam] *inserted above*   synfulle] n
altered from h *by erasing ascender*   134 Wæl] *erased letter before* w

129–34 (*Bede, 121–33*) Si autem quaerit aliquis quid uestimenta domini quae facta sunt
alba sicut nix typice designant, possumus recte intellegere sanctorum eius ecclesiam
per haec esse monstratam de quibus Esaias ait: 'Omnibus his uelut ornamento uesti-
eris'; et apostolus: 'Quotquot enim', inquit, 'in Christo baptizati estis Christum induis-
tis'; qui in tempore resurrectionis ab omni labe iniquitatis simul et ab omni mortalitatis
obscuritate castigantur. Unde pulchre de uestimentis domini dicit euangelista Marcus:
'Quia facta sunt splendida nimis uelut nix, qualia fullo super terram non potest candida
facere' (*Mark ix*); quia quod omnibus patet nemo est qui sine corruptione ac dolore
uiuere possit super terram, quod omnibus sapientibus patet licet heretici contradicant.

134–40 (*Bede, 133–9*) Nemo est qui sine adtactu alicuius peccati uiuere possit super
terram. Sed quod fullo, id est doctor animarum siue mundator aliquis sui corporis
eximius super terram non potest dominus faciet in caelo emundans ecclesiam uestem
uidelicet suam 'ab omni inquinamento carnis et spiritus' insuper et aeterna carnis ac
spiritus beatitudine ac luce reficiens.

oððe on þonce. Ac þeah hit iwurð æt þisre weorlde endunge on domes
dæз þæt Drihten his halзæ laþung and alle haliзe зeclænsæþ and
alyseð fram alle wemme, and heom þenne swa wlitiзe and swa
140 unwemmed into his rice lædeþ.

þe godspellere sæde þæt 'ðær æteowden Moyses and Heliæs, and
þær wið Drihtin speken'. Leofe men, hwylce s[c]awedon heo heom?
oððe hwæt specon heo to him? Lucas þe godspellere hit sæзð зyt
cyðlycor. He sæзð: Moyses and Helias wæron isæзene on þrymme
145 and on wuldre, and heo speco[n] to Criste embe his þrowungæ þe hæ
eft on Ierusalem зefulde. Hwæt tacnæð Moyses and Helias þa ðe
þærup on ðære dune wið Drihten specon embe his þrowunge buton
þa drihtenlice æ and þa haliз witegæn þa ðe mid Godes Gaste
itrymede wæron, þe alle imænelice mycel ær biforen Cristes
150 þrowungæ sæden? And God heom unwreah alle þa ðing ðe towearde
weron, ærest bi Cristes tocyme hider on middæneard, and bi his
þrowunge, and bi his upriste, and bi his upstiзe þe he on heofene
astah, and alle þa ðing þe us haliзe bec nu зyt towearde secgæð, bi
domes dæз and bi Drihtines cyme æft hyder on middænearde, and bi
fol. 162 alles mon|cynnes upriste, and bi þam toweardæn liue. Buton tweon all
156 þis sceal iwurðæn. Witerlice eac Moyses þurh þas men tacnedo hu he
mennisce deaþ underfeng, and forðferde and iburiзed wæs. Rihtlice
þa men maзen beon þurh Moyses bitacnod, þa ðe nu on domes dæз of
deaþe arisæð and ær forþifarene wæron. Eliæs næfre зyt deaþ ne
160 þolode, ac he is зyt on lichame libbende on þam stowe þe God him
hæfð isæt; and he sceal þær abidæn sundfullice his martyrdomes,
oððet Drihten asende hine æft hider on middænearde ær worldes
ende, þæt he sceal þenne secgæn and cuþæn moncynne Godes lare,

---

144 cyðlycor] cy *written over erasure*   154 and¹] *inserted above later by same hand*
161 abidæn] n *altered from another letter*

141–50 (*Bede, 141–51*) Quales apparuerint et quid locuti sunt cum eo Lucas manifestius scribit dicens: 'Erant autem Moyses et Helias uisi in maiestate et dicebant
excessum eius quem conpleturus erat in Hierusalem.' Moyses ergo et Helias qui locuti
sunt cum domino in monte et passionem eius ac resurrectionem dicebant oracula legis
et prophetiae designant quae in domino conpleta et nunc doctis quibusque patent et
electis omnibus in futuro manifestius patebunt. Qui bene uisi in maiestate dicuntur
quia tunc apertius uidebitur quanta ueritatis dignitate omnis diuinorum eloquiorum
non solum sensus sed et sermo fuerit prolatus. . . .

[*OE homilist does not follow Bede here, but expands the material independently.*]

150–6 (*Independent of sources*)

156–66 (*Bede, 152–5* [*Expanded greatly by OE homilist*]) In Moyse quidem qui mortuus
ac sepultus est hi qui in iudicio resuscitandi a morte in Helia uero qui necdum mortis
debitum soluit hi qui in aduentu iudicis uiui inueniendi sunt in carne.

and his martyrdom for Cristes lufæ þrowæn on Antecristes daȝum.
Rihtlice þa men beoð þurh Helias itacnode, þa þe nu ær domes dæȝ 165
libbende beoð imette. Ealle men, æȝþær þa ðe ær forðiwitene wæron,
ȝe þa ðe þenne on lichame libbende | beoð, sceolen beon ahofene up Bf. 118
ofer þysne luftlice heofen on anes eaȝ(æn) beorhtnes, comende to þam
dome toȝeane ure Drihten; and syððæn bið þe mycele dom rædlice
iendod, and alle Godes halȝæn beoð þenne to þam ece lif iledde.   170
    Leofæ men, we sceolen æfre mid þankiende mode understonden
and þencen hwæt þe heofenlice Kyng for us ðrowode, and þæt we
sceolen þanken him a mid worde, mid dæda, and mid alle heortæ. For
ylc mon swa he mare lufe hæfð to þam Almihtiȝæ Gode, swa him lust
swiðor þe lufe; and a swa mycele swiðor swa he þa swetnesse þæs 175
heofenlice lifes on his mode ifeleð, swa mucele swiðor him biteriæð
and unswetiæþ alle þas eorðlice þing. For þam sanctus Petrus, þa ðe
he Cristes ansyne swa briht and swa wlitiȝe iseah and þæt wuldor
þare tweȝræ monnæ Moyses and Helias, þa forȝeat he sone alle þas
eorðlic þing þe he ær on wæs, and wace heo him þuðten for þa murhþe 180
þe he þa iseah. 'þa cwæð he for þon: Drihten, god is us þæt we her
beon, ȝyf þu wult þæt we her wurchen þreo leafselæs, þe an, and Moysi
an, and Helie an.' Sanctus Petrus wæs swiðe mid þam wuldre ofercumen þe he þær iseah, þæt he for þon ne þohte hwæt he speke, swylc he
mynte þæt he sceolde timbriæn eorðlic hus on þam heofenlice blisse. 185
Ne bið þær on þare heahe eadiȝnesse sundries huses neod, be þam

165 Helias] *inserted above by same hand*   168 eaȝæn] eaȝū   174 Gode]
erasure of ascender above g   179 þa] a *altered from* o   182 þreo] þre'o'
184 þæt] *added later at end of line*

166–70 (*Bede, 155–8*) Qui utrique pariter in uno eodemque momento rapti 'in nubibus
obuiam domino in aera' mox peracto iudicio ad uitam inducuntur aeternam.
171–3 (*Bede, 161–6*) Conuenit et hoc quod excessum eius quem conpleturus erat in
Hierusalem dixisse memorantur quia nimirum unica laudis materia fidelibus sui fit
passio redemptoris qui quanto magis meminerint absque gratia illius se saluari
nequiuisse tanto maiorem eiusdem gratiae memoriam deuoto semper in pectore
uersant deuota confessione testantur.
173–81 (*Bede, 166–71*) Verum quia quo amplius quisque uitae caelestis dulcedinem
degustat eo amplius fastidit omnia quae placebant in infimis merito Petrus uisa domini
et sanctorum eius maiestate repente cuncta quae nouerat terrena obliuiscitur solis his
quaeuidet perpetuo delectatur adhaerere (dicens . . .).
181–91 (*Bede, 172–81*) 'Domine bonum est . . . et Heliae unum.' Et quidem Petrus
sicut alius euangelista testatur nesciebat quid diceret in eo quod caelesti conuersatione
tabernacula facienda putauit. In illa namque caelestis uitae gloria domus necessaria non
erit ubi diuinae contemplationis luce omnia pacificante aura aduersitatis alicuius
timenda nulla remanebit testante apostolo Iohanne qui eiusdem supernae ciuitatis
claritatem describens dicit inter alia: 'Et templum non uidi in ea; dominus enim
omnipotens templum illius est et agnus.'

sæde sanctus Iohannes þe apost(ol), þæt Drihten s[c]æwæde him eft
oðre siðen þa gastlice sihðe. þa he þa heofenlice eadiȝnesse iseah and
sceawode, þa sæde he felæ þingæ bi þare feȝernesse þe he iseah. þa
190 sæde he: Ne seah ic þær nan temple, ne nan sundrie hus, ac Drihten
sylf is þare ceastre and þæs æþeles tempelhus. Ac þeah sanctus
Petrus þæt word mearcode, þeah he mid þam wuldre ofercumen
wære, þa he sæde: Drihten, god us is [þæt we her beon], þæt we to
Gode mid gode dæde earniæn þæt we moten mid him beon and his
195 haliȝe ansyne ecelice iseon a buton ende. Ða ðe sanctus Petrus Cristes
ansyne iseah swa briht and swa wlitiȝ, and þæt wuldor þare tweȝræ
monnæ mid him, þa þuhte him, swa ic ær sæde, þæt nan oðer blisse ne
murhðe nære buton þæt. Hwæt secgæ we, leofæ men, hwylc |
Bf. 120 eadiȝnesse underfoð þa men, þe nu mid gode dæde earnæþ þæt heo
200 ecelice iseon moten þone þrym and þæt wuldor ures Drihtines
eadiȝnesse? Hwylc mon is þæt mid worde sæcgæn maȝæ, oððe mid
mode þencean, hu mycele and hu monifealde beoð þa murhðe and þa
fol. 162ᵛ feȝernesse þare soðfæste monnæ, þenne þe | heofenlice Kyng lædeþ
heom to his rice, þær heo moten iseon on ecenesse his godcundæn
205 þrymme? And na þæt an þæt heo þær twæȝræ monnæ wuldor iseon
swa swa Petrus and his feren dudon uppon þare dune, ac swylce þæs
unrimedlicen werodes Godes engl(æ) and alle his halȝæn, and eac heo
moten ecelice loken on Cristes anwlite mid alle murhðe and mid alle
blisse. þær hæfð ælc to oðre unasecgendlic lufæ, and ylc blissæþ on
210 oðres gode and on oðres murhðe swa on his aȝene.

187 apostol] apła   189 he¹] *inserted above later, perhaps by another hand*
194 and his] *erasure between these two words*   206 Petrus] u *altered from another letter*
whose ascender is erased   207 englæ] englū

191-209 (*Bede, 182-202*) Sed bene nouerat quid diceret cum ait, 'Domine bonum est
nos hic esse', quia re uera solum hominis bonum est intrare in gaudium domini sui et
huic contemplando in aeternum adsistere. Unde merito nihil umquam boni ueri
habuisse putandus est cui reatu suo exigente contigit numquam sui faciem uidere
creatoris. Quod si beatus Petrus glorificatam Christi humanitatem contemplatus tanto
afficitur gaudio ut nullatenus ab eius intuitu uelit secerni, quid putamus, fratres
carissimi, esse beatitudinis qui diuinitatis eius altitudinem uidere meruerint? Et si cum
duobus tantum sanctis Moyse uidelicet et Helia transfiguratam in monte hominis
Christi speciem uidere bonum maximum duxit, qui sermo explicare, qui sensus ualet
conprehendere quanta sint gaudia iustorum cum accesserint 'ad Sion montem et
ciuitatem Dei uiuentis Hierusalem et multorum milium angelorum frequentiam'
ipsumque ciuitatis eiusdem artificem et conditorem Deum non 'per speculum et in
enigmate' sicut nunc sed 'facie ad faciem' conspexerint? De qua uisione dicit ipse
Petrus loquens de domino fidelibus: 'In quem nunc quoque non uidentes creditis quem
cum uideritis exultabitis laetitia inenarrabili et glorificata.'
209-10 (*Independent of sources*)

'Ða sanctus Petrus þas word þus to Criste spec, þa com þær feringæ
swiðe briht wolcn and heom alle uten embwreah; and wæs þa an
stæfne clypiende of þam brihte wolcne, þus cwæðende: þis is mi
leofe sunæ þe me wel licæð; ȝeihæreð him,' þæt heo wisten and
underȝeton þæt swa swa he wæs soð mon þurh his menniscen cynde,   215
swa eac he is soð God þurh his godcunde ȝecynde, and anes blisses,
and anre mihte; for þon alle soðfeste men on him ifulled standeþ. For
mucele arfestnesse Crist sceawde his leorningcnihtæs þa godcunde
sihðe, for þon þe he ȝeare wiste þæt ðeo tid neahlæchede þæt he for
monnæ hæle þrowiæn wolde. þa wolde he for þon her on worlde   220
heoræ bileafæ festlycor trymmen and heom cuþan, mid þam heofenlice murhðe þe heo þær isæȝen, hu wlitiȝ his haliȝ lichame beon
sceolde æfter his upriste.

'þa haliȝ for heoræ mennisce tydernesse ne mihten þæt wuldor
aberon, ac heo feollen on þa eorðe. þa dude Crist swa þe arfeste   225
larþeow don sceal, æȝþer ȝe heom mid his honden up arærde, and eac
mid his worde frofrede, and sæde to heom: Arisæð and ne ondredæþ
eow. þa þe heo heoræ eaȝæn up ahofen, þa n[e] isæȝen heo þær
nenne mon buton Crist ane, ac wæs þeo gast[l]ice sihðe þe heo ær
iseȝen eft all aweȝ iwiten. Ða þe heo nyðer of þam dune eoden þe   230
Thabor hatte, þa bead Crist heom þæt heo nane men þæt brihtlice
sihðe ne sæden þe heo þær isæȝen, ær þam þe he for | monnæ hæle   Bf. 122
iþrowod hæfde, and eft wære of deaþe arisen.' For hwon forbeat Crist
his þeiȝnum þæt heo ne sceolden cuþæn ne sæcgæn nane men þæt

---

214 leofe] *erasure of top of ascender above* f   225 arfeste] *glossed by* treowe (*in same*
hand)   228 n[e] isæȝen] ni sæȝen   232 he] *inserted above later by same hand*

211–17 (*Bede, 215–20*) Quia resplendentem filii hominis faciem cernere desiderabant
adfuit pater in uoce docens eundem esse filium suum dilectum in quo sibi bene con-
placuisset ut discerent ab humanitatis eius gloria quam uidebant ad diuinitatis quae
aequalis est illi contemplandam suspirare praesentiam.

217–28 (*Bede, 232–43*) Et quidem pia dispensatione fides discipulorum ne crucifixo
domino titubet solidatur dum inminente crucis articulo et humanitas eius qualiter per
resurrectionem sit sublimanda caelesti luce monstratur; et quia coaeternus sit in diuinitate patri filius caelesti eiusdem patris uoce probatur quatenus adueniente hora passionis minus morientem dolerent quem post mortem mox glorificandum in homine in
diuinitate autem semper a Deo patre glorificatum meminissent. Verum discipuli quasi
carnales adhuc substantiae fragilis audita Dei uoce timentes ceciderunt in faciem.
Dominus autem quasi pius per omnia magister uerbo simul eos et tactu consolatur et
erigit.

233–47 (*Bede, 246–52*) Visionem ostensae suae maiestatis ad tempus taceri praecepit
ne, si palam uulgaretur in populos, aut dispensationem passionis illius idem populi
principibus repugnando impedirent et sic humanae salutis effectus qui per sanguinem
eius erat futurus, retardaretur aut certe hi qui eandem uisionem audientes credidissent
uiso crucis obprobrio scandalizarentur.

235 brihtlice sihðe, buton for twam þingum? þæt oðer is for þan þe he
    wiste ȝif hit þam folce isæd wære, þæt all þæt folc were þenne þe
    mycele wiðerweardre þam ealdermonnum, (and) him þene teone
    iþafien nolden þe heo syððæn wið Crist ȝefremedon. Ac þa nolde
    Crist þæt ðe halȝe ȝeleafæ þe þam monnum þurh his blod and þurh
240 his ðrowunge sceolde (i)wurðæn, þæt he æniȝe hwile ȝeiwoned stode;
    ac hit sceolde nede gan all æfter his aȝene wille, swa he hit ær iset
    hæfde. þenne wæs hit eac for oðre þinge þæt heo þa sihðe sæcgen ne
    mosten. For þam ȝyf hit þenne sone monnum cyþ wære, þenne wære
    moniȝ mon þurh þæt to his ileafen ærest æt frymþe sone ichærred. Ac
245 he wiste þæt hit þuhte eft æfter þam moniȝe tyddrum modum swiðe
    eȝeslic þenne heo his hearde þrowungæ seȝen, and all þæt
    edwit and þa erfoðnesse þe he for monnæ hæle þolede. þa wolde he
    forþan þæt heo abiden þæs sæles, hwænne hit ware monnum
    nytlucost to cuþænne and to sæggene. He wolde þæt his haliȝe
250 þrowung ær ifulled wære, þæt eft his haliȝe apostolas, æfter þam þe
    heo mid þam Haliȝe Gaste itrymede wæron, þæt heo þenne sceolden
fol. 163 cuþæn | and sæcgæn openlice alle monnum, æȝþer ȝe his haliȝe
    þrowungæ, and his upriste, and his upstiȝe on heofene, and eac þas
    brihtlice sihðe þe heo þær mid heoræ eaȝnen isæȝen, and herden hu
255 þeo fæderlice stæfne his ece eadiȝnesse cydde.

    Nu, leofæ men, we habbæð isæd eow be summe dæle þæs
    godspellice word. Uten we nu mid alle ure heorte, and mid alle ure

---

237 wiðerweardre] wiðerweard`r´e   and] þe   240 sceolde iwurðæn] isceolde
wurðæn   hwile] h *altered from* þ (*descender erased*)   243 hit] *added in margin, its*
corrcct position in the text denoted by 77   246 eȝeslic] e¹ *formed from another letter* (*curved*
descender erased)

247–55 (*Bede, 252–9*) Oportunius autem conpleta passione resurrectione et ascensione eius in caelum repletis spiritu sancto apostolis praedicata est quatenus omnes qui
sacramentis eius initiari uoluissent non solum effectum resurrectionis credere sed
etiam modum eiusdem resurrectionis ab his qui uidebant potuissent ediscere nec nonet
aeternitatem diuinae natiuitatis quam a patre audierant cunctis pariter credendam
amandamque praedicarent.
256–68 (*Bede, 260–73*) Exposita lectione dominicae transfigurationis ad nostram,
fratres carissimi, conscientiam reuertamur et, si domini gloriam uidere delectat,
transitis carnalibus desideriis subeamus in montem uirtutum. Si ad uestimenta domini
candidissima pertinere uolumus, 'mundemus nos ab omni inquinamento carnis et
spiritus perficientes sanctificationem in timore Dei'. Si uocem Dei patris audire, si con-
substantialis eius filii maiestatem desideramus intueri, studeamus solliciti peruersa et
inutilia mortalium declinare studeamus a superuacuis saeculi fallentis oculos auertere
spectaculis quatenus resurrectionis nostrae gloria coruscante et ipsi quidem quae modo
nequimus magnalia nostri conditoris uidere simul et dicere mereamur praestante ipso
qui uiuit et regnat cum patre in unitate spiritus sancti Deus per omnia saecula
saeculorum. Amen.

mæӡne, cyrren to ure Drihten and earniæn mid gode dæde þæt we on heahnesse stiӡæn mote[n]. And ӡyf we wullæð lufiæn þæt we iseon moten ure Drihtines ansyne swa wundorlic and swa wlitiӡ, þonne 260 sceole we nu forlæten unrihtlicæ dædæ and lichamlice lustæs, and tilien æfre þæt we clæne beon and libben moten beforen ure Hælende, and healde we ure muð wið unnytte spece, and ure heorte wið yfele þoðtæs, and earniӡe we mid gode dæde þæt þenne all moncynnes uprist bið þæt we þenne moten to þam ece murhðe bicomæn, and þæt 265 ece eadiӡnesse æt ure Hælende underfon, and his ansyne ecelice iseon, and iheren; and þær þenne þæs blisses brucæn mid þam heofenlice Kynge, þe leofeð and rixæð on alræ worldæ world. AMEN.

NOTES

15. *ætsceawede*: This compound (meaning 'appeared') is not found else-where in OE. It is cited in Campb. *Suppl.*, but not in BT.

16. *prophetæ*: Prophet- is rarely used in OE: *witega* is the more common word. The Microfiche Concordance cites only five other instances of *prophet-* in the OE corpus. The word is common, however, in ME (it is of Old French as well as Latin derivation) and its use here may be a twelfth-century scribal substitution.

19. *inn*: The word *inn* is commonly used with the meaning 'tabernacle' (BTS cites one example). Interestingly at 182, where Matth. xvii. 4 is trans-lated for a second time, the unique compound *leafselæs* is used rather than *inn* to translate 'tabernacula': see my note to that line.

41. *bileafe*: OE *geleafa* has here been replaced by a form close to the ME form *bileve*.

66, 158. *bitacnæd, bitacnod*: The verb *betacnian* (cited in Campb. *Suppl.*, but not in BT) was frequent in OE, as the numerous entries in the Microfiche Concordance show.

89, 90, etc. *brihtre, brihtnesse*: The Anglian form *briht-* is more commonly used in this homily than West-Saxon *beorht-* (nineteen instances of *briht-* compared to ten of *beorht-*). In the other homilies edited here, iii uses *beorht-* once, and vii uses *briht-* twice. The form *briht-* may reflect a move towards the ME spelling *bright*.

123. *atwa*: The spelling of this word reflects the ME form *atwo* rather than the OE *on twa*.

142. *hwylce s[c]awedon heo heom?*: MS *sawedon* might possibly be a misspell-ing of *sawon* ('[they] saw'). The context, however, makes a scribal omission of *c*

more likely, making the word a pret. pl. form of the verb *sceawian* meaning 'show' (Campb. *Suppl.*). The nom. pl. *heo* then refers both in this phrase and in the next (143) to Moses and Elijah, and *heom* acts as a reflexive dative object ('in what way did they show themselves?'). Compare *s[c]æwæde* in 187.

152, 155. *upriste*: This word, meaning 'resurrection', is not found elsewhere in the OE corpus. (It is cited in Campb. *Suppl.* but not in BT.)

157. *iburiȝed*: Campb. *Suppl.* adds the form *gebyrgan* (to BT's *byrgan*), and cites the example of Pope vi, l. 43.

168. *luftlice*: The adjective *luftlic* or *lyftlic* is used only twice elsewhere in the OE corpus (one cited in BTS, the other in Campb. *Suppl.*).

177. *unswetiæþ*: BT cites *swetian* (verb) and *unswete* (adj.); the verb *unswetian* is cited in Campb. *Suppl.* only, and does not occur elsewhere in the OE corpus.

182. *leafselæs*: This compound, meaning literally 'leaf-halls', is cited in Campb. *Suppl.*, but not in BT. It combines two Old English words, *leaf* (leaf (of tree)) and *sele* (hall). See MED *s.v. lef* for other usages in Middle English. The translation of 'tabernacula' earlier in this homily is *inn* (19) (a word used elsewhere in Old English to render 'tabernacle'). In the West-Saxon Gospels, 'tabernacle' is translated by *eardung-stowa*, in the Lindisfarne Gospels by *huso*, and in the Rushworth Gospels by *sele-scotu*.

191. *tempelhus*: This compound (cited in Campb. *Suppl.* but not in BT) does not appear elsewhere in the OE corpus. The homilist may have coined *tempelhus* to distinguish the meaning from *temple* in 190 (although the Bible does not make this distinction).

192-5. The scribe has apparently skipped from one *þæt* to another, omitting the phrase *þæt we her beon*. The sense is that although Peter did not think what he spoke, when he referred to constructing earthly dwellings in heaven, yet he did give heed to his words when he said 'Lord it is good for us that we may be here', in that we may deserve by good deeds to dwell in heaven forever.

212. *embwreah*: This compound (cited in Campb. *Suppl.* but not in BT) is not used elsewhere in the OE corpus.

VII

THE TRANSIENCE OF EARTHLY DELIGHTS

STRUCTURE OF THE TEXT

This homily, unlike the others edited here, does not expound a gospel-text, nor does it derive its material from one main Latin patristic source (although all its parts may derive originally from Latin material). It belongs to the corpus of Old English composite homilies, homilies made up from an amalgamation of passages drawn from other vernacular writings.[1] The homily is unique in its present form, but its two separate parts (dividing at l. 94, approximately the half-way mark) probably both derive from earlier English originals.

The second part of the homily certainly derives from a version of an extant homily, Vercelli x; it contains the last third of that homily.[2] Vercelli x, like other Vercelli homilies (such as ii and ix), seems to have been used frequently by scribes and compilers of composite homilies. Vercelli x survives complete in three manuscripts: Vercelli, Biblioteca Capitolare CXVII, dating from the second half of the tenth century; CCCC 421, dating from the first half of the eleventh century; CCCC 302, dating from the eleventh to twelfth century.[3] Fragments of what may originally have been complete copies survive in two manuscripts: the Blickling Homilies, Princeton University Library, W. H. Scheide Collection, dating from the tenth to eleventh century, which has only the early part of the homily and its last few words, and Oxford, Bodleian Library, Junius 85 and 86, dating from the mid-eleventh century, where the manuscript begins imperfectly so that only the last few lines of the homily survive.[4]

The section of Vercelli x most often drawn on by compilers is its

---

[1] For a discussion of some other composite homilies, see M. R. Godden, 'Old English composite homilies from Winchester', *ASE* iv (1975), 57–65.

[2] Szarmach, p. 14, ll. 150ff.

[3] Ker, *Catalogue*, no. 394, item 12; no. 69, item 9; no. 56, item 33.

[4] Ker, *Catalogue*, no. 382, item 9 (Ker suggests that the loss of nine leaves from the manuscript accounts for the missing material); no. 336, item 1.

second half. This exists as an independent homily in two manuscripts: BL, Cotton Faustina A. ix, dating from the first half of the twelfth century, and CCCC 302, dating from the eleventh to twelfth century (the latter also has a complete copy of Vercelli x).[1] Furthermore, excerpts from the second half of Vercelli x occur in some composite homilies. Homily vii, as I noted above, includes the last third of Vercelli x. Oxford, Bodleian Library, Hatton 113, dating from the mid-eleventh century, contains two separate short extracts from the same section of Vercelli x.[2]

The excerpt from Vercelli x in homily vii is, as Scragg has noted, textually closest to the full version in CCCC 302, with which it has occasional additions in common (CCCC 302 occasionally preserves a better reading than the Vercelli Book, which is generally the most conservative).[3] According to Cross, homily vii is in some respects independent of all the other versions and perhaps more conservative, since it provides satisfactory readings where the earlier texts are at fault.[4] It is therefore possible that the excerpt of Vercelli x in homily vii derives ultimately from an exemplar closer to the original than all the other copies of Vercelli x.

It is possible that the second half of Vercelli x was originally independent and that Vercelli x is itself composite, but this seems extremely unlikely. The earliest surviving copies of Vercelli x (in the Vercelli Book, CCCC 421 and the Blickling manuscript) clearly had the full homily. The second half of Vercelli x is not found independently until the latter part of the eleventh century, nor do excerpts survive before that time.[5] Textually, moreover, the Vercelli Book is generally the most conservative, and the full version in CCCC 302, though late, is an independent witness to the original complete state of the text, since it occasionally preserves a better reading than the earlier manuscripts.[6] All the evidence points to Vercelli x being an original homily, whose second half later circulated separately, and became particularly popular with scribes and compilers of composite homilies.

---

[1] Ker, *Catalogue*, no. 153, item 6; no. 56, item 12.

[2] Ker, *Catalogue*, no. 330, item 23. This homily is Napier xxx; the excerpts from Vercelli x which it incorporates are Szarmach p. 14, ll. 151–4 and p. 15, ll. 168–83.

[3] Scragg, 'The corpus of vernacular homilies', p. 230 (including n. 6).

[4] 'Ubi Sunt Passages in Old English', p. 31.

[5] The copy in Bodleian Junius 85 and 86 cannot be used as evidence either way, since only the few closing lines survive.

[6] Scragg, 'The corpus of vernacular homilies', p. 230.

There is no other extant copy of the first half of homily vii. But it almost certainly derives from another vernacular composition, probably the last part of another homily. Immediately preceding the section drawn from Vercelli x, the compiler has included a characteristic closing formula for homilies ('and heo mid him and mid his halȝan libbæþ, and rixæð a on eccenesse', ll. 92–3), which must be the result of slavish copying of an exemplum. Moreover, although the two parts of homily vii are closely connected in theme (the need to renounce the transitory goods of this world, and to look for eternal bliss in heaven), the actual juxtaposition of one to the other is rather clumsy. The first sentence of the extract in homily vii from Vercelli x reads as follows: 'Hwæt we maȝen bi þissum underȝytæn and icnawon þæt þe Almihtiȝ Drihten nele þæt mon his ȝefenæ nænne þanc nyte' (ll. 94–5). In Vercelli x, 'bi þissum' follows naturally from a long speech by God in which He berates men for not appreciating that all things come from Him, for loving earthly things, and for not thanking Him. In homily vii, however, 'bi þissum' has no appropriate antecedent, and the statement has no substantial relationship with the preceding material. The compiler has apparently yoked together two extracts from already existing homilies without even attempting to create any logical link between them.

CONTEXT AND DATE

The homily was probably not composed for any particular occasion. No rubric is provided in Bodley 343, and it belongs to the final section of the manuscript, whose criteria for selection apparently comprised homiletic material not previously included (a *quando volueris* set may have been the compiler's immediate source). It is preceded by two Lenten homilies (v and vi above). Probably it was intended to be appropriate for a lay audience within the periods of both Lent and Rogationtide. It fits well with Godden's description of another composite homily: 'that combination of general exhortation with accounts of death and judgement which is characteristic of the many anonymous homilies in Old English produced for Lent and Rogationtide'.[1] The compiler of homily vii seems to have used the themes of man's death, transitoriness, and Doomsday as his criteria for selection. Vercelli x, from which the second half of the homily is excerpted, was clearly associated with Rogationtide in manuscript tradition.

[1] Godden, 'Old English composite homilies', p. 58.

Bazire and Cross justify excluding Vercelli x from their edition of Rogationtide homilies on the grounds that 'it is doubtful that it was originally composed for the festival', since 'there is no statement within the text indicating special connections with Rogations', and since Junius 85 and 86, which includes Vercelli x, may well have been a collection for Lent.[1] Like Vercelli x, homily vii was probably produced as a *quando volueris* within Lent and Rogationtide.

Some indication is provided about the homily's origin and date from its vocabulary. Hans Schabram, in his study of the Old English vocabulary used for the concept of *superbia*, points out that homily vii renders the concept of 'pride' on six occasions: 'worldprude' (l. 4), 'oferhydo' (l. 11), 'ofermetto' (l. 12), 'modiȝæn' (l. 72), 'oferhudiȝen' (l. 72), 'ofermedo' (l. 128).[2] Schabram works from the premise that 'oferhygd' is Anglian and 'ofermetto' West-Saxon. Of the vocabulary for 'pride' from homily vii, the last, 'ofermedo', is contained within the section of Vercelli x used by the compiler. This, Schabram suggests, is a West-Saxon substitute for an Anglian original (Vercelli x has 'oferhygd'). From the other words for 'pride', Schabram surmises that the first half of homily vii also began as Anglian, then passed through a West-Saxon stage before being copied by a twelfth-century scribe. In two cases, the two words for pride appear as a pair: 'to hwam þu on oferhydo þe sylf up ahæfst on ofermetto' (ll. 11–12), and 'þa modiȝæn and þa oferhudiȝen' (ll. 71–2). According to Schabram, the Anglian original would have had only 'oferhydo' and 'oferhudiȝen', and a West-Saxon scribe has added later 'ofermetto' and 'modiȝæn' (perhaps originally as glosses) to clarify the meaning. The other word used for 'pride', 'worldprude', may be significant for dating. It derives from an Old French adjective which appeared in England in the two forms 'prut' and 'prud'.[3] The word 'prut-'/'prud-' was formerly thought to have appeared in England as a mid tenth-century inter-linear gloss 'prede' to the Latin adjective 'superbe'. Walter Hofstetter, however, shows that this gloss should read 'spede' and that the first instance of 'prut-'/'prud-' is in fact half a century later: the substantive 'pryte' in CH II xii, 530 (Godden dates the original version of the Second Series to 994).[4] After this, the word is quite commonly used;

[1]   *Eleven Old English Rogationtide Homilies*, ed. Bazire and Cross, p. xx.

[2]   *Superbia: Studien zum altenglischen Wortschatz*, I (Munich, 1965), pp. 83–4.

[3]   Schabram, *Superbia*, p. 14. Also see Hermann M. Flasdieck, 'Studien zur Laut-Und Wortgeschichte', *Anglia*, lxx (1951), 225–84, pp. 257–71.

[4]   Walter Hofstetter, 'Der Erstbeleg von AE. *pryte/pryde*', *Anglia*, xcvii (1979), 172–5. For the date of the Second Series, see CH II, pp. xci–xciii.

Hofstetter cites two examples in Byrhtferth's *Manual* (AD 1011), and eighteen in the Old English translation of the *Rule of Chrodegang* (dating from about 1000). The use of 'worldprude' in homily vii suggests that this first section of the homily may have been written after (or contemporaneously with) Ælfric's homilies, and therefore that the whole of the homily was compiled at that later date. The compound 'worldprude' is clearly an Old English rather than a Middle English formation, however; it appears in London, Lambeth Palace 427, dating from the second half of the eleventh century: 'mid ofermettum afylled, ne mid worldprydum'.[1]

SOURCES AND ANALOGUES

The work opens with the familiar homiletic idea of the transitoriness of earthly riches, which is animated by a powerful and evocative image: the rich man's bones warning his living counterpart of his prospective fate as a mortal. As Cross has shown, the passage derives from Caesarius of Arles' sermon *De Elemosinis*.[2] The same passage occurs with only slight differences in a Pseudo-Augustinian sermon *Ad Fratres in Eremo LXVI*,[3] but the Old English homily is closer to Caesarius than to Augustine; only Caesarius, for example, includes the comparison with shadows which is made in homily vii (ll. 4–5). Other Old English homilists, also attracted by Caesarius' illustration, rendered it into the vernacular. The passage must have this source in common with Vercelli xiii and probably also with Blickling x, though there is no direct connection between any of the Old English versions. In Vercelli xiii, very little has been altered from Caesarius. In Blickling x, however, the homilist has incorporated Caesarius imaginatively into his text, transforming the already powerful image into an elaborate exemplum. He creates particular fictional characters and invests them with motives and actions: the protagonist is the rich man's kinsman who lives abroad out of grief for his relative's death; on his return he is addressed by the rich man's bones and, consequently turning to God, saves his kinsman's soul. The mourner is an entirely good man, hence he cannot be exhorted to leave his evil desires, as the passer-by is in

[1] Max Förster, ed., 'Die altenglischen Beigaben des Lambeth-Psalters', *Archiv*, cxxxii (1914), 328–35, p. 334.
[2] 'The Dry Bones Speak—A Theme in Some Old English Homilies', *Journal of English and Germanic Philology*, lvi (1957), 434–9. Caesarius' sermon is found in CCSL 103, no. xxxi, p. 135.
[3] PL 40, cols. 1352–3.

homily vii, but is instead urged to turn to God for comfort.[1] Despite
the development of Caesarius' image by the Blickling homilist, its
original derivation is clear: both context and content, as Cross has
shown, reveal the debt to Caesarius.[2] Although neither Vercelli xiii
nor Blickling x have any direct connection with the Bodley text, all
three versions almost certainly derive independently from the same
source.

Homily vii shows a fairly close correspondence with its source here.
Following Caesarius, the Old English author initially exhorts his
audience to consider the fate of earthly wealth which belonged to rich
men now in their tombs. In his list of vanished earthly things pertaining to rich men, the Old English homilist prefers a few broad categories, writing 'heore gold, and heore þeʒenscypæs, and heore
worldprude þære ydelnesse' (ll. 3–4) for Caesarius' longer and more
specific inventory: 'ubi ornamenta, ubi anuli vel inaures, ubi diademata pretiosa, ubi honorum vanitas, ubi luxoriae voluptas, ubi spectacula vel furiosa vel cruenta vel turpia'. As Cross notes, it is common
for an Old English writer to add to and vary the 'ubi sunt' phrases of a
Latin original. Hence in this passage a category in the Old English
may represent one item or more in Caesarius, for example, 'heore
gold' may represent 'ubi ornamenta, ubi anuli vel inaures, ubi diademata pretiosa'.[3] It is also possible, however, that the Old English
author here has departed from any close adherence to Caesarius,
choosing his own phrases from a traditional stock. Like Caesarius, the
Old English author replies to the 'ubi sunt' list by comparing the transience of these riches to shadows, although he applies it specifically to
'monnes sceadu' instead of shadows in general (ll. 4–5). The following
point made by Caesarius is omitted by the Old English author
(Caesarius first establishes that without penitence, only disgrace and
reproach remain, and then comments on the human body inside the
tomb, of which only 'cineres et foetidae vermium reliquiae' survive).
The Old English homilist picks up Caesarius' account with the speech
of the passer-by as he looks on the grave (ll. 6–8). By abbreviating the
speech, however, he bestows a different character on the entombed
man. Caesarius' dead man 'pro cupiditate currebat' and 'libidini
serviebat'; the Old English homilist's merely 'iu on þissre worlde

---

[1] In its pattern of elegiac narrative opening leading to the specific revelation of the
comfort to be found in God, the exemplum can be compared to poems like *The Wanderer*
and *The Seafarer*.

[2] 'The Dry Bones Speak', pp. 438–9.

[3] Ibid., p. 439.

wunsumlice lyfede'. The pejorative emphasis of the Latin is completely lacking in the Old English homilist's adaptation. The homilist also omits Caesarius' explicit statement (in the mouth of the hypothetical passer-by) that nothing but foulness and dust remain of the dead man.

Like Caesarius, the Old English homilist then turns to the bones themselves and their instructive capacity. For Caesarius, the bones could speak to his audience if they wished to hear; for the Old English homilist, however, the bones would speak 'ʒif heo specen mihten' (l. 10), that is, the power of the bones to speak is deliberately denied. This point is repeated at the conclusion of the bones' warning: 'þenne, leofe men, þeah þe ða deade ban of þare buriʒnes specon ne maʒon, þeah we maʒen us sylfæn bi þam læren' (ll. 16–18). The homilist, adapting Caesarius in Vercelli xiii, also implies that the bones are powerless to speak: they would call to us 'ʒif hie sprecan meahton of þære byrgenne'. Cross concludes from these similar but independent insertions that 'these sermons in the vernacular were modified to suit a less sensitive (but yet hard-headed) audience than the people who heard Caesarius's Latin exhortation'.[1] The Old English comments may also have been made in the light of contemporary theology. The nature of belief in miracles, for example, would have allowed certain saints to perform miraculous deeds from their tombs, but certainly would not have allowed a formerly wealthy and evil man to speak from his tomb. Various analogies can be found elsewhere in Old English literature to support this. *The Seafarer* stresses the complete inertia of the body in its grave:

> Ne mæg him þonne se flæschoma, þonne him þæt feorg losað,
> ne swete forswelgan ne sar gefelan,
> ne hond onhreran ne mid hyge þencan.[2]

In *Soul and Body I*, the Soul expresses a similar idea in its address to the Body:

> Ligeð dust þær hit wæs,
> ne mæg him ondsware ænige gehatan
> geomrum gaste, geoce oððe frofre.[3]

Clearly the writer of homily vii considered that Caesarius' ambiguous phrasing, 'si velis . . . audire', would be too easily misunderstood by his audience.

---

[1] Ibid., p. 437.   [2] *The Exeter Book*, ed. Krapp and Dobbie, p. 146, ll. 94–6.
[3] *The Vercelli Book*, ed. Krapp, p. 57, ll. 105–7.

The actual speech made by the bones corresponds closely to Caesarius. The first question implicitly rebukes the listener for covetousness, the next for pride, evil practices, and sinfulness (the words 'oferhydo', 'ofermetto', 'unþeawæs', 'sunne', correspond to 'superbiae vel luxuriae', 'vitiis', 'criminibus', though the Old English homilist omits the image of serving the cruellest masters). As in Caesarius, the speaker (the pile of bones) then exhorts his audience to behold him, to abhor evil thoughts, and to consider their moral condition. The idea is emphasized by immediate repetition, and repetition at the conclusion of the speech. The Old English homilist translates closely Caesarius' idea, 'quod tu es, ego fui; quod ego sum, tu eris', as 'iu ic wæs swylc þu nu eart, and ᵹyt þu iwurðæst swulc ic nu eom' (ll. 14–15). He then omits a short piece from Caesarius in which the dead man ironically contrasts himself and his listener (perhaps again he feared that its subtlety would be lost on his audience): 'Si in me permansit vanitas, vel te non consumat iniquitas; si me luxuria corrupit, vel te castitas ornet.' The speeches both close with repetition of the exhortation to look on the bones and relinquish evil desires. Whereas the Latin now concludes, 'rebus ergo ipsis ad nos clamat mortuus de sepulchro', the Old English notes that the bones can instruct us 'þeah þe ða deade of þare buriᵹnes specon ne maᵹon' (ll. 16–17). From this point, the two homilies diverge permanently, although both initially include an oblique reference to a potential reward after death.

With the Old English homilist, the reference to death, and the disclosure of rewards and former deeds, lead immediately to an imaginative depiction of Doomsday. The bulk of the material derives ultimately from the Bible, but in selection and organization of biblical passages the homilist for the most part was probably conforming to a contemporary Anglo-Saxon standard. Although there are no direct connections between this depiction and that of any other homily, the similarities between them are often striking.

The homilist first defines Doomsday as that time 'þonne Drihten mid þam heofenlice weredo englæ þisne middæneard sæcð to weane and to wrace synfulle monnum, and eac haliᵹe monnum his fultum to bringenne' (ll. 23–5). Clearly he is interested in Doomsday as a general concept rather than simply its contemporary relevance: neither here nor elsewhere is there any reference to the imminence of Doomsday which is found in the homilies of Ælfric and Wulfstan, and in the Blickling collection. The homilist implies here that the Judgement will be executed on earth. He does not seem to have any consistent conception of this, however, since his subsequent commentary suggests that the earth will be destroyed before the arrival of the Lord. Both views are tenable (see pp. 159–61 above), but to find both expressed within one passage or indeed within one homily is curious.

The homilist then addresses the resurrection of mankind. He does not attempt to explain to his audience how resurrection is possible, even for decayed or maimed bodies.[1] Nor does he refer to the interim between death and Doomsday, or to the fate of the soul as opposed to that of the body; consequently the notion that souls receive their bodies again on Doomsday is not raised. In stating that the bodies and bones 'mid synnæ deopnysse ifestnode wæren' (l. 27), the homilist differs from the usual depiction of the fate of the soul and of the body in the period between death and Doomsday. The image of the burden of sins is usually applied to the soul rather than the body. *Soul and Body I*, for example, suggests that the dead body is separated altogether from sins:

> ac her sceolon onbidan ban bereafod,
> besliten synum, ond þe þin sawl sceal
> minum unwillum oft gesecan,
> wemman þe mid wordum, swa ðu worhtest to me.[2]

In this poem, it is the soul that is associated with sin, and the soul which must revisit the body at regular intervals as a penance. The homilist of vii has avoided any mention of the soul, and has imaginatively combined the non-physical concept of sin with the corpse itself.

The notion that mankind, once resurrected, shall see the world consumed by flames is biblical (2 Petr. iii. 10, 12; Ps. xlix. 3), and is commonly included in Old English depictions of the Last Judgement.[3] The ordering of events is not always identical; in Pope xi, for example, the flames precede rather than follow the universal resurrection. The Bodley homilist dwells on the image of the burning world at some length, using various different phrases to portray it: 'heo þenne iseoð þas world sweliȝende, mid fure brastlende and bærnende, ant þone heahroder on reade liȝeum' (ll. 28–30).

---

[1] The homilist differs here from Ælfric, who attempts to clarify this on several occasions. See, for example, CH I xvi (First Sunday after Easter) and xiv (Palm Sunday); CH II xxvii (Seven Sleepers). For further discussion of Ælfric's eschatology, see Gatch, *Preaching and Theology*, chs. 6–9.   [2] *The Vercelli Book*, ed. Krapp, p. 56, ll. 61–4.
[3] See, for example, Pope xi, 296–307; CH I xl, p. 616.

The account of the Lord's arrival (ll. 30–5) is based fairly closely on Matth. xxv. 31 onwards. The Lord comes from the clouds of heaven (Matth. xxiv. 30) surrounded by His heavenly angels (Matth. xxv. 31), and the righteous and the sinful will be gathered before Him and the Lord will separate them into two halves (Matth. xxv. 32, with the homilist omitting the simile of sheep and goats), and He will set the righteous on the right hand and the sinful on the left (Matth. xxv. 33). With the speech of the Lord to the righteous (Matth. xxv. 34 ff.), the homilist diverges from the gospel-text. The speech begins 'Cumeð, ȝe iblesode', but immediately plunges into a description of the joy of heaven, closing with praise of the good for their obedience and good works (ll. 36–44). Bazire and Cross suggest that 'the speech of Christ has become a topos of Doomsday descriptions, its base being Christ's words in Matthew 25 . . . , which can be verbally changed as needed'.[1] One particularly close analogue to homily vii's speech by Christ is found in Vercelli viii, where His words to the righteous also consist of a description of the joy of heaven:

Cumað ge to me; wuniað mid me in minum rice, þæt ge ge-earnod hæfdon. 7 ge ðonne scinaþ swa biorhte swa sunne, þonne hio æfre on midne dæg fægerost scineð 7 biorhtost. þær is symle ece blis 7 soð syb 7 gefea; 7 þær is singalic Godes lof gehyred; 7 þær is lufu 7 smyltnes 7 syngal lioht 7 swete stenc.[2]

Interestingly, this description has no equivalent in that homily's source, Caesarius, *Sermo* lvii.[3] Both the Vercelli and Bodley homilists must be working from a common variant of the topos of Christ's Doomsday speech. The Bodley homilist alters the scriptural tone by emphasizing the reward to come and specifically mentioning obedience rather than concentrating on the deeds of charity performed by the righteous.

The speech by God to the sinful (ll. 45–54) also diverges from its biblical counterpart. Again the opening words are scriptural: 'Gewitæþ, ȝe awariȝede, from me on þane mycele æðm, and on þæne ece brune'; but the homilist quickly moves to a long and vivid depiction of the horrors of hell. The features included are all of biblical origin: hell's everlasting fire (Matth. xxv. 41); dragons tearing the

[1] *Eleven Old English Rogationtide Homilies*, ed. Bazire and Cross, p. 137.
[2] Förster, p. 158.
[3] See Rudolph Willard, 'Vercelli Homily VIII and the *Christ*', *PMLA*, xlii (1927), 314–30, and Joseph B. Trahern Jr., 'Caesarius of Arles and Old English Literature: Some Contributions and a Recapitulation', *ASE*, v (1976), 105–19.

bodies of the sinful (Mark ix. 44–6); weeping and gnashing of teeth (Matth. xiii. 42, 50, xxii. 13, xxv. 30, etc.), and darkness (for example, Matth. xxv. 30). Clearly these features constituted a standard iconography of hell, for other Old English homilists combine the same themes. Ælfric, for example, describes the torments of hell in similar terms in his homily for the Third Sunday after Epiphany:

þa earman forscyldegodan cwylmiað on ecum fyre, and swa-ðeah þæt swearte fyr him nane lihtinge ne deð. Wurmas toslitað heora lichaman mid fyrenum toðum, swa swa Crist on his godspelle cwæð, 'þær næfre heora wyrm ne swylt, ne heora fyr ne bið adwæsced.' þær beoð þonne geferlæhte on anre susle, þa þe on life on mandædum geðeodde wæron ... þær bið wop and toða gebitt, forðan ðe ða eagan tyrað on ðam micclum bryne, and ða teð cwaciað eft on swiðlicum cyle.[1]

Much rarer, however, is the placement of this depiction of hell within the context of God's speech to the sinful on Doomsday. Vercelli viii is the only homily I have found which offers the same context. After presenting a long condemnation by God of the sinful for their wicked deeds, the Vercelli homilist continues:

Gað ge nu, awyrgedan, in þæt ece fyr 7 in þa ecean forwyrd, þe gefyrn ærest wæs ðam diofle Satane 7 his geferum geearwod. þær ne bið næfre ænig lioht gesewen ne nænig wynsumnes gemeted. Ac þær syndon þa wyrrestan wildeor, þa wundiað eowre sawle; 7 þær syndon þa undeaðlican wyrmas, þe næfre ne sweltað. 7 þæt fyr ne bið næfre adwæsced, ac hit to widan feore byrneð; 7 eowra synna on eowrum sawlum þær byrnað. And þær is eagena wop 7 toða grist-bitung. And þær syndon þa unmætan þystro; 7 þær is egesa 7 fyrhto; 7 þær is swið hreownes; 7 þær is unriht-wisnes, 7 þær is hunger 7 næcedu; 7 þær is yrmðo 7 nearones; 7 þær is un-mæte cyle 7 unahefendlic hæto gemeted; nis nænig ge-met-fæstnes. Ac ðær is sio wyrreste adl 7 se bitera wop 7 a in ecnesse celnes.[2]

Again this particular passage is not found in the homily's main source (Caesarius Sermo lvii). This passage and the Bodley equivalent can be compared in the way they have converted standard features into forceful and terrifying visions of hell by, for example, repetition of ideas and anaphoric repetition of 'þær'.

The homilist closes God's speech to the sinful by explaining their torments: 'for þam þe ȝe mine lare on eowre mode oferhoȝoden, and

---

[1] CH I viii, p. 132. Compare also Assmann xiv, p. 168; Napier xxix, pp. 138–9; *Eleven Old English Rogationtide Homilies*, ed. Bazire and Cross, xi, p. 142.

[2] Förster, pp. 156–7. The preceding passage in Vercelli viii in which God condemns the sinful for their wicked deeds is discussed by Willard in 'Vercelli Homily VIII and the *Christ*'.

ȝe recelease nolden mine bodu healdon'. He stresses the need to obey God's word rather than the importance of voluntary acts of charity.

The wicked are now driven weeping into hell, and at this point the homilist observes: 'heo iseoð þare soðfestræ and englæ murhðe and isæliȝe monnæ hwit werod heriȝende ure Drihten' (ll. 56–7). This idea is extremely unusual amongst available sources and analogues: most stress that although the righteous can see the sinful in torment (whereby their joy is unimpaired), those condemned in hell cannot see the joy of the holy. Julian of Toledo, in a passage drawn on by Ælfric in his homily *In Octavis Pentecosten Dicendus*, distinguishes the situation before and after Doomsday:

Credendum vero est quod ante retributionem extremi iudicii iniusti in poenis quosdam iustos in requie conspiciunt, ut eos videntes in gaudio, non solum de suo supplicio sed etiam de illorum bono crucientur. Post iudicium autem nesciunt quid agatur in gaudio beatorum; boni tamen sciunt quid agatur in suppliciis miserorum.[1]

Following Julian of Toledo, Ælfric writes:

Ne magon þa fordemdan, ne furðon ða deoflu,
þa blisse geseon þe bið mid ðam halgum,
syððan hi gebrohte beoð on þam bradan fyre,
ac hi ðær beclysede cwylmiað on eccnysse.[2]

In another homily based on the story of the rich man and Lazarus (Luke xvi. 19–31), Ælfric does show a sinful man seeing a righteous one in glory (the rich man sees Lazarus in Abraham's bosom).[3] Ælfric stresses, however, that only in the period between death and Doomsday, and not beyond, will the sinful see the chosen in glory, though the righteous will always see the unrighteous suffering. The Bodley homilist is not entirely at variance with vernacular tradition, since the same idea is expressed in the poem *Christ*:

Ðonne bið þæt þridde þearfendum sorg,
cwiþende cearo, þæt hy on þa clænan seoð,
hu hi fore goddædum glade blissiað,
þa hy, unsælge, ær forhogdun
to donne þonne him dagas læstun;
and be hyra weorcum wepende sar
þæt hi ær freolice fremedon unryht.
Geseoð hi þa betran blæde scinan.[4]

[1] Gatch, *Preaching and Theology*, p. 145 (Appendix).
[2] Pope xi, 504–7.   [3] CH I xxiii, p. 334.
[4] *The Exeter Book*, ed. Krapp and Dobbie, pp. 38–9, ll. 1284–91.

Clearly this poem and homily vii are drawing on a similar tradition of commentary.

The homilist then paraphrases Matth. xxv. 46, elaborating on the notion that the sinful shall proceed to hell and the righteous to the joy of heaven (ll. 59–62). Turning once again to his audience, he concludes that God's commands must be kept in order to earn the joys of heaven and avoid the pains of hell (ll. 63–5). He returns at line 65 to a discussion of the transitory nature of man's life, emphasizing that death seizes all men whatever their circumstances. The Bodley homilist observes the futility of clinging to life, noting that death sunders man from his possessions. He reminds his readers that their lives are diminishing day by day (ll. 67–9, 77–8), and contrasts this transience with the eternity of torments.

The homilist then compares the human body to plants, which flourish, then become desiccated and shrivelled in the sun's heat; he applies the image specifically to the decline of human youth and beauty (ll. 79–83). The image resembles the parable of the sower and the seed, particularly Matth. xiii. 6 (cf. Mark iv. 6): 'sole autem orto aestuaverunt, et quia non habebant radicem, aruerunt'. It relates closely too to the discussion of the lilies of the field in Matth. vi. 28–30:

Et de vestimento quid solliciti estis? Considerate lilia agri quomodo crescunt: non laborant, neque nent. Dico autem vobis, quoniam nec Salomon in omni gloria sua coopertus est sicut unum ex istis. Si autem foenum agri quod hodie est et cras in clibanum mittitur Deus sic vestit, quanto magis vos modicae fidei?

The image and its application have a close analogue in Blickling v:

We witon þæt Crist sylfa cwæþ þurh his sylfes muþ, 'þonne ge geseoþ growende & blowende ealle eorþan wæstmas, & þa swetan stencas gestincað þara wuduwyrta, þa sona eft adrugiaþ & forþ gewitaþ for þæs sumores hæton.' Swa þonne gelice bið þære menniscan gecynde þæs lichoman, þonne se geogoþ-had ærest bloweþ & fægerost bið, he þonne raþe se wlite eft gewiteþ & to ylde gecyrreþ, & he þonne siþþon mid sare geswenced bið, mid mislicum ecum & tyddernessum.[1]

A passage by Ælfric, expounding Matth. vi. 28 ff., is also very similar, though here the image is not related specifically to the human body:

Wyrta sind eaðelice gesceafta. and ðurh winterlicne cyle symle forseariað. swa ðeah þæs ælmihtigan cystinys. hi geglencð mid swa wlitigum blostmum. þæt hi oferstigað. mid heora fægernysse ealle eorðlice gebleoh; Ne mihte se

---

[1] Blickling, pp. 57–9.

wuldorfulla Salomon ne nan eorðlic cyning. swa wlitige deagunge his
hræglum begytan. swa swa rose hæfð. and lilie. and fela oðre wyrta þe
wunderlice scinað; Ða wyrta beoð nu todæg blowende on wynsumnysse. and
tomerigen beoð forbærnde; Merigen is geteald on bocum for toweardre tide.
þeah ðe ge ða bysne ne cunnon;[1]

Ælfric's source, according to Förster, is Pseudo-Bede's commentary
on Matthew (PL 92, col. 35), but Ælfric is not very close to that source,
nor does the similar passage from homily vii show any significant
similarity to the Latin.[2]

The Bodley homilist sees the passing away of youth's beauty as
further grounds for loving Christ's countenance, and hence exhorts
his audience again to aim for the kingdom of heaven (in contrast with
the Blickling homilist who proceeds to describe the body after death
and leads thus into a short 'ubi sunt' passage). Heaven is here defined
as a series of negatives of attributes appropriate to earthly life: old age,
childhood, death, birth (ll. 86–90).[3] The passage also has remin-
iscences of stock characteristics of hell, particularly weeping and
grinding of teeth.

This part of homily vii ends with the characteristic closing formula,
suggesting that it was originally separate from the rest of the homily.

At this point the compiler has turned to the last section of Vercelli x
for his material. Although, as I showed earlier, the two sections are
rather clumsily conflated, thematically they fit together rather well,
with the Vercelli x piece building on the theme of the first part of the
homily: the need to renounce the transient things of this world, and
look to eternal happiness in heaven.

The homilist exhorts his audience to show gratitude to God for His
gifts, then explains that God demands much in return for His gifts and
that every high honour in the world is fraught with danger. He
illustrates this with 'sume bysne' and an 'ubi sunt' passage. The source
for this material has been traced by Cross to Isidore of Seville's
Synonyma de lamentatione animae peccatoris.[4] Isidore's *Synonyma*, as
Cross shows, is by far the most popular source for the frequent
adaptations of the 'ubi sunt' formula in Old English literature. This

---

[1] CH II xxxi, 67–76.

[2] 'Über die Quellen', p. 26.

[3] Gatch, 'Eschatology', p. 134, notes that in the Blickling homilies the joys of heaven
are the reverse of the pains of hell and are thus usually described negatively.

[4] '"Ubi Sunt" Passages in Old English', pp. 30 ff. For the source in *Synonyma*, see PL
83, cols. 825 ff.

particular version and the various passages closely connected with it (that is, the other copies of this extract from Vercelli x) constitute over a third of the 'ubi sunt' passages in Old English. Cross shows that the Bodley 343 version, although much later than the other three, 'derives from an independent copy of the O.E. archetype and is valuable for readings where the three older manuscripts differ'.[1]

The borrowing begins with the quotation of Luke xii. 48 (*Synonyma*, §89): 'Cui multum datur, multum ab eo quaeritur; cui plus committitur, plus ab eo exigitur.' The Old English homilist's following sentence (ll. 101–3) represents accurately two phrases in Isidore: 'Honores secum pericula gerunt ... Quanto major honor, tanto majora pericula.' In his illustrations of this idea, the homilist continues to follow Isidore, though tending always towards expansion and prolixity. Mostly these expansions develop, and often vivify, one word or phrase: 'alta arbor' becomes 'þæt treow þe weaxeð on þam wude be ar up ofer alle þa oðre treon' (ll. 103–4); 'fortius agitatur' becomes 'swiðor iwæʒed and iswenced þene þe oðer wudæ' (ll. 105–6)—the homilist here omits direct translation of Isidore's 'et rami ejus citius in ruina confringuntur'—'turres' becomes 'torræs and clifæs þe heaʒæ stondæþ ofer alle oþre eorðæ' (ll. 106–7); 'feriuntur' becomes 'iþread and iþreste, and mid liʒe toslaʒene' (l. 111). The Old English homilist's declaration that earthly power and wealth are destroyed and 'wurðæþ to soreʒæ' (l. 113) makes explicit what is only implied in the Latin but omits Isidore's reference to envy and ill-will as an explanation for such destruction. When he states that however richly one dresses one must still 'ece ende abidæn' (l. 116), the Old English homilist clearly relies on Isidore for expression as well as idea: 'mid þam rædeste golde and mid þam hwiteste seolfre' (ll. 113–14) corresponds to 'purpura auroque', and 'mid þam feʒereste ʒymstanes' (ll. 114–15) corresponds to 'cultu pretioso'. The Old English homilist, however, has omitted a piece from Isidore expounding the futility of trying to defend oneself from the inevitable fate, and has greatly abbreviated him in the last phrase: 'þeah þe mon sceal ece ende abidæn' (ll. 115–16) translates 'semper tamen in poena est, semper in angustia, semper in moerore, semper in discrimine'. Again at lines 116–22, the homilist has derived his material from the Latin, converting it however into another 'although ... yet ...' construction, and expanding it considerably. He particularly emphasizes the passing away of all these possessions, using a wide range of vocabulary to do

---

[1] '"Ubi Sunt" Passages in Old English', pp. 30–1.

so: death 'todæleþ all þæt'; the riches are 'aӡotene'; the glory is 'tobrocen'; the jewels are 'toglidene'; the gold is 'tosceaken'; the body is 'todroren and to dyste iwordon'.

The Old English homilist then concludes that the beauty of the world is nothing, but is rather 'hwilwendlic, and feallendlic, and brosnodlic, and drosendlic, and brocenlic, and yfellic, and forwordenlic' (ll. 124–5). These adjectives correspond to and augment Isidore's 'brevis . . . modica . . . caduca . . . fragilis', but the Old English homilist creates further emphasis by linking them in one long final catalogue. The 'ubi sunt' passage follows this. The homilist translates Isidore's 'ubi sunt' phrases and also adds material of his own. His first questions, 'Hwær beoð þæ rice caseres, and þa kyngæs, þe we iu cuþæn? Hwær beoð þa ealdormen þe boden setten?' (ll. 126–7) are clearly based on Isidore's 'Dic ubi sunt reges? ubi principes? ubi imperatores?'. The next series of questions, however, are interpolated by the homilist: 'Hwær is domeræ domselt? Hwær beoð heoræ ofermedo, buton mid molde beþeaht, and on wite wræcen?' (ll. 127–9). He independently warns his audience: 'Wa byð weorldscryftum buton heo mid rihte ræden and tæcæn. Swa bið eac þam læwæde monnum buton heo heore scriffte lusten and heræn, and þa haliӡe lare healden' (ll. 129–31). The following two phrases, 'Hwær com middaneardes ӡestreon? Hwær com weorlde welen?' (ll. 131–2), correspond to the Latin 'ubi locupletes rerum? ubi potentes saeculi? ubi divites mundi?', but the final two questions are the homilist's own: 'Hwær com folce feӡernes? Hwær comen þa men þe ӡeornlucost eahte tyloden, and oþrum ofte yrfe læfden?' (ll. 132–4). This homilist, then, treats his 'ubi sunt' material in the way Cross has shown to be typical of Old English homilists: 'where the source of a section including an "ubi sunt" passage is clear the writer adds to and varies the "ubi sunt" phrases in his Latin original'.[1] Elsewhere, Cross suggests that 'Archbishop Wulfstan's Commonplace Book', which includes a collection of statements on the transience of life, 'reveals one reason why so many O.E. homilies can extend the "ubi sunt" phrases though the context proves that they draw on one main source'.[2] Clearly the 'ubi sunt' phrases added by the Bodley homilist were thematically conventional since they appear in other vernacular homilies. The homilist of Blickling viii, for example, refers to earthly judges: '& [hwær com] se þe þa

---

[1] '"The Dry Bones Speak"', p. 436. Compare my discussion of 'ubi sunt' earlier in this introduction.

[2] '"Ubi Sunt" Passages in Old English', p. 38.

gebregdnan domas demde?', and Blickling x's homilist asks 'hwær
beoð þonne his wlencea & his anmedlan?'.[1] The one striking distinction between this text and other 'ubi sunt' passages is the interpolated
exhortation to confessors to advise rightly and to the laity to obey their
confessors. This does not fit the 'ubi sunt' pattern, nor is it directly
inspired by what precedes or follows. The piece is appropriate
thematically since it concerns preparation for death. It also anticipates
the last section of the homily where men are exhorted to love God,
keep His commands and hear the teaching in church. It has a particularly fatalistic tone and gains emphasis by its interpolatory position. It
may well have been included because of its appropriateness for the
period of Lent.

Having completed his 'ubi sunt' passage, the homilist abandons
Isidore who continues to discourse on the dangers of riches in general
terms and then on the mental torment of those who care for earthly
things. The Old English homilist initially constructs an elaborate
simile by which earthly possessions are compared to smoke or heavy
rain-showers which are quickly dispersed and followed by bright sun
(ll. 135-7). I have not found a Latin source for this simile, and the
closest analogue is another simile in the same context in Blickling v:

Hwær beoþ þonne þa symbelnessa, & þa idelnessa, & þa ungemetlican
hleahtras, & se leasa gylp, & ealle þa idlan word þe he ær unrihtlice ut forlet?
Ealle þa gewitaþ swa swa wolcn, & swa swa wæteres stream, & ofer þæt
nahwær eft ne æteowaþ.[2]

These two passages must derive from an original common image of a
sudden storm of cloud and rain, which both Old English authors have
slightly altered or muddled. The two images of calm after a storm and
of vanishing like smoke were clearly proverbial from at least the early
Middle English period onwards, as the following examples show:
'Thu laverd, the makest stille efter storm' (*Ancrene Wisse*, c. 1200); 'After
sharpe shoures . . . most shene is the sonne' (*Piers* B); 'Forðon dages
mine gedroren syndan Smece gelice' (*Paris Psalter*, c. 900).[3]

The homilist then dwells on the uncertainty of the soul's fate when
death divides it from the body in order to exhort his audience to love
God with all their might. As evidence, he introduces two biblical

---

[1] Blickling viii, p. 99, l. 32; Blickling x, p. 111, l. 34.
[2] Blickling v, p. 59, ll. 17-21.
[3] Bartlett Jere Whiting, *Proverbs, Sentences, and Proverbial Phrases From English Writings
Mainly Before 1500* (Cambridge, Mass., 1968), items S734, S278, S414.

ideas. The first is that God is merciful to those who love and pray to Him. Since this is a notion frequently expressed in the Old Testament (for example, Ps. lxviii. 36, cxviii. 132; Neh. i. 5), the homilist is probably not referring to any particular instance. The second is a long statement attributed to Christ in which He promises mercy and heavenly bliss to those who repent and confess. Again this does not seem to be an accurate quotation of any biblical passage, but the idea is probably derived and developed from the Sermon on the Mount (Matth. v. 3). The homilist then moves to another biblical theme (ll. 153–7), derived this time from Matth. xvi. 26: 'Quid enim prodest homini si mundum universum lucretur, animae vero suae detrimentum patiatur? Aut quam dabit homo commutationem pro anima sua?' Even 'þusend wintræ' in this life would not profit a man in the end, adds the homilist, if he is to be eternally tormented in hell. The homilist then utters a series of concluding exhortations: his audience should obey God, attend church, pray in silence and thus earn salvation. The second concluding formula of the homily follows, which this time signals its completion.

Ic eow bidde, leofe men, þæt swa ofte swa ȝe faren bi ricre monnæ burines þæt ȝe sceawiæn and asmeȝen hwær heoræ wælan beoð bicumene, and heore gold, and heore þeȝenscypæs, and heore worldprude þære ydelnesse. Hwi nyte ȝe þæt all þæt tofaræð and toglit swa swa monnes sceadu dæþ, and heore worldþrym swa rice 5 ȝedwæscte, and ȝedwan, and aidlode, and afulode? Ac loca þenne on þa buriȝnes and sæȝ to þe sylfum: Hwæt, þæs mon iu on þissre worlde wunsumlice lyfede þe ic ær cuðe. þenne maȝon þa ðyrle ban us læren, and þæs deaden dust of þare buriȝnes to us cwæðon wolden, ȝif heo specen mihten: To hwan, þu earme, on þisse worlde 10 ȝytsungum swinces? Oðer to hwam þu on oferhydo þe sylf up ahæfst

Bodley 343, fols. 163–164ᵛ; Belfour, pp. 124–35.

---

2 wælan] *glossed by* ł æhte *in the same hand*

SOURCES. The sources of two sections of this composite homily have been identified, 1–21, and 99–138.

The main source for the first is Caesarius, CCSL 103, *Sermones I*, xxxi, pp. 134–8, entitled *De Elemosinis. Ex Parte Sancti Salviani. Satis et Conpuncta*, here denoted by [C]. The section occasionally has echoes of a later rendering of Caesarius: Pseudo-Augustine, *Ad Fratres in Eremo*, *Sermo lxvi*, PL 40, cols. 1352–3, entitled *De Agenda Poenitentia*, here denoted by [A].

The source for the second section is: Isidore, *Synonyma de Lamentatione Animae Peccatoris*, PL 83, cols. 825–68, lib. II, here denoted by [I].

(1) 1–21 (*C, p. 135; A, col. 1352*)

1–4 [C] Rogo vos, fratres, aspicite ad sepulchra divitum, et quotiens iuxta illa transitis, considerate et diligenter inspicite, ubi sunt illorum divitiae, ubi ornamenta, ubi anuli vel inaures, ubi diademata pretiosa, ubi honorum vanitas, ubi luxoriae voluptas, ubi spectacula vel furiosa vel cruenta vel turpia.

[A] Iterum rogo vos, fratres, quoties juxta sepulturam divitis transitis, ut diligenter inspiciatis ubi sint eorum divitiae vel ornamenta, ubi gloria, ubi vanitas, ubi luxuriae, ubi voluptas, vel ubi eorum sunt spectacula.

4–5 [C] Certe transierunt omnia tamquam umbra; et si paenitentia non subvenerit, sola in perpetuum obprobria et crimina remanserunt.

5–6 [C] Considerate diligentius et videte superborum sepulchra, et agnoscite quia nihil in eis aliud nisi soli cineres et foetidae vermium reliquiae remanserunt.

[A] Considerate diligenter et videte et agnoscite, quia nihil aliud in eis est, nisi cinis et fetor et vermis.

6–8 [C] Haec ergo, homo, diligenter adtende, et dic tibi, tu ipse loquere tecum: O miser, et iste aliquando pro cupiditate currebat, et iste dum viveret in saeculo libidini serviebat; et ecce nunc nihil ex illo nisi foetidi et horribiles pulveres remanserunt.

8–10 [C] Si velis, o homo, audire, ipsa tibi ossa arida poterint praedicare. Clamat ad te pulvis alterius de sepulchro:

10–11 [C] Ut quid, infelix, tantum pro saeculi cupiditate discurris?

11–12 [C] Ut quid superbiae vel luxuriae infelicia colla submittis? Ut quid te ad serviendum crudelissimis dominis, id est, vitiis et criminibus tradis?

on ofermetto and on unþeawæs, and sunne to swyðe fyliзedest?
Beheald me, and onscyne þine yfelæ þoncæs and onзit þe sylfum.
Sceawe mine ban her on þissere molde and biþeng þe sylfen. Iu ic wæs
15 swylc þu nu eart, and зyt þu iwurðæst swulc ic nu eom. Geseoh mine
ban and mi dust, and forlæt þine yfele lustæs. þenne, leofe men, þeah
þ(e) ða deade ban of þare buriзnes specon ne maзon, þeah we maзen
us sylfæn bi þam læren; for þam þe we sceolen æfre зemunen þen[n]e
ures heonensiþes, and we næfre æft ne wendæþ hider on worlde, þæt
20 we æniз god don, ac þenne beoð þa edlean and þa ær idone weorc
isceawod.

Beþence we eac æfre þone endedæз þissre worlde, þæt is domes
dæз, þonne Drihten mid þam heofenlice weredo englæ þisne
middæneard sæcð to weane and to wrace synfulle monnum, and eac
25 haliзe monnum his fultum to bringenne. þenne arisæþ of þam ealde
buriзnes alle þa lichame and þa ban þe fæle зeare ær deade on swefete
læзen and mid synnæ deopnysse ifestnode wæren. And þenne arisæþ
all moncynn togædere, and heo þenne iseoð þas world sweliзende,
fol. 163ᵛ mid fure brastlende and bæ(r)nende, | ant þone heahroder on reade
30 liзeum; and all þæs middæneard byð mid fure aræred. þonne cymð þe
soðfestæ demæ of heofenæs wolcnu[m], and he byð ymbþrungæn mid
þam heofenlice weredo; and þenne beoð alle igæderæde þe soðfæste
Bf. 126 and þa | synfullæ ætforen þæs strecen demen heahsetle, and Drihten
heom þonne sceadæþ on twa healfæ. And he sæt þa soðfestæ on þam
35 swiðere healfe, and þa synfulle on þam wunstren healfe, and he þenne
sæð to þam soðfestæn: Cumeð, зe iblesode, on þenne roderlice
æþe(l), and þær symle wuniæð, and on blisse and on murhðe efne
englen ilice, and þider зe beoð ibrohte mid muriзe lofsongum, and
þær зe beoð mid me wuniende on heofene rice murhþe on (eowre)
40 Drihtines ansyne. þær eow na(n) wiðerweardnes ne deræð, ac on
sundfulnesse þæs brihte lihtes зe þær bliþe wuniæð, for þam þe зe
lustlice mine æ and mine lare heolden, and alle þa ðing þe ic eow bead

---

17 þe] þa   23 weredo englæ] weredo 7 englæ   29 bærnende] bænnende
35 swiðere] *letter erased between* i *and* ð   37 æþel] æþele   39 eowre] ure
40 nan] nanes

13 [C] Clamat ad te mortuus de sepulchro: Adtende ad me, et agnosce te;
14 [C] considera ossa mea, et vel sic tibi horreat luxuria vel avaritia tua.
14–15 [C] Quod tu es, ego fui; quod ego sum, tu eris.
15–16 [C] Vide pulverem meum, et relinque desiderium malum.
16–18 [C] [*Contrast OE homilist*] Rebus ergo ipsis ad nos clamat mortuus de sepulchro.
18–21 [C] Et ideo quantum possumus auxiliante domino laboremus, ut aliorum
vulnera nobis conferant sanitatem, et pereuntium mors nobis proficiat ad salutem.

to healden. Alle ic heom eft iseah last on eowre gode weorcum, swa ic
heom ær sæde. þenne syððæn bisihð Drihten to þam synfullæn
monnum, and þus to heom cwæð: Gewitæþ, ȝe awariȝede, from me on 45
þa(n)e mycele æðm, and on þæne ece brune, and on þene bittræ
þrosm hælles fures, þær þe leiȝ reþelice bærneð, and þær þa dracæn
þa synfullen teræð mid heoræ toþum. And þær þa scyldiȝe bærnæþ,
and þa wurmæs heom mid weallende muðes forswolȝeð; and heoræ
ansyne bið þær mid teares oferfleowen, and þær bið eȝeslic toðene 50
grind. And þær næfre ne ateoræð þeo swearte niht, ne þeo þystre
dymnes, ne heom þær nefre ne bið isceawed lihtes leome, for þam þe
ȝe mine lare on eowre mode oferhoȝoden, and ȝe recelease nolden
mine bodu healdon. þenne æfter þam þe þa manfulle beoð isceofene
wepende on þæt ece fyr þær heo on pine and on ece yrmþe wuniæð, 55
heo iseoð þare soðfestræ and englæ murhðe and isæliȝe monnæ hwit
werod heriȝende ure Drihten. And þ(a ð)ær cumeð þe her man
wrohten and Godes lare iheren nolden. Heo beoð bisencede on þa
hate liȝæs þær heo þrowiæð on ecere seoreȝe. þenne faræþ þa haliȝe
men and þa soþfeste mid sweȝe to life, ant samod siþiæð mid englæ 60
werod to þam upplice rice, þær heo bliþe wuniæð on ece eadiȝnesse;
and heo næfre ne beoð isceadde fram þare ece murhðe.

þenne is us mucel neod, leofe men, þæt we Godes bodu ȝeorne
healden and earniæn þæt we moten mid heofenwaræ lifes brucen, and
þæt we ne weorþæn aweorpen | on þa deopestæ helles grunde. For Bf. 128
þam þe we iseoð þis læne lif mid fræcednesse and mid mycele 66
earfoðnesse ifulled, and ylce dæȝ þis lif wonæð and wursæð; and na
lifiende mon ne þurhwune(ð) on þisse weorlde, ne nan eft to lafe ne
wurð. Al moncyn is ilice on þas weorld icenned, þeah heore lif beo
syððæn unilic; and heo æft on ende alle ȝewitæð. Ne nan swa longe 70
her on weorlde ne leofæð, þæt eft þe deaþ hine ne ȝenime, and þa
modiȝæn and þa oferhudiȝen deaþes gneornung gripð. And þæt heo
her for Godes lufe syllen nolden heoræ sawle to hælpe, heo hit rædlice
forlæteð, and oðre þerto foð, þa heo for Criste hit letæn | nolden, þa fol. 164
hwile þe heo lifedon. Ac þenne þe deaþ cymæð, þenne sceolen heo 75
forlæten heoræ æhtæ heoræ unðancæs, and heo his þenne nan þing
nabbæð. Ylce dæȝ þis andwearde lif wonæð þe we lufiæð, ac þa pine
ne woniæð þam monnum þe heom nu æfter earniæð.

46 þane] þare   on þene] *inserted above*   52 isceawed] d *altered from* ð *by erasure*
of cross-stroke   54 healdon] e *altered from another letter*   57 þa ðær] þa þe ðær
67 earfoðnesse] f *altered from* t   68 þurhwuneð] þurhwuned, *with letter erased after* d
(e?)   71 hine ne] hine, *with stroke between* hi *and* ne   78 earniæð] ea'r'niæð

Uton we þenne, leofe men, þas þing alle ȝemunen and iþencean
80 þæt þæt mennisce lichame is swa blowende wurten, þe for þare sunnæ
hæte fordruȝiæð and forscrincæð. Swa eac þæs monnes ȝeoȝeþæ and
feȝernes dæþ. þenne þeo ælde on him siȝæð mid unhæle, all þare
ȝeoȝeðe feȝernes aweȝ awit and forwurð. Ac Cristes ansyne is to
lufiȝenne ofer alle oðer þing mucele swiðor þenne þes lichames
85 ȝeoȝæðhad. Ac habbæþ eowre heorte on þisse eorþlice ȝewinne and
earniæþ eow þæt heofenlice rice, þær is ece eadiȝnesse: þær eald ne
graneð, ne child ne scræmeð. Ne bið þær þurst, ne hungor, ne wop, ne
teoðe ȝegrind, ne morþer, ne man, ne þær nan ne swæltæð, for þam ðe
þær ne byð nan acenned; ne þer ne byð sar, ne seoreȝæ, ne nan
90 longing, ne unlustes ȝewin. Ac þær is þæs hestæn kynges kynerice,
and þær wuniæþ alle þa þe Godes bodu heolden on ece murhðe; and
heo dæȝhwamlice þene heofenlice kyng bliðne iseoð, and heo mid
him and mid his halȝan libbæþ, and rixæð a on eccenesse.

Hwæt we maȝen bi þissum underȝytæn and icnawon þæt þe
95 Almihtiȝ Drihten nele þæt mon his ȝefenæ nænne þanc nyte. Ne þearf
us na tweoȝean þæt he us næle eft þare læna muneȝiæn þæs þe he us
Bf. 130 her on weorlde to | forlæt. Æfre swa he us merlucor ȝyfð, swa we him
swiðer þonciæn sceolen; and swa þrymlicor ar, swa beo þær maræ
eadmodnesse. þam ðe Drihten mycel sylþ, myceles he him eft æt
100 biddæþ; and þam þe he her on worlde mucel to forlæteþ, mucel he to
þam eft seceð. Æȝh[w]ylc heah ar her on worlde bið mid frecednesse
bewund(en); and swa þeo ar bið mare, swa beoþ þa frecednesse
swiðræn. Be þam we wullæð eow sume bysne sæcgen: þæt treow þe
weaxeð on þam wude be ar up ofer alle þa oðre treon, and hit þenne
105 feringæ strang wind wi(ð)stont, þenne bið hit swiðor iwæȝed and
iswenced þene þe oðer wudæ. Eac þa heahȝæ torræs and clifæs þe
heaȝæ stondæ(þ) ofer alle oþre eorðæ, heo eac þe mare rune nimæð
ȝyf heo feringæ to eorðe fællæþ. Swy[l]ce eac þa heaȝæ muntæs and
dunæ þa ðe heaȝe stondæþ and torriæð ofer alne middæneard,

102 bewunden] be wundū   beoþ] be`o´þ   105 wiðstont] widstont
106 heahȝæ] *erasure below* h²   107 stondæþ] stondæþ

(2) 99–138 (*I, col. 865*)

99–101 'Judicium enim durissimum in iis qui praesunt fiet' (*Luc. xii. 48*). Cui multum
datur, multum ab eo quaeritur; cui plus committitur, plus ab eo exigitur.

101–3 Honores secum pericula gerunt, cito periclitatur potestas, cito ruinam patitur.
Quanto major honor, tanto majora pericula.

103–11 Alta arbor a ventis fortius agitatur, et rami ejus citius in ruina confringuntur;
excelsae turres graviori casu procumbunt. Altissimi montes crebris fulminibus
feriuntur.

þeahhwæðere heo habbæð wite þæs ealderdomes, þæt heo beoð mid 110
heofenlice fure iþread and iþreste, and mid liჳe toslaჳene. Swa eac þa
heaჳæ mihtæ her on worlde fællæð and drosæð and to lure wurðæþ.
And þisre weorlde welæ wur(ð)æþ to soreჳæ. þeah we us scrydæn mid
þam rædeste golde and mid þam hwiteste seolfre, and we mid þam
feჳereste ჳymstanes all uten embihangene beon, þeah þe mon sceal 115
ece ende abidæn, and þeah þa mihtiჳe men and þa ricostæn haten
heom ræste wurcean of marmanstane and of goldfretewum, and heom
hate(n) mid ჳymmum and mid seolfrene | r(u)wum þæt bed al wreon, fol. 164ᵛ
and mid þe deorewurðeste godewebbe al uton ymbhon, þeah cymeð
þe bitter deaþ and todæleþ all þæt. þenne beoð þa welæn and þa 120
glenჳæ aჳotene, and þe þrym tobrocen and þa ჳymmæs toglidene, and
þæt gold tosceaken, and þe lichame todroren and to dyste iwordon.
For þam nis þissere weorlde wlite noht, ne þisses middaneardes
feჳernes, ac he is hwilwendlic, and feallendlic, and brosnodlic, (and)
drosendlic, and brocenlic, and yfellic, and forwordenlic. Swa swa ricu 125
beoð her on worlde. Hwær beoð þæ rice caseres, and þa kyngæs, þe
we iu cuþæn? Hwær beoð þa ealdormen þe boden setten? Hwær is
domeræ domselt? Hwær beoð heoræ ofermedo, buton mid molde
beþeaht, | and on wite wræce[n]? Wa byð weorldscryftum buton heo Bf. 132
mid rihte ræden and tæcæn. Swa bið eac þam læwæde monnum buton 130
heo heore scriffte lusten and heræn, and þa haliჳe lare healden. Hwær
com middaneardes ჳestreon? Hwær com weorlde welen? Hwær com
folce feჳernes? Hwær comen þa men þe ჳeornlucost eahte tyloden,
and oþrum ofte yrfe læfden? Swylc bið þeo oferlufe eorþlice

---

113 wurðæþ] wurdæþ   114 golde] *erasure of* d *between* o *and* l   118 haten]
hatem   ruwum] rawum   124–5 and drosendlic] 77drosendlic

111–13 In potentem cito cadit invidia, cito patet insidiis gloriosus. Gloria enim
invidiam parit, invidia vero pericula.
113–16 Quamvis quis in saeculi gloria fulgeat, quamvis purpura auroque resplendeat,
quamvis cultu pretioso redimitus emineat, . . . semper tamen in poena est, semper in
angustia, semper in moerore, semper in discrimine;
116–20 in sericis stratis cubat, sed turbidus; in pluma jacet, sed pallidus; in lectis
aureis, sed turbatus.
120–22 (*Not in source, but extends ideas of source.*)
123–6 Brevis est hujus mundi felicitas, modica est hujus saeculi gloria, caduca est et
fragilis temporalis potentia.
126–7 Dic ubi sunt reges? ubi principes? ubi imperatores?
127–31 (*Not in source.*)
131–2 ubi locupletes rerum? ubi potentes saeculi? ubi divites mundi?
132–4 (*Not in source.*)
134–8 quasi umbra transierunt, velut somnium evanuerent. Quaeruntur, et non sunt;
divitiae usque ad periculum ducunt, divitiae usque ad exitium pertrahunt, multi propter

135 ȝestreonæ. Efne heo bið smeke ilic, oððe rænæs scuræs, þonne heo of
heofenne swiðost reosæð, and raþe eft toglidene wurðæþ, and cymð
þenne fæȝer wæder and brihte sunnæ. Swa wace and swa tealte beoð
eorðlice dreames, and swa wace beoð eahtæ mid monnum. Swa bið
todæled lichame and sawle, þenne heo bið of þam lichame ilæd; and
140 bið syððæn ful uncuþ hu þe deme embe þa sawle wule. Ðenne nis us
nan þing bætere ne sælre buton þæt we lufien ure Drihten mid alle
mode, and mid alle mæȝne, and mid alle inþoncæ. Swa hit bi þam
iwriten is: þe ðe his Drihten lufæð, and his bene to him sendeþ, he
iheræð him eafre, and his mildse on him sendeþ. Swa Crist sylf sæde:
145 þa ðe to me cerræð from heoræ gyltæs, and heoræ synnæ andedtæð
on mine nome, and dæðbote doþ mid fæstene and mid teare gute, and
mid clæne ȝebedum and mid ælmes, ic ȝea(t)e heom mine milse, and
sylle heom forȝefenesse, and alyfe heom mine rice, and to heofene
wæȝ tæche, þær beoð alle gode and þeo singale blis and þeo mucele
150 mede. Ic sylle for þisse eorþlice swinke þæ heofenlice reste, and for
þisse læne rice þa heofenlice ȝife, and for þissum earme life þæt eadiȝ
and þæt æȝendlice rice. Ealæ, iseliȝe beoð þa men þe þæt rice lufæð;
and unlæde beoð þa ðe him wiðsacæð. Hwæt fremæþ þam men, þeah
he al middæneard on his aȝene æht istreone, ȝif þe deofel nimæþ eft
155 his sawle? Oððe hwæt, þeah he libbe her on life a þusend wintræ? Al
hit bið him unnyt ȝyf he æfter his deaþe bið into hælle ilædd, and þær
on pine wunæð a buton ende.

Uton we wenden us nu to þam beteræ and cerræn to ure Drihten, and
him ȝeorne iheræn, and his bodum healdon. And secea we ure
160 chyrceæn mid clænnesse, and þær ȝeorne lystæn þare halȝæ lare. And
þerinnæ nane spece ne spæken, buton þæt we mid stilnesse ure bedu
singæn, and earniæn us þæt uplice rice. Þær is Kynges þrym isyne, and
Bf. 134 þær is feȝer englæ werod, and | apostola song, and Godes lof, and þæs
heahsten kynges herung. Þer þa soðfeste men scinæð swa sunne, and
165 men rixiæð swa englæs on heofene rice. We beoð ihatene and ilaðode to
þam haliȝe hame and to þam kynelice friðstole, þær ðe Almihtiȝ Drihten leofæð ant rixæð mid alle his halȝæn a a buten ende. AMEN.

147 ȝeate] ȝeafe   150 mede] *followed by an erasure, perhaps of punctuation*
164 þer] þe`r´

opes periclitaverunt. Multi propter divitias in discrimen venerunt; multis exitiabiles
fuerunt divitiae, multis mortem generaverunt opes.
 [*The OE author's subsequent passage with its reference to division of body and soul, its exhortation
to love God, and the rewards to be gained from this, is not from Isidore, who proceeds to discuss the
mental torment which besieges those who care for earthly things.*]

NOTES

4. *worldprude*: The word occurs only once elsewhere in OE, in MS Lambeth 427 dating from the second half of the eleventh century: '. . . mid ofer-mettum afylled, ne mid woruld-prydum' (see Max Förster, 'Die altenglischen Beigaben des Lambeth-Psalters', *Archiv* 132 (1914), 328–35, p. 334). For a discussion of the words for 'pride' in homily vii, see pp. 182–3 above.

5. *worldprym*: This compound (cited in Campb. *Suppl.* but not in BT) is not found elsewhere in the OE corpus.

6. *ʒedwæscte*: The intransitive meaning of this verb is not cited in BT.

55, 77, 157. *pine*: This form probably represents a ME gloss to the OE word *wite*. The OED states that 'it is notable that the substantive has not yet been found in OE, where the derived verb *pinian* was common from an early period'. The word is not cited in BT, but is cited in Campb. *Suppl.*, which also includes a use of the word in Cotton Vespasian D. xiv (another late twelfth-century manuscript). The OED includes examples from the Peterborough Chronicle (dated 1154), the Hatton Gospels of *c.*1160 and the Lambeth Homilies of the end of the twelfth or early thirteenth century. The word is well attested in ME, as the MED shows. See also my note to iii. 161.

39. *eowre*: MS *ure* presents an inherent contradiction between the speaker *Drihten* (34) and His promise to the righteous of life in heaven *on ure Drihtines ansyne*. It is conceivable that the reading *ure* is correct if the homilist was intending to distinguish between *Drihten* meaning 'Christ' in 33 and *Drihten* meaning 'God' in 40 (compare Matth. xxv. 31 ff. where the Judge is 'Filius hominis' who addresses the blessed as 'benedicti Patris mei'). However it seems unlikely that the homilist did intend this semantic distinction between two uses of the same word within such close proximity of one another. *Eow* and *eowre* are used frequently throughout the two speeches by *Drihten* (40, 42, 43, 53), and *eowre* seems a more convincing reading.

43–4. *swa ic heom ær sæde*: This phrase attributed to Christ by the homilist must refer not to material within the homily but to Christ's words in Matth. xxv. 35–6. It is also possible that the phrase refers to an earlier section of the original vernacular homily whence the first part of vii is derived; this earlier section could then have included an account of man's good works.

68. *lafe*: A possible emendation would be to *life*. The repetition of the word *lif* in the preceding lines would make this emendation justifiable in literary terms. It also makes sense in the context.

72–7. The direct object of *syllen* (73) is *þæt* (72) meaning 'that which'. This is picked up by the pronoun *hit* in 73 and 74, and by the partitive genitive *his* in 76. Its meaning is made explicit in *heoræ æhtæ* (76).

87. *scræmeð*: The word does not occur elsewhere in the OE corpus. Campb. *Suppl.* notes that it derives from the Old Norse *skræma*.

107. *rune*: This word (not cited in BT) is cited in Campb. *Suppl.* under *ruine* (f.) 'fall'.

109. *torriæð*: The word (cited in Campb. *Suppl.* but not in BT) does not appear elsewhere in the OE corpus.

125. *drosendlic*: This word is cited as *drosenlic* in BT, deleted in BTS, then replaced by *drosendlic* in Camp. *Suppl.* It does not appear elsewhere in the OE corpus.

125. *brocenlic*: The word (cited in Campb. *Suppl.* but not in BT) does not occur elsewhere in the OE corpus. Campb. *Suppl.* cross-refers to *tobrocenlic* in BT.

129. *weorldscryftum*: *Scrift* usually appears as a separate word meaning 'confessor'. In the other copies of this part of the homily, *worulde* and *scriftum* are two separate words. The compound appears once elsewhere (in Cotton Faustina A. ix).

152. *æȝendlice*: The word does not appear elsewhere in the OE corpus. It is cited in the MED, with this instance only. OE prefix *æ-* is here used to mean 'un-'.

GLOSSARY

All English words that occur in the texts are listed, including proper names. All forms of the stems of nouns and adjectives are given (except, occasionally, for common orthographical variations occurring in unstressed syllables, for example, *æ* and *e*), but the inflected forms are excluded if they follow a regular Old English pattern or conform to the pattern of inflections outlined in the general introduction. In the case of verbs, I have given every form of every verb to provide an accurate picture of the scribe's usage. Verb types and classes have not been included: although in general the Old English strong and weak conjugations are retained, twelfth-century orthographical changes and inconsistencies are frequent enough to suggest that the Old English verb system, like the system of inflections, was breaking down. The verb forms are entered under their infinitives (in square brackets when they follow the infinitive is not recorded in Old English). I have aimed to supply all the meanings of prepositions, but to discuss them as briefly as possible. Quantitative changes at the end of the Old English period make any attempt to mark the vowel-length of syllables impractical, and I have therefore omitted such markings.

The occurrences of a word are listed by homily and line after the main entry in numerical sequence. Consideration of space has led me to include only the first few examples of a word or form. The list is then cut off with 'etc.'. For a form very common both in Old English and in these texts, sometimes only one or two occurrences are listed. All the occurrences of a word are listed if they are not too numerous. Where there are a large number of occurrences of a word or form in the first part of homily iv (from CUL Ii.1.33), occurrences in homilies v, vi, and vii are listed in preference to all the examples in iv. Since all spellings are given, reference to the Microfiche Concordance can be made for details when 'etc.' has been used.

Entries are alphabetically arranged, and spelt as they appear in the text, but all words beginning with the prefix *ȝe-*, *i-* or *ȝei-* are listed according to their unprefixed forms. Preference is generally given to the Old English spelling if it occurs in the texts. With common words like *all* and *sæcgan*, however, which occur with the Old English spellings *eall* and *secgan* only rarely or only in the first part of iv, preference is given to the twelfth-century spellings. When a word and a compound including that word are spelt differently, the spelling is standardized, for example, *worldprude* (VII. 4) appears under *weorldprud* alongside *weorld* and other compounds with *weorld*. In all cases, thorough cross-reference is used to refer the reader to the main entry. The diagraph *æ* is treated as *ae*, following *ad*. The letters *ð* and *þ* are interchangeable; the first occurrence in the texts generally determines which letter is used in the head-word. *Ð* and *þ* are treated as a separate letter between *t* and *u*. The letters *g* and *ȝ* are treated as two separate letters, with *ȝ* following *g*. The manuscript providing the first part of homily iv (CUL Ii.1.33) differs from MS Bodley 343 in that it almost invariably uses *ȝ*, including in words where the Bodley scribe uses *g*. Where a word overlaps with a Bodley 343 usage, the Bodley 343 form is preferred for the main entry. The interchange of *g* and *ȝ* is not cross-referenced (though the other spelling is given in the list of forms.) An ordinary *G* is used for the capital of *ȝ* in MS Bodley 343. Only *Ȝit*, *Ȝif/Ȝyf* and occasional words with prefix *Ȝe-* are affected, and again these are not cross-referenced to the form with *ȝ*. The suffix *-nys(s)*, *-nis(s)*, *-nes(s)*, is not standardized (though only one form is given for each noun).

When a word appears only with an unusual spelling, the usual dictionary form or a form indicating its Old English origin is placed immediately after it in quotation marks and brackets, e.g. *ætrine* ('æthrine'). Where a word is close to a form appearing elsewhere only in Middle English, the Middle English word is given (in brackets and preceded by 'ME'). Words or usages of particular interest, for example rare words, have 'n.' placed after the homily and line reference, to indicate that a note on that word will be found in the relevant textual notes.

Emendations to the text are not generally marked in the Glossary (as far as possible emended words are not chosen to illustrate a particular form.)

The abbreviations used in the Glossary are as follows:

A verb is indicated by *v.*, infinitive by *infin.*, inflected infinitive by *infl.infin.*, imperative singular by *imper.s.*, the plural by *imper.p.* The finite forms are indicated by tense, person and number, e.g. *pres.3s.* for present third person singular, *pret.1s.* for preterite first person singular (without person in plural, e.g. *pret.p.*), and *subj.* is added if the mood is subjunctive not indicative. The participles are connoted by *pres.pt.* for present, and *pp.* for past. When a past participle is declined because it is being used as an adjective or a substantive, *decl.* is put in brackets before the relevant forms. When a verb takes a genitive or a dative object, *v.w.g.* and *v.w.d.* are used respectively. *Refl.* indicates that the verb is used reflexively.

Nouns are indicated by a following *m.*, *f.*, or *n.* for masculine, feminine or neuter; a noun is declined strong unless indicated otherwise by a *wk.* before the gender. The other parts of speech are indicated by the usual abbreviations such as *adj.*, *adv.*, *pron.* Inflexions of nouns are indicated by case and number: *ns.* for nominative singular, *gp.* for genitive plural, etc. Inflexions of adjectives are indicated by gender, case and number: *mns.* for masculine nominative singular, *fap.* for feminine accusative plural, etc. Where any confusion is possible, I give the fuller *sg.*, *pl.*, *nom.*, *acc.*, *gen.*, *dat.* (e.g. see *twezen*). For the strong and weak declensions of adjectives, *str.* and *wk.* are used. A comparative form is indicated by *comp.*, a superlative by *sup.* An adjective used as a substantive is indicated by *sb.*

a *adv.* always, ever. I.202, II.131, 222, 222, III.369, IV.282, *etc.*

aberan *v.* (*a*) to bear, produce. *pret.3s.* **aber** IV.306; (*b*) to bear, suffer. *infin.* VI.25, 225

abidan *v.* to await. *infin.* VI.161, VII.116; *pret.subj.p.* **abiden** VI.248

ablendan *v.* to blind. *pp.* **ablend** (*decl.*) I.185, III.116, 125

Abraham Abraham. II.115

abugan *v.* to bow, bend, incline. *infin.* IV.53

ac *conj.* but. I.65, 81, 96, 111, 130, 131, *etc.*, **ah** V.101

acennan *v. Only as pp.* **acenned**, born. II.127, III.6, 8, 11, 52, 57, *etc.*, **accenned** III.55

acennednyss *f.* nativity. I.40, II.115

acsoð *see* **axian**

acwellan *v.* to kill, destroy. *infin.* IV.25, 29; *pret.3s.* **acwalde** I.49

Adam Adam. II.111, 122, III.116, 119, *etc.*

adon *v.* to take away, remove. *pres.p.* **adoþ** V.181

adræfan *v.* to drive out, expel. *pret.p.* **adræfdon** III.94

adreozan *v.* (*a*) to act, perform. *pret.p.* **adruzon** III.252; (*b*) to pass, spend (time). *pres.subj.p.* **adreozon** III.203; *pres.3s.* **adrihð** V.32; *pret.p.* **adrozon** III.248

adun *adv.* down, downward. II.15, 23, V.98

adwæscan *v.* to quench, put out. *infin.* IV.14; *pp.* **adwæsced** IV.20, 315

æ *f.* law. I.164, III.274, IV.142, V.173, VI.148, VII.42

æarmun *see* **earm**

æblæc *adj.* pale, wan. IV.130, 214

ædlean *see* **edlean**

æfen *m.* evening. III.223

æfre *adv.* ever, always. I.76, II.111, 123, 198, 201, III.225, 252, *etc.*, **æffre** III.183, IV.366, **eafre** III.186, V.56, VII.144

æft *see* **eft**

æfter *prep.w.d.* after, according to. I.40, III.199, 201, 205, 238, 274, IV.54, *etc.*, **æftær** V.44

æze *m.* fear. II.190

æzendlic *adj.* eternal, endless. VII.152 n.

æzhwær *adv.* everywhere. I.75, 81

æzhwylc *adj.* every. VII.101

æȝðer *pron.adj.* each (of two), both. **æȝðer ȝe ... ȝe/and ...** *conj.* both ... and ... I.42, III.360, V.122, 152, 186, 188-9, VI.226, 252-3, **æȝþær (ȝe) ... ȝe ...** VI.38, 166-7

æht *f.* possessions, property. VII.76, 154, **eaht-** VII.133, 138

æhte *see* **agan**

ælc *pron.adj.* each, any, every. *as adj.* I.67, 75, 77, 79, 201, II.47, *etc.*, **ealc** V.31, 102, **elc** V.102, **ylc** V.173, VI.5, 36, 174, VII.67, 77; *as pron.* I.53, 55, III.123, 284, V.10, 76, *etc.*, **ylc** VI.209

ælcian *v.* to put off, delay. *imper.s.* **ælciȝe** II.182

ælde *f.* age, old age. VII.82

ælfremed *adj.w.* **fram** estranged, alienated. II.68 n., 76

ælle *see* **all**

ælles *adv.* else, otherwise. II.192

ælmesse *wk.f.* alms, almsgiving. IV.345; **ælmes** V.12 (*as.*), VII.147 (*ds.*)

ælmesdæd *f.* gift of alms, charitable deed. V.186

ælmihtig- *see* **almihtiȝ**

ȝe-ælnian *v.* to strengthen. *pret.ȝs.* **ȝeælnode** *in the phrase* **ȝeælnode ... hine up,** picked himself up. II.26 n.

æm *see* **beon**

æniȝ *adj.* any. I.190, III.46, 88, 337, V.8, 27, *etc.*, **eniȝe** IV.347

ænne *see* **an**

ær *adv.* before. II.74, 121, 155, 187, III.73, 89, *etc.*; *comp.* **æror** IV.268; *sup.* **ærest,** earliest, first. II.61, 100, 185, IV.37, 88, V.142, *etc.*; **on ær,** at an earlier time, before. II.197

ær *adj.* early. *comp.* **ærran** IV.166; *sup.* **ærest,** first. VI.80, **ereste** V.60, 63

ær *prep.w.d.* before. III.209, VI.81, 162, 165. **ær þan(þam) ðe** *conj.* before. I.17, 90, III.146, 164, IV.271, 337, *etc.*

ærist *m.* resurrection. III.199

ærming *m.* miserable being, wretch. III.92

æs *n.* food, carrion. IV.236

æt *prep.w.d.* at. I.13, 60, 104, II.90, 187, IV.25, *etc.*

æt (*v.*) *see* **etan**

ætberstan *v.* to escape from, break away from. *infin.* IV.267; *pres.subj.s.* **ætberste** IV.151; *pret.ȝs.* **ætburste** IV.268

ætbredan *v.* to take away. *pp.* **ætbroȝdon** III.200 n.

æteowan *v.* to appear. *pret.p.* **æteowden** VI.141

æteowian *v.* to show, display. *pret.ȝs.* **ætywde** VI.39

ætforen *prep w.d.* before, in the presence of. VII.33

æthiwian *v.* to present as an illusion. *pp.* **æthiwod** V.126 n.

ætleanes *see* **edlean**

ætrinan ('æthrinan') *v.* to touch. *infin.* V.84

ætrine ('æthrine') *m.* touch. V.96

ætsceawian *v.* to appear. *pret.ȝs.* **ætsceawede** VI.15 n.

ætywde *see* **æteowian**

æð *see* **eaðe**

æþel ('eþel') *m. or n.* country, native land. VI.191, VII.37

æðele *adj.* noble, distinguished, excellent. IV.41

æðm *m.* blast (of fire). VII.46

æðryt *adj.* wearisome, tedious. I.35

afedan *v.* to feed, nourish. *pret.s.* **afedde** IV.65, 247; *pp.* **afedd,** brought up. IV.4

afeormian *v.* to cleanse. *pres.ȝs.* **afeormæð** II.177

afliȝan *v.* to expel, put to flight, *pret.ȝs.* **afliȝde** IV.243

afulian *v.* to become foul, be defiled. *pret.ȝs.* **afulode** VII.6

afyllan *v.* to fell, beat down, overturn. *pp.* **afulled** V.141

afyllan *v.* to fill. *pp.* (*decl.*) **afyllede** IV.30

afyrhtan *v.* to affright, terrify. *pp.* (*decl.*) **afyrhte** IV.196, 198, VI.24

agan *v.* to have, owe. *pret.ȝs.* **ahte** II.8, 22, **æhte** V.61; *pret.p.* **ahton** I.38

agyltan *v.* to offend, sin against. *pres.p.* **agyldtæþ** II.105, **agyltæð** II.178, **aȝyltæð** II.83, 102; *pret.ȝs.* **agylte** II.167, **aȝulte** II.213, **aȝylte** II.47, 81; *pret.p.* **agulten** VI.81

aȝean ('ongean') *adv.* again, back. III.23

aȝeldan *v.* to pay, render. *imper.s.* **aȝeld** II.25

aȝen *adj.* own. II.21, 54, 158, 190, III.9, 11, *etc.*

aȝeotan *v.* to consume, destroy. *pp.* (*decl.*) **aȝotene** VII.121

ȝe-aȝnian *v.* to possess, inherit. *imper.p.* **iaȝniæð** III.241

ah (*conj.*) *see* **ac**; (*v.*) *see* **agan**
ahebban *v.* to lift up, raise. *pres.2s.*
　ahæfst VII.11; *pret.3s.* **ahof** VI.27;
　pret.p. **ahofæn** VI.28, **ahofen** VI.228;
　pp. (*decl.*) **ahofene** VI.167
ahnexian *v.* to soften. *infin.* IV.125
ahof(-) *see* **ahebban**
ahon *v.* to hang. *infin.* IV.158, V.92;
　imper.p. **ahoð** IV.99
aht *adv.* at all, by any means. II.80
ahte, ahton *see* **agan**
ahwær *adv.* anywhere. V.28
aidlian *v.* to become idle, useless. *pret.3s.*
　aidlode VII.6
aldan *see* **eald**
aldor *m.* prince, chief. **hundredes aldor**,
　centurion. I.102, 108, 124, 133
alecgan *v.* to suppress, lay aside. *infin.*
　II.192
alesan *v.* to redeem. *infin.* V.10
alesend *m.* redeemer. III.182
al(l) *adj.sb.* all. I.31, 39, 39, 65, 67, 77, 82,
　etc., **eall** IV.100, 173, 259, *etc.*, VI.166;
　ofer all, everywhere. V.7
al(l) *adv.* fully, entirely. I.105, II.196,
　III.92, VI.54, 230, 241, VII.115, 118, 119,
　155, **eall** IV.160, 179; *before* **swa**, just.
　I.115, II.45, 52, 59, 104, 132, *etc.*
alles *adv.* entirely, altogether. I.63, II.150
allungæ *adv.* entirely, altogether. V.126
almihtiȝ *adj.* almighty. I.79, 84, III.78,
　159, 179, 182, 331, *etc.*, **ælmihtiga(-)**
　IV.144, 245
alyfan *v.* to grant, allow. pres.1s. **alyfe**
　VII.148
alysan *v.* to free, deliver, redeem. *pres.3s.*
　alyseð VI.139; *pres.p.* **alysæð** II.86;
　pret.3s. **alysde** III.154, 297; *pp.* **alysed**
　III.161
alysednyss *f.* deliverance, redemption.
　III.159
am *see* **beon**
Amen Amen (*concluding formula at end of
　each homily*). I.203, II.223, 223, III.370,
　etc.
amyrran *v.* to injure, destroy. *imper.s.*
　amyr IV.149
an *pron.adj.* (*a*) *as adj. before noun*, one,
　single. I.112, 161, 172, II.5, III.20, *etc.*;
　mas. **ænne** II.8, 64, V.101, **anne** IV.145;
　mds. or nds. **anum** IV.235, 261, 371; *fgs. or
　fds.* **anre** IV.24, 48, 370, VI.217; (*b*) *as
　adj. after noun or pron.*, alone, only.

I.193, 197, II.92, IV.183, 210, 288, *etc.*; (*c*)
　as pron. II.47, 167, VI.19, 19, 20, *etc.*; **on
　an** *adv.* continuously. I.158
and *conj.* and (represents *MS* 7). I.5, 8, 11,
　12, 21, 21, 23, *etc.*; *MS* **ant** II.40, 65, 78,
　80, 114, 220, *etc.*
anda *wk.m.* enmity, envy. IV.84, **onde**
　III.119
andetnyss *f.* confession. II.152, IV.146,
　162, 174, 204, **-dæt-** IV.45
andettan *v.* (*a*) to confess, *pres.p.*
　andetteð II.174, **andedtæð** VII.145;
　(*b*) to acknowledge, declare belief in.
　pres.1s. **andette** IV.144; *pret.3s.* **andette**
　III.64
andȝit *n.* sense, meaning, understanding.
　I.33, 34, II.48, III.267, 311, IV.298,
　anȝit(e) III.107, 108
andȝitleast *f.* want of understanding. I.91
andrædlice ('ondrædendlic') *adv.* fear-
　fully. III.340
andswarian *v.* to answer. *infin.* **-swyr-**
　III.60; *pres.3s.* **andswaræþ** I.176;
　pret.3s. **andswarde** I.14, 16, 61, 89, 172,
　182, **andswerede** V.110, **andswarede**
　III.80, **andswyrde** III.30, 96, 98, 347;
　pret.p. **andswyrdan** III.45, **andsware-
　don** III.91
andswaru *f.* answer. I.26, 147, 180, III.10,
　72, 169, 315, IV.214, **andswyre** III.68
andweald *see* **anweald**
andweard *adj.* present. IV.336, VI.70,
　VII.77
(ȝe)andweard(e) *see* **(ȝe-)andwyrdan**
andweardnyss *f.* presence, present time.
　V.46
andwlita *wk.m.* face, countenance. IV.59,
　130, 173, VI.62, **anwlite** VI.208
(ȝe-)andwyrdan *v.* to answer. *imper.s.*
　andweard IV.79; *pret.3s.* **ȝeand-
　wearde** IV.70
anfeald *adj.* one-fold, simple, single.
　II.94, III.107
anfenge ('anfenge') *adv.* acceptable, fit.
　V.164
anginn *n.* beginning, enterprise. III.242,
　336, **anȝinne** III.87, IV.35
anȝit(e) *see* **andȝit**
ȝe-anȝsumian *v.* (*a*) to vex, make
　anxious. *pp.* **ȝeanȝsumod** IV.213, 252;
　(*b*) to be vexed. *pret.3s.* **ȝeanȝsumode**
　IV.95 n.
anlicnesse *f.* likeness, image. I.129,
　VI.129

anræde *adj.* constant, resolute. IV.79, 129
anseone *see* **ansyn**
ansund *adj.* sound, unimpaired, in good health. IV.60, 61
ansyne ('ansyn') *f.* face, countenance. VI.46, 65, 73, 77, 105, 107, *etc.*, **anseone** VI.12
ant *see* **and**
Antecrist *m.* Antichrist. VI.164
anweald *m.* power, rule. I.38, 112, 201, IV.28, 33, V.115, **andweald** I.55, 171
anwlite *see* **andwlita**
apostol *m.* apostle. II.168, 216, III.130, V.157, 163, VI.55, 97, 127, 187; *gs.* **apostolas** III.214; *np.* **apostolas** VI.250, **apostoli** III.7, 204; *ap.* **apostlæs** I.163, **apostolas** V.143; *gp.* **apostola** VII.163; *dp.* **apostolis** II.100
ar *f.* honour, glory, dignity. V.136, VII.98, 101, 102, 104
aræran *v.* (*a*) to raise (from the ground), lift up. *pret.s.* **arærde** VI.226; (*b*) to excite, disturb. *pp.* **aræred** VII.30
aras *see* **arisan**
Archelaus Archelaus (*son of Herod, king of Judea*). I.48
ardlice *adv.* quickly. IV.205
arfest *adj.* merciful, gracious. VI.225
arfestnyss *f.* mercy. VI.218
arfoþ- *see* **earfoþe**
arian *v.* to spare, have mercy. *pres.3s.* **aræð** II.206
arisan *v.* to arise, rise up. *imper.p.* **arisæð** VI.27, 227; *pres.p.* **arisæð** VI.159, VII.25, 27; *pret.3s.* **aras** III.296, IV.11; *pret.subj.s.* **arise** VI.32; *pret.p.* **arison** VI.28; *pp.* **arisen** VI.233
arleas *adj.* wicked, impious. III.252, IV.11, 79, 82, 95, 205, 251, **arlesa** IV.225
arleasnyss *f.* wickedness. II.43
arwurðian *v.* to honour, reverence, worship. *infin.* I.126; *pres.3s.* **arwurðað** IV.295, **arwurðæþ** IV.358, **arwyrðæð** IV.360
arwyrðe *adj.* honourable, venerable. *ds.* **arwyrðam** IV.78
arwyrðnyss *f.* reverence. IV.278
asæton *see* **asittan**
asawan *v.* to sow. *pp.* (*decl.*) **asawene** IV.301
asendan *v.* to send forth or out. *imper.s.* **asend** V.98; *pres.subj.s.* **asende** VI.162; *pret.3s.* **asende** III.177, 184, IV.246; *pp.* **asend** III.21, 157, 158, 160, 165, 178

asittan ('onsittan') *v.* to fear, be afraid. *pret.p.* **asæton** III.61
asmeagan *v.* to consider, contemplate, judge. *infin.* IV.207, **asmeʒ-** VI.45, VII.2
aspendan *v.* to spend entirely, squander. *pres.3s.* **aspent** IV.330
astigan *v.* to proceed, climb, descend. *pret.3s.* **asteah** III.147, **astah** VI.153
astreccan *v.* to stretch out. *imper.p.* **astreccað** IV.99, 180; *pret.3s.* **astræhte** III.101; *pp.* **astreht** III.225, (*decl.*) **astreahtum** III.354, **astrehtum** IV.161
ateorian *v.* (*a*) to fail, come to an end. *pres.3s.* **ateorað** IV.219, **ateoræð** VII.51; (*b*) to become exhausted. *pret.p.* **ateoŕodon** IV.127
ateoriendlic *adj.* failing, fleeting. VI.54
atwa ('on twa') *adv.* in two. VI.123
aðwean *v.* to wash. *infin.* III.32; *pret.3s.* **aþwoh** III.22, 156
aðyan *v.* to press. *pp.* **aðyd** IV.302
Augustinus St. Augustine. II.50, 107, 189, **Auʒust-** III.109
awæʒ *adv.* away. V.150, **aweʒ** IV.243, VI.230, VII.83
awariʒed *adj.* (*pp. of* awariʒan, 'awyrgan') accursed. III.249, 250, 316, V.15, 62, 110, *etc.*
awat *see* **awitan**
awendan *v.* to turn, change. *pret.3s.* **awende** I.5; *pp.* **awend** II.196, IV.211
aweorpen *see* **awurpan**
awitan ('gewitan') *v.* to go, depart. *pres.3s.* **awit** VII.83; *pret.3s.* **awat** V.150
awritan *v.* to write down, record. *pret.3s.* **awrat** II.169, III.109, 322; *pp.* **awriten** IV.142
awurpan, -weorp-, -wyrp- *v.* to throw down, cast out. *imper.p.* **awurpað** IV.262, **awyrpað** IV.235; *pret.p.* **awurpan** IV.265, **awurpon** IV.239; *pp.* **aweorpen** VII.65
axian *v.* (*a*) to ask. *infin.* II.96; *imper.p.* **axiæð** III.59; *pres.3s.* **acsoð** II.103; *pret.3s.* **axode** II.69, 96, IV.63, IV.130; *pret.p.* **axoden** I.188, III.29; **axodon** III.35, 39, 48, 71; (*b*) to learn, discover. *pret.3s.* **axode** I.9 n.

bæddræda *adj.* bedridden. I.132.
bæd(e) *see* **biddan**
bæran *see* **beran**

bærn *n.* barn. IV.309
bærnan *v.* to burn. *pres.3s.* **bærneð**
VII.47; *pres.p.* **bærnæþ** VII.48; *pres.pt.*
bærnende VII.29
bætere *see* **betera**
bæð *n.* bath. VI.133
ban *n.* bone. IV.279, VIII.8, 14, 16, 17, 26
bar ('bær') *adj.* bare, naked. IV.160
be, bi *prep.w.d.* (*a*) about, concerning,
with respect to. I.186, 194, II.108, III.49,
51, 130, 137, 302, *etc.*; (*b*) according to.
I.34, 47, II.86, 131, 142, 179, III.109,
VI.186; (*c*) along, beside. II.212, VII.1;
(*d*) by, by means of. V.77, 78, VII.18, 94;
(*e*) by, in (*indicating degree of difference or
fulfilment*). II.93, 94, VI.256
bead *see* **beodan**
beæ3ðan ('egeþe, egþe') *v.* to harrow. *pp.*
beæ3ðæd IV.287, **beæ3ðed** IV.289 n.
bealo *n.* harm, evil, mischief. *ds.* **bealowe**
IV.30, 88
bearn *n.* child. II.193, III.134, 135, 136,
V.161, VI.93
bearnteam *n.* progeny, offspring. III.137
beatan *v.* to beat, strike. *pret.3s.* **beot**
IV.159
bebod *n.* command. II.142
bebyrgan *v.* to bury. *pp.* **bebyrged**
IV.276, **bebyriged** IV.278
bec *see* **boc**
becuman, bicuman *v.* to come to, visit,
arrive at (*w.* **to** +*d. of person*, **to** *or* **on** +
d. of thing). *infin.* IV.209, V.160, VI.57, 67,
265; *pret.3s.* **becom** III.120, 205, IV.271,
V.33; *pp.* **becumen** IV.132, (*decl.*) VII.3
bed (II.213) *see* **(3e)betan**
(-)bed- (*v.*) *see* **biddan**
(3e)bed *n.* prayer. II.99, IV.342, V.12, 187,
VII.147, 161
bedælan *v.* to deprive. *pp.* **bedæled**
III.117, IV.184
bed(d) *n.* bed. IV.184, 217, 224, VII.118
beddian *v.* to prepare a bed. *pp.* **3ebed-
dod** IV.192
bedding *f.* bedding, bed. IV.192, 206
bediglian *v.* to conceal. *pp.* **bediglod**
IV.260
bedyrnan *v.* to hide, conceal. *infin.*
IV.138
beforen, biforen *prep.w.d.* before, in
front of. VI.13, 133, 149, 262, **before**
V.129; **her biforen**, earlier than. V.37
befrinan *v.* to ask, question. *pres.1s.*

befrine IV.67; *pret.3s.* **befran** I.24, 145,
III.314, IV.66; *pret.p.* **befrunnon**
III.166, **befrynnon** III.7, **bifrynnon**
I.168
be3en *adj.pron.* both. IV.30, 49, 59
be3enga *wk.m.* worshipper. III.85
be3innan *v.* to begin (*w.* **to** + *infl.infin.*).
pret.3s. **be3an** IV.35, 115
be3itan *v.* to obtain. *pret.3s.* **be3eat**
IV.25; *pres.subj.s.* **bi3ete** V.11, **bi3yte**
VI.49
behatan *v.* to promise. *pret.3s.* **behet**
III.226, 235, IV.230, **bihet** II.28, VI.65,
67; *pret.subj.s.* **behæte** IV.368
behealdan *v.* to behold. *imper.s.* **beheald**
VII.13
belifan *v.* to remain, be left. *pret.3s.* **belaf**
IV.168
belucan *v.* to enclose, shut, lock. *infin.*
IV.49; *imper.p.* **belucað** IV.183; *pret.p.*
belucon III.93
ben *f.* prayer, request. III.84, V.167,
VII.143
benæman *v.* to take (sth.) away from
(s.o.) (*w.d. of pers.*). *pret.3s.* **benæmde**
IV.84
bend *m.* bond, fetter. IV.201
beniman *v.* to deprive. *pp.* (*decl.*) **benumene** VI.87
beodan *v.* to command. *pres.3s.* **beodeþ**
V.99; *pret.3s.* **bead** II.129, VI.30, 231,
VII.42; *pp.* **iboden** V.173
beon *v.* to be. *infin.* II.124, 127, 131, III.74,
105, 314, *etc.*; *imper.s.* **beo** III.76, 315,
IV.198, *etc.*; *pres.1s.* **am** I.109, 112, III.16,
æm III.16, 196, **eam** III.196, **eom**
IV.110, 202, VII.15, **heom** IV.198, **beo**
III.230, IV.92, 294; *pres.2s.* **eard** V.97,
eart III.92, V.65, VII.15; *pres.3s.* **bið**
I.111, II.70, 88, 89, *etc.*, **byð** IV.20, 21,
etc., VII.30, 31, *etc.*, **is** I.32, 36, 75, 78,
etc.; *pres.subj.s.* **beo** I.80, 80, 175, 181,
II.68, *etc.*; *pres.p.* **beoð** I.135, II.85, 113,
125, *etc.*, **beo we** IV.308, **sund** IV.201,
synd IV.176, 215; *pres.subj.p.* **beon**
II.210, 215, VI.18, 262, VII.115, **beo**
V.167, **be** IV.257, 261; *pret.1s.* **wæs**
III.70, *etc.*; *pret.3s.* **wæs** I.7, 46, 54, 57,
132, *etc.*, **wes** III.308; *pret.subj.s.* **wære**
I.94, 131, 189, III.27, 54, 305, *etc.*, **were**
III.26, 28, 50, 52, *etc.*, **ware** VI.248;
pret.p. **wæron** I.37, 45, 185, II.119, 151,
III.111, *etc.*, **wæren** I.52, V.50, 90, 143,
VI.24, 123, *etc.*, **weron** II.148, 218,

III.133, *etc.*, **wæran** IV.133; *pret.subj.p.*
weren V.71; *negative forms, pres.3s.* **nis**
II.79, 80, III.44, *etc.*; *pret.3s.* **næs** I.63,
II.123, III.11, 24, *etc.*, **nes** III.172, 174,
264; *pret.subj.s.* **nære** II.157, III.292, 299,
IV.169, V.155, VI.198, **nere** III.160

beorht, briht *adj.* bright. **beorht(-)**
III.200, IV.191, VI.20, 79, **briht(-)**
VI.129, 133, 178, 196, 212, 213, VII.41,
137; *comp.* **briht(t)r-** VI.90 n., 99, 100,
108

beorhtlice, brihtlice *adv.* clearly, distinctly, splendidly. **beorhtlice** VI.46,
brihtlice VII.231, 235, 254

beorhtnys, brihtnys *f.* brightness,
splendour. **beorht-** VI.77, 82, 87, 96, 96,
109, 168; **briht-** VI.89 n., 90, 98, 106, 107,
127

beot *see* **beatan**

beran *v.* to bear, carry. *imper.p.* **beraŏ**
IV.216; *pret.3s.* **ber** V.59; *pret.p.* **bæran**
IV.220

ȝeberan *v.* to bear, bring forth. *pp.* **ȝe-/
iboren** III.24, 114, 125, 359, IV.4

besencan *v.* to (cause to) sink. *pp.* **be-
senced** IV.257, *(decl.)* VII.58

besittan *v.* to surround. *pret.3p.* **besæton**
IV.188

besiwian *v.* to sew together. *pp.* **besiwod**
IV.261

beswican *v.* to deceive. *pret.3s.* **beswac**
III.119, **biswaac** V.60, 63

(ȝe)betan *v.* (*a*) to improve, amend,
correct. *infin.* II.209; *imper.s.* **bet** II.211,
bed II.213; (*b*) to make amends for.
infin. II.154, III.288, V.9

betera *comp.adj.* better. **bætere** III.305,
V.135, VI.102, VII.141; **þæt beteræ** *n.*
the better. VII.158

betwyx *prep.w.d.* between. I.174, II.82,
150, III.47

beþeccan *v.* to cover. *pp.* **beþeaht**
VII.129

beþencan *v.* (*a*) to take thought for, plan.
pres.subj.p. **beþence** VII.22; (*b*) *refl.*, to
consider, take heed. *imper.s.* **biþeng**
VII.14

beweaxan *v.* to overgrow, cover over.
pret.p. **beweoxon** III.122

bewendan *v.* to turn. *pres.subj.3s.*
bewende IV.181

beweorpan *v.* to cast, throw. *pp.* **beworpen** IV.275

bewerian *v.* to guard, protect, defend.
pret.3s. **bewerode** IV.242

bewindan *v.* to wind about, surround. *pp.*
bewunden VII.102

bewyrcan *v.* to cover. *pret.2s.* **bewrohtest** VI.62

bi *see* **be**

ȝebicnung *f.* indication. IV.273

bicom-, bicum- *see* **becuman**

(ȝe)biddan *v.* (*a*) to ask, entreat (s.o.,
acc.) for (sth., *gen.*). *infin.* V.147 n. (*thing
sought introduced by* **to**); *pres.1s.* **bidde**
IV.177, 216, VII.1; *pres.2s.* **bist** II.90 (*person from whom thing is sought introduced by*
æt); *pres.3s.* **biddæþ** VII.100 (*person
from whom thing is sought introduced by*
æt), **bit** I.80; *pres.p.* **biddæþ** I.169,
II.98; *pret.2s.* **bæde** II.37; *pret.3s.* **bæd**
I.11, 59, 64, II.16, (i)**bed** I.72, III.329;
pret.subj.s. **(ȝe)bede** I.133, III.354;
pret.p. **bedon** III.363; *pres.pt.* **biddende**
II.27; *pp.* **ibeden** I.131; (*b*) *w.* **to**. to
pray to, worship. *infin.* V.140, 144, 145,
148.

biforen *see* **beforen**

bifrynnon *see* **befrinan**

ȝebiȝan *v.* to turn. *infin.* IV.39

biȝete, biȝyte *see* **beȝitan**

biȝspel(l) *n.* parable. II.3, 4, 73

bihet *see* **behatan**

bihydan *v.* to hide, conceal. *pres.2s.*
bihuddest VI.61, **bihydest** II.184; *pp.*
bihud V.73, **bihyd** V.121

bileafa ('geleafa', ME bileve) *wk.m.*
belief, faith. VI.41 n., 75, 221

bilimpan ('belimpan') *v.* to concern,
belong. *pres.3s.* **bilimpŏ** V.103

ȝebindan *v.* to bind. *pp.* (*decl.*) **ȝe-
/ibundene** IV.48, V.51

binnon *prep.w.d.* within. III.329

bipæcan ('bepæcan') *v.* to deceive. *pres.p.*
bipæceŏ II.173

bireowsunge ('behreowsung') *f.* lament-
ing, repentance. II.152

bisæcgan ('besecgan') *v.* to announce.
pret.3s. **bisæde** VI.130

bisceop *m.* bishop. IV.8, 36, 40, 66, 70, 75,
78, 97

bisencede *see* **besencan**

bisene, bisne *see* **bysen**

biseon ('beseon') *v.* to look. *pres.3s.*
bisihŏ VII.44

bist *see* **biddan** (II.90), **beon** (IV.113)

biswaac *see* **beswican**

bit *see* **biddan**

bitacnian *v.* to signify. *pp.* **bitacnæd** VI.66, **bitacnod** VI.158 n.

bitæcan ('betæcan') *v.* to deliver, commit, entrust. *infin.* II.40; *pret.3s.* **bitæhte** II.136; *pp.* **bitæht** II.161

biterian *v.* to embitter, make sharp. *pres.p.* **biteriæð** VI.176

bitter *adj.* bitter, sharp, severe. VII.46, 120

biþeng *see* **beþencan**

blætsung *f.* blessing. III.317

bletsian, bledsian *v.* to bless. *pp.* **ibledsod** I.196, (*decl.*) **iblætsedon** III.240, **iblesode** VII.36

blind *adj.* (*a*) blind. III.6, 8, 11, 24, 52, 55, *etc.*, *as sb.* III.19, 151, 293, 312; (*b*) dark. IV.177, 187, 191, 216

blindnyss *f.* blindness. III.127, 150, 194, 368

bliss *f.* bliss, joy. I.23, 144, IV.269, V.120, VI.43, 56, 57, 67, *etc.*, **blis** VII.149

blissian *v.* to rejoice. *pres.1s.* **blissiȝe** IV.200, 201; *pres.3s.* **blissæþ** VI.209; *pres.p.* **blissiæð** VI.72

bliðe *adj.* joyous, glad. IV.59, 173, VII.92; *adv.* joyously, gladly. IV.193, VII.41, 61

bliþelice *adv.* gladly, joyfully. IV.220; *comp.* **bliþelycor** V.189

blod *n.* blood. IV.170, 222, VI.239

blowan *v.* to blossom, flower. *pres.pt.* **blowende** VII.80

blysa *wk.m.* torch. IV.160

boc *f.* book. I.157, III.254, 327; *np.* **bec** II.208, IV.21, 27, 281, VI.153; *ap.* **bec** V.101; *gp.* **bocæ** V.117, 175; *dp.* **bocum** III.109, 137, IV.248, VI.69

bocere *m.* writer, scribe. I.168, 174, 185

bod *n.* command, order. *ap.* **bode** V.79, **bodu** V.162, VII.54, 63, 91, **boden** VII.127; *dp.* **bodum** VII.159

iboden *see* **beodan**

bodian *v.* to preach. *pret.3s.* **bodede** I.4, 157

-boren *see* **ȝeberan**

bot *f.* help, remedy. V.3

brad *adj.* broad. IV.163

bræd *n.* table, tablet. V.40

brastlian *v.* to crackle. *pres.pt.* **brastlende** VII.29

breost *n.* breast. IV.163 (*pl. for sg.*)

briht(-) *see* **beorht(-)**

(ȝe)bringan *v.* to bring. *infin.* IV.47, 54; *infl.infin.* **bringenne** VII.25; *imper.p.* **ȝebrinȝaþ** IV.97; *pres.3s.* **bringæð** IV.289, 308, V.137; *pres.p.* **ȝebrohten** IV.200, **ȝebrohton** IV.187; *pret.3s.* **brohte** V.43; *pret.p.* **brohten** I.41; *pp.* (*decl.*) **ibrohte** VII.38

brocenlic ('tobrocenlic') *adj.* frail, perishable. VII.125 n.

brohte(n) *see* **bringan**

brosnodlic ('gebrosnodlic') *adj.* corrupted, decaying. VII.124

(ȝe)broðor *m.* brother. II.61, 64; *coll.p.* **(ȝe)broðræ**, Christians or men generally (*i.e.* brothers of Christ). II.46, 166, III.197, 261

brucan *v.w.g.* to enjoy, partake of. *infin.* IV.365, VI.38, 267, VII.64; *pres.1s.* **bruce** IV.206

bryne, brune *m.* burning. III.258, VII.46

buȝan *v.* to submit. *infin.* I.56

-bundene *see* **ȝebindan**

burȝan ('beorg', ME berwen) *v.w.d.* to protect. *infl.infin.* **burȝene** V.107

burȝen *f.* burying-place, tomb. *ds.* **buriȝene** I.95

burh *f.* city, town. *ds.* **buriȝ** I.7, 60, 158, IV.48, V.81

bur(i)ȝan *v.* to bury. *pp.* **iburiȝed** VI.157

buriȝnes *f.* burying-place, tomb. VII.2, 7, 9, 17, 26

butan, buton, buten *prep.w.d.* (*a*) without. I.63, 192, 201, II.199, III.172, 203, 221, 294, *etc.*; (*b*) except. III.232, V.53, 182, VI.29, 131, 147, 198, 229; *conj.* (*a*) unless (*w.subj.*). I.15, 62, 199, III.90, 160, 339, VII.128, 129; (*b*) (*co-ordinating, after negatives*) but, except. III.342, IV.362, V.49, 146, 148, VI.107, 235, VII.132, 144, 165

ȝebyld ('gebyldan') *adj.* bold, courageous. IV.75

bylȝan *v.* to offend, anger. *infin.* V.167

bysen, bisen *f.* pattern, example. **bys-** V.5, 115, VII.103, **bis-** V.10, 29

Capharnan Capernaum (*city in Galilee*). I.7, 60

casere *m.* emperor. I.36, 37, 45, 47, 48, 56, IV.25, 27, 69, VII.126

ceaster *f.* city. *gs.* **ceastre** VI.191

cene *adj.* bold, brave. IV.153

cennan *v.* to conceive. *pp.* **icenned**, born. VII.69

ceosol *m.*(?) gravel, sand. IV.272, 275

cerran *v.* to turn, change, convert. *infin.* VII.158, **cyrren** VI.258; *pres.p.* **cerræð** VII.145; *pp.* **ichærred** VI.244

Chanan Cana. I.3

child(-) *see* **cild**

chinan ('cinan') *v.* to gape, break into chinks. *pres.3s.* **chinæð** IV.301

chyrceæn *see* **cyrce**

cild, child *n.* child. *ns.* **child** VII.87; *ap.* **childræn** I.49; *dp.* **cildrum** II.13, **childum** II.190

clæne *adj.* clean, pure. IV.304, V.170, VI.262, VII.147

clænness *f.* cleanness, purity, chastity. IV.343, V.169, VII.160

ʒeclænsian *v.* to cleanse, purify. *pres.3s.* **ʒeclænsæþ** VI.138; *pp.* **iclænsod** IV.316

clænsung *f.* cleansing, purifying. V.4

claþ *m.* cloth, (*in pl.*) clothes. VI.14, 130

clif *n.* cliff. VII.106

clut *m.* piece (of metal). IV.163

clypian *v.* to cry out, call. *infin.* II.35; *pres.3s.* **clypæð** III.239, 245; *pres.p.* **clypiæð** I.77; *pret.p.* **clypodon** III.53; *pres.pt.* **clypiende** IV.175, VI.213

cnapa *wk.m.* boy, young man. I.73 n., 104, 111, 120, 123, 132

ʒecnawan *v.* to know, perceive, understand, recognize. *infin.* I.190, VII.94; *pret.subj.s.* **cneowæ** V.154

cniht *m.* young man, retainer. I.113 n.

com(-) *see* **cuman**

ʒecoren *adj.* (*pp. of* 'ʒeceosan') chosen, beloved. (*as sb.*) III.239

corn *n.* corn. IV.286, 301, 304, 316

costnian *v.* to tempt, try. *infin.* V.23, 26

costung *f.* temptation. V.59, 59, 63

creft ('cræft') *m.* art, skill. II.207

Crist *m.* Christ. I.40, 57, 63, 71, 99, 121, *etc.*

Cristen *adj.* Christian. III.316, IV.13, 26, 29, 34

cristendom *m.* Christianity, christendom. III.318, IV.5

cruma *wk.m.* crumb. III.260

cucu *adj.* alive. IV.186, 234

cuman *v.* to come. *infin.* V.85, 104; *imper.s.* **cum** I.115; *imper.p.* **cumæð**

III.240, **cumeð** VII.36; *pres.1s.* **cume** I.107; *pres.3s.* **cymæð** I.115, III.14, IV.331, VI.92, VII.75, **cymeð** VII.119, **cymð** III.189, VII.30; *pres.p.* **cumæð** V.106, **cumeð** VII.57, **cymð** (*for s.?*) VII.136; *pret.3s.* **com** I.3, 10, 57, 102, 140, *etc.*; *pret.3s.subj.* **come** I.73, III.201, V.28; *pret.p.* **comen** I.22, 43, 143, VII.133, **comæn** III.121, **comon** IV.59; *pret.subj.p.* **comen** III.263; *pres.pt.* **cumende** VI.9, **comende** VI.168; *pp.* **icumen** III.79

cunde *see* **(ʒe)cynd**

cunnan *v.* to be acquainted with, know (how to), understand. *pres.subj.s.* **cunne** V.186; *pres.p.* **cunnon** I.128, III.79; *pret.1s. and 3s.* **cuþe** III.327, VII.8; *pret.p.* **cuþæn** VII.127; *pret.subj.p.* **cyðen** I.190

cuð (*adj.*) *see* **fulcuþ**

cuþ- (*infin. forms*) *see* **cyðan**; (*pret. forms*) *see* **cunnan**

cuðlice *adv.* certainly, manifestly. V.22

ʒecwæman *v.* to please. *pret.p.* **icwæmdon** III.244

cwæmlic *adj.* agreeable. V.176

(ʒe)cwæðan *v.* to say, speak, call, interpret. *infin.* VII.9; *pres.1s.* **cwæðe** I.114, II.106; *pret.3s.* **cwæð** I.18, 29, 99, 103, 106, *etc.*, **ʒecwæð** III.17; *pret.subj.s.* **icwæde** V.67; *pret.3p.* **cwæden** I.180; *pres.pt.* **cwæðende** I.174, II.16, 24, *etc.*, **cweðende** IV.131; *pp.* **icwæden(-)** II.135, III.21, 64, V.161, **icwædon** III.138, 157

cwalu *f.* violent death, destruction. IV.344

cweartern *n.* prison. II.30, IV.49, 177, 187, 191, **cwærterne** IV.216

cwellere *m.* killer. IV.11, 32, 101, 122, 131, 186, *etc.*

cweðende *see* **(ʒe)cwæðan**

cwician *v.* to make alive, quicken. *pret.3s.* **cwicede** IV.310

cwide *m.* sentence, saying. V.102

cwylman *v.* to suffer torment. *pret.3s.* **cwylmde** III.254, **cwylmode** III.258

cwylmynʒ *f.* torture, suffering. III.263

(-)cydd(-) *see* **cyðan**

cym(-) (*v.*) *see* **cuman**

cyme *m.* approach, coming, advent. VI.154

(ʒe)cynd *n.* nature, kind, condition. I.127, III.121, 133, 154, IV.371, V.152, VI.215, 216, **cunde** VI.86

cynedom *m.* royal power. I.38
cynehelm *m.* crown, diadem. IV.44
cyninga *see* **kyng**
cyrce, chyrce *wk.f.* church. *ds.* **cyrcan**
    IV.277; *ap.* **chyrceæn** VII.160
cyrren *see* **cerran**
cyssan *v.* to kiss. *pret.p.* **cystun** IV.222
cyst *f.* excellence, virtue, goodness. II.58
cyð (*adj.*) *see* **cuþ**
(ȝe)cyþan *v.* to make known, tell, relate.
    infin. I.136, **cuþ-** V.113, VI.3, 163, 221,
    234, 252; *infl.infin.* **cuþænne** VI.249;
    imper.s. **cyð** II.61; *imper.p.* **cyþaþ**
    IV.205; *pres.p.* **cyþaö** IV.27; *pret.3s.*
    (ȝe)cydde I.48, IV.34, VI.255; *pret.p.*
    cydden I.23, **cyddon** I.144, II.34,
    IV.212; *pp.* **ȝecydd** IV.251
cyþere *m.* witness. IV.148
cyðlice ('cuþlice') *adv.* certainly, mani-
    festly. *comp.* **cyðlycor** VI.144
ȝecyðnes *f.* testament. III.280

dæd *f.* deed. III.252, 291, IV.138, V.86,
    VI.102, 134, 173, *etc.*
dæȝ *m.* day. I.27, 148, 158, II.98, III.14,
    189, 191, *etc.*
dæȝhwamlice *adv.* daily. VII.92
dæȝþerlic *adj.* daily, present. V.17
dæl *m.* part, portion. I.53, IV.168, V.174,
    178, 182, VI.114, *etc.*
dæþ (*v.*) *see* **(ȝe)don**
dæþ (*n.*) *see* **deaþ**
dæþbot ('dædbot') *f.* repentance, penit-
    ence. II.151, VII.146
ȝedafenian *v.* to be fitting. *pres.3s.* **ȝe-/
    idafenæö** III.13, 177; *pret.3s.* **ȝeda-
    fenode** III.180
ȝedafenlic *adj.* becoming, fit. III.353
Datianus Datianus. IV.23, 32, 46, 95, etc.,
    Dacianus IV.157
dead *adj.* dead. I.94, IV.234, 253, 310,
    VII.9, 17, 26
dearne *see* **dyrne**
deaö *m.* death. III.296, 297, IV.87, 307,
    V.90, 94, *etc.*
deaþelic *adj.* deadly, mortal. VI.84
dema *wk.m.* judge. IV.60, 266, VII.31, 33,
    140
deman *v.* to judge. *infin.* VI.6; *pret.p.*
    demdon V.91
deofol, deofel *m.* devil. III.119, 141, 141,
    250, IV.14, 228, V.15, *etc.*
deofollic *adj.* devilish. IV.20, 32, 46, 232

deofollice *adv.* devilishly. IV.114
deop *adj.* deep, profound. II.3, 132,
    IV.260; *sup.* VII.65
deopnyss *f.* depth, profundity. VII.27
deor *n.* animal. IV.244
deorc *adj.* dark. III.14, 189, 201, 232
deorewurðe *adj.* precious, dear. IV.307;
    sup. VII.119
derian *v.* to injure. *pres.3s.* **deræö** VII.40
dest, (ȝe)deþ *see* **(ȝe)don**
diacon *m.* deacon. IV.7, 72, 77
diȝelic ('digol') *adj.* secret, hidden.
    III.112
diȝol, diȝle *adj.* secret, private, hidden.
    II.211, IV.138
diȝollice *adv.* secretly. II.209, 211
dim *adj.* dim, dark. III.245
dimnes, dymnes *f.* dimness, darkness.
    III.232, VII.52
discipul *m.* disciple, scholar. II.3
dom *m.* judgment. III.103, 246, 356, VI.2,
    79, 88, *etc.*
domere *m.* judge. VII.128
domsetle *n.* judgment-seat. III.239, **-selt**
    VII.128
(ȝe)don *v.* (*a*) to do. *infin.* I.71, 87, 109,
    II.95, 153, *etc.*; *infl.infin.* **donne** V.176;
    imper.s. **do** I.116, II.104, III.67, 298;
    imper.p. **doö** II.89; *pres.2s.* **dest** II.186,
    IV.68; *pres.3s.* **deþ** I.116, II.45, 165, *etc.*,
    ȝedeþ VI.128, **dæþ** I.152, VII.5, 82 (*for
    p.?*); *pres.p.* **doö** IV.345, VII.146, **do we**
    V.3; *pres.subj.p.* **don** VII.20; *pret.3s.*
    dyde I.69, 93, II.32, *etc.*, **dude** V.29,
    VI.225; *pret.p.* **dudon** VI.206, **dydon**
    IV.186, 237, 264; *pp.* **idon** II.34, (*decl.*)
    VII.20; (*b*) to take off (from) (*w.* **of**).
    infin. IV.157; (*c*) to make (s.o. sth.)
    (*w.adj.*). *pp.* **ȝedone** IV.56
dorston *see* **durran**
draca *wk.m.* dragon. VII.47
dræfedness ('gedrefednyss') *f.* trouble,
    tribulation. V.169
dranc *see* **drincan**
dreaȝan ('dreogan') *v.* to endure, suffer.
    pres.p. **dreaȝæö** VI.94
dream *m.* joy, pleasure. VII.138
dreccan *v.* to afflict, torment. *infl.infin.*
    dreccenne IV.35
drenc *m.* drink. IV.64
Drihten (-in) *m.* Lord, God, Christ. I.16,
    89, 104, 109, 196, III.3, *etc.*

drihtenlic *adj.* divine. I.94, III.224, VI.105, 107, 110, *etc.*

drincan *v.* to drink. *pret.3s.* **dranc** IV.88

drosan ('dreosan') *v.* to fall, perish. *pres.p.* **drosǣð** VII.112

drosendlic *adj.* fragile, brittle. VII.125 n.

drunceness *f.* drunkenness. IV.330, V.14

drycræft *m.* magic art, sorcery. IV.136

drypan *v.* to moisten. *pret.3s.* **drypte** III.257

dud- *see* **don**

dun *f.* mountain, hill. V.38, 119, VI.11, 30, 59, *etc.*

duneweard *adv.* downward. II.115

[durran] *v.* to dare, presume. *pres.subj.s.* **durre** IV.68; *pret.s.* **durste** IV.367, V.85, 153; *pret.p.* **dorston** IV.63

durstiness ('dyrstignes') *f.* boldness, presumption. V.26, 84, 92

dust *n.* dust. VII.9, 16, **dyste** VII.122

ȝedwæscan *v.* to be extinguished, fade. *pret.3s.* **ȝedwæscte** VII.6 n.

dwelian *v.* to err. *pret.p.* **dweloden** I.188

ȝedwinan *v.* to dwindle, waste away. *pret.3s.* **ȝedwan** VII.6

dwyld *n.* error, heresy. IV.315

dwymorlice ('gedwimorlice') *adv.* deceptively. V.128

dyd- *see* **don**

dymnes *see* **dimnes**

dyrne *adj.* secret. IV.136, **dearne** III.63

dyrstiȝ *adj.* presumptuous, daring. IV.35

dysiȝ *n.* error, foolishness. II.192, 194

dyste *see* **dust**

eac *adv.* also, likewise. I.43, 125, 182, II.168, 175, *etc.*

ȝe-eacnian *v.* to make greater, increase. *pret.p.* **ȝeeacnodon** IV.165; *pp.* **ȝeeacnod** IV.21

eadiȝ *adj.* blessed. IV.40, VII.151

eadiȝness *f.* happiness. V.160, VI.186, 188, 199, *etc.*

eadleanes *see* **edlean**

eadmedan *v.* to humble. *pres.3s.* **ȝeeadmodeþ** V.134; *pret.3s.* **eadmedede** V.47

eadmod *adj.* humble, meek. *as sb.* I.126

eadmodlic *adj.* humble. *comp.* V.86, 95

eadmodness *f.* humility. I.125, 136, VI.118, 122, 128, VII.99

eafre *see* **æfre**

eaȝe *wk.n.* eye. III.19, 22, 31, 59, 82, 89, *etc.*; *dp.* **eaȝum** V.129, VI.134, **eaȝan** III.360, **eagan** III.364, **eaȝnen** VI.254

eahringas ('eaghringas') *mp.* eyebrows, eyelids. III.41

eaht- *see* **æht**

eala, (-æ) *interj.* O, lo. I.104, II.36, IV.67, V.85, *etc.*; **elæ** V.133

ealc *see* **ælc**

eald *adj.* old. V.36, 39, 173, VII.25, **ald-** III.274; *as sb.* VII.86

ealdordom *m.* sovereignty, authority. IV.31, VII.110

ealdormann *m.* ruler. VI.237, VII.127

ealicum ('eallic') *adj.* universal, general, catholic. II.134

eall *see* **al(l)**

eam, eard *see* **beon**

eardlice ('arodlice') *adv.* quickly, immediately. IV.43

earfoþe *adj.* hard, difficult. *sup.* **arfoþeste** III.267

earfoþlic *adj.* irksome. V.177, 185

earfoðness *f.* difficulty. V.66, VII.67, **erfoðnesse** VI.247

earm *adj.* poor, miserable. III.260, IV.105, VII.151; *as sb.* VII.10

earm *m.* arm. *dp.* **æarmun** IV.220

earmlice *adv.* miserably, wretchedly. III.116

(ȝe)earnian *v.* to earn, merit. *infin.* V.13, 159, 165, VI.258; *imper.p.* **earniæþ** VII.86; *pres.3s.* **ȝe-/iearnæð** III.143, 144; *pres.p.* **earnæþ** VI.199, **earniæð** VII.78; *pres.subj.p.* **earniæn** VI.194, VII.64, 162, **earniȝe we** VI.264; *pret.3s.* **(ȝe)earnode** I.142, IV.86

eart *see* **beon**

eaðe *adv.* easily, readily. V.112; *comp.* **æð** V.87

eaðelice *adv.* easily. IV.58, V.30

eaðfynde *adj.* easy to be found. II.80

eawfæstnyss *f.* religion, piety. IV.69

eawfest *adj.* religious, pious. IV.354

ece *adj.* eternal. II.92, III.117, 249, 297, IV.229, 292, *etc.*

ecelice *adv.* eternally. VI.126, 195, 200, 208, 266

ec(e)nyss *f.* eternity. I.202, III.369, IV.282, 369, 371, V.190, *etc.*, **ecce-** VII.93

ȝe-ecgode *adj.* edged. IV.180

edlean *n.* reward, retribution. III.242, 251, 264, VII.20, **æd-** VI.6, 103, **ead-** III.238, **æt-** III.236

edwit *n.* reproach, disgrace, scorn. VI.247
efestan *v.* to hasten. *imper.s.* **efest** I.89; *pret.s.* (*for p.*) **efste** IV.40
efne *adv.* even, just. VII.37, 135; **efne þa**, just then. II.20; **efne swa**, just as. VI.98; *interj.* lo, behold (*cf. Lat. 'ecce'*). III.230
eft *adv.* again, then. I.16, 91, 115, II.64, 80, *etc.*, **æft** V.74, 106, 135, VI.70, 88, 154, 162, VII.19, 70
eȝeslic *adj.* terrifying, terrible, awesome. VI.246, VII.50
ehtan *v.w.g.* to persecute. *pres.1s.* **ehte** IV.254
ehtere *m.* persecutor. IV.23, 28, 46
ehtness *f.* persecution. IV.11, 15, 20, 254
elæ *see* **eala**
elc *see* **ælc**
Elias Elijah. IV.245, V.41, VI.159, **Heli-** V.49, VI.16, 29, 141, 144, *etc.*
embe *prep.w.a.* about, round, around. I.9, II.33, VI.9, 145, 147, VII.140; **æfre embe**, every. V.174
embhon *v.* to drape, clothe, deck. *pp.* (*decl.*) **embihangene** VII.115
embspecan *v.* to speak about (sth.). *pret.3s.* **embespæc** IV.304
embwreon *v.* to enwrap. *pret.3s.* **embwreah** VI.212 n.
ende *m.* end. I.118, III.225, 253, IV.152, *etc.*
endeburdness ('endebyrdnes') *f.* order, method, manner. V.18
endedæȝ *m.* last day. VII.22
endemes *adv.* equally, likewise, together. I.82
(ȝe)endian *v.* to end. *infin.* IV.58; *pp.* **iendod** III.223, VI.71, 170
endlyfæn *num.* eleven. II.150, 151
endlyfænfeald *adj.* elevenfold. II.145
endung *f.* ending, end. III.231, 237, VI.4, 88, 137
engel *m.* angel. V.42, 99, 104, 105, 109, 130, *etc.*
engellic *adj.* angelic. IV.199
Englelond *n.* England. I.43
Englisc *adj.* English. I.32, II.52, 74, III.106, *etc.*
eniȝe *see* **æniȝ**
eode(n) *see* **gan**
eom *see* **beon**
eornan *v.* to run. *pres.pt.* **eornende** III.33
eornestlice *adv.* therefore. II.77
eornost *n.* earnest, seriousness. *Only in*

phrase **on eornost**, in earnest, earnestly. II.186
eorðe *wk.f.* earth, ground. III.17, 18, 31, 152, *etc.*
eorðlic *adj.* earthly. III.154, V.122, VI.51, 54, *etc.*
eow *see* **þu**
eower *poss.adj.* your. I.34, 78, III.54, IV.132, *etc.*
ereste *see* **ær**, *adj.*
erfoðnesse *see* **earfoþness**
estfulness *f.* devotion, zeal. IV.43
etan *v.* to eat. *pret.3s.* **æt** V.42
Eua Eve. III.343, V.60, VI.81

fæder *m.* father, God the Father, religious elder. I.24, 28, 145, 153, II.45, *etc.*, **Fader** III.179
fæderlic *adj.* fatherly, paternal. VI.24, 255
fæȝer *adj.* fair, beautiful. IV.62, VI.12, VII.137, **feȝer** VII.163; *sup.* **feȝereste** VII.115
fæȝerness *f.* fairness, beauty. VI.95, 121, **feȝernes(-)** V.125, 127, VI.105, 109, 189, 203, VII.82, 83, 124, 133
fæla (-e) *see* **fela**
fællæþ *see* **feallan**
fær *f.* journey. I.9
færde *see* **feran**
færinge *adv.* suddenly. VI.20, **fering-** VI.12, 211, VII.105, 108
færlic *adj.* sudden, unexpected. IV.196
færð *see* **faran**
fæstan *v.* to fast. *pres.subj.s.* **feste** V.178, 185; *pret.3s.* **fæste** V.8, 33, **feste** V.9, 37, 41, 44, 48, **festæ** V.6; *pret.p.* **festen** V.37
fæste *adv.* fast, firmly, securely. IV.183
fæsten *n.* fast, fasting. V.2, 4, 44, 44, 48, 182, 185, VII.146, **festen(-)** V.9, 12, 37, 41, 169, 180
(ȝe)fæstnian, festnian *v.* to make fast, confirm, fasten. *infin.* VI.41, 75; *pret.p.* **ȝefæstnodon** IV.101; *pp.* (*decl.*) **ifestnode** VII.27
fæt *n.* vessel, cup. *ap.* **fate** I.6
fallen, ȝefalleð *see* **feallan**
fandian *v.* to try, tempt. *infin.* V.15, **fondi-** V.112, 153; **fanden** V.49, **fonden** V.59; *pret.3s.* **fondode** V.49; *pp.* **ifondod** V.20
faran *v.* to go, proceed. *infin.* I.12, 122, II.19, IV.350; *infl.infin.* **farenne** I.132; *imper.s.* **far** I.90, 100, 114, 118, **fare** I.17,

19, 30, 155; *pres.3s.* **færð** I.114; *pres.subj.s.* **fare** II.194; *pres.p.* **faræð** V.106, VI.53, VII.59; *pres.subj.p.* **faren** VII.1

faru *f.* journey, expedition, passage. I.113, V.27

fate *see* **fæt**

feallan *v.* to fall. *infin.* **fallen** V.133; *pres.3s.* **3efalleð** V.134; *pres.p.* **fællæþ** VII.108, 112; *pret.s.* **feol** II.15, 27, III.352; *pret.p.* **feollen** VI.25, 225; *pres.pt.* **feallende** IV.287

feallendlic *adj.* perishable, transitory, frail. VII.124

feawa *adj.* few, a few. I.167

fedan *v.* to feed. *infin.* IV.64

fefor *m.* fever. I.27, 28, **feof-** I.148, 153

fe3er(-) *see* **fæ3er(-)**

fela *pron.adj.indecl.* much, many. *as adj.* I.41, II.103, 139, III.5, 204, V.128, VI.189, **fæl-** II.113, VII.26; *as pron.* I.44

3efelan *v.* to feel, perceive. *pres.3s.* **ifeleð** VI.176

feld *m.* field. IV.235, 238

feofer, -or *see* **fefor**

feoh *n.* money. II.17, 19, 28, 31, 42; *as.* **feo** II.13 (*elsewhere* **feoh**); *gs.* **feos** II.9

feohtan *v.* to fight. *pres.subj.s.* **feohte** IV.90

feol(len) *see* **feallan**

feondlic *adj.* devilish, fiendish. IV.90

feor *adv.* far. VI.60, 105

feorran *adv.* from afar. I.41

feorða *adj.* fourth. I.53

feower *num.* four. I.52, 95

feowerti3 *num.* forty. V.6, 6, 34, 37, 41, 180; *as adj. ap.* **feowerti3æ** V.48

(3e)fera *wk.m.* companion. II.21, 38, 158, VI.206

(3e)feran *v.* to go, journey. *pret.3s.* **ferde** I.11, 141, V.6, 25, **færde** III.4; *pret.p.* **3eferedan** IV.238; *pp.* **3eferod** IV.277

feringæ (-e) *see* **færinge**

feste(-), -æ(-) *see* **fæst-**

festlice ('fæstlice') *adv.* firmly, constantly. *comp.* **festlycor** VI.221

festn- *see* **(3e)fæstnian**

fet *see* **fot**

fif *num.* five. V.179, **fiue** VI.70

(3e)findan *v.* to find. *infin.* V.136, VI.108; *pret.3s.* **funde** II.112

finger *m.* finger. III.257, V.39

fiðere *n.* wing. IV.243

fiðerrica *m.* tetrarch. I.52

fix *m.* fish. IV.263

fleogan *v.* to fly. *pret.3s.* **fleah** IV.241

flit *n.* contention, strife. III.47

flowan *v.* to flow. *pret.3s.* **fleow** IV.170; *pres.pt.* **flowende** IV.222

folc *n.* people. I.167, 178, II.54, 137, *etc.*

fol3ian *v.* to follow. *infin.* III.323; *pres.3s.* **fol3æð** III.138; *pres.subj.s.* **fol3ie** III.318; *pret.p.* **fol3edon** III.321, **fol3odon** III.320

fon *v.* to take, succeed to. *pres.p.* **foð** VII.74

fond- *see* **fandian**

for *prep.w.a.d.* (*a*) because of, on account of. I.51, 91, 125, II.43, 58, 92, 92, 95, 151, 152, III.5, 8, *etc.*; (*b*) in place of. I.51, VII.150, 150, 151; (*c*) before, in front of. VI.100; **for þan (þam, þon) ðe** *conj.* for, because. I.53, 95, 162, 179, 190, 198, II.57, 75, *etc.*

forbeodan *v.* to forbid. *pret.3s.* **forbeat** VI.233

forberan *v.* to endure, suffer. *infin.* V.117; *pret.3s.* **forbær** IV.173

forbu3an *v.* to avoid, shun. *infin.* III.286

forcostian *v.* to tempt. *pret.3s.* **forcostode** V.60 n.

fordon *v.* to destroy. *pp.* **fordon** II.202

fordru3ian *v.* to dry up. *pres.p.* **fordru3iæð** VII.81

foresæcgan *v.* to foresay. *pp.* (*decl.*) **for(e)sæd-** III.114, 289, IV.24, 66

foresceawung *f.* foresight, providence. IV.240

for3æ3ednyss *f.* transgression. II.146; **for3ea3ed-** II.145

for3efenesse *see* **for3ifen(n)yss**

for3eldæn *see* **for3yldan**

for3ifan, -3yfan *v.* (*a*) to give. *pret.3s.* **for3eaf** IV.85; (*b*) to forgive. *infin.* II.38, 69, 97, 157, 178; *imper.s.* **for3if** II.105, 186; *imper.p.* **for3ife 3e** II.88; *pres.1s.* **for3ife** II.185; *pres.3s.* **for3yfæð** II.176; *pres.subj.s.* **for3ife** II.84, 101, 103, 129; *pres.p.* **for3ifæð** II.46, 102, 106; *pres.subj.p.* **for3ifan** II.83; *pret.1 and 3s.* **for3eaf** II.19, 37, 43, 155, 187; *pp.* **for3ifen** II.88, 124, 159, (*decl.*) II.125, 131

for3ifen(n)yss, -3yf- *f.* forgiveness. I.152, II.98, **-3efen-** VII.148

for3itan *v.* to forget. *pret.3s.* **for3eat** VI.179

forȝyf- *see* forȝif-
forȝyldan, -ȝeldan *v.* to repay. *infin.*
-ȝeld- II.28; *pres.1s.* forȝylde II.17;
pret.3s. forȝylde II.31, 42, 163;
pret.subj.s. forȝylde II.11; *pp.*
forȝolden II.14, 93
forhæfdness *f.* restraint, abstinence. V.2,
13
forlæran *v.* to deceive, seduce. *pret.3s.*
forlærde IV.83
forlætan *v.* (*a*) to leave, let go, forsake.
infin. VI.36, 261, VII.76; *imper.s.* forlæt
VII.16; *imper.p.* forlæteð IV.97; *pres.p.*
forlæteð VII.74; *pret.3s.* forlet I.27, 28,
148, 153, V.150; *pret.p.* forleton III.66,
forleetan IV.225; (*b*) to leave, allow.
pres.3s. forlæteð VII.100; *pret.3s.* forlæt
VII.97; (*c*) to omit, neglect. *pp.*
forlæten II.123
forleosan *v.* to lose. *pres.3s.* forlosæð
IV.320, forlyst IV.290; *pres.subj.s.* forleose IV.327; *pret.p.* forluron IV.312
forliger *n.* adultery, fornication. IV.136
forma *wk.adj.* first, earliest. V.102
forniman *v.* to waste, destroy. *infin.*
IV.256; *pp.* (*decl.*) fornumene IV.55
forsædon *see* foresæcgan
forscrincan *v.* to shrink up, dry up,
wither. *pres.p.* forscrincæð VII.81
forscyldegod *adj.* (*pp. of* 'forscyldigian')
condemned, guilty. IV.134
forseon *v.* to despise, scorn, neglect.
infin. IV.76; *pret.s.* forseah III.256;
pret.p. forsæȝen III.345, IV.335,
forsæȝon III.253, forseȝon III.365
forstelan *v.* to steal, rob, deprive. *pp.* forstolen V.121
forswolȝan ('forswelgan') *v.* to devour,
swallow up. *pres.p.* forswolȝeð VII.49
forð *adv.* forth, into view, on, onward.
I.96, II.100, 137, III.230, IV.289, VI.70
forþan *adv.* for that reason, therefore.
I.142, V.8, VI.248, forþon V.100; *for*
conj. for þam (þan, þon) þe, *see* for
forþan *adv.* ('furþum') even. VI.45,
forðen V.85, forþon IV.253
forðfaran *v.* to die. *pret.3s.* forðferde
VI.157; *pret.p.* forðfærdon I.44; *pp.*
forðfæren VI.16, (*decl.*) forþifarene
VI.159
forðfor *f.* departure, death. Only in the
phrase to forðfore, at death's door. I.8
forþgan *v.* to go forth. I.97

forðsið *m.* departure, death. Only in the
phrase æt forðsiðe, at death's door.
I.13, 60
forþsteppan *v.* to proceed. *pres.3s.*
forþstepð V.76
forþy, forþyȝ *adv.* for that cause, therefore. I.72, II.148
forwel *adv.* very. I.44
forwenednyss *f.* presumption, arrogance. I.51
forð(ȝe)witan *v.* to depart, die. *pp.* (*decl.*)
forðiwitene VI.166
forwordenlice *adj.* corrupt. VII.125
forwundian *v.* to wound badly. *pp.* forwundod II.205
forwurþan *v.* to perish, be destroyed.
pres.3s. forwurð VII.83
forwyrnan *v.* to deny, refuse. *pret.3s.* forwyrnde III.260; *pp.* forwyrnd III.259
forwyrnedlice *adv.* with restraint,
abstemiously. V.184
fot *m.* foot. V.100; *ap.* fet IV.222; *dp.*
fotum I.110, II.15, 27, III.101, etc.
fræcedness, freced- *f.* danger, peril.
II.194, VII.66, 101, 102
fram, from *prep.w.d.* from. I.10, 101, II.68,
76, 110, 112, 115, 117, *etc.*
frefran *v.* to comfort, console. *infin.* I.87;
pp. ȝefrefrod IV.198
fremian *v.* to avail, benefit. *pres.3s.*
fremæþ VII.153
(ȝe)fremman *v.* to do, perform. *infin.*
I.198; *pres.subj.s.* ȝefræmme II.147;
pret.p. ȝefremedon VI.238; *pp.* (*decl.*)
ȝefremede III.111
freolice *adv.* freely. III.340
freols *m.* feast, festival. III.279
freolsdæȝ *m.* feast-day, festival-day.
III.272
freolsian *v.* to celebrate. *pret.p.* freolsoden III.278, 289
friðstol *m.* sanctuary, refuge. VII.166
frofrian *v.* to comfort. *pret.3s.* frofrede
VI.227
from *see* fram
frumsceapen *adj.* first-created, first.
IV.83, 87
frymð *m.* beginning. V.68, VI.244
fugel *m.* bird. IV.236, 242, 247, 250, 263
ful *adj.* foul. III.124, IV.236
fulcuð, ful cuð *adj.* well known, public.
IV.248, V.35
fule *adv.* foully. I.96

fulfremed *adj.* complete, perfect. V.184

full *adj.* full, filled. I.6, III.164, IV.62, VI.89

ful(l) *adv.* fully, to the full, completely, very. III.67, 301, 340, V.68, 74, 153, VII.140

ifulled *see* **(ʒe)fyllan**

(ʒe)fullian *v.* to baptise. *pret.ʒs.* **fullode** II.120; *pp.* **ifullod** II.109, III.164

fullice *adv.* fully. IV.287

fulluht *n.* baptism. I.173, 175, 177, 181, 187, II.117, 118, *etc.*, **fuluhte** V.5

fultum *m.* help, support. I.87, III.108, V.104, 105, 147, 157, VII.25

fultumian *v.* to help. *pres.pt.* **fultumiende** V.189

funde *see* **findan**

fur(-) *see* **fyr**

fyl(i)ʒean *v.* to follow. *infin.* IV.349, V.117; *pres.subj.s.* **fyliʒe** IV.293, 339, 348; *pret.2s.* **fyliʒedest** VII.12

(ʒe)fyllan *v.* to fill, fulfil. *pret.ʒs.* **(ʒe)fulde** VI.64, 146; *pp.* **ifulled** V.45, VI.217, 250, VII.67, **ifylled** II.144, VI.61, 71

fyr, fur *n.* fire. III.249, VII.29, 30, 47, 55, 111

fyrmest *sup.adj.* best. I.6, IV.317

ʒefyrn *adv.* formerly. **ʒefurn** IV.83, **ifyrren** VI.15

fyrst *m.* time, respite. II.17, 27, 29, IV.54, 226

fyrwytnyss *f.* curiosity. I.145, **fyrwet-** I.24

gæderian *v.* to gather, collect. *pret.p.* **ʒaderoden** IV.223; *pp.* *(decl.)* **igæderæde** VII.32

gædering ('gaderung') *f.* gathering, assembly. VI.132

gafol *n.* tribute. I.42

Galilea Galilee. I.10

Galileisc *adj.* Galilean. I.4

gan *v.* to go, walk, proceed. *infin.* III.20, 32, VI.241; *imper.s.* **ga** V.138; *imper.p.* **gað** IV.199; *pret.1 and ʒs.* **eode** II.20, III.22, 34, 213; *pret.p.* **eoden** VI.30, 230; *pp.* **igan** VI.70

gast *m.* spirit, Holy Spirit. I.150, III.206, 250, *etc.*

gastlic *adj.* spiritual. III.108, 279, 311, IV.298, VI.40, 188, 229

glenʒ *f.* ornament. VII.121

gneornung *f.* grief, lamentation. VII.72

God *m.* God. I.75, 79, 129, 159, 187, 192, *etc.*

god *adj.* good. III.244, 311, V.32, 159, VI.18, 113, 181, *etc.*

god *n.* good thing, good deed(s), virtue, benefit. I.190, II.89, 91, III.15, 190, 233, 262, V.187, *etc.*

godcund *adj.* divine. V.113, VI.204, 216, 218

godcun(d)lic *adj.* divine. V.30, 73

godcundness *f.* divine nature, divinity. III.153, IV.370, V.115

godeweb *n.* precious cloth. VII.119

godspel(l) *n.* gospel. I.32, 59, II.44, 155, 164, 216, III.106, *etc.*

godspellere *m.* evangelist. II.110, 114, 168 (-**spæll**-), V.17, VI.1, *etc.*

godspellic *adj.* evangelical. V.22, VI.257

gold *n.* gold. VII.3, 114, 122

goldfretewe ('goldfrætwe') *fp.* gold ornaments. VII.117

grama *wk.m.* anger, rage, trouble. II.30, IV.66

granian *v.* to groan, lament. *pres.ʒs.* **graneð** VII.87

gremian *v.* to provoke, irritate. *pret.p.* **gremoden** III.247

grim *adj.* fierce, cruel. *comp.* V.137

(ʒe)grind *n.* grinding, gnashing. VII.51, 88

gripan *v.* to grasp, seize. *pres.ʒs.* **gripð** VII.72

grund *m.* depth, abyss. VII.65

grymetian *v.* to rage, cry out. *pret.ʒs.* **ʒrymetode** IV.121

grymness *f.* grimness, fierceness. V.109

gult(-) *see* **gylt(-)**

gute ('gyte') *m.* shedding, flood. VII.146

gylt, gult *m.* guilt, sin, crime. II.84, 208, 211, V.51, VII.145, **ʒylt(-)** II.156, III.116

gyltan *v.* to commit guilt or sin, to be guilty. *pres.ʒs.* **gulteð** VI.136; *pret.p.* **gylten** VI.83

ʒe *see* **þu**

ʒeaf *see* **ʒifan**

ʒealʒa *m.* gallows. IV.158

ʒear *n.* year. I.41, III.148, VII.26

ʒeʒearcian *v.* to prepare. *pp.* **iʒearcod** III.241, 250

ʒeare *adv.* well, perfectly, for certain. III.67, 301, V.24, 46, 153, VI.219

ȝearu *adj.* ready, prepared. I.132, IV.73, 110, 182

ȝearwian *v.* to make ready, prepare, *pres.subj.p.* ȝearwie V.167; *pret.ȝs.* ȝearwode VI.68

ȝeatan *v.* to grant. *pres.1s.* ȝeate VII.147

ȝefenæ *see* ȝifu

ȝeldan *v.* to pay. *infin.* II.25; *infl.infin.* ȝeldene II.8, 77; ȝeldenne II.22

ȝeman *v.w.g.* to care for, regard, heed. *pres.ȝs.* ȝemð III.234

ȝeoȝeþ *f.* youth. IV.149 (-uþe), VII.81, 83

ȝeoȝeðhad *m.* youth. VII.85

ȝeond *prep.w.a.* through, throughout. III.4, IV.12, 179, V.142

ȝeorne *adv.* eagerly, earnestly. I.11, II.16, III.288, V.79, *etc.*; *comp.* V.136

ȝeornlice *adv.* earnestly, zealously. II.174, IV.223; *sup.* ȝeornlucost VII.133

ȝif *conj.* if. I.74, 80, 175, 177, 190, II.46, 61, *etc.*, ȝyf V.65, 79, 132, 184, VI.182, *etc.*

ȝifan, ȝyfan *v.* to give. *infin.* III.342, V.26; *pres.1s.* ȝyfe V.132; *pres.ȝs.* ȝyfð VI.88, VII.97; *pret.ȝs.* ȝeaf I.171, III.206; *pp.* iȝifen II.89, iȝyfen V.161

ȝifernes *f.* gluttony. V.14, 61

ȝifu, ȝyfu *f.* gift, grace. I.88, 151, VII.151; ȝefenæ (*gp.*) VII.95

ȝinȝra *wk.m.* vassal, follower. IV.96

ȝit *see* ȝyt

ȝlowan *v.* to glow. *pres.pt.* ȝlowende IV.164

ȝyf- (*v.*) *see* ȝifan

ȝyfe (*n.*) *see* ȝifu

ȝylp *m.* boasting, pride. V.62

ȝylt(-) *see* gylt

ȝymm *m.* gem, jewel. VII.118, 121

ȝymstan *m.* gem, jewel. VII.115

ȝyrd *f.* rod. IV.115, 123

ȝyrstandæȝ *adv.* yesterday. I.26, 147

ȝyt *adv.* still, yet (*alone or with other adverbs, e.g.* þa) III.71, 327, V.72, 73, *etc.*, ȝit II.132; þa ȝyt *adv.* still. I.71

ȝytsung *f.* covetousness, avarice. V.61, VI.51, VII.11

habban *v.* to have. *infin.* II.187, III.255, IV.324, 334, V.80; *imper.s.* hafe II.63; *imper.p.* habbæð VII.85; *pres.1s.* habbe I.113; *pres.ȝs.* hæfð II.78, III.60, 135, 266, *etc.*, hafð V.161; *pres.subj.s.* habbe IV.182; *pres.p.* habbæð I.129, 135, III.76, 118, V.100, *etc.*, habbað V.3,

habbeð VI.83; *pret.ȝs.* hæfde I.53, II.6, *etc.*; *pret.p.* hæfdæn VI.82, hæfden V.52, hæfdon III.64

(ȝe)hadian *v.* to ordain, consecrate. *pp.* ȝehadod IV.6, (*decl.*) IV.36

hæ *see* he

(ȝe)hælan *v.* to heal. *infin.* I.12, 68, 72, 93, II.207, III.88, 337, V.10; *pres.1s.* hæle I.107; *pret.ȝs.* (ȝe-/i-)hælde I.64, 70, III.71, 151, 216, 293; *pret.subj.s.* hælde I.73; *pp.* ihæled I.120, 149, II.204, III.38, *etc.*, (*decl.*) III.48, 72, 80, *etc.*

hæle *wk.f.* health, safety, salvation. I.142, IV.223, V.96, VI.32, 220, 232, 247

Hælend *m.* Saviour, Christ. I.3, 9, 11, 14, 18, *etc.*, Healend VI.26, Helend(-) IV.7, 18, 175

hælle(-) *see* hell

hælp *f. or m.* help. V.156, VII.73

(ȝe)hælpan, helpan *v.* to help. *infin.* I.76 (*w.d.*), II.197 (*w.g.*); *infl.infin.* hælpe V.107 (*w.d.*)

hælu *f.* health, safety, salvation. I.59

hænum *see* hean

hær *see* her

hæren *adj.* made of hair. II.151

ȝeihæreð *see* (ȝe)hyran

hæs *f.* command, behest. I.68

hæt *see* hatan

hæte *f.* heat. VII.81

hæðen *adj.* heathen. I.163, II.68

hal *adj.* whole, well. I.101, 111, III.214, 361

hald- *see* (ȝe)healdan

halȝa *wk.m.* saint. IV.18, 47, 116, 227, 265, 365, V.147, VI.15, 47, 62, *etc.*

halȝian *v.* to hallow, consecrate. *pres.p.* halȝiæð III.295; *pp.* ihalȝod III.308

haliȝ *adj.* holy. I.150, 150, 163, II.60, 67, 218, III.38, 50, *etc.*

halwende *adj.* salutary, healing. V.164

ham *m.* home. VII.166; *in phrase* æt ham I.104; *as adv.* I.30, 70, 121, 155, III.332

hamweard *adv.* homeward. I.21, 118, 138, 141, IV.269

hand *f.* hand. IV.133, V.99, honden V.94, VI.226

hat *adj.* hot. VII.59

hatan *v.* (*a*) to bid, order, command. *infin.* V.72, VII.116, 118; *imper.s.* hat V.65; *pret.ȝs.* het II.12, 35, 95, III.20, *etc.*, hæt I.97, V.92, VI.3; (*b*) to call, name. *pp.* i-/ȝehaten I.36, 58, II.53, III.30,

IV.23, *etc.*, (*decl.*) VII.165; (*c*) **hatte**, was called. III.21, IV.3, VI.231

hate ('hete') *m.* hatred, enmity, malice. V.116

hatian *v.* to hate. *pres.3s.* **hatæð** IV.291, 321; *pres.p.* **hatiæð** IV.332

hatung *f.* hate, hatred. II.196, 199

he *m.*, **heo** *f.*, **hit** *n. pron.3p.* I.4, 5, 8, 10, 11, *etc.* [*The following forms are found:* *sg.m.nom.* **he, hæ** VI.145, *acc.* **hine**, *gen.* **his**, *dat.* **him**; *sg.f.nom.* **heo**, *acc.* **heo**, *gen.* **hire**, *dat.* **hire**; *sg.n.nom.* **hit**, *acc.* **hit**, *gen.* **his**, *dat.* **him**; *pl.nom.* **heo, hyo** VI.27, *acc.* **heo, hi** II.65, *gen.* **heoræ, -a, -e, hore** VI.53. *See also p. lxxiv above.*]

heafod *n.* head. V.88, 89

heafodburh *f.* chief city. IV.24

heafodmann *m.* elder, leader. IV.37

heah *adj.* high. VI.52, VII.101; *str.fas.* **heahne** V.119, *str.np.* **heaȝæ** VII.107, **heaȝe** VII.109; *wk.fas.* **heaȝe** VI.58, *wk.fds.* **heahe** VI.186, *wk.np.* **heaȝæ** VII.108, 112, **heahȝæ** VII.106; *sup.* **heahsten** VII.164, **hestæn** VII.90

hea(h)lic *adj.* high, very great. IV.269, 318

heahness *f.* high place. VI.259

heahroder *m.* lofty sky. VII.29

heahsetl *n.* throne, judgement-seat. VII.33

(ȝe)healdan *v.* to hold, keep, protect. *infin.* V.79, 162, VI.135, VII.43, 54, 159, **hald-** III.280, 310; *pres.3s.* **heald** III.271, IV.292, **healt** III.44, IV.322; *pres.p.* **healdaþ** IV.231, **healdæþ** V.109; *pres.subj.p.* **healden** VII.64, 131, **healde we** VI.263; *pret.3s.* **(ȝe)heold** III.293, IV.249; *pret.p.* **heoldon** III.272, **heolden** VII.42, 91

Healend *see* **Hælend**

healf *f.* side, half. VII.34, 35, 35

hean *adj.* low, poor, humble. VI.6; *dp.* **hænum** VI.38

heap *m.* host, multitude, crowd. III.246, VI.132

heard *adj.* hard, firm. III.365, IV.51, 102, 151, 158, V.108, VI.246

heardheort *adj* hard-hearted. III.80, 335

heardlice *adv.* harshly. V.183

hefiȝ *adj.* heavy. IV.261, 266

(ȝe)hefiȝian *v.* to oppress, burden. *pp.* **ȝehefeȝode** IV.51

Helend- *see* **Hælend**

Heli- *see* **Elias**

hell *f.* hell. III.144, 144, 161, 232, VII.65, **hælle(-)** VII.47, 156

hengen *f.* rack. IV.99, 102, 124, 157

heo *see* **he**

heofen, -on *m.* heaven. I.173, 175, II.5, 53, 119, *etc.*

heofenlic, -onlic *adj.* heavenly. II.45, 165, III.86, 184, 300, IV.190, *etc.*

heofenware *pl.* inhabitants of heaven. VII.64

heold(-) *see* **healdan**

heom *see* **he**

heom (IV.198) *see* **beon**

heonensiþ *m.* departure, death. VII.19

heonon *adv.* hence. **heonne** V.138; **heonon forþ**, henceforth. III.230

heora (-æ, -e) *see* **he**

heorte *wk.f.* heart. II.47, 167, 180, 182, 188, *etc.*

her *adv.* here. I.91, II.48, 94, 109, 127, III.147, *etc.*, **hær** I.59, V.106, VI.18; **her biforen**, *see* **beforen**

(ȝe)her- (*v.* to hear) *see* **ȝehyran**

heræfter *adv.* hereafter. V.16

heretoȝa *wk.m.* leader. III.77, IV.22

herian *v.* to praise. *pres.pt.* **heriende** IV.194, **heriȝende** VII.57; *pp.* (*decl.*) **iherode** II.219

Herod Herod. *gs.* **Herodis** I.49

herto *adv.* for this purpose. II.49

herung *f.* praise. VII.164

hestæn *see* **heah**

het *see* **hatan**

hetelice *adv.* savagely, fiercely. IV.99, 102

hetol *adj.* hostile, evil, malignant. IV.23, 133, 212; (*as sb.*) IV.141

hi, him, hine, hire *see* **he**

hider, hyder *adv.* hither. III.103, 165, 356, V.156, 158, VI.4, *etc.*

hingrian *v.* to hunger. *infin.* V.36; *pret.3s.* **hingrede** V.35

hired *m.* household. I.31, 156, 160

hiredmann *m.* member of a household. II.32

his, hit *see* **he**

hiwæs *see* **hyw**

hlaforde *see* **laford**

hnesce *adj.* soft. IV.192

hnesce *adv.* softly. IV.202

honden *see* **hand**

hopian *v.* to trust, have confidence (in). *pret.3s.* **hopode** I.21, 138, IV.52

hore *see* **he**

hraðe *see* raðe

hrem, hræm *m.* raven. IV.241, 246, 250

hryman *v.* to rave, cry out. *pret.3s.* hrymde IV.121

hu *adv.* how. I.47, 79, 81, 86, 165, II.32, *etc.*; ȝehu . . . þæt, how. III.137; hu ne is that not. III.24

humeta *adv.* how, in what manner. III.29, IV.63

hund *m.* hound, dog. IV.236

hund *n.* hundred. I.41

hundfeald *adj.* hundredfold. II.93

hundred *n.* hundred. V.179. *In phrase* hundredes aldor. I.102, 108, 124, 133

hundseofenteoða *adj.* seventieth. II.128

hundseofentiȝ *num.* seventy. II.72, 107, 113, 122

hundteontiȝ *num.* hundred. II.14c, -tentiȝ II.22

hungor *m.* hunger. VII.87

huru, hure *adv.* at least, at any rate, indeed. II.14, 186, III.257, IV.140, 151, 152, 260, 267, V.185, hyre V.177

hus *n.* house, family. I.70, 121, VI.185, 186, 190

huxlice *adv.* ignominiously, disgracefully. III.91, 307, 365

hwa *m.f.*, hwæt *n.* (*a*) *interr.pron.* who, what. *mns.* hwa I.171, *etc.*; *mgs.* hwæs I.170, III.8, 167; *nns. or nas.* hwæt I.135, 135, II.106, *etc.*; to hwam, hwan, hwon *or* for hwam, hwan, hwon, why. V.48, VI.106, 233, VII.10, 11; (*b*) *indef.pron.* someone, something. *nas.* hwæt III.288; swa hwa swa, whosoever. III.64, IV.346

ȝehwa *m.f. indef.pron.* each one, everyone. III.138

hwænne *adv.* when. VI.248

hwær *adv.* where. III.35, IV.274, VII.2, 126, *etc.*, hwar IV.132

ȝehwær *adv.* everywhere. IV.280

hwærfan *v.* to turn, change. *pp.* ihwærfod VI.78

hwæs, hwæt *see* hwa

hwæt *interj.* what! indeed! III.197, IV.32, V.76, 95, *etc.*

hwæten *adj.* wheaten. IV.286, 304, 316

hwæðer *conj.w.subj.* whether. III.314; hwæðer þe . . . oððe . . ., whether . . . or . . ., III.9, 168

hwanon *adv.conj.* whence. I.181, 189, III.79, 81

hwar *see* hwær

hwene *adv.* a little, somewhat. II.74, III.73

hwi *adv.conj.* why. I.176, VI.73, VII.4

hwil *f.* a while, space of time. VI.44, 240; þa hwile þe *conj.* while. III.14, 16, 189, 196, V.77, VI.49, 135, VII.74–5

hwilc, hwylc *pron.adj. as interr.* what, which. *interr.pron.* III.97, 191, 348, II.195, VI.142; *interr.adj.* I.25, 146, 183, IV.206, 206, 360, V.21, *etc.*

(ȝe)hwilc, (ȝe)hwylc *adj.* each, any. I.42, 86, hwylc(-) V.176, 183, 184

hwilon *adv.* (*a*) at times, for a time. I.43, II.191, 191, III.133, V.129; (*b*) once, some time ago. I.3, 5, 103, 168, 194, II.4, 6, 60, III.277, IV.246

hwilwendlic *adj.* temporary. VII.124

hwit *adj.* white. VI.14, 131, 132, 133, VII.56; *sup.* VII.114

hwon *see* hwa

ȝehwylc(-) *see* ȝehwilc

hyder *see* hider

hyht *m.* hope, joy. VI.53

hyo *see* he

(ȝe)hyran, -heran *v.* to hear, listen to. *infin.* -hyr- III.86, 178, 325, IV.353, -her- VI.267, VII.58, 159; *infl.infin.* herenne V.83; *imper.p.* ȝehyræð VI.23, ȝeihæreð VI.214; *pres.3s.* ȝehyrð II.65, 67, hereð V.136, iheræð VII.144, ihyræð II.62, 63; *pres.subj.s.* ihere I.79, ihyre V.135; *pres.p.* ȝehyrað IV.143, ihyræð II.215, iheræð VI.71; *pres.subj.p.* iheren VI.41, heræn VII.131; *pret.s.* ihyrde III.94; *pret.p.* ihyrdon I.124, ihyrden VI.76, ihærdon VI.24, (i)herdon II.179, VI.39, herden VI.254; *pres.pt.* (*as sb.*) ȝehyrendan IV.143; *pp.* iheræd III.73, ihyred III.87, 336

hyre *see* huru

ȝehyrsumian *v.w.d.* to obey. *pret.p.* ȝehyrsumodon IV.85

hyw *n.* appearance, form. V.130, hiw- IV.62

hywian *v.* to form, fashion, feign. *infin.* V.129

ȝehywian *v.* to transform. *pres.3s.* ȝehywæð VI.128

hywung *f.* forming, feigning, dissimulation. V.128

Iacobus the apostle James. VI.11
ic *pron.1p.* I. *Forms same as OE* (*ns.* **ic**, *as.*, *ds.* **me**, *np.* **we** (*once* **wæ** V.10), *ap.*, *dp.* **us**, *gp.* **ure**, *see* **ure**)
idel *see* **ydel**
Ierusalem Jerusalem. VI.146
ilc- *see* **ylca**
in, inn *adv.* in. IV.178, 199
incund *adj.* inward, heartfelt. IV.194
ingangan *v.* to go in, enter. *pres.subj.s.* **in3onge** I.110
in3ehyd *n.* thought, mind. II.183
inn *n.* dwelling, lodging. VI.19 n.
innan *adv.* within. IV.278
inneweard *adj.* inward, internal. II.180, 188
innoþ *m.* inside of the body, vitals. IV.167, 171
into *prep.w.d.* into. III.249, IV.48, 167, 190, 309, VI.140, VII.156
inþonc ('in3eþonc') *m. or n.* thought, mind, heart. VII.142
Iohannes (*a*) John the Baptist. I.173, 179, 181, 186, II.120; (*b*) John the Evangelist. II.168, VI.11, 187
is *see* **beon**
isen *n.* iron. IV.51
isen *adj.* of iron. IV.163
Ispania Spain. IV.2, 9
Israel Israel. I.196
iu *adv.* formerly. II.218, VII.7, 14, 127
Iudei *np.* the Jews. III.91; *np.* **Iudeus** V.90; *gp.* **Iudea** I.10, 54
Iudeisc *adj.* Jewish (*often as sb.*, the Jews). I.165, 168, III.51, 63, 272, *etc.*

kyne3yrd ('cyne-') *f.* royal wand, sceptre. I.56
kynelic ('cyne-') *adj.* royal. VII.166
kynelice ('cyne-') *adv.* royally. I.40
kynerice ('cyne-') *n.* kingdom. VII.90
kynestol ('cyne-') royal throne. I.50
kyng ('cyning') *m.* king. I.20, 39, 48, 52, 57, 63, 71, *etc.*

la *interj.* lo, O, then. I.16, 89, II.17, III.24, 55, *etc.*
lac *n.* gift. I.42
3elæccan *v.* to take, seize. *pret.3s.* **ilæhte** II.23; *pret.p.* **ilæhten** IV.312

læce *m.* doctor. II.203, 206
læcnian *v.* to heal, treat. *pres.3s.* **læcnæð** II.203
lædan *v.* to lead, take. *infin.* II.12; *pres.3s.* **lædeþ** VI.52, 140, 203; *pres.p.* **lædeþ** V.171; *pret.3s.* **lædde** V.25, 118, VI.11, 58, **ledde** IV.163; *pret.p.* **lædden** III.211, **læddon** III.36; *pp.* **ilæd** V.20, 21, VII.139, **ilædd** VII.156, (*decl.*) **ilædde** VI.125, **iledde** VI.170
læfan *v.* to leave, leave behind. *pret.p.* **læfden** VII.134
læ3d- *see* **(3e)lecgan**
læ3(en) *see* **licgan**
læ3erbedd *n.* sick-bed. III.212
ilæhte(-) *see* **3elæccan**
læhtræs *see* **leahter**
læn *f.* loan. VII.96, **lan(e)** II.11, 14
læne *adj.* transitory, temporary. VI.36, 38, VII.66, 151
læran *v.* to teach, instruct. *infin.* VI.48, VII.9, 18; *pres.2s.* **lærst** III.93; *pres.3s.* **læreð** VI.34; *pret.3s.* **lærde** II.75, V.7, 163
læs *adv.* less. *Only in* **læs þe**, lest. V.167
læssa *comp.adj.* less. II.159; *pl. as noun*, **þa læssan**, the weaker, the lesser. IV.39
lætan *v.* (*a*) to let, allow, permit. *infin.* II.29; *imper.s.* **let** II.17, IV.50; *pret.3s.* **læt** II.19, 40; (*b*) to leave, forsake. *infin.* **letæn** VII.74; *pret.p.* **letæn** I.184
læwede *adj.* lay, unlearned. VII.130
laf ('hlaf') *m.* loaf, bread. V.65, 66, 72, 75
laf *f.* what is left. *In* **to lafe wurþan**, to be left, to remain. VII.68
laford ('hlaford') *m.* lord. II.11, 12, 15, 18, 40, *etc.*
la3e ('lagu') *f.* law. II.133, 144, 146, 153, V.36, 39, 175
lam *n.* clay, mud. III.18, 19, 31, 41, 152, 155
-lamp *see* **3elimpan**
lan *see* **læn**
land, langlice *see* **lond, longlice**
langsum *adj.* long, taking a long time. III.266, IV.54
lar *f.* teaching, instruction, doctrine. I.159, II.86, III.320, 321, IV.5, *etc.*
lareow *m.* teacher. II.218, III.76, 319, IV.9, **larþeow** V.143, 166, VI.226
larþeawsetle ('lareowselt') *n.* seat of a teacher. V.82

lastan ('læstan') *v.* to do, perform, carry out. *pp.* **last** VII.43

laõ *adj.* hateful, grievous. IV.105, 172, 184

laõian *v.* to invite, call. *pret.3s.* **laõode** I.121; *pp.* (*decl.*) **ilaõode** VII.165

laõian *v.* to be hateful. *pres.subj.s.* **laõiჳe** IV.299

(ჳe)laõung *f.* congregation, church. II.54, 56, 66, 67, VI.131, 138

Lazarus (*a*) Lazarus, brother of Mary and Martha. I.93, 95; (*b*) Lazarus, beggar in Christ's parable of the rich man and Lazarus. III.256, 260

ჳeleafa *m.* belief, faith. I.63, 65, 117, 139, III.5, 96, 100, *etc.*, **leafæ** III.362

ჳeleafful *adj.* believing, faithful, holy. I.85, 141, III.126, IV.272, 277, **leafulle** III.211

ჳeleafleas *adj.* faithless. IV.60

leafsele *m.* tabernacle. VI.182 n.

leah *see* **leogan**

leahter *m.* offence, sin, vice. III.121, 124, 126, IV.326, **læhtræs** VI.35

lean *n.* reward. IV.353

leasung *f.* lying, falsehood. V.102, 124

(ჳe)lecgan *v.* to lay, place, set. *pret.s.* **læჳde** II.23; *pret.p.* **ჳeleddon** IV.224, **lægdon** III.212

Leden *n.* Latin, the Latin tongue. II.135

Leden *adj.* Latin. IV.10

Ledenspæc ('-spræc') *f.* the Latin tongue. II.51

ilef- *see* **(ჳe)lyfan, lifan**

leiჳ *see* **liჳ**

leng *adv.* (*comp. of* **lange**) longer. III.309, IV.128

leod *f.* people (of a country). IV.2

leof *adj.* beloved, dear. I.16, 89, 92, 104, VI.22, 33, 80, *etc.*, *used absolutely in vocative,* dear (one), (dear) sir. II.17; *comp.* dearer, more pleasing. IV.108 (**leofre**), IV.336 (**leofere**); *sup.* **leofest(-)** V.1, VI.1

leofaõ, leofæõ, leofed(-), leofode *see* **libban**

leogan *v.* to lie, say falsely. *pret.3s.* **leah** V.102, VI.68

leoht(e-) *see* **liht**

leohtleas *adj.* without light. IV.49

leoma *m.* light, radiance, ray or beam of light. I.82, 85, VII.52

leorningcniht *m.* scholar, disciple. III.74, 76, 77, 166, *etc.*

let(æn) *see* **lætan**

libban *v.* (*pret. and one form of pres.pt. as from* 'lifian, leofian') to live. *infin.* V.77, 78, 166, 184, VI.262, **lybbæn** V.189; *pres.3s.* **leofæõ** I.19, 30, 100, 155, III.142, *etc.*, **leofaõ** IV.282, 369, **leofeõ** VI.268; *pres.subj.s.* **libbe** VII.155; *pres.p.* **libbæõ** III.150, VI.127, VII.93; *pres.subj.p.* **libban** IV.333; *pret.3s.* **leofede** I.23, 98, III.294, **leofode** I.144, **lyfede** VII.8; *pret.p.* **leofedon** III.243, **lifedon** VII.75, **lyfedon** V.41; *pres.pt.* **lifiჳend(-)** I.66, II.55, IV.324, **lyfiჳend(-)** III.369, **lifiende** V.58, VII.68, **libbende** VI.160, 166, 167

lic *n.* body. IV.160, 235, 238, 242, *etc.*

ჳelic *adj.* (*a*) like (+ *d. of object*). II.5, III.27, V.162, VI.95, VII.38, 135; (*b*) alike. VII.69

licgan *v.* to lie. *infin.* **liggan** IV.50; *pres.3s.* **liõ** I.104, III.124, **liჳeõ** II.205; *pres.subj.s.* **licჳe** IV.183; *pret.3s.* **læჳ** I.8, 13, 60, 95, IV.274, **ჳelæჳ** IV.272; *pret.p.* **læჳen** VII.27; *pres.pt.* **licჳendæ** I.123

lichama *wk.m.* body. IV.60, 105, 168, 170, 274, V.36, 55, *etc.*

lichamlic *adj.* bodily. III.310, V.13, 14, VI.261

lichamlice *adv.* bodily, in the flesh. III.4 (**-chom-**), 310, V.91, 94

lician *v.* to please. *pres.3s.* **licæõ** VI.22, 214; *pres.subj.s.* **licie** II.195

(ჳe)licness *f.* likeness, image. II.56, 75

lif *n.* life. I.13, II.80, 92, 92, 109, 127, *etc.*, **liue** VI.155

lifedon, lifi(ჳ)ende(n) *see* **libban**

liggan *see* **licgan**

liჳ *m.* flame. VII.30, 59, 111, **leiჳ** VII.47

liht *n.* light. III.16, 117, 146, 192, 196, 200, *etc.*, **leoht(-)** IV.178, 184, 190, *etc.*

lim *n.* limb. III.354, IV.100, 161, V.88, 89, 90, 91, 94

ჳelimpan *v.* to befall. *pres.3s.* **ilimpõ** VI.87; *pret.3s.* **ჳe-/ilamp** IV.226, 240, V.155

litel *adj.* little. IV.226

liõ (*v.*) *see* **licgan**

liþ *m. or n.* joint. IV.100, 172

liõe *adj.* gentle, mild. II.220

liõnyss *f.* mildness, gentleness. II.219, 220

liue *see* **lif**

loca *interj.* look, look you. *Only in*
loca(-æ) hu, however, whatever. I.47
n., 86
locian *v.* to look, see. *infin.* **lokiæn**
VI.113, **loken** VI.208; *imper.s.* **loca**
VII.6; *pres.subj.s.* **loci3e** II.195; *pres.pt.*
lokinde III.23
lof *n.* praise. III.287, IV.282, 345, VII.163
lofsong *m.* song of praise, hymn. VII.38
3elo3ian *v.* to place, put. *pret.3s.*
3elo3ode II.51
lok- *see* **locian**
lomlic *adj.* frequent. V.12
long *n.* land, country, region. I.10, 42, 54,
82, 86, 141, *etc.*, **land(-)** III.4, IV.2, 9, 24,
271
long *adj.* long. III.266
longe *adv.* long, a long time, far. I.98,
VI.38, VII.70
longing ('-ung') *f.* longing, desire. VII.90
longlice *adv.* long, at length, for a long
time. I.35, **lang-** IV.299
losian *v.* to perish, be lost. *pres.3s.* **losæ͞o**
II.205; *pret.subj.p.* **loseden** II.76
Lucas Luke the Evangelist. II.110, 117,
121, *etc.*
lufian *v.* to love. *infin.* VI.259; *infl.infin.*
lufi3enne VII.84; *imper.s.* **lufe** IV.326;
pres.3s. **lufæ͞o** II.221, IV.290, 320,
VII.143; *pres.p.* **lufia͞o** IV.230, **lufiæ͞o**
III.226, IV.368, VII.77, 152; *pres.subj.p.*
lufien VII.141
luftlic *adj.* of the atmosphere, aerial.
VI.168 n.
lufu *f.* love. II.76, 95, 176, 190, *etc.*
lure ('lyre') *m.* loss, destruction. V.113,
VII.112
lust *m.* desire. V.14, VI.50, 261, VII.16
lustan ('lystan') *v.* to please. *pres.3s.* **lust**
VI.174
lusten *see* **lystan**
lustlice *adv.* gladly, willingly. VII.42
lybbæn *see* **libban**
lyfan *v.* to allow. *pp.* **ilyfed** V.129
(3e)lyfan, lifan *v.* to believe. *infin.* I.15,
66, 92, III.51, V.24, 87, **ilef-** I.62, 176;
infl.infin. **lyfene** V.83; *pres.1s.* **ilyfe**
III.100, 351; *pres.2s.* **ilefest** III.346, **ilyfest** III.96; *pres.3s.* **3elyfæ͞o** III.148, 150,
ilefæ͞o II.55; *pres.subj.s.* **ilefe** III.348,
ilyfe III.97; *pres.p.* **(i)lyfæþ** I.162,
IV.311; *pret.2s.* **ilyfdest** I.119; *pret.3s.*

(3e/i)lyfde I.20, 31, 74, 137, 156, 160,
IV.175; *pret.p.* **(3e/i)lyfdon** I.159, 167,
III.321, IV.17
lyfede, lyfedon *see* **libban**
ly3e *m.* lie, falsehood. V.102
lystan ('hlystan') *v.* to listen to, hear.
infin. V.79; *pres.subj.p.* **lystæn** VII.160,
lusten VII.131
lyt *indecl.adj.* few, little. VI.42
lytlian *v.* to lessen, diminish. *pp.* **ilytlod**
I.54

ma *indecl.sb.* more. IV.16, 17
macian *v.* to make, do, act. *infin.*
maki3en I.191; *pres.1s.* **maki3e** I.183;
pres.3s. **makæ͞o** I.200; *pres.subj.s.*
maky3e I.171; *pret.3s.* **macode** III.152,
makede III.18
mæde *see* **med**
mæ3 (*v.*) *see* **ma3an**
mæ3 *m.* kinsman. *np., ap.* **ma3as** III.56,
61, 66, **mæ3es** III.53; *gp.* **ma3a, -æ, -e,**
III.9, 11, 168, 170, 174; *dp.* **ma3um** IV.4
mæ3en *n.* might, virtue. IV.132, V.171,
VI.258, VII.142
mæ3enörym(m) *m.* majesty, glory.
IV.371, VI.5
mæ3racu *f.* genealogy. II.126
mæ3ö *f.* generation. II.113, 122, 123, 128,
128
mældian *v.* to inform against, accuse.
imper.s. **mælde** II.212
(3e)mænan *v.* to mean. *pres.3s.* **3emænö**
II.106; *pret.3s.* **mende** III.333
3emænelice *adv.* commonly. V.3, VI.149
mænniscæ *see* **mennisc**
mære *adj.* great, famous. III.319, IV.8, 9
mæsseþenung *f.* service of mass. IV.342
mæte *see* **mete**
mæ͞o *f.* (*a*) extent, degree. I.34; (*b*) (extent
of) power, ability. V.27
ma3an *v.* to be able, may. *pres.1 and 3s.*
mæ3 I.67, 76, 84, 88, 198, II.192, *etc.*;
pres.subj.s. **ma3e** IV.178, 207, 209, V.136,
188, *etc.*, **ma3æ** VI.201; *pres.p.* **ma3en**
III.178, IV.353, V.151, VI.119, 158, *etc.*,
ma3on III.268, 287, IV.139, VII.8, 17,
ma3e 3e/we II.96, III.221, IV.215, V.87;
pret.3s. **mihte** I.68, 71, 93, 191, 198,
III.82, *etc.*; *pret.p.* **mihton** IV.128, 138,
mihten I.190, III.104, 357, VI.25, 77,
224, VII.10
mak- *see* **macian**

man *n.* shameful action, crime. VII.57, 88

mandæd *f.* evil deed, crime, sin. VI.35

manful(l) *adj.* evil, wicked. III.173, 246, IV.74, VI.35; *as sb.* III.328, VII.54

manian *v.w.d. of person, g. of thing,* to claim what is due. *pret.3s.* **manode** II.9

man(n-) *see* **monn**

mansliht *m.* manslaughter, murder. IV.135

mara, -e *comp.adj.* greater, more. III.210, IV.57, 366, V.2, 2, 86, *etc.*; *as sb.* more. IV.215, VI.103

marȝen *m.* morning. *ds.* **mareȝen** *in the phrase* **þæs on mareȝen**, the next morning. I.22, 143

marmanstan *m.* marble. VII.117

martyr, martir *m.* martyr. IV.3, 16, 128, 335

martyrdom, (-tir-) *m.* martyrdom. IV.41, 44, 72, 209, 228, VI.161, 164

Matheus Matthew the Evangelist. II.114, V.17, VI.1

me *see* **ic**

me (III.162) *see* **monn**

mearcian *v.* to give heed to. *pret.3s.* **mearcode** VI.192 n.

med *f.* meed, reward. VII.150, **mæd-** VI.103

mende *see* **(ȝe)mænan**

(ȝe)mengan *v.* to mix, mingle. *pp.* **imeind** VI.55

men(n) *see* **monn, mann, man**

mennisc *adj.* human. V.50, 114, VI.44, 86, *etc.*, **mænnisc-** V.31

menniscness *f.* humanity. III.153, 198

merlice ('mærlice') *adv.* greatly, magnificently, splendidly. *comp.* **merlucor** VII.97

ȝemetan *v.* to find, meet, encounter. *pret.3s.* **imette** II.20, III.95; *pp.* **imette** VI.166

ȝemetan *v.* to measure. *pret.3s.* **ȝemet** VI.106

mete *m.* meat, food. IV.236, 239, 246, 263, V.43, 77, **mæte** V.42

meteleast *f.* want of food, famine. IV.50, 56

mi *see* **min**

mic(e)l-, miccl- *see* **mycel**

mid *prep.w.d.* with, among, by means of. I.6, 23, 24, 68, 70, 72, 98, *etc.*; **mid þam þe** *conj.* when, as. II.207, III.17, 292, IV.68 (**mid þam þæt**), 189

mid(d) *adj.* mid, middle. IV.238; in phrase **midne dæȝ** I.27, 148

middaneard *m.* earth, world. I.39, II.116, III.16, 16, 103, *etc.*

midwunung *f.* dwelling with others, fellowship. III.224, 235

miht *f.* might, power. I.76, 94, 127, 170, 183, 189, *etc.*

mihte(-), mihton *see* **maȝan**

mihtiȝ *adj.* powerful, mighty. VII.116

mihtleas *adj.* powerless. IV.56

milde *adj.* mild, merciful. II.201

mildelice *adv.* graciously, mercifully. II.156

mildheort *adj.* kind-hearted, meek. III.3, 146

mildheort(ed)ness *f.* mercy, compassion. II.201, 221, IV.210

milds *f.* mercy, kindness. VII.144, **milse** VII.147

(ȝe)mildsian, (-)miltsian *v.* to have pity (on s.o.), show mercy. *infin.* II.39, 181, IV.156, **milscian** IV.211; *imper.s.* **ȝemilsa** IV.149, **mildsæ** II.90; *pres.3s.* **mildsæð** II.58; *pres.subj.s.* **mildsiȝe** II.180, III.331; *pres.subj.p.* **mildsien** II.59; *pret.3s.* **mildsode** II.18, 39

mildsung *f.* mercy. I.80, II.85, 90

milse *see* **milds**

min *poss.pron.adj.* my, mine. I.17, 90, 104, 111, 116, II.45, *etc.*

mislic *adj.* various. IV.26

mismacian *v.* to misuse, squander. *pres.3s.* **mismaky** III.123 n.

mist *m.* mist, dimness. VI.22

mod *n.* mind, heart. I.185, II.184, III.125, 129, IV.125, *etc.*

modiȝ *adj.* proud. *as sb.* VII.72

molde *wk.f.* ground, earth. IV.301, VII.14, 128

mona *wk.m.* moon. VI.82, 89

ȝemong *prep.* among. *In* **imong þæt**, while. VI.20

monhata *wk.m.* man-hater. II.217 n.

moniȝ *pron.adj.* many. *as adj.* I.113, 166, III.173, IV.340, 342, *etc.*, **monie** V.20, VI.134; *as pron.* I.162

moni(ȝ)feald *adj.* manifold. II.106, VI.202

monn, mann, man *m.* (*ds., np., ap.* **men(n)**) (*a*) man. I.22, 79, 85, 98, 112, *etc.*; (*b*) *as indef.pron.*, one, *ns.* only.

(man, mon) I.41, 66, II.146, 189, 198, III.137, *etc.*, me III.162 n.

mon(n)cynn *n.* mankind. III.115, IV.306, V.7, 9, *etc.*

monð *m.* month. V.174, 179, 183

morþdæd *f.* murder, deed of violence. IV.135

morþer *n. or m.* murder. VII.88

mot ('ʒemot') *n.* meeting. II.6

[motan] *v.* to be permitted, may, must, can. *pres.3s.* mot VI.110; *pres.subj.s.* mote IV.362, VI.39, 115; *pres.p.* moten IV.355, V.160, 161, 188, VI.91, 126, *etc.*; *pres.subj.p.* moten IV.334, VI.265; *pret.3s.* moste IV.25, 29, V.85, 93; *pret.p.* mosten III.276, VI.243

Moyses Moses. II.136, 149, III.77, 78, *etc.*

mucel(-) *see* mycel(-)

-munan, munæð, etc. *see* (ʒe)mynan

munt *m.* hill, mountain. II.136, VII.108

murhð *f.* pleasure, joy. IV.334, V.11, 125, VI.43, 55, 56, *etc.*

muriʒe *adj.* pleasing, agreeable. VII.38

muð *m.* mouth. IV.82, V.76, VI.263, VII.49

mycclum *adv.* greatly, much. micclum IV.51

mycel *adj.* (*a*) great. I.76, 88, 166, 189, II.58, 108, III.328, mucel(-) II.48, III.81, V.160, 168, VI.84, 87, *etc.*, mic(-) III.246, 276, 333, IV.306; (*b*) much. II.94, 141, IV.5, 335, VI.149, VII.99, 99, mucel- VI.102, VII.100, 100

mycele *adv.* (*is. of* mycel), *w. comparatives* (by) much. I.84, II.159, VI.101, 103, 175, 237, mucele V.86, 95, VI.82, 100, 176, VII.84, mycel IV.314

(ʒe)mynan, -munan *v.* to remember, remind. *infin.* V.162, VI.51, 55, VII.18, 79, muneʒiæn VII.96; *pres.3s.* munæð VI.34; *pret.3s.* munede V.163 n.

ʒemynd *n. or f.* mind. III.261

myntan *v.* to intend. *pret.3s.* mynte VI.185

na *adv.* not, no. I.35, 109, 127, 135, 181, II.71, 92, *etc.*

nabban ('ne habban') *v.* not to have, have not. *pres.subj.s.* næbbe II.79, 81; *pres.p.* nabbæð VII.77, næbbæð II.172; *pret.3s.* næfde I.65, II.10

nædre *wk.f.* snake, serpent. IV.82

næfre *adv.* never. III.303, IV.20, V.52, 54,

103, 108, VI.67, *etc.*, næffre III.87, nefr- III.336, VII.52

næʒl *m.* nail. VI.116

næʒlian *v.* to nail. *pp.* inæʒlod VI.116

næle *see* nellan

nænne *see* nan

nære, næs *see* beon

naht, noht *n.* nothing. III.15, 190, 233, V.120, 167, VII.123

nam *see* niman

nama *wk.m.* name. III.165, IV.337, nom- I.192, IV.313, VII.146

nan *pron.adj.* not one, none, no. *as adj.* I.191, 198, 198, II.10, 79, 80, *etc.; mas.* nænne II.29, VI.29, 117, VII.95, nenne III.216, V.166, VI.119, 229; *fgs.* nare V.57; *as pron.* III.160, VI.108, VII.68, 70, 88, 89; *in phrase* nan þing, nothing. III.221, IV.108, 208, VII.76, 141

nat *see* nytan

nateshwon *adv.* not at all, by no means. I.122, II.212

naþor *adv. in correl. constr.* naþor ne ... ne ... neither ... nor ... V.145, neoþer VI.28, nowþre III.323

ne *particle* not. I.35, 69, 109, 128, 133, 182, *etc.*

neahʒebur *m.* neighbour. III.23

neahlæcan *v.* to approach. *pret.3s.* neahlæchede V.64, VI.26, 219; *pret.p.* neahlæcedon V.151

neawist *f.* nearness, neighbourhood. *ds.* neawiste V.28, 85, neawiste VI.60

nebb *n.* face, countenance. IV.214

ned *see* neod

nefr- *see* nefre

nellan, nyllan *v.* to be unwilling, will not. *pres.1s.* nelle IV.110, 112, 218; *pres.2s.* nelt II.197; *pres.3s.* nele III.325, VII.95, næle VII.96, nyle II.206; *pres.p.* nelle ʒe I.15, nylle ʒe I.62; *pret.2s.* noldest II.38, IV.152; *pret.3s.* nolde I.122, 131, II.29, 76, 157, 160, V.48, 72, VI.238; *pret.p.* nolden I.186, III.51, VI.238, VII.53, 58, 73, 74, noldon, III.323, IV.263, nolde ʒe I.176

nenne *see* nan

neod, ned *f.* need. VI.186, VII.63; sceolde nede gan, must needs go. VI.241

neorxnawang *m.* Paradise. VI.81

neoþer *see* naþor

neowen *see* niwe

nere, nes *see* **beon**
niht *f.* I.95, III.14, 189, 191, 201, 202, *etc.*
(3e)niman *v.* to take, seize. *pres.3s.*
  nimæþ VII.154; *pres.subj.s.* **3enime**
  VII.71, *pres.p.* **nimæð** II.49, VII.107;
  pret.3s. **nom** VI.10, **nam** V.81, 118
3enip *n.* mist, cloud. VI.21
nis *see* **beon**
niþ *m.* envy, hatred, spite. V.109, 116
niðer *adv.* down, beneath, below. III.147,
  nyðer VI.29, 230
niðerweard *adv.* downwards. II.116
niðfull *adj.* rancorous, malicious. IV.84
niwe, neowe *adj.* new. **neow-** III.280,
  niw- V.175
3enoh *adj.* enough. **inoh** II.70
noht *see* **naht**
nold- *see* **nellan**
nom *see* **niman**
nomæ(-e) *see* **nama**
nowþre *see* **naþor**
nu *adv.* now. I.19, 30, 32, 57, 78, 100, 112,
  etc.; *conj.* since. V.21
nuste, nute *see* **nytan**
nyl(l)- *see* **nellan**
nytan ('ne witan') *v.* not to know. *pres.1s.*
  nat III.69; *pres.p.* **nyten** III.58, 81,
  nyton III.333, **nute we** I.181, **nyte 3e**
  VII.4; *pres.subj.p.* **nyten** II.184; *pret.3s.*
  nyste I.71, **nuste** III.36; not to feel (*in*
  phrase **þanc nytan**). *pres.subj.s.* **nyte**
  VII.95
nytlic *adj.* useful, profitable. *sup.* VI.249
nyðer *see* **niðer**

of *prep.w.d.* of, from, out of, off. I.34, 42,
  50, 162, 163, 167, *etc.*
ofdredd ('ofdrædd') *adj.* terrified, afraid.
  VI.26
ofer *prep.w.a.* (*a*) over, above. I.39, 39, 164,
  III.19, 41, IV.34, 170, *etc.*; **ofer all,** *see*
  al(l); (*b*) after, beyond (*w.* **swa**). I.27,
  148
ofercuman *v.* to overcome. *infin.* IV.39,
  V.32, 62; *pret.3s.* **ofercom** V.30, 114; *pp.*
  ofercumen VI.183–4, 192
oferflowan *v.* to overflow, run over. *pp.*
  oferfleowen VII.50
oferglidan *v.* to glide over. *pret.3s.* **ofer-**
  glad III.213 n.
oferho3ian *v.* to despise, scorn. *pret.p.*
  oferho3oden VII.53

oferhudi3 ('-hydig') *adj.* proud, arrogant.
  as sb. VII.72
oferhyd *f.* pride, arrogance. VII.11
oferi3endlice ('oferhygdlice') *adv.* arro-
  gantly, presumptuously. V.111 n.
oferlufu *wk.f.* excessive love. VII.134
ofermede *n.* pride. VII.128
ofermetto *f.* pride, arrogance. VII.12
ofersceadwian *v.* to cover with a shadow,
  overshadow. *pret.3s.* **ofersceadewæde**
  VI.21
oferscinan *v.* to cover with light, illumine.
  pres.p. **oferscinæð** VI.96, **-scineð** VI.98
oferstigan *v.* to surpass, excel. *pres.3s.*
  oferstihð IV.319, VI.105 (*sg. for pl.*), 110
  (*sg. for pl.*)
oferswiðan *v.* to overpower, overcome.
  infin. IV.38, 139, 233, 253; *pp.* (*decl.*)
  oferswið(e)d- IV.71, 76, 94, 147, 176,
  215, 228
ofsceamian *v.* to put to shame. *pp.*
  ofsceamod IV.233
ofseon *v.* to see, observe. *pret.3s.* **ofseah**
  III.6
ofsettan *v.* to afflict, oppress. *pret.p.*
  ofsettan IV.166
ofslean *v.* to slay. *pret.3s.* **ofsloh** IV.16
oft(e) *adv.* often. II.2, 69, 97, 129, IV.134,
  258, V.155, 156, VII.1
oftorfian *v.* to stone. *infin.* I.178
ofþryccan *v.* to press, oppress. *pret.3s.*
  ofðryhte II.24
ofwundrod (*pp. of* 'ofwundrian') *adj.*
  astonished. IV.61
on *prep.w.d.a.* on, in. I.4, 5, 7, 19, 22, 25, 29,
  32, *etc.*; **on an,** *see* **an; on ær,** *see* **ær**
onbrurdness ('-bryrd-') *f.* stimulus,
  inspiration. III.328
oncnawan *v.* to know, realise, understand. *pres.1s.* **oncnawe** IV.133;
  pres.subj.s. **oncnawe** IV.147; *pres.p.*
  oncnawaþ IV.185; *pret.3s.* **oncneow**
  I.28, 153, III.352
onde *see* **anda**
ondrædan *v.* often *with refl.dat.pron.* to
  fear, dread. *imper.s.refl.* **ondræed**
  IV.325; *imper.p.refl.* **ondredæþ** VI.27,
  227; *pres.1s.refl.* **ondræde** IV.154, 210,
  not *refl.* 155; *pret.3s.* not *refl.* **ondredde**
  V.57
onfon *v.* to take, receive, undergo. *infin.*
  VI.8, 86

ongean *prep.w.a.* against. IV.13, 13, 69; *as adv.* again, in return. IV.164, 171
onginnan *v.* to begin, set about. *pret.3s.* **ongon** II.114, V.23, 26, **ongan** II.118, V.101
on3itan *v.* to perceive, recognize, judge. *imper.s.* **on3it** VII.13
onhende *adj.* on hand. III.20
onhinderling *adv.* back. V.138, 141
onlihtan *v.* to illumine, make bright. *pres.3s.* **onliht** III.128, 194; *pres.p.* **onlihtæð** I.151; *pret.3s.* **onlihte** III.149; *pp.* (*decl.*) **onlihte** III.368
onræs *m.* attack, assault. IV.244
onscynian *v.* to abhor. *imper.s.* **onscyne** VII.13
onsi3an *v.* to descend. *pres.pt.* **onsi3endum** III.223
onstellan *v.* to institute, set. *infin.* **-stæll-** V.10; *pret.3s.* **onstealde** V.5, 116
onsundrum *adv.* (*a*) especially. V.2 (**-dren**); (*b*) apart. II.61 (**-dron**), VI.12 (**-dræn**), 59 (**-dron**)
ontendan *v.* to set fire to. *pret.3s.* **ontende** IV.160
(3e-)openian *v.* to open; disclose, expound. *infin.* III.82, 89, 338, 341, IV.298; *pret.3s.* **3eopenode** III.59, IV.171; *pp.* **iopenod** V.74, (*decl.*) II.119
openlice *adv.* openly. II.66, 210, 213, 213, V.7, 23, 151, VI.252
ordfryma *wk.m.* source, origin. III.118
ormæte *adj.* immense, excessive. IV.126, **ormet-** III.258, IV.15
oð *prep.w.a.* until. III.225, 231, 237, 253, IV.231
oðer *pron.adj.* (*str.decl. only*) other, another. *as adj.* I.52, 103, II.21, 59, 78, 81, 89, 90, *etc.*; *as pron.* I.115, II.26, 33, 112, 123, 210, 215, *etc.*; **oþer ... oþer ...**, one ... another ... III.236
oððæt, oððet (*a*) *conj.* until. II.31, 42, 163, III.156, IV.6, 272, VI.162; (*b*) *prep.w.a.* until (*cf.* **oþ**). II.115
oððe *conj.* or. I.171, 173, 192, II.64, III.9, 11, *etc.*, **oðer** V.85, 121, *etc.*; *as correl.* **oþþe ... oþþe**, either ... or ... IV.135-6, VI.136-7

paralisim paralysis, palsy. I.105 n.
paternoster the Lord's Prayer. II.99
Paulus St. Paul the Apostle. III.130, IV.331, VI.97

pene3 ('peni3') *m.* penny. *gp.* **pene3æ** II.22, 140
Petrus St. Peter. II.60, 69, 96, III.213, VI.10, *etc.*
Pilatus Pontius Pilate. V.91
pin *f.* pain, torment. III.161, 251 n., VII.55, 77, 157
pinian *v.* to torment, torture. *pres.3s.* **pinæð** II.204
pistol *m.* epistle, letter. II.169, III.130
preost *m.* priest. IV.36
prophete *m.* prophet. VI.16 n.
psalm, psealmsong *see* **sealm, sealmsong**
pund *n.* pound (of money). II.9, 139

racu *f.* account, narrative, exposition. VI.42
racenteah *f.* chain, fetter. *dp.* **racentea3um** IV.48
rædan *v.* (*a*) to read. *pres.p.* **rædæþ** V.101, **rædeð** VI.69; (*b*) to advise. *pres.subj.p.* **ræden** VII.130
rædeste *see* **read**
rædlice ('hrædlice') *adv.* quickly. VI.14, 169, VII.73
ræn ('ren') *m.* rain. VII.135
ræst- *see* **rest(-)**
ræðe *see* **raðe**
ræðnesse *see* **reðness**
ran *see* **rinan**
raðe, ræðe ('hraþe') *adv.* quickly, soon, at once. I.30, 155, II.25, IV.264, VII.136
read *adj.* red. VII.29: *sup.* **rædeste** VII.114
reccan *v.* (*a*) to explain, expound. *infin.* V.101; (*b*) to rule, direct. *pres.3s.* **reccæð** V.123
3erecednyss *f.* narrative. IV.10
receleas *adj.* reckless. VII.53
re3ol *m.* rule. III.84
3ereord *n.* language. IV.10
reosan ('hreosan') *v.* to fall. *pres.p.* **reosæð** VII.136
reowan *see* **rowan**
repung ('hrepung') *f.* touch. III.215
rest *f.* (*a*) rest, quiet. VI.93, VII.150; (*b*) bed, couch. **ræste** VII.117
restan *v.* to rest. *infin.* VI.91; *pres.subj.s.* **reste** IV.217
restanda3 *m.* day of rest, Sabbath. III.271, 293, 306, 308, **-ræst-** III.38, 44, 269, 285, 289, 291

reðe *adj.* fierce, savage. IV.131, 244, 264
reþelice *adv.* fiercely. VII.47
reðnyss *f.* cruelty, severity. IV.31, 121, 156, ræð- II.202
ribb *n.* rib. III.343
rice *n.* kingdom, realm. I.53, II.5, 53, III.241, IV.331, V.119, 120, *etc.*
rice *adj.* mighty; rich (in wealth). VI.6, 38, VII.1, 5, 126; *sup.* VII.116; *as sb.* I.130, III.255
riht *n.* what is right, the right. III.326; mid rihte, justly. VII.130
rihtlæcen *v.* to correct, rectify, amend. *infin.* II.199; *pres.subj.s.* ȝerihtlæce II.65; *pp.* irihtlæht II.202, 214
rihtlic *adj.* right, fitting. V.176, VI.106
rihtlice *adv.* rightly, justly, correctly. I.74, II.55, III.243, IV.316, V.165, VI.157, 165
rihtwis *adj.* righteous, just. II.175, III.243
ȝerihtwisian *v.* to justify. *pp.* irihtwisod III.332
rihtwisness *f.* righteousness. IV.351, V.31, 32, 114–5
rinan ('hrinan') *v.* to touch. *infin.* V.93; *pret.s.* ran VI.26
rixian *v.* to rule, govern, reign. *pres.3s.* rixæð I.36, V.190, VI.268, VII.93, 167; *pres.p.* rixiæð VII.165; *pret.p.* rixoden I.40
rod *f.* the cross, rood. VI.116
roderlic *adj.* celestial, heavenly. VII.36
rof ('hrof') *m.* roof. I.110
Rom Rome. I.37
rowan *v.* to row. *pret.p.* reowan IV.269
rune ('ryne') *m.* running, course, orbit. VI.91
rune ('ruine') *f.* fall. VII.107 n.
ruwa *wk.m.* rug, covering, tapestry. VII.118

sæ (*pron.*) *see* þe
sæ *f.* sea. IV.260, 262, 265, 267
sæcc ('sacc') *m.* sack, bag. IV.261
sæcgan *v.* to say, speak. *infin.* I.33, 186, III.107, VI.201, *etc.*, sægg- V.1, VI.41, secg- III.267, V.16, VI.76, 163; *infl.infin.* sæcgenne I.181, sæggene VI.249, sec-gene IV.323; *imper.s.* sæȝe I.169, II.66, sæȝ VII.7; *imper.p.* sæcgð I.172, secgað IV.185, 281; *pres.1s.* sæcge I.182, II.71, secge IV.286; *pres.2s.* sæȝest II.104, seȝst IV.104; *pres.3s.* sæȝð I. 59, 157, II.44, 107, *etc.*, sæð

III.328, VII.36, seȝð IV.10; *pres.p.* sæcgæð I.175, 177, II.52, *etc.*, secgæð III.54, VI.153, seȝað IV.21, sæcge we VI.129, secgæ we VI.198; *pret.1 and 3s.* sæde II.4, 44, 70, 73, *etc.*, sæȝde V.34; *pret.p.* sæden I.26, 147, II.74, IV.338, VI.150, sædon II.121, III.26, 27, *etc.*; *pret.subj.p.* sæden VI.31, 232; *pp.* isæd I.32, III.106, IV.297, VI.236, 256, iseid V.103, isæid VI.58
sæcð *see* secan
sæd *n.* seed. IV.317
isæȝe(-) *see* seon
sæl *m.* time, occasion. VI.248
sælic *adj.* of the sea. IV.257, 275
ȝesæliȝ *adj.* happy. IV.42, VII.56, iseliȝe IV.332, VII.152
sælra ('selra') *adj.comp.* better. VII.141
(i)sæt *see* settan
Sæteresdæȝ *m.* Saturday. III.273, 278
sæð *see* sæcgan
sagol *m.* club, cudgel. IV.123, 159
Salomon Solomon. III.329
Samaria Samaria. *gs.* I.158
(ȝe)samnung *f.* meeting, assembly. III.62, 65, VI.132
samod *adv.* together. VII.60
sanctus *adj.* saint. V.17, VI.1, 97, 177, *etc.*
sang (*v.*) *see* singan
sang *m.* song, singing. IV.201, song VII.163
sar *n.* bodily pain, wound. VI.115, 119, VII.89
sarlice *adv.* sorely, painfully. V.134
sawan *v.* to sow. *pret.p.* seowon I.164; *pp.* (*decl.*) isawene IV.286
sawol *f.* soul. I.151, IV.290, 291, *etc.*
scæde *see* sceadu
scæwæde, scawedon *see* (ȝe)sceawian
ȝescead *n.* reason, discretion, reckoning. II.7, 209
(ȝe)sceadan *v.* to separate, divide. *infin.* VI.50; *pres.3s.* sceadæþ VII.34; *pp.* ȝeiscead VI.123, (*decl.*) isceadde VI.59, VII.62
sceadu *f.* shade, shadow. VII.5, scæd-III.214, 215, 216
(ȝe)sceaft *f.* created being. I.83, IV.319, V.69, 70, 123
sceal, scealt *see* sceolan
sceamian *v.* (*impers.w.d. of person*) to cause shame to, make ashamed. *pres.3s.* sceamiȝe IV.258

scean *see* **scinan**
isceapen *see* **ӡescyppan**
scearp *adj.* sharp, piercing. IV.140
scearpe *adv.* sharply, keenly. IV.180
(ӡe)sceat *m.* property, goods, wealth.
II.37, 159, 163
(ӡe)sceawian *v.* (*a*) to look at. *imper.s.*
sceawe VII.14, **ӡesceawæ** I.81; *imper.p.*
sceawiað IV.199; *pres.subj.p.* **sceawiæn**
VII.2; *pret.ӡs.* **sceawode** VI.189; *pp.*
isceawod VII.21; (*b*) to show. *infin.*
sceawen VI.46; *pres.ӡs.* **sceawæð** V.130;
pret.ӡs. **sceawde** VI.218, **sceawede**
V.119, **s[c]æwæde** VI.187; *pret.p.*
s[c]awedon VI.142 n.; *pp.* **isceawed**
VII.52
scencan *v.* to give drink, pour out drink.
pret.ӡs. **scencte** IV.87
sceocca *m.* evil spirit, devil. V.139
isceofene *see* **scufan**
sceolan *v.* (*a*) shall, must, ought. *pres. 1
and ӡs.* **sceal** I.66, II.69, *etc.*; *pres.2s.*
scealt II.25, 71, 214; *pres.subj.s.* **sceole**
I.109; *pres.p.* **sceolon** I.134, II.97, 178,
etc., **sceolen** I.126, II.131, IV.349, *etc.*,
sceole we V.145, 166, VI.261; *pret.ӡs.*
sceolde I.12, 74, 92, *etc.*; *pret.p.* **sceoldon** I.55, **sceoldan** IV.58, **sceolden**
II.41, 162, VI.8, *etc.*; (*b*) owe. *pres.ӡs.*
sceal II.78; *pret.ӡs.* **sceolde** II.139, 141,
158
-sceop *see* **ӡescyppan**
sceort *adj.* short. IV.328
sceortlice *adv.* briefly. I.32, III.329,
IV.297
scinan *v.* to shine. *pres.ӡs.* **scinæð** VI.100,
scynæð I.81; *pres.p.* **scinæð** VI.127,
133, VII.164, **scineð** VI.79; *pret.ӡs.*
scean VI.13, 74; *pres.pt.* **scinendæ**
VI.74, 126
scir *f.* district, province. I.4
iscop *see* **ӡescyppan**
scræman *v.* to scream. *pres.ӡs.* **scræmeð**
VII.87 n.
scrift *m.* confessor. **scrifft-** VII.131
scrydan *v.* to clothe. *pres.subj.p.* **scrydæn**
VII.113
scufan *v.* to shove, push. *pp.* (*decl.*) **isceofene** VII.54
scur *m.* shower, storm. VII.135
scyldan *v.* to shield, protect. *pres.p.*
scyldæþ V.107; *pret.2s.* **scyldest** VI.63
scyldiӡ *adj.* guilty. (*as sb.*) VII.48

scynæð *see* **scinan**
scyncreft ('scincræft') *m.* magic, deceptive art. V.124
ӡescyppan *v.* to form, create. *pret.ӡs.*
(ӡe)isceop III.342, V.69, **iscop** V.70;
pp. **isceapen** I.83, VI.68
Scyppend *m.* the Creator. III.129, 287
ӡescyrtan *v.* to shorten. *imper.s.* **ӡescyrt**
IV.150
se *see* **þe**
iseaӡen, (i)**seah** *see* **(ӡe)seon**
sealde(-) *see* **syllan**
sealm *m.* psalm. IV.193, **psalm-** VI.61
sealmsong *m.* psalmody. **psealm-** V.186
sealmwurhta *wk.m.* psalmist. I.194
secan *v.* to seek, visit. *infin.* **sechon** VI.4;
imper.p. **secaþ** IV.177; *pres.ӡs.* **sæcð**
VII.24, **seceð** VII.101; *pres.subj.p.* **secea
we** VII.159
secg- *see* **sæcgan**
sechon *see* **secan**
seӡað, **seӡst**, **seӡð** *see* **sæcgan**
(i)seӡen *see* **(ӡe)seon**
iseid *see* **sæcgan**
iseliӡe *see* **ӡesæliӡ**
sellice *see* **syllic**
selost *adv.sup.* best. III.287, V.185
seluen *see* **sylf**
sendan *v.* to send. *infin.* **senden** I.85,
V.113; *pres.ӡs.* **send** I.82, **sendeþ**
VII.143, 144; *pret.ӡs.* **sende** I.50, III.13,
V.40; *pp.* **isend** VI.125, (*decl.*) **isende**
V.156, 158
seo *see* **þe**
seoc *adj.* sick, ill. I.8
seocnyss *f.* sickness, illness. I.101
seofan, -en, -on *num.* seven. II.70, 71, 72,
etc.
seofonfeald *adj.* sevenfold. I.151
seofoða *adj.* seventh. I.149
seolf(-) *see* **sylf**
seolfor *n.* silver. VII.114
seolfren *adj.* made of silver. VII.118
(ӡe)seon *v.* to see. *infin.* III.104, 129, 357,
IV.364, V.127, VI.47, *etc.*; *imper.s.*
ӡeseoh VII.15; *pres.1s.* **iseo** III.70;
pres.2s. **isixt** III.29; *pres.ӡs.* **ӡesyhð**
IV.91, **isihð** II.183, III.55, 58, 163; *pres.p.*
i-/ӡeseoþ III.105, 358, 367, IV.143, 259,
VI.72, *etc.*; *pres.subj.p.* **iseon** I.15, 62,
III.104, 357; *pret.1 and ӡs.* **(i)seah** II.120,
III.34, 42, 359, V.55, VI.178, *etc.*; *pret.2s.*
isæӡe III.99, 350; *pret.subj.s.* **iseӡe**

III.39; *pret.p.* **isæȝen** I.165, II.32, VI.17, 24, 222, 232, *etc.*, **iseaȝen** III.25, **(i)seȝen** III.364, VI.8, 28, 31, 43, 76, 232, 246, **iseȝon** III.362, 366; *pres.pt.* (*as sb.*) **ȝeseondan** IV.143; *pp.* (*decl.*) **isæȝene** VI.144

seoreȝ- *see* **sorȝ**

seowon *see* **sawan**

seruian *v.* to serve, minister to. *pret.p.* **seruedon** V.151 n.

ȝesetnyss *f.* ordinance, decree, law. II.147

(ȝe)settan *v.* (*a*) to set, put, set down, appoint. *pres.ȝs.* **sæt** VII.34; *pret.ȝs.* **(ȝe)sette** I.50, 51, II.30, 82, 99, 143, V.81; *pret.p.* **setten** VII.127; *pp.* **iset** I.112, IV.317, 328, VI.241, **isæt** VI.161, **isett** II.133, (*decl.*) **isette** IV.341; (*b*) to settle (a case). *infin.* II.7

siȝan *v.* to sink, descend. **siȝæð** VII.82

siȝe *m.* victory. IV.73, 258

siȝefæst *adj.* victorious. IV.204, 228

(ȝe)sihð *f.* sight. III.342, 366, IV.259, VI.31, 40, 188, 219, *etc.*

Siloe, Syloe (the pool of) Siloam. III.21, 33, 157

simle *see* **symle**

singal *adj.* continual. VII.149

singan *v.* to sing. *pres.subj.p.* **singæn** VII.162; *pret.ȝs.* **song** I.194, **sang** IV.164, 193; *pp.* **isungen** V.104

sittan *v.* to sit. *infin.* III.25

siþ *m.* time, occasion. II.70, 71, 72, 72, V.155, VI.90, 188; **tyn siðes tene**, ten times ten. II.140

siðian *v.* to journey, go, travel. *infin.* I.131; *pres.p.* **siþiæð** VII.60, *pret.ȝs.* **siðode** I.69

six *num.* six. I.6, V.179, 180, 182, VI.9, 64, 69

sixta *ord.num.* sixth. VI.70

sixtiȝ *num.* sixty. V.179

slæp *m.* sleep. IV.189

slean *v.* to strike. *infl.infin.* **sleanne** IV.115; *pres.pt.* **sleande** IV.122

smeagan *v.* to consider, meditate, inquire, deliberate. *pret.p.* **smeadan** I.174

smek ('smec') *m.* smoke. VII.135

smercian *v.* to smile. *pret.ȝs.* **smercode** IV.141

smirian *v.* to smear, anoint. *pret.ȝs.*

smirede III.19, **smirode** III.31, 41, 155; *pp.* (*decl.*) **ismirode** III.163

snaw *m.* snow. VI.14, 131

softe *adj.* soft. IV.217, 224

sona, -æ, -e *adv.* immediately, at once. I.24, 96, 115, 145, *etc.*

song (*v.*) *see* **singan**; (*n.*) *see* **sang**

sorȝ *f.* care, anxiety, sorrow, grief. *ds.* **sore3-** VI.54, VII.113, **seore3-** VI.94, VII.59, 89

soð *adj.* true. I.136, II.57, 85, 176, III.128, 149, *etc.*

soð *n.* truth. I.179, 186, II.45, 165, IV.300; *as adv.* (translating 'amen'), truly, verily. IV.286, 286

soðfæst, -fest- *adj.* true, faithful. III.83, 302, IV.19, VI.59, 79, 124, *etc.*; *as sb.* VII.32, 34, 36, 56, 60

soðfæstness, -fest- *f.* truth. II.173, III.324, IV.86, 351

soðlice *adv.* truly, in truth, surely, indeed. III.55, 56, 83, 111, 149, *etc.*

spæc ('spræc') *f.* speech. I.20, 137, II.7 n., III.132, 207, 220, 229, **spec-** V.38, VI.263, VII.161, **sprece** II.52

spæc- *see* **specan**

spætan *v.* to spit. *pret.ȝs.* **spætte** III.17, 152

spatle *n.* spittle, saliva. III.18, 152

specan, spæcan ('sprecan') *v.* to speak. *infin.* II.2, VII.10, 17; *pres.ȝs.* **spæcð** III.99, **spæky** III.350, **specð** IV.82; *pres.subj.p.* **spæken** VII.161; *pret.ȝs.* **spæc** II.8, III.78, 313, 340, **spec** V.74, 114, VI.2, 211; *pret.subj.s.* **speke** V.126, VI.184; *pret.p.* **spæcon** III.307, **specon** VI.16, 143, 145, 147, **speken** VI.20, 142

Speonisc *adj.* Spanish. IV.2

sprece *see* **spæc**

spurnan ('spyrran') *v.* to strike, spar. *infin.* V.100; *pres.p.* **spurneð** V.108

stæfne *see* **stefn**

stæȝer *adj.* steep. VI.52

stænen *adj.* stone, made of stone. II.134, V.40

stæppan *v.* to step, go, proceed. *pret.ȝs.* **stop** I.96; *pret.p.* **stopon** IV.271

stan *m.* stone. I.178, IV.261, 266, V.65, 66, 72, 100, 108

standan *v.* to stand. *pres.p.* **standeþ** VI.217, **stondæþ** VI.69, VII.107, 109; *pret.subj.s.* **stode** VI.240

stefn, stæfne *f.* voice. VI.21, 24, 213, 255
steor *f.* (*a*) guidance, direction. II.137, 143; (*b*) punishment, penalty. II.215
steoran, styran *v.* to steer, guide; to reprove. *infin.* steor- II.189, 197, 198, -styr- II.200, 214, 217; *pres.3s.* steoræð II.220, styreð V.124; *pp.* (*decl.*) isteoredæ II.210, istyrede II.215
steorra *wk.m.* star. VI.98
sti3an *v.* to ascend. *infin.* VI.259
stilness *f.* tranquillity. VII.161
stincan *v.* to stink. *pres.pt.* stincende I.96
stiþ *adj.* stiff, hard, stern. II.41, 162
stiðlice *adv.* severely. II.200
stiðness *f.* severity, strictness. II.154, 206
stode, stondæþ *see* standan
stop(-) *see* stæppan
stow *f.* place. I.67, 75, 77, 103, II.53, VI.160
stræt *f.* road. III.212
strand *n.* shore (of sea). IV.271, 274
strang *adj.* strong. IV.174, VII.105
(3e)strangian *v.* to strengthen, confirm. *infin.* strengæn VI.75; *pp.* 3estrangod IV.202, istrongæd V.43
strec *adj.* strict, severe. VII.33
strengæn *see* (3e)strangian
3estreon *n.* treasure. VII.132, 135
istreone *see* (3e)strynan
strewian *v.* to strew. *imper.p.* strewiað IV.179
stronge ('strange') *adv.* strongly. V.74
(3e)strynan *v.* to gain, acquire. *pres.2s.* strynest II.62; *pres.subj.s.* istreone VII.154
stunt *adj.* foolish, stupid. II.198
-styr- *see* steoran
sum *pron.adj.* some, a certain, one. *as adj.* I.7, 33, 43, 102, *etc.*; *as pron.* I.78, *etc.*
sunbeam *m.* sunbeam. IV.191
sund *see* beon
sunderhal3a *wk.m.* Pharisee. III.270, synd- III.37, 39, 43, 47
sunderlice *adv.* apart, separately. V.103
sundfullice *adv.* safely. VI.161
sundfulness *f.* safety. VII.41
sundri3 ('syndrig') *adj.* separate. VI.186, 190
sunegode *see* syngian
sunful(l) *see* synful
sunn- *see* synn
Sun(n)andæ3, -nend- *m.* Sunday. III.273, V.181

sunne *wk.f.* sun. I.81, VI.13, 80, 82, 89, 90, *etc.*; synne VI.74
sunu *m.* son. I.8, 12, 17, 19, 23, 25, *etc.*
susl *f. or n.* torment. IV.150
suwian *v.* to be silent. *pres.3s.* suwige IV.140
swa *adv.conj.* so, as, thus. I.54, 70, 71, 87, 101, 109, *etc.*; swa ofer, just after. I.27, 148; swa swa *conj.* so as, just as. I.59, 66, 69, 93, 119, 124, *etc.*; swa þeah *adv.* however, nevertheless. I.35, 65, 122, 167, II.26, 200, *etc.*; swa þæt, so that (*expressing purpose, result*). I.38
swælt(-) *see* sweltan
3eswæncan *see* 3eswencan
swær *adj.* heavy, grievous. *comp.* IV.93
swæsende *n.* food. V.181
swang *see* swingan
swarte *see* sweart
swaðeah *adv.* however, nevertheless. II.182, IV.161, 233
swaðu *f.* trace, vestige. VI.116
sweart *adj.* black, dark. IV.241, 246, VII.51, swart- III.202
swefet ('sweofot') *n.* sleep. VII.26
swe3 *m.* song, melody. VII.60
swelan *v.* to burn (*intrans.*). *pres.pt.* sweli3ende VII.28
sweltan *v.* to die. *infl.infin.* swæltanne IV.336, -ænne IV.325; *pres.3s.* swæltæð VII.88; *pret.subj.s.* swælte I.17, swelte I.90
3eswencan *v.* to afflict, oppress. *infin.* IV.117 (-swænc-), *pp.* iswenced VII.106
3eswencednyss *f.* affliction, tribulation. IV.94
swetnes *f.* sweetness. VI.175
3eswican *v.* (*a*) to cease. *pres.subj.s.* 3eswice IV.110; (*b*) *w.g.* to cease from, desist from. *infin.* IV.155
swilce *see* swylce
swincan *v.* to work, labour. *pres.2s.* swinces VII.11
swingan *v.* to flog, beat. *pret.3s.* swang IV.159
swingel *f.* stroke, scourging. II.191
swink ('swinc') *n.* labour, hardship. VII.150
swiðe *adv.* very, much, greatly. II.25, 33, 175, III.122, 173, 278, IV.12, *etc.*, swyðe I.188, VII.12; *comp.* more greatly, rather. swiðer VII.98, swiðor IV.21, 117, 121,

122, *etc.*, **swyðor** I.84, IV.91; *sup.* chiefly, especially. **swiðost** IV.109, 210, VII.136, **swyðest** I.4

swiðlic *adj.* very great, intense, severe. II.30; *comp.* IV.254

swiðra *comp.adj.* (*a*) right (hand or side). VII.35 (**-ðere**); (*b*) stronger, greater. VII.105

swulc *see* **swylc**

swutel *adj.* clear. IV.273

(ʒe)swutelian *v.* to make clear, show, declare. *pret.3s.* **ʒeswutelode** II.130, **swytelode** V.45; *pret.subj.s.* **(ʒe)swutelode** I.125, 134; *pp.* (*decl.*) **iswutelode** III.176, **iswytelode** III.12, 171

swutelice *adv.* clearly. III.111, 364, **swytellice** II.183, III.106

swylc *pron.adj.* such. *as adj.* I.171, 191, III.84, 334; *as pron.* I.188, VI.99, VII.15, 134, **swulc** VII.15

swylce (*a*) *conj.* as if. III.316, **swilce** IV.69, 120, 191, 211, 276, **swylc** III.125, 299, VI.184; (*b*) *adv.* likewise, also. VI.206, VII.108

(i)swytelode, swytellice *see* **(ʒe)swutelian, swutelice**

swyð- *see* **swiðe**

ʒesyhð *see* **(ʒe)seon**

sylf *pron.adj.* (*decl.str. in agreement w. noun or pers. pron.*) (*a*) self, myself, himself, *etc.* I.31, 75, 112, 129, 135, 136, 156, 157, *etc.*, **seluen** V.130, **syluen** V.142, **seolf(-)** II.42, 214, III.282, 307, IV.352, V.165; *in ns. agreeing w. subj. sometimes preceded by refl.d.pron.* **me sylf** I.107, IV.294, **him sylf** I.200, III.192, IV.288, 303, VI.3, 79, **him seolf** III.28, **us sylfe** I.135, V.167–8, **us sylfæn** VII.18, **eow seolfe** III.268; (*b*) same, very, own. II.86, IV.109

sylfwill *n.* free-will. V.25

syllan *v.* (*a*) to give. *infin.* V.175, VI.6, VII.73; *pres.1s.* **sylle** V.132, VII.148, 150; *pres.3s.* **sylþ** VII.99; *pret.3s.* **sealde** IV.305, V.39, 93; *pret.p.* **sealden** IV.344; (*b*) to sell (**wið**, for). *infin.* II.13

syllic ('seldlic') *adj.* strange, extraordinary, wonderful. I.170, IV.207, **sellic(-)** III.37)

Syloe *see* **Siloe**

symle *adv.* ever, always. I.126, IV.255, V.117, VII.37, **symble** IV.182, **simle** III.25, 286, IV.351

Synai, Synay Mt. Sinai. II.136, V.38

synd *see* **beon**

synderhalʒan *see* **sunderhalʒa**

ʒesyne *adj.* visible, evident. VII.162

synful(l) *adj.* sinful. III.46, 68, 69, 301, 334, *etc.*, **sunful(-)** V.89, 94, VI.111

syngian *v.* to sin. *pres.3s.* **synegæð** II.61; *pret.3s.* **sunegode** V.53; *pp.* **isyngod** V.51

synlic *adj.* sinful. VI.50

synn *f.* sin. I.152, II.79, 98, 101, 103, 124, 125, *etc.*, **synum** III.92, **sunn(-)** V.8, 9, 54, VII.12

synne *see* **sunne**

syððan *adv.* afterwards, since. I.98, II.73, 100, 129, 186, III.32, *etc.*, **syðan** (**-æn**, **-on**) V.140, 141, 142, 143, VI.83, 126

tacn, tacen *n.* token, sign. I.15, 62, 165, 191, III.46, 113, 204, *etc.*

(ʒe)tacnian *v.* to signify, betoken. *pres.3s.* **tacnæð** IV.305, VI.59; *pres.p.* **tacnæð** VI.146; *pret.3s.* **tacnode** III.115, 277, **tacnedo** VI.156; *pret.p.* **(ʒe)tacnoden** III.112, VI.130; *pp.* (*decl.*) **itacnode** VI.165

(ʒe)tacnung *f.* signification, token. II.108, III.276, IV.317, **tacnuncg** II.132

tæcan *v.* to show, direct, teach. *pres.1s.* **tæche** VII.149; *pres.3s.* **tæcæð** II.207, 216, **tæcð** III.162; *pres.subj.p.* **tæcæn** VII.130; *pret.3s.* **tæhte** II.221, V.163

tæcing *f.* teaching, doctrine. V.166, 175, **teachunge** V.117

ʒetæl *see* **ʒetel**

ʒetæld *n.* tent, tabernacle. *ds.* **itælde** II.148

teachung *see* **tæcing**

(i)tealde *see* **(ʒe)tellan**

tealt *adj.* unstable, precarious. VII.137

tear *m.* tear. VII.50, 146

teart *adj.* sharp, severe. IV.165

(ʒe)tel, (ʒe)tæl *n.* number. I.150, II.106, 131, 138, 142, 144

(ʒe)tellan *v.* (*a*) to count, reckon. *infl.infin.* **tellenne** II.114; *pret.3s.* **tealde** II.110, 116, 117, 121, 126; (*b*) to consider. *pp.* (*decl.*) **itealde** III.134; (*c*) to ascribe, assign. *pret.3s.* **tealde** III.183, *pp.* (*decl.*) **itealde** II.148

teman ('timan') *v.* to resort to, appeal to. *prep.p.* **temdon** III.319

tempel *n.* temple. III.329, V.82, VI.190

tempelhus *n.* temple. VI.191
ten(-) *see* **tyn, tynfeald**
teona *wk.m.* injury, insult. VI.237
teonfull *adj.* grievous, causing hurt. III.134
teoða *wk.adj.* tenth. V.174, 178, 182
teoðe (*n.*) *see* **toþ**
teran *v.* to tear. *pres.p.* **teræð** VII.48
Thabor (Mount) Tabor. VI.231
tid *f.* time, hour, season, period. I.25, 29, 120, 146, 149, 154, *etc.*
tiȝele *wk.f.* tile, brick. IV.179
tihtan *v.* to stretch, draw out. *pres.ȝs.* **tiht** IV.103; *pret.p.* **tihton** IV.102
tilian *v.* to strive for. *infin.* VI.262; *pres.subj.s.* **tilie** V.185, **tylie** V.177; *pret.p.* **tyloden** VII.133
tima *wk.m.* time, hour. I.37, III.236, 236, 237, 238, 264, 285, IV.341
timbrian *v.* to build. *infin.* VI.185
ȝetimian *v.* to happen, befall. *pres.subj.s.* **ȝetimiȝe** I.119; *pret.ȝs.* **ȝetimode** IV.108
tintreȝ *n.* torture. IV.154, 172, 221
tintreȝian *v.* to torment, torture. *infl. infin.* **tintreȝienne** II.161
tintreȝunȝ *f.* torment, punishment. IV.127
to (*a*) *prep.w.d. noun or pron.* to, for, as, in. I.3, 5, 8, 10, 11, 17, 18, *etc.*; **to þam þe**, in what. I.46, *etc.*; *preceding an infl.infin.* I.132, 181, II.8, *etc.*; (*b*) *as adv. qualifying an adv. or adj.* too. I.35, 167, II.200, III.122, *etc.*
tobrecan *v.* (*a*) to shatter, overthrow, break down. *pp.* **tobrocen** VII.121, (*decl.*) IV.179; (*b*) to infringe, violate. *pres.ȝs.* **tobræcð** II.153; *pres.subj.s.* **tobræce** II.146; *pret.p.* **tobrecon** III.288
tobrutan ('tobritan') *v.* to destroy. *pp.* **tobrut** IV.80
tocnawan *v.* to discern, distinguish, understand. *infin.* I.134, IV.65, 74
tocyme *m.* coming, advent. VI.151
todælan *v.* to distribute, divide. *pres.ȝs.* **todæleþ** VII.120; *pp.* **todæled** VII.139, (*decl.*) IV.279
todreosan *v.* to decay. *pp.* **todroren** VII.122
tofaran *v.* to go away, depart. *pres.ȝs.* **tofaræð** VII.4
toforen *prep.w.d.* ahead of, above. VI.102

togædere *adv.* together. V.7, 34, 125, VII.28, **-gad-** V.48, 127, **-ged-** V.38
togan *v.* to be sundered, to part. *pres.subj.p.* **togaan** IV.100
toglidan *v.* to be dispersed, pass away, slip away. *pres.ȝs.* **toglit** VII.5; *pp.* (*decl.*) **toglidene** VII.121, 136
toȝeane(s) *prep.w.d.* towards. I.22, 143, VI.169
tolysan *v.* to loose, undo. *pp.* (*decl.*) **tolysede** IV.201
tomiddes *prep.w.d.* in the midst of, amidst. I.166
torr *m.* projecting rock, tor. VII.106
torrian *v.* to tower. *pres.p.* **torriæð** VII.109 n.
toȝescead ('toscead') *n.* distinction, difference. VI.111
tosceakan ('tosceacan') *v.* to shake to pieces. *pp.* **tosceaken** VII.122
toslean *v.* to shatter. *pp.* (*decl.*) **toslaȝene** VII.111
toslupan *v.* to slip apart. *pret.p.* **toslupon** IV.172
tosomne *adv.* together. V.42
toþ *m.* tooth. VII.48, 50, **teoð-** VII.88
toweard *adj.* at hand, approaching, future. V.2, 45, VI.60, 150, 153, 155
traht *m.* exposition, commentary. III.266
trahtnung *f.* exposition, commentary. I.34, II.49
treow *n.* tree. VII.103, 104
ȝetreowe *adj.* true, faithful. II.175
truwa *wk.m.* belief, confidence. IV.90
truwian *v.* to trust. *pres.p.* **truwiæð** II.50
(ȝe)trymman *v.* to confirm, strengthen. *infin.* VI.221; *pp.* (*decl.*) **itrymede** VI.149
tun *m.* town. I.3, 5
tunge *wk.f.* tongue. III.257
tungla *wk.f.* heavenly body, star, planet. VI.82, 85, 95
turnan *v.* to turn. *pp.* **iturnd** VI.78
tweȝen *m.*, **twa** *f.n.* two. *m.nom.acc.* **tweȝen** I.158, II.64, **twæȝe** V.37, **twea** V.180; *f.n.nom.acc.* **twa** II.85, IV.323, VII.34; *gen.* **twæȝræ** VI.205, **tweȝræ** VI.179, 196; *dat.* **twam** II.134, V.40, VI.235
twelf *num.* twelve. V.174, 178, 183
tweo *m.* doubt. *Only in phrase* **buton tweon** V.23, VI.155
tweoȝan *v.* to doubt. *infin.* VII.96

tweonian *v.* (*a*) *impers.w.d.* of *person*, to cause doubt. *pret.3s.* **tweonode** I.91; (*b*) to doubt. *pres.p.* **tweoniæð** V.21

twynung *f.* doubt, uncertainty, hesitation. I.140

tyddre *adj.* weak, frail. VI.245

tyderness *f.* weakness, frailty. VI.224

tylie, tyloden *see* **tilian**

tyn *num.* ten. II.134, 138, 140, 142, **ten** II.9, **tene** II.140

tynan *v.* to vex, irritate. *pres.3s.* **tynð** IV.98

tynfeald *adj.* tenfold. II.138, **tenfeald-** II.144

(ʒe)tyðian *v.* to grant. *infin.* II.160; *imper.s.* **tyðæ** II.91; *pres.2s.* **tyðæst** II.94; *pp.* **ityðod** II.160

þa *adv.* then. I.7, 8, 9, 11, 13, 14, 20, 22, *etc.*; **þa þa** *conj.* (then) when, since. I.64, 97 (**þa ðe**), 186, 188, II.109, 127; **þa ʒyt** *see* **ʒyt**

þa (*pron.adj.*) *see* **þe**

ðæ *see* **þe**

þæʒen *see* **þeʒen**

þæh *see* **þeah**

þæne *see* **þe**

ðær, ðer *adv.* there. I.44, 73, II.132, III.20, 47, *etc.*, **þar** IV.239, 278; *conj.* where. I.80, II.93 (**ðær ðe**), III.265; **ðær ðær** *conj.* (there) where. I.4, III.213 (**ðer ðer**), IV.294

þæra, þære *see* **þe**

þæron *adv.* thereon. IV.180

þærup *adv.* up there. VI.147

þæs *see* **þe**

þæsne *see* **þes**

þæt *conj.* that, in that, so that. I.10, 12, 23, 27, 28, 31, *etc.*, **ðet** III.353, IV.303; *for* **swa þæt** *see* **swa**

þæt (*pron.*) *see* **þe**

ʒeþafi(ʒ)an *v.* to permit, allow. *infin.* VI.238; *pres.subj.s.* **iðafiʒe** II.193; *pret.3s.* **ʒeðafede** V.29

þam, þan, þane, þare, þara *see* **þe**

þanc *m.* (*a*) thanks, gratitude. *In phrase* **þanc nytan** not to feel gratitude. VII.95; (*b*) thought. V.170, VI.137, VII.13

þancfull *adj.* thankful, grateful. **þoncfull** VI.123

þancian *v.* to thank. *infin.* III.300, **þanken** VI.173; **þonciæn** VII.98; *pres.pt.* **þankiende** VI.171

þanon *adv.* thence. II.121, 126

þar *see* **þær**

þas *see* **þes**

þe (se) *m.*, **þeo (seo)** *f.*, **þæt** *n.* *pron.adj.def.art.* that one, that, the. [*Forms, one example each except for rare spellings where all occurrences are cited:* sg.m.nom. **þe** I.9, **sæ** I.140 (*one only*), *acc.* **þone** I.66, **þonne** III.86, 151, 271, 273, 293, V.118, **þene** II.203, **þenne** V.112, VII.36, **þæne** VII.46 (*one only*), *gen.* **þæs** I.9, *dat.* **þam** I.3; *sg.f.nom.* **þeo** I.157, *acc.* **þa** I.58, **þæ** VII.150 (*one only*), *gen.* **þare** II.85, *dat.* **þare** I.29, **þære** III.233, **þere** III.212; *n.nom.* **þæt** I.150, *acc.* **þæt** I.31, *gen.* **þæs** I.53, **þes** III.234, *dat.* **þam** I.6, **þan** I.21, **þe** IV.309, 327, VII.119; *pl.nom.* **þa** I.45, **þæ** VII.126 (*one only*), *acc.* **þa** I.49, *gen.* **þare** I.243, **þære** V.187, *dat.* **þam** I.130. *See also* p. lxxv above.] *For* **ær þan ðe** *and* for **þan ðe**, *see* **ær** *and* for *respectively. For* **þæs on mareʒen**, *see* **marʒen**

þe *indecl.rel.part.* (*a*) *as substitute for relative pron.* I.13, 29, 77, 88, 151, *etc.*; (*b*) *as sign of the relative in combination with the demonstrative.* **sæ ðe** I.140, **þe ðe** I.193, 197, 200, **ðæ** V.90, **he ðe** II.6; (*c*) *as element in various compound conjunctions.* **for, ær, to þan ðe, ðeah ðe,** *etc.*, *see* **for, ær, to, ðeah,** *etc.*

ðe *pers.pron. see* **þu**

ðeah *conj.* (*with* **þe**) though, even if. I.69, 94, 131, 133, II.157, 184, *etc.*, **þæh** (*without* **ðe**) V.73; *adv.* nevertheless, yet. I.83; *for* **swa þeah**, *see* **swa**

þeahhwæðere *adv.conj.* yet, nevertheless, however. V.148, VI.43, VII.110, **-hweð-** V.130

þearf *see* **þurfan**

þearfa *adj.* destitute, poor. III.256

ðeaw *m.* custom, usage. III.310

ðeʒen, þeʒn *m.* servant. II.10, 18, 20, 29, 32, 141, 156, *etc.*, **þæʒen** II.12, 15, 139, **þei(ʒ)n-** V.168, VI.17, 23, 58, 65, 234

þeʒenscyp *m.* body of thanes. VII.3

þeʒnian *v.* to serve. *infin.* **þeiniʒen** V.158, **þeniæn** IV.351; *pres.3s.* **ðenaþ** IV.295, **ðenæð** IV.293, 339, 347, 348, 358, 361; *pres.p.* **þeniæð** IV.340, 349, 354; *pret.p.* **þenedon** V.154

þeʒniendlic ('þegnian'/'þegenlic') *adj.* ministering, attendant. V.157

(ȝe)þencan v. (a) to think of, consider. infin. V.86, VI.36, 172, 202, VII.79; pres.p. ðencþ VI.53; (b) to think, mean, intend. pres.3s. þenceþ VI.49, ðencþ V.11; pret.3s. þohte IV.125, V.58, VI.184; pret.p. þohtan IV.42

þene (pron.adj.) see þe

þene (conj. w. comparatives) see þonne

þenne (adv.) see þonne

þenne (pron.adj.) see þe

þenung f. service, ministry. IV.199, 247

þeo see þe

ðeod f. nation, people. I.163, 196, III.207

þeoht ('þeaht') f. counsel. III.63

þeon v. to thrive, flourish. pres.pt. þeonde IV.6

þeos see þes

þeostru fp. darkness. IV.178

ðeow m., þeowa wk.m. servant. str. I.116, III.284; wk. II.36

ðeowdom m. service (of the church). IV.341

þeowian v. to serve. infin. V.140, 144; pres.pt. þeowiende IV.7

ðeowtlic adj. servile. III.275, 281, 309

ðer see þær

þeræfter ('þæræfter') adv. thereafter. V.41

þere see þe

þerinne ('þærinne') adv. therein. VII.161

þerrihte ('þærrihte') adv. straightaway. II.18

þerto adv. thereto, about it. I.33, VII.74

þes m., þeos f., þis n. dem.pron.adj. this. [Forms, one example each, except for rare spellings where all occurrences are cited: sg.m.nom. þes I.57, þæs III.8, acc. þesne I.171, þisne III.79, þæsne V.142, VI.110, þysne VI.168 (one only), gen. þisses III.193, dat. þissum I.114; f.nom. þeos II.56, acc. þas I.81, þis V.47 (one only), gen. þisre VI.137, VII.113, þissere III.87, þissre VII.22, dat. þisse III.303, þissere II.49, þissre VII.7, þissen VI.51, þissum V.22; n.nom. þis I.32, acc. þisse VI.84, þis V.185, gen. þisses I.78, þysses V.121, dat. þisse III.110, þissum II.16, pl.nom. þas V.171, þæs V.65, acc. þas I.170, dat. þissum II.169. See also p. lxxv above.]

þes (dem.pron.gs.) see þe

ðet see þæt (conj.)

ðider adv. thither. III.263, V.25, VII.38

þin poss.pron.adj. your, yours. I.19, 19, 30, 100, 100, 111, 155, II.17, etc.

þince, þing see þyncan

þing n. thing. I.67, 88, 171, 172, II.77, 78, III.112, etc.

þingung f. intercession, intervention. V.147

þis(-) see þes

þoht- see (ȝe)þencan

þolemodness f. patience, endurance. V.170

þolian v. to suffer, endure. pret.3s. þolede V.15, VI.247, þolode VI.160

þon see þe

þonc(-) see þanc(-)

ðone see þe

ðonne, ðenne adv. then. I.74, 176, 177, 178, II.66, 67, 68, etc.; conj. when. I.187, II.106, III.162, V.71, 106, etc.; conj.w. comparatives, than. II.159, III.15, 190, 239, 245, VI.44, etc., þene VI.99, 103, VII.106

þonne (asm. pron.) see þe

þoðt ('þoht') m. thought. VI.264

þreaȝan v. to reprove, rebuke, reproach. imper.s. ðrea II.64; pp. iþread VII.111

þrem, þreo(m) see þry

þrestan v. to torment, afflict. pp. iþreste VII.111

þrittiȝ num. thirty. V.182

þrosm m. smoke or darkness. VII.47

þrowian v. to suffer. infin. IV.93, V.95, VI.85, 164, 220; infl.infin. þrowienne IV.111; pres.1s. þrowiȝe IV.119; pres.3s. þrowæð I.105; pres.p. þrowæð VI.92, 94, þrowiæð VII.59; pret.3s. þrowode V.96, VI.172; pp. iþrowed VI.32, iþrowod VI.233

þrowung f. suffering. III.209, 308, VI.122, 145, 147, etc.

þry m., þreo, þre f.n. num. three. V.179, VI.10, 19, 182; dat. þrem V.63, þreom VI.30, þrym VI.13

ȝeþryccan v. to suppress. pp. iþryht IV.314

þrymlic adj. glorious, magnificent. comp. VII.98

þrymlice adv. magnificently, splendidly, gloriously. VI.47

þrym(m) m. glory. VI.144, 200, 205, VII.121, 162

þrystru ('þeostru') fp. darkness. IV.200

ðu *pron.2p.* you. *Forms same as OE.*
þuhte *see* þyncan
þuld ('geþyld') *n. or f.* patience. V.168
þuldelice ('geþyldelice') *adv.* patiently.
V.74, 114, 117
þuncþ *see* þyncan
[þurfan] *v.* to need. *pres.3s.* þearf VII.95;
pres.subj.s. ðurfe V.100; *pres.p.* ðurfon
III.309; *pret.3s.* þurfte V.9
þurh *prep.w.a.* through. I.31, 76, 88, 94,
150, 156, *etc.*, þurðh I.83, þur IV.240,
247, þurð V.127, þyrh IV.17
þurhwunian *v.* to persevere, continue,
remain. *pres.3s.* þurhwuneð VII.68;
pret.3s. þurhwunode IV.129, 162;
pret.p. þurhwunedon III.368
þurst *m.* thirst. VII.87
þus *adv.* thus. I.14, 18, 61, 103, 116, 174,
II.24, *etc.*
þusend *n.* thousand. *undecl.* II.9, 139,
VII.155; *decl. as p.subst.* II.138
þusne *see* þes
þuðten *see* þyncan
ӡeþwærlæcan *v.w.d.* to comply with,
observe. *pres.2s.* ӡeþwærlæcst IV.109
ӡeþyld *f.* patience, resignation. II.193
þyncan *v.w.d.* to seem to (s.o.). *pres.3s.*
þing IV.104; þuncþ V.82; *pres.subj.s.*
þynce I.35, V.177, þince V.185; *pret.3s.*
þuhte VI.197; *pret.subj.s.* þuhte VI.245;
pret.p. þuðten VI.180
ðyrel *adj.* perforated, fretted. VII.8
þyrh *see* þurh
þysne, þysses, þysum *see* þes
þystre *adj.* dark. VII.51

Ualerius Bishop Valerius. IV.8, 67
Uincentius St. Vincent. IV.3, 40, *etc.*,
Uincencius IV.338
unasecgendlic *adj.* unutterable. VI.209
unaseӡenlice ('-secgen-') *adv.* unspeak-
ably, indescribably. III.186
uncuð *adj.* unknown, uncertain. VI.37,
VII.140
under *prep.w.d.* under. I.36, 110, 113
underfon *v.* to receive, get. *infin.* II.91,
VI.103, 266; *pres.3s.* underfehð VI.89;
pres.p. underfoð III.251, VI.93, 199;
pret.3s. underfeng III.153, 345, IV.273,
VI.157; *pret.p.* underfengon IV.43; *pp.*
underfangen IV.33
underӡytan *v.* to perceive. *infin.* V.152,

VI.77, VII.94; *pret.3s.* underӡeat V.50;
pret.p. underӡeton VI.215
underkyng *m.* dependent or tributary
king. I.7, 9, 14, 16, 36, 45, *etc.*
underniman *v.* to take (into the mind),
receive. *pret.3s.* undernam I.139
understandan *v.* to understand. *infin.*
III.268, -stond- VI.171; *infl.infin.*
understandenne II.188
understreowod *adj.* under-strewn.
IV.202
underðeod *adj.* (*pp. of* 'underþeodan')
subject, subordinate. I.45
uneaðelic *adj.* difficult. V.83, 177
unhæl *f.* bad health, disease. VII.82
unhersumness *f.* disobedience. VI.83
unlæd *adj.* miserable, wretched. VII.153
unlaðod *adj.* (*pp. of negative of* 'laðian')
uninvited. I.123
unleafful ('ungeleafful') *adj.* unbelieving.
III.40
unӡeleaffullice *adv.* without belief.
III.124
unleaffulness ('ungeleaf-') *f.* unbelief,
incredulity. III.127
unӡelic *adj.* unlike. V.55, VII.70
unlust *m.* evil desire, sensuality. VII.90
ӡe-unnan *v.w.d. of pers.* to grant. *pret.3s.*
ӡeuþe IV.27
unnyt(t) *adj.* useless, unprofitable.
VI.263, VII.156
unriht *adj.* unrighteous, unjust. III.291
unrihtlic *adj.* unjust, unrighteous. VI.261
unrihtlice *adv.* unrighteously. III.142
unrihtwisness *f.* unrighteousness,
iniquity. II.177, III.120, 142, 248
unrimedlic ('ungerimedlic') *adj.* innum-
erable. VI.207
unrodsian ('unrotsian') *v.* to be sorrow-
ful. *pret.p.* unrodsoden II.33
unsceapen ('ungesceapen') *adj.*
unshapen, unformed. III.341
unswetian *v.* to become bitter. *pres.p.*
unswetiæþ VI.177 n.
untrum *adj.* sick. III.211
untrumness *f.* sickness, illness. III.215
unðances *adv.* unwillingly, against
(one's) will. I.55, II.31, VII.76
unþeaw *m.* evil custom, vice. VII.12
unþongful ('ungeþancfull') *adj.* ungrate-
ful. *comp.* VI.118
unwæne *adj.* without hope (for), despair-
ing (of). I.13

unwemmed *adj.* unspotted, undefiled.
VI.140
unwreon *v.* to reveal. *pret.3s.* unwreah
V.45, VI.150
up *adv.* up. II.26, VI.27, 28, 58, 167, *etc.*
up(p)lic *adj.* upper, on high. VII.61, 162
uppon *prep.w.d.a.* upon, on. VI.11, 206
uppon (*n.*) *see* yppe
uprist *f.* resurrection. VI.152 n., 155 n.,
223, 253, 265
upsti3e *m.* ascension. II.118, III.199, 201,
205, VI.152, 253
upweard *adv.* upwards, up. II.111, 117,
122, 126
ure *poss.pron.adj., 1p.* our. I.3, 97, 151, 152,
II.84, *etc.*
us *see* ic
ut *adv.* out. I.50, II.20, III.94
utdrifan ('ut' + 'drifan') *v.* to drive out,
expel. *pret.p.* utdrifon III.344
uten, uton (*w.infin.*) let us. V.162, VI.55,
257, VII.79, 158
uten, uton *adv.* without, on the outside.
VI.212, VII.115, 119
3e-utla3ian *v.* to outlaw. *pp.* iutla3od
III.65, (*decl.*) III.62
3e-uþe *see* 3e-unnan

wa *inter.* (*a*) woe, alas. IV.176, 176; (*b*)
w.d. woe (to). VII.129
wac *adj.* weak, degraded, base. VI.180,
VII.137, 138
wæ *see* ic
wæbb *see* web(b)
wæcce *wk.f.* watching, watch. V.169, 187
wæder ('weder') *n.* weather. VII.137
wædlian *v.* to beg. *pres.pt.* wædliende
III.25
wæ3 *m.* way. I.19, 100, VI.52, 53, VII.149,
we3- IV.350
wæ3an *v.* to harass, afflict. *pp.* iwæ3ed
VII.105
wæl *adv.* well. I.187, II.50, 217, VI.22, 134,
wel IV.6, 64, VI.58, 214
wælan *see* wela
wælded ('weldæd') *f.* good deed. IV.355
wældend *see* wealdend
wælhreow *adj.* cruel. IV.22, 28, 154, 221,
237; *as sb.* IV.70, 103, 106
wælhreownyss *f.* cruelty. IV.119
wæli3 ('welig') *adj.* wealthy, rich. III.255
wære, -en, -on, -an *see* beon
wæredo *see* werod

wæs *see* beon
wæscan *v.* to wash. *pret.1s.* weosc III.34,
42
wæsten ('westen') *m. or n.* desert, wilderness. II.149, V.6, 15, 20, 25, 33, westen
V.21
wæstm *m.* fruit, produce. IV.289, 306,
308, 316
wæt *n.* moisture. III.259
wæter *n.* water. III.33, 156, water I.5
wæterscipe *m.* piece of water. III.20
wakian ('wacian') *v.* to stay awake, watch.
pres.pt. wakigende IV.188
walde *see* willan
wanian *v.* to diminish. *pres.3s.* wonæð
VII.67, 77; *pres.subj.s.* wani3e IV.112,
208; *pres.p.* woniæð VII.78; *pp.*
3eiwoned VI.240
wann *see* (ge)winnan
ware *see* beon
wari3an ('wirgan') *v.* to curse. *pret.p.*
wari3edon III.75, 312; *pp.* (*decl.*)
wari3ede, accursed. V.22
wari3ung ('wirgung') *f.* cursing, curse.
III.317
warnian *v.* (*a*) to warn. *infin.* III.262; (*b*)
to take heed of. III.281; *pres.subj.p.*
warniæn VI.34
wat *see* witan
3ewat *see* 3ewitan
water *see* wæter
waxende *see* weaxan
we *see* ic
weane ('wea') *wk.m.* woe, misery. VII.24
weald *n.* power. V.61, 123
wealdend *m.* ruler, God. I.84, wældend
III.86
weallan *v.* to foam or blaze. *pres.pt.* weallende VII.49
weardmann *m.* watchman, guard. IV.63,
189, 195
weardung *f.* guardianship. IV.250
wearð *see* (3e)wurþan
weaxan *v.* to grow. *pres.3s.* weaxæð
IV.303, 313, weaxeð VII.104; *pres.pt.*
waxende V.141
weaxbræd *n.* tablet. II.134
web(b) *n.* web, piece of woven material.
II.150, IV.103, wæbb II.150
wedan *v.* to rage. *pret.3s.* wedde IV.122
we3as *see* wæ3
wel *see* wæl

wela *wk.m.* wealth, riches. I.130, VII.113, 120, 132, **wæl-** VII.2

welwillende *part.adj.* benevolent. IV.229

wem(m) ('wamm') *m. or n.* stain, spot. V.57, VI.139

ʒewemman *v.* to stain, defile, pollute. *pret.p.* **ʒewemdon** III.290

wen *f.* expectation, likelihood. **wen is þæt...,** it is likely that... I.78

wenan *v.* to think, believe. *pres.p.* **wene we** III.197; *pret.3s.* **wende** IV.55; *pret.p.* **wendon** III.304, 361

wendan *v.* to take (one's) way, go, turn. *infin.* VII.158; *pres.p.* **wendæþ** VII.19; *pret.3s.* **wende** I.21, 138, III.332

weorc *n.* work, labour, deed. II.85, III.13, 113, 141, 177, 180, *etc.*, **weorcc-** III.111, 134

weorld *f.* world. III.336, IV.333, V.13, :06, *etc.*, **weoruld-** III.87, 225, 231, 237, *etc.*, **world(-)** IV.12, 227, VI.15, 46, 117, *etc.*, **worulde** I.202, III.207

weorldæht *f.* worldly possession. V.174

weorldlic *adj.* worldly, earthly. V.125, 127, VI.37, **weoruldlice** III.222, 290

weorldprud ('-pryd') *f.* worldly pride. **worldprude** VII.4 n.

weorldscryft *m.* earthly judge, earthly confessor. VII.129 n.

weorldþing *n.* worldly thing. IV.300

weorldþrym *m.* worldly glory. **worldþrym** VII.5 n.

weorpan *v.* to cast, throw, fling. *pret.3s.* **weorp** VI.84

weorþæn *see* **wurþan**

weoruld- *see* **world-**

weosc *see* **wæscan**

wepan *v.* to weep. *pres.pt.* **wepende** VII.55

wer *m.* man. II.218, IV.106, 118, 124, 141, 187, *etc.*

were, -en, -on, wes *see* **beon**

werod (-ed) *n.* host, troop. VI.207, VII.23, 32, 57, 61, 163, **wæred-** VI.5

westen *see* **wæsten**

wide *adv.* widely. IV.12, 279

widgil *adj.* extensive, spacious. IV.235, 262, 265

wif *n.* woman, wife. II.13

wilde *adj.* wild. IV.242

wildeor *n.* wild beast. IV.237, 239

will *n.* will, pleasure. VI.241, **wyll-** V.61

willa *wk.m.* will, purpose, desire. I.47, III.85, IV.346, V.123

willan *v.* to desire, wish, intend. *pres.1s.* **wulle** II.187; *pres.2s.* **wult** V.133, VI.182, **wylt** II.91, IV.324, VI.19; *pres.3s.* **wille** III.86, **wule** I.178, II.59, *etc.*; *pres.subj.s.* **wille** IV.120, 211, **wylle** II.181, IV.155, **wulle** I.86; *pres.p.* **willæð** III.107, **wullæð** I.33, V.1, 16, 86, *etc.*, **wyllæð** IV.298, V.159, **wylle ʒe, we** III.74, 267; *pret.3s. and pret.subj.s.* **wolde** I.46, 47, 123, *etc.*, **walde** III.255, V.9, 29, 58, *etc.*; *pret.p.* **wolden** III.314, VII.9

(ʒe)wilnian *v.* to desire, ask for. *infin.* IV 366, 367; *pret.1s.* **ʒewilnode** IV.107

ʒewilnung *f.* desire. IV.109

win *n.* wine. I.5, 6

wind *m.* wind. VII.105

(ʒe)win(n) *n.* conflict, strife. IV.89, VI.91, 94, VII.85, 90

winnan *v.* (*intrans.*) to fight, contend, strive. *infin.* **winne** IV.68; *pres.subj.s.* **winne** IV.89; *pret.3s.* **wann** IV.126

winter *m.* winter. VII.155

wis *adj.* wise. II.50, III.109

ʒewis *adv.* for certain, surely. II.72, 93 (**iwiss**)

ʒewiscan *v.* to wish, desire. *pret.1s.* **ʒewiscte** IV.107

wisdom *m.* wisdom. V.44

wise *f.* way, manner. I.58, III.274, IV.323, 340, 347

wissian *v.* to direct, rule. *pres.3s.* **wissæð** V.122

(ʒe)wis(s)lice *adv.* certainly. III.70, IV.333, V.68, 153

wissung *f.* guidance, instruction. IV.276

wist *f.* sustenance, food, provisions. IV.64

wist- *see* **witan**

ʒewita *wk.m.* witness. II.63

witan *v.* to know. *infin.* I.74; *infl.infin.* **witenne** II.48, V.24; *pres.1s.* **wat** III.69; *pres.p.* **witen** III.78, 301, V.76, 178, VI.134, **witæn** I.179, VI.104, **witan** III.56, 67, 83, **witon** IV.300; *pres.subj.p.* **witen** V.10; *pret.3s.* **wiste** V.46, 67, VI.219, 236, 245; *pret.p.* **wiston** I.187; *pret.subj.p.* **wisten** V.29, VI.48, 214

(ʒe)witan *v.* to go, depart. *imper.p.* **ʒewitæð** III.249, VII.45; *pres.p.* **ʒewitæð** VII.70; *pret.3s.* **ʒewat** IV.227; *pp.* **iwiten** VI.230; *pres.pt. as adj.,* transitory, fleeting. **witende** VI.37, **witiʒendæn** V.121

wite *n.* punishment, torment. III.307, IV.15, 26, 29, 38, 52, *etc.*

witega *wk.m.* prophet. I.179, III.50, V.41, VI.148, **wite3-** IV.245, VI.61

witegung *f.* prophecy. III.322

witnere *m.* punisher, tormentor. II.41, 162, IV.96, 116

(3e)witnian *v.* to punish, torment. *infin.* II.41, 162, IV.57, 123, 128; *imper.s.* **witna** IV.146; *pres.1s.* **witni3e** IV.234; *pres.2s.* **witnast** IV.113; *pres.3s.* **witnaþ** IV.92; *pret.p.* **(3e)witnodon** IV.116, 134, 221; *pp.* **3ewitnod** IV.92, 113, 219

witnung *f.* punishment, torment. IV.169

witodlice *adv.* indeed, surely, truly. IV.42, 142, 290, 320, 324, 329, **witollice** I.128, **witolice** III.317, 323, **witerlice** V.35, 120, VI.156

wið *prep.w.a.* with, in return, against. II.6, 8, 13, 61, 81, 83, *etc.*

wiðcwæðan *v.* to contradict, gainsay, oppose. *pret.p.* **wiðcwædon** III.292

wiðercora *wk.m.* rebel. IV.98, 181

wiðerweard *adj.* hostile, adverse. *comp.* VI.237

wiðerweardness *f.* adversity. VII.40

wiðerwinnan *v.* to oppose, resist. *infin.* IV.31

wiðinnan *prep.w.d.* within. II.182

wiðsacan *v.* to deny, reject. *pres.p.* **wiðsacæð** VII.153; *pret.subj.p.* **wiðsocen** IV.337

wiðstandan *v.* to withstand, resist. *pres.3s.* **wiðstont** VII.105

wiðuton *adv.* without, outside. III.93

wlite *m.* aspect, appearance; brightness (of aspect). VI.13, 78, 95, 96, 104, *etc.*

wliti3 *adj.* beautiful. VI.129, 139, 178, 196, 222, 260; *comp.* VI.108

wodlic *adj.* mad, furious. IV.31

wodlice *adv.* madly, furiously. III.75, 312, IV.12

wodnyss *f.* madness. IV.34, 80

wolcn *n.* cloud. VI.212, 213, VII.31

wold- *see* **willan**

wolice ('wohlice') *adv.* wrongly, unjustly. I.130

-woned, wonæð, woniæð *see* **wanian**

wop *m.* weeping. VII.87

word *n.* word. I.72, 111, 117, 139, *etc.*

(i)worden, -on *see* **(3e)wurþan**

3eworhtan *see* **wurcan**

world(-), worulde *see* **weorld(-)**

wracu *f.* pain, suffering, misery. VII.24, *gp.* **wracane** III.143, **wræc-** III.143

wræcan ('wrecan') *v.* to drive. *pp.* **wræcen** VII.129

wræcsið *m.* exile, banishment. I.50

wrat *see* **writan**

3ewrecan *v.* to take vengeance. *infin.* IV.120; *pres.2s.* **3ewrecst** IV.118

wreon *v.* to cover, clothe. *infin.* VII.118

wreðian ('gewraþian') *v.* to make angry. *pret.p.* **wreðædon** VI.81

writan *v.* to write. *pret.3s.* **wrat** V.17, 39, VI.2; *pret.subj.s.* **write** VI.42; *pp.* **iwritæn (-en)** II.133, V.5, 36, 75, 98, 104, 111, 139, VII.143

wroht- *see* **wurcan**

wruht ('wyrht') *f.* doing, work. VI.7

wudewa *wk.f.* widow. IV.272

wudu *m.* wood, tree. VII.104, 106

wuldor *n.* glory. I.201, II.222, III.67, 183, *etc.*

wuldorful(l) *adj.* glorious. IV.44, 73, 111, 218, 255

wule, wull-, wult *see* **willan**

3ewuna *wk.m.* custom, wont, manner. II.2

wund *f.* wound. II.204, 207, IV.166, 166, VI.115, 120

3ewundian *v.* to wound. *pret.p.* **3ewundodon** IV.167; *pp.* **3ewundod** IV.169

wundor, -er *n.* wonder, miracle. I.161, III.81, 333, V.92, VI.17, 23, 39, *np., ap.* **wundræ, -a** I.170, 183, 193, 197, *etc.,* **wyndræ** III.12, 204; *dp.* **wundrum** I.189

wundorlic (-er-) *adj.* wonderful. III.113, V.83, VI.30, 74, 260; *comp.* VI.100

wundorlice (-er-) *adv.* wonderfully. IV.313, VI.12, 65, 111

wundrian *v.* to wonder at. *imper.p.* **wundriað** IV.203; *pres.subj.s.* **wundri3e** I.78; *pret.3s.* **wundrode** I.117, IV.195 (*for pl.*)

3ewunelic *adj.* usual, ordinary. III.222

3ewunelice *adv.* commonly. III.122

wunian *v.* to dwell, remain. *infin.* IV.355, 362; *pres.3s.* **wunæð** III.126, IV.288, 303, VII.157; *pres.subj.s.* **wuni3e** IV.326; *pres.p.* **wuniæð** IV.343, VII.37, 41, 55, 61, 91; *pret.3s.* **wunode** III.147, IV.86; *pres.pt.* **wuniende** VII.39, **wuni3ende** III.4, 145

wunstre ('wynstre') *adj.* left. VII.35

wunsumlice *see* **wynsumlice**

wunung *f.* dwelling. IV.309

(ʒe)wurcan, (-)wyrcan *v.* to work, do, perform, make. *infin.* **wyrc-** III.46, 190, 233, 262, *etc.*, **wurc-** VII.117; *infl.infin.* **wyrc(c)enne** III.13, 177, 180; *pres.1s.* **wyrce** IV.255; *pres.2s.* **wurcæst** I.170; *pres.3s.* **wurcæð** I.197, **(ʒe)wyrcæð** III.85, 284, **wurcð** I.193, **wyrcð** III.141; *pres.subj.s.* **wurce** I.199; *pres.p.* **wurcæð** III.210; *pres.subj.p.* **wurcean** VI.19, **wurchen** VI.182; *pret.3s.* **wrohte** I.161, 165, II.149, III.31, *etc.*, **iwrohtæ** V.71; *pret.subj.s.* **wrohte** V.66; *pret.p.* **wrohten** III.204, 208, VII.58, **wrohton** III.305, **ʒeworhtan** IV.18; *pres.pt.* **wyrcende** III.5

wurde, wurdon *see* **(ʒe)wurþan**

wurhʒiæn *see* **wurþian**

wurm *m.* serpent. VII.49

(ʒe)wurpan, -wyrpan *v.* to recover from illness. *pret.3s.* **(ʒe)wurpte** I.25, 26, 146, **wyrpte** I.147

wursian ('wirsian') *v.* to get worse. *pres.3s.* **wursæð** VII.67

wurt ('wyrt') *f.* plant. VII.80

wurð *n.* worth, value. V.120

(ʒe)wurþan *v.* (*a*) to become, be. *pres.2s.* **iwurðæst** VII.15; *pres.3s.* **wurð** V.137, VII.69; *pres.subj.s.* **(ʒe)wurðe, -æ** II.204, IV.80, V.69; *pres.p.* **wurð** VI.123, **wurðæþ** VII.112, 113, 136; *pres.subj.p.* **weorþæn** VII.65, **wurðen** V.65, 72; *pret.3s.* **wearð** I.101, 120, 149, II.161, III.47, 87, *etc.*; *pret.subj.s.* **wurde** II.14, IV.71, **wyrde** III.52, 65, 160, 200; *pret.p.* **wurdon** III.214, 368, *etc.*, **worden** VI.87; *pret.subj.p.* **wyrden** III.62, **wyrdon** III.12, 171, 176; **bið iworden (-on)** becomes. VI.132, VII.122 (*in pl.*); **wearð, wæs iworden,** became. VI.12–13, 14, 73–4, 130–1; (*b*) to come to pass, happen. *infin.* VI.156, 240; *pres.3s.* **iwurð** VI.137; **(bið) wæs iworden,** (is) was done, occurred. V.67, 70, VI.21, 92, 111

ʒewurþan *v.* to be fitting for. *pres.3s.* **ʒewurð** II.56

wurðe *adj.* worthy. I.109, II.157, **wyrðe** III.136

wurðian *v.* to value, esteem, honour, worship. *infin.* I.127, 128, **wurhʒiæn** V.133; *pres.3s.* **wurðaþ** IV.203, **wyrðaþ** IV.280; *pres.p.* **wurðiæþ** I.130

wurðmynt (-ment) *n.* honour. I.202, II.222, **wyrð-** IV.360, 362, 366

wurðscip *m.* honour, glory. I.46, V.160

ʒewyldan *v.* to conquer, subdue. *pret.p.* **ʒewyldon** IV.137

wyll- *see* **will-**

wylt *see* **willan**

wyndræ *see* **wundor**

wynsum *adj.* pleasant, agreeable. IV.195, 309

wynsumlice *adv.* gladly, joyously. **wunsumlice** V.24, VII.8

wynsumness *f.* pleasantness, agreeableness. IV.364

(-)wyrc- *see* **wurcan**

wyrde, -en, -on *see* **(ʒe)wurþan**

wyrp- *see* **wurpan**

wyrðaþ *see* **wurþian**

wyrðe *see* **wurþe**

wyrðmente *see* **wurþment**

ydel *n.* emptiness, vanity. *Only in phrase* **on idel,** in vain. IV.126

ydel *adj.* idle, vain. V.62

ydelness *f.* idleness, vanity. VII.4

yfel *n.* evil, ill. V.109

yfel *adj.* evil, bad. II.36, 193, III.247, V.116, VI.60, 63, *etc.*

yfele *adv.* evilly, badly, ill. I.105, II.205, III.117

yfellic *adj.* foul, rotten. VII.125

yfelness *f.* evilness, wickedness. III.145

ylc, ylce *see* **ælc**

ylca, ilca *pron.adj.* same. *as adj.* I.29, 58, 120, 154, II.131, 142, III.26, 28, 291, *etc.*; *as pron.* III.99, 135, 350, IV.249

yld *f.* (*a*) age, time of life. III.60; (*b*) age, period of time. VI.70

ymbhon *v.* to hang round, drape. *infin.* VII.119

ymbþringan *v.* to crowd round, surround. *pp.* **ymbþrungæn** VII.31

yppe *wk.f.* raised place. V.82, **uppon** V.98

yrfe *n.* inheritance, property. VII.134

yrmþ *f.* poverty, misery. V.137, VII.55

yrre *n.* anger. II.36, III.134, 135, 135

yrsian *v.* to be angry, rage. *pret.3s.* **yrsode** II.40, IV.114; *pret.p.* **yrsodan** III.344

ytemest *sup.adj.* latest, last. V.47

yþ *f.* wave. IV.257, 275